"'THE FAU...
OUR STA...
MONES, OU...
CYCLES O...
INTERNAL SPACES, BUT IN
OUR INSTITUTIONS AND
OUR EDUCATION.'

This is what *Woman in Sexist Society* is about. It is a collective attack on the anti-female culture created by a patriarchal society that stratifies people by sex, class and race, and defines woman "not by the struggling development of her brain or her will or her spirit, but rather by her child-bearing properties and her status as companion to men who make, and do, and rule the earth. . . . An important book because it is an intelligent attack on an antiquated, oppressive culture . . . a useful book for Women's Studies courses on women in literature, the socialization of women—in fact, for any course that teaches that the quest is not for the Holy Male, but for self-definition."
—Roberta Salper, *Ramparts*

"Women have always been treated as a subordinate sex, the editors proclaim, because this was supposedly the 'natural' order of things. Actually, they reply, this is no more 'natural' than slavery or the divine right of kings. The balance of the book is a closely reasoned, heavily documented, sometimes passionately argued statement of that case. . . . Speaking as a male, I found it meaty, argumentative, mostly persuasive . . . insightful."
—John Barkham, *Saturday Review Syndicate*

"THE FAULT LIES NOT IN

"*I AM NOT REAL TO MY CIVILIZA-
TION. I AM NOT REAL TO THE CUL-
TURE THAT HAS SPAWNED ME
AND HAS MADE USE OF ME. I AM
ONLY A COLLECTION OF MYTHS.
I AM AN EXISTENTIAL STAND-IN.
THE IDEA OF ME IS REAL—THE
TEMPTRESS, THE GODDESS, THE
CHILD, THE MOTHER—BUT I AM
NOT REAL.*"

"For the most part the essays in *Woman in Sexist
Society* are so well argued, so passionate, so honest, that I feel the collection provides emotional
support to help its readers begin to break out of
the traditional sex roles for themselves. The writers
have a serious cause in common: to illuminate the
political nature of woman's condition, to describe
the structure of our sexist society. As the editors
say in their stirring introduction, 'Sexism has made
of woman a race of children, a class of human
beings utterly deprived of self-hood, of autonomy,
of confidence—worst of all, *it has made the false
come true.* . . .' Single voices by themselves can
be enormously effective, and surely Kate Millett
has succeeded in breaking the back of the Freudian mythology with *Sexual Politics.* Yet there is
something equally exhilarating when many powerful voices are raised in the feminist cause. An anthology, moreover, is a most appropriate vehicle
to present the feminist point of view, since the
women's movement is a collective action representing a variety of individuals. In that regard, too,
Woman in Sexist Society is a particularly impressive addition to the writings from the women's liberation movement."

—Margaret Lichtenberg, *The Nation*

"ANY LOOK AT CULTURE AND LITERATURE WILL CONFIRM THAT THE LIFE OF A WOMAN IS OFFERED AS SACRIFICE."

". . . stimulating reading for many women indeed, and for men who are open-minded on the issues of feminism. These are articulate, sometimes eloquent and nearly always closely reasoned essays that refuse to substitute impassioned rhetoric for keen analysis. Outstanding . . . A feminist latecomer but a good one."

—*Publishers' Weekly*

"This big collection offers great catholicity of perspective, topics, and levels of analysis. Women's ascribed nature, acculturated dispositions, and actual potentialities are examined with a natural emphasis on family relations . . . in range and quality, it remains a standout."

—*Kirkus*

". . . the best try to date at undermining the conventional wisdom about women . . . so full of new facts and moving insights, so reasoned, so free from rancor, so uniformly intelligent, that it makes for totally absorbing reading."

—Joanne Von Blon, *Minneapolis Star*

". . . a lively, challenging anthology of current writing and research by women scholars, authors, and activists . . . combines scholarship and imagination with commitment to social change."

—*Library Journal*

SIGNET Non-Fiction Books
You Will Want to Read

WOMAN
IN
SEXIST SOCIETY

Studies in Power and Powerlessness

Edited by VIVIAN GORNICK
and BARBARA K. MORAN

A SIGNET BOOK from
NEW AMERICAN LIBRARY
TIMES MIRROR

SIGNET TRADEMARK REG. U.S. PAT. OFF. AND FOREIGN COUNTRIES
REGISTERED TRADEMARK—MARCA REGISTRADA
HECHO EN CHICAGO, U.S.A.

SIGNET, SIGNET CLASSICS, SIGNETTE, MENTOR AND PLUME BOOKS
are published by The New American Library, Inc.,
1301 Avenue of the Americas, New York, New York 10019

FIRST PRINTING, JUNE, 1972

PRINTED IN THE UNITED STATES OF AMERICA

The Authors

SIDNEY ABBOTT is a free-lance writer and an active worker in the women's and gay liberation movements. She is a member of Columbia University Women's Lib, Radical Lesbians, and the Gay Liberation Front.

MARGARET ADAMS is consultant in social work to the interdisciplinary training program, Eunice Kennedy Shriver Center, at the Fernald State School of Massachusetts. She was senior social worker and coordinator of social work at Brooklyn Jewish Hospital and before that served at the London Community Mental Health Service. She is author of *Mental Retardation and its Social Dimensions* (1971) and of numerous other publications on social work and children.

ALTA lives in Berkeley, California. She is the author of *Freedom's in Sight* and *Letters to Women*.

JUDITH M. BARDWICK is Assistant Professor of Psychology at the University of Michigan. She is the author of *The Psychology of Women: A Study of Bio-Cultural Conflict* (1971).

PAULINE B. BART holds a joint appointment as Assistant Professor of Sociology in Psychiatry at the University of Illinois Medical Center and as Assistant Professor of Sociology at the Chicago Circle Campus of the University of Illinois. She is the author of numerous studies on the sociology of psychiatry.

JESSIE BERNARD is Research Scholar in Sociology at Pennsylvania State University. Her most recent publications are *Women and the Public Interest: An Essay on Policy and Protest* (1971) and *The Future of Marriage* (1971). Among her many other publications, those relating most directly to women are *American Family Behavior* (1942), *Remarriage* (1956), *Dating, Mating, and Marriage* (1958), *Academic Women* (1964), *Marriage and Family among Negroes* (1966), and *The Sex Game* (1968).

PHYLLIS CHESLER is Assistant Professor of Psychology and Coordinator of the Female Studies Workshop at Richmond College of the City University of New York. Her articles have appeared in *Science, The Radical Therapist, The Village Voice*, and in professional publications. She is the author of a forthcoming book on women and the mental health professions.

NANCY CHODOROW is a graduate student and teaching assistant in the Department of Sociology at Brandeis University. A 1966 graduate of Radcliffe College, Harvard University, she is a member of Bread and Roses and Boston Area Women Social Scientists.

ANSELMA DELL'OLIO is Director and founder of the New Feminist Repertory Theatre and a member of the Advisory Council of the National Organization for Women (NOW).

ELIZABETH DOUVAN is Professor of Psychology at the University of Michigan and the author of *The Adolescent Experience* (with Joseph Adelson, 1966) and *Adolescent Development* (with Martin Gold, 1969).

SHULAMITH FIRESTONE was co-editor of *Notes from the Second Year* and has been an active member of the women's movement in New York City. She is the author of *The Dialectic of Sex: The Case for Feminist Revolution* (1970).

DORIS B. GOLD is a freelance writer and editor and has been an active community service volunteer on Long Island, New York. She taught English at the State University of New York (Farmingdale) and is the editor of a magazine, *The Young Judaean*, for children.

VIVIAN GORNICK is a staff writer for *The Village Voice* in New York City. She taught English at Hunter College of the City University of New York and at the State University of New York at Stonybrook.

LUCY KOMISAR is a journalist whose work has appeared in *New York Magazine, The Saturday Review, Washington Monthly,* and *The Mississippi Free Press.* She was a reporter and producer for WBAI radio, Special Assistant in the New York City Human Resources Administration, and Vice President for Public Relations of the National Organization for Women (NOW).

MYRNA LAMB'S musical, *Mod Donna,* produced by Joseph Papp, was presented at the New York Shakespeare Festival in 1970. Her feminist plays, notably *But What Have You Done for Me Lately?* and *The Serving Girl and the Lady,* have been performed at Off-Broadway theatres, on television here and abroad, and at universities across the country.

RUBY R. LEAVITT is Assistant Professor of Social Sciences at Manhattan Community College in New York City. She is the author of *The Puerto Ricans: Culture Change and Language Deviance* (1971).

BARBARA LOVE is an editor and writer with a special interest in women and the media. She lives and works in New York City.

WENDY MARTIN is Assistant Professor of English, Queens College, City University of New York. Her studies of American literature have appeared in *Eighteenth Century Studies* and in *William and Mary Quarterly*. She is presently preparing a source book on the American feminist movement from colonial times to the present.

KATE MILLETT is the author of *Sexual Politics* (1970). While writing *Sexual Politics*, she taught philosophy and literature at Barnard College. She is at present Lecturer in the Department of Sociology at Bryn Mawr College, and active in the women's movement in New York City.

BARBARA K. MORAN is an editor of *Woman's Day Magazine*, where she has written on women's rights.

LINDA NOCHLIN is Professor of Art History, Vassar College. She is the author of *Realism and Tradition in Art* (1966) and *Impressionism and Post-Impressionism* (1966). Her articles have appeared in *Art News, Art Bulletin*, and professional journals.

CYNTHIA OZICK is the author of the novel *Trust* (1966) and of *The Pagan Rabbi and Other Stories* (1971). Her fiction, criticism, reviews, essays, poetry, and translations have appeared in *Commentary, Hudson Review, Midstream*, and other periodicals.

CHRISTINE PIERCE is a Fellow in Law and Philosophy at Harvard University and Assistant Professor of Philosophy at the State University of New York at Oswego.

"A REDSTOCKING SISTER" is the name taken by a woman who holds that pride of authorship must not interfere with the goals of sisterhood and social change.

LIZ SCHNEIDER is a law student at New York University and a planner of the Vera Institute of Justice Project on Women in the Criminal Justice System. She studied political sociology at the London School of Economics and is active in the women's rights and legal education reform movements in New York City.

ELAINE SHOWALTER is an Assistant Professor of English at Douglass College, New Brunswick, New Jersey, with a special interest in Victorian literature and women in the nineteenth century.

ALIX SHULMAN is a writer whose feminist stories and essays have appeared in *Aphra, Up From Under*, and in *Women: A Journal of Liberation*. She is the author of four books for children, of a biography, *To the Barricades: The Anarchist Life of Emma Goldman* (1971) and of a novel (in press).

UNA STANNARD is the author of a feminist novel, *The New Pamela* (1969), and of numerous studies of sex and society including "The Male Maternal Instinct" (*Trans-Action*, November, 1970) and "Clothing and Sexuality" (*Sexual Behavior*, April, 1971). She was Assistant Professor of English at the University of California, Berkeley, from 1959 to 1965.

CATHERINE R. STIMPSON is Assistant Professor of English at Barnard College in New York City. She is the author of *J.R.R. Tolkein* (1969).

ETHEL STRAINCHAMPS is a freelance writer, editor and lexicographer. Her articles have appeared in *Harper's, Saturday Review,* and other magazines. She is the author (with Porter Perrin) of *Index to English* (in press).

MARJORIE B. U'REN taught English at Stanford University from 1968 to 1970 and is now completing her doctorate in English at the University of California at Berkeley. She is a member of the National Organization for Women (NOW).

NAOMI WEISSTEIN is Associate Professor of Psychology at Loyola University in Chicago, Illinois. She is the author of numerous scientific papers on perception, cognition, information science, memory, and the psychology of differences between men and women. She is also a member of The Chicago Women's Liberation Rock Band and a student of Karate.

ROSLYN S. WILLETT is president of Roslyn Willett Associates, consultants in marketing, communications, and food services in New York. She has worked in "a man's world," as an editor of McGraw-Hill, editor of a number of magazines, and executive officer in charge of technical service and development for food products at Stein, Hall & Company.

Contents

INTRODUCTION

Vivian Gornick and
Barbara K. Moran

The political nature of woman's condition has only rarely been recognized and never fully understood. Woman has lived, almost always, as the subordinate member of the species, defined as biologically and physically limited—to be given, at best, a place of protection or of benign neglect. This relationship of women to men has been readily accepted by civilization after civilization as one whose inherent justice has been decreed, not by the rough approximations of the laws of man, but rather by the profounder exactitude of the laws of nature; a relationship having nothing, really, to do with the evolutionary dictates of political or cultural decisions, but rather to do with the fulfillment of a logic determined by the cosmological order of things.

The perception of the categorical inferiority of one group of humans by another group of humans is as old as recorded time, and in each instance of its occurrence it is described as "natural," as being in accordance with the cosmic will of things. The ancients said it was "natural" for slaves to be slaves and for free citizens to be free citizens. The nobility of the middle ages claimed "natural" or divine right for the rule of royalty and the subsequently subhuman status of serfs. In modern times white men have claimed that the subjugation of blacks is merely proof that whites rule by virtue of their "natural" superiority. And, unfailingly, in each and every instance, when those who occupy the inferior space on the board begin the long push upward toward the announcement of their full humanity, the hue and cry ensuing from those in the position of thoughtless and essentially unearned superiority is that the "natural" order of things is being challenged—and surely the earth must open and the heavens will fall if things are permitted to go on much longer like this.

Woman is just about the last category of human on earth to challenge civilized life for her humanity. Perhaps this is only "natural." Certainly she has been more totally invisible in the history of human life than any other category of person; therefore, why should she not be the last to surface in the centuries' long move toward full egalitarianism? Why should she not be the last to stand up and say: "You who rule the earth and everything that is on it, I am as human as you are. I need exactly what you need. I suffer from the deprivation of that initial *recognition* even as you would suffer from it should you find yourself where I am now." It is very understandable that she should have taken so very long to come center-front and make her little speech. Certainly there is good reason why she herself, as well as man, her master, should have had serious doubts about the actual nature of her being. Certainly there is nothing in the great structural myth of our common life to indicate that woman is indeed fully human. For in the tale of the creation it is stated clearly that God made the earth, the elements, the animals, the vegetables, and then—as the final, fulfilling justification for the entire creation—he made man. It was only after he made man that he realized he had given him nothing to reproduce himself with—and then he made woman.

In every real, as well as metaphorical, sense, woman was absent at the creation. The great biblical tale recording man's growing consciousness was created by men, to tell the story of men, to other men, about the world in which men grow and discover themselves and come to power by virtue of their particular perceptions of reality. Nowhere in all this tale is woman present. Nowhere in the subsequent structures of law, morality, and religion, in the systems of science, philosophy, and aesthetics, in the developing expressiveness of the arts that mark man's struggle to identify himself is woman's presence or being or perception of reality fully felt. As man lives his life, observing it as he goes, he is substantially creating it; at this creation woman is consistently absent.

The powerful inequities inherent in this state of affairs have never gone completely unacknowledged by those in authority. That women—like blacks and other deprived categories of humans—existed and were growing more and more restive as modern civilization progressed was certainly duly noted within a specific context. It was always The Woman Question—just as it was always The Negro Problem and, before that, The Labor Problem. The implications of that euphemism being: "Yes, no doubt about it. There's a little problem there. We simply must get around to it one of these days. Throw them a bone or we may have a bit of a mess on our hands. But don't worry. The company's in no real danger." That mistake was a fatal one. The company *was* in danger: the bones were thrown too late and too small, and indeed they had a mess on their hands. In the exemplary case of labor, for instance: one day the workers not only struck, they organized. In a flash, they became the Labor Movement, and suddenly they themselves constituted Labor Power. Then all was out of the dark, and a significant truth beneath the relations, one to another, of labor and capital was visible; the true politicalness of their odd marriage came to the surface, and they were openly locked in the struggle for power that had lain so long beneath the naive surface of their common life.

In the 1960s The Negro Problem became racism; from there to Black Power was only a very short distance to travel. In 1970 The Woman Question became sexism, and the distance to travel to the open realization of the political nature of woman's condition in society is but very brief, indeed. For as it is in psychoanalysis, so it is in social-political life: to name the thing by its rightful name is instantly to begin to alter its power. To *recognize* the political nature of woman's condition, to see that it constitutes one-half of a binding relation of power to powerlessness, to see further that the power conceives of itself as predicated on the continuing life of the powerlessness, is vital to any understanding of women's liberation and of the women's liberation movement.

This movement, like the civil rights movement, began with libertarian, "educational" efforts aimed at overcoming inequities assumed to be at least partially the result of ignorance. Both movements began in an atmosphere of "freedom," but very quickly the participants began to understand a peculiar mechanism of their economic and political isolation. Not only were the white male keepers of the culture prepared to defend their privilege, they believed it was theirs by right. They had won it, and blacks and women had not. Evidently blacks were "culturally deprived" or even genetically inferior, and women were naturally unsuited for power or responsibility. These groups found that the "freedom" of the individualist ethic, while it, on the one hand, served them very little in breaching the wall of prejudice that prevented their sharing the society's rewards, on the other hand, left them foundering in guilt and self-reproach generated by the assumption that not only one's achievements and one's rewards but *even one's happiness* were the fruits of one's own effort.

Here Freudianism, though it promised freedom and seemed to challenge Puritanism, had been subverted to a privatism that served the status quo only too well. Unhappiness—whatever it's source—was hygienically quarantined as a form of sickness. "Misery is pathology" had taken its place beside the only slightly less vicious "anatomy is destiny."

As blacks and women explored their own weaknesses and failures, they found that their misery was not individual but common to their class. They began to see that beyond electoral politics, beyond even the politics of money, prestige, and real power, there were the politics of role and relationship, and more subtle, and perhaps more final, the politics of personality.

Women were last to reach this realization largely because women were so thoroughly isolated—cut off from society within the confines of the family, each dependent for security upon her own male, in aggressive competition with one another, and prevented from articulating many of her grievances by the tacit understanding that there is nothing more unpleasant, unworthy, and unattractive than an unhappy woman.

Nevertheless, the facts of her political disadvantage were clear. Without the protection of a man, she could only with difficulty achieve either the freedom or the security necessary for simple comfort. Income statistics revealed a strong order of priorities. Among full-time workers in 1966, white males were paid an average of $7,396, black males $4,777, white females $4,279, and black females $3,194. The black woman college graduate earned less than her white woman counterpart, who earned less than a black male high school graduate, who in turn earned less than a white male high school dropout. The average female head of family in 1966—when the U.S. Department of Labor defined $7,000 per year as a family income of "modest adequacy"—supported her family on a total yearly income of $4,010. The individual woman, struggling against *her* poverty, *her* failure, *her* helplessness, may have felt her situation as personal, but it was not.

Although there are thirty million women in the labor force and these women have exactly the same average education—12.2 years—as men, only 4 percent of federal employees in the highest grades and 2 percent of all business executives listed in Standard and Poor's Directory are women. Women comprise only 22 percent of faculty and professional staff of colleges and universities; 1 percent of federal judges; 1 percent of the U. S. Senate.

Because women are not represented in decision-making positions, law and public policy have never reflected their needs—nor, often, the needs of their children. Although some six million preschool children have working mothers, the total number of places for these children in day-care homes and centers, both public and private, is 640,000. Mothers who are the sole support of their children in many cases have to leave their children at home with no care at all. Even if places are available, their cost is not tax-deductible as a legitimate business expense. Abortion law as well has borne very little relation to the real situation of women. Five years ago, when one out of five women was reported to have undergone an abortion at some time during her life, abortion was virtually illegal in every state of the Union.

This book is a collection of essays gathered together for the purpose of demonstrating that woman's condition, here and now, is the result of a slowly formed, deeply entrenched, extraordinarily pervasive cultural (and therefore political) decision that—even in a generation when man has landed on the moon—woman shall remain a person defined not by the struggling development of her brain or her will or her spirit, but rather by her childbearing properties and her status as companion to men who make, and do, and rule the earth. Though she is a cherished object in her society, she shall remain as an object rather than becoming a subject; though she is exposed to education, wealth, and independence, apparently exactly as though she were an autonomous being and the equal of men, every genuine influence in her life is actually teaching her that she may educate herself only in order to be a more fit companion to her husband. She may use wealth but not make it; she may learn about independence only so that she can instill it in her male children, urge it forward in her husband, or admire its presence or despise its absence in her father. Her sense of these characteristics of adult life is sharply and distinctly *once removed:* it never really occurs to her that these necessities are there for her, as well as for those to whom she is attached. Everything in her existence, from early childhood on, is bent on convincing her that the reality of her being lies in bearing children and creating an atmosphere of support and nurturance for those who aggress upon the world with the intent of asserting the self, grasping power, taking responsibility—in other words, those who are living life as it has always been defined by human principle. Woman shall never be allowed to forget that her ego is passive and her will to independence lies fallow; that the urgent desire for self-assertion that spurs the development of intellect, genius, and complex capacities is, in her, a weak and flickering mechanism; that, in reality, woman is a differently made creature, one whose proportions are more *childlike,* if you will, less given to maturity than are the proportions of men.

This is the substance of sexism. This is the creation of thousands of years of thought and reinforced patterns of behavior so deeply imprinted, so utterly subscribed to by the great body of Western conviction, that they are taken for "natural" or "instinctive." Sexism has made of women a race of children, a class of human beings utterly deprived of self-hood, of autonomy, of confidence—worst of all, it has *made the false come true.* Women have so long shared acquiescently in society's patriarchal definition of them as beings composed of warmth, passivity, nurturance, inert egos, and developed intuition, that they have become the very thing itself and can no more see themselves in that mirror of life that declares independence, aggression, intellectual abstraction, and primary responsibility to be the silhouette of human development than can men. As a result, women have long suffered from an image of the self that paralyzes the will and short circuits the brain, that makes them deny the evidence of their senses and internalize self-doubt to a fearful degree. They have been raised to be the bearers of children by other bearers of children. They have been treated primarily as bearers of children by everyone they have ever known: parents, teachers, friends, lovers, busdrivers, landlords, employers, policemen, culture heroes. . . . Should they reveal strong wishes that their lives form themselves around an altogether other definition, they are branded unnatural.

Sexism, like any other cultural characteristic, lives through institutions—those that blindly perpetuate it and those that depend upon it for their very life. Altogether, the essays in this book form a detailed examination of these institutions—these attitudes, these responses, these ignorant convictions about woman's nature, and these religiously blind observations about her need—that, petrified by custom, have determined woman's unchanging position throughout the patriarchal centuries.

And the greatest of these is marriage. Woman's situation is harshest when she is alone. When she is safely under the protection of a male, her position is secondary, but it is secure. If she is fortunate, she is indulged, pampered, and happily relieved of the responsibilities (read *powers*) of their joint life. But even though marriage is her natural demesne and the model for all her other relationships, it does not appear to serve her as well as it does her husband. As Jessie Bernard's "The Paradox of the Happy Marriage" shows, despite the fact that marriage is more important to women than to men, despite the fact that women are willing to make more adjustments and sacrifices for it, they are less happy within it than their husbands. Furthermore, despite the advantages of relative security, married women are more likely to be depressed, phobic, and passive than single women; in fact, at least one-half of all married women were one of the three.

More astonishing than these findings themselves is the attitude of those who have made the findings. The mental ill-health of married women is considered normal and is actually encouraged by counsellors and analysts. A survey of clinicians reported by Bernard showed that they judged characteristics that would be considered pathological in the male normal in the female.

In marriage, as in the economy, woman's position is essentially subservient and supportive. Within the home and without, she performs the services of the society without sharing in its decisions or in the freedoms it grants other adults. Women perform the day-to-day tasks of maintaining humanity—preparing food, keeping up the home, caring for children, and giving emotional support. These functions to a large degree determine the social definition of femininity. "Feminine" women are supportive, nurturative, kind, gentle, selfless, and giving and—in the bargain—pliant and stupid enough never to resent their subservient position. In short, they have variously all the virtues of an ideal servant or an ideal companion. The qualities one might well wish for *oneself*—intelligence, bravery, ingenuity, creativity, or mastery—are neither necessary nor desirable.

Within marriage the relationship that is most clearly understood and assumed by society is the disposition of money, power, and services. Here the duties of both partners are clear. The superposition of the sentimental—the notion that the arrangement is primarily a mutual exchange of affection and sexuality—is very often confusing and frustrating to the participants since it beclouds the underpinnings of the relationship.

When sexual relationships conform to the disposition of power, as they do in patriarchal culture, then power rules sexuality. Eroticism is cathected to conquest and surrender. Confined to powerlessness and dependence, the woman glories in subservience, manipulates from beneath, and calculates a dominion of submission, sacrifice, and acceptance.

Myrna Lamb's "Two Plays on Love and Marriage" are paradigms of this sexual *realpolitik*. Her lady and maid servant are ruled by a lust beyond love. Though her male characters are often puzzled, even frightened, when the workings of the struggle for sexual mastery are made clear, her women—who engage in the struggle not for pleasure, but for survival—understand the exchange so well that they can move from one sexual role to the other with perfect virtuosity. They can adopt the submissiveness that draws and holds power or the dominance that power confers. Since she shares her husband's wealth, the lady, like her husband, can exact surrender, can elicit from the servant girl those sexual cries, "Anything, anything you want, anything to make you happy."

Playing counterpoint to Lamb's visionary view of the economics of sexuality is the deadly force of taped reality in Kate Millett's "Prostitution: A Quartet for Female Voices." Four women are speaking. Two are prostitutes (one black, one white) and two are movement women (both middle class and white). The subject here is the *overt* purchase of female flesh—and the revelations of anxiety, spiritual numbness, detached observation of the

disintegrating self, the humanist preoccupation with surrogate selves are amazing in that they produce a series of
unexpected and startling confusions of identity among the
four women that reveal clearly the deep emotional solidarity between the prostitutes and the movement women.

What is perhaps sadder and more frightening than any
other single aspect of woman's condition is the spectacle
of the women who have done exactly as they were told to
do: those who ardently believed in marriage and in motherhood as legitimate vessels in which to pour the substance
of their lives and became dutiful wives and passionately
attentive mothers. In "Depression in Middle-Aged Women"
sociologist Pauline Bart describes interviews with twenty
women interned in a Los Angeles hospital for depression,
suffering from what is known as the "empty-nest" syndrome. These are all middle-aged women whose children
have grown up, married, left home, whatever; they are
gone, that is all that counts, the children are gone. And
now what? Now, nothing. Now, a hospital full of "depression."

How do women become like that? How is it that so
shortsighted a view, so ignorant a sense of self, so hum-
bling an expectation should come to full life in so many,
many women? In "Ambivalence: The Socialization of
Women," Judith M. Bardwick and Elizabeth Douvan
demonstrate all too thoroughly how women are made.
They show that society dictates that boys must achieve
masculinity, whereas femininity is a given attribute until
puberty. Independence or dependence and aggression or
passivity are determined in the individual by social pressure, with independence and aggression permitted in the
male and gradually proscribed in the female. After puberty certain kinds of behavior—such as strong academic
competitiveness—are forbidden the female, for any qualities that might threaten the success of the heterosexual relationships that are to be prime in her life must be abandoned. Girls then enter a period of unhappy ambivalence
in which they fear both failure and success. The net result
is that although girls are not forbidden to enter masculine
fields of competition, they are psychologically ill-equipped
to succeed in them.

Furthermore, it is abundantly apparent to them that
the society values those qualities it encourages in males,
and derogates those qualities it instills in females. Thus,
women are made to feel forever inferior. What else on

this earth are they fitted for—nay, happy and *grateful* to nestle into—than marriage, that very same marriage their forty-eight-year-old mothers are urging them anxiously, but confusedly, not to rush into.

Cross-cultural studies suggest further that societies that distinguish strongly between "male" and "female" characteristics and value the latter highly perpetuate an unfortunate cycle in which the attainment of sexual identity is made equally difficult for males and females. As Nancy Chodorow points out in "Being and Doing," those cultures—chiefly the developed Western societies—where "assertive," "egoistic," male behavior is most strongly encouraged are also those where the change from childhood to male adulthood is most difficult because there are so few opportunities for male children to perform useful work. In these societies, child-rearing is directed toward "forming character" rather than teaching roles. The precise nature of the male child's eventual masculine role is unclear to him—although the overriding importance of his assuming a masculine role and stance is not. Since he is socialized almost entirely by the mother in her socially dictated "feminine" role, he is in the unhappy position of being able to attain masculine identity almost solely through efforts to distinguish himself from the person closest to him, with whom he might most naturally identify. His efforts commonly take the form of a rather primitive rejection of all that is "feminine" in women and in himself. Thus women are condemned to bringing up "sons whose sexual identity depends on devaluing femininity inside and outside themselves, and daughters who must accept this devalued position and resign themselves to producing more men who will perpetuate the system which devalues them."

When the proper socialization of the female does not "take," women may become lesbians. The question of the relation between lesbianism and feminism is of paramount importance, for it touches on one of the most complicated strands in the entire tapestry of sexism and the sex-role system: the question of full and open self-possession; the question of how and when and if women will be able to define themselves in whatever terms they themselves choose without suffering the consequences of being told they are not women if their sexual-emotional choices seem unorthodox, without feeling the need for self-denial in order to "pass for white"—which is how the lesbian actually lives, and how all women fundamentally live. In "Is Women's Liberation a Lesbian Plot?" Sidney Abbott and Barbara Love explore the connection between the woman's movement and homosexual liberation.

The power of mere experience to triumph over the stubborn determination of cultural stereotypes to flourish and reinforce themselves is as nothing. The truth of woman's life and of her actual experience is engulfed again and again by those institutions of our society, owned and operated by men, that act as a kind of policing force to keep her in line, to keep her believing that she is what men say she is, that she wants what men say she wants, that she knows only what men say she knows.

If feminist analysis is often flawed, ragged, or naive, this is precisely *because* it is so necessary. There is a whole universe of meaning to be rescued and redefined. The sexist clichés are so well-worn, so familiar—the unacknowledged cornerstone of so many articles of faith— that it takes more than simple evidence of error to demystify them. As Ethel Strainchamps shows in "Our Sexist Language," even our language, praised by philologists for its "masculinity," complicates any efforts at redefinition of woman's place by its implicit bias. It characterizes things feminine as diminished and diminutive, childish or childlike, and even at its clearest and most idealistic, reinforces the view of man and his activities as central and women and hers as peripheral and secondary. Even the scholarly disciplines are infected with sexism, which Jessie Bernard so aptly defines as

the unconscious, taken-for-granted, assumed, unquestioned, unexamined, unchallenged acceptance of the belief that the world as it looks to men is the only world, that the way of dealing with it which men have created is the only way, that the values which men have evolved are the only ones, that the way sex looks to men is the only way it can look to anyone, that what men think about what women are like is the only way to think about what women are like.[1]

In nearly every discipline, the assumptions and explanations that are made about women are mechanical and unempirical. When attention is turned to them, they are usually found to be flimsy and unworkable models. Unfortunately, attention is rarely turned to them. In general, our social scientists have happily enshrined the most simplistic of old husband's tales without ever a second glance. "The world as it looks to men" quite naturally has men at its center, and women and other foreigners at its periphery. Once women are viewed as separate, distinct, and "other," they are liable to redefinition at will, whim, or need.

In "Psychology Constructs the Female," psychologist Naomi Weisstein demonstrates that psychologists—like many other scientists—find what they want to find, what they *expect* to find. Dr. Weisstein describes in detail the faulty methods of research upon which so many of psychology's absolute dicta rest and shows that psychologists accept almost wholesale Freud's unempirical, socially determined notions about woman's nature as their starting point—and from there proceed to speculate as "experts" on woman's needs, conflicts, and inabilities to resolve the fundamental neurosis of her existence, that is, that she is not a man.

In "Patient and Patriarch," another psychologist, Phyllis Chesler, denounces the practice of psychotherapy as one of the major institutions—the prime one being marriage—whereby women are kept as children throughout their adult lives. The relationship between female patient and male analyst mirrors the stereotypical relationship of woman to man in patriarchal society—that of wife to husband or girl child to father. The patient's position is passive, subsidiary, and dependent, whereas her analyst's role is actively authoritative, expert, and protective. Not unexpectedly, the very psychology of the women patients studied conformed to the classic pattern of the psychology of subjugated or slave classes. Her psychiatrist treats her plight, however, as individual, discouraging action to change it, enforcing conformity to prevailing social expectations, and promoting adjustment and "understanding" rather than self-fulfillment.

Since woman is the sexual partner of the dominant class, she is expected to be beautiful, sexy, and above all, young. Una Stannard, in "The Mask of Beauty," argues that "woman's beauty is largely a sham, and women know it. That is why they obediently conform every time the fashion masters crack the whip. A woman conforms to all the whims of the cosmetic and fashion industries so that she will not be singled out from the mass of women, so that she will look like every other woman, and thus manage to pass as one of the fair sex." The inordinate emphasis on her physical beauty ends by making her a narcissist, a state which men from the ancients to Freud have accepted as natural—for women.

Higher status for women is not, as is so often asserted, dependent upon the economic or technological development of the culture. Many simpler and less developed cultures than ours have granted women higher status than Western society has and have, in fact, been generally more egalitarian. As Ruby R. Leavitt's "Women in Other Cultures" shows, Western colonialization introduced repressive patriarchal prejudices as it brought economic progress to Burma and parts of Malaysia and Africa. In imposing technological values, it also promulgated and often enforced Puritanical sexual taboos and the exclusion of women from their traditional economic and civil status. Leavitt's account of the gradual subjugation of African and Burmese women under Western rule leaves little doubt that any cultural force but virulent prejudice is at work.

Where skills and training cannot be denied women, male privilege is often guarded by rigid enforcement of a double standard. In nineteenth-century England, as Elaine Showalter documents in "Women Writers and the Double Standard," literary critics chose to consider even the greatest women writers as women first and writers second. They stigmatized what in a man might have been considered "sensitivity" as feminine weakness, and at the same time, attacked as unwomanly and immoral the "masculine" vigor of any woman writer who ventured beyond the spiritual confines of home and family. They refused women participation in the larger world of masculine affairs and then claimed that woman's scope as a writer was forever bounded by her lack of experience. When a woman's accomplishment was beyond question, as George Eliot's was, they attacked her on personal grounds as unwomanly and unnatural. This "Ovarian Theory of Literature" still pertains today, as Cynthia Ozick shows in "Women and Creativity: The Demise of the Dancing Dog." In a year spent teaching undergraduates in a prominent university, Miss Ozick found her male and female students alike in their "illiteracy, undereducation, ignorance and prejudice"—and in their unshakable conviction that the writing, and even the minds, "of men and women are entirely unlike."

Women painters, like women writers, have been more harshly judged and more quickly consigned to the storage rooms of history than their male counterparts. In "Why Are There No Great Women Artists?" Linda Nochlin shows that women artists have not only been given less serious attention, but have been faced with serious handicaps that have been largely disregarded by critics and scholars. Denied special education, unable to avail themselves of such necessary conventions as nude models, women were isolated from the mainstream of artistic production and then criticized for the "triviality" of the work they produced in effective exile.

Women professionals in the modern working world are similarly judged by a harsh double standard. If they are not entirely ignored, Roslyn Willett's "Working in 'A Man's World'" shows, they are subject to closer scrutiny and harsher criticism than their male colleagues. They must prove that they are different from and better than the "average" female, but must never threaten their male coworkers by surpassing them. They must be feminine in appearance and passive, submissive, and sympathetic in situations that require aggressiveness and cunning. They must demonstrate their femininity, but never use it. They are excluded from business clubs and inner councils and then excluded from responsibility because they cannot be privy to these councils. Amid the general assumption that they are the more emotional and weaker sex, they are expected to endure continual belittlement and unthinking insult with objectivity and restraint beyond the reach of the ordinary mortal.

Popular literature, advertising, children's literature, and even textbooks reinforce bias against women. When Marjorie U'Ren surveyed "The Image of Woman in Textbooks" used by the California school system, she found that 75 percent of the main characters in the stories were male. In all, only 20 percent of the space was devoted to females. Male and female children were presented very differently. Boys were shown as independent and adventurous, seeking and gaining real rewards in the real world. Little girls, on the other hand, were confined by their creators to the close keep of home and family; their rewards were intangible.

In advertising, where popular fantasy reigns most freely, the picture of women is even more fanciful. Adorable in her not-very-bright submissiveness, charming in her childlike delight in shiny floors, even forgivable in her spiteful competition for the whitest, brightest wash, Madison Avenue's girl-next-door is all the American male could wish for—unless, by some miscarriage, he should fancy human companionship. In "The Image of Woman in Advertising," Lucy Komisar takes on the image-makers, lays many a White Knight to rest, and concludes in the process that advertising's blatant distortions can serve to raise rather than obscure woman's consciousness of her low status.

In our literature as well, women's predicament conforms to masculine fantasy. Throughout the American novel, as Wendy Martin shows in "Seduced and Abandoned in the New World," women of independent thought and action are severely punished—they either die or are cast out or go mad—while women who submit are rewarded as the safeguarded objects of matrimonial protection.

Even in those special professions where they dominate, social prejudice against women has its effect. For whatever women touch is instantly considered "feminine" and is kept trivial by social pressure and the denigration of its being "woman's work." Thus, when these professions are ineffective by virtue of being held in check by male hands and by general social neglect, the stereotypes of female ineptness are further reinforced. In "The Compassion Trap," Margaret Adams discusses the frustrations and limitations that are imposed upon social work by virtue of its being considered woman's work. As Doris Gold's "Women and Voluntarism" shows, voluntarism is the very model of women's work. Volunteers are almost without exception women; they work without pay or status and very often become volunteers rather than paid workers in order to avoid competing with their husbands or casting any shadow on their husband's status. The work they do is an important social subsidy that does not appear on the balance sheets and provides for a part of the economy that is probably, of all sectors, worst provided for by free enterprise. They serve the young, the poor, the aged, and the sick. Unfortunately, in serving them without pay, they may serve them ill. Volunteer work gets very little respect, and volunteers are unable to effect even the most unimportant changes in policy. Then, too, as Margaret Adams argues, women are often reluctant to take up the cudgels on behalf of their clients because they accept the notion that aggressiveness is unfeminine and improper.

It is difficult to look upon this recital of female subjugation and not feel that clearly this cannot be some accidental societal formation; clearly, there is some grand patriarchal scheme here; clearly, woman in modern times fulfills the same purpose as the slave in ancient Greece: to perform all those odious and necessary tasks and services so that Greek male democrats could pursue the active and reflective life that was their unparalleled civilization; clearly, the ritualized sexual roles into which men and women are guided from birth serve to sacrifice women's lives to a notion of civilization that men decide upon and profit by.

The accomplishment of women's liberation represents in some sense the end point of the individualist ethic—freedom and self-determination for the last group of adults to whom it has been denied. This is a frightening prospect for many. To them it represents the disappearance of the last ascribed rather than earned position, the demise of the family, and the destruction of the last haven from competitiveness—indeed, the last reservoir of amity—in the society. When women are free, what will become of the special virtues with which they have been entrusted? Where will we find gentleness, motherliness, supportiveness, the nurturative arts, womanly selflessness? The answer is simply, "We must each find them in ourselves." These virtues are too important to our happiness and our survival to be the sole responsibility of a powerless underclass.

Women in this country do not want to be free for ruthless competition. They want to be freed from private curatorship of the happiness of individuals—too often victims themselves—to joint trusteeship of the common good. They want a place in public life for the values they have been forced to cherish in private for too long. They want an end to the political distribution of character traits. They want an end to the perverted morality that says one sex must be weak and good and the other strong, selfish, and violent.

Women must yet fight a bitter fight for justice, as those in power never relinquish power willingly: the specter of powerlessness is a real and vivid terror for those who have never known the condition. And yet it is true that men suffer from the oppression of women nearly every bit as much as women do, for not only the *death* of another, but also the denial of his humanity, diminishes us. If one is suppressed and the other suppressing, the behavior of both is circumscribed (it was Abraham Lincoln who said: "If you want to keep a man down in the dirt, you've got to get right down there with him"). In order to oppress women, men must act as oppressors. To act as an oppressor is to have only certain forms of behavior open to you. To have only certain forms of behavior open to you, it is necessary to suppress or destroy any impulses that cannot be expressed within those prescribed forms of behavior. To have certain parts of the self, therefore, cut off from the release and growth of full expression is, in a sense, to be wounded, to be deprived of the use of one's own properties.

Two of the most moving essays in this collection are Shulamith Firestone's "On American Feminism" and Catharine Stimpson's "Thy Neighbor's Wife, Thy Neighbor's Servants." Coming at it from two very different angles—one concentrating on the relation between black civil rights and the women's movement, the other analyzing the hundred-year-old elements of American feminism, then and now—both writers evoke with splendid feeling the life and times of the great nineteenth-century feminists, and there on the page before us are the living voices of Lucretia Mott, Elizabeth Cady Stanton, and Susan B. Anthony. The thrill of recognition is profound—as they speak in *exactly* our accents—but the internal excitement that mounts, following in its wake, is tinged with fear and sickness. For here we are in 1971 saying exactly what they were saying (for their radicalism was right down to the bone: with no equivocation they knew the heart of the matter was marriage and the family and woman's fixed and central role in those institutions) and saying it as though for the very first time; saying it as though those women had never lived and fought and died, having given their youth, their age, their spiritual entirety to the cause of justice for women; saying it because their long struggle has been erased from the living record of this country's history so that sixty-year-old women as well as eighteen-year-old girls have to be told who the Grimké sisters were. One could weep with the shame and frustration of it, with the history of ourselves that we have lost, with the cumulative power that might have been ours. But we can also hear the reassuring voices of those great ladies who showed such extraordinary grace under pressure, telling us not to regret the lost years: We are here now, and the future is surely ours.

NOTE

1. Jessie Bernard, unpublished letter to *Playboy* magazine.

I:

BEAUTY, LOVE AND MARRIAGE: THE MYTH AND THE REALITY

1

"PRETTY"

Alta

You know, Alta, your roommate
may be pretty, but you have that inner
beauty that counts!—BARRY, 1960

and here we are again, folks, a table of women, 7 of us,
and the first thing i do to assess my coworkers on *Tooth
&Nail* is look around at all of you to see who is prettier
than i. my lover used to say how i was prettier than the
other women in my women's liberation group and i would
feel better while feeling worse and wish it weren't even a
consideration in anybody's mind, including mine, because
it drives me crazy and actually prevents me from enjoying
social situations. like i used to hate to go to martha's
house because she is, and i quote, perfectly beautiful. she
doesn't even bite her nails. how can i compete with that/
munch, munch. then i got to know her and the bitterness
is real, cannot be measured; that we really like each other
and could have been friends all that awful lonely year but
i was afraid to be around her and have him look at my
lousy skin and big nose and bitten nails next to her perfect
complexion and little nose and nice nails. how could he
possibly want me more than her? everything becomes a
handicap: every time i take a pill i think jesus no man
loves a sick wife (to quote mother). men don't make
passes at girls who wear glasses. blondes have more fun.
fat ass. big boobs, clear skin. sheeit.

then i got so that i could count on being the second
prettiest woman in any given situation! sitting at the
mediterraneum i would always be able to find one woman
who was prettier and usually not more than one. at any
given party i could always see one woman who was
prettier and feel prettier than the rest. even on busses.
even in classes. doctors offices, restaurants. dances. no
doubt it could have carried over to skating rinks, art

shows, family reunions, funerals. we tried grading our
looks one time. i gave myself 90 and my therapist asked
what would john rate you and i said lower and can you
imagine the bottom of that horrible fear/ that each year i
could only become more afraid because now i've nursed 2
children; now my throat is getting creapy (or whatever it's
called); & my thighs will never again be size 10 unless i
get emaciated. a horrible fear that drove me to a plastic
surgeon who said all he could do with my big nose was
hook it, drive me to try on 7 different bras to nurse with
so my boobs wouldn't hang low (do your boobs hang low?
do they wobble to and fro?), drove me to dermatologists
to smooth out my skin, drove me to cover my face with
makeup, eyeliner, lipstick, mascara. drove me to curl and
bleach my hair, drove me to diet, drove me to sit with my
fists clenched so no one could see my nails. tell me i'm not
oppressed. ask me what i want. tell me you don't like my
methods. listen to my life and see that it has been intolerable and leave me the fuck alone.

2

TWO PLAYS ON LOVE AND MARRIAGE

Myrna Lamb

These two powerful short plays by Myrna Lamb, while continuing to explore the ravages worked on our humanity by a patriarchal system (like the rest of *Scyklon Z*),[1] are especially interesting in their differences. Each shows a complementary but sharply different facet of the author's temperament.

At first glance *The Serving Girl and the Lady* seems to be yet another confirmation of that recurring (and cherished) male canard that women are their own worst enemies. A closer look shows that while women do indeed inflict great harm on one another, this is merely another example of the kind of divisiveness and self-destruction that members of most oppressed groups practice upon each other.

There are many reasons for this, not the least of which is that it is safer to express one's hostilities toward one's own kind than to strike at the powerful master class. Thus, the poor most often steal from and kill one another,

From *Mod Donna, Scyklon Z: Plays of Women's Liberation* (New York: Pathfinder Press, 1969). © 1969 by Myrna Lamb. Caution: All rights for both professional and amateur performances are strictly reserved, and no portion of these plays may be performed without written authorization. Enquiries should be directed to Howard Rosenstone, William Morris Agency, Inc., 1350 Avenue of the Americas, N.Y., N.Y. 10019.

and so do American blacks. Imbued from their earliest years with the belief in their own inferiority and unworthiness, they re-create a form of pecking order or caste system that pitifully but cruelly mirrors the archetype.

And so we arrive at the mistress–maid or lady–serving girl relationship. Because their husbands are defined and divided by their different economic class memberships, it is often assumed that wives correspond to the same general categories and that their relationships with one another can be analyzed in the same way. But I believe this is a superficial assumption, and closer scrutiny of the women's lives reveals a vastly more complex network of motivating forces.

In *The Second Sex* Simone de Beauvoir writes, "a housewife has more intimate relations with her maid than any man—unless he be homosexual—ever has with his valet or chauffeur; they exchange confidences, at times they are accomplices; but there exists also a hostile rivalry between them, for the mistress, while avoiding the actual work, wishes to have responsibility and credit for it; she wants to be thought irreplaceable, indispensable."[2] And although the housewife wants to appear vital and unique to the whole family, it is above all the male, the head of the household, whom she wishes to impress. Men are divided by, and compete for, money. It is money that gives them their social standing in the world. Women only *acquire* their husband's status. Their money and social standing are derived from the man they belong to. Their emotional *and* their economic well-being and security depend on him. Thus, my belief that women are divided by, and compete for, men.

In the light of these observations, it is interesting that a frequent comment about *The Serving Girl and the Lady* has been: "It was difficult to figure out which one was the lady and which the serving girl." In fact, the differences between them are not great. If they were to be divorced and remarried to each other's husband, the serving girl would become the lady and vice versa, while the husbands' roles would not change at all. Marriage does not generally affect a man's *financial* or *social* status in the eyes of the world—at least not automatically as with women.

The play has a fascinating blend of forms that rise quickly to an arresting climax and end with a punch in the stomach. The opening section of the play takes the shape of counterpoint solos or monologues, punctuated by a long, memorable aria belonging to the serving girl. To continue the operatic analogy, the voices then turn to a dialogue-recitatif confrontation which is resolved with the triumph of the male through the lady, who relishes her "victory" with seductive, but bone-chilling repetition.

A frequently heard comment about Myrna Lamb's work, and about this play in particular, is that it is written in a highly complex verbal shorthand—that her plays are in fact full-length works compressed into a time slot of well under a half-hour. In truth, the shortest of Lamb's one-act plays contains more dramatic meat than most three-act plays. However, I do not believe that this is from a lack of desire to develop the play's theme. In *The Serving Girl and the Lady,* Lamb offers us a ritual which has been reenacted countless times throughout (patriarchal) history around the world; she offers us this ritual in its essence. She spares us the slow torture of a two-hour reenactment of our habitual follies and in return asks that we follow her fast, deft strokes carefully. Her language is complex because her subject is complex. But just pay attention: since we've all been through this routine so many times before, close attention will reveal that the labyrinth of her experience is more startlingly familiar to us than we might initially have thought.

But What Have You Done for Me Lately, while further illustrating the fabric of female oppression and equally charged with dramatic tension and unforgettable images, shows us the author's skill from yet another vantage point.

In this play the author is working with two dramatic conventions which present especially dangerous terrain for the playwright: role reversal and agit-prop. Role reversal has, of course, been with us a long time: but I would venture to say that rarely has it been used more skillfully, or to greater effect, than here. A lawmaker, pregnant against his will, is given the legitimate opportunity to voice every imaginable feminist argument in favor of abortion. A female surgeon, perpetrator of the unwanted pregnancy, is offered the equally legitimate opportunity to give voice to every conceivable paternalistic and pseudohumanist rebuttal. The play is undeniably political, unceasingly and unabashedly feminist; the speeches are long and often strident in tone; it is difficult to stage as there is little movement directly called for in the script. Yet during

every performance (and there have been hundreds before
every kind of audience and under every conceivable condition, favorable and unfavorable) presented by the New
Feminist Repertory,[3] attention was riveted upon the
stage throughout the twenty-odd minutes running time.
Clenched fists, gnawed knuckles, heads cocked to catch
every word, these were a common sight. After every
performance there was inevitably a crush of people back-
stage, some with eyes filled with tears, others merely
shaken individuals who only wanted to express a few
halting words of gratitude—and to share their intense involvement.

What I am trying to say is that the theatre of agitation
and propaganda, normally a didactic and boring dramatic
form to be avoided like the plague, has here been raised
to a high artistic level. This is the author's achievement.
Without ever having received a fully financed production
But What Have You Done for Me Lately has acquired a
widespread popularity and an international reputation; it is
the most requested piece in the New Feminist Repertory.
It is already an underground classic and will undoubtedly
confirm its position overground as well. Many people have
returned to see it again and again.

As an actress, I am hard put to think of a role I would
rather perform than the female surgeon. Both the male
and the female roles are *tours de force* which present a
challenge to an actor and an actress difficult to equal in
one-act plays. On the other hand, *The Serving Girl and
the Lady* presents two actresses with a challenge possibly
unparalleled in one-act plays, with the brilliant exception
of Strindberg's *The Stronger*, with which *The Serving Girl
and the Lady* easily ranks.

Both plays were first produced, together with a third
play from *Scyklon Z, In the Shadow of the Crematoria,*
by the New Feminist Repertory Theatre in March-April
1969. That Myrna Lamb had to await the existence of a
feminist theatre in order to be produced is a shameful
indictment of our society—and especially of our complacently male-chauvinist theatrical establishment. For years
now we have been subjected to the seasonal laments over
the woeful state of "The Fabulous Invalid." And for many
of those years, a playwright of the stature of Myrna Lamb
was given short shrift. I shudder to think that but for the
renaissance of the feminist movement she (and who
knows how many others there might be like her) might

never have been produced. Fortunately, that is not the case. Nor is it any longer true that she has only been produced by a feminist theatre company. Of course, I have mixed feelings about this, because I would have liked to retain exclusive rights to produce every play she might care to write. Although I retain proprietary feelings about Lamb's work and am not a little jealous that it has not always been possible to produce each one "first," I am naturally delighted and gratified that the American theatre is finally, if slowly, coming of age.

Anselma Dell 'Olio
Director, New Feminist Repertory Theatre

NOTES

1. *Scyklon Z* is the collective title of a larger cycle of one-act plays by Myrna Lamb, designed to be performed together.
2. Simone de Beauvoir, *The Second Sex* (New York: Bantam, 1961).
3. The New Feminist Repertory Theatre made its debut in New York City in March–April 1969 at the Martinique Theatre.

BUT WHAT HAVE YOU
DONE FOR ME LATELY

TIME: whenever.
PLACE: a space, silent, encapsulated. A man lies with his head angled up and center stage, feet obliquely toward audience. His couching, which is by all means psychiatric in flavor, should also be astronautic and should incline him acutely so that he almost looks as though he is about to be launched. An almost perpendicular slantboard comes to mind or a simple sliding pond or seesaw.

There is a simple table or desk, angled away from man, and a chair placed toward desk that will keep the occupant's back toward man in orthodox (approximate) psychiatric practice, but will give profile or three-quarter view to audience.

At rise man in business suit is situated as delineated. Woman in simple smock (suggestive of surgical smock) comes on upstage and crosses without looking at man. He does not see her. She sits silently. Some time elapses. A soldier, in green beret outfit, complete with M-1 rifle, comes to stage center. He faces audience.

MAN: Where am I? What have you done to me? Where am I? What have you done to me? Where am I? What have you done to me?
    (*Soldier stands at attention.*)
WOMAN (*her voice dehumanized by amplification*): Don't worry. Don't worry. We have not done that to you.
MAN: That? What do you mean, "that"?
WOMAN: We have not taken anything.
MAN: Oh. (*Pause.*) But where am I? What have you done to me?
WOMAN: Are you in pain?
MAN: Yes. I think I am in pain.
WOMAN: Don't you know?
MAN: I haven't been able to consider it fully. The whole

procedure . . . strange room—anesthetic—nurses? Sisters in some order?

WOMAN: Nurses. Sisters. In some order. Yes, that would cover it. Yes, anesthetic.

MAN: Anesthetic.

WOMAN: Yes. We didn't want you thrashing about. Or suffering psychic stress. Yet.

(*Soldier executes left turn and salute.*)

MAN: I am suffering abominable psychic stress now.

(*Soldier stands at attention through next speeches.*)

WOMAN: Yes, I know. But the physical procedure is at an end. You are in remarkably good health. Arteries. Heart. Intestinal tone. Very good. Good lungs too. Very good. I suppose that's due to the electronically conditioned air and the frequent sojourns to unspoiled garden spots of nature.

MAN: What has that to do with it? Was I too healthy? Was that it? Did some secret-society deity decide I should be given a handicap to even up the race?

WOMAN: Well, that is an interesting conjecture.

MAN: It can't be! That I was considered too healthy? That's preposterous.

WOMAN: Yes, it is. You couldn't really have been too healthy.

MAN: Then . . . what have you done? Was there a handicap?

(*Left turn and salute by Soldier.*)

WOMAN: To even up the race. I believe that was your phrase. I approve. Very compressed. Very dense. The race that we run . . . the race of man, as we shorthandedly express it . . . and somewhere in my memory, a line about the race going to the swift . . . yes, and then the association with handicap . . . a sporting chance for the less swift.

MAN: Handicap . . . some kind of tumor . . . some kind of cancer . . .

(*Young woman hereafter referred to as Girl crawls onstage.*)

Is that it? What have you done to me?

WOMAN: No, no. Calm yourself. No cancer. No tumor. Not parasitic death, my friend. Parasitic life.

MAN: I don't understand you. What have you done to me? Parasitic life? (*Pause.*) Parasitic life. Pseudoscientific claptrap. Parasitic life. Witchdoctor mumbo-jumbo.

Parasitic life. Wait a moment. There is a meaning to
that phrase. It can't apply to me—not to me—not—
    *(Girl pulls on Soldier's leg. She is still in crawling
position. Soldier stands at rigid attention throughout
next speeches with no obvious awareness of Girl. She
rises and approaches him, reaching out to him.)*

WOMAN: Yes, it can apply to you. We have given you an
impregnated uterus. Implanted. Abdominal cavity. Yours.
Connections to major blood vessels were brought in very
quickly. As a matter of fact, it was destined for you. It
has achieved its destiny.

MAN: I don't believe it. I can't believe this nightmare.

WOMAN: Well, that is how many people feel upon learning
these things. Of course, most of those people have been
considered female. That made a difference, supposedly.
We've managed to attach a bit of ovary to the uterus. I
don't think it will do any real good, but I will give you a
course of hormonal and glandular products to maintain
the pregnancy.

MAN: Maintain the pregnancy, indeed! How dare you
make that statement to me!
    *(Using outreaching arm of Girl and foot leverage,
Soldier flips her over and throws her to floor.)*

WOMAN: I dare. There is a human life involved, after all.

MAN: There is a human life involved? You insane creatures, I'm fully aware that there is a human life involved.
My human life. My human life that you have decided to
play with for your own despicable purposes, whatever
they are.

WOMAN: Do you think you are in the proper frame of
mind to judge? My purposes?
    *(Soldier does pushups with sexual-soldier connota-
tions over outstretched body of Girl.)*
Your ultimate acceptance of what you now so vocifer-
ously reject? The relative importance of your mature
and realized life and the incipient potential of the life
you carry within you? Your life is certainly involved.
But perhaps your life is subsidiary to the life of this
barely begun creature which you would seek to deny
representation.

MAN: Why should I give this . . . this thing representation?
    *(Soldier rises and kicks Girl aside. Walks to rifle.
Walks around Girl, pacing, right shoulder arms.)*
It is nothing to me. I am not responsible for it or where
it is nor do I wish to be. I have a life, an important life.

I have work, important work, work, I might add, that
has more than incidental benefit to the entire population
of this world—and this—this mushroom which you have
visited upon me—in your madness—has no rights, no
life, no importance to anyone, certainly not to the
world. It has nothing. It has no existence. A little group
of cells. A tumor. A parasite. This has been foisted upon
me and then I am told that I owe it primary rights to
life, that my rights are subsidiary! That is insanity! I do
not want this thing in my body. It does not belong there.
I want it removed. Immediately. Safely.

WOMAN: Yes, I understand how you feel. But how would
it be if every pregnancy brought about in error or ignorance or through some evil or malicious or even well-
meaning design were terminated because of the reluctance or the repugnance of the host? Surely the population of the world would be so effectively decimated as
to render wholly redundant the mechanisms of lebens-
raum, of national politics, of hunger as a weapon, of
greed as a motive, of war itself as a method.

(*Soldier lunges and stabs at the invisible enemy, accompanying movements with the appropriate battle
grunts and cries. There is hatred and despair in the
sounds.*)

Surely if all the unwilling human beings who found
motherhood forced upon them through poverty or
chance or misstep were to be given the right to choose
their lives above all else, the outpouring of acceptance
and joy upon the wanted progeny of desired and deliberate pregnancies would eliminate forever those qualities of aggression and deprivation that are so necessary
to the progress of society.

After all, you must realize there are so many women
who find themselves pregnant and unmarried, pregnant
and unprepared, with work that cannot bear interruption, with no desire to memorialize a casual sexual
episode with issue. So many human beings whose incidental fertility victimizes them superfluously in incidents
of rape and incestuous attack.

(*Following the lunges, stabs, and grunts, Soldier
slams the rifle against the stage in vertical butt
strokes.*)

So many creatures confounded by sexual desire or a
compelling need for warmth and attention who find

themselves penniless, ill, pitifully young and pregnant too.

(Finally Soldier simply stands, lifts rifle to shoulder.)

And so many women who with the approval of society, church and medicine have already produced more children than they can afford economically, psychically, physically. Surely you can see the overwhelming nature of the problem posed by the individual's desire to prevail as articulated by you at this moment. If one plea is valid, then they might all be. So you must learn to accept society's interest in the preservation of the fetus, within you, within all in your condition.

MAN: Do you know that I want to kill you? That is all I feel. The desire to kill you.

(Soldier points rifle at Girl's head.)

WOMAN: A common reaction. The impregnated often feel the desire to visit violence upon the impregnator. Or the maintainers of the pregnancy.

MAN: You are talking about women.

(Soldier spreads Girl's legs with butt of rifle. Nudges her body with rifle.)

Pregnancy, motherhood is natural to a woman. It is her portion in life. It is beneficial to her. It is the basic creative drive that man seeks to emulate with all his art and music and literature. It is natural for a woman to create life. It is not natural for me.

(Soldier kicks and rolls Girl's body in sharp rhythm corresponding with beginning of Woman's sentences in next speech so that Girl, in 3 movements, is turned from her back to her stomach to her back again. Soldier then turns away. Freezes.)

WOMAN: The dogma of beneficial motherhood has been handed down by men. If a woman spews out children, she will be sufficiently exhausted by the process never to attempt art, music, literature or politics. If she knows that that is all that is expected of her, if she feels that the fertility, impregnation, birth cycle validates her credentials as a female human being, she will be driven to this misuse of nature as a standard of her worth, as a measure of the comparative worthlessness of those who breed less successfully. That will occupy her sufficiently to keep her from competing successfully with male human beings on any other human basis.

MAN: You cannot dismiss natural as an inappropriate

term. My body cannot naturally accommodate a developing fetus. My body cannot naturally expel it at the proper moment.

WOMAN: Females cannot always naturally expel the infant at term.

(Soldier turns, rests butt of rifle on Girl's stomach, and presses. Girl pants.)

The pelvic span is a variable. Very often, the blood or milk of a natural mother is pure venom to her child. Nature is not necessarily natural or beneficial. We know that. We alter many of its processes in order to proceed with the exigencies of our civilizations. Many newly pregnant women recognize that the situation of egress is insufficient in their cases. In your case, there is a gross insufficiency. The Caesarian procedure is indicated.

MAN: But that is dangerous, terribly dangerous even to contemplate. I tell you I am terrified almost to the point of death.

WOMAN: Others have experienced the same sense of terror. Their kidneys are weak, or they have a rheumatic heart, or there is diabetes in the family. As I have told you, you are quite healthy. And you will have excellent care. You will share with others a lowered resistance to infection. But you will not go into labor and you will not risk a freak occurrence in which strong labor produces a suction through the large blood vessels that bring particles of placental detritus and hair and ultimate suffocation to the laboring woman's lungs. . . .

MAN: Your comparisons are obscene. My body isn't suitable for carrying a child. There isn't room.

(Soldier slams rifle between Girl's legs. Hard.)

WOMAN: Many female bodies are as unsuitable for childbearing as yours is.

(Soldier stands at attention again.)

Modern science has interceded with remedies. Your internal circumstance will be crowded. Not abnormal. Your intestines will be pushed to one side. Your ureters will be squeezed out of shape. Not abnormal. Your kidneys and bladder will be hard pressed. All within the realm of normality. Your skin will stretch, probably scar in some areas. Still not abnormal.

MAN: But I am a man.

WOMAN: Yes, to a degree. That is a trifle abnormal. But not insurmountable.

MAN: But why should anyone want to surmount the fact

of my being a man? Do you hate all men? Or just me?
And why me?

(*Soldier executes present arms maneuver.*)

WOMAN: At one time I hated all men.

MAN: I thought so.

WOMAN: I also hated you most particularly. I am not
ashamed of it. (*She turns toward him.*) You may guess
the reason.

MAN: I recognize you, of course.

    (*Soldier comes violently to attention and slams rifle
against stage, vertical butt.*)

WOMAN: And you understand a little more.

MAN: But that was so long ago. So—so trivial in the light
of our lives—your life—mine—so trivial! Surely your
career, your honors, the esteem in which you are held
. . . surely all of this has long since eclipsed that—that
mere episode. Surely you didn't spend all those years
training—research—dedication—to learn how to do this
. . . to me!

    (*Soldier adopts caricature of at ease position.*)

WOMAN: Surely? No, I cannot apply that word to any
element of my life. Trauma is insidious. My motives
were not always accessible to me. That mere episode.
First. Then certain choices. Yes. Certain directions.
Then, witnessing the suffering of others which reinforced memories of suffering. Then your further iniquities, educated, mature, authoritative iniquities in your
role of lawmaker that reinforced my identification of
you as the . . . enemy. All those years to learn how to
do this . . . to you.

MAN: You really intend to go through with this, then?

WOMAN: (*silence . . . looks at him . . . even through him*)

MAN: What will become of me? I'll have to disappear.
They'll think I've died. Absconded. My work. Believe
me, lives, nations, hang in the balance. The fate of the
world may be affected by my disappearance at this
moment. I am not stating the case too strongly!

    (*Soldier squats, staring out at audience.*)

WOMAN: I recognize that. However, those arguments are
not held valid—here.

MAN: Why not? They are valid arguments anywhere. Here
or anywhere.

WOMAN: I think you are rather confused.

MAN: Wouldn't you be under these circumstances?

    (*Realizes.*)

(*During speech that follows Soldier and Girl circle counter-directionally in blind panic, looking to see where the danger is coming from as Soldier aims rifle fruitlessly in several directions.*)

WOMAN: Yes. Would be and was. So were many others. Couldn't approach friends or relatives. Seemed to run around in circles. Time running out. Tried things. Shots. Rubber tubes. Tricky. Caustic agents. Quinine. Wire coat hanger. Patent medicine. Cheap abortionist. Through false and real alarms, through the successful routines and the dismal failures, our minds resided in one—swollen—pelvic—organ. Our work suffered. Our futures hung from a gallows. Guilt and humiliation and ridicule and shame assailed us. Our bodies. Our individual unique familiar bodies, suddenly invaded by strange unwelcome parasites, and we were denied the right to rid our own bodies of these invaders by a society dominated by righteous male chauvinists of both sexes who identified with the little clumps of cells and gave them precedence over the former owners of the host bodies.

(*Girl drops to ground, her face hidden in her arms. Soldier simply stands.*)

MAN: Yes. I understand. I never thought of it in that way before. Naturally . . .

WOMAN: Naturally. And yet, you were my partner in crime, you had sex with me and I had sex with you when we were both students. . . .

MAN: Did you consider it a crime?

WOMAN: Not at the time. Did you?

MAN: I never did.

WOMAN: When did the act between two consenting adults become a crime—in your mind?

MAN: I tell you—never.

WOMAN: Not your crime?

MAN: Not anyone's crime. . . .

WOMAN: So you committed no crime. You did not merit nor did you receive punishment.

MAN: Of course not.

WOMAN: Of course not. You continued with your studies, law, wasn't it?

(*Soldier pushes Girl all the way down with rifle. He gets up and kisses rifle.*)

You maintained your averages, your contacts. You pleased your family, pursued your life plan. You prospered. Through all of this, you undoubtedly had the opportunity to commit many more noncrimes of an interestingly varied nature, did you not?

MAN: Noncrimes? Your terminology defeats me. Yes. Yes to all of your contentions. I led a normal life, with some problems and many satisfactions. I have been a committed man, as you know, and have done some good in the world. . . .

(*Soldier kisses own arms.*)

WOMAN: Yes. I know. Well, the noncrime that you and I shared had different results for me. Do you remember?

MAN: I do remember . . . now. But I wasn't in a position then. . . . I wasn't sure. I recognize my error, my thoughtlessness now . . . but I was very young, I had so much at stake. . . .

WOMAN: And I? Everything stopped for me. My share of the noncrime had become quite criminal in the eyes of the world.

(*There is a shot offstage. Soldier cries out. He is wounded in the belly. He falls. The Girl falls and cries out simultaneously.*)

Wherever I went for help, I found people who condemned me and felt that my punishment was justified, or people who were sympathetic and quite helpless. I had no money, no resources. My parents were the last persons on earth I could turn to, after you. I dropped out of sight; for a while I hid like an animal. I finally went to a public institution recommended by a touch-me-not charity. I suffered a labor complicated by an insufficient pelvic span and a lack of dilation. I spent three days in company with other women who were carried in and out of the labor room screaming curses and for their mothers.

(*Soldier and Girl are lying head to head on their backs. They are wounded and they cry out inarticulately for help as the amplified voice overpowers their cries. Their downstage arms reach up and their hands clasp.*)

My body was jostled, invaded, exposed as a crooning old man halfheartedly swept the filthy floor. Many of my fellow unfortunates would come fresh from their battles to witness the spectacle of my greater misfortune. Three days and that cursed burden could not be released from the prison of my body nor I from it.

(*The Girl screams. She begins to pant loudly as*

though she can not catch her breath. The Soldier moans.)

Finally there was a last-ditch high forceps, a great tearing mess, and the emergence of a creature that I fully expected to see turned purple with my own terrible hatred, and ripped to shreds by the trial of its birth. What I saw, instead, was a human being, suddenly bearing very little relationship to me except our common helplessness, our common trial. I saw it was a female, and I wept for it. I wept and retched until my tired fundus gave way and there was a magnificent hemorrhage that pinned me to that narrow bed with pain I shall never forget, with pain that caused me to concentrate only on the next breath which seemed a great distance from the one before. Some kind fellow-sufferer and my own youth saved me. I awoke to tubes spouting blood from insecure joints. The splattered white coats of the attendants made it a butcher shop to remember. I never held that baby.

(*The arms drop. They lie still to end of speech.*)

For some days I was too ill. And then the institution policy decreed it unwise. There was a family waiting to claim that female creature, a family that could bestow respectability and security and approval and love. I emerged from that place a very resolved and disciplined machine. As you know. I worked. I studied. I clawed. I schemed. I made my way to the top of my profession and I never allowed a human being to touch me in intimacy again.

MAN: It was—it was criminal of me to have been the author of so much suffering . . .

(*Soldier sits up.*)

to have been so irresponsible . . . but I was stupidly young. I never could have imagined such things. Believe me.

WOMAN: Yes, you say you were young. Stupidly young. But what was your excuse when you were no longer young and stupid?

MAN: I'm sorry. I'm tired. I don't understand you.

WOMAN: Your daughter and mine grew to womanhood. And she and all her sisters were not spared the possibility of my experience and those of my generation.

(*Girl sits up. Girl and Soldier face each other. Soldier stands and becomes speechmaker, rifle arm behind his back, other hand "sincerely" across his heart.)*

Because there you were. Again. This time, not perpetrating unwilling motherhood upon a single individual, but condemning countless human females to the horrors of being unwilling hosts to parasitic life. You, for pure expediency, making capital of the rolling sounds of immorality and promiscuity which you promised accession upon relaxation of the abortion laws. Wholesale slaughter, you said, do you remember? Wholesale slaughter of innocent creatures who had no protection but the law from the untimely eviction from their mother's sinning wombs.

(Girl crouches at his feet, in attitude of supplication. She rests her head on his boot-tops and lies still.)

You murdered. You destroyed the lives of young women who fell prey to illegal abortion or suicide or unattended birth. You killed the careers and useful productivity of others. You killed the spirit, the full realization of all potential of many women who were forced to live on in half-life. You killed their ability to produce children in ideal circumstances. You killed love and self-respect and the proud knowledge that one is the master of one's fate, one's physical body being the corporeal representation of it. You killed. And you were so damned self-righteous about it.

MAN: I cannot defend myself.

(Girl crawls off to stage right.)

WOMAN: I know.

MAN: But, I beg you, is there no appeal from this sentence?

(Soldier cradles rifle.)

WOMAN: As it happens, there is. We have a board before whom these cases are heard. Your case is being heard at this moment, and their decision will be the final one. The board is composed of many women, all of whom have suffered in some way from the laws which you so ardently supported. There is a mother who lost her daughter to quack abortionists. There is a woman who was forced to undergo sexual intercourse on the examining table by the aborting physician. There is a woman who unwittingly took a fetus-deforming drug administered by her physician for routine nausea, and a woman who caught German measles at a crucial point in her pregnancy, both of whom were denied the right to

abortion, but granted the privilege of rearing hopelessly
defective children. There is an older woman who spent
a good part of her childrearing years in a mental
institution when she was forced to bear a late and
unwanted child. There are others. You won't have too
long to wait, now. For the verdict.

MAN: I promise you, that if I am spared, that I will be
able to do much to undo the harm I have ignorantly
done. This experience has taught me in a way that no
other learning process could. I am in a position to . . .
For the first time I can truly . . . identify . . . it would
be to the advantage of all. . . .

(*Soldier leaves rifle and stands as a human being,
without pose.*)

WOMAN: That is being taken into account.

(*Someone brings report or Woman goes to side of
stage where she emerges with it from a cubicle.*)

MAN: Is that the decision?

WOMAN: Yes. The board has decided that out of compassion for the potential child—

MAN: No, they can't!

(*Soldier turns to audience.*)

WOMAN: Out of compassion for the potential child, and
regarding the qualities of personality and not sex that
make you a potentially unfit mother, that the pregnancy
is to be terminated.

BLACKOUT

THE SERVING GIRL
AND THE LADY

TIME: The Present.

PLACE: A Stage (Empty or with Things).

AT RISE: An androgynous figure strides on stage; slender, tall, hair slicked or pulled back tightly from face. Perhaps dressed in tights and leotards.

Following her at some distance is a dark, short, full-figured female, maybe "natural" haircut or wig, barefoot. If Things depicted on stage, can be carrying cartons, pails, or whatever. Dropping them. Pick them up.

Activity during long speeches, if preferred, can include dressing of leotarded figure by herself or "serving girl" in wig, padded bra, waist-cincher, fluffy apron, jewelry (or whatever is deemed symbolically feminine), and/or bustling sweeping, scrubbing, sewing (or whatever is deemed essentially female) by the serving girl.

THE SERVING GIRL: For the man I drew, it was the end of hope. Rigidity. Rigor mortis before death. A decapitated chicken moving through life by reflex but never any possibility of life any more. My marriage was weighted like some intolerable mathematical proposition, the gross weight of the injustice increasing with each area of diminished returns.

> (*Pause. Looks at Lady. Indicates her. Lady looks back at her.*)

On the other hand, what she has, the Lady that is, is this Big Man. Big. Big enough for two was what they suggested. Big head, Big hands, Big brain, Big ambition. Big. A couple of million in five years if he lives. Instantly, if he dies. He might actually be worth more alive than dead. To replace him, what he is to his wife, you would have to hire a policeman, a babysitter, a loving carpenter, a lawn boy, a nurse, a furniture mover, a shopper, a cook, a house boy, an escort, a circumspect frigger—and above all, a Provider. Capital P.

THE LADY: (*Looks at Serving Girl for some time*) The serving girl's husband is bored by himself. He knows his own incapacity too well. Therefore, his only diversion is to never make love to her. (*Pause*) So the lovegiver is the lovestarved. (*Pause*) And yet the serving girl is a very desirable woman. If I wished to solve the mystery of her desirability, among other mysteries, I might—I just might—approach her husband. Yes. If, however, he is wholly occupied in maintaining his minus manipulation—I might send my own boy to do a man's job— (*Pause*) So what? Everyone uses these methods. We want to get the cheese without the trap springing shut, don't we? And there *are* ways to keep the trap from springing shut, are there not?

THE SERVING GIRL: The Lady lives at some distance from most traps, with sculpture in her—kitchen, and books lining her—living room. Music is piped into bathrooms and bedrooms. The children spring gleaming from the belly of an appliance.

(*Picks up oversized telephone receiver or sense memory*)

Memo to the Spic'n'Span Accommodation Agency— Flash! Mobilize all your sensual impetuous self-destructive teenage girls. Alert your tall-highly-intelligent-with-promising-careers-before-them-but-horny-as-hell college boys. Position them felicitously. Go!

(*Stares at oversize wristwatch as nine loud clicks or bells are counted off.*)

Stop! (*Exceedingly rapid delivery from this point to indicated stop*) Mr. and Mrs. Pure have been our acquaintances for several years and intimate friends for a few years. Stop! We have been associated with them in enterprises that reflect their highly developed social consciousness. Stop! They are outgoing, intelligent, and conscientious members of the community. Stop! They are home-oriented. Stop! Mrs. Pure is very interested in the interior of the home, implementing her creative approach with solid participation in painting of rooms and furniture. Stop! She knits and sews. Stop! Mr. Pure is a talented wood worker, able to finish off basements, install cabinets and provide toys and furniture for cooperative nurseries. Stop! The Pures are both interested in sports and travel. Stop! Mr. Pure is an excellent squash player. Stop! Mrs. Pure is an excellent spectator. Stop! Let's hear it for the Pures!—Stop!

(*Stop rapid delivery*)

(*Calling*) Reply requested!

The children, a boy with muscles and a girl with charm are given rooms appropriate to their needs. Mr. Pure kisses the little boy on the mouth. A lot. He pulls the little bugger's pants down, playfully, on almost any opportunity. Mrs. Pure watches with—triumph—as the little girl lies on her back on the pink bathinette, her little legs akimbo and a silent tiny freshet wells up *uncontrollably* from the pink little sugarplum between the plump little thighs. The kimona gets wet but Mrs. Pure doesn't care.

THE LADY: In our Bacchic rites for social fertility there was love in a cage, love in a box, love in a dirty hotel room where the sheets were only slightly used. Anything, I said. Anything to make you happy. The man was very dark and shorter than I, a croupier in Pleasureland who performed as programmed. Who delivered. Who could go on, to serve my husband his propulsive reaming at the crap table. Afterward.

THE SERVING GIRL: Sexual fantasy, in extremis, should be stored like oxygen, in hospital or hotel rooms, not in the properly maintained home because of its explosive nature and potential danger to—the children.

THE LADY: My husband and I watch fondly, are fond of watching the little tiny ever-so-feminine girl as she plays enthusiastically with the green shoot on the young brother tree, testing its firmness and resiliency as manly little brother stands, oh so still—tolerating it.

THE SERVING GIRL: Tolerating it.

THE LADY: That is what I said.

THE SERVING GIRL: The children do learn by example. They are exemplary children.

THE LADY: I try.

THE SERVING GIRL: To exemplify?

THE LADY: In a manner of speaking.

THE SERVING GIRL: And what is the manner of your speaking?

THE LADY: That is none of your concern. Haven't you something to do?

THE SERVING GIRL: Watch Mama, now. Children, see Mama.

THE LADY: Some dusting? A seam? The dishes!

THE SERVING GIRL: See how mama *tolerates* it, children?

THE LADY: Hold on, there. Who are you? (*Suspiciously*) I'm not sure I recognize you—after all—

THE SERVING GIRL: Oh, I'm just an old—gymnasium.

THE LADY: An old—gymnasium—

THE SERVING GIRL: A business lunch? A fraternity brother?

THE LADY: Oh, yes.

THE SERVING GIRL: Yes?

THE LADY: Yes. Now that I've looked at you more closely, I find I do recognize you after all. But I remember you differently. I remember you as a whisper of crisis, a thrill of competition, the proof that he was attractive to someone—else.

THE SERVING GIRL: What was it you said to your croupier?

THE LADY: Anything. Anything you want.

THE SERVING GIRL: I said that to your husband. Anything. Anything you want

THE LADY: And did you give it to him?

THE SERVING GIRL: And he gave it to me.

THE LADY: Really? Anything you wanted?

THE SERVING GIRL: I wanted what he gave me. You wouldn't understand.

THE LADY: You poor thing. I wouldn't understand?

THE SERVING GIRL: I don't think you would.

THE LADY: Just between us girls, is the name of the game—Passion—?

THE SERVING GIRL: It can only be a joke to you.

THE LADY: And you? Are you proud? Proud of your passion?

THE SERVING GIRL: (*Pause*)—yes.

THE LADY: (*Abrupt*) Don't be. It's only a species of myth to ensure the perpetuation of the species—A specious myth to keep you forever in a convenient position—convenient for us. The Big Man and I—on your back, on your knees—and enjoying it in the bargain.

THE SERVING GIRL: (*Pause*) But you've got the real bargain.

THE LADY: Yes.

THE SERVING GIRL: Feeding. Clothing. Housing. Honoring. Not dependent on the myth of passion.

THE LADY: Definitely dependent on the myth of passion. The myth of your passion. The myth of his passion for your passion. The myth of his passion for *my* passion. Here, you naughty boy. You dear sweet naughty boy. I forgive you. I will give you some. Here, for being a good naughty boy. Here for the house. Here for the money. Here for the kitchen, the car, the trip to Puerto Rico, the insurance if you shuffle off this currency-packed coil—

(*Each "here" accompanied by a "bump"*)

THE SERVING GIRL: And he thought he was a man.

THE LADY: Yes. Didn't he though?

THE SERVING GIRL: He thought that three times from his head to his toes—proving, proving—meant the final confirmation of his manhood. Do squirrels believe the myth too? Have you seen the female squirrel, drawn up, waiting, while the male flattens himself against a redwood bench, his caution temporarily winning over the compelling little lust? Have you heard the agony of the mythic sexual urgency propelling those sounds out of them, those attack and defend sounds? In sun-heated smoke have you made my body the incubator of your passionate pretense, so that it might be carried warmed and ready into your winning threshold? Artificial heat. Artificial light. Forced blooming. Wigs. False eyelashes. Fake fingernails. Padded bellies. Grated passions. All myths. All efficacious.

THE LADY: That's really enough. Quite enough. Rather too much catharsis for one day. When you speak to me next, remember the reality. Tolerance is terminated. Come to terms. What do you say to me, Serving girl?

THE SERVING GIRL: I say—.

THE LADY: You say what?

THE SERVING GIRL: I say—

THE LADY: What do you say to me? Come now, you must remember—you know how to say it—you love to say it—it was only a rehearsal with him, the myth belongs to him, but this is the *real thing,* little peasant, *the real thing.*

THE SERVING GIRL: But will you shut me out?

THE LADY: Perhaps.

THE SERVING GIRL: No protection?

THE LADY: None guaranteed.

THE SERVING GIRL: I won't! *I don't have to!*

THE LADY: You will. I'm the only hope you have, the only possible hope.

THE SERVING GIRL: (*Dully*) Anything—

THE LADY: The Big Man will love this. It's what he wanted all along—

THE SERVING GIRL: Anything you want.

THE LADY: That's right. Louder please.

THE SERVING GIRL: Anything to make you happy— (*Shouts*)

THE LADY: Oh, perfect—Just perfect—Say it—Say it again —keep on saying it—but, as I say,—Perfect.

END

3

PROSTITUTION: A Quartet for Female Voices

Kate Millett

INTRODUCTION

It is my impression that emerging peoples have great difficulty with form. Baldwin's novels are very conventional. Edna St. Vincent Millay and Elizabeth Barrett's poems have the sound of borrowed Keats or Shakespeare, dressed up to appear "classical," and affecting the manners of the very best male poets. They *are* actually saying something different, something new. But they are saying it in an old way. Their derivative character makes it easy for the male academic establishment to denigrate and even overlook their substance. There are also rare eccentric figures, such as Gertrude Stein, saying new things in such novel ways that no one hears them at all. Then there is Virginia Woolf who combines both approaches in good measure. I never chose between the two, but if I had to, I would choose to admire Stein the more.

I should like to see the new movement give women in the arts a confidence in the value of their own culture (in the sense that females are a class with a subculture of its own) and a respect for its experience, together with the freedom, even the spontaneity, to express this in new ways, in new forms. I say this because I really love to see form become content. And if, indeed, we are saying something new, it does seem to me we ought to say it in new ways.

I have a strong feeling for the spoken language, for

oral English. And women talk. Like the members of any repressed group, they are verbal persons, talking because they are permitted no other form of expression. When the prestigious intellectual and artistic media—be they traditional, such as poetry and philosophy, or contemporary, such as film or rock lyrics—are in the hands of those who govern, those out of power must settle for talk. One observes, for instance, a quite fantastic verbal ability in blacks. But women's talk has always been deliberately trivialized. And yet over the past five years, years I have spent in the women's movement, I have experienced a great change in such talk. There is a new cogency and direction, a clarity and rising consciousness in the speech of women now. I hear it in the conversation of women outside the movement as well as those within. And I attribute a good measure of this to the movement's acting as a cultural catalyst for numbers of women, many of whom are scarcely conscious, even unconscious, of its source.

What I have tried to capture here is the character of the English I heard spoken by four women and then recorded on tape. I was struck by the eloquence of what was said, and yet when I transcribed the words onto paper, the result was at first disappointing. Some of the wit of M's black and southern delivery had disappeared, gone with the tang of her voice. Liz's sincerity, her pain and concern, made an exact transcription digressive and repetitious. J's difficulty in speaking of things so painful that she had repressed them for years required that I speak often on her tapes, hoping to give her support, then later, edit myself out. My own transcripts read like the raving of an illiterate so I sometimes gave up on them and fell back into composition. As I grew more and more earnest about the project, I found the complexities of written English more appropriate in some places, a loose oral narrative more fitting in others. For all the voices it took a good deal of work to transform spoken to linear-language, and I know I have not been successful in satisfying the demands of both. But I did learn a great deal about language: to respect the spoken word and to love its rhythms. Even to respect the tape recorder. For without this device to preserve the very sound of language, we should have no idea of how people *really* talk: their pauses, inflexions, emphases, unfinished sentences, short periods. All attempts to mimic spoken language seem

terribly mannered, and one comes to respect Stein still
more, and to admire how carefully she must have listened.

My options in this project—writing on prostitution—
were to invent something myself, knowing nothing of the
subject matter, or to eke it out of books, or else to begin
the long and difficult process of finding women who could
teach me. I took the latter course through a long and
traumatic summer of intermittent work on the piece or of
solemn anxiety during moments I was unable to work on
it. Although I experienced for months a curious, defensive
uneasiness over my inadequacy, never having been a prostitute as the term is generally understood, I did not finally
succumb to the temptations of class guilt and delete my
own voice or that of Liz Schneider, my collaborator, from
the text. I decided instead on a four-cornered conversation
encompassing very different persons, whose voices were
instruments expressing their diverse experience. Without
becoming fanciful, this reminded me of the quartet form.
It is my hope that Liz and I contributed something by way
of focus to balance the depth and validity of personal
knowledge that M and J provided. Reading the piece in
columns as one reads a score, I can hear J's voice, a first
violin leading my own more subjective meander, then Liz's
voice telling of her bitter experience in the courts, poignant as the viola, then M's resonant cello, vibrant, full.*

Seeing how the columns would read across the page, I
winced to realize my own would commence with a remark
on Baudelaire, M's with a reminiscence of a policeman
accosting her as a prostitute and a junkie, then forcing his
hand into her shirt. But these are in fact the directions
from which we did approach the subject, and it would be
pointless to hide this truth. Looking at the four columns
on the page, Liz's and my own to one side, J's and M's to
the other, the voices of two movement women merging
with those of two women who have lived the prostitute's
life and now either belong to the women's movement as
does J, or are beginning to organize for it as is M, I could
feel a certain gratification that, on paper at least (the reality is yet to come and will not be on paper but in the courts
and on the streets), women are coming together from very

---

* In case the reader is curious as to what we are doing this year:
J will finish graduate school; Liz will begin law at New York University; after having worked as a director of a drug rehabilitation
center for some time now, M will be resigning her post to begin
college.

different points of personal history or social origin. That is not, I hope, to disguise those differences in a fraudulent "sisterhood." Indeed, it is our very differences that make us unique and fascinating to each other as we join together in this movement, openly recognizing those differences —class, color, region, the varieties of our experience.

Loving someone is wanting to know them. Insofar as we are able to learn and know of each other, we can acknowledge, and even in part assimilate into our own imaginative life, the thousand differences that have always been used as wedges to drive us apart. So that the experience of all women everywhere becomes, in a sense, our communal property, a heritage we bestow upon each other, the knowledge of what it has meant to be female, a woman in this man's world.

J

K

The way that I got into it was like this. I was just broke and I had never liked to be in debt to anyone. I have a thing about it—being in debt. I've never liked to be financially dependent on anyone. I've always had this thing. What happened was I borrowed ten dollars from someone, and then I realized, after I borrowed it, that I couldn't pay it back. I had no way of knowing that I'd ever be able to pay it back—it was a man that I'd slept with too. So that's how I got into it. I just decided fuck it, man, I'm not going to be poor any more. I'd never been poor and I wasn't used to it. I was an undergraduate on a scholarship. My father was doing the worst he'd done in years. He couldn't afford to give me any money. They would have gone out of their way to give me money—my folks—especially if they'd known what I was doing to get it.

So I just went on the street. The thing that broke the ice had actually happened years before at a concert of Miles Davis. Davis was playing in a club, and someone outside wanted to take me. You know, asked me if I wanted

Prostitution is something I've had on my mind all this year. Last fall I did some reading on it with my students in the experimental college, first defining prostitutes as a social group, then studying their collective behavior. When the American Philosophical Association asked me to talk at their Western Meetings this spring, I offered to discuss prostitution, homosexuality, and abortion as three instances where the law infringes upon sexual freedom. Whereupon their enthusiasm waned and the invitation seemed somehow to evaporate. Then Vivian asked me to do something for this book. I chose to write on prostitution, and I chose it with some determination.

Everything I've read on prostitution, even the way it is discussed, pisses me off: the statistical approach of sociological texts, the cheerful rationalizations of popular accounts, the romanticized versions of literature. One is slowly forced to realize that for centuries a tremendous moral and sociological confusion has surrounded the entire issue, a phenomenon one can account for only by considering the monumental sex-

L

Just to remember that year in the courts brings back my depression, the futility I knew every day, the impotence. . . . Last year I was with the Vera Institute of Justice, trying to provide civil rights counsel at arraignments. I had felt that if I were to be working with accused persons, I wanted to be working with women. From the time I started, even when I was up in the Bronx, the women I saw in the court were just so much more sad, really wasted people than the men. Somehow the kinds of crime men were involved in did not seem to devastate them as much. Crime has in it a curiously gratifying element of macho for a man: a hustler, con, hood. To a woman crime is a terrifying sort of breakthrough, degrading to a kind of ingrained self-image of femininity.

Logically, I started to see prostitution as the form of criminal activity not only most prevalent among women in the numbers arraigned, but also as representing the most awful kind of life a woman might have. Or so it seemed at the time. I would never say it is the most honest life for a woman because that implies a value judgment on

M

Now I'm off the street. And if a cop comes up to me and sticks his hand in my shirt, feeling me up to look for something, you can believe it baby I'm gonna call a lawyer or the ACLU or something. But in those days it was pretty different. I was holding then and likely to carry heroin in my bra. And when you got that shit on you, you don't argue. If they don't get you for drugs, they'll get you for whoring. And you gotta be scared all the time. Now I can tell him to get his fucking hand off me. I got myself together now.

You can say whoring is business. Or a means to an end. But it's not that cut and dried. It's important for you to know that most women who turn tricks have to be loaded on something. You don't have any woman out there selling this commodity and doing this trading who's not loaded on something. They're not that hip to business. And they're not that void. Like you gotta have something. If you're not high on dope it's something else. Every time I went to turn a trick I had to fix before and after. There's a price a woman pays.

One of the problems we

J

to go in. And I knew that if I went in with him I'd have to sleep with him. But I figured it was worth it; I wanted to see Miles Davis. I had no feeling for this guy; I just wanted the ticket to get in there. I realized I'd whored—there was no way of denying the truth to myself. So when the time came a few years later and I was absolutely broke, I was ready.

I had talked to somebody and gotten a connection. I was living in an S.R.O.* over on Ninety-fifth Street, and there was this woman and one night she came down the hall and she said, "I'm going out hustling tonight." I couldn't have started by myself if I hadn't had a connection. And you make connections very fast if you're into it or want to get into it. She said she'd take me out and show me what to do, how to watch out for the cops, everything.

I didn't know I'd make really good money. But she told me to ask for fifteen dollars, "take ten dollars if you have to, and if you're really broke, go down to seven dollars." So I started off kinda slow, down Sev-

* Single room occupancy.

K

ual repression within our culture, and its steady inability, after having created both the prostitute and her plight, to recognize her as human in any meaningful sense at all. The smug stupidity with which people are accustomed to discuss the subject is fairly outrageous: the victim, the prostitute, rather than the institution that victimizes her, is condemned. Prostitution is regarded as humorous, inevitable or convenient, the prostitute is derided, castigated, or pharisaically informed that her situation is of her own choosing and "her own fault." As the causes of female prostitution lie in the economic position of women, together with the psychological damage inflicted upon them through the system of sex-role conditioning in patriarchal society, this conventional satisfaction with the prostitute's fate is not only unjust, but simplistic.

Lately, apologists for that custom of trafficking in persons which we call prostitution have overhauled the tired machinery of the double standard, and hailed this enslavement of women as "sexual freedom." This is to subvert the

L

M

my part about what is honest. But it is surely the most obvious way in which women sell themselves: using themselves as commodity, being used as commodity. Really being just that—and that being the most appropriate possible metaphor for our whole condition. I think of crime itself as a notion, a concept representing those things a society holds most dear and yet is most afraid of. The fact that sex is directly linked to money only through prostitution represents the devious way in which society deals with its truths.

I started thinking what it would be like to be a prostitute, what it would be like to be in prison for it, what it would be like to live as a prostitute. I started reading things—stuff written mostly by men. Except for Sara Harris who argued that women were able to separate sex and love, that prostitution was simply a business, and claimed that there was no higher incidence of homosexuality among prostitutes, that it was just another way that a woman could live. And deep, in some very basic woman's part of me, I said, "No, that's not true. It's as degrading for them as it is

deal with in drug rehabilitation is to get women to have a little pride, get up off the floor. We have to cope with the feeling of having turned a trick. This is one thing that stays with women and makes them feel very bad about themselves. The fact that at one time in their lives they were in a position where they were out selling their bodies. They really have one hell of a time forgetting about that.

Prostitution goes with addiction. Because it's a means of supporting a habit. Something that'll sell when nothing else will. I don't think you ever get too sick or too ragged or too ugly or too beat up to turn a trick. There's always someone out there buying. But you can get too beat up or raggedy to go to a store and try to boost something. They chase you out. And whoring is also a fast way to make enough money for a bag.

When I was using it, about eight or nine years ago, heroin was five dollars. Now it's gone up. And there's no limit on the bags you need. You need as many bags as you can get, depending only on the amount of money you can find. I used about a $100 a

J

enty-second Street, in high heels, and I must have looked inexperienced because no one made an offer. I walked until four in the morning and ended up in a coffee shop, exhausted. I'd walked all the way from Ninety-fifth Street down to Seventy-second, ending up in this coffee shop called The Laundry Chute. I don't know if anyone remembers it. This was pretty far back. But it was really nice. They had all these left-wing people, folk singers too, and I enjoyed that. Then I felt I ought to go back on the street and make some money. I'd gotten all dressed up and I had decided to do it. So I started to walk back. This guy came up in a gray car, and I got in. I was a little scared getting in the car. I didn't know what he would do. I think I brought him back to my place, and I think he offered me ten dollars. I might have asked for fifteen dollars. I don't remember how it went down. But he was very nice. I think he took my number, or something. I don't remember what we did either—I mean, in bed. I can't remember whether he wanted to pay my rent or not. I know there was

K

promise of sexual liberation into a tawdry license to exploit women further through state brothels complete with a medical assurance that the males who patronize them do so without risk. This is to foster and acknowledge the prostitution of women as a privilege of the state. It is even more vicious than the present system, general throughout the United States, of harassing and persecuting the prostitute with summons, fines, and imprisonment, punishing in the female an offense society does not think to punish in the male. (Male prostitutes sell themselves to other males and are a parallel case here, not a contradiction).

It is a further irony that our legal ethic prosecutes those who are forced (economically or psychologically) to offer themselves for sale as objects, but condones the act of buying persons as objects. Yet the system of exploited labor called voluntary servitude, practiced under the indentured-servant code of colonial America and clearly analogous to prostitution, would never be permitted today and was outlawed even before the abolition of

L

for me to sleep with someone I don't care about and wake up in the morning next to him." Then I began to realize that the difference lay in my expectation about what might happen when I woke in the morning; my expectations were very different from those of a woman who was selling herself, a woman who was hustling. The fact that she was turning a trick on him, rather than being turned and exploited by her own emotions, came home to me. Because in her case nothing would ever meet those expectations of intimacy the act presupposed—and this made it very different: she could not be disappointed, and I could. So when I first started to write about prostitution, the distance that I felt between her condition and my own was enormous.

Months in the courts gave me an idea for a project of my own, a rehabilitation center for women convicted of crime and run by such people themselves, as the drug rehabilitation centers are. I finally succeeded in convincing the Vera Institute to let me draw up such a plan and work out its details. But it too became a disappoint-

M

day. If you've got $15 a day, you use that; if you've got $50, you use that; if you've got $100, you use $100. You use whatever you make. It's a trap.

There's usually something left for a place to sleep and some food, unless you're living with a man. Around this neighborhood if you can get enough together for a bag, you can just sleep on a roof someplace. But most junkies live in rooms. You can scrape enough up for a room most days. And you live on hero sandwiches, Yoo-Hoos, candy bars, that kind of thing—cupcakes, kid food. The food of regression; addiction itself is a form of regression. The drug becomes the nourishment you receive through your veins.

You can say prostitution feeds a drug habit. Which comes first? Perhaps it's a kind of circle. You need the shit to kill the pain of prostitution; you need the prostitution to kill the pain of needing the drug. Around and around. But generally addiction comes first in most cases. Most people come to find themselves associated with drugs, the underworld, and so they naturally find themselves associated with prostitution,

J

another guy who definitely wanted to pay my rent.

I can never remember one job from another, but I do remember the first two. They all merge in a gray mass. A few of them stick out, like the one who gave me a bad check. I was turned on to him by someone who did take checks. I wouldn't take checks. I wasn't that stupid. But there are exceptions like this. Some guys always pay call girls in checks and they're always good.

There are guys who come back time and time again because they can't afford to keep a call girl. They can only afford the ten or twenty dollars a week, so they come back because they can't afford anything else. I don't think they want all that, you know, a mistress. It becomes like a business relationship, time after time—a relationship like you might have with someone at the corner grocery.

There was one guy who wanted to pay me to beat him. It turns me on just to talk about it. I never thought I wanted to beat somebody, but when I did it, I felt I really liked it. I learned something that way—I learned that I real-

K

Negro slavery. Rather than state regulation or repression of prostitution, the course of justice would appear to lie in another direction: namely, in removing prostitution from the criminal code altogether. This would in no way increase the incidence or availability of female prostitution, but it would frustrate the exploitation of prostitutes by the two classes of men who are their chief predators: pimps and police. The latter function in the same manner as pimps, since the fat earnings of members of the vice squad are acquired through methods of coercive protection. One defines a pimp as a male who lives on the earnings of a prostitute. Since the prostitute is a lucrative source of police graft, forced to endure either extortion or arrest, government has a vested interest in prostitution's illegality, rivaled only by those states that in "regulating" (e.g. institutionalizing) prostitution, make it a state monopoly. Oddly enough, the other chief opponent of the legalization of prostitution is not organized religion, but powerful hotel interests, who see the prostitute's patronage as insufficiently lucrative to out-

L

M

ment—restricted by its very nature: establishment funding and the process of remanding women from the court which would make the women prisoners of the program. What I have now is a nearly settled conviction of impossibility, a knowledge it is impossible to relate to women this way. Finally perhaps impossible to relate at all. I see these women in the court every day, and I feel they are my sisters. But how deep the barriers are, how deep their defenses. And so ingrained in our sense of ourselves as women, is the idea of sexual objectification that I see these women and I don't even begin to know how to speak with them. And I feel not only that my presuppositions, but even my analysis and judgments on prostitution, come out of something I can't act on, something I'm prevented from realizing in any way.

The actual situation in the city is that prostitution is accepted by everyone—police, judges, clerks, and lawyers. Arrest and prosecution are purely gestures that have to be made to keep up the façade of public morality. The method of dealing with it is sim-

prostitutes, and pimps. I was into drugs first. When you start on drugs you start hanging out in certain places and with a certain kind of people.

I lived the first twenty years of my life around nuns and a convent. And the first heroin I ever saw in my life I used. I don't think I was rebelling. It was the point in my life when my family broke into pieces—like my father and about the fifth wife he'd had during the twenty years I'd lived with him finally separated. We had a house and a car and that whole bit, and it all went down the drain.

My father pretty much raised me. And I think I was kinda thrown, disappointed and rollin'. My father was a drinker and not too well put together. I think my stepmother just couldn't take him anymore. So they separated. And for the first time in my life I felt I was some sort of outcast. She didn't take me with her. Most of my father's women spent all their time resenting my relationship with him. Like I say, I felt myself thrown out in the street, depressed and upset about the whole thing, the separation. I had to learn to take care of my-

J

ly got pleasure from it. It wasn't sexy—it was not a sexual excitement at all. I guess I was getting back at all the men who'd done me wrong. I never get sexually excited in any relationship with a john. I've never made love with another woman. Now I guess I'm sort of neuter. I don't have sexual relationships now with anyone.

At that time, though, I'd have boy friends I really liked to sleep with. But as soon as somebody paid me any money, that changed the whole thing; made it the other thing. I see them as something else when they give me money. They might be the nicest people in the world, but it's something else, and you don't mix business with pleasure. I make a tremendous division between love and money. I don't get sexually turned on by somebody who gives me money. I didn't feel consciously degraded when somebody gave me money, but desire, affection, sex, feeling for the person, never entered into it.

And if you're on the street you have to take anybody who comes along, no matter what they look like—as long as they are

K

weigh her possible threat to the public image of the more expensive hotels affluent enough to dispense with her custom.

To educated women the prostitute is probably only familiar through literature. The woman as whore is a literary archetype of greater frequency than the actual prostitute population would ever warrant, a version of female existence insisted upon by the men who create our high culture. It is difficult not to find the literary man's impressions of prostitution particularly annoying. Baudelaire and his zest for "evil" come to mind. The glorification of the golden-hearted whore is a cheap and easy stunt: in identifying with her the poet feeds his self-pity; in condescending to her he congratulates himself on his humanity, his special insight in perceiving the suffering Magdalene in a mere woman of the people, a creature of the street. And in sugaring her situation, or clothing it in sentiment, he perpetuates it as surely as French tourism does. There is a perfection in all this: the liberal fellow has found moral credit through patronage . . . and

L

ply a form of harassment, not a form of prevention, abolition, or punishment. There is no conviction at any level that prostitution is a crime on anyone's part, only a total and satisfied acceptance of the double standard, excusing the male, accusing the female. There is also a curious fascination with the prostitutes, "the girls" a geniality toward them, friendliness even, in the sense of familiarity.

What was most frightening to me in court was not only my own sense of distance, of separation from the women arraigned, but the very familiarity, as I said, between the clerks, the judges, the women themselves, everyone in the court. Everyone accepts the fact that each woman who comes in will be in again and again, will go through the same routine, maybe stay in the pens overnight, but she knows all the cops and they know her, they accept her and they fuck her and she pays them and gets off: that's how the relationship is defined, clear and simple. And I play no part in the scheme at all. It's obvious to all that prostitution should be made legal, obvious to the women themselves that prostitutes

M

self. That's what was going down with me. Nobody had ever taught me how to make it in the street. I grew up in the convent instead. Did you ever hear that song of Bobby Dylan's —"Like a Rolling Stone?" It was like that.

How does it feel to be on your own
No direction known
Like a rolling stone
Nobody ever taught you how to make it on the street
Now you'll have to get used to it.

Well, nobody ever taught me how to make it in the street. I just did it on my own. And I made my way. I really don't believe in the bullshit they teach you in the Catholic Church— that if you do good you get good, love your neighbor, and you're your brother's keeper and all that bullshit. You're a mark for everybody. They laugh at you, and they lay you. I was a marked woman. I mean like when I started using drugs, I didn't know the price of a bag. I didn't even know how to hit myself with the needle.

And I was stealing at that point. Compared to

J   K

reasonably clean. I didn't walk the street after that first time. I don't have to take just anybody. And if someone asks me to do something I don't want to do, I can refuse. I can refuse anybody because there were so many people. New York is crawling with johns. And, what's very important, I wasn't dependent on any *one* man.

I was always scared to get into a car with somebody. I knew, second or third hand, of women who have been hurt by sadists, but I never got that kind. And I've seen women with marks and bruises that they got from their pimps. But I never knew anyone who was beaten up by a john. Of course it's different on the street. On the street you take anybody. On the street it's anything and anybody and, to a certain extent, whatever his sickness is, you're at his mercy. After that first time, I always worked through connections, but the first time it was a man in a car. This was an older man, with gray hair, and he was driving an old, gray car. A ten-dollar john. After that I didn't walk the streets any more because I was still waitressing and getting

he is still fucking the whore while congratulating himself on noticing her misery.

But I am a woman, so there are more personal motives behind my interest in prostitution. I remember the tenor of the first conversations I had with Liz Schneider on the subject. We both felt we had no real right even to speak. We had been to college; we had never sold for cash. Not bound by the same economic iron maiden many prostitutes are, nor even well-informed on the call girl's life, we felt presumptuous as well as ignorant. And yet, we argued, here was a great informational blank since one does not hear honest accounts from the subjects themselves, but suborned nonsense invented either *by* men or *for* their satisfaction (see the glowing accounts of the party girls found in men's magazines). Nearly all other information on the subject is limited to male sources. Someone, we agreed, must begin getting some truth out, if only because people have been misinformed so long and the misrepresentation continues.

L

suffer for the supposed crimes of other people, yet the guilt and shame are part of their lives as well, their isolation too: all this is made clear in talking to them. The distance I feel from the women when I'm in court, the familiarity with which they relate to the men—the clerks, the judges, the cops—is so heartbreaking to me that I don't know how to bear it.

I feel utterly paralyzed as I sit in the arraignment part computing the numbers of women who are getting fucked over for one thing or another, and a prostitute walks in, heavily made up, heavily wigged, wearing supposedly seductive clothes, open, friendly and warm, flirting with all the rest of the people—all the men. There's my sister and I'm so far removed from her.

When it is understood that I am one of the women who wishes to work with prostitutes, the attitude I am received with becomes one of incredulous ridicule on the part of every member of the court, ranging all the way from male clerks to male Legal Aid people. Even women Legal Aid people and the other women around, the women who are legal secretaries.

M

boosting, I was a lousy whore. I was really a lousy whore. That wasn't my stick at all. I was a good thief though. I used to make $200 a day, then give it all to some guy. I used to take orders, like Petricelli suits—that's an Italian name-brand suit. Got them from men's clothing stores. But you can't boost with no shopping bag. That's not cool. You have to wear something loose. You wear something very very loose, not some tight-fitting dress. Like you have to put it between your legs and under your arms. First thing, you have to roll it to make it very small and compact so you can stash it on the body. I used to take orders from people. They used to tell me what they wanted and I'd go get it.

Boosting didn't frighten me too much. I guess in the beginning I was a little worried. A girl friend and I used to go boosting for fun, just daring. I was nervous too. Stuff like mink stoles, stuff like that. I got busted. I got busted a couple of times but it don't freeze you up. Because you've got to make money. So you change territories.

I could dress well enough so I could pass in those places. That's very impor-

J

K

referrals from 80 Warren Street. Michael Harrington talks about 80 Warren Street in *The Other America*. It's an employment agency dealing in waiters and waitresses, cooks and things like that. I went down there one day to get a job. I was going to get a job before Saturday and this was a Friday afternoon. So there weren't any jobs and I was just hanging around. I ran into a guy there who was also looking for a job. He was trying to pick me up. It was a wild thing: I ended up going over to Brooklyn. He didn't want to buy me. I got scared he was a cop or something. He was pretty nice: a black guy. He wanted to set up a thing where he'd see me every week and go twice. His thing was going twice—for twelve fifty. And he wanted to pay my rent. Going twice—that means he screws me twice. It's a very bad deal because they take forever going the second time. That going twice business, I got out of that.

I think the next connection I made was, I was riding on the bus. I got off at 102nd Street—somebody came up to me. I think I'd been in a bar trying to pick

I knew, or I thought I knew, how difficult it would be to find informants, to acquire and deserve their trust, to forge past the prostitute's habitual defenses—the product of her social and legal persecution. But I underestimated the difficulties, just as I never foresaw the depth of my eventual involvement, my growing feeling of commitment to (and ultimately, identification with) a group of women whom I came to know through friendship with a few of them. So wronged, so utterly exploited—it made me furious. Or afraid. Because like all women, I know the prostitute exists as an object lesson to the rest of us. Like the squaw in the Westerns, docile and on foot behind her master, an example even if purely fictitious, the whore is there to show the rest of us how lucky we are, how favored of our lords, how much worse it could go for us.

Staying up all night talking with J, chilly with fatigue 'though it was summer, making a new pot of coffee to keep us awake, or broad leaves of a courtyard sitting in M's apartment in the early evening, the

L

Everyone assures me I'll fail; everyone is eager to set me straight: "You'll never be able to relate to them. How could they want to give it up when they make so much money? How could you ever talk to them?" And for months my innate sense of idealism and sisterhood said "No, that's not true. There's a solidarity among us that can break through that." Yet sitting in the court everyday, or interviewing women in the pens and feeling paralyzed while interviewing, in dread even about what this may tell you of how hopeless I feel it is, knowing that the shell these women have developed about their lives as women, about their relationships to men, about their relationships to the pimps (who are there with them, bailing them out) goes so much deeper than any sense of potential solidarity I feel or that the woman's movement could give now.

Finally I've come to feel that the whole legal system backs men up, confirms their power. In court I've been watching what happens to women who are picked up for prostitution. There are some judges who will just dismiss it. The district attorney will charge

M

tant. Also you've got to have a car. Very important to have a car when you're boosting. You dress nice, you have a car. Very "bouge" looking, which is an accomplishment because usually when you walk into a store, if they're looking, you're *black*, no matter how well dressed you are. Very often I'd team up with some white girl and then the heat was off. Then you could clean up.

They don't say, "Excuse me, lady, are you shoplifting?" They usually say, "Can I help you please?" And are very insistent about it. It's frightening, but I think the most important thing is that you can't panic. You have to remember never to panic because the moment you panic, you're dead. You have to be very cool, you have to defend yourself. Of course you deny everything, that you're not copping nothing. As long as they don't catch you with the goods on you. Even if they catch you with the goods on you in the store, you can still cop out. But what they usually do is let you get outside, and if they get you outside you're dead. You've had it at that point. Still, you can pretend like you don't know what's happening. "Who, me?"

J

somebody up or something. It's very vague—all the sequences—but this guy, I took him home, and he gave me fifteen dollars. He was also black and said he could help me out. He introduced me to a lady who was in the life and who would show me around. This was the woman he was living with. He wasn't a pimp, no. He was a wonderful person. He was a numbers banker, and the woman he lived with was a whore, and they lived together. He was a really good guy. I don't see anything wrong with that. She had a boy friend whom she slept with because she wanted to. She eventually left him. I see him as a victim really. And this man really did me a lot of favors and directed me to a lot of connections. He was my boy friend for a while. He always either gave me money or he got me connections. While he was getting me connections he always gave me money whenever I saw him. He wasn't flashy; not at all. But then in a way he was. He was such a good hustler, you know, and such a good con man. I never really knew him. But he was such fun to be with, such a

K

tree filling the white room with a cool green serenity—we were women talking about things women go through, things that physically happened to these two women, yet in a sense, psychically happen to all of us. For there are more immediate reasons behind any woman's interest in prostitution, that come to mind more quickly than mere academic interest. Or even a women's liberation version of prostitution, highly analytical, drenched in rhetoric and superior theoretical insight. Or a Marxist table of wage scales balancing the oldest profession with the less remunerative categories of woman's work. There are better and more homely reasons why all women are conscious, or paradoxically, refuse to be conscious, of prostitution.

A woman does not really need all that much imagination to have some insight into the prostitute's experience. I found a recess in my mind, a "closet" I call it, which, probably like most of us, I had always dimly perceived yet hesitated to approach, a fantasy mesmerizing me for half a lifetime, the fifteen or twenty years since ado-

L

M

the woman with loitering for the purposes of prostitution, and the judge will respond with, "Forget it, this is pointless." Other judges will send prostitutes up for fifteen to ninety days. It is a system which says that women who are making it with men for money, selling their body when it is the best, the only, commodity they have, are commiting a victimless crime, but, nonetheless, we're going to get them for it. And for me, there's no clearer indication than prostitution that all women are a potential species of social or political prisoner. Prostitution is really the only crime in the penal law where two people are doing a thing mutually agreed upon and yet only one, the female partner, is subject to arrest. And they never even take down the man's name. It's not his crime, but the woman's.*

Anyone who believes to some extent in the basic tenets of women's liberation has probably also believed that in some way

* The recent New York statute, which declares the male client (the "john") guilty too, in an act of female prostitution, is simply not enforced and may therefore be disregarded in such discussions.

And then you have a lawyer who you keep and pay, that you can call and you get away with a fine.

Having a lawyer, being smart, this makes it easier. You get out of jail faster and you can make more money. But I didn't always do that good. Like the last year when I was into addiction, I was grimy, came out of the bottom of the barrel. You can't keep it up. Because the heroin becomes too demanding, and you can't have time for all that bullshit, for making the rounds, being cool, and so on. You don't have time for all that. You have to work something out. But there's a trap you fall into once you get started and you're doing really good. I used to hang around uptown a lot, like at Minton's. It's a bar at 118th Street at St. Nicholas and Seventh Avenue. That's where Charlie Parker, Miles Davis, and a lot of those guys hung out. It's a place where all the real hustlers are, guys that blow $1,000, you know—pimps and everything. I've been in and out of there a lot and I was young. They used to like me and spent a lot of money on me. The pimps. Pimps spend money on some women. Sure they do.

J

good guy. He was an older guy—he was about forty-six—and he'd been in jail fourteen years, off and on, for everything. And it made him very difficult to know and very hard. I never really knew him. I never saw him without the façade. Soft he was, yes, but still I never knew him. Soft, in a special way.

There was one thing, though, and I think I've repressed it because I like to see him as a nice guy. It's not 'cause he's black he's a bastard. I don't have that white liberal hangup at all. Black people can be the biggest bastards in the world. Black people can be horrible people. I've seen more black sons-of-bitches than anything, and every pimp in the city's black. There are very few white pimps. And so it isn't his blackness that I was trying to protect in repressing what I'd remembered about him. It's that I like to see him as a nice guy. Now that I think of it—of course I don't know whether I'm paranoid or not—there was one funny thing that happened during the time I knew him. It was when I was in jail. That night I got busted, he wasn't around. And I was

K

lescence. It occurs to me to wonder if the night riders hold any of this hypnotized value for blacks. Or would it be the New Orleans Market? In any case, what is it like to stand on Broadway tonight . . . ? Perhaps the rest of us are merely deceiving ourselves—it is ultimately an experience we all share. But diluted. I think many of us, maybe all of us, are really selling and not knowing we're doing it. The question lies then in who among us *could* stand, or will *have* to stand, on Broadway tonight.

The watered-down character of our own prostitution occurred to me and to Liz the moment we remembered dates and dinners. I kept thinking back to a time when I first got my Bowery studio. The girl I lived with then had split and I was very alone. I was broke too, living on the forty dollars a month my mother sent me out of what she earned selling life insurance to people who didn't want it. The loft was cold as hell. I was sick all the time. Bronchitis. The only heat was a little pot-bellied stove; used to sleep with the damned dog to

L

prostitutes are the most exploited of women. And there has been much rhetoric on how prostitutes are the most oppressed among us, how in a sense they are models for the movement because most exploited, because engaged in work that is the most direct and honest expression of our general condition, prostitution putting the economic relationship between the sexes "right out front" and so forth. All of this, in an abstract way, does make sense to me. But I know too that when I go down every day to those pens below the court where the women are kept, all this no longer makes sense to me at all. Because all I see are the wrecks of what society has done to these particular individuals. I could rap to them about women's lib stuff for hours. And they are so out of touch with themselves, they cannot hear. Even if you assume that there's a sense of rage which develops, you can scarcely continue with that assumption when you see their terrible passivity, their remoteness from any consciousness of their condition.

Since I've been in court, I've seen cases of women

M

They used to give me a lot of coke—a lot of cocaine. But once you start on that heroin, they don't have anything to do with you after that. But the whole point was I really thought I was into something, boosting, and it was going to go on forever that way. I was always going to be like really into something cool and high rollin' and everything. But that's not true. Not with that heroin. Heroin's not like amphetamines. I think speed affects your brain and stuff like that. Heroin doesn't have that kind of effect on you. Heroin's just the opposite—I mean it's real down. That's why when people take an overdose their heart stops beating and it slows down your heart like to nothing—poop, poop, poop. Like nothing's happening.

It's a groove. If you were rich and could afford it and didn't have to work in the street and do things. . . . You see, heroin doesn't get you arrested; it's what you have to *do* to get the heroin that gets you arrested. Heroin's not bad for your body. There's no physical defect as a result of using heroin. What happens to people's bodies is that if they're reefing her-

J

more worried about him than I was about me. He was busted, too; I was afraid he'd get prison. But what happened was, he didn't have to go away at all; he got off. And it could be that he might have turned me in and got off. Of course, I had no way of knowing because he was downtown and I was uptown. I was at Fourteenth Street then. And I didn't think of it until much later. I did wonder why I got busted, and I couldn't imagine who would have turned me in. But I didn't know anyone else who could have. Because someone had turned me in, and there were only two people who could have—this guy and a woman, and she'd got busted before me. Maybe her thing was to get off her sentence too, but this guy had been sure he was going to be sent away. And so I was so surprised when he wasn't.

He'd even been in for murder. I don't know if he'd ever killed anyone. I never knew. He never told me. But I assumed he'd done it. You know, he might have had good reason to do it. I never thought of it, but he might have killed me too, if he'd

K

keep warm. And there was a young doctor chasing me around for a few months. I suppose there's some popular masculine belief that women artists are something special, you know, "liberated women." An interesting or an easy lay. This Brooks Brothers suit, Doctor John, began giving me a big rush. He took me out to dinner for a couple of weeks running. Then I began to think I had to make it with him. What was I putting out? He was putting out dinner. I needed the dinners, but I really could have used the cash. Sixty, maybe one hundred dollars; a whole month's rent was only fifty. John wouldn't buy sculpture. And he didn't seem to find my art interesting, still less to care about my soul. Would I have taken advantage of J's "connection" into prostitution if I'd had it then? Or did the garbage I made out of plaster in those days give me so much purpose and satisfaction I could pass up cash money? So I got five or six steak dinners in four weeks, held aloof from the doggie bag, and got laid for free.

Then I thought of the time when I really did plan

L

M

who have been arrested for years and years for nothing but prostitution—thirty-five, forty arrests in a year, maybe. Just back and forth, coming in and out. There's one lawyer I've seen do all the expensive prostitution grabs, an old, gray-haired, greasy, pin-stripe-suited guy, making all his money off women. But he's always the one they want. I don't know whether his offices are in the court and he just sits there and waits, or whether he goes into the pens and picks up cases, or whether he's known to all, or what the situation is, but he deals with all the prostitution cases where a lawyer is hired, all the cases that Legal Aid doesn't get, all the cases where a woman wants to get out quickly.

Few women actually go on trial for prostitution. Charged only with loitering, most simply plead guilty at arraignment and pay their fine, ranging from fifteen to one hundred dollars. Almost none of the women I've seen, maybe two, have had to go to the House of Detention because they were unable to pay their fine right on the spot. And a good three-quarters of the time cases are simply dismissed.

The charge of prostitu-

oin they don't go to the dentist. They don't go to the doctor. If you're rich and went to the doctor and you kept yourself up and you could afford heroin, it'd be a real groove. You could be totally out of it all the time. Not feeling, not knowing.

People do feel high on heroin. And you can even get a lot done. You know, musicians play. Charlie Parker played better. You can write on it. I know some actors who're acting on it, but they won't be for very long. 'Cause if you're rich and have somebody there to take care of you— be O.K. If the stuff cost just as much as cigarettes and was legal, be no problem.

There was a panic five years ago when there was no drugs in the street. I never knew the details, heard it through the grapevine. There was a whole thing going between Genovese and Robert Kennedy. Bobby was trying to get him. Genovese said something like "I'll show you what'll happen if I take all the stuff out of the street. Try to put a stop to it." During a panic you really find out who's on dope. Because everyone comes out looking for a bag—

J

killed someone else. I never thought of it. He didn't seem especially violent; no more violent than most guys. I think maybe I romanticized his crimes a bit. I always imagined he committed murder in self-defense. Yet I never did ask him so I never did know.

He was in the numbers. I don't care though. There was one time, one thing he did, that did get to me, that was when he broke up a crap game and stole the money in the pot from a lot of poor black people playing. Of course, the numbers is a racket played off the black poor too. It isn't until now that I see how exploitative he was. But in those days I was always concerned with his being a nice guy.

When prostitutes put down other women, women like housewives, it's really only out of self-defense. Prostitutes feel that housewives are very moralistic people who even know that their husbands are cheating on them. While they're cheating on them they're seeing us. We're really not a threat to them; not at all. I wouldn't mind if I had a husband who went to see

K

a sale. It was when I had just finished college. I was going on to Oxford, the rich relatives having swooped in at this juncture, offering the money to send me. I was not going alone, but with someone I liked, loved actually. A woman. The relatives didn't take to this at all ... true tragedy ... a *pervert* in the family. They held a tribal council just to discuss my crime, aunts and uncles flying in from all parts. The upshot was that I had to renounce my friend or give up Oxford. Didn't do either: I lied to them and went to Oxford with her. But before she could go, we had to find the money. I worked in a factory all summer and there still wasn't enough saved up. My friend was a graduate student with a place in the ghetto near the university. We lived in a rooming house, ate the food she brought home from waiting on tables, and kept a Dalmation who turned out to be deaf and capable of resisting our every effort at house training. Mother broke out in Sophie Portnoy tears upon seeing the place. It was the happiest summer of my life.

But by summer's end

L

tion itself, which was once merely a violation, is now a misdemeanor in New York, a heavier charge with a longer maximum sentence. The change was made at the recommendation of the Mayor's Committee on Prostitution. It is interesting that the only woman who served on this committee was a person connected in some capacity with the House of Detention. The committee's justification in lengthening the maximum penalty for prostitution was that there would be a longer period for rehabilitation in prison, the old sentence of fifteen days being far too short a time to affect change. Originally, in fact until two or three years ago, there was a separate court called Women's Court. But prostitutes are now arraigned in the regular arraignment part of the Criminal Court, like all other criminals.

In actual practice; raising the charge of prostitution to a misdemeanor has, paradoxically, actually softened it. What happens is this: the district attorney, who in the Complaint Room has the discretion (given the evidence that the policeman will submit) to charge a woman with a particular crime, is astute

M

chauffeur-driven Cadillacs, Mercedes Benzes, People you never thought was using heroin before, you find out: they come out like dogs. So it's a simple matter of a bag and who can afford it. If you can afford it you got it made, and you're not going to have to hustle or go uptown trying to get it. If you don't have money, somebody's gonna come and get you. Put you in jail. And then you don't have money for someone to get you out. And then you become a statistic.

You can say—well, if they didn't make a racket out of it. Well, can I tell you something? There's a lot of money involved in heroin, so they'll never make it legal and it'll never be abolished. And when there's that much money involved, forget it.

I'll bet legalizing prostitution would take a lot of wind out of its sails too. But in Nevada prostitution *is* legal and they have more murders and. . . . No, I don't think they should legalize prostitution. Anyway, I don't dig those state whore houses. In Reno they have legal whore houses, and they have them in Hamburg too. Everyone walks around with a li-

J

whore. It wouldn't bother me. But then, if he had an affair with somebody, that would bother me—if he loved someone, if he got involved, then that would be a threat. The difference between being a prostitute and being a wife is the security a wife's got. But it's also the difference in having a lot of men versus having just one. If you have a lot of men—like if you have ten a day—then you're not dependent on any *one* of them. They can always be replaced; if one of them gives you trouble, you can just say "fuck you." But you can't do that if you're married and you can't do that if you're being kept. Of course, you can't depend on any john either. If the stock market falls, it's just like any other business. But that's the thing I wanted—never to be dependent. I spent the night with a john only once and I wouldn't even go out to dinner.

A lot of them wondered —they want to take you out to dinner, want to talk to you; they wanted to mimic the behavior of lovers. Maybe that's what they want. Some of them really do want that—to be lovers. They fall in love with you.

K

there still wasn't enough money. So I got a brilliant idea. I would sell myself for no less than a fortune and make us rich quick. I was younger than she and fervent after love's heroism. She left me four years later for someone else. By a fine irony, it was the same midwinter that my lie came to light and the Milletts all invited me for Christmas just so they could disown me. That summer I can't remember whether I was planning on five hundred or a thousand dollars—but it was awfully goddamned ambitious. Had my john all picked out, friend of my rich aunt, owned a Cadillac agency, and was loaded, and, I thought, lecherous. Betting on the fresh youth angle. I never did get around to revealing my great scheme to him, but I did have the details pretty well worked out. I guess I was chicken: I was afraid he'd tell my folks. The factory was so monotonous, the assembly line such a nightmare, I woke up jibbering and sweating: I'd worked all summer and was still so far away from the $800 needed. There had to be a lot of money at once for passage and to satisfy customs.

L

M

enough to know that if his office overcharges—if for instance, his office charges a woman with prostitution, when the only evidence it has is for loitering—the judge will raise hell and throw it out of court. So the practice has simply been to lay a charge of loitering rather than one of prostitution. And in nearly every loitering case I've watched, the district attorney dismisses charges. What this means is that a woman may be picked up and literally come into court and walk right out. Generally, however, she is picked up at night and locked up in the pens overnight until arraigned. Even when she escapes the fine through dismissal of charges, she has been harassed. When she is fined in addition, she has contributed to the support of the system that oppresses her. It also means that there is no systematic attempt to enforce the new prostitution law with its intention of longer periods of rehabilitation. Instead, the effect is only a continuous intimidation and inconvenience placed upon prostitutes—and a continuous fleecing.

Almost none of the women I've seen actually committed to the House of

cense. If you ever tried to get another job, forget it. They've got you on the police books, and the state is making a lot of money on prostitution. Cool. Got it? And then the second thing is, like you're in there. You're really in a box, because they've got you licensed and ticketed and you can't do anything else. In Hamburg you can't appear on the streets in the rest of the city, in the nice part, after 8 P.M. so you're on a reservation, in a cell. In the Near East the brothels are literally cages, and whores have to turn twenty to thirty tricks a day.

My first experience with prostitution was in a whorehouse, and you're in a cage no matter which way you look at it. That was a real dragged-out horror; I'll never forget that as long as I live. I was taken there by some old woman who was a prostitute, who was teaching me to be a prostitute. She'd been a prostitute since she was about thirteen years old; her name was Djuna Mae. So she was going to teach me to be a prostitute. She went through the whole thing of taking me to her room, showing me how to give head and all that. So

J

That's very hard to take. I never liked that. Because that was crossing the boundary—it wasn't business any more. And this was business; it wasn't love.

Johns are full of self-pity. They come on with this line about their wife doesn't understand them, and we follow right along with it. Or they turn us on to being good sports. And, you know, that made me feel great—that they'd say I was a good sport. They make you feel for a moment that you're somebody special, not a whore. When they would tell me I was special, I wanted to say; "Baby, I'm just a plain whore. Forget that crap." And the old line about "How could a nice girl like you get into a business like this?" That's really said a lot. It's said a lot, especially by people who seem educated or middle class. And then sometimes they tell you that you aren't really a whore. I had a guy who I was seeing—about a month ago—I actually couldn't take it any longer. I saw him every week or every two weeks; he gave me a lot of money. Every time I saw him he gave me about sixty dollars, and I would see him for about an hour.

K

Harebrained scheme that it was, I was smart enough to know my body was all I had to trade on. I met a girl the other day who had actually sold herself for a woman she loved. Was the kid a better lover than I was (wit and determination enough not to settle on a friend of the family as her patron)—or was her beloved only a better tyrant?

It seems to me that prostitution is somehow paradigmatic, somehow the very core of the female's social condition. It not only declares her subjection right in the open, with the cash nexus between the sexes announced in currency, rather than through the subtlety of a marriage contract (which still recognizes the principle of sex in return for commodities and historically has insisted upon it), but the very act of prostitution is itself a declaration of our value, our reification. It is not sex the prostitute is really made to sell: it is degradation. And the buyer, the john, is not buying sexuality, but power, power over another human being, the dizzy ambition of being lord of another's will for a stated period of time—the euphoric abili-

L

M

Detention have been charged with prostitution, but with other crimes. They may and do hustle, but that isn't what they're being picked up for. And every woman I've seen who comes in to pay bail comes in with a man, so one may be sure there is still a very active pimp trade. What is being done lately, however, is a good deal more sinister than jailing whores. Prostitutes are being imprisoned through a kind of preventive detention on other grounds than prostitution itself: namely petty theft and drugs, the two areas where prostitutes are most likely to have previous records or might "reasonably" be expected to be future offenders—the two crimes prostitutes most often resort to to supplement or to palliate their prostitution. So while prostitution itself is hardly prosecuted, prostitutes themselves are imprisoned and subject to the specious, and unjustifiable—often even capricious—methods of preventative detention.

In the court itself the women concentrate their attentions upon the men who will judge or release them, the battery of male officials at whose mercy

she finally took me to this whorehouse in Trenton, New Jersey. This place was too much to believe. The police, the detectives used to come every day for their payoff. They used to talk to the madam of the house; they'd pick up their money and leave. Only white men came into this place. Right in the middle of Trenton.

The girls were all black, with a few exceptions. Not entirely all black. There were a few exceptions. Variety. Very important—variety in a whorehouse. And you'd just sit there. A guy would come in; he'd look everybody over and he'd pick you and you'd go off to the room. You could never see your money. The madam would demand the money, and when you got ready to leave she would give you your half. I decided after three days it wasn't for me. I didn't like it, and I wanted to leave. And she didn't have my money. She'd gambled it away. Later found out that if I had a pimp she would have given me my money. He would have threatened her. I didn't have any protection. I didn't have a man who was a pimp who could kick her ass, or whatever they do.

So I didn't get my mon-

J

K

He was a very, very old guy—about sixty-seven. He was in love with me, and he would keep telling me, "You're not a whore." He was so hung up. Poor man. You have to feel sorry for someone who's that screwed up.

Johns go into this whole thing like, "I want to leave her but if I divorce her, she'll take all my money." And they come on screaming and yelling about their alimony. I don't believe in alimony, but I certainly believe in child support. When you look into it, that's usually all they're paying, if that. And the wife, who's stuck taking care of the children, is doing him a service. In waiting on the child she's doing his work too because a child is something between two people.

You wouldn't have prostitution in a utopia. But you might still have it somewhere halfway between what we have now and a utopia. Prostitution might even, in a certain sense, be a reasonable service to be sold—sexual attention. But as it is now, I see it as a symptom, a symptom of the kind of sex we have here now. I think

ty to direct and command an activity presumably least subject to coercion and unquestionably most subject to shame and taboo. This is a very considerable impression of power to purchase for ten or fifteen dollars. When the bargain is struck, the prostitute will, like labor in any exploitative relationship, try to do the least she possibly can to earn it. But at the same time the bargain *is* struck, and the very fact that it *can be* demonstrates the relative position of male and female, his place as master, hers as slave, outlined in a manner gross enough, enlarged enough, to evoke an earlier, more open mastery. Prostitution is, in a sense, antique, a fossil in the social structure, pointing, as all fossils do, to an earlier age. But the correct metaphor must be social, not phenomenological; must remind us, as Lévi-Strauss emphasizes, that men have traded in women throughout most of human history and have regarded her as currency in every country of the world, in societies where a monetary system was never arrived at. Little wonder that the origins of prostitution lie in temples converted from fertility

L

they are—the Man who will decide their fate. It is only in the pens, the cages in the basement of the building, that the women are together as women, and the pens reveal the way women relate to each other. In the pens there is a strange hilarity; the women rap and talk to each other. The comfortableness between the women there is a stark contrast to the way they ignore each other when upstairs in the court itself. They seem open to each other, apparently familiar with each other too. It's a kind of laughing, giggling, crazy high scene, like when they are outside, or just paying their fine, finished and on their way out. There are many who are arrested in bunches, two or three together, and as they leave it's hard to know how they are connected to the men around—whether they are all one stable or couples of individual pimps and whores. These are the two occasions when the prostitutes I see are open and jovial—paying their fines or waiting in the pens. Then they seem together, giggling about the whole thing, walking around together. There is something about the way they relate to each other

M

ey, but I really wasn't uptight for money because I still had money in the bank, you know what I mean. Didn't really need to go to this whorehouse 'cause I had money in the bank, but I was doing something *different*. It was a whole different *scene* for me. I wasn't on the street. I was getting experience. I romanticized this sort of shit.

I was real impressed with Djuna Mae and this homosexual Bernard. I used to stop by their house every morning. They lived between my house and my church. After a while I'd start for Djuna Mae's, and they'd give me grass and then they'd talk about the money they made and doing their thing. They were very cool people and I was very impressed. Djuna Mae made it sound so groovy to go to this whorehouse. I could make money and that was where it was at. And besides, I was trying very hard to impress her. To show her that I had guts. I dug her. I liked Djuna Mae. I gave her the first heroin she ever had in her life. She was an older woman. She'd never used heroin in her life. She's been in the street for years. She stuck with it. I

J   K

as long as you're going to have compulsive marriage and compulsive families, I think you're going to have prostitution. If I had a husband who wanted variety, it would be better if he had prostitutes than lovers. That's my hangup: I'm very possessive. I have this demanding possessiveness and insecurity. I wish I weren't so hung up on monogamy myself; I think it's idiocy. Monogamy and prostitution go together. There are lonely women all over New York, women sitting in bars, who would go with a guy, take him back to their place, make it with him, treat him well too—and be glad to do it. But instead men go to prostitutes on Seventh Avenue, Fifty-Seventh Street, and Broadway, because there are no strings attached to a whore. And if you're married, that's a consideration. There isn't even that much chance that she'll be clean if she's from the street. But there are no strings, absolutely no strings attached.

I don't know why they go with girls from the street, unless they don't have connections. And there's always the chance of getting rolled. I really

rites to the cult of patriarchy.

Somehow every indignity the female suffers ultimately comes to be symbolized in a sexuality that is held to be her responsibility, her shame. Even the self-denigration required of the prostitute is an emotion urged upon all women, but rarely with as much success: not as frankly, not as openly, not as efficiently. It can be summarized in one four-letter word. And the word is not *fuck*, it's *cunt*. Our self-contempt originates in this: in knowing we are cunt. That is what we are supposed to be about—our essence, our offense.

Both the rewards and the punishment of accepting this definition are extravagant. J told me that in her prime, when she was really operating a business, she made $800 a week. With a Ph.D. and after ten years' experience in teaching, I was permitted to make only $60 a week. Since J and I are both academics, this amused us enormously. And we saw in it other kinds of prostitution such as those the academic world requires, the sycophancy due to department chairmen, the psychic blow

L

M

that I haven't seen among women in a long time, not since I was a child. It's a wild, silly kind of camaraderie. But I cannot trust it much: the best-friend routine, the effusiveness of our childhood, girlhood chumming was pretty phony. This has the same quality for me, the same nervous superficiality, the same illusory solidarity—longed for and impossible, therefore counterfeited, parodied. I cannot believe in the reality of this intimacy because I know that many of the women talking to each other, seemingly such good buddies, don't even know each other. Except that they've seen each other in the pens often, maybe spent time in the House of Detention together, or just seen each other around the court a lot. But in their lives, this is probably one of the few ways in which they enjoy the company of other women—the rest of the time isolated from each other by the pimps and the johns.

It is only in the pens that I can get attention or response from the women I try to work with; in court all their attention is riveted on the men. In court they are uninterested in me because I am a woman, and

never thought of it as revenge. I was turning her on like she was turning me on.

A lot of people go into the street on a dare, or for kicks, or to prove something. I mean, like when I think about how goddamned naive I was. I went from the convent to the streets. But they aren't that far apart, because evil had a glamour for me. And I thought Djuna Mae was cool. But you can bet that was some ugly whorehouse. Oh god, it was horror. I wound up burning that goddamned whorehouse down. And going to jail. I actually burned it down. It was a matter of principle. I wanted my money. Every time I went back and asked for my money, she was never there. And I thought: "The bitch is in there and she's coming out!" I watched the fire. It was a real groove. The flames were leapin' out all over. I didn't want to kill her; I just wanted to see her come out. They knew I did it. Arthur knew it. I had a lawyer. The DA was a Catholic. It was a "house of sin." I was facing five to twenty years. But I got out of it pretty cool.

This place looked very legitimate from the outside. A friend of mine says half

J

don't know why they go to the street. I think that it must be because there is nothing asked of them, even so far as spending the night. And then there are no games: You don't have to play seduction or anything. It's right on the table. And if they're worried about their masculinity, well, they're taking a chance with a girl if she's going for free. You don't know if she'll let you get laid or not. You might have to go through a lot of changes to get laid. And you might have to spend money and spend time. And a prostitute can't say, "Well, I don't suck," whereas another woman might. She's got to do what he says or the deal is off. A pickup doesn't have to. You make the deal with her when you pick her up, you may do it without even speaking of it. But if she's chicken, well, you lose the whole thing—the time and effort. But with a whore, there's no risk, no gamble. Somehow you always pay for what you get, one way or another.

But what they're buying, in a way, is power. You're supposed to please them. They can tell you what to do, and you're supposed to

K

jobs we call faculty meetings. But I know what the years in sexual prostitution have cost J too, can see it in the damage in her eyes, at moments their blueness as dead as glass. It is no melodious or pietistic bullshit to see prostitution as a particular crime against her humanity. Her suffering comes back when I remember our long halting talks, both her admissions and her denials, the long pained hours, her sensitive face. How much it has all hurt her: the years of silence and repression, the secrecy so deep it forbade her even to remember for some years after. And at the time, how deeply the pain required that she utterly anesthetize herself, passive even to the point of numbness. Now too bitter to love anyone. That's a lot to pay even for $800 a week; it's a still more terrible sum for which to hold men liable.

For the prostitute, probably the ultimate oppression is the social onus with which she is cursed for accepting the agreed-upon social definition of her femaleness, her sexual abjectification. A Marxist analysis here is quite inadequate, as it fails to take psychologi-

L

therefore, by definition, powerless. It's not a put down, not hostility, only their conviction that my sex makes me impotent to help them and they must relate to those in power over them. Then too, the only image of "straight" women they have, of nonprostitutes, is one of contemptuous, moralistic, jealous, or disapproving respectable women. So there is little to encourage them to speak with me. But in the pens it is possible to relate to them somewhat, to interview them, to try to help.

I never use the phrase "women's liberation." I did once or twice early on and people sort of nodded unresponsively. So I gave that up. What I do now is simply tell the women why I'm talking to them, and sometimes they may end up mentioning women's lib. But I don't start off announcing I'm in women's lib and trying to relate to you because I think you're my sister. What I try to do is come on as straight, as direct, and as open as I can, and not go through any legal junk, but just begin to talk to them about their lives, what they've done, when they were married, when they've had kids and where their kids are,

M

of the air-conditioned apartments in New York are whorehouses. I could have made a lot of money. Eight hundred dollars, or half of that—if she'd paid up.

If you're gonna whore you need protection: a man's protection from other men. All men are in the protection business. We don't need protection from women: if men didn't beat us up we wouldn't need half the husbands we got. You know, most whores don't even get laid by their pimps. Most of them in a stable never get laid at all. There's usually one who does. He usually has a favorite; if he doesn't have a favorite in the stable he usually has a favorite across town some place. There's always a woman some place he spends money on. But there has to be a lesbian or someone in a stable to take care of you sexually.

Pimps got to save themselves for driving their Cadillacs. They cheat on us. They're women-haters. They have a very low opinion of the women in the stable. Who ever respected his slaves? And I think probably a lot of them have a very difficult time getting it up anyway. Be-

J

please them, follow orders. Even in the case of masochists who like to follow orders themselves, you're still following *his* order to give him orders. Prostitution not only puts down women, but it puts down sex—it really puts down sex. Often I really couldn't understand the customer, couldn't understand what he *got* out of this, because I really felt I was giving nothing. What he got was nothing. I could never see myself in his position, doing what he was doing. I would think it would be humiliating to buy a person, to *have* to offer somebody money. I felt the poor guy's gotta buy it; I felt sorry for him. He's really hard up. But then I remember he could be not so hard up as to have to buy, really; he wanted instead to have something so special you gotta buy it. I did not always see the gesture of buying someone as arrogance because I did not feel that controlled by the customer. I felt I was the boss because I could say no to the deal. I didn't want even the involvement of being a kept woman because then it's control again. When you're living with someone—when I was

K

cal factors such as shame into account. For there *is* a crucial element quite beyond the economic. Perhaps it might be described as a kind of psychological addiction, to self-denigration, an addiction I feel all women are socially conditioned to accept. In a sexual culture as unhealthy as our own, it is reiterated again through the manner of our sexual acts that the female is carnality, a thing—cunt. It is as though cunt were posed as the opposite of ego or selfhood, its very antithesis, the negative pole of selfhood or spirit. The sale of women in prostitution reinforces this attitude more powerfully than any other event.

There is much cant about female masochism. One hears from males in general and Freudians in particular that it is congenital. One can recognize this as a hoax, a rationalization, knowing that any atrocity performed upon women is likely to be justified this way, with claims that self-defeating behavior observed in women is organic, constitutionally female, inseparable from the x chromosome, and so forth. I am as annoyed as anyone

L

M

how long they've been in the House of Detention, and what they've been picked up for before. It's very rare, in fact it only happened twice, that a woman began to talk to me without my asking, really began to talk to me about her feelings about it all. Generally, when I've talked to them awhile, they do become responsive. But then, you know, considering all the thousands of women who go through these pens, I really haven't talked to that many. What I have done more than others is to see and carefully observe the way that they are treated here. But the feeling of distance is so enormous, the conditions themselves so impossible, you feel uncomfortable—you do not really have an opportunity to talk. You can't really talk to somebody when you're in front and they're behind bars. Even if you can come on in a way that will open them up, you can't talk to somebody about that kind of stuff if the situation is one where they're the ones that are getting fucked over and you're not. Immediately there is an inequality very hard to bridge. The only women I've talked to who had been in prostitution

cause that's a very important thing with a pimp— you do *not* fuck. You do not fuck. You just make money. You don't fuck women: you make money off of them. Like women are like employees. What if the pimp really had to satisfy the whole stable?

Say, she comes in and she needs a little loving— like to be loved—that takes a couple of hours. Say he had to do that five times a night. The bastard would be dead in the morning. And anyway, he's got to drive his Cadillac. Heavy work. He's got to brag to the other pimps and that takes some energy. Hang around in bars. Pimps look and act like most other men. They're the same as any men are with each other. When men get together men are like men. They flex their muscles, talk about their conquests, and their bitches. The language might vary from place to place or the words might be a little different, but they do the same thing when they get together at Small's as they do at the Playboy Club.

And pimps make and spend a lot of money. They spend a helluva lot of money. I mean, to spend $1,-000, $2,000 a day is noth-

J   K

living with someone, that's when I really felt controlled. Then you can't refuse. People I've lived with, men I've lived with—I really felt that they had power because I couldn't say no to them. Because then I could lose them and, if I did, I would lose my whole life—lose my whole reason for living.

And with men I lived with, it wasn't just sex with which they controlled me. It was like pushing me around, giving me orders, unreasonable jealousy. There was one guy—I think of him all the time. When I think of a male chauvinist, I think of him. He's a black guy. He actually got me out of the business. He told me, "Either you quit or I'll leave you," so I quit and that's how I got out of it. It was a *man*, actually, who got me out of it. I got into it myself.

I felt freer of men as a prostitute than I would as a wife or a mistress or a beloved. Because he isn't there all the time—the john. Like for half an hour and that's all. And then someone else comes in. They really can't control you very much. You don't have the oppression that comes because you love the

when I hear such twaddle, and the very term irritates me as a deliberate misunderstanding. Yet I know that I behave "masochistically" myself; I know that I continually make myself suffer in ways that men wouldn't think of. And I do it because masochism is part of the female role. It's feminine and I have been trained into it, even unconsciously. But this being the case, masochism is an inaccurate term altogether. If such utterly self-destructive behavior is urged upon us, it is because our society is bent upon destroying something in its females, destroying their ego, their self-respect, their hope, their optimism, their imagination, their self-confidence, their will. "Masochism" in such a group is, in fact, only the behavior of accommodation, forced upon any oppressed group that it may survive. Because if members of this group do not so cooperate in their own oppression by interiorizing their oppressor's hatred and contempt, their insubordination will become apparent, and they will be punished and perhaps die. This is really not very difficult to understand if one observes

L

and who were interested and really cared about women's liberation were the women at Phoenix House, the drug rehabilitation center. Elsewhere, what happens is that we talk of things that concern women, things women undergo, and strong feelings of sisterhood, closeness, concern, and strength just come out—not couched in the terms and jargon of the movement—but spontaneously emerging out of this shared experience. There is a communion of emotion, even if at this point politicized discussions of it only interfere.

Prostitution arrests vary enormously from day to day: one day thirty-five arrests for prostitution and none for drugs; the next day only ten prostitution arrests and fifteen for drugs. You really get the feeling that when the police do go out, they do a whole armful, probably because somebody called up and said, "West Forty-Fourth Street is bothering me, would you go over and clean it up." The cops delicately refer to the vice squad, the plain clothes unit that does all the prostitution arrests, as the Pussy Brigade. And that's just the

M

ing for a pimp. They party. A pimp's whole life is a party. They do most of their partying with other pimps. The *real* people. Not the broads who make the money, mere employees. Pimps go play golf together. They have fun with one another. A lot of them are some of the most handsome, intelligent guys. They have to be. You can't be an idiot and be a pimp. An idiot can't be a pimp and pull it off successfully. He's going to get it. And it's true, any guy who's a good pimp would be a good banker. They're in business. And the best pimps come from the South. It's very interesting; they make the best hustlers too. Guys from the South, they make the best con men. I think it's because nobody suspects them; everyone thinks they're stupid. It's a fence game. They even fool black people with that shit, the country boy act. But that whole pimp-whore thing is something else. I didn't ever have a pimp. No, I can't say that. Yes I did. I rationalize mine away because he was my man. Because there was nobody else but me that I know of—no stable. I selected him without making him my pimp. But I guess I

J

K

person and are so afraid of losing them. When you're a whore and somebody rejects you and says they want to see another girl, well, that's just part of the business. That's the reason he's coming to you in the first place—because he wants variety. It's much safer to do it for money, much safer.

You know, often it wasn't that a guy wanted to take over and invade my life so much. But that I would let them. I don't know if I'm still that way. I haven't tried lately. But in those days, I would let them do it. They didn't even have to want to. Like sometimes the guy might even resent it; he might want me to be more independent.

I don't think you can ever eliminate the economic factor motivating women to prostitution. Even a call girl could never make as much in a straight job as she could at prostitution. All prostitutes are in it for the money. With most uptown call girls, the choice is not between starvation and life, but it is a choice between $5,000 and $25,000 or between $10,000 and $50,000. That's a pretty big

the behavior of other socially subordinate groups.

Prostitutes are bitter toward men and will often say they hate them. Given their relationships with men, how could they love them? It is difficult to see the prostitute's subjection to the measured sadism of the pimp pass for love by any criterion of emotional sanity. And so it is fairly common for prostitutes to love other women; women neither buy nor brutalize them (though it is not unknown for a prostitute to keep another woman as a pimp is kept, mimicking the heterosexual roles prevalent throughout society). In women, prostitutes seek the human acknowledgment men deny them and the tenderness our every custom denies men even learn. I'm told that in the House of Detention the women feel a curious serenity, often confessing that they enjoy going back. However absurd, this is a fantasy to which I find myself sympathetic. Somehow this fits our habit of self-abuse, happy when we are all locked up safe in our misery together. The prison is a secret home, asylum away from the pimp, away from the cop, away from

L

way they see it; it's just picking up the cunt, bringing it in, and letting it go loose again. Obviously, there's a lot of graft going on, a lot of give and take between the women and the cops; they've known each other for a long time and they're known to watch out for each other. There's not even the sembalance of hostility between them. In fact, there may be something quite opposite, a total passivity on the part of the woman in relation to the police, but there is also a whole lot of what sociologists call "accommodating" behavior too. The scene in court is astonishing: the woman is absolutely flirting throughout the whole proceedings. She's doing it when she comes in; she does it when she's going out with the cops and clerks. It doesn't break down for a minute. That interchange is very weird to watch, and it's something that would take a long time to explain, but you know the woman's security and advantage lies in maintaining this relationship.

There was a woman who came in Tuesday, and like most of the women who come in, she wore a wig (a trivial item but I find it significant, basic to the whole

M

made him into my child instead.

It's a whole game. When a pimp is trying to pull a girl into the stable, I think he does a bit of romancing and spending and everything like that. And once he gets her, he keeps on promising. There's a book based on interviews with a pimp called Iceberg Slim, very accurate account of the whole scene. Prostitutes admire pimps. They'll kill for them. Then they'll turn around and kill the pimp too. They do kill pimps sometimes. There's always a great amount of fear in a pimp. There's a terrible amount of fear when you have slaves about. Fear of what will happen to you.

Pimps do rotten things. I guess they have to. That life is kind of bitter. And if you're in that life, how else are you gonna be a pimp? And live up to it? You've got to prove everything all over every day, right? You've got all the guys watching you. What do they do? What kinds of really raunchy things do they do? What are they capable of, these cats? I saw a girl walk into a bar and hand the pimp a $100 bill. He took it and burned it in her face and turned around and knocked her down on

J

K

choice: a pretty big difference. You can say that they're in this business because of the difference of $40,000 a year. A business man would say so. Businessmen do things because of the difference of $40,000 a year. Call girls do go into capitalism and think like capitalists. But you can't say, even of the call girl, that she has so many other ways to earn an adequate living. Even with an undergraduate degree, chances are that she couldn't do better than earn $5,000 or $6,000 a year, outside of prostitution. Because it's very *hard* for women to earn an adequate living and so we do not have much economic choice—even the call girl. And the minority woman on the street—the poor woman—she has no choice at all.

For white women you usually can't say that there's no choice but prostitution. There is. But the choice itself is a choice between working for somebody else and going into business for yourself. Going into business for yourself and hoping to make a lot of money. There's that choice. Prostitution on those terms is a kind of laissez-faire capitalism. But

dependency (you get fed in the House, and whenever you get fed you don't have to hustle). And there one is with other women, the one group of persons we flee most till we are confined together—at last a circumstance intervenes that justifies our hidden desires for association. Intimacy in inmateship. Even the defeatism of so arranging your life that the only time you are with other women is in prison is congruent with the repugnance for each other imposed on us by our training and situation. Yet for all one observes of it, one can still be overwhelmed at what women will do to themselves. Habits as well-learned as ours can be practiced anywhere—proficiently, at home or away.

This has been the most difficult bit of writing I've ever done, the most costly in time and psychic energy. Only to bring the people together was exhausting. It took most of the month of June; days and days of phoning; Byzantine diplomacy. Almost every woman knows someone in the life or someone who knows someone. But for people to come and talk is very very

L

sense of remoteness, of self-distancing that goes on, the escapism). This woman was truly beautiful, with a really beautiful face, a black woman, wearing an enormous blond wig, a halter top with lots of empty space around the belly-button, with a high chest and wearing a very short skirt. From what I could tell (and I tried to watch her closely during the twenty-five minutes she was there rapping with everyone) she seemed to be enormously attached to the cop who had arrested her. She was flirting with him, even trying to talk to him, but not in the usual manner, that casual back and forth I hear everyday: "Hey, Tina, glad to see you again. What's it this time baby? Sure. See you around." This time it seemed different. She really cared: she looked sorry to leave. She kept on looking back at him—and that tore me up.

Ultimately I have come to understand the legal treatment of prostitution is only a farce. The court is merely a machine, processing an average of thirty women a day on loitering and prostitution charges, spitting out people like paper wads. The women I

M

the floor and kicked her and said, "I told you, bitch, $200. I want $200, not $100." Now she's gotta go out again and make not another hundred, but two hundred. I know of some pimps who killed a whore with an overdose of heroin and then fucked her dead body. They're sick. Half the time they're not in their right minds—out on coke or something. It's a special world they live in.

Getting into turning tricks after the way I grew up, the convent and all—I was always aware of a certain amount of guilt. Always guilty. All that guilt. But once I started I was kind of like *in* it. After the first time it was all over. 'Cause then I had lost face, so what the hell. Everybody knew. And when I burned down that whorehouse I made the Trenton papers. I was scared and guilty, but I got a kick out of it too. Both emotions at once. Got a real bang out of it. Got arrested: never been arrested before. Like a movie. Me and my girl friend. Set the fire and called the fire department. Then this big deal of getting out of town in the back of a car, and policemen. I was eighteen. I have no idea

J

it's also slavery, psychologically. And it's also feudalism, where the protection of a pimp is offered in return for services. Unless you're starving so bad you literally have no choice—as some women do—the choice is between a lower-middle income and a really good one, lots of money. Lots of whores are on junk: it's expensive. A junkie has very little choice. For the junkie the only choice is getting off junk, a tough thing to do. Then too, a junkie off junk wouldn't be a junkie anymore. Prostitution is a kind of addiction too. It's an addiction to money. I felt that.

The worst part about prostitution is that you're obliged not to sell sex only, but your humanity. That's the worst part of it: that what you're selling is your human dignity. Not really so much in bed, but in accepting the agreement—in becoming a bought person. When I really felt like a whore was when I had to talk to them, fucking up to them really while only talking. That's why I don't like to go out to dinner and why I don't like to spend the night. Because when

K

difficult; to ask them is difficult too. This summer's conversations were a long, strange experience, at first only puzzlingly traumatic. Fumio and I quarreled with a terribly acrimony every night I held them, as if some inordinate resentment had taken hold of me and some overwhelming and surly defensiveness had found him, neither of which we understood. When the tapes were made I regarded them as precious. Then I found I could not even bear to listen to the tapes for two weeks after their completion. The experience had to settle down; I was very shaken by it. I found that it changed me a lot. I can hear it in the tapes, a continuous process from the first tapes where I talked all the time to the latter ones where I learned to listen a little. And there's a change in my voice from the usual excited voice one has at meetings, reserved for moments when everyone's trying to shout each other down, to a quieter voice, much quieter.

During the weeks we met at my studio I went along, day after day, driving myself, working twelve or twenty hours on an hour

L

M

saw while doing statistical work in the court clerk's office, arraignment section, are very different from the group below in the pens, if only because they are sufficiently well off to get bailed out. Such women are not the committed cases, not the addicts, not the petty thieves. The rest down below stairs I remember most as being totally drugged out, their passivity a wall between us, between themselves and the world. But the group who come to court after bail, dressed up and eager to deal their way out of charges, look well kept and they usually show up with this unctuous lawyer, who's really a pig. What takes place in court is just the machine part of it, the racket part of it, how it actually works, coming in and going out. And it's nothing. Just like going to the doctor. Just as quick and just as routine.

The real reasons why the law was changed and the prostitution charge raised to a misdemeanor have obviously nothing to do with the stated intention given out at the time, namely the need for longer periods of rehabilitation, but only reflects the varying pressure the city feels from businessmen to clean up

where she is now, my girl friend.

She was from Perth Amboy. I go to Asbury Park and I still see people I knew when I was in the streets. Occasionally here in New York I meet somebody I knew when I was in the streets. I still see some gay guy I used to hustle with when I was in Connecticut. I haven't seen him in a while. I wonder what happened to him. He was a friend of mine. There were a few people who were real friends. But there isn't much room for friendship in that world. Though there are some people who are all right no matter what. Not much space for love either.

People can't trust each other much in that world. You need the drug so badly you'll do anything. And there are so many games and roles; mommy and daddy and kid games. You need each other only 'cause there's nobody and nothing else.

It's going to be hard to change this system. Black men are into a special macho thing now that goes well with the system of exploitation we call pimps and whores. It may not be "legitimate" for white women rather than black

J   K

they talk about "niggers," you've just got to go "uh-huh, uh-huh" and agree with them. That's what I really couldn't stand. It was that kind of thing. That's when I really felt I was kissing their ass—*more* than when I was literally kissing their ass. That's when I really felt that I was a whore. That's the most humiliating thing—having to agree with them all the time because you're bought.

That's why it's not as easy as just saying "prostitution is selling a service." That's why it's selling your soul and not selling a service. In business people sell their souls too, and that's why business destroys people—how would you feel about selling encyclopedias to poor people? But there's a special indignity in prostitution, as if sex were dirty and men can only enjoy it with someone low. It involves a type of contempt, a kind of disdain, and a kind of triumph over another human being. Guys who can't get it up with their wives can do it with whores. They have to pay for it. For some of them, *paying* for it is very important.

But a lot of them didn't make me feel degraded.

or two of rest, often none at all. Later I understood why I did it, and why the experience was so strangely unsettling. I think it wasn't only a feeling that we'd embarked on a great and possibly even dangerous project, but one that affected me at a level far deeper than conscious understanding. I mention all this because I venture that it has some larger meaning than just my own response, the emotions of an individual woman. You see, I began by saying I had an interest in prostitution because of this or that intellectual, social, or political concern. But it emerged in time that it was more than that—that prostitution was what I've called one of my "closets." Everyone has such closets in their mind that they're afraid to look into because they're terrifying. The notion of standing on Broadway offering myself to strangers, the idea of being that brave or desperate terrified me—terrifies me more than anything else I can think of. And the women who have been there and can tell me they've been through it do more than command my respect or imaginative understanding. It's almost as

L

M

hotels. This is also the major block to legalization.

Since no one takes it seriously the entire legal aspect of prostitution is just bullshit, based on nothing but some kind of out-of-nowhere sense that they just must get this show into production over and over again, not because it matters or because it'll change anything or because anyone believes there is anything wrong with it at all—but because it is essential to keep up appearances. It's clear that prostitutes are the greatest spectacle in the court, every day's choicest entertainment. What happens to them matters to no one. They're no threat, but the law keeps on picking them up. They have relationships with the cops, and the judges know them too; the whole system bleeds them sexually and economically. They put out and they pay their fines. Public decorum is satisfied because whores are arrested. This is the justice men bestow on women.

M

women to approach the black liberation guys with this. But that's where their heads are at now. They'd listen to white women fast-

er. Black men might do a lot about prostitution if they thought they could stop white men from coming uptown and turning a trick. They could stop putting black women out on corners. The women they are calling whore, the women they hate, the women who they say got no class, and are all the things they don't want, those are the women they keep sticking out on the corner. Most of those guys uptown that keep sticking black women out on corners get into their El Dorado and go downtown, and spend most of her money on some eighteen- or nineteen-year-old little white girl. She's a lady 'cause she went to a fancy school and her folks are white bread. That's racism. Doing Whitey's thing. Charlie's nigger. Fucking Charlie's daughter. And you know he ain't doing that white girl no good either. Getting back at Charlie through women. Putting both women down. Since childhood that's what he's seen Charlie do. Can't do nothing else, 'cause Charlie's his role model. He has no other. The white man is the *only* man. And that's why he tries to get a Cadillac and a white woman. Then

J

Most of them didn't. If they had, I wouldn't have stayed. Some of them did—for example, the southerners. They were awful. And there's something about some men—the way they fuck—they lean on you and poke you with their bones. I'm sure they're not conscious of it. I found that so much more with southerners. They hurt me. And they've got to use all the *words*—all the words they can't say to their wives, covering you with the language of their shame. And their anger. That was another thing I didn't like either. When you're doing prostitution—if only in order to cope—you've got to have tremendous defenses. You've just gotta turn off, somehow. Drugs or will power, you've got to cut yourself off.

I think that the conviction that females are dirty, that their genitals are dirty, really sticks to us. I think that's why I don't like men to go down on me. Because I think I'm dirty. I just don't like it because I think I must be dirty—and I think they're not. Maybe they clean themselves. A lot comes from this belief in our dirt—like I was douching all the time. Some

M

he'll have everything Charlie got.

You give a black woman to a black man and she'll remind him of his mother who he wanted desperately to get away from. She' spent a great part of her time doing what he calls "suppressing" him, that is, keeping him from being a white man. It's all about power and all about Charlie. Charlie runs everything, runs the white women too. He owns it all.

K

though they came back from having perpetuated the worst fantasy the rest of us harbor: our own nightmare.

The summer changed even my vision of the street and neighborhood where I've lived for ten years. I can never see Third Avenue with the same indifferent innocence. One very hot day my ridiculous, elderly convertible chose to break down at the corner of Third Avenue and Thirteenth Street. While the transmission cooled I had a full hour to observe pimps, whores, and johns: what I had learned earlier in the summer made it like watching a foreign film a second time, after the dub-

J

of them like you to be dirty. One guy said to me, "I would like it if you didn't douche for a week." They want to go down on you and, another thing, they want you to come. That was another thing that I didn't like. Here I go, thinking about all the things I didn't like. And now I'm really getting into it. I know I didn't like it and I don't want to get into it again. One of the worst things about it was the faking. You had to fake orgasm. They expect it because that proves their masculinity. That's one of the worst things about it. That's really being a whore, being so dishonest. I don't know how they believe it. I really don't know how they believe it—johns. Some of the ones I've had were even bachelors—good-looking guys with a lot of money, eligible young men. Very good-looking with a lot of money, didn't want to marry, wanted to go to whores. They had a tremendous fear of getting involved because that's giving something.

When I wanted to get out of it, one of the things which made it very difficult was that I wanted to get

K

bing had been added and one is able to understand the language. The pimps lean against a car smoking and overseeing trade; one fat and ugly, one with a shaved head, elegantly vicious. A great black woman jiggles herself on the threshold of a crummy bar. She is huge, ungainly. But she has a magnificent head. Young black culture hero in political costume, jacket and shades, strolls past, catches sight of her, and with a superior turn of the head calls out an insult to the effect that she is a ton of meat, a heap of cunt.

She is stung, hurt out of the somnolence of her mindless and comforting dance of sale, and yells back "sonofabitch," "motherfucker." But her clichés have no striking power, and he continues to taunt her, ridiculing the object for sale, cheapening it, defiling it, declaring it altogether valueless. All she has. Her outrage and frustration, the overpowering indignity make her shake. It's blown her cool altogether; she looks ashamed to live. The shouting has wakened a white hippie girl from her permanent high of down and she even throws out a

J

married. This was one of the reasons I got out of it— I thought I was going to get married. And you can't go on if you want to get married, unless there's a pimp who wants to marry you and put you to work. I think the worst thing about prostitution was the way it spoiled my relationship with men. It's very hard to be common property like that, hard to find a man who'll put up with it. They either want you to quit or they want to take all your money, and there're very few men who don't fall into either one of those categories. Most of the ones I'd like would want me to quit. The other ones want my money. The only exceptions I've been able to find are gangsters. And the guys who want you to quit, they want you to be true, like they feel you're cheating if you're whoring. Very few men will understand that when a woman screws for money, she has no involvement at all. Yet *they* can just go out and get laid and feel no involvement. But they don't understand how you can do it for money and feel nothing. They think you're cheating and they can't take that. And the guy who wants you to

K

curse at the guy. I astonish myself by yelling out at him, from the car, "fuck off." So we are a trio of women against this piece of arrogance. But he is untouched altogether (women are so contemptible) and saunters on, so righteous, so better, that it protects him like a celluloid covering.

Two big black birds on a black car, the pimps have never moved their eyelids. The whore is beaten. Later her master awards her a popsicle. The orange child-food glittering against her black shape in its black dress, she jiggles on. It was the fat guy who gave her the ice, but it was with the shaved head that I saw her again in Philadelphia at the Panther Conference. She was only along for the ride. It was the pimp, however, whom it was astonishing to meet at a "Constitutional Convention of Revolutionary Peoples," resplendent in black beret, black leather jacket, complete with Panther badges. They are for sale—anyone can buy them—but the pimp as revolutionary is a repellent image. Yet not all that surprising either during that nightmare Philadelphia weekend when Panther

J

quit: he's seeing you as property; he's changing you, from like currency, which passes from hand to hand, to something like real estate. *Real* property. There's an *owning* thing about wanting you to quit, especially if the guy is poor.

And I don't want to be kept. I don't care how much I love somebody, I don't want to be kept. Because anyone who keeps me has power over me. To ask someone for money to buy something, that would be so demeaning. I couldn't do that. I'll tell you what it is with the money and not wanting to be kept. If I loved someone and were dependent emotionally, then to be economically dependent too would be terrible. At least let me be financially independent because I'm so dependent emotionally. I have a tremendous thing about this; I had it with my parents too. I'm getting a little better about it with them. Because I feel so helplessly at someone's mercy.

Yet dating, for example, I found so much more humiliating. It's the same thing as prostitution—they're buying you and you know they're buying you, but they're doing it indirectly.

K

swagger reached a fever pitch of macho bully.

Back to that scorched day on Third Avenue. One of the white prostitutes in the stable, unbelievably blank on heroin, walks back and forth almost blind. She uses herself like soiled kleenex, dabbling at the traffic of uncurious males: a suit with a briefcase, two carpenters who snicker, a Puerto Rican whose cock-rank dictates that he bargain and then grandly refuse. It is 2:30 in the afternoon; the whores have eternity before them.

Another moment on Third Avenue, as the cab passes the Pocket Theatre at Twelfth Street, I thought I saw my younger sister, Mallory. I have a painful, surely overprotective obsession with Mallory's eventual victory over circumstances. This week she has another impossible job, taking tickets at the theatre. I look again. A quick cut: Mallory is transformed into a fourteen-year-old Puerto Rican whore standing by the entrance. Today might be Mallory's day off, but not this kid's. How easily has this child's slavery come about, how acceptable people find it—her fel-

J

K

And we're all pretending that this isn't happening. You see I can't pretend. Because I know what it's about; that's why I can't do it.

Men think that sex once is sex always, on demand. If you go out with them and make it, you're their thing. Maybe you haven't got laid in six months, but they don't consider that. It's a terrible disappointment. I feel like sleeping with somebody sometime. Then he turns out to be a real son of a bitch—like he'll introduce me to his friends. His friends I don't feel like sleeping with; I just want to say "fuck off." But the friend is so sure he's going to get laid because you slept with his pal—as if they felt they could *loan* us or "fix us up." And if you don't put out, they call you a lesbian or else they'll say, "Are you prejudiced because I'm black?" You're getting cornered all the time. But when you whore, at least you're getting something back—you're getting cash. So in a sense whoring is less oppressive. And with the cash you can do anything that you want to. Cash—you can get it from a southern racist and give it

lowmen. It's 11:30 in the morning. Will a john have her for lunch? My older-sister's fury feeds on his gizzard.

Then one fine summer evening when things were going splendidly, the tin can even a joy to drive, and some happy meeting with a friend lighting my euphoria, I pulled up at the corner of Third and Thirteenth. That first corner. Both women were there. I'm recognized by two prostitutes' long stare. Suddenly I feel extremely derelict in duty; just what duty I have no idea. But it seems criminal to be in such a mellow mood, so rich feeling, even though I'm broke, the movie having consumed every cent I can get my hands on. Even the uncertain mobility of this old car seems a luxury, wildly extravagant. What's expected of me anyway—saintly fanaticism? What new absurdity am I getting myself into, I wonder, recognizing the traps of white liberal and middle-class guilt spread out before me. I've enough lower-mid in me to encumber my life with an infatuation for a real greaser's car. And I am not forced to recover from a Seven Sister's education

J

to the Black Panthers; you can do what you want to with it. With the dinner and the date, what can you do? Just get fat. And they force you to eat a lot or drink too much so they can lay you.

I would so much rather turn a trick with somebody than go out on a date. Turning a trick is not anxiety-producing. But going out on a date, I just freak out. Of course, on a date you may kid yourself that it's your personality they like. But when you're whoring, it's sometimes your personality they like too. There's one guy who comes to the studio regularly, he does other things with other people, but he gives me ten dollars just to talk to me. For shrinking too, you get ten dollars while they talk. And that's why I think I'm going into it. When I was in therapy I saw such parallels between the two things —prostitution and psychiatry—kinds of therapy. And then all the money they make. Like, I thought, here's a way I can legitimately do all this. I felt always that my analyst was doing the same thing I'd been doing, but respectably.

Psychology today is really into keeping us in our

K

through courses in home explosives like Bryn Mawr's poor dead child.

I've seen class guilt send movement women into frenzies of divisiveness all year, poisoning the hopes of unity with a self-righteous missionary trip, which maunders on about the Third World and proletarian woman, using it as an opportunity for endless recriminations among former friends, all of them middle-class. The animosity we practice upon each other is ultimately little better than a form of self-mutilation. It is a habit now among that social group who might be described as bourgeoisie in origin transformed into the masses upon arrival into the New Left. A righteous political asperity or a dedication to violent means and manners is here a guarantee of sincerity, even atonement, for the comfort of one's upbringing. This sort of meddling folly would delight in converting the prostitute into flag and symbol, a movement idol. Where scores are kept, with the highest Oppression Rating awarded the most acrimonious effusion, the whore's penultimate suffering could be quickly and

J

little cages, but I still hope that that isn't all there is to it. I can't even be that sure about my analysts. My first analyst I'm not too sure of; nor my second. But the second did a lot for me. After all, I was in prostitution before I got into therapy. In fact, I couldn't afford analysis until I was a prostitute. And therapy is what got me back into school, into graduate school, and out of prostitution. And the parallel between therapy and prostitution is a parallel that I often draw even to the analyst. It was freaky, comical. I certainly hope he didn't do less work than I did—because I want to get *my* money's worth. I want to *get* something for my money, and I know those johns didn't. The analyst sells a service which does not degrade him, but makes him distinguished and respected.

When I try to think of prostitution as selling a service, I have to remember that most people don't sell services to others. They just trounce all over them and call it competition. Then when I think, how did the john get the money he pays me? By exploiting another woman—a secretary, or

K

facilely converted into a superrating.

But the two prostitutes are still staring at me. And whatever that stare means, it's recognition. They know me from last time, know I watched and saw their experience, know I know whatever little I know. Ignorance may be a lousy excuse, but at least it's something. When you lose it you gain responsibility. And if you have knowledge of something as wrong as their wrongs and do nothing, you take on some culpability, even complicity.

The traffic light changes color and the car turns home. But I have felt that stare and registered it. M says there is danger in continuing the project, swears the pimp is smart enough to figure out the economic threat women's liberation could offer him if we had any success in reaching prostitutes. She warns that like any capitalist he'll be uptight if hit in the pocket. And since like any pimp he specializes in beating up women, some of us might be attacked if we were successful. I'm a fairly frank physical coward, and the prospect of being worked over sometime by a couple of pimps does terrify me. It is for that reason (among

J

someone like that, a wife. The boss is likely to sleep with his secretary on the side. She's doing it for nothing and that's really horrible. Secretaries and women in sweat shops— places like that—are put in the position where they feel that if they don't put out, they'll lose their job.

I don't feel that I'm a whore now, but the social stigma attached to prostitution is a very powerful thing. It makes a kind of total state out of prostitution so that the whore is always a whore. It's as if— you did it once, you become it. This makes it very easy for people to get locked into it. It's very hard to get married; then too, most of the people who do it are not that well educated, not that many of them could do any other job. You get locked into it simply because you get hooked on luxuries. You can get hooked on consumerism, or even just on living decently. You can get hooked on a certain kind of freedom, where you can go where you want to without being beholden to someone who supports you. For me prostitution didn't even offer good hours 'cause I had this work hang-

K

others, but the others are only variant dreams of an end to black male chauvinism) I look forward to the possibility of Panther support, counting on one muscle man against the other, hoping they cancel each other out, so that women, black and white, may be able to come together, free of the bully pimp. And of course the Panthers could do it if they chose—could pass the word that pimping was out, over, unacceptable, uncool. If they really felt that way.

Beyond acting as a catalyst I know I can do little myself. There are a number of women who have worked with me on this project and who now care about it quite a lot; the women who compose the quartet, of course, but others too who came to our raps and contributed a knowledge of persons, or prisons, or law. I feel very strongly that the discussions must be continued and enlarged. It will be the prostitutes themselves, the persons involved and informed, who are best qualified to direct the decisions and strategy of such a campaign and its targets: the vice squad, city hall, the legislature. At present prostitutes are subject to arrest at any

J

up. I worked about twenty-four hours a day—I was into making so much money—obsessive about it. I can also see how people could be trapped in it because it's so hard for them literally, objectively, so difficult to do anything else, let alone to do as well economically.

But however underpaid a woman factory worker or a typist may be, she still has something the whore doesn't have. Even I wanted to have a legitimate front. I had to do something else too. Lots of call girls have done secretarial work from time to time. I don't put women down who have straight jobs. I wanted a straight job more than anything and I'm going into a straight job. I'm not going to make any more money. I may even, as an intern, make less than the average secretary and a great deal less than I made when I was in the life. Yet I'm looking forward to it. Because you are selling *a lot* when you are being a whore. You're giving up a lot. One thing you're giving up is a chance to have a normal relationship with a man.

As a prostitute you're alienated, isolated even, not

K

moment, stigmatized in any area of employment by a record and fingerprints, and offered no protection against the assaults of pimps or police. Again, it would be the prostitutes themselves who are in the best position to direct young movement lawyers, law students, and legal assistants toward those incidents in the prostitute's life that would make the most promising test-case material in a long-range legal struggle, not only to change the present laws so oppressive to prostitutes, but to extend every form of civil rights to a group so long and so generally denied them.

Prostitution has flourished always and made fortunes, counting on and aided by the state. Considering the weight of this tradition, one gets a notion of how heavy a job actual social revolution is: bigotry, habit, moneyed interest, physical force, even indifference are so solid. How unshakably based in these things our man's world really is. To look ahead nearly takes one's breath away—the difficulty of the thing. Just the mess our sick culture has made of sexuality. Yet one can think of a love that's free based on re-

J

only from yourself but from the rest of society because you can't talk to people about it. And when I was doing it, I only had friends that I could tell about it, people in the life. For the power of straight society to oppress prostitutes—for that to—disappear—prostitution has to be legalized. Right now you can't even tell people because of the law. And the cops are very scary, very hard to spot. Ugliest bastards in the world driving around in old Plymouths. They are frightening because they can pick you up. If you were able to tell people, that that's what you do, if it weren't assumed that that's what you're always going to do, you would be able to leave it and do something else. Imprisoned in it—you shouldn't be imprisoned in it all the rest of your life. Having done it now prevents you from doing anything else in the future. You're vulnerable if you quit—I am myself—in regard to my fellowship. I probably will be even after I finish my degree and internship. Yet you ought to be able to go straight whenever you want to.

Funny—that expression,

K

spect, affection, understanding, tenderness. How great to live that way. And to love many people and love them well. To have the joy of that, of what love is without possessiveness, exclusiveness, jealousy, property, economic dependence, ego conflict. How full of flowers, music, highs, conversation, fantastic love making ... all of it could be. And I think it's worth it. But never let it prevent you from the knowledge and expectation of how hard it's going to be, how scary—until we can live that way. And it's not only the hedonist but the pragmatist that urges we practice for living the revolution, since surely there won't be one unless we've made some progress at living the new way. And it must be new: revolution's got to be a better way to live, lovingly even. Not hate: we have such a sickening amount of that already.

But all of it will hardly be easy. I had a glimpse of that this spring. It was after the abortion rally and some of us went down to the Women's House of Detention. The Panther women are being held there, and the custom had grown up over the winter of ending

J

K

"go straight"—same expression that's used for gay people. I wonder what's the opposite of going straight. Crooked? I wonder what is synonymous with going straight—being perfect, I guess. It's funny that both those worlds should use that expression. The underworld too—"going straight." All three groups are outsiders.

If you tell me that being in the life is beating yourself up psychologically, I can't help but resent that. Because psychologically I've suffered so much more in other situations, been humiliated much more in other situations. I think the money had a lot to do with my feeling freer. I didn't feel I was taking nearly so much shit when I was in the life as I do now that I am a teaching assistant. As a teaching assistant I am really put down and I don't make nearly as much money. True, it carries a certain social status that's a lot higher than that of a prostitute, but you pay for it, you really pay for it. I worked long hours for little money and I took shit. I was in tears so much more in graduate school, infuriated and sick. I didn't get an ulcer when I was a pros-

most demonstrations in the city there. It was strangely exciting—even the walk from Union Square—you knew so well where you were going that you picked up a feeling for it as you went along. It was a feeling for what we'd see there. Not just the cops all lined up making trouble, but the place itself. We were headed for the big place our lives are supposed to be spent not heading for, going to it by a new route.

I can remember asking some of my friends among the women at the rally if they were going down. Some said yes, some said not this time, next time, or I'll be there soon. Kidding about it. But aware it may not be a joke long. Robin and Ti-Grace and some others have already been there, busted at a peaceful sit-in against Grove Press. In a sense one somehow expects the House of D. eventually; a premonition, a sense of foreknowing, we'll get together there someday. Most days I remember this is paranoia and that a claustrophobe like myself is bound to be fascinated and frightened of places like this. But that late afternoon in March after the rally and the march and the crowds and the

J

titute. That happened when I was in graduate school.

And I'll tell you, I have not cried nearly as much being a prostitute as I have being a student. It's different somehow. When I was a prostitute it wasn't *me* somehow. I didn't get put down in the same way. I didn't feel it as much. You just don't get that put down in the same way. Maybe because you're down so far, you just can't get put down any further when you're a prostitute. The street is the street and you expect nothing from it. The academic world I did expect something from. You're always defensive with johns. You never invest your ego with them. But I did with the university. After all, this was going to be my profession. The university was going to be my way out from the street—from being a prostitute. What a disappointment. School just doesn't have to be that way—they just don't have to humiliate you that way. They should just treat you with respect, for God's sake. All I want is respect, for God's sake. I don't want unconditional love, just respect.

As for me, I feel better about being a prostitute

K

chanting it all made a curious logic.

So we arrived. We're on the far side of the street so we can see up at the walls. The prostitutes, the shoplifters, and the addicts in the House of Detention are on the other. And the cops between us. Two groups of women with men and walls intervening. We're yelling, of course. But so are they across the street. The most astonishing thing: they're yelling political stuff. It blew my mind. "Free our sisters," we're chanting. And they're echoing it back. Then they're chanting it and we're echoing it back. But they're talking to us: we're communicating at last. And in between us, between the two groups, the men, the police.

Look up and the women are all at the windows. I once worked in a lock-up, had a job in a mental hospital the summer I was eighteen. I've carried my bunch of keys, and I know that when everybody's at the windows like this—everything's out of control. They are keeping them inside the building, but it seems sure that they're beyond the pale in there—way out of hand. They're all there at the windows

J

than being married to somebody I can't stand and being locked into that. If I were the slave of a pimp and getting beat up all the time, I would see that not as prostitution but as another kind of marriage. It's very hard to find a prostitute who hasn't got a pimp, and so I'm not really representative of prostitutes. I not only didn't have a pimp, but my education also makes me unrepresentative. But I'm not so different either—consider the devotion I had to whoever my lover was. And the dependence I had is the same devotion that the average whore has to a pimp except I wouldn't let him take my money or beat me. With me it's got to be more subtle—but it's the same goddamn thing.

I'm terribly messed up as far as sex is concerned— that's why I could become a prostitute. I've always been messed up as far as sex is concerned. Now I don't relate to men at all. It's easy to go along with what most people say about prostitution 'cause they read it all in a book. But I'm not going to say it's true unless I feel it. And I do hate prostitution—I do hate it. That's why I'm not

K

where we can hear them and see them. Not just a random voice heard by a shopper on Sixth Avenue carrying groceries along, the prisoner yelling something for the crowd to laugh at. Every single woman in the place seems to be at the windows, shouting.

I looked up at this building. It's so big and so strong and so made out of stone. I begin to see how hard revolution is. Because we can shout free our sisters till we crumble and there's still that stone wall between us, the iron security entrance, and all those cops. They won't crumble. You get a notion of what you're up against.

Seeing it all, a strange perception came over me. That prostitutes are our political prisoners—in jail for cunt. Jailed for it, for cunt, the offense we all commit in just being female. That's sexual politics, the stone core of it.

J

doing it now. I spent all these years in school just to get out of it. If I liked it I'd be there now. At the time I was so numb that I felt nothing. I hate it now because now I feel. I just can't stand it now when

J

J

people touch me. I just can't stand being put there. Here I've had all these years of education and I should still have to do this and I'm still expected to put out. And now it's for a lousy dinner. Even with my Ph.D. Now I hate it but I won't project about how I felt about it then or failed to feel. I did, I must have hated it then. But I wasn't aware of it or I couldn't admit it. I think I'm getting better now, now that I realize that I hated it so much. But now I'm getting so I hate men. I'm getting so that I avoid men. What I am is I'm becoming aware of how much I always hated it. And I know now how it has ruined all my relationships with men. We are so afraid to say that we hate men. So the prostitute finds a pimp and says this is the one man I can love. And he treats her like dirt. I've become aware of hating men, and I've been afraid to say it for a long time. I'm becoming aware of how the whole experience just freaked me out. They put you down for what they have made of you. I learned this lesson too well—first when I got put down in school, then you get put down for hav-

ing done prostitution so you learn the lesson all over again. Say you come out and do it honestly and sell yourself for money. And then you're put down for that.

When I became a prostitute I didn't feel my will being broken. To become a prostitute was just the easiest thing in the world— I was ready for it. Because sex had never meant much to me at all. So I could make money with it; might as well use it for that. Most of the time it just didn't mean anything at all: I guess that's what made me ready. And that didn't change when I was in the life. I felt nothing, a lack of feeling in sex. Except with special people. And with the special people there was this terrible emotional dependency which is really the way a prostitute is— although she doesn't feel anything when she's out hustling. And they're just hung up and depend on their pimp—so I was into that. That I could screw all kinds of guys and not care. Screw. Maybe get screwed by is the right word.

Long before I got into prostitution I would go to bed with guys, because I thought I owed it to them,

J

J

because I'd "led them on" or some bullshit. I let them con me into that. And when that happens you just lay back and say, "Okay, I got myself into this. Go ahead, I don't care—do it. Go ahead, do your thing." Passive. Even being passive is a way of resisting. It says, yes, you can have my body, but you won't get me excited. Neither angry nor sexually excited. The scary thing about it is the way I put myself out, asleep inside. Now if you're actually making love to a guy you get tired, use up energy. But if you're passive as I was, you use up little, you suppress it all. When I was a whore I never got tired, never exerted myself.

I could anesthetize myself so that I didn't suffer that much. But a lot of whores can't. They're really in conflict all the time. I had a friend like that become a junkie. She wouldn't *be* a whore. She refused. But then she became an addict. She had an old man who put her out on the street. And she hated it. If I'd been like that I would have gotten myself out of poverty some other way. It was because it wasn't painful that I

could do it. I think I couldn't take it now.

I didn't have a bad life in prostitution. Primarily, I didn't have a pimp. To organize prostitutes the hardest thing about it will be to get around the pimp. You're gonna have the pimp down on you; after all, his livelihood and his interests are threatened. I saw some pimps today—two black guys with Texas plates—I'll say they had guts. There they were with those Texas plates on a 1970 Cadillac with a blue-flowered convertible top. Man, those guys had class. Ever seen a Cadillac with a flowered top? Nothing but a pimp or possibly a rock 'n' roll star would ever sport that—but they're usually pimps on the side or whores of one kind or another before they got to be stars.

Pimps really do nothing. They don't get you dates. They provide no service at all and do nothing at all all day. They gamble, they drink, they beat you up. They ride around in them Cadillacs. They look pretty. They stink from perfume. Pimps don't do a damn thing for you. They spend all your money. That's what they do for you.

J

They'll bail you out of jail only 'cause you're their money. But you can bail yourself out of jail and you can keep your own money. You don't need a pimp.

Most prostitutes do have pimps. I can understand where they're at. Because I was into the same thing, the same type of dependency. I just didn't give the pimps my money. It's this love thing—the dependency. For most prostitutes the pimp fulfills the romantic ideal of true love. For me it was different—a poor scroungy student was my true love. And I wanted to give him my money—I really wanted to. But he wouldn't take it. True, I was a student too and just as scroungy. But I didn't see myself in the same romantic light I saw him in. He was a leader, a revolutionary. He wouldn't take my money. I tried to force it on him but he wouldn't take it. I was his suffering proletariat, his Mary Magdalene. Then he went off and married someone else. He married a good girl. I felt he had a mind and was important: the idealist, the rebel. He was always better than me. I felt lucky to know a great fellow like that. Yes, and

J

the dangers and temptations of the leadership trip: I saw them. Most of these guys take care of themselves. A few years after college they're in a law firm or they're out hustling like Jerry Rubin. Everybody hustles. They hustle the revolution. They prostitute it. Off on their ego trip.

I'm not free of this guy yet. I was still in love with him last summer. And I'm not sure I wouldn't go to bed with him again if he came to New York—I can't say for sure that I'd be able to tell him to fuck off. I did say no to him last fall. He wanted to come to New York and I said no. At least as a prostitute you can say, "Yes but—yes but I want fifteen dollars." If you're a good chick all you can say is yes. One thing I did accomplish: he wanted me to go back with him and I refused. That's probably why we're not together now. He wasn't going to stay here with me—that hadn't occurred to him as an option.

I think I only once had a john who was a college boy, a student like myself. But once I told a professor I was doing prostitution. I told him half jokingly. And he set up a bachelor party

J

J

for me. He was going to do it, anyway, and thought he'd hire someone he knew. He wasn't actually my teacher—I wasn't in his course. He could have said no. You do occasionally meet guys who say no. But that's very rare, because it's the men who initiate it. I can't put this guy down especially, just 'cause he's a professor. All jobs are alike really—a john's a john. It wasn't like he was corrupting me or something. This was my business. If he'd come on moralistic with me I would have really hated him. If he'd started giving me that crap I would have been mad. I lead my own life. I'm not going to let any john tell me. I may have hated prostitution but I had the *right* to do it. I don't like people telling me not to do it. Gets me mad, when they tell me not to do it—that I'm too good for it and so on and so forth. I feel that's a "superior" kind of attitude, morally superior. I get very tired of the people with that "healthy" nonsense—the argument that prostitution's not psychologically healthy. They have a double standard about prostitution, you know. I could be doing all

kinds of self-destructive things and they wouldn't mind. They wouldn't criticize me for self-destructiveness if I were just as compliant or masochistic outside of prostitution, as a girl friend or wife. I could be doing much worse things to myself, and they would approve. When they tell me, "You shouldn't do it, it's bad for you." I hear, "You shouldn't do it, it's bad." And I hear them saying, "I'm superior, what a wonderful person I am to speak to you and lift you up, you fallen woman."

I like to believe I have some kind of free choice. Some choice in my life. That I chose a lesser evil. I wanted to do it. And somehow I want that to be respected. I *wanted* to do that. Somehow their pity deprives me of my freedom of choice. I don't want to be saved; saved by the Christians or saved by the shrink. Whatever the rationale is, it's the same: condescending, patronizing. Something in me just resents this moralism, their uplifting. I'd like so much to have the illusion that I had some freedom of choice. Maybe it's just an illusion, but I need to think

J

I had some freedom. Yet then I realize how much was determined in the way I got into prostitution, how determined my life had been, how fucked over I was to have no confidence in myself. But I had to get myself out of it somehow. So I believed I'd chosen it. What's most terrifying is to look back, to realize what I went through and that I endured it.

When I look back on prostitution, I have so much ambivalence. I'm not even sure how I feel about it. It's not all negative. In

J

remembering it, I was so afraid to come off with the ready answers the shrink had demanded. It's really more complex. So there was much that I denied, because it was only too painful to remember. Also I had seen how much conformity there was in the therapist's way of regarding it so I resisted that kind of pat answer. I denied at first what I can remember feeling—how in the beginning I just hated the men, just wanted them to stop touching me. To just get away.

4

WOMAN AS OUTSIDER

Vivian Gornick

By any definition woman is an outsider. A difficult notion genuinely to digest, as woman occupies one-half of the race, constitutes an entire sexual category, cuts across all cultures, classes, and conditions, and often occupies positions of honor within those very circumstances in which total rule is exercised, it nevertheless is true.

The literary concept of the outsider speaks to the idea of a human being who, for mysterious reasons and in mysterious ways, is outside the circle of ordinary human experience. Rather than mingling with his fellows within the circle's embrace, he stands beyond it, and because of his distance he is able to see deeply into the circle, penetrating to its very center, his vision a needle piercing the heart of life. Invariably, what he sees is intolerable, and further, what he sees makes *living* intolerable. For while he shares the characteristics and recognizable elements of all other human beings, the mere distance of the outsider has acted as a force for an economical kind of perception, a perception that is trained on the irreducible; thus, the outsider is denied the filtered vision that allows men to live without too troubling an insight.

The outsider's experience, therefore, continually exposed to the glaring light of his special perception, becomes an agony, his responses a kind of grotesquerie, his behavior profoundly unsocialized. His is the humanness that is carried to the edge of what it means to be human. Outside, standing there utterly alone, looking in, the proportion of his thought, his feelings, his very being becomes metaphorical in size. His anguish is the ultimate human anguish, his violence the ultimate human violence, his numbness, his cruelty, his fear, his hatred, as well as his awe, his love, his religiosity, his courage, his compassion all become larger than life. He becomes, in all his parts, a symbolic container of elemental humanness. His life, paradoxically extraordinary, nevertheless makes grand statements about the nature of human experience.

The most famous outsider in literature—Herman Hesse's *Steppenwolf*—and the most famous outsiders in history —among them Van Gogh and Nijinsky and Nietzsche —are men of tragically unfiltered vision, distended emotion, unbearable spiritual honesty; men alone, hated, primitive sacrifices to self-understanding, driven ultimately either mad or suicidal. These figures have become our surrogate selves, our symbolic representations of the stunning aloneness, the dazed sense of disorder and madness, the wild kind of accompanying violence we have all— at least once in our lives—felt characterize human existence. Theirs has been the symbolic pain of the symbolic individual.

The pain of the individual, however, is ultimately the pain of a culture, a civilization, a politics. Sometimes that pain is the torment of the existential *one*, and sometimes it is that of a cultural *one*. The tension wire upon which these two realities move creates a flowing current, one that pushes each of them interchangeably back and forth, between the pole ends of the wire, one glowing first at one end, then at the other end. Thus, the existential sense of "outsidedness" gathers mythic pain and mythic impact as it is translated into the experience of a subculture, as it were, a group of human beings whose national or racial characteristics have put them forever beyond the pale of ordinary human experience, have made of them beings who must eternally *become* but never simply are, beings whose existence is dominated by an overriding sense of cultural distance, and who therefore become, not by virtue of their individual experience, but by virtue of their culturally accidental lives, existentially symbolic. Hence, the most famous culturally prototypic outsiders of all: the Wandering Jew and the Noble Savage. In these cultural outsiders we have gathered, in a peculiar dimension, the properties of that other single, existential outsider. We see in their behavior, in their idiom, in their dreams and fears,

those particularities of human response that attest to lives
dominated by a baffling sense of distance between men
and world, between men and being, between men and
self-realization. Thus, the Jew cringes and the Negro kills;
the Jew retreats into isolated thought, and the Negro
lashes out in maddened action; the Jew defends his besieged existence by numbing himself to his sexuality, and
the Negro defends his by abandoning himself to his. Both
kinds of behavior are exaggerated, "half" behaviors. Both
represent a kind of infantilism, the infantilism of reduction. Both are the painful, disproportionate, *metaphorical*
responses of human beings deprived of suffrage.

Very few writers speaking for either of these groups of
hounded outsiders have described the true meaning of
their condition as well as have Richard Wright and James
Baldwin. In his autobiography, *Black Boy*, Richard Wright
describes a scene between his exploding sixteen-year-old
self and his strong, ignorant, intelligent, Baptist aunt. She
slaps the rebellious Richard across the face and announces
fiercely that he should thank God every day of his life that
he was born black, that it was a blessing, a token of
favoritism on God's part that he had visited upon the
black people the privilege of truly understanding human
pain. . . . And then again, Baldwin, writing out a wild and
beautiful power of needle-heart understanding about the
violence of the black man, a violence that springs directly
from his insupportable knowledge of his outsidedness, a
violence that reveals that at the heart, life is irrational and
suicidal whenever autonomy is withheld. . . .

In every real sense woman also is an outsider, one in
whom experience lives in a metaphorical sense, one whose
life and meaning is a surrogate for the pain and fear of
existence, one onto whom is projected the self-hatred that
dogs the life of the race. Only a brief look at the cultural
and religious myths and the literary projections of woman
that surround the female existence—smothering it, depriving it, manipulating it, and in the final irony, creating it
and then reflecting it—will instantly reveal the essential
outsidedness of woman: her distance from the center of
self-realizing life, the extremity of her responses to experience, her characteristic femaleness incorporating (very
much as a black man's blackness does) a distillation of
human behavior that grows directly out of the excluded
nature of her destined life. Further, a look at culture and
literature will confirm that the life of woman, like the life

of every outsider, is determinedly symbolic of the life of the race; that this life is offered up, as every other outsider's life is offered up, as a sacrifice to the forces of annihilation that surround our sense of existence, in the hope that in reducing the strength of the outsider—in declaring her the bearer of all the insufficiency and contradiction of the race—the wildness, grief, and terror of loss that is in us will be grafted onto her, and the strength of those remaining within the circle will be increased. For in the end, that is what the outsider is all about; that is what power and powerlessness are all about; that is what inclusion and exclusion are all about; that is what the cultural decision that certain people are "different" is all about: if only these *Steppenwolfs*, these blacks, these Jews, these women will go mad and die for us, we will escape; we will be saved; we will have made a successful bid for salvation.

Man's life is pervaded by a mixture of elements that sets up for him an obstacle course which he must perpetually run. A complication of circumstances elaborated from within insures both the magnitude of his longing and the bitterness of his failure. Man's condition has been described for thousands of years by religion as an internal war between the spirit and the flesh, and then again by Freud as an internal war between the desire to live and the desire to die, and now yet again by Arthur Koestler—who seeks to demonstrate that all is evolutionary physiology—as a conflict within man's physical being between two brains, evolved at different times, predicated upon different principles of life, both still exerting influence. The manifestations of the condition remain eternally the same: man is intellectually brave and emotionally craven, spiritually daring and biologically fearful. Thus, he speaks of brotherhood and makes war, he adores reason and is a slave to passion, he fawns upon moral courage and repeatedly falls to moral cowardice.

One of the most fully realized characters in English literature to embody these painfully contradictory elements is the woman, Sue Bridehead, in Thomas Hardy's *Jude the Obscure*. A powerful tale of nineteenth-century England in which the rural Jude comes to the city to begin a lifelong attempt to gain entrance to the university, the story is one of false seduction and cruel abandonment. The cohesive farm life out of which Jude comes is slowly being sucked by the Industrial Revolution into the urban restlessness. There, all of its good is lost and all of its deficiency prevails. The city life is a misery—and yet they cannot stay away. It is the fatal lot of men that they are irresistibly drawn by complication. The farm life that is going is also the simple life; the city life that is growing is also the life of mental and spiritual complexity. Jude is drawn by it all, spends his life wrestling with it all, and in the end is desperately defeated by it all. However, his struggle is but a pale reflection of the struggle of Sue—his cousin, his sweetheart, his destiny—whose life parallels his and whose pain and defeat are an incredible agony, drawn in fevered lines, as though she were meant to be the heroine in a medieval morality play, and he the shadowy life copy that lends credence to the parable.

Sue is a marvelous creature, a woman of dimension and enormous appeal, full of terrible longings and terrible anxieties—alive with intellectual courage and emotional cowardice. In nineteenth-century England she lives "platonically" with a young student, she rearranges the Bible chronologically, she brings naked Greek statuary into her boarding-house room, she instructs and bewilders and arouses Jude with all that seductive mental longing. On the other hand, out of emotional fear and sexual immaturity, she is helpless to resist a loveless Victorian marriage. When its full horrors break on her, and she does leave her husband for Jude, she struggles continually against an irrational conviction of retribution that haunts her, a conviction that goes directly counter to every thing she intellectually *knows* to be right, a conviction that finally overcomes her, sending her toppling from spiritual and intellectual enlightenment down into the most slavering, primitive, utterly mad religiosity imaginable: she ends her days a groveling, half-lucid creature. Both she and Jude are utterly destroyed by her compulsive, self-imposed fall from grace, a fall surely as determinedly low as her rise was high. She is impaled upon the cross of spiritual boldness and emotional terror that marks her being.

Now, the point of all this is that Sue is the most brilliantly recognizable *female* in all of Hardy's literature, and it is within the context of her femaleness, almost as a function of it, that this ancient dilemma of the human construct is played out. Jude could never bring down on them the mayhem she causes. In the ultimateness of their lives, he is too rational, too modest, too decent in his soul to be brought to this screaming, life-destroying edge.

There is in him some vital center, some sense of self that *holds*, that resists the disaster of utter emotional abandonment, that cannot go back entirely on things it already knows. For Sue this is not true. For Sue extremity is the familiar condition: she swings wildly from one clutched principle of life to another, eradicating one entirely as she embraces the other.

Sue is the quintessential female. Everything that she is and everything that she does and everything that happens to her is seen within the circle of her femaleness. Her behavior is emotional, impetuous, illogical, uncontrollable. (A thread runs through the story—Sue always treats Jude cruelly, then overcome with remorse, sends him tearful notes of regret with strict promises that it will never happen again. Of course, nothing changes. She continues to treat him to her unpredictable responses to the end of his miserable life.) She is spineless in most of her behavior; incapable of making the best of a bad bargain or of ever taking the consequences for her action. She is a rather hysterical female as a mother, as well as an incompetent and compassionate female as an intellectual dreamer. And, of course, she is most female when she goes mad.

Madness. It runs through the mythic life of woman like a stream running down through a rain forest, seeking the level of the sea. Women go mad. Men shoot themselves bravely, but women go mad. Hamlet dies, but Ophelia goes mad. Macbeth dies, but Lady Macbeth goes mad. Jude dies, but Sue goes mad. Our men die, but our asylums are overflowing with madwomen: women who become depressed—and go mad.

And, indeed, is it not more to the point to go mad than to commit suicide? Is it not truer of life that we do not escape it, that we are not released, that we cannot simply end it all? Caught as we are, thrashing around inside a skin that wishes simultaneously both to conquer existence and simply to walk away from it, we are driven ever more deeply *into* ourselves. *In* is the true direction of life; to penetrate that circle, to get to the heart of it all, to free ourselves by struggling inward. To be defeated by the effort. To lose the battle on a grand scale. To go mad. Much more than suicide, madness is the symbolic illness of life. And fighting so much harder, traveling from so much further a distance toward that magical center, women—more than men—go mad. Madness is in the female vein. Antonioni, that master moviemaker, knows what he is about when he portrays twentieth-century angst in repeated female nervous breakdowns. Monica Vitti, in movie after movie, is seen as beautiful, wealthy, beloved: rolling her eyes wildly in her head, stuffing her hand in her mouth, unable to articulate the cause of her misery, unable to name the beast in the jungle that is eating at her vitals, while her affluent lovers and husbands go about their business—clothing her ample flesh while her spiritual bones crumble.

In *Boesman and Lena*, a contemporary South African play about two Cape coloreds, it is Lena, the woman, who goes mad. Boesman and Lena are two homeless drifters, continually on the run. Although both are strong and capable of enduring, something always goes wrong and there they are again—with pots and pans and mattresses on their heads and on their backs—walking. They spend their lives out on the mud flats of the river Swartkops which links up the cities they spend their lives madly veering toward, madly veering away from. Inevitably, they wind up pitching a desperate camp, by turns cowed and defiant, shivering at the prospect of regrouping.

When the play opens Lena is mad. Lost in a hallucination of fatigue and startling hopelessness, she apparently has lost her wits trying to remember the sequence of their wanderings. "Let's see now," she muses, "when were we at Redhouse? Before Missionvale? After the dog died? Before Boesman blacked this eye? Just now? Yesterday? Last month? Two years ago? When? Oh God, *when?*" Boesman is infuriated by her lapsing reason, her endless talking to herself, her frightening withdrawal. He threatens, he pleads, he punishes, he cajoles. To each of his actions she responds, but her responses are rather like those of a half-dead body that nevertheless twitches convulsively at the touch of an electric prod.

Boesman and Lena are startlingly reminiscent of the two characters in Fellini's film *La Strada;* the wild man, Zampano ("he's like a dog; he wants to talk but all he can do is bark") and the girl whose name I cannot remember but whose anxious, funny, expressive face Giulietta Masina stamped indelibly upon my memory. They too were the dreadfully castoff of the world, those who lived a wild, peripheral existence, lurking at the edges of other people's lives, living a grabbing, biting, violent, hand-to-mouth life of the spirit, the woman taking on the added burden of being whipped daily not only by the world but by Zampano as well. She too, it will be remembered, went mad.

In *Boesman and Lena* the condition of being cast out is carried to the nth power, held as it is beneath the powerful light of being black, as well, in a country that unyieldingly holds black to be ahuman. Deprived as they are, the equation of their despair is that much closer to the bone than is the despair of the two in *La Strada*—but the models are unmistakably the same. In a life that is not to be borne, a life that *must* end either in madness or suicide, it is Lena, the woman, who assumes the burden of madness for both of them; it is Lena who allows Boesman the luxury of fury while taking on the necessity of annihilation herself. It is she who raves on and on, mixing up the past and the present, refusing the moment coherence, renouncing the cogency of chronology, refusing to remember—although she can remember every detail of the event —when or where their child died. Boesman lashes out at her dementia, but clearly, it is tantamount to bloodletting for him. Clearly, the scorn her madness induces in him reduces the pressure of his fear. Clearly, the woman, who is the only living thing *beneath* him, relieves him of his stunning sense of powerlessness, and utter powerlessness— a recognizable root of madness—devolves upon her. Clearly, then, her madness is intimately tied to her femaleness, that condition of reduced meaning than which there is none greater.

The myth of violence, no less than the myth of madness, also haunts the race. Violence at all times, in all places, under all conditions, in numberless variations. It is a measure of life, a reflection of self-value, the world one comes gaspingly up against; the threat, the challenge, the real and imagined fear; the long dream of guilt. Coming up against potential violent death is coming up against life. From the very first recognition of parental power and childish helplessness, the male dreams often—as befits a child—of conquering through violence. It will be a long time before he understands that that primitive, lifelong violence is not a response to external circumstance; rather, the violence is in him, built into him, a force of expression which lives always in him and threatens always to destroy him at the same time that its release is also one of the crucial ways in which he experiences himself. Violence brings man to the edge of death, and it is there, at that edge, that he feels most keenly the thrill of life

running through him, there he discovers—if he lives
through it—a sense of himself unavailable anyway else.
Thus, from Achilles and the Trojan War to Dr. Strange-
love and the Bomb, men demonstrate the profound pull of
violence: a force that kills, yet without which we are only
half alive. Men go to war, fight wild animals, undergo
challenges of all sorts, pitting themselves against an external world in order to come violently up against that
irresistible urge to live while yet challenging death to
come and get them.

In woman the myth of violence takes form through the
fantasy of rape. Women, who are also both terrified of
violence and drawn to it, shiver in excited fear over the
prospect—real or imagined—of rape. Rape looms in their
dreams, in their contradictory desires, in their fears both
real and imagined. Women who wish to live and at the
same time wish to walk the white line down the center of
the road are continually—in the ordinary course of social
existence—in the presence of that possible danger. Sometimes they flirt with it, sometimes they court it, sometimes
they flee from it. Always, they are aware of it. Always, in
actuality, it is a possibility. Always, an apparently harmless situation may actually flare suddenly and end in annihilation. Always, there is the possibility that at the next
street corner after dark, or in some taxi with the driver
gone beserk, or in some inescapable elevator, or on some
subway platform at four in the afternoon, or out for a
casual evening with a man met just last week . . . suddenly, rape.

The level of fear that is experienced at the prospect of
actual rape has been developed by the fantasy of rape that
has been blooming in the hothouse of woman's mind. Just
as the man facing an African jungle for the first time with
a gun in his hand begins to sweat long before he sees
anything moving because he has fantasized about this so
long, so women live with an exaggerated anxiety about
rape because they have fantasized about *it* so long. A
number of years ago, when the roots of racism first began
to be explored psychoanalytically, much was made of the
fact that white middle-class women dream of being raped
by black men, that this archetypical male incorporated in
his being all the repressed sexual longings and provocative
fears of the race. The emphasis was wrong, all wrong. It
was on the blackness of the man when it should have been
on the idea of rape. Of course, for racial purposes the

blackness was all-important, but the fact is, women fantasize most, not of being raped by some nameless, faceless, unknown man, but rather of being raped by their fathers, their brothers, their uncles, their lovers, their husbands, their sons, their family friends. The danger that is dreamed of will come from the violence that is provoked by closeness; by the love-hate of what is *known;* by the desire to protect and the desire to abandon that lives simultaneously in those to whom our care is entrusted; by the passionate, trembling, exhausting awareness that—always—our lives are barely under control, that the terror lies right here in the bosom of the known circle, not out there in some nameless, faceless black man.

Rape is the ultimate death wish. It is the death wish operating at a level of self-sealing internalization. Men must come up against the external to give life to their expressive longing for violence, but women, in the grip of that same longing, come up against themselves. The woman's dream of rape is that of being pierced, torn, violated, challenged for her very existence by man, her enemy; man, her brother; man, her lover; man, her other self.

Implicit in the dream of rape is woman's true sense of herself, her true subconscious understanding of the actual position of value which she occupies in the life of the culture, her dread, long-felt conviction that she is not real to men. Her fantasies of rape are a culmination of the fact that she has always *been* raped. She is preeminently an object of lust; a creature upon whom the darker desires are realized; a source of release, of tension gathered and tension exploded; a creature with whom the agony of passion and the morbid fear of sexuality are associated. As man is desperate in his fear of himself, he externalizes that in himself which he fears most, projecting onto the outside universe the causes for his frenzy. Thus, woman becomes the *cause* of his lust, the seducer of his reason, the fabled temptress who calls into being his ignoble passions and causes him to wrestle in torment for all that is noble in himself, for his very soul.

For thousands of years woman has been characterized as the temptress. In every modern religion she lives as the source of sexual challenge in this earthly life. In the fierce unjoyousness of Hebraism, especially, woman is a living symbol of the obstacles God puts in man's way as man strives to make himself more godly and less manly. An orthodox Jewish woman must cut off her hair upon marriage and wear a wig all her life long because her hair, her crowning glory, is a chief source of sexual temptation; and now that she has fulfilled her obligation to marry and beget children she must tempt men no longer. An orthodox Jewish man may have no physical contact with his wife while she menstruates. An Orthodox Jew may not look upon the face or form of a woman—ever—and he daily thanks God that he has not been born a woman. These strictures are not a thing of some barbaric past, they are a living part of the detail of many contemporary lives. Today, on the Lower East Side of New York, the streets are filled with darkly brooding men whose eyes are averted from the faces of passing women, and who walk three feet ahead of their bewigged and silent wives. If a woman should enter a rabbinical study on Grand Street today, her direct gaze would be met by lowered eyelids; she would stand before the holy man, the seeker of wisdom, the worshipper of the spirit, and she would have to say to herself: "Why, in this room I am a pariah, a Yahoo. If the rabbi should but look upon my face, vile hot desire would enter his being and endanger the salvation of his sacred soul; when my body discharges its monthly portion of blood and waste, he dare not even pass over to me an object that will touch my hand, much less sleep with me if I am his wife, for that monthly waste in me is disgusting, and it makes me disgusting. It is offal, dung, filth. It reminds him of what no holy man ever wishes to be reminded: that he is matter as well as spirit. So he has made a bargain with God and constructed a religion in which *I* am all matter and *he* is all spirit; I am (yet!) the human sacrifice offered up for his salvation. Even as Agamemnon offered up his virgin daughter, Iphigenia, to the gods so that the strength of the elements would enter into him and he would triumph at Troy, so this rabbi is still sacrificing the female so that the strength of concentrated spirituality will course through his veins. I am to live as a Yahoo so that the rabbi can play at being a Houyhnhnm. . . . But, rabbi, listen: once a Jew created by a Gentile had to come before the world and *announce* his reality. 'If you cut me,' he said, 'do I not bleed?' Now I must say to you: rabbi, do I not also have a soul that is endangered by the perils of the flesh? Rabbi, am I not also humiliated by lust? If my body grows hot, does my soul not burn even as yours does? Oh rabbi, I am grown numb beneath the double weight of centuries of sexual denial, I

have not been able to struggle up even far enough to tell
you that I am made even as you are, that I carry the same
freight of sexual fear and hope that you do, that if there is
no salvation for me there is certainly none for you, that
the bargain you struck is false, that your religion is a
measure of your fear not of your courage, that you'll
never get out of this world alive, rabbi, not so long as
your women wear wigs and you avert your eyes from
them."

The terror of felt sexuality is the terror of our lives, the
very essence of our existence. It pervades the culture,
manifesting itself not only in the bodies of relgious codes
but in every aspect of moral law, every nuance of custom,
every trace of human exchange, soaking through social
intercourse: it is there in restaurants, on busses, in shops,
on country roads, and on city streets; in university ap-
pointments and government decisions and pleasure trips
and the popular arts. Everywhere—like some pernicious
covering—can be felt the influence of that fear of the
sexual self that has destroyed our childhoods, scarred our
adolescences, forced us into loveless marriages, made of us
dangerously repressed and corrupt people, and sometimes
driven us mad. And deeply interwoven in the fabric of this
cultural cloak is the image of woman: woman, the temptress; woman, the slut; woman, the heartless bitch—luring
men eternally toward spiritual death, making them come
up against what they most fear and hate in themselves,
pulling them down, down, down into the pit of themselves. Sensuous Circe luring Ulysses onto the rocks of his
worst self, sluttish Mildred in *Of Human Bondage* man-
gling crippled Philip still further, heartless Marlene Die-
trich casually destroying the weak, decent professor in The
Blue Angel—the list is endless and the lesson is always the
same. Woman herself is not locked in this profound struggle with the self; she is only the catalyst for man's struggle
with himself. It is never too certain that woman has any
self at all. What *is* certain is that onto woman is projected
all that is worst in man's own view of himself, all that is
primitive, immature, and degrading. In woman man has a
kind of reverse reflection of himself: all of his sloth and
weakness is there in full vibrance, and only a shadow of
those higher emotions that will flame into full life in
himself alone.

Othello's ill-fated Desdemona carries almost whole,
within her frail, confused, weakly existent being, the bur-

den of the foregoing argument. Without a shred of actuality, Desdemona is a total projection of Othello's fears and
self-hatred, a direct reflection of his great longings and his
melancholy sense of humiliated defeat. When Iago first
comes to Othello with his dramatic tale of Desdemona's
perfidy, Othello, feeling very much satisfied with Desdemona's love, quite sensibly says: "But why on earth would
she do *that?*" Iago, hesitating not an instant, announces:
"Lust!" "Oh," says Othello, and Desdemona's fate is
sealed. He accepts in a shot that Desdemona is a craven
female, absolutely helpless before an onslaught of lust.
Should it overcome her, clearly there is an immediate end
to love, loyalty, survival instinct, the lot—all, all are as
nothing before the raging lust of the female. At that
moment, it is remarkably clear that Desdemona is, and
always has been, without any reality for Othello, for his
capitulation is the bow to destiny of a man gripped by a
fearful and intimate knowledge of his *own* volatile passions. Immediately, we remember Othello's description of
how he won Desdemona. He told her stories! He told her
stories of his own military glory and she came to adore
him. She has never been anything but a receptacle for his
own dreams and his own fears; when fears outstrip
dreams we perform acts of violence and sacrifice, so
unbearable are we then to our exposed selves.

Desdemona aside, the painfully abundant proof of the
cultural effectiveness of this myth of the lustful and arousing female can be found in the statistics of sexual-
psychopathic murders. The number of women who have
been butchered to death in a frenzy of psychopathic lust
and fear (and we all know that a psychopath's obsessions
are not atypical of a culture's hallucinations, but rather
archetypical) would no doubt populate a small country.

Of course, there is also an opposite value to this exaggerated mythic projection of woman—equally exaggerated, equally mythic, equally difficult to bear. The man who
reviles the slut slavers at the feet of his mother. If woman
is not temptress, then she is goddess. She is all, then, that
breast-beating man would be if he were not the craven
creature that he is. Woman-the-mother is the golden ideal,
the convenient repository for man's most unexamined,
unwanted, sentimentalized, suffocating, ahuman notions
about his own composite being. She too is a creation of
his adolescent dreams, of his frightened longing that life
should only prove not to be what he deeply suspects it is.

I was a twenty-five-year-old graduate student of English literature when I first read George Washington Cable's *The Grandissimes,* an 1870 novel about New Orleans. This story of a racially mixed family was the first important work in America literature to recognize the Negro question as a deep spiritual curse that would hover over the South, eventually taking a violent retribution. Although the novel is written in the stilted language of self-conscious nineteenth-century Americanese, an undeniable underlying power emerges in the delineation of the book's black and white male Grandissimes, never through its women. The major male characters are two Honores—black and white —both powerful, interesting, oddly believable. The heroine, on the other hand, is Aurora. She is thirty-five years old, a young widow and mother struggling financially (and in every other damn way too). She is magnificently, touchingly, incredibly beautiful, brave, true, soft, good, loyal, courageous, quiet, need I go on? She is the quintessential Victorian fantasy female. As I continued to read of Aurora, I felt a strange, sickening feeling developing in my chest and stomach. I felt heavy and anxious each time I came back to her. It was a long time before I realized that I was feeling panic. Who *was* Aurora? I thought. *What* was she? And what on earth did she have to do with *me?* With any woman? In what skin on what earth in what time could Aurora ever have lived? In *no* skin, on *no* earth, at *no* time, I said fiercely to myself. Aurora, you are *destroying* me! If you live, I surely cannot!

Here, then, the double sexual image of woman: Circe on the one hand, Aurora on the other. All that is evil, all that is ideal. Like a compress for drawing fever, woman is endowed with the sexual unreality the race longs for, burdened with a life-destroying innocence (for make no mistake: her evil is certainly as innocent of genuine knowledge as is her goldenness) that makes of her, at one and the same time, obsessively sexual and extraordinarily asexual.

And, of course, in the end that's it: the final mythic outsidedness of woman is that ultimately she is beyond sex. Steeped in sex, drugged on sex, defined by sex, *but never actually realized through sex,* she has gone beyond it, she has gone through it, she is on the other side.

Woman has been defined primarily in her society as a sexual object—either one of lust or one of chastity. She has been allowed to be nothing else, essentially. Whatever else she reaches for, or appears to have gained, or however far from this definition she seemingly has traveled, the fact is—all superficially deceptive appearances to the contrary—there isn't a woman alive who is not obsessed with her sexual desirability. Not her sexual *desire*. Her sexual *desirability*. Her inner life—no matter *who* she is—is, in many senses, ruled by the continual measure she is taking of her ability—on a scale of one to ninety million—to attract men. When she feels this power waning she literally feels that life is leaving her. The multiplicity of needs attached to this condition long ago produced a kind of deadening panic in which her own sexuality was never even acknowledged, much less fulfilled. No one understands this better than D. H. Lawrence. Lawrentian women only discover their own sexuality in their mid-thirties; then it is gut-ripping trauma, an upheaval that destroys the ordered life around them—something along the lines of crucifixion and resurrection. The average woman, however, preoccupied all her life with everything that her sexuality has been a stand-in for, never realizing herself in simple human sexual terms, is exhausted, in her mid-thirties, and she continues to lie back in bed, never taking, always being taken, never absorbed by her own desire, preoccupied only with whether or not she is desired.

Valerie Solanas' remarkable *SCUM Manifesto* is a perfect illustration of what I mean. A virulent and extraordinarily imaginative piece of man-hating, the Manifesto circulated, with much heated debate, throughout the underground of the women's liberation movement for a long time before surfacing. The Manifesto is mainly a description of society as Solanas sees it in the hands of men, whom she considers walking abortions (literally). In the last analysis, though, the piece is a startling portrait of the horrors of the sexual role system, even though Solanas thinks it is a denunciation of men alone, and a defense of women. However, Solanas understands full well that the enemy is not really men, but women against themselves; she understands that the revolution will not occur until women simply refuse to play their customary roles, and against this understanding she constructs a revolutionary female whom she calls the SCUM female, the female who will lead the struggle, the female who is, indeed, the irreducible Liberationist woman, the SCUM female who has been driven by her own experience to take the position she now takes, and it is in describing this experience Solanas now becomes important to us. Listen:

Sex is the refuge of the mindless. And the more mindless the woman, the more deeply embedded in the male "culture," in short, the nicer she is, the more sexual she is. The nicest women in our society are raving sex maniacs. But, being most awfully, awfully nice they don't, of course, descend to fucking—that's uncouth—rather they make love, commune by means of their bodies and establish sensual rapport; the literary ones are attuned to the throb of Eros and attain a clutch upon the Universe; the religious have spiritual communion with the Divine Sensualism; the mystics merge with the Erotic Principle and blend with the Cosmos, and the acid heads contact their erotic cells.

On the other hand, the females least embedded in the male "culture," the least nice, those crass and simple souls who reduce fucking to fucking, who are too childish for the grown-up world of suburbs, mortgages, mops and baby shit, too selfish to raise kids and husbands, too uncivilized to give a shit for anyone's opinion of them, too arrogant to respect Daddy, the "Greats" or the deep wisdom of the Ancients, who trust only their own animal, gutter instincts, who equate Culture with chicks, whose sole diversion is prowling for emotional thrills and excitement, who are given to disgusting, nasty, upsetting "scenes," hateful, violent bitches given to slamming those who unduly irritate them in the teeth, who'd sink a shiv into a man's chest or ram an icepick up his asshole as soon as look at him, if they knew they could get away with it, in short, those who by the standards of our "culture," are SCUM ... these females are cool and relatively cerebral and skirting asexuality.

Unhampered by propriety, niceness, discretion, public opinion, "morals," the "respect" of assholes, always funky, dirty, lowdown, SCUM gets around ... and around ... and around. . . . they've seen the whole show—every bit of it—the fucking scene, the sucking scene, the dick scene, the dike scene—they've covered the whole waterfront, been under every dock and pier—the peter pier, the pussy pier ... you've got to go through a lot of sex to get to anti-sex, and SCUM's been through it all, and they're now ready for a new show; they want to crawl out from under the dock, move, take off, sink out. But SCUM doesn't yet prevail; SCUM's still in the gutter of our "society," which, if it's not deflected from its present course and if the Bomb doesn't drop on it, will hump itself to death.[1]

Solanas has stumbled onto the fact that sex, in a curious way, is to women what alcohol is to the alcoholic or drugs to the addict. Forced to live her life within the incomprehensible shadow of unrealistic sexual terms, saddled with the whimpering male fear, stemming from the mother, that has projected onto woman the image of lady or slut, woman herself—numb and confused—has become dangerously lost. Never—in all of this—realizing her own self through her sexuality, she becomes obsessed with sexuality, and finally, perhaps, must pass beyond it in order to live. For in woman the *mythic* sexual sense, the sexual need, the sexual preoccupation has been so pervasive, so confused, so multiple in definition, so grotesquely unfiltered that she has suffered the fate of the compulsive: in order to live perhaps she must remove herself from sex *entirely*.

Once again, in this hideous charade of female masks, a deadly perfect opposite appears: Miriam of the luxuriant *Sons and Lovers*. Miriam of the Spirit (I feel an old familiar pain in my chest)—true sister to the SCUM female, every bit as much beyond sex as that lady of the thousand bodies; Miriam, growing up amid the slop and crudity and backbreaking labor of the English farmlands of the 1890s; Miriam, servant to men who were servants to the earth, taught to love what was beautiful and to shun what was ugly by a mother who could save her own soul only through the retreat into romance: the spirit was beautiful, the flesh was ugly. (How many women, faced with the terror of the masculine earth, become just such "spiritual" creatures? How many? Who could even begin to count?) Thus, Miriam grows, arrested nearly in prepuberty, worshipping the spiritual, repulsed by the carnal, displacing her erotic impulses onto nature, never growing to feel the force of sexuality fusing in her own self; when she comes to love Paul Morel she is drawn, numb with fear, into a bed she cannot share. For her sex can never be a path to self-realization; for her sex is a card to be thrown into the game of chance, gambling on the win: possession of the man. For him, of course, it is otherwise. For him that bed is a marvel of revelation through abandon; for him it is the ecstasy of biology, the moment of ultimate daring, of total exposure, total risk. For him the great and voluptuous pleasure is to lose all sense of himself, as such, and all sense of her, as such, and to feel them both as marvelous mindless embodiments of the sexual principle alive in each of them. For her, ah, for her—it is death. No desire, only a grim and continual struggle to hold onto herself, not to drown in the inundation of his desire, and above all, at all times, to be *recognized*. At the very point of his orgasm she cries: "Do you love me? Paul! Do you love me?" Me! Me! It's Miriam here. It is I giving myself to you, not some faceless nameless female. Do you realize what I am doing for you? Do you? Reward me. Love me. Take care of me. Treat me as if I were precious, of great value, as if you *appreciate* what I am doing, don't abandon me along with yourself, to these disgusting emotions, these animal actions, this sex I cannot feel, I cannot touch, I only know is my mortal enemy. . . .

Not too long ago I sat across a luncheon table from a man who is intelligent, educated, urbane, and somewhat famous. As coffee was being poured, he leaned back, lit a cigarette, narrowed his eyes against the smoke, flicked an ash from his arm, and casually said: "Of course, you realize that if Women's Liberation wins, civilization will simply be *wrecked*."

I put my trembling hands in my lap and stared silently at him. This very same man had once—also apropos women's liberation—said something to me about the "fear of female sexuality" being at the bottom of it all; he had said it with the same shrewd, amused, conspiratorial expression in his eyes that was there now, as if he was admitting that we both shared this knowledge (I because I was the clever exception) of fearful female sexuality and female liberation threatening civilization, very much as someone else, a Protestant I knew, had once leaned across another table and said to me: "Jews really *are* smart, aren't they? *You* know what I mean. *Smart!*"

I thought when my Protestant friend had spoken, and I thought now as my worldly male friend spoke: "To whom is he speaking? Could it be *me*? No, that is impossible. I couldn't be real to him. No one speaks to a human being who is *real* in this manner. Now here am I, a living breathing woman, what's more a living breathing woman this man has known for many years, and he tells me now that I am petitioning my civilization—out of the very need of my soul—for full recognition of my humanness that I am about to wreck that civilization. . . . And he speaks to me of "fearful female sexuality" . . . Is that *me* he is speaking of? Dear God, where am *I* in all of that? Where is *my* life in all of that? Me at the typewriter, me talking, me in bed, me struggling to write, me fearful of love and wanting everything, me squirming inside my skin, alive with terror and ambition. Could it be that I am flesh and blood to this man? Could it be that my life is as real to him as it is to me?

No. It cannot be. I am not real to him. I am not real to my civilization. I am not real to the culture that has spawned me and made use of me. I am only a collection of myths. I am an existential stand-in. The *idea* of me is real—the temptress, the goddess, the child, the mother— but *I* am not real. The mythic proportions of woman are recognizable and real; it is only the human dimensions that are patently false and will be denied to the death, our death. James Baldwin once wrote: "The white man can deal with the Negro as a symbol or as a victim, but never as a human being." It was given to the black in the second great wave of black civil rights to understand that he lived as a symbolic surrogate, as a deliberate and necessary outsider, as an existential offering in his own civilization. Now, in the second great wave of feminism, the same understanding is being granted to women.

Wherever it is possible subjugation takes place: the reduction of power for some will increase the power for others. The race *knows* better; of course, it does. But so great is the need—so great—that waves of helpless delusion wash over civilization after civilization, and the process continues, unheeded—and wherever it does, subjugation is accompanied by mythic structures that mingle with and confuse the luminous pain of the outsider.

Life, from beginning to end, is fear. Yes, it is pain, yes, it is desire, but more than anything it is fear; a certain amount rational, an enormous amount irrational. All political cruelties stem from that overwhelming fear. To push back the threatening forces, to offer primitive sacrifices, to give up some in the hope that others will be saved . . . that is the power struggle. That is the outsidedness of the poor, the feeble, the infantile. That is the outsidedness of Jews. That is the outsidedness of blacks. That is the outsidedness of women.

NOTE

1. Valerie Solanas, *S.C.U.M. (Society for Cutting Up Men) Manifesto* (New York: Olympia Press, 1971), pp. 30-31. Preface by Maurice Girodias, Introduction by Vivian Gornick.

5

THE PARADOX OF THE HAPPY MARRIAGE

Jessie Bernard

THE STRUCTURE OF AMERICAN MARRIAGE

In 1840 Alexis de Tocqueville analyzed the American marriages:

> In America the independence of woman is irrecoverably lost in the bonds of matrimony: if an unmarried woman is less constrained there than elsewhere, a wife is subjected to stricter obligations. . . . The Americans . . . require much abnegation on the part of women, and a constant sacrifice of her pleasures to her duties which is seldom demanded of her in Europe. . . . When the time for choosing a husband is arrived at, that cold and stern reasoning power which has been educated and invigorated by the free observation of the world, teaches an American woman that a spirit of levity and independence in the bonds of marriage is a constant subject of annoyance, not of pleasure; it tells her that the amusements of the girl cannot become the recreations of the wife, and that the sources of a married woman's happiness are in the home of her husband. As she clearly discerns beforehand the only road which can lead to domestic happiness, she enters upon it at once, and follows it to the end without seeking to turn back. . . .
>
> Nor have the Americans ever supposed that one consequence of democratic principles is the subversion of marital power, or the confusion of the natural authorities in families. They hold that every association must have a head in order to accomplish its object, and that the natural

head of the conjugal association is man. They do not
therefore deny him the right of directing his partner; and
they maintain, that in the smaller association of husband
and wife, as well as in the great social community, the
object of democracy is to regulate and legalize the powers
which are necessary, not to subvert all power. This opinion is not peculiar to one sex, and contested by the other;
I never observed that the women of America consider
conjugal authority as a fortunate usurpation of their rights,
nor that they thought themselves degraded by submitting
to it. It appeared to me, on the contrary, that they attach
a sort of pride to the voluntary surrender of their own
will, and make it their boast to bend themselves to the
yoke, not to shake it off.[1]

In 1912 Mary Roberts Coolidge speculated *Why Women
Are So:*

> Mastery . . . was the natural ambition of men not fully
> civilized; but, in a brutal, competitive world, they found it
> difficult to achieve over other men and contrary circum-
> stances. All the more, therefore, they desired mastery in
> their households—it was easier to begin at home. The head
> of a family who spent his days even in mere commercial
> contest with other men, would naturally expect subservi-
> ence in his wife and children, just as he did in his
> employees; nor would he be likely to tolerate in them
> original opinions and independent action. . . . In the past
> century, by far the larger number of women were well
> broken; and, in proportion as they were, they lost the
> power of thinking and deciding for themselves in any
> matter outside the household affairs for which they were
> responsible.[2]

THE WIFE'S MARRIAGE

A substantial body of research shores up Émile Durkheim's conclusion that "the regulations imposed on the
woman by marriage are always more stringent [than those
imposed on men]. Thus she loses more and gains less
from the institution."[3] Considerable well-authenticated
data show that there are actually two marriages in every
marital union—his and hers—which do not always coincide. Thus, for example, when researchers ask husbands
and wives identical questions about their marriages, they
often get quite different replies even on fairly simple
factual questions.[4] Although in nonclinical populations

roughly the same proportion of men and women say they are happy (Table 5-1), by and large when husbands and

TABLE 5-1

*Summary of Studies of Happiness and
Unhappiness by Sex*

STUDY	PERCENT "VERY HAPPY"		PERCENT "NOT TOO HAPPY"	
	MARRIED MEN	MARRIED WOMEN	MARRIED MEN	MARRIED WOMEN
Gurin, Veroff, Feld[a]	36	43	8	7
Bradburn and Caplovitz[b]	27	27	14	11
Bradburn[c]	35	38	9	7
Knupfer et al.[d]	39	39	7	10

[a] Gerald Gurin, Joseph Veroff, and Sheila Feld, *Americans View Their Mental Health* (New York: Basic Books, 1960); a nationwide sample studied in 1957; 908 married men, 963 married women.
[b] Norman M. Bradburn and David Caplovitz, *Reports on Happiness* (Chicago: Aldine, 1965), p. 9; a study of four rural Illinois communities made in 1962; 794 married men, 824 married women.
[c] Norman M. Bradburn, *The Structure of Psychological Well-Being* (Chicago: Aldine, 1969), p. 149; a study of five urban and suburban communities made in 1963; 1,009 married men, 1,171 married women.
[d] Genevieve Knupfer, Walter Clark, and Robin Room, "The Mental Health of the Unmarried," *American Journal of Psychiatry* 122 (February 1966): 842; study made in 1962; of 374 married men, 375 married women.

wives are asked about specific items in their relationships, the wives' marriages look less happy than their husbands'. For as Durkheim found, marriage is not the same for women as for men; it is not nearly as good.

Half a century ago, G. V. Hamilton found women more dissatisfied with marriage than men. J. K. Folsom, analyzing marital discord, found that in 58 percent of the cases where there were sufficient data on which to base a judgment, the wives were more frustrated than their husbands. Among happily married couples, Harvey Locke found husband-wife agreement on family matters reported by fewer wives than husbands on ten out of eleven items; fewer wives than husbands reported "no difficulties at all."[5] Boyd Rollins and Harold Feldman found that although general marital satisfaction varied over time, wives reported it somewhat less frequently, negative feelings somewhat more, and positive companionship and present satisfaction slightly less.[6] Gerald Gurin, Joseph Veroff, and Sheila Feld found that more wives than husbands reported marital problems.[7] And, what is equally if not more interesting, more husbands as well as more wives mentioned the husband rather than the wife as creating the problems.[8] A recent study, which was particularly impressive because of the size of the sample (6,928 persons twenty years of age and over plus never-married persons sixteen to nineteen years of age) and because such a large number of the respondents—2,480—were couples, found that more women (23 percent) than men (18 percent) reported marital dissatisfaction. More wives (7 percent) than husbands (4 percent) considered their marriages unhappy; more wives (9 percent) than husbands (6 percent) had recently considered separation or divorce; more wives (34 percent) than husbands (30 percent) had at some time regretted their marriage.[9] Even when the marriage was better than had been expected, more wives than husbands expressed dissatisfaction. It is understandable, therefore, that more women than men show up in marriage counsellors' offices[10] and that more wives than husbands initiate divorce proceedings.

These findings on the wife's marriage are especially poignant because marriage in our society is more important for women's happiness than for men's. "For almost all measures, the relation between marriage, happiness and overall well-being was stronger for women than for men," one study reports.[11] In fact, the strength of the relationship between marital and overall happiness was so strong for women that the author wondered if "most women are equating their marital happiness with their overall happiness."[12] Another study based on a more intensive examination of the data on marriage from the same sample notes that "on each of the marriage adjustment measures ... the association with overall happiness is considerably stronger for women than it is for men."[13] Karen Renne also found the same strong relationship between feelings of general well-being and marital happiness: those who were happy tended not to report marital dissatisfaction; those who were not, did. "In all probability the respondent's view of his marriage influences his general feeling of well-being or morale";[14] this relationship was stronger among wives than among husbands.[15] A strong association between reports of general happiness and reports of marital happiness was also found a generation ago.[16]

Because women have to put so many more eggs in the one basket of marriage, they have more of a stake in its stability. Because their happiness is more dependent on marriage than men's, they have to pay more for it. All the studies show that women make more concessions.

> The preponderance of replies of husbands and wives in our interviews was that the wives made the greater adjustment in marriage. This finding is in agreement with the theory advanced by Burgess and Cottrell in their study of success or failure in marriage. They point out that in both their study, and in Terman's investigation of marital happiness [in the 1930s], the background scores of husbands have a greater correlation than those of wives with marital success. . . . With many couples, the husband upon entering marriage maintains his routine with no expectation of modifying it in relation to his wife's wishes. Often she submits without voicing a protest. . . . In other cases the wife may put up a contest, although she generally loses. . . . Wives appear, on the average, to make the greater adjustment in marriage according to their own testimony and that of their husbands.[17]

Finally, in a study of lower-class marriage, Lee Rainwater found that when differences existed between husbands and wives with respect to role expectations, especially the affectional, it was "probably easier for the wife to go along with her husband than . . . for her to persuade him to interact more affectionately—both because it is difficult for one person to force affection from another and because the wife already is persuaded that the parental and work roles are important, while the husband may be quite insensitive to the wife's affectional needs."[18]

Wives are, therefore, reflecting objective circumstances when they report more problems and dissatisfactions in their marriages than their husbands do. *Their* marriages are more problem-laden and dissatisfaction-prone than their husbands' are. The psychological costs to women of the happiness achieved by thus adjusting to the demands of marriage have been not inconsiderable.[19]

How Happy Is the Happy Housewife?

When radical women indict marriage as it is now insti-

tutionalized, invariably at least one listener indignantly
challenges them. The charges cannot be true because she
is perfectly happy with present arrangements; she enjoys
her status as wife and mother; she would not have anything different; she does not want the boat rocked; she
rebukes the radical women for raising such threatening
issues. Only sick women would want things changed . . .

It is true that a considerable proportion of married
women judge themselves as happy. Although several
studies differ somewhat, by and large a sizable proportion
of married women report themselves as happy (Table
5-1), a considerably larger proportion of married than of
single women (Table 5-2). Since there is a close relationship between evaluation of one's marriage and of one's
marital happiness,[20] especially, as we have just seen, for
women, they also report their marriages as happy (Table
5-3).

TABLE 5-2

*Happiness and Unhappiness of Women
by Marital Status*[a]

	PERCENT "VERY HAPPY"		PERCENT "NOT TOO HAPPY"	
STUDY	MARRIED WOMEN	SINGLE WOMEN	MARRIED WOMEN	SINGLE WOMEN
Gurin, Veroff, and Feld	43	26	7	11
Bradburn and Caplovitz	27	27	11	15
Bradburn	38	18	7	14
Knupfer et al.	39	24	10	12

[a] Source same as Table 5-1.

But how happy is the happy housewife? Examination of
specific personality and behavioral items reported by
women and surveys of mental-health impairment raises
doubts. In such studies[21] married women appear to be
more damaged than single women. Thus, for example, in
one study more married than single women were bothered
by feelings of depression (50, 30); did not feel happy
most of the time (17, 15); disliked their present jobs (19,
11); sometimes felt they were about to go to pieces (44,
24); were afraid of death (53, 19); were terrified by

TABLE 5-3

Happiness Ratings of Marriage by Sex

STUDY	VERY HAPPY HUSBANDS	WIVES	AVERAGE HUSBANDS	WIVES	VERY UNHAPPY HUSBANDS	WIVES
Terman[a]	66.3	70.5	29.2	23.9	1.7	2.6
Terman[b]	54.9	55.2	37.9	33.7	7.2	11.1
Burgess and Cottrell[c]	80.1	79.3	11.9	12.3	8.0	8.4
Gurin, Veroff, and Feld[d]	71.0	65.0	26.0	32.0	3.0	3.0

[a] Lewis M. Terman et al. *Psychological Factors in Marital Happiness* (New York: McGraw-Hill, 1939), p. 78. A nonrandom set of 792 marriages; the categories were: extraordinarily happy (29.5 and 34.6 percent for men and women respectively); decidedly above average (36.8 and 35.9 percent); somewhat above average (16.3 and 14.7 percent); average (12.9 and 9.2 percent); somewhat less than average (2.9 and 3.0 percent); decidedly less than average (1.6 and 1.8 percent;) and extremely unhappy (0.1 and 0.8 percent).

[b] A random sample of 902 men and 644 women. Same categories as in above sample, same source. The proportions of men in the several categories were: 25.5, 29.4, 13.1, 18.2, 6.6, 3.2, and 4.0; of women: 27.2, 28.0, 10.1, 16.3, 7.3, 4.0, and 7.1.

[c] E. W. Burgess and Leonard S. Cottrell, *Predicting Success or Failure in Marriage* (Englewood Cliffs, N. J.: Prentice-Hall, 1939), p. 39. Based on 526 young marriages, largely urban or small town in background.

[d] Gerald Gurin, Joseph Veroff, and Sheila Feld, *Americans View Their Mental Health* (New York: Basic Books, 1960), p. 102.

windstorms (34, 24); worried about catching diseases (30, 19); sometimes thought of things too bad to talk about (30, 20); were bothered by pains and ailments in different parts of the body (17, 10).[22] Overall, more married than single women were reported to be passive, phobic, and depressed, at least half of the married women falling into one or another of these three categories (Table 5-4). Although the total number was small, almost three times as many married as single women showed severe neurotic symptoms (11, 4), and, except in the menopausal decade, there were more married than single women with mental-health impairment (Table 5-4).

Married women also show up less well than married men (Table 5-5).

TABLE 5-4   *Some Personality Dimensions of Single and Married Women (Percent Scoring High)*[a]

PERSONALITY DIMENSION	MARRIED (289)	SINGLE (45)
Passivity	74	57
Phobic tendency	55	44
Depression	54	35
Severe neurotic symptoms	11	4
Mental health impairment:		
20-29	13.4	11.2
30-39	22.1	12.1
40-49	18.1	24.6
50-59	30.6	25.6

[a] Genevieve Knupfer, Walter Clark, and Robin Room, "The Mental Health of the Unmarried," *American Journal of Psychiatry* 122 (February 1966): 841-851, copyright 1966 American Psychiatric Association. Mental health impairment data from Leo Srole, Thomas S. Langner, Stanley T. Michael, Marvin K. Opler, and Thomas A. C. Rennie, *Mental Health in the Metropolis* (New York: McGraw-Hill, 1962), pp. 177, 178.

TABLE 5-5 *Some Personality Dimensions of Married Women and Married Men (Percent Scoring High)*[a]

PERSONALITY DIMENSION	MARRIED MEN (301)	MARRIED WOMEN (289)
Passivity	50	74
Phobic tendency	30	55
Depression	37	54
Severe neurotic symptoms	17	11
Mental health impairment:		
20-29	11.7	13.4
30-39	19.6	22.1
40-49	19.0	18.1
50-59	25.7	30.6

[a] Sources same as Table 5-4.

Twice as many married women (25 percent) as married men (12 percent) have felt that a nervous breakdown was impending;[23] many more women than men experience psychological anxiety, physical anxiety, and immobilization.[24] More wives than husbands, especially among college women, have feelings of inadequacy in marriage. Except among college women thirty-five to fifty-four years of age, many more women than men have negative or ambivalent self-perceptions.[25] Many more wives than husbands mention their physical appearance as a shortcoming,[26] reflecting the enormous emphasis put on youth and beauty among women in our society. Except among young college women, many more women than men mention their lack of general adjustment as a shortcoming.[27] Their husbands may create the problems, but women feel their own inability to adjust to them to be a shortcoming on their part.[28]

A SHOCK THEORY OF MARRIAGE

Can we accept de Tocqueville's contrast between the unmarried American woman, "less constrained" than women anywhere else, and the abject wives who "attach a sort of pride to the voluntary surrender of their own will," who "make it their boast to bend themselves to the yoke, not to shake it off." Did they really? Or were they really as "well broken" as Mary Roberts Coolidge reported them to be?

In 1942, on the basis of data far less abundant than today's, I proposed what I called a shock theory of marriage.[29] It was suggested by a study using a forty-item questionnaire of 1,400 preponderantly urban men and women of upper socioeconomic status, higher than the average in education and intelligence. Comparing married women and spinsters, the author concluded that "either a calm type of woman remains unmarried or that marriage has disturbing effects upon women."[30] Since the differences between married and unmarried women tended to be slight in younger age brackets and to increase with age, I concluded that "the hypothesis that marriage is selective of more emotional women seems less tenable than the alternative hypothesis, that marriage has disturbing effects upon some women. . . . The data suggest that marriage has a traumatic effect on personality."[31] As the structure of marriage lags farther and farther behind the needs of the kind of women modern life calls for, the theory seems increasingly apt. "Shock" may have been too shocking a term to use; researchers tend to use the less frightening term "trauma." But whatever the term used, it refers to both commonly reported phenomena and others less likely to find recognition in the literature.

Some of the shocks to which marriage subjects women have been widely recognized. The "rape" of the bride on the honeymoon used to be a common folk stereotype. The let down in personal appearance is a shock for both men and women: the unshaven face and neglect of personal cleanliness on his side and the cold cream and curlers on hers. The relaxation of general manners—that is, no longer seeing the other always on best behavior—is another shock. Increasingly, the shock implicit in the wife's change in occupation upon marriage has been recognized. From being a secretary, sales girl, teacher, or nurse in her own right she becomes a housekeeper, an occupation that is classified in the labor market and in her own mind as menial and of low status. The apologetic "I'm just a housewife" that she tenders in reply to what she does illustrates how low her self-evaluation of her occupation is, no matter how loudly and defensively she proclaims her pleasure in it. Although the young wife feels secure among her peers because now she has succeeded in a goal—marriage—common to all of them, in other relationships she finds herself ciphered out as an individual. She is no longer the young woman who was an individual in her own right, entitled to ideas, opinions, preferences of her own, but only a shadow;[32] it is assumed that her husband represents her. Employers now see her as bound to another loyalty and hence not to be taken seriously. She is shocked to learn that her husband's work is likely to win out over her in competition for his time and attention; she had thought before marriage that she was the most important component in his life; she learns now that his work is likely to come first when a choice has to be made. Furthermore, he "is involved in more stimulating activity in adult concerns and with adults, while ... [she] is involved with small children. ... There is apt to be differential personal growth, with the husband and wife having less and less satisfying interaction with each other."[33]

In addition to these "conventional" shocks, well documented in the literature, there is another only recently recognized—discovering the fallacy of the sex stereotypes that the wife has been socialized into accepting and around which she has built her life. Her husband is not the sturdy oak on whom she can depend. There are few trauma greater than the child's discovery of the fallibility of his parents; than the wife's discovery of her husband's dependencies; than the discovery of her own gut-superiority in a thousand hidden crannies of the relationship; than the realizations that in many situations his judgment is no better than hers; that he does not really know more than she; that he is not the calm, rational, nonemotional dealer in facts and relevant arguments; that he is, in brief, not at all the kind of person the male stereotype pictures him to be. Equally, if not more, serious is her recognition that she is not really the weaker vessel, that she is often called upon to be the strong one in the relationship. These trauma are the more harrowing because they are interpreted as individual, unique, secret, not-to-be-shared with others, not even, if possible, to be admitted to oneself.

There are doubtless many ways of meeting the situation. One is to hide it, to refuse to recognize it, to go on believing that the husband really does conform to the stereotype, that he really is superior, to learn, as de Tocqueville reported, to glory in her lowly status. Even, if necessary, to trim her sails so that she really becomes inferior to him, dependent on him (an incubus at middle age, in fact).[34] That approach at least prevents facing the situation. Another way to meet it is to reinterpret it. "Men are just little boys grown tall" is the reassuring cliché that saves older women from the disillusionment. This redefinition—or inversion—of the cultural stereotype helps salve the wound by making the situation sharable with other women; they are not alone.

If the structure of marriage is so unfavorable to women as compared to both married men and single women, why do married women report themselves as happy? It is difficult to reconcile the depressed, fearful, passive-dependent women in Table 5-4 with the happy woman in Table 5-1.[35] Why do women who present such a far-from-happy picture nevertheless think of themselves as happy? What is back of the happy housewife's judgment?

HAPPY OR RECONCILED?

In order to adjust to a relationship structured as marriage has been until now, the character and personality of women have had to be socialized according to a specific pattern. Just as the feet of traditional Chinese gentlewomen had to be bound, the wings of Western women have had to be clipped. If some young Katharine did manage to arrive at marriageable age before she had been properly tamed, there was always a willing Petruchio ready to take on the task.

The pattern of socialization that in the United States

transformed de Tocqueville's free and unconstrained girl
into a self-abnegating wife has been unquestioned even by
clinicians. Only now, in fact, is it coming to be seriously
challenged by them. The challenge raises disturbing questions. For example, could it be that women report themselves as happy because they are oversocialized, overcul-
turated, or too closely integrated into the norms of our
society? We know from the Burgess-Cottrell data that
conventional people, conforming people, people shaped
for our institutions, fit them and are comfortable in them.
Could it be that because married women thus conform
and adjust to the demands of marriage, at whatever cost
to themselves, they therefore judge themselves to be happy? Are they confusing adjustment with happiness? For, as
de Tocqueville reminded us, until recently women were
indoctrinated with the idea that their happiness lay in
devoting their lives to their husbands and children.[36] They
are doing just that; they are living up to the prescribed
norms. Everyone defines feminine happiness in these terms
so, ipso facto, they must be happy. By definition, having
managed to adjust to the demands of marriage, they are
convinced that they are happy; they interpret their conformity as happiness. Conforming to the standards of femininity fits women for marriage.

When few if any alternatives existed for women, there
may have been a defensible rationale for this happiness-as-
adjustment point of view. Healthy people do bow to the
unchangeable. They do come to terms with the inevitable,
or what they accept as inevitable.[37] The talented woman
who as a girl dreamed of becoming a singer, dancer, actress, author, musician, nurse, even doctor, lawyer, mer-
chant, or chief may look back with tender secret nostalgia
at her dreams, but she dismisses them—with a sigh—as
childish fantasies and resumes her vacuum cleaning. Without options, without alternatives, many married women do
thus achieve a kind of reconciliation that is easy to interpret as happiness. Their standards for marriage are low.
They have no idea how exciting, joyous, and delightful a
relationship between a man and a woman can be when
they can share their minds as well as their bodies and
when they can appreciate one another's ideas as well as
one another's sexuality. For many women, untrained for
independence and "processed" for wifehood, marriage,
even if not up to their expectations, is preferable to the
alternatives. They will settle for a "good provider." Only

when attractive alternatives become available do many find they want more.

But as radical women have been pointing out and as clinicians themselves now agree, the standards of femininity, however suitable they may have been in the past, may now be dysfunctional. They are not standards of good mental health; in fact, adjustment to the demands of marriage may greatly impair mental health.

HAPPY OR SICK?

Some clinicians are now seriously questioning whether the qualities that are associated with marital happiness for women may not themselves be contrary to good mental health. Is it possible that many women are "happily married" *because* they have poor mental health?[38] A generation ago, Winnifred Johnson and Lewis Terman noted that happily married women were, among other things, docile rather than aggressive, indecisive, cautious rather than daring, and not very self-sufficient.[89] They were, in brief, women who had achieved an "adjustment" standard of mental health. They fit the situation they had been trained from infancy to fit and enjoyed conformity to it.

Few people challenged this Hausfrau concept of marital happiness. Indeed, therapists and clinicians encouraged it. Psychoanalysts, in fact, measured their success with women patients by the degree to which they could help them achieve reconciliation with their inferiority and accept the standard described by Terman.[40] Even a generation later, some clinicians were still thinking in terms of a "healthy" feminine woman as one far below the standards of adult mental health. Thus, for example, in one experiment male and female clinicians were given lists of traits. On one they were told to specify those that characterized a healthy adult, sex unspecified; on another, those that characterized a healthy adult male; and on still another, a healthy adult female. Analysis showed that the first two coincided, but that the third was different. The clinicians were more likely to attribute traits characteristic of healthy adults to men than to women. They had, in fact, a "double standard of health for men and women ... [which stemmed] from the clinicians' acceptance of an 'adjustment' notion of health."[41]

... clinicians are more likely to suggest that healthy women differ from healthy men by being more submissive, less independent, less adventurous, more easily influenced, less aggressive, less competitive, more excitable in minor crises, having their feelings more easily hurt, being more emotional, more conceited about their appearance, less objective, and disliking mathematics and science. This constellation seems a most unusual way of describing any mature, healthy individual.[42]

The authors of this study called for alternative definitions of mental health and maturity that would include self-actualization, mastery of the environment, and fulfillment of potential. They recognized that these drives were "in conflict with becoming adjusted to a social environment with associated restrictive stereotypes."[43] Nevertheless, they felt that "the cause of mental health may be better served if both men and women are encouraged toward maximum realization of individual potential, rather than to any adjustment to existing restrictive sex roles."[44] In terms of these updated standards of mental health, the happy housewife, depressed, phobic, passive, does not seem very well.

Radical women now appeal to psychiatrists to review their past orientation. The Women's Caucus of the Radical Caucus of the American Psychiatric Association in 1969 resolved that "research and therapy should at this time in history view women's mental health problems as arising from: (1) the unequal power relationship between men and women in which women are at the bottom and (2) the woman's position as legal domestic in the home or exploited public worker" and urged psychiatrists to stop rationalizing the situation of women by labeling its victims neurotic rather than oppressed.

In terms of the present structure of society, this new orientation is completely subversive. But it may well be a *sine qua non* for the kind of structuring now called for. It may come to seem increasingly anomalous that we must make women sick in order to fit them for marriage.

Could it be that marriage itself is "sick"?

NOTES

1. Alexis de Tocqueville, *Democracy in America, Part the Second, The Social Influence of Democracy* (New York: J. & H. G. Langley, 1840), pp. 212-213, 227.

2. Mary Roberts Coolidge, *Why Women Are So* (New York: Holt, 1912), p. 171, 177.

3. Émile Durkheim, *Suicide*, trans. J. A. Spaulding and George Simpson (Glencoe: Free Press, 1951), p. 271.

4. See Jessie Bernard, *The Sex Game* (Englewood Cliffs, N. J.: Prentice-Hall, 1968), chap. 10, for a summary of some examples. See also Jessie Bernard, *The Future of Marriage* (New York: Macmillan, 1971), chap. 1 for a discussion of "discrepant replies." There is usually agreement on the number of children and similar facts. But not on, say, frequency of intercourse, where conceptions or collective representations play an important part in actual perceptions. Because men are popularly thought to have greater sexual drive than women, even if women show greater interest, they attribute more to men than to themselves, and so do their husbands.

5. Harvey J. Locke, *Predicting Adjustment in Marriage: A Comparison of a Divorced and a Happily Married Group* (New York: Holt, 1951), pp. 68-69. The consistency of the wife's greater sense of difficulties rather than the percent reporting them seemed significant.

6. Boyd C. Rollins and Harold Feldman, "Marital Satisfaction over the Family Life Cycle," *Journal of Marriage and the Family* 32 (February 1970): 20-28. In the later stages of the marriage, as many as 40 percent of the wives report low general marital satisfaction. Another study also reported relative marital satisfaction of husbands and wives in six areas over the life cycle: in two (children and finances) the wife reported more satisfaction than the husband; in one (satisfaction with tasks), less; and in the other three (social activities, companionship, and sex), the relative satisfaction of husbands and wives varied over the life cycle. Wesley R. Burr, "Satisfaction with Various Aspects of Marriage over the Life Cycle: A Random Middle Class Sample," *Journal of Marriage and the Family* 32 (February 1970): 29-37.

7. Gerald Gurin, Joseph Veroff, and Sheila Feld, *Americans View Their Mental Health: A Nationwide Interview Survey* (New York: Basic Books, 1960), p. 102.

8. *Ibid.*, p. 110. Women worry more than their husbands also (p. 42), but the authors believe that worrying implies "an investment in life, the absence of worrying a lack of involvement and aspiration" (p. 30).

9. Karen S. Renne, "Correlates of Dissatisfaction in Marriage," *Journal of Marriage and the Family* 12 (February 1970): 56.

10. One study of couples undergoing counseling found 30 percent of the wives and 18 percent of the husbands unhappy in the first year of marriage. More wives than husbands had been unhappy from the very beginning. After the first several years, half were unhappy, especially the women. "A larger percentage of wives than husbands (14 percent compared to 4 percent) had expressly turned negative. For these wives, despair or hopelessness was the main theme running through their responses." Emile L. McMillan, "Problem Build-up: A Description of Couples in Marriage Counseling," *The Family Coordinator* 18 (July 1969): 261.

11. Norman M. Bradburn, *The Structure of Psychological Well-Being* (Chicago: Aldine, 1969), p. 150.

12. *Ibid.*, p. 159.

13. Susan R. Orden and Norman M. Bradburn, "Dimensions of Marriage Happiness," *American Journal of Sociology* 73 (May 1968): 731.

14. Renne, *op. cit.*, p. 64.

15. Among white couples, 71 percent of the wives and 52 percent of the husbands who were "not too happy" expressed marital dissatisfaction; 22 percent of the wives and 18 percent of the husbands who were "pretty happy" expressed marital dissatisfaction; and 4 percent of the wives and 2 percent of the husbands who were "very happy" expressed marital dissatisfaction. *Ibid.*, p. 63.

16. Gordon Watson, "Happiness among Adult Students," *Journal of Educational Psychology* 21 (1930).

17. E. W. Burgess and Paul Wallin, *Engagement and Marriage* (New York: Lippincott, 1953), pp. 614, 618.

18. Lee Rainwater, *And the Poor Get Children* (Chicago: Quadrangle Books, 1960), pp. 67-69.

19. The costs to men are discussed in Bernard, *The Future of Marriage.*

20. "An individual's own assessment of his marriage is a reasonably valid and stable measure of happiness in marriage." Orden and Bradburn, *op. cit.*, p. 730.

21. Hospital studies deal with different populations and the results do not always conform to those of noninstitutionalized populations.

22. Genevieve Knupfer, Walter Clark, and Robin Room, "The Mental Health of the Unmarried," *American Journal of Psychiatry* 122 (February 1966): 844. In any comparison of married and never-married subjects, allowances must be made for selective biases. In the case of women the bias tends to favor the never-married; in the case of men, the married. For more detailed discussion of this complex matter, see Bernard, *The Future of Marriage.* Also mothers have more to be worried and anxious about than single women.

23. Gurin, Veroff, and Feld, *op. cit.*, p. 42.

24. *Ibid.*, p. 190.

25. *Ibid.*, p. 108. But in frequency of feelings of inadequacy, there were no sex differences (p. 102).

26. *Ibid.*, p. 70.

27. *Ibid.*, p. 74.

28. *Ibid.*, p. 72.

29. Jessie Bernard, *American Family Behavior* (New York: Harper, 1942), p. 453.

30. Raymond R. Willoughby, "The Relationship to Emotionality of Age, Sex, and Conjugal Condition," *American Journal of Sociology* 43 (March 1938): 923. Willoughby reported that more married women than unmarried women were troubled by an idea that people were watching them on the street; were afraid of falling from high places; had their feelings easily hurt; were happy and sad by turns without apparent reason; regretted impulse statements; cried easily; felt hurt at criticism; sometimes felt miserable; found it hard to make up their minds; sometimes felt grouchy; were burdened by a sense of remorse; worried over possible misfortune; changed interests quickly; were bothered when people watched them perform a task; would cross the street to avoid meeting people; were upset when people crowded ahead of them in a line; would rather stand than take

a front seat when late; were self-conscious about their appearance; felt prevented from giving help at the scene of an accident. The unmarried women came through as quite different. They presented a picture of rejected, not traumatized, personalities; defined as failures because they were not married they seemed to withdraw from confrontations. Thus, more often than wives they lacked self-confidence, felt inferior, preferred quiet amusements, avoided crowds, expressed themselves better in writing than in speech, kept in the background at social occasions, felt shy, liked to be alone, avoided meeting the important people at a tea, hesitated to express themselves in a group, and felt self-conscious before superiors (pp. 920-931).

31. Bernard, *American Family Behavior*, p. 453.
32. The assumption made by the unsophisticated that a woman who engages in activities as an individual in her own right has to be unmarried was illustrated when male hecklers shouted to women participating in the Women's Strike, August 26, 1970, "get married!" They were nonplussed when the women shouted back that they were married. That situation violated the males' conception of wifehood, of marriage itself.
33. Floyd Mansfield Martinson, *Family in Society* (New York: Dodd, Mead, 1970), p. 177.
34. Pauline B. Bart, "Depression in Middle-Aged Women: Some Sociocultural Factors," paper presented to Society for Study of Social Problems, 1968, Table 3.
35. The data in the study by Knupfer et al. were derived from a reinterview in 1964 of 979 persons from an area probability sample in San Francisco first interviewed in 1962. The reinterview sample was biased in the direction of heavy drinkers, but "this bias is not sufficiently great to render the sample appreciably different from San Francisco as a whole in its distribution on any of the common demographic variables." Knupfer et al., *op. cit.*, p. 841. Intrasample controls—sex and marital status (Tables 5-4 and 5-5)—are not invalidated by such overrepresentation. For between-sample controls (comparisons with Tables 5-1 and 5-2) the proportions in Tables 5-4 and 5-5 might have to be stepped down somewhat.
36. "The only honorable career for a woman is marriage. She is required by public opinion to devote herself to a particular man and to defer to men in general. She has been trained from birth to do this. Any 'personal' ambitions are secondary, and if she goes against this she is flaunting values held universally by society and internalized by her. . . . Not only have they been taught to lack self-confidence, taught that they are thoroughly inadequate and incompetent in all important things, they have not been trained to pursue a career, and often have left off their education early. And why not, since getting and keeping a man was the only important thing? . . . Stepping out of her role . . . goes against the woman's own values and sense of the rightness of things. . . ." Dana Densmore, "The Slave's Stake in the Home," *Journal of Female Liberation* 2 (February, 1969): 14-15.
37. The Catholic Church built its doctrine on divorce on this principle. Indoctrinate people with the conviction that their marriage is indissoluble, that there is no way out, that whatever the nature of the relationship, it is for keeps and they will become reconciled to it.

38. Sick standards are by no means new phenomena. In the nine-teenth century, consumption was a romantic trait in women; the most famous heroine of the stage was Camille, romantically dying of consumption. Girls fainted adorably on any appropriate occasion and earthy good health was even embarrassing. Dora's helplessness was enthralling to David Copperfield—at first. Epileptic seizures, hallucinations, and visions are reported by anthropologists as valued characteristics in some cultures.

39. Winnifred Burt Johnson and Lewis M. Terman, "Personality Characteristics of Happily Married, Unhappily Married, and Divorced Persons," *Character and Personality* 2 (June 1935): 304-305.

40. Even psychoanalysts are now coming to recognize that "it is possible that the analyst's view of a successful analysis may be skewed if he feels that he has reached the core of a woman's femininity when he has been able to get her to share with equanimity his belief that she is really an inferior form of male." Robert J. Stoller, *Sex and Gender* (New York: Science House, 1968), p. 63.

41. Inge K. Broverman et al., "Sex-Role Stereotypes and Clinical Judgments of Mental Health," *Journal of Consulting and Clinical Psychology* 34 (February 1970): 6.

42. *Ibid.*, p. 5.

43. *Ibid.*, p. 6.

44. *Ibid.*, p. 7.

6

DEPRESSION IN MIDDLE-AGED WOMEN

Pauline B. Bart

> A young man begs his mother for her heart, which a betrothed of his has demanded as a gift; having torn it out of his mother's preferred breast he races away with it; and as he stumbles, the heart falls to the ground, and he hears it question protectively, "Did you hurt yourself, my son?"—JEWISH FOLK TALE.

> I'm glad that God gave me . . . the privilege of being a mother . . . and I loved them. In fact, I wrapped my love so much around them . . . I'm grateful to my husband since if it wasn't for him, there wouldn't be the children. They were my whole life. . . . My whole life was that because I had no life with my husband, the children should make me happy . . . but it never worked out.—DEPRESSED MIDDLE-AGED WOMAN

We have all read numerous case histories in which a child's neurosis or psychosis was attributed to the mother's

Much of this chapter appeared, in a somewhat different form, under the title "Portnoy's Mother's Complaint," *Trans-action* (November-December 1970). © 1970 by Trans-action, Inc.

behavior. Only recently has the schizophrenogenic family replaced the demon double-binding schizophrenogenic mother in theories about the causes of schizophrenia. This inquiry deals with the reverse situation—how given the traditional female role, the children's actions can result in the mother's neurosis or psychosis. This is a study of depressed middle-aged women in mental hospitals. The story of one such woman follows.

THE SUPERMOTHER AND HER PLIGHT

Mrs. Gold is a youthful Jewish housewife in her forties. Her daughter is married and lives about twenty miles away; her hyperactive brain-damaged thirteen-year-old son has been placed in a special school even farther away. After his departure she became suicidally depressed and was admitted to a mental hospital.

I asked her how her life was different now and she responded:

> It's a very lonely life, and this is when I became ill, and I think I'm facing problems now that I did not face before because I was so involved especially having a sick child at home. I didn't think of myself at all. I was just someone that was there to take care of the needs of my family, my husband and children, especially my sick child. But now I find that I—I want something for myself too. I'm a human being and I'm thinking about myself.

She was dissatisfied with her marriage; their mutual concern for their son held the couple together, but when their son entered an institution, this bond was loosened, although they visited him every Sunday. "My husband is primarily concerned with only one thing, and that is making a living. But there's more to marriage than just that [pause] you don't live by bread alone." Mrs. Gold states that she is not like other women for whom divorce is simple, but she is considering divorcing her husband if their relationship does not improve. Yet, another patient I interviewed later told me Mrs. Gold had cried all the previous night after her husband came to the hospital to tell her he was divorcing her.

Although she believes her life was "fuller, much fuller,

yes much fuller" before her children left, she used to have crying spells:

> ... but in the morning I would get up and I knew that there was so much dependent on me, and I didn't want my daughter to become depressed about it or neurotic in any way which could have easily happened because I had been that way. So I'm strong minded and strong willed, so I would pull myself out of it. It's just recently that I couldn't pull myself out of it. I think that if there was—if I was needed maybe I would have, but I feel that there's really no one that needs me now.

She is unable to admit anger toward her children and makes perfectionist demands on herself. "It was extremely hard on me, and I think it has come out now. Very hard. I never knew I had the amount of patience. *That child never heard a raised voice.*"

While she is proud of her daughter and likes her son-in-law, an element of ambivalence is apparent in her remarks. "Naturally as a mother you hate to have your daughter leave home. I mean it was a void there, but, uh, I know she's happy. . . . I'm happy for my daughter because she's happy." Since she had used her daughter as a confidant when the daughter was a teenager, a pattern also present among other women I interviewed, she lost a friend as well as a child with her daughter's departure. Mrs. Gold said she did not want to burden her daughter with her own problems because her daughter was student teaching. The closeness they had now was "different" since her daughter's life "revolved around her husband and her teaching and that's the way it should be." They phone each other every day and see each other about once a week.

Like most depressives she feels inadequate: "I don't feel like I'm very much." Since her son's departure she spent most of her time in bed and neglected her household, in marked contrast to her former behavior. "I was such an energetic woman. I had a big house, and I had my family. My daughter said, 'Mother didn't serve eight courses. She served ten.' My cooking—I took a lot of pride in my cooking and in my home. And very, very clean. I think almost fanatic." She considers herself more serious than other women and could not lead a "worthless existence" playing cards as other women do. She was active in fund-raising for her son's institution, but apparently without the maternal role, the role that gave her her sense of worth, fund-raising was not enough. Formerly, her son "took every minute of our lives" so that she "did none of the things normal women did, nothing." "I can pardon myself for the fact [that he was placed in a school] that I did take care of him for twelve years and he was hyperactive. It was extremely hard on me ... I never knew I had that amount of patience."

Like most of the women I interviewed, Mrs. Gold is puritanical and embarrassed about sex.

> I think anything that gives you pleasure or enjoyment, oh, is good as long as it's, uh, decent, and uh, not with us [slight embarrassment] some women I imagine do things that they shouldn't do, but I'm not referring to anything like that. It's just that I'm not that kind of woman.

Where she is at psychologically and sociologically is dramatically apparent in her response to the question in which she had to rank the seven roles available to middle-aged women in order of importance. She listed *only one role:* "Right now I think *helping my children,* not that they really need my help, but if they did I would really try very hard." Thus, she can no longer enact the role that had given her life meaning, the only role she considered important for her. Her psychiatrist had told her, and she agreed, that a paying job would boost her self-esteem. But what jobs are available for a forty-year-old woman with no special training, who has not worked for over twenty years?

Mrs. Gold combines most of the elements present in the depressed women I interviewed, elements considered by clinicians to make up the preillness personality of involutional depressives: a history of martyrdom with no payoff (and martyrs always expect a payoff at some time) to make up for the years of sacrifice; inability to handle aggressive feelings, rigidity; a need to be useful in order to feel worthwhile; obsessive, compulsive supermother and superhousewife behavior; and generally conventional attitudes.

WHY STUDY MRS. PORTNOY AND HER COMPLAINTS

Some of my hip friends ask, "Pauline Bart, what are *you* doing studying depressed middle-aged women?" The question itself, implying that the subject is too uninteresting and unimportant to be worth studying, indicates the unfortunate situation in which these women find themselves. But a nation's humanity may be measured by how it treats its women and its aged as well as by how it treats its racial and religious minorities. This is not a good society in which to grow old or to be a woman, and the combination of the two makes for a poignant situation. In addition, there are practical and theoretical reasons why such a study is important. Women today live longer and end their childbearing sooner than they did in the last century. In other words women are more likely now to reach the "empty-nest" or postparental stage (a term used by those investigators who do not consider this life-cycle stage especially difficult). Depression is the most common psychiatric symptom of adulthood, but, like middle age, it too has been generally ignored by sociologists.[1]

Such a study is theoretically important for several reasons. First, it can illuminate that important sociological concept, role—the concept that links the individual to society—because at this stage a woman loses certain roles and gains others; some roles contract, others expand. Moreover, there is contradictory evidence as to whether middle age *is* a problem for women. Knowing the conditions under which these women become depressed helps us explain these contradictory theories. Why is it that one woman whose son has been "launched" says, "I don't feel as if I've lost a son; I feel as if I've gained a den," while another thinks the worst thing that ever happened to her was

when I had to break up and be by myself, and be alone, and I'm just—I really feel that I'm not only not loved but not even liked sometimes by my own children. . . . they could respect me. If—if they can't say good things why should they, why should they feel better when they hurt my feelings, and make me cry, and then call me a crybaby, or tell me that I—I ought to know better or something like that. My worst thing is that I'm alone, I'm not wanted, nobody interests themselves in me . . . nobody cares.

The *best* times of her life were when she was pregnant and when her children were babies.

One clue to the differing views of middle age is that many of the problem-oriented studies are written by clinicians who are generalizing from their patients, while the studies showing that the postparental stage is no more difficult for most people than any other life-cycle stage, that many people like "disengaging," come from surveys and interviews conducted by behavioral scientists. The patients clinicians see are not a random sample of the population; they are more likely to be middle class and Jewish. This is precisely the group in which I would expect the departure of children to cause stress because the departure of children is more difficult for women whose primary role is maternal—the situation in the traditional Jewish family. If this hypothesis is correct, the difference between the two approaches to middle age may result from clinicians' generalizations about a population that is more susceptible to the stresses of middle age—the Jewish mother.

THERE IS NO BAR MITZVAH FOR MENOPAUSE

Émile Durkheim sheds light on the stresses that a mother may feel when her children leave. His concepts of both *egoistic* and *anomic* suicide are relevant to the problems of "the empty nest." According to Durkheim, marriage does not protect women from egoistic suicide, as it does men; rather, the birth of children reduces the suicide rate for women, and immunity to suicide increases with the "density" of the family. "Density" diminishes as the children mature and leave. Few clear norms govern the relationship between a woman and her adult children; consequently, when her children leave the woman's situation is normless or anomic. This normless state is apparent in the responses to my question, "What do people expect a woman to do after her children are grown?" Mrs. West said that while a married woman is supposed to make a home for her husband, she did not know what was expected from a divorced woman like her. "I don't think they expect anything special . . . you just mind your own business. Let them mind theirs . . ." Another woman said, "My mission in life is completed. I have no place to go." All women verbally denied the obligations of adult children toward their parents. When asked what their children owed them, all the women say "nothing," even though, in fact, they are apparently dissatisfied with their present situation and want more from their children. Much as some of the mothers want to live with their children, they cannot openly state this as a *legitimate* demand.

As financial crises lead to anomic suicides because individuals must change their expectations, women whose children leave must also change their expectations. But not only have these expectations been given legitimacy through years of interaction, there are no guidelines, no *rites de passage* for the mother herself to guide her through this transaction. *There is no bar mitzvah for menopause.*

David Riesman, following the Durkheimian tradition, notes that autonomous persons have no problems when they age, but both the "adjusted," who find meaning in their lives by carrying out culturally defined tasks, and the anomic, whom the culture has been "carrying" but then drops, have difficulties as they grow older and these external "props" are no longer available. Thus, the woman's position dramatically changes; from being overintegrated into society through the props of domestic and maternal roles, she becomes unintegrated or anomic. It is true, as Marvine Sussman claims, that urban kin networks do exist, and that the concept of the isolated nuclear family is false, since kin are turned to in time of trouble.[2] But it is precisely *because* kin, that is, children, can be called upon in time of trouble that secondary gain is possible from depression. When a woman becomes depressed, once again she gets the attention, sympathy, and control over her children she had before they left.

Durkheim constructed a theory of social control and the pathological effects of its breakdown. The basis of social control is norms, the factors that control and constrain. However, Durkheim lacked an explicit social psychology, failing to posit any mechanism that could account for the manner in which these constraints are internalized. Role theory furnishes us with such a mechanism.

ROLE

The most important roles for women in our society are wife and mother. For example, one woman stated that getting married was the only thing she ever did that made her parents think she was worthwhile, compared to her younger brother, a doctor. The wife role may be lost at any time during the adult life cycle through separation, divorce, or widowhood, although the last is most common during old age. However, during the years between forty and fifty-nine, the maternal role is the one most frequently lost.

Two postulates from Ralph Turner's monograph, "Role Theory—A Series of Propositions," are illuminating. "Almost any stabilized role expectation contains some elements of latent feeling that the other ought to continue the same role and role behavior as before. ... There is a tendency for stabilized roles to be assigned the character of *legitimate expectations*."[3] While ideally a mother should be flexible and change her expectations of her children as they mature, if a woman's personality is rigid, as these women's personalities are, she may expect adult children, even if married, to act largely as they did when they were children and dependent on her. To the extent that they no longer act this way, she is likely to feel resentful; since, as Yehudi Cohen suggests, a woman is not "allowed" to be hostile toward her children, she may turn the resentment inward and become depressed.[4] Turner's second postulate states: "The degree to which ego can legitimately claim the privileges of his role tends to be a function of his degree of role adequacy" since "the actor who performs his role more adequately than could be legitimately expected raises thereby the legitimate expectations of other actors. The mother, for example, by being more patient or working harder than could reasonably be expected, places a moral debt on husband and children which is not satisfied by normal adequacy."[5]

KLAYNE KINDER, KLAYNE TSURUS; GRAYSE KINDER, GRAYSE TSURUS[6]

Since the women that I predict will be most affected by the departure of their children are the supermothers, the martyrs, the self-sacrificing women who have devoted their lives to their children, they can legitimately expect their children to be more devoted to them, more considerate of them, bring them more satisfaction, than would otherwise be the case. The literature on the Jewish mother quite clearly portrays her as this type of supermother; this supermother is especially likely to be severely affected if her children fail to meet her needs, either by not making what she considers "good" marriages, or by not achieving

the career aspirations she has for them, or even by not
phoning her every day. The moral debt Turner refers to
results in the child's feeling guilty. Therefore, if his mother
does become depressed, he is particularly vulnerable, and
he may expiate his guilt by becoming the "good" child
again. Greenburg's best-selling satire, *How to Be a Jewish
Mother*, refers to guilt as the mother's main method of
social control;[7] it is no accident that his second book,
How to Make Yourself Miserable, begins with the sentence: "You, we can safely assume, are guilty."

Not only is the traditional Jewish mother overinvolved
with or overidentified with her children, obtaining narcissi-
tic gratification from them, but the children are viewed as
simultaneously *helpless* without the mother's directives and
powerful—able to kill the mother with "aggravation." As
one depressed empty-nest woman says, "My children have
taken and drained me." In a sentence completion test, she
filled in the blank after the words "I suffer" with "from
my children."

Overprotection and overidentification is apparent in the
case of another depressed Jewish woman, Mrs. Berg, who
moved from Chicago to Los Angeles with her husband
four months after her daughter, son-in-law, and
granddaughter did "because my daughter and only child
moved here, and it was lonesome for her, you know. And
I figured we had nobody," except a brother, and "you
know how it is. My granddaughter was in Los Angeles. I
missed them all." Mrs. Berg and her daughter are "inseparable." "She wouldn't buy a pair of stockings without me."
However, the daughter had written to the hospital; in her
letter she stated that much as she loved her mother, her
need to be kept continually busy was destroying the
daughter's own private life, and she had to enter psychotherapy herself.

Mrs. Berg thought that the worst thing that could happen to a woman of her age was for her children to leave
home. "Children leaving home to me is a terrible thing,
but mine didn't. She waited until she got married." When
her daughter did not have a date, this supermother would
say to her husband, "Oh, I don't feel so good tonight," so
that she and her husband would stay home in case her
daughter was lonesome.

I was one of those old-fashioned mothers. I thought that
you have to stay home and take care of your child, or

when she has a date see what kinda fellow she's going out with. . . . today the mothers are a little bit different. We manage a building now and we could write a story—write a book about our life there. The way twenty, twenty-one and twenty-two year olds leave home. Even younger, and share an apartment in Hollywood. I—I oughta write a book on that, when I get the time and the health back.

She thought the best time for a mother was from infancy till the child was eleven or twelve "because after that they become a little self-centered . . . they think about good times and go bowling, go this and that, you know." The best thing for a woman after her children are raised is working. "Keep your hands occupied. Don't think too much. Just be occupied." Her greatest concern is her granddaughter. "It will be the greatest joy of my life when my granddaughter meets somebody and she'll get married."

ROLE AND SELF

Role and self-concept are intimately interconnected. When people are given the "Who Are You" test to get at their self-concept, they usually respond in terms of their various roles—wife, doctor, mother, teacher, daughter, and so forth. As a person moves from one life-cycle stage to another, or from one step in a career to another, he or she must change their self-concept because the relevant or significant others, the people with whom they interact, change. A loss of significant others can result in what Arnold Rose called a "mutilated self."[8] Some roles are more central for one's self-image than others; self-esteem comes from role adequacy in these more salient roles. For most people, the social structure determines which roles these are. Because the most important roles for women in our society are the roles of wife and mother, the loss of either of these roles might result in a loss of self-esteem— in the feeling of worthlessness and uselessness that characterizes depressives. For example, one woman said:

I don't. I don't, I don't feel liked. I don't feel that I'm wanted. I don't feel at all that I'm wanted. I just feel like nothing. I don't feel anybody cares, and nobody's interested, and they don't care whether I do feel good or I don't feel good. I'm pretty useless. . . . I feel like I want somebody to feel for me but nobody does.

Another woman stated: "I don't feel like I'm doing anything. I feel just like I'm standing still, not getting anywhere."

Since mental health or a feeling of well-being is dependent on a positive self-concept, it is therefore dependent on the roles felt to be available to the individual. Women whose identity, whose sense of self, is derived mainly from their role as mothers rather than their role as wives and workers, women whose "significant others" are limited to their children, are in a difficult situation when their children leave. These women's self-conceptions must change; some of these women cannot make this change. They are overcommitted to the maternal role and in middle age suffer the "unintended consequences" of this commitment.

INTEGRATION OF PSYCHIATRIC AND SOCIOLOGICAL THEORY

Psychiatric as well as sociological theory is relevant to a discussion of depression. Depression is usually considered a response to loss, loss of an ambivalently loved person or object by the psychoanalytically oriented, loss of a goal or self-esteem by ego psychologists, and loss of meaning by existentialists such as Ernest Becker.[9] Role loss is consistent with all of these approaches.

One possible way of combining the Freudian position which considers depression anger directed inward, the existential position concerning loss of meaning, and the sociological theory I am presenting may be the following. People who are intrapunitive, who turn anger inward against themselves rather than express it, are conforming to the cultural norms, especially if they are women. Since they have been "good" they expect to be rewarded. Therefore, when their husbands or children leave them their lives may seem meaningless; their world may no longer "make sense." Thus introjected anger leads to "proper" behavior which in turn leads to expectations of reward; when this reward does not materialize, but in fact tragedy strikes, they suffer from a loss of meaning and become depressed.

Clinicians use the term "defense mechanism" to describe the way an individual characteristically copes with the problems of living. This construct can be refined by the addition of sociocultural factors. There is a relationship between the utility of a defense and the person's stage in the life cycle. Withdrawal as a defense in a society valuing instrumental activism is likely to cause problems early in life. However, if one *defends by doing*, one can manage very well in our society, barring physical illness, until retirement for men or the departure of children for women. My interview data and certain comments on the hospital charts, for example, "She needed to keep busy all the time," indicated that many of the women had such defense systems. This system had been rewarded by the society at earlier stages in the woman's life cycle; however, later when many women were physically ill, and there was little for them to do, this life style was no longer effective.

METHODS: CROSS CULTURAL, EPIDEMIOLOGICAL, AND INTERVIEW

I used three kinds of data in this study: anthropological, epidemiological, and interviews with projective tests. First, in order to test the hypothesis that depression in middle-aged women was the result of the hormonal changes of menopause, I conducted a cross-cultural study of thirty societies, using the Human Relations Area Files, and intensively studied six cultures, using the original anthropological monographs (becoming the Margaret Mead of menopause).

After I completed this cross-cultural study of the roles available to women after childbearing ceased, I examined the records of 533 women between the ages of forty and fifty-nine who had had no previous hospitalization for mental illness. I used five hospitals, ranging from an upper-class private hospital to the two state hospitals that served people from Los Angeles County. I compared women who had been diagnosed "depressed" (using the following diagnoses: involutional depression, psychotic depression, neurotic depression, manic depressive depressed) with women who had other functional (nonorganic) diagnoses.

Five methods were used to overcome diagnostic biases. First, the sample was drawn from *five* hospitals. Second, "neurotic depressives" were merged with the "involutional," "psychotic," and "manic depressives" since I suspected that patients who would be called "neurotic depressed" at an upper-class hospital would be called "involutional depressed" at a lower-middle-class hospital, a suspicion that was borne out. Third, a symptom check list was used in the analysis of data, and I found that depressed patients differed significantly from those given other diagnoses for almost all symptoms. Fourth, a case history of a woman with both depressive and paranoid features was distributed to the psychiatric residents at the teaching hospital for "blind" diagnosis. The woman was called Jewish in half the cases and Presbyterian in the other half. The results showed no differences between the "Jews" and "Presbyterians" in number of stigmatic diagnoses since the most and least stigmatic diagnoses (schizophrenia and neurotic depression) were given to "Presbyterians." Fifth, thirty-nine M.M.P.I. profiles were obtained at one hospital and given to a psychologist to diagnose "blind." He rated them on an impairment continuum. The results supported the decision to combine psychotic, involutional, and neurotic depressives, because the ratio of mild and moderate to serious and very serious was the same for all these groups. But all the schizophrenics were rated serious or very serious.

Next, I conducted twenty intensive interviews at two hospitals to obtain information unavailable from the patients' records, to give the women questionnaires used in studies with "normal" middle-aged women, and to administer the projective biography test—a test consisting of sixteen pictures showing women at different stages in their life cycle and in different roles. These interviews provided an especially rich source of information. I did not read their charts until *after* the interviews so as not to have my perception affected by psychiatrists' or social workers' evaluations.

Maternal role loss was recorded when at least one child was not living at home. I considered an overprotective or overinvolved relationship present when a statement such as "my whole life was my husband and my daughter" was written on the woman's record, or if the woman entered the hospital following her child's engagement or marriage. Ratings of role loss and relationship with children and husbands were made from a case history that omitted references to symptomatology, ethnicity, or diagnosis; high intercoder reliability was obtained for these variables (an interesting serendipitous finding was that the Jewish coders were more likely to call a parent-child relationship unsatis-

factory than non-Jewish coders. The categories were
refined so that this difference no longer occurred). A
woman was considered Jewish whether or not she was
religious if she had a Jewish mother. The attitudes and
values I am discussing need not come from religious
behavior. For example, Mrs. Gold did not attend religious
services and was unsure of her belief in God, but she
taught her daughter that "we just don't date Gentile
boys," and considered herself very Jewish, "all the way
through, to the core."

RESULTS: YOU DO NOT HAVE TO BE JEWISH TO BE A JEWISH MOTHER, BUT IT HELPS

Before embarking on the cross-cultural and epidemiological studies and the interviews and projective tests, I had
made a number of hypotheses; some were confirmed and
others were refuted.

Depressions in middle-aged women are due to their lack
of important rules and subsequent loss of self-esteem,
rather than the hormonal changes of the menopause. The
cross-cultural studies indicated that women's status frequently rose at this life-cycle stage, that the two societies
in which women's status decreased were similar to our
own, and that, since middle age was not usually considered an especially stressful period for women, explanations
of such stress based on the biological changes of menopause could be rejected.[10]

Role loss *is* associated with depression; middle-aged
depressed women are more likely to have suffered maternal role loss than nondepressed women. Because we are
symbolic creatures in which the past and future are ever
present, even impending role loss can bring on depression.

I had hypothesized that certain factors—intrinsically
satisfying occupations; satisfactory marriages; some children still at home; and children's residence near the mother—would make it easier for the mother when her children left. I had also felt that women who suffered other
role loss in addition to maternal role loss and women who
had unsatisfactory relationships with the departing children would find role loss much harder to bear. However,
neither of these hypotheses was confirmed. Role loss is
apparently an all or nothing phenomenon since predictions
based on the assumption that such loss is a matter of

degree and can be compensated for by the expansion of other roles were not supported.[11]

Certain roles appear to be structurally conducive to increasing the effect of the loss of other roles (see Table 6-1). Women who have overprotective or overinvolved

TABLE 6-1 *Conditions under Which Role Loss Is Increasingly Associated with Depression*

CONDITION	PERCENT DEPRESSED	TOTAL N (BASE)
Role loss	62.0	369
Maternal role loss	63.0	245
Housewives with maternal role loss	69.0	124
Middle-class housewives with maternal role loss	74.0	69
Women with maternal role loss who had overprotective or overinvolved relationships with their children	76.0	72
Housewives with maternal role loss who have overprotective or overinvolved relationships with their children	82.0	44

Women with Maternal Role Loss

TABLE 6-2

Effect of Overprotective or Overinvolved Relationships with Their Children on Depression for

RELATIONSHIP	PERCENT DEPRESSED	TOTAL N (BASE)
Overprotective	76.0	72
Not overprotective	58.0	88

NOTE: No information on 83, of whom 47 were depressed.

relationships with their children are more likely to suffer depression in their postparental period than women who do not have such relationships (see Table 6-2). Housewives have a higher rate of depression than working women since being a housewife is really, as Parsons put it, a "pseudo occupation."[12] Not only do housewives have more opportunity than working women to invest themselves completely in their children, but the housewife role is cut down once there are fewer people for whom to shop, cook, and clean. Middle-class housewives have a higher rate of depression than working-class housewives, and those housewives who have overprotective relationships with their children suffer the highest rate of depression of all when the children leave home.

Depression among middle-aged women with maternal loss is related to the family structure and typical interactive patterns of the ethnic groups to which they belong. When ethnic groups are compared, Jews have the highest rate of depression, Anglos an intermediate rate, and blacks the lowest rate. Since in the traditional Jewish family the most important tie is between the mother and the children and the mother identifies very closely with her children, the higher rate of depression among Jewish women in middle age when their children leave is not surprising. Table 6-3 shows that Jewish women are

TABLE 6-3
Relationship between Ethnicity and Depression

ETHNICITY	PERCENT DEPRESSED	TOTAL N (BASE)
Jews	84.0	122
Non-Jews	47.0	383

roughly twice as likely to be diagnosed depressed than non-Jewish women; in addition there was a higher ratio of depression to other mental illness among Jewish women than among non-Jewish women.

However, when family interactive patterns are controlled, the difference between Jews and non-Jews sharply diminish (Table 6-4). Although vertical frequencies show

TABLE 6-4 *Relationship between Depression and Overprotection or Overinvolvement with Children for Jewish and Non-Jewish Housewives with Maternal Role Loss*

| | JEWS | | NON-JEWS | |
RELATIONSHIP	PERCENT DEPRESSED	TOTAL N (BASE)	PERCENT DEPRESSED	TOTAL N (BASE)
Overprotective	86.0	21	78.0	23
Not overprotective	75.0	8	60.0	25

NOTE: No information for 8 Jews, of whom all were depressed and for 38 non-Jews, of whom 21 were depressed.

that overprotection or overinvolvement with children is much more common among Jews than among non-Jews, it is clear that *you don't have to be Jewish to be a Jewish mother.* For example, one divorced black woman, who had a hysterectomy, went into a depression when her daughter, her only child, moved to Oregon; the depression lifted when she visted her and recurred when she returned to Los Angeles.

The very small group of Jewish women whose mothers were born in the United States had a depression rate midway between that of Jewish women with mothers born in Europe and Anglo women. One of my hypotheses, that the departure of a son would be more closely associated with depression than the departure of a daughter, could not be tested because in every case when the Jewish women had sons who were only children, the sons still lived with their mothers. As one such woman told me, "My son is my husband, and my husband is my son." Such was not the case for Jewish-only daughters or for sons or daughters in non-Jewish families. (The hypothesis had to be tested with only children because of the way the cards had been punched.)

Black women had a lower rate of depression than white women. The patterns of black female-role behavior rarely result in depression in middle-age. Often, the "granny" or "aunty" lives with the family and cares for the children while the children's mother works; thus, the older woman suffers no maternal role loss. Second, since black women traditionally work, they are less likely to develop the extreme identification, the vicarious living through their children, that is characteristic of Jewish mothers. In addition, there is no puritanical idea in black culture equivalent to that in Anglo and Jewish cultures, that sex is evil and primarily for reproductive purposes or that older women are inappropriate sex objects. The famous black blues singers—women such as Bessie Smith—reached the height of their popularity when they were middle-aged.

Of course, one cannot entirely overlook the possibility that the low black depression rate simply reflects the black community's greater unwillingness to hospitalize depressed black women. Depressives are not likely to come to the attention of the police unless they attempt suicide. Therefore, if the woman or her family do not define her condition as psychiatric, she will remain at home. Only a

prevalence study can fully test any hypothesis about the
black family.

There were too few Mexican families in the sample to
test my hypothesis that Mexican women would have a
lower depression rate because Mexican women have larger
families and the extended family is very much in operation; in addition, there is a shift in actual, though not in
formal, power to the mother from the father as they
become middle-aged.

INTERVIEWS

The interviews dispelled any of my doubts about the
validity of inferences from the hospital charts that these
women were overprotective, conventional, martyrs. Even
though they were patients and I was an interviewer and a
stranger, one Jewish woman forced me to eat candy,
saying, "Don't say no to me." Another gave me unsolicited
advice on whether I should remarry and to whom, and a
third said she would make me a party when she left the
hospital. Another example of the extreme nurturant patterns was a fourth patient who insisted on caring for
another patient who had just returned from shock while I
was interviewing her. She also attempted to find other
women for me to interview. The vocabulary of motives
invoked by the Jewish women generally attributed their
illness to their children. They complained about not seeing
their children often enough. The non-Jewish women were
more restrained and said they wanted their children to be
independent. All the women with children, when asked
what they were most proud of, replied "my children";
occasionally, after this, they mentioned their husbands.
None mentioned any accomplishment of their own, except
being a good mother.

Two of the Jewish women had lived with their children
and wanted to live with them again; their illness was
precipitated when their children forced them to live alone.
However, living with children was not a satisfactory arrangement for the women in the epidemiological sample,
since the few women having this arrangement were all
depressed. For example, one woman complained: "Why is
my daughter so cold to me? Why does she exclude me?
She turns to her husband ... and leaves me out. I don't

tell her what to do, but I like to feel my thoughts are wanted."

Table 6-5 shows the conventionality and the rigidity of

TABLE 6-5
Frequency of Ranked Choice

ROLE	1	2	3	4	5	6	7
Being a homemaker	5	—	3	2	2	—	—
Taking part in church, club and community activities	—	1	3	4	1	—	—
Companion to husband[a]	2	2	1	—	1	—	1
Helping parents	1	1	—	1	1	—	—
Sexual partner	—	1	2	—	—	1	—
Paying job	1	3	—	—	—	1	—
Helping children	4	5	2	1	1	—	—

[a] Not including the two unmarried women who ranked this item first.

the women interviewed. In middle age it is necessary to be flexible so that new roles can be assumed. The mother role, "helping my children," is most frequently ranked first or second, although only one of the seven women whose children were all home ranked it first, and one ranked it second. Since it is difficult to help children who are no longer home, women who value this behavior more than any other are in trouble; they are frustrated in behaving in the way that is most important to them. Items that were not chosen are as interesting as those that were; only one woman ranked "helping my parents" first. Her hospitalization followed her mother's move to Chicago after she had remodeled her apartment so that her mother could live with her. No woman listed "being a sexual partner to my husband" first, and only one woman listed it second. Three married women did not include it in their ranking, indicating its lack of importance or their embarrassment or rejection of this role. It is apparent that although eight of the women worked, the occupational role was not important to them; three did not even list it. In short, the women view as important precisely the roles of homemaker and mother that become contracted as the women age. Conversely, they do not consider as important the roles that could be expanded at this time: the sexual partner role, the occupational role, and the organizational role (taking part in church, club, and community activities).

The women interviewed were given the projective biography test—sixteen pictures showing women in different rolls and at different stages in their life cycles. The clinical psychologist who devised the test analyzed the protocols "blind" without knowing my hypothesis. He said they were "complete mothers," showing total identification with the maternal role. I content analyzed the responses to the sexy picture, the pregnancy picture, the old age picture, and the angry picture; Table 6-6 shows the responses to the old age picture.

TABLE 6-6

Response to Old Age Picture

RESPONSE	IN STORY	IN INQUIRY
Positive	1	1
Negative	6	4
Denial	2	—
Neutral	2	1
Not used	9	—

The old age picture shows an old woman sitting in a rocking chair in front of a fireplace. The nine women who did not include this picture in their stories of a woman's life do not want to grow old and inactive. Only one woman used the picture in the story and responded positively to it. Two used it, but denied the aging aspects of it. An example of such denial is the following response: "Here she is over here sitting in front of the fireplace, and she's got her figure back, and I suppose the baby's gone off to sleep and she's relaxing." This woman interpreted every picture with reference to a baby.

Six women did not like the picture (two responses were uncodeable). One woman who used the picture in the story said, "And this scene I can't stand. Just sitting alone in old age by just sitting there and by some fireplace all by herself [pause] turning into something like that. And to me this is too lonely. A person has to slow down sometime and just sit, but I would rather be active, and even if I would be elderly, I wouldn't want to live so long that I wouldn't have anything else in life but to just sit alone and you know, just in a rocking chair." Another woman who was divorced and had both her children away from home said, "This could look very much like me. I'm sitting, dreaming, feeling so blue." When she chose that as the picture not liked, she said, "Least of all, I don't like this one at all. That's too much like I was doing. Sitting and worrying and thinking . . ."

In the inquiry period, one more gave a positive response, four gave a negative response, and one response was uncodeable. One empty-nest woman who was divorced and living alone did not use the picture in her story. After listing eight other pictures which were like her life, she said, "I don't like to point to that one." One person liked this picture best, but did not perceive the woman as old, while six women included this picture among the ones they liked least.

How about Men

Does this theory explain depression in men? I think it does. Men who have involutional psychosis are usually in their sixties, the retirement age; these are probably men whose occupational roles were "props." Men whose identity comes from their work role will also be depressed on retirement. For example, the director of admissions at the teaching hospital reported that it was not unusual for army officers to have involutional depressions on retirement. Rafael Moses and Debora Kleiger's study of involutional depression in Israel found loss of meaning a factor among old pioneers who believed "that the values so dear to them were rapidly disappearing. Current ideals and expectations were now alien to them and the sense of duty and sacrifice as they knew it seemed to exist no longer. They felt different, isolated and superfluous."[18]

What Is to Be Done?

It is very easy to make fun of these women, to ridicule their pride in their children and concern for their well-being. But it is no mark of progress to substitute Mollie Goldberg for Stepin Fetchit as a stock comedy figure. These women are as much casualties of our culture as the children in Harlem whose I.Q.'s decline with each additional year they spend in school. They were doing what they were told to do, what was expected of them by their families, their friends, and the mass media; if they deviated from this role they would have been ridiculed (ask any professional woman). Our task is to make their sacrifices pay off, though in a different way from what they expected. As their stories are told, other women will learn the futility of this life style.

Two psychoanalysts, Therese Benedek and Helene Deutsch, state that menopause is more difficult for "masculine" or "pseudo masculine" women. Benedek describes the "masculine" woman as one whose "psychic economy was dominated—much like that of man's—by strivings of the ego rather than by the primary emotional gratifications of motherliness."[14] Deutsch states that "feminine loving" women have an easier time during climacterium than do "masculine-aggressive ones." While she believes in the desirability of "good sublimations" in addition to erotic and maternal qualities, "if their social and professional interests have taken excessive hold of them, these women are threatened in the climacterium by the danger that I call Pseudomasculinity."[15] However, my data show that it is the women who assume the traditional feminine role—who are housewives, who stay married to their husbands, who are not overly aggressive, in short who "buy" the traditional norms—who respond with depression when their children leave. Even the M.M.P.I. masculine-feminine scores for women at one hospital were one-half a standard deviation *more* feminine than the mean. These findings are consistent with Cohen's theory of depression; he considers depression, in contrast to schizophrenia, an "illness" found among people too closely integrated into the culture.[16]

Ernest Becker's theory of existential depression among middle-aged women is borne out because these martyr mothers thought that by being "good" they would ultimately be rewarded. When there was no pot of gold at the end of the rainbow, their life pattern seemed meaningless. As one woman said:

> I felt that I trusted and they—they took advantage of me. I'm very sincere, but I wasn't wise. I loved, and loved strongly and trusted, but I wasn't wise. I—I deserved something, but I thought if I give to others, they'll give to me. How could they be different, but you see, they be different, but you see those things hurted me very deeply and when I had to feel that I don't want to be alone, and I'm going to be alone, and my children will go their way and get married—of which I'm wishing for it and then I'll still be alone, and I got more and more alone, and more and more alone.

The norms of our society are such that a woman is not expected to "fulfill" herself through an occupation, but rather through the traditional feminine roles of wife and mother. More than that, she is not *allowed* to do so. The great discrimination against "uppity women"—women professionals—the cruel humor, not being taken seriously, the lower pay scale, the invisibility (literally and metaphorically), make it suicidal for a woman to attempt to give meaning to her life through her work. (We are told that women are not hired because they put their personal life first, and leave with the first available man. I think the sequence is reversed. It is only after she learns what her situation really is, after she has been treated as a nonperson, that she turns to a more traditional role. If she's lucky she still has that option.)

Until recent years, a common theme of inspirational literature for women, whether on soap operas or in women's magazines, was that they could only find "real happiness" by devoting themselves to their husbands and children, that is, by living vicariously through them. If one's satisfaction, one's sense of worth comes from other people rather than from one's own accomplishments, one is left with an empty shell in place of a self when such people depart. On the other hand, if a woman's sense of worth comes from her own accomplishments, she is not so vulnerable to breakdown when significant others leave. This point is obscured in much of the polemical literature on the allegedly castrating, dominant American female who is considered to have lost her femininity.

It is, after all, *feminine* women, the ones who play the traditional roles, not the career women, who are likely to dominate their husbands and children. This domination, however, may take more traditional female forms of subtle manipulation and invoking of guilt. If, however, a woman does *not* assume the traditional female role and does not expect her needs for achievement or her needs for "narcissistic gratification," as psychiatrists term it, to be met vicariously through the accomplishments of her husband and children, *then* she has no need to dominate them since her well-being does not depend on their accomplishments. In an achievement-oriented society it is unreasonable to expect one sex not to have these needs.

The women's liberation movement, by pointing out alternative life styles, by providing the emotional support necessary for deviating from the ascribed sex roles, and by emphasizing the importance of women actualizing their *own selves*, fulfilling their *own* potentials, can help in the development of personhood for both men and women.

NOTES

1. See my forthcoming chapter on "The Sociology of Depressive Disorders," in *Current Perspectives in Psychiatric Sociology*, eds. Paul Roman and Harrison Trice (Science House, 1971) for a further discussion of this point.
2. Marvine B. Sussman, "Relationships of Adult Children with Their Parents in the United States," in Ethel Shanas and Gordon Streib, eds., *Social Structure and the Family: General Relations* (Englewood Cliffs, N.J.: Prentice-Hall, 1965).
3. Ralph Turner, "Role Theory—A Series of Propositions," *Encyclopedia of the Social Sciences* (New York: Macmillan and the Free Press, 1968). These ideas are incorporated in "Role: Sociological Aspects," *Encyclopedia of the Social Sciences*.
4. Yehudi A. Cohen, "The Sociological Relevance of Schizophrenia and Depression," in Cohen, ed., *Social Structure and Personality* (New York: Holt, Rinehart and Winston, 1961), pp. 477-485.
5. Turner, *op. cit.*
6. Small children, small troubles; big children, big troubles.
7. Dan Greenburg, *How to Be a Jewish Mother* (Los Angeles: Price, Stern, Sloan, 1964).
8. Arnold Rose, "A Social-Psychological Theory of Neurosis," in Rose, ed., *Human Behavior and Social Processes* (Boston: Houghton Mifflin, 1962), pp. 537-549.
9. Ernest Becker, *The Revolution in Psychiatry* (Glencoe: The Free Press, 1964).
10. These results are presented in greater detail in my "Why Women's Status Changes in Middle Age: The Turns of the Social Ferris Role," *Sociological Symposium* 1 (Fall 1969).
11. See *Society, Culture, and Depression* (Cambridge: Schenkman forthcoming) for elaboration of these and subsequent findings.
12. Talcott Parsons, "Age and Sex in the Social Structure of the United States,"*American Sociological Review* 7 (1942): 604-606.
13. Rafael Moses and Debora S. Kleiger, "A Comparative Analysis of the Institutionalization of Mental Health Values: The United States and Israel," unpublished manuscript presented at the American Psychiatric Association meetings, New York, 1965.
14. Therese Benedek and Boris B. Rubenstein, "Psychosexual Functions in Women," in *Psychosomatic Medicine* (New York: Ronald Press, 1952).
15. Helene Deutsch, *The Psychology of Women: A Psychoanalytic Interpretation* (New York: Grune & Stratton, 1945), vol. 2.
16. Cohen, *op. cit.*

7

THE MASK OF BEAUTY

Una Stannard

Women are the beautiful sex. Who doubts it? Among birds the male may have the pretty plumage, but among human beings it is the female who wears the peacock feathers.

Whatever else is denied women, no one denies that they are better looking than men. Little boys are made of frogs and snails, but little girls are made of sugar and spice, that is, potential cheesecake. When the first baby born in the New Year is a girl, the newspaper predicts that in twenty years she will be Miss America, for just as all men are created equal, all women are created beautiful. Of course, occasionally an unfortunate woman may be an exception, but isn't she the exception that proves the rule? Or rather, just as all men have different I.Q.s, so all women have different Beauty Quotients; although all women are beautiful, some women are more beautiful than others.

When a mother unwraps the pink blanket from her tiny bundle, we say, "My, isn't she pretty." And as the little girl grows up and looks about her, she sees models of female beauty everywhere. As she sits in front of the television set, every deodorant and soap powder is in the hand of a fair lady. The actresses on TV and in the movies are always beautiful, or at least the young ones who get the men are. When the little girl travels on an airplane, the stewardess who gives her a balloon is lovely, and when she peeks over her father's shoulders as he reads a magazine, she sees the beautiful paper dolls in *Playboy*.

When she walks beside her mother in the supermarket, her eyes are level with the beautiful women on the covers of the magazines and with the beautiful half-naked women on the covers of the paperback books. When she rides in the family car, her eyes rise to the gigantic beautiful girls papered on billboards; when she is taken to a museum, she sees mostly women in stone and paint, their naked beauty displayed for all to see and admire. Perhaps on the coffee table at home is a heavy book with glossy photographs of beautiful women. On TV every year, she can watch dozens of beauty contests—Miss Peaches, Miss Salt Lake City, Miss Rodeo, Miss Tall San Francisco, Miss Junior Miss, Miss Teen-Age America. From Alabama to Wyoming, every year without fail a new Miss Prettiest in the state is selected, from which crop of beauties Miss U.S.A. is chosen, who may then honor all American womanhood by being selected as Miss Universe, The Most Beautiful Woman in the World.

Little girls not only look endlessly at beautiful women, they hear and read about them too. In the newspapers women are almost always described as the beautiful Miss ——, or the pretty coed, or the attractive Mrs.——, and, of course, all the brides on the society page are beautiful. All the songs are about beautiful girls too; in stories the fairy princess and later, all the heroines, always overwhelm men with the power of their beauty; the poets too, every last one of them, are forever exclaiming, "O fair is she," "so divinely fair," "the fairest of creation."

Then the little girl looks in the mirror. But she has read the story of the ugly duckling who turns into a swan, and when she visits her relatives they all smile at her and say, "What a sweet face!" and her father is always telling her what a knockout she is going to be when she grows up. She decides that beauty, like menstruation, is something that happens to girls at adolescence. She will wait. When she becomes a woman, she again looks at herself in the mirror—long and hard.

She then begins woman's frantic pursuit of beauty, for she has read in innumerable ads that "every woman has the right to be beautiful. Make-up is magic! It can transform you, create the illusion of perfect feminine loveliness that every woman longs for." In every new jar of face cream, box of powder, tube of lipstick, mascara, eyeliner, she expects to find the magic formula that will transform her into a beauty. Every change of hairdo, every padded bra, every girdle, every pair of high heels or sandals, every mini skirt or midi skirt, every tight sweater or sack dress will somehow make her glamorous, captivating. She never gives up. Her blue hair waved, circles of rouge on her wrinkled cheeks, lipstick etching the lines around her mouth, still moisturizing her skin nightly, still corseted, she dies.

For centuries, in the pursuit of beauty, Chinese women used to bind their feet, trying to compress them to the ideal three inches. To achieve this ideal beauty, no suffering was too great. At about the age of four, a girl's feet were bandaged; the toes were pulled backward so tightly that blood and pus later oozed from the bandages, a toe or two might fall off, and death from gangrene was possible. If the girl survived, she would never be able to walk freely again without a cane or the support of attendants. But the excruciating pain and the loss of freedom were worth it, for the tinier her feet, the richer the husband she might get. She might also win first prize in one of the many tiny-foot beauty contests. All ladies had bound feet; it was fashionable; natural feet were ugly; only tiny feet were beautiful.

Not long ago when narrow-toed shoes were fashionable, many women had their little toes amputated so their feet would more comfortably fit the shoes. These women were like Cinderella's sisters, one of whom cut off her big toe and the other the back of her heel in order to fit the glass slipper. These are extremes, perhaps, but few women alive today have not subjected themselves to the discomfort of high heels, which produce such deformities as calluses, corns, bunions, clawed toes, unduly high arches, and secondary shortening of the calf muscles, deformities different only in degree from those of the bound foot.

In China it used to be said that a girl had to suffer twice—she had to have her ears pierced and her feet bound. But today a girl in her first pair of high heels will rarely admit that her feet hurt; almost every girl begs to have her ears pierced and does not think of it as suffering or mutilation. Apparently, the pursuit of beauty is a great anesthetic. Older women used to wince bravely as they plucked their eyebrows, and who can doubt that if it became fashionable many women would pluck out every eyebrow hair, as Japanese women did not long ago. As it is, women merely razor off the "unfeminine" hair on their legs and under their arms. The women unlucky enough to

have "masculine" facial hair endure the pain of electroly-
sis; millions of women undergo surgery to have their
freckles burnt off, their skin peeled, their faces lifted, their
noses reshaped, their breasts filled with silicone. Millions
of women wear tight girdles, live for weeks on celery and
beef broth, or sweat in gyms, or if rich, subject themselves
to the luxurious rigors of a beauty farm, just to keep thin.
It is now fashionable to be thin, but if it were fashionable
to be fat, women would force-feed themselves like geese,
just as girls in primitive societies used to stuff themselves
because the fattest girl was the most beautiful. If the
eighteen-inch waist should ever become fashionable again,
women would suffer the tortures of tight lacing, convinced
that though one dislocated one's kidneys, crushed one's
liver, and turned green, beauty was worth it all.

When Rudi Gernreich predicted that women in the
future would shave their heads and wear wigs, everyone
laughed, but in ancient Egypt women did precisely that.
And though at present women increase the size of their
breasts with internal or external falsies, if it became fashionable to be flat-chested women would, as in the 1920s,
flatten their breasts with bandages, or, if rich, have a
plastic surgeon transform their breasts into the fashionable
size. Is it too much to predict that if the ideal became
long pendulous breasts, women would, as Nigerian women
used to, spend hours pulling at their breasts to make them
droop? Black teeth were once considered beautiful in
Japan, so all fashionable women blackened their teeth, just
as actresses and models now have their teeth filed down to
points and capped with shining white porcelain. Because
America is the world's most powerful nation, rich Oriental
women have their eyelids straightened; if China should
become the great world power, American women would
have their eyelids lifted.

In the past men pursued beauty as avidly as women; in
fact in most primitive societies (just as among animals)
the male sex is believed to be the fair sex; only the men
wear beads, feathers, flowers, perfumes, and bright colors.
In an East African tribe the men wear huge cone-shaped
headdresses; when a woman marries she traditionally
shaves off her hair and gives it to her husband to pad out
his headdress. Among the Tchambuli in New Guinea,
women also shave their heads and do not adorn themselves; the men are graceful and charming, curl their hair,
and wear bird of paradise headdresses. Similarly, in ancient

Greece, men were considered the beautiful sex. Originally, nude statues were all male; even as late as the fifth century B.C., the great period of Greek art, nude statues of women were extremely rare. It was not until a century later that nude statues of women became common, but they did not predominate. We can explain the Greek preference for the male nude by the bisexuality of Greek culture, yet in Italy and other heterosexual Western European countries during the Renaissance, female beauty was not more celebrated than male beauty in painting and sculpture. It was only with Raphael that the female nude began to predominate, and it took 200 years before it was a *fait accompli*. It was not until the nineteenth century that "the nude" in art almost always meant a female nude.

The exclusive identification of women with beauty occurred at the same time that men stopped being sex objects. Around the end of the 1830s men gave up wearing bright colors, silks, laces, earrings, and perfumes and stopped setting their hair. Men no longer showed off their legs; instead they wore trousers so loose that a man's sex can only be assumed from the presumptive evidence of the fly; they also covered their chests with loose jackets. Men became modest; they now conceal everything and signify their maleness only by a symbol—the necktie.

Since the Victorian period men have projected all sexuality onto women, whose dress has obediently conformed to whatever aroused men. One hundred years ago the Victorian woman tried to look like Miss Innocent: she wore no make-up except for a touch of rice powder, fluttered her lowered eyelids, and floated about in crinolines as if she lacked legs to walk on. She looked angelic because men were sexually aroused by innocence. Victorian brothels always kept a fresh supply of virgins, who were often extremely young—until 1885 the age of consent was twelve. Adult prostitutes tried to look like children. "You find the women dress like children, and it pays better. Children used to dress like women in the streets and now women dress like children," said an English clergyman testifying before a committee investigating child prostitution.

Men, having tired of innocence, now require women to look sexy. As Caitlin Thomas, wife of Dylan Thomas, once said, the woman who wants to keep a man must continually emphasize "bust, bum, legs, lips." Clare Booth Luce, in a speech given in 1969, advised women who wanted husbands to turn their bodies into a "man-trap" by wearing mini skirts and plunging necklines. Even after marriage, the good woman is supposed to continue to look sexy. Columns in the women's pages instruct them in the art of dressing and undressing sexily; not long ago a New York disc jockey suggested that the really good wife would greet her husband at the door dressed only in Saran wrap, and at least one good woman followed his advice.

Woman's present state of undress, therefore, is not an indication of her own sexiness; it is merely the current way of arousing men, who now like women to look sexually aggressive. But only to look it. A woman must still be innocent of active sexual aggressiveness. The woman in a mini skirt and plunging neckline must never ask a man to bed, and in bed she must surrender, not assert her sexuality. The modern woman's liberty to expose her legs and most of her body does not signify women's sexual liberation but only her obsessive desire to please men. Women are "free" to start wearing padded bras at the age of nine and to spend forty-eight million dollars annually on eye make-up alone. Women are free to be Playboy bunnies or to be topless and bottomless waitresses. Women are not free *not* to be sexy.

Women are not free to stop playing the beauty game, because the woman who stops would be afraid of exposing herself for what she is—not the fair sex. And yet the woman who does play the beauty game proves the same thing. Every day, in every way, the billion-dollar beauty business tells women they are monsters in disguise. Every ad for bras tells a woman that her breasts need lifting, every ad for padded bras that what she's got isn't big enough, every ad for girdles that her belly sags and her hips are too wide, every ad for high heels that her legs need propping, every ad for cosmetics that her skin is too dry, too oily, too pale, or too ruddy, or her lips are not bright enough, or her lashes not long enough, every ad for deodorants and perfumes that her natural odors all need disguising, every ad for hair dye, curlers, and permanents that the hair she was born with is the wrong color or too straight or too curly, and lately ads for wigs tell her that she would be better off covering up nature's mistake completely. In this culture women are told they are the fair sex, but at the same time that their "beauty" needs lifting, shaping, dyeing, painting, curling, padding. Women are really being told that "the beauty" is a beast.

In the eighteenth century Swift described a "fair nymph" preparing for bed by taking off her artificial hair, false eyebrows, false teeth, the rags she used to "prop her flabby dugs," her corset, and her hip bolsters. How different is she from the twentieth-century woman who at bedtime takes off her wig, peels off her false eyelashes, creams off her eyeliner, eyebrow pencil, and lipstick, and removes her girdle and padded bra? If women were indeed the fair sex, why would they need all these improvements? Why couldn't they simply be as nature made them?

Women's beauty is largely a sham, and women know it. That is why they obediently conform every time the fashion masters crack the whip. A woman conforms to all the whims of the cosmetic and fashion industries so that she will not be singled out from the mass of women, so that she will look like every other woman and thus manage to pass as one of the fair sex. Clothing and cosmetics are the means by which society tries to prove that all women are beautiful, but it is one of our great cultural lies.

Women are the false peacocks of the species. The average woman—and that means a good 95 percent of them—is not beautiful in the way the culture pretends. Look at women and try to see them without their symbols of beauty. How many beautiful women are there then? Then picture men fully adorned—in bright colors, with their hair curled and with eye make-up. How unsettlingly attractive most of them become.

Beauty is rare in either sex. In most species in the animal kingdom, one sex *is* more colorful or attractive than the other; more often than not it is the male. But in the human species neither sex, *au naturel,* is more attractive than the other. But a strong case could be made for considering woman the less attractive sex, at least if we maintain our present standards of beauty. Schopenhauer described women as "that undersized, narrow-shouldered, broad-hipped and short legged race." If he had added that their waists are usually large and their bosoms small or, if full, tend to droop, he would have described the average woman's body fairly well. The average woman does not resemble at all the naked women in *Playboy*. And even those beauties were not meant merely for male contemplation but for impregnation, and the pregnant woman is not beautiful. During pregnancy a woman's face may be radiant (and that belief is by and large a myth too), but what of her body?—the breasts swollen, the nipples brown,

the belly distended and shiny with stretch marks, the belly
button protruding. Are women beautiful then? And after
pregnancy the breasts of millions of women collapse, the
stretch marks remain, the belly sags, and the nipples stay
brown.

However beautiful one may think women are, their
beauty leads to the nonbeauty of pregnancy. Woman's
body is functional. Since the man does not have to carry a
child within him, he is better fitted to keep whatever looks
he was born with. There are, of course, some people who
would insist that the pregnant woman is beautiful because
whatever is natural is beautiful. Certainly prehistoric men
admired natural women, as their squat, hippy, swollen-
bellied, swollen-breasted figurines testify.

But the modern cult of women's beauty has nothing to
do with what women naturally look like, which is why
Playboy doesn't run pictures of pregnant women or average women, and heavily airbrushes its carefully selected
beauties. For even the small percentage of women who
fulfill the modern ideal of beauty are not allowed to be
natural. They too are creatures of artifice. The women
who compete in the Miss U.S.A. contest are required to
wear false eyelashes, and, like all the other beauties who
dazzle us in the media, must be well-groomed, carefully
curried like expensive horses, with full make-up, elaborate
hair-dos, and the latest fashionable attire. Their beauty is
kept at the highest level of artificial polish because they
are performing an essential service in our society.

Glittering and smiling in the media, looked at by millions, envied and ogled, these ideal beauties teach women
their role in society. They teach them that women are
articles of conspicuous consumption in the male market;
in other words, that women are made to be looked at, and
that females achieve success in the world by being looked
at. "My face is my fortune," said the pretty maid in the
nursery rhyme, by which she meant that her pretty face
would enable her to get a husband—the prettier the face,
the richer the husband. The prettiest faces in our society
angle for the biggest fortunes. Why else is the office
beauty the front office secretary? Why else are airline
stewardesses, models and actresses chosen solely for their
looks? Why, if not to put them in the most visible places
in the market so that the richest men can see and buy
them? Men have so structured our society that the most

beautiful women, like all other valuable property, can go to the highest bidder.

In the eighteenth century Swift said that a rich man was able to buy "the finest clothing, the noblest houses, the most costly meats and drinks and have his choice of the most beautiful females." The world has always served up its most beautiful girls to its richest men. In Edwardian days an exceedingly rich man decided to test the claim of Maxim's of Paris that it would serve a customer any dish he desired, no matter how exotic. The rich gentleman ordered a naked girl covered with cherry sauce. He got her, silver platter and all, in one of Maxim's private dining rooms.

What the rich gentleman obtained in private is now procured for rich men by society, and in public, for we live in a democracy. Therefore, there is no silver platter and the girls are usually only partially naked, but they are on display everywhere—on TV, in movies, ads, and planes—waiting to satisfy the rich man's palate.

Although only the rich can afford these ideal beauties, the not-so-rich man can ogle them and daydream, and the average woman can imitate them. Since the ideal beauties are obviously not quite as nature made them, the average woman is encouraged to artificially aspire. So she pads herself and copies their make-up, hair styles, and clothes, and walks with her breasts and ass jiggling, dangling herself before every man in the street. In our twentieth-century democracy men do not have to be rich to be polygamists. A man may only be able to marry one woman at a time, but every woman bedizens herself and constantly entices him. Every woman in our society, like the few beautiful ones in the media, is a flesh peddler in the harem of this man's world.

The ideal beauties teach women that their looks are a commodity to be bartered in exchange for a man, not only for food, clothing, and shelter, but for love. Women learn early that if you are unlovely, you are unloved. The homely girl prepares to be an old maid, because beauty is what makes a man fall in love. "As fair thou art, my bonnie lass, So deep in love am I," wrote Robert Burns. A man's love is beauty deep. Beauty is man's only and sufficient reason for lusting, loving, and marrying a woman. Doesn't a man always say you're beautiful before he says I love you? Don't we all think it strange when a man marries a girl who isn't pretty and not at all strange when

he marries a dumb beauty? Is it therefore surprising that
even the great beauty fears a man's love will not survive
her looks, and the average woman is convinced that no
man can really love her? How can he love her when she
lacks what is needed to produce love? That is why she so
desperately keeps up her looks and feels that although all
the kids have the measles, she ought to greet her husband
with her beauty mask on. In France there are beautymo-
bils that dash to the bedside of a newly delivered mother
lest papa see her when she isn't beautiful. To keep their
men in love, women spend billions on creams and moistur-
izers so their skin will continue to look youthfully beautiful. To keep their men in love, women read book after
book telling them *How To Be Thirty for Forty Years, The
Art of Staying Young, Beauty Is Not an Age,* and take the
love potions prescribed by modern witchdoctors who
devise special hormone therapies to help women stay
"feminine forever," which means, of course, beautiful forever.

However, the ideal beauties in the media do remain
young forever. They are always there to keep women
permanently insecure about their looks, and that includes
the great beauties as well. Indeed, the more beautiful a
woman, the more she dreads time and younger beauties;
for generally the beautiful woman's opinion of herself has
depended almost solely on her looks. Elizabeth of Aus-
tria, who in the nineteenth century was regarded as the
most beautiful woman in Europe, said when she was
approaching forty: "Nothing could be more terrible than
to feel the hand of time on one's body, to watch the skin
wrinkling, to wake and fear the morning light and know
that one is no longer desirable. Life without beauty would
be worthless to me." In the 1960s when Grace Kelly,
Princess of Monaco, turned forty, she said that though
forty was a marvelous age for a man, it was torture for a
woman because it meant "the end."

Certainly it means the end if a woman's value depends
upon her looks and her looks succumb—as they must—to
age. The only road to glory this culture offers women is
one that cannot last, one that must perish long before they
do. The culture discourages women from achieving the
kind of glory that does last, the glory that results from
using one's mind. The little boy is asked what he's *going to
become* when he grows up; the little girl is told she
is—pretty. A girl's potential is only physical. Like an ani-

mal, she is expected to create only with her body, not her mind. The quickest and easiest way for a woman to get ahead (besides hitching her body to a man's star) is by displaying her body, like an animal in a zoo, as a topless waitress, a belly dancer, a model, an airline stewardess, a Miss U.S.A., or that ultimate glory, a Raquel Welch, who at present embodies the height of woman's attainments.

Women are supposed to be bodies, not differentiated complex minds. Who would think of talking to the virtually indistinguishable, vacuous faces in *Playboy?* Women are supposed to be a man's sexual outlets, not his work colleagues, not his intellectual companions. The girl who tries to show off her mind instead of her body is penalized. On a date the girl who stops listening and starts talking is considered rude and aggressive; the girl who presumes to argue, disprove, and refute is not asked out again. In the eighteenth century Mary Wortley Montagu advised her daughter to hide her learning "like a physical defect." No one minded Jayne Mansfield's 160 I.Q. because she kept it hidden well behind her bosom. Men want their women dumb, their beautiful lips sealed. "No dress or garment is less becoming to a woman than a show of intelligence," decreed Martin Luther.

Men feel threatened unless they are with a woman who is less intelligent than they are. Accordingly, men, in order to keep their egos inflated (at least in the presence of the fair sex), for centuries excluded women from schools and colleges, and then sneeringly discoursed on woman's stupidity: "A woman has the form of an angel . . . and the mind of an ass" (German proverb). "No woman is a genius; women are a decorative sex" (Oscar Wilde). Max Beerbohm felt that a woman couldn't be charming who had a "masculine-styled brain," which is male for "a powerful intellect."

The woman who, in spite of cultural disapproval and the difficulties of acquiring an education, pursues learning is regarded by men as a sexual freak. Nietzsche said that "when a woman inclines to learning there is usually something wrong with her sex apparatus." Women seem to feel the same way, for when they do use their brains they tend to fear that they have unsexed themselves. In 1787 when Dorothea von Schlözer took her doctorate of philosophy at Göttingen, she dressed herself in white, with a veil on her head and roses and pearls in her hair; that is, she dressed like a bride to reassure herself that she was a

woman. Today even female professors, doctors, and lawyers dress sexily and still modestly pretend to know less
than they do; they act like dumb blondes and enjoy being
mistaken for them.

It is protective covering, for the intelligent woman is
disliked, and if she cannot pass as at least "attractive," she
has to endure constant adverse comments about her appearance. It took the press about twenty years to stop
joking about Eleanor Roosevelt's looks. A journalist recently explained the phenomenon of Bernadette Devlin,
M.P., as a compensation for her lack of beauty, the
implication being that if Miss Devlin had been prettier she
would not have had to be an M.P. but would long ago
have happily become Mrs. SomeMan. George Eliot, who
was among the two or three greatest novelists of the
nineteenth century, was forced by society to agonize about
her looks. Even so serious a journal as the *London Times
Literary Supplement* recently captioned a review of her
latest biography, "Magnificently Ugly," and devoted almost half the review to a discussion of the problem of
her looks. But George Eliot was no worse looking than
Emerson or Dante; she was ugly only in terms of the
beauty ideal artificially set up for women. Critics still like
to talk so much about her looks because they do not want
to think of her as a mind, but rather as a woman.

In 1966 when a woman was appointed vice president of
a corporation, journalists were impressed not by her competence with financial statistics but by her own statistics—
34-24-36—which they published so all the world could
marvel at the anomaly: a brainy woman who was built
too. What they were in reality doing was reducing the
vice-president of a corporation to a beautiful body. Similarly, when a woman is appointed a judge, we sometimes
see the exclamation, "She's pretty too!" When a good-
looking man is appointed a judge, the press rarely ex-
claims, "He's handsome too!" Men are astonished by the
combination of beauty and brains in a woman because
they really cannot understand why a good-looking woman
should have brains. What does she need them for? In 1837
Alexander Walker, in his discourse on *Beauty; Illustrated
Chiefly by an Analysis and Classification of Beauty in
Woman,* concluded that the ideal beauty's head ought to
be small "because the mental system in the female ought
to be subordinate to the vital . . . sensibility should exceed
reasoning power." Or as a twentieth century song put it,

"Why does a beautiful girl need an I.Q. to say I do?" On the same either/or principle is a watch ad in which the woman's watch is described as beautiful, the man's as accurate.

Society has so overvalued beauty that most women, given the choice between unusual intelligence and great beauty, would choose beauty. Charlotte Brontë was so angry at fate for not making her pretty that her publisher believed she would have given "all her genius and all her fame to have been beautiful." How many girls given the choice between Raquel Welch or Maria Goeppert-Mayer, the woman who won a Nobel prize for physics in 1963, would choose to be the physicist?

At present men seem to object somewhat less to the woman who uses her brains. Occasionally one does find an article in the Sunday supplement that tells young girls that it is okay to use their brains. But, why? Because husbands would have no objections to having both an attractive and intelligent wife for entertaining their business friends or a shrewd silent partner with whom they could discuss business strategy. Husbands also do not mind if their wives entertain them in the evening by telling them about something interesting they have been reading. So long as a woman's brains are used in the service of a male, men will permit her to display them. But her brains must be kept subordinate. Even the most enlightened men and women suspect the manliness of a man married to a doctor or a professor. It somehow does not seem right. Men are supposed to marry their intellectual inferiors; if by some unlucky chance, the wife is the husband's intellectual superior, she is always advised to play down her brains and play up her sex appeal if she wants her marriage to last.

Whether a woman has an I.Q. of 60 or 160, whether she is young or old, her first duty is to keep herself attractive. Men have taught women to regard themselves exactly the way men do—as sex objects. A woman's body, accordingly, becomes her lifelong sex object, the physical object she cherishes most. All babies begin by loving their physical selves, but the male baby is encouraged to stop loving just himself and to transfer some of his self-love to the outside world. Girls, on the other hand, are encouraged to continue obtaining gratification the way a baby does—from reveling in and showing off their bodies. A baby's pride is centered in its physical being, not in its accomplishments, and so it is with women. They are never supposed to grow up, but to remain fixated in infantile narcissism. And most women do continue to overvalue their physical selves; this is why all evidence to the contrary notwithstanding, every woman is pleased and secretly believes a man when he tells her she is beautiful. Because women are infant narcissists, they like to be treated like queens, for whom doors are opened and cigarettes lighted, and toward whom the whole male world moves as toward a magnet. These attentions make women feel good about themselves, because they are repetitions of infancy, when one's helplessness forces the whole world to wait upon one.

As narcissists women are incapable of loving anyone but themselves. When a beautiful woman falls in love, it generally only means that she has found a man who overvalues her physical self as much as she does. For the average woman the process of falling in love is more complicated. Since every baby thinks of itself as the greatest thing ever created, the average-looking woman at first overvalues herself the way everyone else does. When she discovers that the ideal image she has of herself is not what society finds ideal, she does not give it up; it remains her secret ideal image, which society encourages her to maintain by the deceptions of clothes and cosmetics. Her real self, which she can't love and which she consequently feels no one else can love, is abandoned, and she typically falls in love by self-abnegation, by unselfishly devoting herself to a man whom she regards as her superior and then living through him, making his life her life. She wants no life of her own because she has no real self. But the superior being she worships is not a real man, but an embodiment of her own self-worship transferred onto him.

Narcissus was so enraptured by his own image reflected on the surface of a lake that he tried to embrace himself. Women, too, are in love with their own body image, are therefore unconscious homosexuals. It would be surprising if they were not, since they grow up in a world in which only the female body is glorified, and in which they are bombarded in all the media with millions of images of beautiful women described as love objects. Far from conditioning women to be heterosexual by holding up for their admiration images of handsome men, the culture keeps women looking constantly at other women. The culture, however, likes to think that women don't look at women in the same way that men do. Psychology textbooks are fond of presenting statistics that prove that men are sexually aroused by looking, but that women are not. The trouble probably is that in their tests psychologists show women only pictures of men. It is pictures of *women* that women are nurtured on, and women do look, and look, and look. Women look at other women with a more intense and discriminating eye than any man does. The culture likes to think that a woman's glance is only critical, to see if the other woman is better looking or better dressed than she is, or that women look because they want to identify with the ideal beauties. But envy is looking at what one desires, and identification is one of the most potent forms of love; one wants to merge, with what one identifies with, become one with the beloved. The almost inevitable rivalry between women, the seeming impossibility of women being friends, may well be an overreaction to an overattraction.

What holds women back from widespread homosexuality? Although the female body is glorified, females are regarded as the inferior sex, and women share this male-created attitude. The very cause of women's glorification—her presumptive beauty—is at the same time the stigma of her inferiority. No matter how much a woman is unconsciously attracted to another woman, she also despises the other woman as she despises herself, because she is of the inferior sex. In this culture a woman can lose her sense of inferiority only when she is loved by a member of the superior sex. To be loved by a woman would mean to be loved by someone as inferior as oneself. So women, though intensely in love with the female body image, recoil from women.

Perhaps the only women in the culture who do not despise themselves because they are women, are the active lesbians—at least those who don't imitate men—the many lesbians who look and act intensely feminine. They have wholly identified with the beauty ideal, so much so that they despise men because men are not women and because men really don't admire women, not the way they wish to be totally admired. They want to continue to live in the one-sexed world of infancy, in the cocoon of their mother's or their own unconditional love. Lesbians are merely more unadulterated narcissists than heterosexual women.

Because women are narcissists, they are also exhibition-

ists, whose exhibitionism, like their narcissism, is approved
by the culture. The male exhibitionist who thrusts his penis
at a female is put in jail, but the female who thrusts her
bosom, behind, and legs at a male is admired. Female
exhibitionism is socially approved because the culture
wants to keep woman infantile, to keep her identity focused on her physical person, not on her accomplishments.
The culture therefore compels a woman to show off her
body, makes her feel unfeminine unless she does so, and
makes the woman who accomplishes something feel unsexed. The accomplished woman feels unsexed because she
has achieved identity the way a man is supposed to—
indirectly, through the active use of his abilities. The male
exhibitionist is put in jail, for trying to achieve his identity
the way women and infants do, directly, by sheer physical-
ity. He wants to prove his masculinity simply by exposing
his penis; he does not want to have to prove it indirectly
through accomplishments.

The normal man proves his physical maleness indirectly—compelling woman to expose herself as unlike him.
The woman with the most exaggerated secondary sexual
characteristics is considered the most beautiful because she
makes a man feel more like a man, that is, unlike a
woman. Men force women to constantly and blatantly
expose themselves as women so that men can constantly
assure themselves they are men. They need that reassurance, because their masculine identity is weak, because all
men have an unconscious desire to be female, to return to
the infancy in which they identified with mother, were not
yet differentiated into boys. That is why man both desires
and despises woman, why he both glorifies her as beautiful
and regards her as a temptress, a *femme fatale*. Woman
is beautiful to man, because she is the image of his
rejected unconscious desire, a desire that he can allow
himself to experience only indirectly, through a woman. In
sex men unconsciously can take what they desire, become
one with their lost female selves, much in the same way
that primitive men ritually partake of their forbidden
totem animal, their "ancestor" whose characteristics they
wish to acquire. That is why men must "take," aggressively, powerfully, dominantly, in order to keep unconscious
the kind of power they envy—the effortless power of the
woman, who, like the infant, is loved simply for her
adorable self.

Young childlike women are preferred in this culture

because they embody most clearly men's projected desires. "Pretty women always seem to appeal to us as more dependent and childlike," admitted William Dean Howells. Children are pretty and dependent, and man wants woman to remain a pretty, dependent child, so that through woman he can reunite himself with his lost childhood when he was still identified with woman and was allowed to be soft, tender, helpless, narcissistic, exhibitionistic, a cuddly, sweet-smelling naked bunny rather than a developed character and mind, a hard-working, responsible, assertive man.

The cult of beauty in women, which we smile at as though it were one of the culture's harmless follies, is, in fact, an insanity, for it is posited on a false view of reality. Women are not more beautiful than men. The obligation to be beautiful is an artificial burden, imposed by men on women, that keeps both sexes clinging to childhood, the woman forced to remain a charming, dependent child, the man driven by his unconscious desire to be—like an infant—loved and taken care of simply for his beautiful self. Woman's mask of beauty is the face of the child, a revelation of the tragic sexual immaturity of both sexes in our culture.

II:

WOMAN IS MADE, NOT BORN

8

PSYCHOLOGY CONSTRUCTS THE FEMALE

Naomi Weisstein

It is an implicit assumption that the area of psychology that concerns itself with personality has the onerous but necessary task of describing the limits of human possibility. Thus, when we are about to consider the liberation of women, we naturally look to psychology to tell us what "true" liberation would mean: what would give women the freedom to fulfill their own intrinsic natures?

Psychologists have set about describing the true nature of women with a certainty and a sense of their own infallibility rarely found in the secular world. Bruno Bettelheim tell us that "we must start with the realization that, as much as women want to be good scientists or engineers, they want first and foremost to be womanly companions of men and to be mothers."[1] Erik Erikson, upon noting that young women often ask whether they can "have an identity before they know whom they will marry, and for whom they will make a home," explains somewhat elegiacally that "much of a young woman's identity is already defined in her kind of attractiveness and in the selectivity of her search for the man (or men) by whom she wishes to be sought. . . ." Mature

An expanded and revised version of "Kinder, Küche, Kirche as Scientific Law: Psychology Constructs the Female" (Boston: New England Free Press, 1968). © 1969 by Naomi Weisstein.

womanly fulfillment, for Erikson, rests on the fact that a woman's ". . . somatic design harbors an 'inner space' destined to bear the offspring of chosen men, and with it, a biological, psychological, and ethical commitment to take care of human infancy."[2] Some psychiatrists even see the acceptance of woman's role by women as a solution to societal problems. "Woman is nurturance," writes Joseph Rheingold, a psychiatrist at Harvard Medical School, ". . . anatomy decrees the life of a woman . . . when women grow up without dread of their biological functions and without subversion by feminist doctrine, and therefore enter upon motherhood with a sense of fulfillment and altruistic sentiment, we shall attain the goal of a good life and a secure world in which to live it."[3]

These views from men who are assumed to be experts reflect, in a surprisingly transparent way, the cultural consensus. They not only assert that a woman is defined by her ability to attract men, but they see no alternative definitions. They think that the definition of a woman in terms of a man is the way it should be; and they back it up with psychosexual incantation and biological ritual curses. A woman has an identity if she is attractive enough to obtain a man, and thus, a home; for this will allow her to set about her life's task of "joyful altruism and nurturance." A woman's *true* nature is that of a happy servant.

Business certainly does not disagree. If views such as Bettelheim's and Erikson's do indeed have something to do with real liberation for women, then seldom in human history has so much money and effort been spent on helping a group of people realize their true potential. Clothing, cosmetics, and home furnishings are multimillion dollar businesses. If you do not like investing in firms that make weaponry and flaming gasoline, then there is a lot of cash in "inner space." Sheet and pillowcase manufacturers are anxious to fill this inner space:

Mother, for a while this morning, I thought I wasn't cut out for married life. Hank was late for work and forgot his apricot juice and walked out without kissing me, and when I was all alone I started crying. But then the postman came with the sheets and towels you sent, that look like big bandana handkerchiefs, and you know what I thought? That those big red and blue handkerchiefs are for girls like me to dry their tears on so they can get busy and do what a housewife has to do. Throw open the windows and start getting the house ready, and the dinner, maybe clean the silver and put new geraniums in the box. *Everything to be ready for him when he walks through that door.*[4]

Of course, it is not only the sheet and pillowcase manufacturers, the cosmetics industry, and the home furnishings salesmen who profit from and make use of the cultural definitions of men and women. The example above is blatantly and overtly pitched to a particular kind of sexist stereotype: the child nymph. But almost all aspects of the media are normative, that is, they have to do with the ways in which beautiful people, or just folks, or ordinary Americans, or extraordinary Americans should live their lives. They define the possible, and the possibilities are usually in terms of what is male and what it female.

It is an interesting but limited exercise to show that psychologists and psychiatrists embrace these sexist norms of our culture, that they do not see beyond the most superficial and stultifying conceptions of female nature, and that their ideas of female nature serve industry and commerce so well. Just because it is good for business does not mean it is wrong. What I will show is that it is wrong; that there is not the tiniest shred of evidence that these fantasies of servitude and childish dependence have anything to do with women's true potential; that the idea of the nature of human possibility which rests on the accidents of individual development of genitalia, on what is possible today because of what happened yesterday, on the fundamentalist myth of sex-organ causality, has strangled and deflected psychology so that it is relatively useless in describing, explaining, or predicting humans and their behavior. It then goes without saying that present psychology is less than worthless in contributing to a vision that could truly liberate—men as well as women.

The central argument of my essay, then, is this. Psychology has nothing to say about what women are really like, what they need and what they want, essentially because psychology does not know. I want to stress that this failure is not limited to women; rather, the kind of psychology that has addressed itself to how people act and who they are has failed to understand in the first place why people act the way they do, and certainly failed to understand what might make them act differently.

These psychologists, whether engaged in academic personality research or in clinical psychology and psychiatry, make the central assumption that human behavior rests on an individual and inner dynamic, perhaps fixed in infancy, perhaps fixed by genitalia, perhaps simply arranged in a rather immovable cognitive network. But this assumption is rapidly losing ground as personality psychologists fail again and again to get consistency in the assumed personalities of their subjects.[5] Meanwhile, the evidence is accumulating that what a person does and who he believes himself to be will in general be a function of what people around him expect him to be, and what the overall situation in which he is acting implies that he is. Compared to the influence of the social context within which a person lives, his or her history and traits, as well as biological make-up, may simply be random variations, noise superimposed on the true signal that can predict behavior.

Some academic personality psychologists are at least looking at the counterevidence and questioning their theories; no such corrective is occurring in clinical psychology and psychiatry. Freudians and neo-Freudians, Adlerians and neo-Adlerians, classicists and swingers, clinicians and psychiatrists simply refuse to look at the evidence against their theory and practice. And they support their theory and their practice with stuff so transparently biased as to have absolutely no standing as empirical evidence.

To summarize: psychology has failed to understand what people are and how they act because (1) psychology has looked for inner traits when it should have been noting social context; and (2) theoreticians of personality have generally been clinicians and psychiatrists, and they have never considered it necessary to offer evidence to support their theories.

THEORY WITHOUT EVIDENCE

Let us turn to the second cause of failure first: the acceptance by psychiatrists and clinical psychologists of theory without evidence. If we inspect the literature of personality, it is immediately obvious that the bulk of it is written by clinicians and psychiatrists whose major support for their theories is "years of intensive clinical experience." This is a tradition started by Freud. His "insights" occurred during the course of his work with his patients. Now there is nothing wrong with such an approach to theory *formulation;* a person is free to make up theories with any inspiration that works: divine revelation, intensive clinical practice, a random numbers table. However, he is not free to claim any validity for his theory until it has been tested and confirmed. But theories are treated in no such tentative way in ordinary clinical practice. Consider Freud. What he thought constituted evidence fell short of the most minimal conditions of scientific rigor. In *The Sexual Enlightenment of Children,* the classic document that is supposed to demonstrate empirically the existence of a castration complex and its connection to a phobia, Freud based his analysis on the reports of the father of the little boy, himself in therapy, and a devotee of Freudian theory.[6] I really do not have to comment further on the contamination in this kind of evidence. It is remarkable that only recently has Freud's classic theory on the sexuality of women—the notion of the double orgasm—been actually tested physiologically and found just plain wrong. Now those who claim that fifty years of psychoanalytic experience constitute evidence enough of the essential truths of Freud's theory should ponder the robust health of the double orgasm. Did women, until Masters and Johnson,[7] believe they were having two different kinds of orgasm? Did their psychiatrists cow them into reporting something that was not true? If so, were there other things they reported that were also not true? Did psychiatrists ever observe anything different from what their theories had led them to believe? If clinical experience means anything at all, surely we should have been done with the double-orgasm myth long before the Masters and Johnson studies.

But certainly, you may object, "years of intensive clinical experience" are the only reliable measure in a discipline that rests for its findings on insights, sensitivity, and intuition. The problem with insight, sensitivity, and intuition is that they can confirm for all time the biases that one started out with. People used to be absolutely convinced of their ability to tell which of their number were engaging in witchcraft. All it required was some sensitivity to the workings of the devil.

Years of intensive clinical experience are not the same thing as empirical evidence. The first thing an experimenter learns in any kind of experiment that involves humans is the concept of the double blind. The term is taken from medical experiments, where one group is given a drug which is presumably supposed to change behavior in a certain way, and a control group is given a placebo. If the observers or the subjects know which group took which drug, the result invariably comes out on the positive side for the new drug. Only when it is not known which subject took which pill is validity remotely approximated. In addition, with judgments of human behavior, it is so difficult to precisely tie down just what behavior is going on, let alone what behavior should be expected, that one must test again and again the reliability of judgments. How many judges, blind, will agree in their observations? Can they repeat their own judgments at some later time? When in actual practice these judgment criteria are tested for clinical judgments, then we find that the judges cannot judge reliably, nor can they judge consistently; they do no better than chance in identifying which of a certain set of stories were written by men and which by women; which of a whole battery of clinical test results were the products of homosexuals and which were the products of heterosexuals,[8] and which of a battery of clinical test results and interviews (where questions are asked such as "Do you have delusions?")[9] were products of psychotics, neurotics, psychosomatics, or normals. Let me stress the implications of these findings. The ability of judges, chosen for their clinical expertise, to distinguish male heterosexuals from male homosexuals on the basis of three widely used clinical projective tests—the Rorschach, the TAT, and the MAP—was *no better than chance.* The reason this is such devastating news, of course, is that sexuality is supposed to be of fundamental importance in the deep dynamic of personality; if what is considered gross sexual deviance cannot be recognized, then what are psychologists talking about when they, for example, claim that at the basis of paranoid psychosis is "latent homosexual panic"? They cannot even identify what homosexual anything is, let alone "latent homosexual panic."[10] More frightening, expert clinicians cannot be consistent about what diagnostic category to assign to a person, again on the basis of both tests and interviews; a number of normals in the Little and Schneidman study were described as psychotic, in such categories as schizophrenic with homosexual tendencies or schizoid character with depressive trends. But most disheartening, when the judges were asked to rejudge the test protocols some weeks later, their diagnoses of the same subjects on the basis of the same protocols differed markedly from their initial judgments. It is obvious that even simple descriptive conventions in clinical psychology cannot be consistently applied; that these descriptive conventions have any explanatory significance is therefore, of course, out of the question.

As a graduate student at Harvard some years ago, I was a member of a seminar that was asked to identify which of two piles of a clinical test, the TAT, had been written by males and which by females. Only four students out of twenty identified the piles correctly; this was after one and a half months of intensively studying the differences between men and women. Since this result is below chance—that is, this result would occur by chance about four out of a thousand times—we may conclude that there *is* finally a consistency here; students are judging knowledgeably within the context of psychological teaching about the differences between men and women; the teachings themselves are simply erroneous.

You may argue that the theory may be scientifically "unsound" but at least it cures people. There is no evidence that it does. In 1952 Eysenck reported the results of what is called an "outcome of therapy" study of neurotics which showed that, of the patients who received psychoanalysis, the improvement rate was 44 percent; of the patients who received psychotherapy, the improvement rate was 64 percent; and of the patients who received no treatment at all, the improvement rate was 72 percent.[11] These findings have never been refuted; subsequently later studies have confirmed the negative results of the Eysenck study.[12] How can clinicians and psychiatrists, then, in all good conscience, continue to practice? Largely by ignoring these results and being careful not to do outcome-of-therapy studies. The attitude is nicely summarized by J. B. Rotter: "Research studies in psychotherapy tend to be concerned more with psychotherapeutic procedure and less with outcome . . . to some extent, it reflects an interest in the psychotherapy situation as a kind of personality laboratory."[13] Some laboratory.

THE SOCIAL CONTEXT

Since clinical experience and tools can be shown to be worse than useless when tested for consistency, efficacy, agreement, and reliability, we can safely conclude that theories of a clinical nature advanced about women are also worse than useless. I want to turn now to the second major point in my essay: even when psychological theory is constructed so that it may be tested, and rigorous standards of evidence are used, it has become increasingly clear that in order to understand why people do what they do, and certainly in order to change what people do, psychologists must turn away from the theory of the causal nature of the inner dynamic and look to the social context within which individuals live.

Before examining the relevance of this approach for the question of women, let me first sketch the groundwork for this assertion. In the first place, it is clear that personality tests never yield consistent predictions;[14] a rigid authoritarian on one measure will be an unauthoritarian on the next. But the reason for this inconsistency is only now becoming clear; it seems overwhelmingly to have much more to do with the social situation in which the subject finds himself than with the subject himself.

In a series of brilliant experiments, R. Rosenthal and his coworkers have shown that if one group of experimenters has one hypothesis about what they expect to find, and another group of experimenters has the opposite hypothesis, both groups will obtain results in accord with their hypotheses.[15] The results obtained are not due to mishandling of data by biased experimenters; rather, the bias of the experimenter somehow creates a changed environment in which subjects actually act differently. For instance, in one experiment subjects were to assign numbers to pictures of men's faces, with high numbers representing the subject's judgment that the man in the picture was a successful person, and low numbers representing the subject's judgment that the man in the picture was an unsuccessful person. One group of experimenters was told that the subjects tended to rate the faces high; another group of experimenters was told that the subjects tended to rate the faces low. Each group of experimenters was instructed to follow precisely the same procedure: they were required to read to subjects a set of instructions and to *say nothing else*. For the 375 subjects run, the results showed clearly that those subjects who performed the task with experimenters who expected high ratings gave high ratings, and those subjects who performed the task with experimenters who expected low ratings gave low ratings. How did this happen? The experimenters all used the same words, but something in their conduct made one group of subjects do one thing, and another group of subjects do another thing.

The concreteness of the changed conditions produced by expectation is a fact, a reality: even in two separate studies with animal subjects, those experimenters who were told that rats learning mazes had been especially bred for brightness obtained better learning from their rats than did experimenters believing their rats to have been bred for dullness.[16] In a very recent study Rosenthal and Jacobson extended their analysis to the natural classroom situation.[17] Here, they tested a group of students and reported to the teachers that some among the students tested "showed great promise." Actually, the students so named had been selected on a random basis. Some time later, the experimenters retested the group of students: those students whose teachers had been told that they were "promising" showed real and dramatic increments in their I.Q.'s as compared to the rest of the students. Something in the conduct of the teachers toward those whom the teachers believed to be the "bright" students made those students brighter.

Thus, even in carefully controlled experiments and with no outward or conscious difference in behavior, the hypotheses we start with will influence the behavior of the subject enormously. These studies are extremely important when assessing the validity of psychological studies of women. Since it is beyond doubt that most of us start with notions about the nature of men and women, the validity of a number of observations of sex differences is questionable, even when these observations have been made under carefully controlled conditions. Second, and more important, the Rosenthal experiments point quite clearly to the influence of social expectation. In some extremely important ways, people are what you expect them to be, or at least they behave as you expect them to behave. Thus, if women, according to Bettelheim, want first and foremost to be good wives and mothers, it is extremely likely that this is what Bruno Bettelheim and the rest of society want them to be.

Another series of brilliant social psychological experiments point to the overwhelming effect of social context. These are the obedience experiments of Stanley Milgram in which subjects are asked to obey the orders of unknown experimenters, orders which carry with them the distinct possibility that the subject is killing somebody.[18] In Milgram's experiments a subject is told that he is administering a learning experiment and that he is to deal out shocks each time the other subject (in reality, a confederate of the experimenter) answers incorrectly. The equipment appears to provide graduated shocks ranging upward from 15 volts through 450 volts; for each of four consecutive voltages there are verbal descriptions such as "mild shock," "danger, severe shock," and, finally, for the 435 and 450 volt switches, a red XXX marked over the switches. Each time the stooge answers incorrectly the subject is supposed to increase the voltage. As the voltage increases, the stooge begins to cry in pain; he demands that the experiment stop; finally, he refuses to answer at all. When he stops responding, the experimenter instructs the subject to continue increasing the voltage; for each shock administered the stooge shrieks in agony. Under these conditions about 62.5 percent of the subjects administered shocks that they believed to be possibly lethal.

No tested individual differences between subjects predicted how many would continue to obey and who would break off the experiment. When forty psychiatrists predicted how many of a group of 100 subjects would go on to give the lethal shock, their predictions were orders of magnitude below the actual percentages; most expected only one-tenth of one percent of the subjects to obey to the end.

But even though psychiatrists have no idea how people will behave in this situation, and even though individual differences do not predict which subjects will obey and which will not, it is easy to predict when subjects will be obedient and when they will be defiant. All the experimenter has to do is change the social situation. In a variant of Milgram's experiment, two stooges were present in addition to the "victim"; these worked along with the subject in administering electric shocks. When these two stooges refused to go on with the experiment, only 10 percent of the subjects continued to the maximum voltage. This is critical for personality theory. It says that behavior can only be predicted from the social situation, not from the individual history.

Finally, an ingenious experiment by S. Schachter and S. E. Singer showed that subjects injected with adrenalin, which produces a state of physiological arousal in all but minor respects identical to that which occurs when subjects are extremely afraid, became euphoric when they were in a room with a stooge who was acting euphoric, and became extremely angry when they were placed in a room with a stooge who was acting extremely angry.[19]

To summarize: if subjects under quite innocuous and noncoercive social conditions can be made to kill other subjects and under other types of social conditions will positively refuse to do so; if subjects can react to a state of physiological fear by becoming euphoric, because somebody else around is euphoric, or angry, because somebody else around is angry; if students become intelligent because teachers expect them to be intelligent, and rats run mazes better because experimenters are told the rats are bright, then it is obvious that a study of human behavior requires, first and foremost, a study of the social contexts within which people move, of the expectations about how they will behave, and of the authority that tells them who they are and what they are supposed to do.

BIOLOGICALLY BASED THEORIES

Two theories of the nature of women, which come not from psychiatric and clinical tradition, but from biology, can be disposed of now with little difficulty. The first biological theory of sex differences argues that since females and males differ in their sex hormones, and sex hormones enter the brain, there must be innate differences in nature.[20] But this argument only tells us that there are differences in physiological state. The problem is whether these differences are at all relevant to behavior. Recall that Schachter and Singer have shown that a particular physiological state can itself lead to a multiplicity of felt emotional states and outward behavior, depending on the social situation.[21] The second theory is a form of biological reductionism: sex-role behavior in some primate species is described, and it is concluded that this is the natural behavior for humans. Putting aside the not insignificant problem of observer bias (for instance, H. Harlow of the University of Wisconsin, after observing differences between male and female rhesus monkeys, quotes Lawrence Sterne to the effect that women are silly and trivial and concludes that "men and women have differed in the past and they will differ in the future"),[22] there are a number of problems with this approach.

The most general and serious problem is that there are no grounds to assume that anything primates do is necessary, natural, or desirable in humans, for the simple reason that humans are not nonhumans. For instance, it is found that male chimpanzees placed alone with infants will not "mother" them. Jumping from hard data to ideological speculation researchers conclude from this information that *human* females are necessary for the safe growth of human infants. Following this logic, it would be as reasonable to conclude that it is quite useless to teach human infants to speak since it has been tried with chimpanzees and it does not work.

One strategy that has been used is to extrapolate from primate behavior to "innate" human preference by noticing certain trends in primate behavior as one moves phylogenetically closer to humans. But there are great difficulties with this approach. When behaviors from lower primates are directly opposite to those of higher primates, or to those one expects of humans, they can be dismissed on evolutionary grounds—higher primates and/or humans grew out of that kid stuff. On the other hand, if the behavior of higher primates is counter to the behavior considered natural for humans, while the behavior of some lower primate is considered natural for humans, the higher primate behavior can be dismissed also on the grounds that it has diverged from an older, prototypical pattern. So either way, one can select those behaviors one wants to prove as innate for humans. In addition, one does not know whether the sex-role behavior exhibited is dependent on the phylogenetic rank or on the environmental conditions (both physical and social) under which different species live.

Is there then any value at all in prime observations as they relate to human females and males? There is a value but it is limited: its function can be no more than to show some extant examples of diverse sex-role behavior. It must be stressed, however, that this is an extremely limited function. The extant behavior does not begin to suggest all the possibilities, either for nonhuman primates or for humans. Bearing these caveats in mind, it is nonetheless interesting that if one inspects the limited set of existing nonhuman primate sex-role behaviors, one finds, in fact, a much larger range of sex-role behavior than is commonly believed to exist. Biology appears to limit very little; the fact that a female gives birth does not mean, even in nonhumans, that she necessarily cares for the infant (in marmosets, for instance, the male carries the infant at all times except when the infant is feeding).[23] Natural female and male behavior varies all the way from females who are much more aggressive and competitive than males (for example, Tamarins)[24] and male "mothers" (for example, Titi monkeys, night monkeys, and marmosets),[25] to submissive and passive females and male antagonists (for example, rhesus monkeys).[26]

But even for the limited function that primate arguments serve, the evidence has been misused. Invariably, only those primates have been cited that exhibit exactly the kind of behavior that the proponents of the biological basis of human female behavior wish were true for humans. Thus, baboons and rhesus monkeys are generally cited: males in these groups exhibit some of the most irritable and aggressive behavior found in primates, and if one wishes to argue that females are naturally passive and submissive, these groups provide vivid examples. There are abundant counterexamples, such as those mentioned above; in fact, in general a counterexample can be found for every sex-role behavior cited, including, male "mothers." The presence of counterexamples has not stopped florid and overarching theories of the natural or biological basis of male privilege from proliferating. For instance, there have been a number of theories dealing with the innate incapacity of human males for monogamy. Here, as in most of this type of theorizing, baboons are a favorite example, probably because of their fantasy value: the family unit of the hamadryas baboon, for instance, consists of a highly constant pattern of one male and a number of females and their young. And again, the counterexamples, such as the invariably monogamous gibbon, are ignored.

An extreme example of this maiming and selective truncation of the evidence in the service of a plea for the maintenance of male privilege is a recent book, *Men in Groups*, by a man who calls himself Tiger.[27] The central claim of this book is that females are incapable of honorable collective action because they are incapable of "bonding" as in "male bonding."[28] What is male bonding? Its surface definition is simple: "a particular relationship between two or more males such that they react differently to members of their bonding units as compared to individuals outside of it."[29] If one deletes the word male, the definition, on its face, would seem to include all organisms that have any kind of social organization. But this is not what Tiger means. For instance, Tiger asserts that because females are incapable of bonding, they should be restricted from public life. Why is bonding an exclusively male behavior? Because, says Tiger, it is seen in male primates. All male primates? No, very few male primates. Tiger cites two examples where male bonding is seen: rhesus monkeys and baboons. Surprise, surprise. But not even all baboons: as mentioned above, the hamadryas social organization consists of one-male units; so does that of the Gelada baboon.[30] The great apes do not go in for male bonding much either. The male bond is hardly a serious contribution to scholarship; one reviewer for *Science* has observed that the book "shows basically more resemblance to a partisan political tract than to a work of objective social science," with male bonding being "some kind of behavioral phlogiston."[31]

In short, primate arguments have generally misused the evidence: primate studies themselves have, in any case, only the very limited function of describing some possible sex-role behavior; and at present, primate observations have been sufficiently limited so that even the range of possible sex-role behavior for nonhuman primates is not known. This range is not known since there is only minimal observation of what happens to behavior if the physical or social environment is changed. In one study different troops of Japanese macaques were observed.[32] Here, there appeared to be cultural differences: males in three out of the eighteen troops observed differed in their aggressiveness and infant-caring behavior. There could be no possibility of differential evolution here; the differences seemed largely transmitted by infant socialization. Thus, the very limited evidence points to some plasticity in the sex-role behavior of nonhuman primates; if we can devise experiments that massively change the social organization of primate groups, it is possible that we may observe great changes in behavior. At present, however, we must conclude that since nonhuman primates are too stupid to change their social conditions by themselves, the innateness and fixedness of their behavior is simply not known. Thus, even if there were some way—which there is not—to settle on the behavior of a particular primate species as being the "natural" way for humans, we would not know whether or not this behavior was simply some function of the present social organization of that species. And finally, once again it must be stressed that even if nonhuman primate behavior turned out to be relatively fixed, this would say little about our behavior. More immediate and relevant evidence, that is, the evidence from social psychology, points to an enormous plasticity in human behavior, not only from one culture to the next, but from one experimental group to the next. One of the most salient features of human social organization is its variety; there are a number of cultures where there is at least a rough equality between men and women.[33] In summary, primate arguments can tell us very little about our innate sex-role behavior; if they tell us anything at all, they tell us that there is no one biologically natural female or male behavior and that sex-role behavior in nonhuman primates is much more varied than has previously been thought.

CONCLUSION

In brief, the uselessness of present psychology with regard to women is simply a special case of the general conclusion: one must understand social expectations about women if one is going to characterize the behavior of women.

How are women characterized in our culture and in psychology? They are inconsistent, emotionally unstable, lacking in a strong conscience or superego, weaker, nurturant rather than productive, intuitive rather than intelligent, and, if they are at all "normal," suited to the home and the family. In short, the list adds up to a typical minority-group stereotype of inferiority:[34] if women know their place, which is in the home, they are really quite lovable, happy, childlike, loving creatures. In a review of the intellectual differences between little boys and little girls, Eleanor Maccoby has shown that there are no intellectual differences until about high school, or, if there are, girls are slightly ahead of boys.[35] In high school girls begin to do worse on a few intellectual tasks, such as arithmetic reasoning, and beyond high school the achievement of women now measured in terms of productivity and accomplishment drops off even more rapidly. There are a number of other, nonintellectual tests which show sex differences; I chose the intellectual differences since it is seen clearly that women start becoming inferior. It is useless to talk about women being different but equal; all of the tests I can think of have a "good" outcome and a "bad" outcome. Women usually end up at the "bad" outcome. In light of social expectations about women, what is surprising is not that women end up where society expects they will; what is surprising is that little girls do not get the message that they are supposed to be stupid until high school; and what is even more remarkable is that some women resist this message even after high school, college, and graduate school.

My essay began with remarks on the task of discovering the limits of human potential. Psychologists must realize that it is they who are limiting discovery of human potential. They refuse to accept evidence if they are clinical psychologists, or, if they are rigorous, they assume that people move in a context-free ether, with only their innate dispositions and their individual traits determining what they will do. Until psychologists begin respecting evidence and until they begin looking at the social contexts within which people move, psychology will have nothing of substance to offer in this task of discovery. I do not know what immutable differences exist between men and women apart from differences in their genitals; perhaps there are some other unchangeable differences; probably there are a number of irrelevant differences. But it is clear that until social expectations for men and women are equal, until we provide equal respect for both men and women, our answers to this question will simply reflect our prejudices.

NOTES

1. B. Bettelheim, "The Commitment Required of a Woman Entering a Scientific Profession in Present-day American Society," in *Woman and the Scientific Professions,* an MIT Symposium on American Women in Science and Engineering (Cambridge, Mass., 1965).
2. E. Erikson, "Inner and Outer Space: Reflections on Womanhood," *Daedalus* 93 (1964): 582-606.
3. J. Rheingold, *The Fear of Being a Woman* (New York: Grune & Stratton, 1964), p. 714.
4. Fieldcrest advertisement in the *New Yorker*, 1965. My italics.
5. J. Block, "Some Reasons for the Apparent Inconsistency of Personality," *Psychological Bulletin* 70 (1968): 210-212.
6. S. Freud, *The Sexual Enlightenment of Children* (New York: Collier Books, 1963).

7. W. H. Masters and V. E. Johnson, *Human Sexual Response* (Boston: Little Brown, 1966).

8. E. Hooker, "Male Homosexuality in the Rorschach," *Journal of Projective Techniques* 21 (1957): 18-31.

9. K. B. Little and E. S. Schneidman, "Congruences among Interpretations of Psychological and Anamnestic Data," *Psychological Monographs* 73 (1959): 1-42.

10. It should be noted that psychologists have been as quick to assert absolute truths about the nature of homosexuality as they have about the nature of women. The arguments presented in this essay apply equally to the nature of homosexuality; psychologists know nothing about it; there is no more evidence for the "naturalness" of heterosexuality than for the "naturalness" of homosexuality. Psychology has functioned as a pseudoscientific buttress for our cultural sex-role notions, that is, as a buttress for patriarchal ideology and patriarchal social organization. Women's liberation and gay liberation fight against a common victimization.

11. H. J. Eysenck, "The Effects of Psychotherapy: An Evaluation," *Journal of Consulting Psychology* 16 (1952): 319-324.

12. F. Barron and T. Leary, "Changes in Psychoneurotic Patients with and without Psychotherapy," *Journal of Consulting Psychology* 19 (1955): 239-245; A. E. Bregin, "The Effects of Psychotherapy: Negative Results Revisited," *Journal of Consulting Psychology* 10 (1963): 244-250; R. D. Cartwright and J. L. Vogel, "A Comparison of Changes in Psychoneurotic Patients during Matched Periods of Therapy and No-Therapy," *Journal of Consulting Psychology* 24 (1960): 121-127; E. Powers and H. Witmer, *An Experiment in the Prevention of Delinquency* (New York: Columbia University Press, 1951); C. B. Traux, "Effective Ingredients in Psychotherapy: An Approach to Unraveling the Patient-Therapist Interaction," *Journal of Counseling Psychology* 10 (1963): 256-263.

13. J. B. Rotter, "Psychotherapy," *Annual Review of Psychology* 11 (1960): 381-414.

14. Block, *op. cit.*

15. R. Rosenthal and L. Jacobson, *Pygmalion in the Classroom: Teacher Expectation and Pupil's Intellectual Development* (New York: Holt, Rinehart & Winston, 1968); R. Rosenthal, *Experimenter Effects in Behavioral Research* (New York: Appleton-Century Crofts, 1966).

16. R. Rosenthal and K. L. Fode, "The Effect of Experimenter Bias on the Performance of the Albino Rat," unpublished manuscript (Cambridge: Harvard University, 1960); R. Rosenthal and R. Lawson, "A Longitudinal Study of the Effects of Experimenter Bias on the Operant Learning of Laboratory Rats," unpublished manuscript (Cambridge: Harvard University, 1961).

17. Rosenthal and Jacobson, *op. cit.*

18. S. Milgram, "Some Conditions of Obedience and Disobedience to Authority," *Human Relations* 18 (1965): 57-76; S. Milgram, "Liberating Effects of Group Pressure," *Journal of Personality and Social Psychology* 1 (1965): 127-134.

19. S. Schachter and J. E. Singer, "Cognitive, Social and Physiological Determinants of Emotional State," *Psychological Review* 69 (1962): 379-399.

20. D. A. Hamburg and D. T. Lunde, "Sex Hormones in the De-

velopment of Sex Differences in Human Behavior," in E. Maccoby, ed., *The Development of Sex Differences* (Stanford: Stanford University Press, 1966), pp. 1-24.

21. Schacter and Singer, *op. cit.*
22. H. F. Harlow, "The Heterosexual Affectional System in Monkeys," *The American Psychologist* 17 (1962): 1-9.
23. G. D. Mitchell, "Paternalistic Behavior in Primates," *Psychological Bulletin* 71 (1969): 399-417.
24. *Ibid.*
25. *Ibid.*
26. All these are lower-order primates, which makes their behavior with reference to humans unnatural, or more natural; take your choice.
27. M. Schwarz-Belkin, "Les Fleurs du Mal," in *Festschrift for Gordon Piltdown* (New York: Ponzi Press, 1914), claims that the name was originally *Mouse*, but this may be a reference to an earlier L. Tiger (putative).
28. L. Tiger, *Men in Groups* (New York: Random House, 1969).
29. *Ibid.*, pp. 19-20.
30. Mitchell, *op. cit.*
31. M. H. Fried, "Mankind Excluding Woman," review of Tiger's *Men in Groups, Science* 165 (1969): 884.
32. J. Itani, "Paternal Care in the Wild Japanese Monkeys, *Macaca fuscata*," in C. H. Southwick, ed., *Primate Social Behavior* (Princeton, N.J.: Van Nostrand, 1963).
33. M. Mead, *Male and Female: A Study of the Sexes in a Changing World* (New York: William Morrow, 1949).
34. H. M. Hacker, "Women as a Minority Group," *Social Forces* 30 (1951); 60-69.
35. Maccoby, *op. cit.*

9

AMBIVALENCE: The Socialization of Women

Judith M. Bardwick and Elizabeth Douvan

"What are big boys made of? What are big boys made of?"

Independence, aggression, competitiveness, leadership, task orientation, outward orientation, assertiveness, innovation, self-discipline, stoicism, activity, objectivity, analytic-mindedness, courage, unsentimentality, rationality, confidence, and emotional control.

"What are big girls made of? What are big girls made of?"

Dependence, passivity, fragility, low pain tolerance, nonaggression, noncompetitiveness, inner orientation, interpersonal orientation, empathy, sensitivity, nurturance, subjectivity, intuitiveness, yieldingness, receptivity, inability to risk, emotional liability, supportiveness.[1]

These adjectives describe the idealized, simplified stereotypes of normal masculinity and feminity. They also describe real characteristics of boys and girls, men and women. While individual men and women may more resemble the stereotype of the opposite sex, group differences between the sexes bear out these stereotypic por-

225

traits. How does American society socialize its members so that most men and women come close to the society's ideal norms?

From infancy children have behavioral tendencies that evoke particular types of responses from parents, older siblings, and anyone else who interacts with the child. Such responses are a function of both individual values—whether the particular person values outgoing extroverted behavior, for example—and widespread social values of acceptable child behavior. Socialization refers to the pressures—rewarding, punishing, ignoring, and anticipating—that push the child toward evoking acceptable responses.

Comparisons between boys and girls in infancy and the earliest childhood years reveal modal differences between the sexes. Boys have higher activity levels, are more physically impulsive, are prone to act out aggression, are genitally sexual earlier, and appear to have cognitive and perceptual skills less well-developed than girls of the same age. Generally speaking, girls are less active physically, display less overt physical aggression, are more sensitive to physical pain, have significantly less genital sexuality, and display greater verbal, perceptual, and cognitive skills than boys.[2]

All impulsive, aggressive children are forced to restrain these tendencies since running away, biting, kicking, publicly masturbating, and other similar behaviors are injurious either to the child and his playmates or the pride of his parents. It is critically important to the development of sex differences that these tendencies are more typical of boys than of girls. In addition, girls' more mature skills, enable them to attend to stimuli, especially from other people, more swiftly and accurately than boys.[3] Girls are better at analyzing and anticipating environmental demands; in addition, they have greater verbal facility. Girls' characteristic behavior tends to disturb parents less than boy's characteristic behavior. The perceptual, cognitive, and verbal skills which for unknown reasons are more characteristic of girls enable them to analyze and anticipate adult demands and to conform their behavior to adult expectations.[4] This all means that if the socialization demands made upon boys and girls were actually the same, girls would be in a better position to cope with the world than are boys.

While these differences in response tendencies would be sufficient to result in group differences between boys and girls, another factor adds to the probability of sex differences. Many characteristic responses are acceptable in girls, ranging from the very feminine through the athletic tomboy. For boys, neither the passive sissy nor the aggressive and physical "bad boy" are acceptable. From around the age of two to two and a half, when children are no longer perceived as infants but as children, more boys than girls experience more prohibitions for a wider range of behavior. In addition, and of special importance, dependent behavior, normal to all young children, is permitted for girls and prohibited for boys. Thus, girls are not encouraged to give up old techniques of relating to adults and using others to define their identity, to manipulate the physical world and to supply their emotional needs.[5]

When people find their ways of coping comfortable and gratifying, they are not motivated to develop new techniques which in the long run might be far more productive. All very young children are dependent on adults for their physical well-being and for the knowledge that they exist and have value. Girls' self-esteem remains dependent upon other people's acceptance and love; they continue to use the skills of others instead of evolving their own. The boy's impulsivity and sexuality are sources of enormous pleasure independent of anyone else's response; these pleasures are central to the early core-self. Negative sanctions from powerful adults against masturbation, exploration, and physical aggression threaten not only the obvious pleasures, but, at heart, self-integrity. Thus, boys are pressured by their own impulses and by society's demands to give up depending predominantly on the response of others for feelings of self-esteem. Adult responses are unpredictable and frequently threatening. Forced to affirm himself because of the loss of older, more stable sources of esteem, the boy begins, before the age of five, to develop a sense of self and criteria of worth which are relatively independent of others' responses. He turns to achievements in the outer and real world and begins to value himself for real achievements in terms of objective criteria.

On the other hand, neither the girl's characteristic responses nor widespread cultural values force her to give up older, more successful modes of relating and coping. Her sexuality is neither so genital nor so imperative,[6] but, rather, an overall body sensuality, gratified by affection and cuddling. Since girls are less likely to masturbate, run away from home, or bite and draw blood, their lives are relatively free of crisis until puberty. Before that girls do not have to conform to threatening new criteria of acceptability to anywhere near the extent that boys do. When boys are pressured to give up their childish ways it is because those behaviors are perceived as feminine by parents. Boys have to earn their masculinity early. Until puberty, femininity is a verbal label, a given attribute—something that does not have to be earned. This results in a significant delay in the girl's search for identity, development of autonomy, and development of internal criteria for self-esteem. Because they continue to depend on others for self-definition and affirmation and are adept at anticipating other people's demands, girls are conformist. Girls are rewarded by good grades in school, parental love, teacher acceptance, and peer belonging. As a result, girls remain compliant and particularly amenable to molding by the culture.[7]

Longitudinal studies which measure the same people from earliest childhood through adulthood reveal that some characteristics remain stable over the life span in both sex groups, while other traits change.[8] While activity level and the tendency to be extroverted or introverted are rather stable in both sexes, other dimensions like passivity-dependence and aggression may remain stable or change depending on sex. There are significant correlations over the life span for aggression in males and passivity and dependency in females; on the other hand, passivity and dependency in males and aggression in females show no consistency over the life span. These psychological dimensions change or remain constant depending on whether individual inclinations threaten idealized cultural concepts of masculinity and femininity.[9] Aggression in boys is permitted and encouraged and only the form is socialized; dependence and passivity in girls is permitted or encouraged, and only the form is altered. Sex differences in infancy and childhood are enlarged through socialization.

Schools are generally feminine places,[10] institutions where conformity is valued, taught largely by conformist women. The course content, the methods of assessing progress, and the personal conduct required create difficulties for boys who must inhibit impulsivity, curb aggression, and restrain deviance. The reward structure of the school system perpetuates the pattern set by relationships with the parents—boys are further pressured to turn to their peers for acceptance and to develop internal criteria and objective achievements; girls are further urged to continue the nondeviant, noninnovative, conformist style of life.

Girls are rewarded with high grades in school, especially in the early years of grammar school. What do girls do especially well in? What are they being asked to master? Grammar, spelling, reading, arithmetic—tasks that depend a great deal upon memorization and demand little independence, assertiveness, analysis, innovativeness, creativity.[11] The dependent, passive girl, cued into the affirming responses of teachers, succeeds and is significantly rewarded in school for her "good" behavior and her competent memorizing skills.

It appears that until puberty academically successful girls evolve a "bisexual" or dual self-concept. Both sexes are rewarded for achievement, especially academic achievement. Girls, as well as boys, are permitted to compete in school or athletics without significant negative repercussions. The girl who is rewarded for these successes evolves a self-concept associated with being able to successfully cope and compete. While there are no negative repercussions and there is a high probability of rewards from parents and teachers as long as her friends are similarly achieving, this girl will also feel normally feminine (although questions of femininity are probably not critically important in self-evaluation of prepubertal girls unless they are markedly deviant). With the onset of the physical changes of puberty, definitions of normalcy and femininity change and come precipitately closer to the stereotype. Now behaviors and qualities that were rewarded, especially successful competing, may be perceived negatively.[12] Femininity also becomes an attribute that has to be earned—this task is made crucially difficult because of the girl's ambivalent feelings toward her body.[13]

The maturation of the girl's reproductive system brings joy and relief, feelings of normalcy, and the awareness of sexuality. Simultaneously, in normal girls the physical changes are accompanied by blood and pain, the expectation of body distortion in pregnancy, the threat of the trauma of birth, and the beginning of sexual desirability. In addition, the physical changes of menstruation are accompanied by significant and predictable emotional cycles sufficiently severe to alter the perception of her body as secure or stable.[14] Simultaneously joyful and fearful, the young adolescent girl must begin to evolve a feminine self-concept that accepts the functions and future responsibilities of her mature body; at the same time these physical changes are cues for alterations in the demands made upon her by the culture.[15] From the very beginning of adolescence girls, as potential heterosexual partners, begin to be punished for conspicuous competing achievement and to be rewarded for heterosexual success. Socialization in adolescence emphasizes the use of the cosmetic exterior of the self to lure men, to secure affection, to succeed in the competition of dating. At the same time the girl is warned not to succeed too much: conspicuous success in competitive dating threatens her friendships with girls. She learns in puberty that she is likely to be punished for significant competition in either of her important spheres.

Thus, for a long time, even the girls who are competitive, verbally agressive, and independent can feel normal, but with the onset of puberty girls are faced with their first major crises: they must come to terms with and find pleasure in their physical femininity and develop the proper psychological "femininity." Since they are still primarily cued to others for feelings of esteem, and largely defined by interpersonal relations, under the stress of their evolving incomplete feminine identity, most girls conform to the new socialization criteria. While girls characteristically achieved in grade school because of rewards for this "good" behavior from others (rather than for achievement's own sake), in adolescence the establishment of successful interpersonal relationships becomes the self-defining, most rewarding, achievement task.[16] When that change in priorities occurs—and it tends to be greatest in the later years of high school, and again in the later years of college—personal qualities, such as independence, aggression, and competitive achievement, that might threaten success in heterosexual relationships are largely given up.

While boys are often afraid of failing, girls are additionally afraid of succeeding.[17] The adolescent girl, her parents, her girl friends, and her boy friends perceive success, as measured by objective, visible achievement as antithetical to femininity. Some girls defer consciously, with tongue in cheek, but the majority, who were never significantly aggressive, active, or independent, internalize the norms and come to value themselves as they are desired by others. The only change from childhood is that the most important source of esteem is no longer the parents but the heterosexual partner.

The overwhelming majority of adolescent girls remain dependent upon others for feelings of affirmation. Unless in early life the girl exhibited the activity, aggression, or sexuality usually displayed by boys, and thereby experienced significant parental prohibitions, there is little likelihood that she will develop independent sources of esteem that refer back to herself. Instead, the loss of love remains for her the gravest source of injury to the self and, predictably, she will not gamble with that critical source of esteem.[18]

In the absence of independent and objective achievements, girls and women know their worth only from others' responses, know their identities only from their relationships as daughters, girl friends, wives, or mothers and, in a literal sense, personalize the world. When we ask female college students what would make them happy or unhappy, when would they consider themselves successful, both undergraduate and graduate students reply: "When I love and am loved; when I contribute to the welfare of others; when I have established a good family life and have happy, normal children; when I know I have created a good, rewarding stable relationship."[19] During adolescence as in childhood, females continue to esteem themselves insofar as they are esteemed by those with whom they have emotional relationships. For many women this never changes during their entire lifetime.

Girls are socialized to use more oblique forms of aggression than boys, such as the deft use of verbal injury or interpersonal rejection. Their aggression is largely directed toward people whose return anger will not be catastrophic to self-esteem—that is, other females. In their relationships with their fathers and later with their boy friends or husbands, girls do not threaten the important and frequently precarious heterosexual sources of love. Instead, aggression is more safely directed toward other women with whom they covertly compete for love. In relationships between men, aggression is overt and the power relationships are clear; female aggression is covert, the power relationships rarely admitted. With the denial and disguise of anger, a kind of dishonesty, a pervasive uncertainty, necessarily creeps into each of a woman's relationships, creating further anxiety and continued or increased efforts to secure affection.

The absence of objective success in work makes girls invest in, and be unendingly anxious about, their interpersonal worth. Women use interpersonal success as a route to self-esteem since that is how they have defined their major task. If they fail to establish a meaningful, rewarding, unambivalent love relationship, they remain cued into the response of others and suffer from a fragile or vulnerable sense of self. Those who are secure enough, who have evolved an identity and a feeling of worth in love relationships, may gamble and pursue atypical, nontraditonal, competitive, masculine achievements.

According to Erik Erikson, the most important task in adolescence is the establishment of a sense of identity. This is more difficult for girls than for boys. Because her sexuality is internal, inaccessible, and diffuse, because she feels ambivalent toward the functions of her mature reproductive system, because she is not punished for her impulsivity, because she is encouraged to remain dependent, a girl's search for her feminine identity is both complex and delayed. To add to her problems, she is aware both of the culture's preference for masculine achievements and of the fact that there is no longer a single certain route for achieving successful femininity. The problem grows even more complex, ever more subtle.

In these affluent times middle-class girls are apparently not punished simply for being girls. They are not prohibited from going to college, seeking school office, or achieving honors. Marriage and maternity are held out as wonderful goals, not necessarily as inhibiting dead ends. Although girls are rewarded for conformity, dependence, passivity, and competence, they are not clearly punished for the reverse. Until adolescence the idea of equal capacity, opportunity, and life style is held out to them. But sometime in adolescence the message becomes clear that one had better not do too well, that competition is aggressive and unfeminine, that deviating threatens the heterosexual relationship.[20] Masculinity is clearly defined and earned through individual competitive achievement. For the girl overt freedoms, combined with cultural ambiguity, result in an unclear image of femininity. As a result of vagueness about how to become feminine or even what is feminine, the girl responds to the single clear directive—she withdraws from what is clearly masculine. In high school and increasingly in college, girls cease clearly masculine pursuits and perceive the establishment of interpersonal goals as the most salient route to identity.[21] This results in a maximization of interpersonal skills, an interpersonal view of the world, a withdrawal from the development of independence, activity, ability, and competition, and the absence of a professional work commitment.

The personality qualities that evolve as characteristic of the sexes function so as to enhance the probability of succeeding in the traditional sex roles. Whether you are male or female, if you have traditionally masculine personality qualities—objectivity rather than subjectivity, aggression rather than passivity, the motive to achieve rather than a fear of success, courage rather than conformity, and professional commitment, ambition, and drive[22]— you are more likely to succeed in masculine roles. Socialization enhances initial tendencies; consequently, relatively few women have these qualities.

Thus, the essence of the problem of role conflict lies in the fact that up until now very few women have succeeded in traditionally masculine roles, not only because of disparagement and prejudice, but largely because women have not been fundamentally equipped and determined to succeed. Some women's tragedy is their desire to succeed in competitive achievement and their contempt for the traditional role for which they are better equipped.

It is probably not accidental, therefore, that women dominate professions that utilize skills of nurturance, empathy, and competence, where aggressiveness and competiveness are largely dysfunctional.[23] These professions, notably teaching, nursing, and secretarial work, are low in pay and status. The routes to occupational success for women are either atypical and hazardous or typical, safe, and low in the occupational hierarchy. (It is interesting to note that in the USSR where over 70 percent of the physicians are women, medicine is a low-status occupation.)

In spite of an egalitarian ideal in which the roles and contributions of the sexes are declared to be equal and complementary, both men and women esteem masculine qualities and achievements. Too many women evaluate their bodies, personality qualities, and roles as second-rate. When male criteria are the norms against which female performance, qualities, or goals are measured, then women are not equal. It is not only that the culture values masculine productivity more than feminine productivity.

The essence of the derogation lies in the evolution of the masculine as the yardstick against which everything is measured. Since the sexes are different, women are defined as not-men and that means not good, inferior. It is important to understand that women in this culture, as members of the culture, have internalized these self-destructive values.[24]

What we have described is ambivalence, not conflict. Conflict is the simultaneous desire to achieve a stable and rewarding heterosexual relationship (and the rest of the female's traditional responsibilities and satisfactions) and to participate fully in competitive achievement and succeed. Conflict, in this sense, is understandable as a vying between traditional and nontraditional roles, between affiliative and achievement motives. (Most women resolve this potential difficulty by defining affiliation as achievement.) Ambivalence is clearly seen in the simultaneous enjoyment of one's feminine identity, qualities, goals, and achievements and the perception of them as less important, meaningful, or satisfying than those of men. Girls envy boys; boys do not envy girls.

The culture generally rewards masculine endeavors and those males who succeed—who acquire money, power, and status, who enjoy an easy and free sexuality, who acquire and produce things, who achieve in competition, who produce, who innovate and create. By these criteria, women have not produced equally. The contributions that most women make in the enhancement and stabilization of relationships, their competence and self-discipline, their creation of life are less esteemed by men and women alike. It is disturbing to review the extent to which women perceive their responsibilities, goals, their very capacities, as inferior to males; it is similarly distressing to perceive how widespread this self-destructive self-concept is. Society values masculinity; when it is achieved it is rewarded. Society does not value femininity as highly; when it is achieved it is not as highly rewarded.

Today we have a peculiar situation in which sex-role stereotypes persist and are internalized by adults and children, yet the labor force includes thirty-one million working women and the college population is almost half women.[25] The stereotype persists because there is always cultural lag, because few women achieve markedly responsible or powerful positions, and because the overwhelming majority of working women preceive themselves as working in order to benefit the family.[26] In general, working women do not see work as an extension of egocentric interests or as the fulfillment of achievement ambitions, but as another place in which more traditional motives are gratified.

Perhaps the percentage of the female population who have had at least some college and who have achieved and been rewarded in the educational system faces the most difficult problems. Some part of this population has evolved—normally and not as a compensatory function—self-concepts and motives that take for granted the value of marriage and maternity, but also include individuality, creativity, independence, and successful competitive achievement. These characteristics become criteria by which the excellence of the self is measured. It is obvious that these characteristics are not highly functional within the traditional role, and moreover, cannot truly be achieved within the traditional female role. There would be no conflict if competitive achievement were the only aspect of these women's self-concept, but it is not. Characteristically, normal girls simultaneously put priority upon successful heterosexual relationships, which lead to the establishment of the nuclear family and traditional responsibilities.[28] Most girls effect a compromise, recognizing the hierarchy of their motivations and the appropriateness of their heterosexual desires. They tend to marry, work for a few years, and then start having babies. Inexperienced and unprepared, they tell themselves that the traditional role is creative and fulfilling. But creativity and fulfillment are hard to distinguish under the unending and repetitive responsibilities of diapers, dishes, and dusting. They tell themselves that when the children enter school they will reenter the labor force or the university. For these women, who have internalized the unequal evaluation of roles, who have developed needs to achieve, who have been rewarded because of their achievements, the traditional role is inadequate because it cannot gratify those nonnurturant, nonsupportive, nondependent, nonpassive aspects of the self.

Very few young women understand the very real limits upon achieving imposed by maternity, because they traditionally have had little experience with traditional role responsibilities before they marry. Typically, girls do not ask why there are so few female role models around who succeed in work while they have young children. While

children are a real achievement, a source of joy and fulfillment, they are also time-consuming and energy-deplet-
ing, a major source of responsibility and anxiety. In
today's child-centered milieu, with the decline of the
extended family and the dearth of adequate child-care
facilities, the responsibility for childrearing falls directly
on the mother alone.

Success in the traditional tasks is the usual means by
which girls achieve feelings of esteem about themselves,
confidence, and identity.[29] In general they have continued, even as adults, to esteem themselves as they are
valued by others; that source of esteem is interpersonal,
best earned within the noncompetitive, nonaggressive traditional role. Without independent, objective competitive
achievements, confidence is best secured within the traditional role—in spite of the priority given to masculine
achievements. Whether or not the woman is achievement-
oriented, her years of major childrearing responsibilities
result in a decline in old work skills, a loss of confidence
that she can work, a fear of failing within a competitive
milieu that she has left. In other words, not only have
specific techniques been lost or new data become unfamiliar, withdrawal from a competitive-achievement situation
for a significant length of time creates the conviction that
she is not able.

The very characteristics that make a woman most successful in family roles—the capacity to take pleasure in
family-centered, repetitive activities, to sustain and support members of the family rather than pursuing her own
goals, to enhance relationships through boundaryless empathy—these are all antithetical to success in the bounded,
manipulative, competitive, rational, and egocentric world
of work.[30] Because they are not highly motivated and
because they are uncertain about what is normal or desirable, many women do not work. Even those who do
continue to feel psychologically responsible for the maintenance of the family and are unwilling to jeopardize
family relationships. Most work at jobs that contribute to
family vacations, college fees, or the general family budget.[31] Even women who pursue a career or profession,
rather than merely holding a meaningless job, assume the
responsibility for two major, demanding roles. Rather than
make this commitment, many women professionalize their
voluntary or club activities, bringing qualities of aggres-

sion, competitiveness, and organizing skills to these "safer" activities.

Women tend not to participate in roles, or seek goals that threaten their important affiliative relationships because in those relationships they find most of their feelings of esteem and identity. This perpetuates psychological dependency which may be functional in the relationships but injurious to the self-concept of those who have internalized the values of the culture. Undeniably, it is destructive to feelings of esteem to know that you are capable and to be aware that you are not utilizing much of your potential.[32] The question of whether nontraditional success jeopardizes feelings of femininity has not yet been answered. Most women today would not be willing to achieve a greater success than their husbands. In this tradition-bound, sex-stereotyped culture, even though millions of women are employed, old values are internalized and serve as criteria for self-evaluation.

Neither men nor women entering marriage expect the sexes to share equally in privileges and responsibilities. Very few couples could honestly accept the wife's having the major economic responsibility for the family while the husband deferred to the demands of her work. Few individuals could reverse roles without feeling that he is not "masculine," and she is not "feminine."[33] Masculinity and femininity are aspects of the self that are clearly tied to roles—which role, how typical or deviant, how well accomplished, the extent of the commitment.

Yet a new reality is emerging today, for this is an era of changing norms. Although the unidimensional stereotype still persists and remains partially viable, it is also simplistic and inaccurate. Both men and women are rejecting the old role allocations which are exaggerated and costly because they push men and women into limited slots solely on the basis of sex. But an era of change results in new uncertainties and the need to evolve new clear criteria of masculinity and femininity, which can be earned and can offer feelings of self-esteem to both sexes.

The socialization model is no longer clear; in its pure form it exists primarily in media, less in life. Since almost half of American women work, the percentage rising with the rising level of education, it is clear that, at least for educated middle-class women, the simplistic stereotype is no longer valid. Similarly we find that more men are rejecting success as the sole source of esteem or masculinity. The male turning toward his family reflects his need not to be bound or limited by a unidimensional role model. For both sexes this is a period of change in which both old and new values coexist, though the visible norms derive from the old model. Today's college students seem to be more aware than the generation that preceded them of the consequences of role choice; they seem to be evolving a goal in which men are more nurturant than they were, while females are freer to participate professionally without endangering the male's esteem.

Both the work and the housewife roles are romanticized, since romanticism is enhanced when reality does not intrude. Women glorify work when and because they do not participate in it. Role conflict for women is largely a feeling of having been arbitrarily shut out from where the action is—a reaction to a romanticized concept of work and a reaction against the reality of the repetitive world of child care. Frustration is freely available to today's woman: if she participates fully in some professional capacity she runs the risk of being atypical and nonfeminine. If she does not achieve the traditional role she is likely to feel unfulfilled as a person, as a woman. If she undertakes both roles, she is likely to be uncertain about whether she is doing either very well. If she undertakes only the traditional role she is likely to feel frustrated as an able individual. Most difficult of all, the norms of what is acceptable, desirable, or preferable are no longer clear. As a result, it is more difficult to achieve a feminine (or masculine) identity, to achieve self-esteem because one is not certain when one has succeeded. When norms are no longer clear, then not only the "masculine" achieving woman but also the nonworking traditionally "feminine" woman can feel anxious about her normalcy, her fulfillment. Many women try to cope with their anxiety by exaggerating, by conforming to stereotyped role images. When one is anxious or uncertain about one's femininity, a viable technique for quelling those anxious feelings is an exaggerated conformity, a larger-than-life commitment to *Kinder, Küche, Kirche.* In this way a woman creates images, sending out clarified and exaggerated cues to others. Thus, the message is clear and she can be more certain that the feedback will assure her of her femininity.

It is easy to be aware of the discrepancy between the stereotyped norm and the reality. People are not simple. Whenever one sees a total investment or role adoption in its stereotyped, unidimensional form, one suspects a flight from uncertainty about masculinity or femininity. During a period of transition one can expect to see increasing numbers of women quelling anxiety by fleeing into a unidimensional, stereotyped femininity. As new norms gain clarity and force, more flexible roles, personalities, and behaviors will evolve. Role freedom is a burden when choice is available but criteria are unclear; under these circumstances it is very difficult to know whether one has achieved womanhood or has dangerously jeopardized it.

NOTES

1. J. Silverman, "Attentional Styles and the Study of Sex Differences," in D. Mostofsky, ed., *Attention: Contemporary Studies and Analysis* (New York: Appleton-Century-Crofts, in press): H. A. Witkin et al., *Personality through Perception: An Experimental and Clinical Study* (New York: Harper, 1954); J. Kagan, "Acquisition and Significance of Sex Typing and Sex Role Identity," in M. L. Hoffman and L. W. Hoffman, eds., *Review of Child Development Research* (New York: Russell Sage Foundation, 1964), 1:137-167; L. M. Terman and L. E. Tyler, "Psychological Sex Differences," in L. Carmichael, ed., *A Manual of Child Psychology,* 2nd ed. (New York: John Wiley, 1954), ch. 19; E. Douvan and J. Adelson, *The Adolescent Experience* (New York: John Wiley, 1966).

2. Silverman, *op. cit.,* Terman and Tyler, *op. cit.;* R. Q. Bell and N. S. Costello, "Three Tests for Sex Differences in Tactile Sensitivity in the New Born," *Biologia Neonatorum* 7 (1964): 335-347; R. Q. Bell and J. F. Darling, "The Prone Head Reaction in the Human Neonate: Relation with Sex and Tactile Sensitivity," *Child Development* 36 (1965):943-949; S. M. Garn, "Roentgenogrammetric Determinants of Body Composition," *Human Biology* 29 (1957): 337-353; J. Kagan and M. Lewis, "Studies of Attention in the Human Infant," *Merrill-Palmer Quarterly* 2 (1965): 95-127; M. Lewis, J. Kagan, and J. Kalafat, "Patterns of Fixation in the Young Infant," *Child Development* 37 (1966): 331-341; L. P. Lipsitt and N. Levy, "Electrotactual Threshold in the Human Neonate," *Child Development* 30 (1959): 547-554.

3. Kagan and Lewis, *op. cit.;* Lewis, Kagan, and Kalafat, *op. cit.* In spite of this initial advantage which might be thought to lead, logically and inevitably to high-achievement investment, girls' socialization ends without realization of this early promise. J. Veroff, "Social Comparison and the Development of Achievement Motivation," in C. Smith, ed., *Achievement Related Motives in Children* (New York: Russell-Sage Foundation, 1969); pp. 46-101, suggests that the period of optimal generalization of the achievement motive is early, about the age of four or five. At this time girls are better at the truly critical tasks of speaking, comprehending, and remembering. But these ac-

complishments are taken for granted by children, who strive rather to tie shoelaces, ride bicycles, climb trees, and jump rope—all physical accomplishments. In other words, at the time when the motive for achievement is learned and generalized, the children themselves define physical tasks as important. Girls' greater cognitive and verbal skills do not, therefore, contribute to the development of a higher achievement motivation.

4. E. Maccoby, ed., *The Development of Sex Differences* (Stanford: Stanford University Press, 1966).
5. J. M. Bardwick, *The Psychology of Women* (New York: Harper & Row, 1971).
6. Helene Deutsch, *Psychology of Women* (New York: Grune & Stratton, 1944), vol. 1: K. Horney, "On the Genesis of the Castration Complex in Women," *International Journal of Psychoanalysis* 5 (1924): 50-65.
7. Douvan and Adelson, *op. cit.*
8. N. Bayley, "Consistency of Maternal and Child Behaviors in the Berkeley Growth Study," *Vita Humana* 7 (1964): 73-95; M. P. Honzik and J. W. MacFarlane, "Prediction of Behavior and Personality from 21 Months to 30 Years," unpublished manuscript, 1963; J. Kagan and H. A. Moss, *Birth to Maturity* (New York: John Wiley, 1962); E. S. Schaefer and N. Bayley, "Maternal Behavior, Child Behavior, and Inter-correlations from Infancy through Adolescence," *Monograph of the Society for Research on Child Development* 28 (1963), serial no. 87.
9. Kagan and Moss, *op. cit.*
10. H. S. Becker, "Social Class Variations in One Teacher-Pupil Relationship," *Journal of Educational Sociology* 25 (1952): 451-465.
11. Maccoby, *op. cit.*
12. M. S. Horner, "Fail: Bright Women," *Psychology Today* 3 (November 1969): 36.
13. Bardwick, *op. cit.*; E. Douvan, "New Sources of Conflict at Adolescence and Early Adulthood," in Judith M. Bardwick et al, *Feminine Personality and Conflict* (Belmont, Calif.: Brooks/Cole, in press).
14. M. E. Ivey and J. M. Bardwick, "Patterns of Affective Fluctuation in the Menstrual Cycle," *Psychosomatic Medicine* 30 (1968): 336-345.
15. Douvan, *op. cit.*
16. J. G. Coleman, *The Adolescent Society* (New York: Free Press, 1961).
17. Horner, *op. cit.*
18. Deutsch, *op. cit.*; Douvan and Adelson, *op. cit.*
19. J. Bardwick and J. Zweben, "A Predictive Study of Psychological and Psychosomatic Changes Associated with Oral Contraceptives," mimeograph, 1970.
20. M. Komarovsky, *Women in the Modern World* (Boston: Little Brown, 1953).
21. *Ibid.*; R. Goldsen, M. Rosenberg, R. Williams, E. A. Suchman, *What College Students Think* (Princeton, N.J.: Van Nostrand, 1961); Coleman, *op. cit.*; N. Sanford, *The American College* (New York: John Wiley, 1962).
22. T. Parsons, "Age and Sex in the Social Structure of the United States," *American Sociological Review* 7 (1942): 604-616.
23. M. Mead, *Male and Female* (New York: William Morrow, 1949).

24. Bardwick, *op. cit.;* Mead, *op. cit.*

25. R. E. Hartley, "Children's Concept of Male and Female Roles," *Merrill-Palmer Quarterly* 6 (1960): 153-163.

26. F. I. Nye and L. W. Hoffman, *The Employed Mother in America* (Chicago: Rand-McNally, 1963).

27. R. Baruch, "The Achievement Motive in Women: Implications for Career Development," *Journal of Personality and Social Psychology* 5 (1967): 260-267.

28. Bardwick, *op. cit.*

29. Douvan and Adelson, *op. cit.*

30. D. L. Gutmann, "Women and Their Conception of Ego Strength," *Merrill-Palmer Quarterly* 11 (1965): 229-240.

31. Nye and Hoffman, *op. cit.*

32. G. Gurin, J. Veroff, and S. Feld, *Americans View Their Mental Health* (New York: Basic Books, 1960).

33. D. J. Bem and S. L. Bem, "Training the Woman to Know Her Place," based on a lecture delivered at Carnegie Institute of Technology, October 21, 1966, revised 1967.

10

NATURAL LAW LANGUAGE AND WOMEN

Christine Pierce

"Nature" or "human nature" must be among the most enigmatic concepts ever used. Often, when the "natural" is invoked, we are left in the dark as to whether it is meant as an explanation, a recommendation, a claim for determinism, or simply a desperate appeal, as if the "natural" were some sort of metaphysical glue that could hold our claims or values together.

Sometimes people arguing both for and against a thing will in each case call it "natural." There are, however, certain reasonably standardized uses such that one can anticipate with some accuracy what will be called "natural." On the whole, for example, natural law language is almost invariably used against women although occasionally an Ashley Montagu appears upon the scene to talk about the "natural" superiority of women. It is a familiar ploy to insist that ones own values, *commonly thought to be unnatural*, are really the natural ones (polygamy is natural, homosexuality is natural). This, we contend, yields nothing except calling more and more things "natural," and hence finding such appeals to be a vague if not vacuous support for our views. We could achieve a refreshing advance in clarity by trading in our uses of "natural" for equivalent phrases so that our value choices and explanatory claims would at least be made explicit.

For centuries people have appealed to the "natural" to

back up their moral and social recommendations. The ordinary uses of the term which everyone hears from time to time demonstrate that such efforts are still very much with us. We are told, for example, that suicide, artificial means of birth control, and sexual deviation are wrong because they are unnatural. Now and then the argument takes a positive form; because monogamy is natural, it is the only proper form of marriage. This particular belief, that only one to one is natural in intimate relationships, lends plausibility to a legal excuse appealed to in cases of passion shooting: that jealousy (at least on the part of men) is natural. Arguments against women's rights to equality often cite the "proper sphere" and the "nature" of women, which supposedly renders them inherently inferior, thus making any just empirical test unnecessary.

Our major intent is to examine the language of "proper sphere," role, or function, showing its relationship to the language of natural law and pointing out the conspicuous absence of any notion of liberty in the discussions of those who use this type of argument against women. As a preface to these specific efforts, however, it is important to stress how difficult it is for anyone in any social or moral context to say what they mean by "natural" and why it recommends itself as good. Two distinct steps are involved here: defining what is meant by "natural" and arguing that what is natural is good. The difficulty created by lumping these two problems together as if they were one can be clearly seen in the case of authors who agree on what the natural is, but disagree on whether the natural is good or bad. Nietzsche argues that since nature or life is essentially exploitation and conquest, this somehow endorses the concept of the "superman" and discredits Christianity, which denies human "instincts." Schopenhauer, on the other hand, with the same empirical evidence at his disposal concludes exactly the opposite; such considerations as "life preys on life" and "man oscillates between desire and boredom" do not encourage ambition, but show the pointlessness of life.

It is often assumed that the word "natural" has an automatic "plus" value tag which does not have to be argued for on independent grounds. In other words, it is taken for granted that if one persuades us that " 'X' is natural," he has also persuaded us that " 'X' is good." The Vatican's position on birth control reflects this: *Humanae Vitae* assumes that it is sufficient to point out that artificial means of birth control interrupt the natural order of things. The most significant question of all, "Why is 'natural order' a good thing?" is never asked. Apparently, what the "natural order" means in this case is that which will happen if untouched by human invention. This definition, however, yields absurd consequences if we try to use it as a prescription. If "natural order" is a good thing, and we must assume it is because we are told not to interrupt it, why isn't shaving a moral issue? Clearly, it is natural for hair to grow on a man's face, and shaving introduces an artificial means to disrupt the natural order of things.

Even if we have guessed wrong on what "natural" means in this case, it is clear that regardless of the case, we cannot discuss whether the natural is good until we are able to state what we mean by the term. Thus far, we have seen that although "untouched by human invention" is one meaning of "natural," it does not seem to be the key to why we think the natural is good. Two other possible meanings of the term "natural" are particularly interesting, not only because of their relevance to arguments for women's inequality, but because both definitions are currently in use and yet clearly incompatible. Human nature is construed to be either what man has in common with the rest of the animal world or what distinguishes man from the rest of the animal world.

One of the most amusing efforts to make the former use work against women is the following comment by Mary Hemingway: "Equality, what does it mean? What's the use for it? I've said it before and I'll repeat: Women are second-class citizens and not only biologically. A female's first duty is to bear children and rear them. With the exception of a few fresh water fish, most animals follow this basic rule."[1] Unfortunately, the most obvious consequence of Hemingway's argument is that a few fresh water fish are immoral! What she meant to say, however, was that human duties somehow can be determined by observing animal behavior. *Prima facie,* it seems odd to claim that the meaningfulness of moral terminology could be derived from a realm to which moral vocabulary does not apply. We must insist that people who talk this way be able to make sense of it. What does it mean, for example, to say that nature intends for us to do certain things? We know what it means to say that "I intend to pack my suitcase," but what sense can it make to say that nature intends for us to do one thing rather than another? The above use of "natural" reduces to saying "this is what most animals do." To the extent that this is the meaning of the term, it will be hard to get a notion of value out of it. The fact that something happens a lot does not argue for or against it.

Interchanging words like "normal" and "natural" illustrates prejudice for the statistically prevalent as opposed to the unusual, the exception. The unusual qua unusual, however, cannot be ruled out as bad; it can be alternatively described as "deviant" or "original," depending on whether or not we like it. Nothing prevents describing the so-called sexual deviant as a sexual original except most people's inability to tolerate any unusual behavior in this area; hence, they use statistical concepts with bad connotations (unnatural, abnormal) to discuss it, instead of those with good connotations (original, exceptional).

The second meaning of "natural," that which distinguishes man from the rest of the (animal) world, reaches back to Plato. For Plato, to state the nature of any given class of things was to state the features of that class which distinguished it from all other classes of things. Man's nature or essence is that which is *essentially* his. Although Plato did not claim that men and women have different natures, but rather referred to human beings as the class with the capacity to reason, his use of "natural" lends itself to the defining of classes of things according to function or role that is frequently used to restrict women. In order to understand how similar our way of talking and explaining things is to the Platonic view, it is first necessary to grasp how the latter has been historically conceived. An increased awareness of the natural law basis of the language of function should help us to be more critical of the language we take for granted, and to see what kinds of philosophical commitment we perhaps unwittingly make.

The Greek method of explanation for questions of the sort, "What is the nature of 'X'?" was teleological; explanations were given in terms of function, role, end, or purpose, as opposed to mechanistic explanations. The difference between these explanations can easily be illustrated by comparing their answers to a simple question such as "What is a lawnmower?" A teleologist will explain: a lawnmower is something that is used to cut grass; a mechanist will explain about pulleys, plugs, and metal "teeth." Manufactured items lend themselves to the former type of explanation because hopefully we have in mind what the function of something is going to be before we start making any of it. Such explanation, however, is not so easily forthcoming for questions like, "What is the nature of man?" However, Plato was interested in this type of question; he wanted to explain the "natural" world. In this realm of nonmanufactured items, functions and roles are discovered, not created.

Although Plato thought he could answer the question concerning the nature of man, for the moment what concerns us is not the content of his answer, but the additional philosophical mileage we can expect from success in providing this type of answer. To be able to say what a thing is in terms of its function or purpose is simultaneously to set up standards for its evaluation. Once we can state the function of any "X," we can say what a good "X" is, or more precisely, we can say that "X" is good to the extent that it fulfills its function. We still have this use of "good" in English; we say, for example, that a good lawnmower is one that cuts grass well, that is, one that fulfills its function.

Plato's effort to apply this teleological framework to man consists of his functional analysis of the soul as reason, spirit, and desire. These are analogous to functioning units in the state, namely, philosopher-kings, soldiers, and artisans. Even as the function of the philosopher-king is to rule the state, implicit in the notion of reason as a function is the ability to rule, govern, or control the rest of the soul or personality. When anything does its work well, we call it virtuous or excellent. In this case, when reason as well as every other functioning unit is working well and working together, we have a harmony or an order of soul to which Plato gives the name of the overarching virtue, justice. Reason, then, is the ordering principle; a good man is one who has an ordered soul, whose personality is controlled by reason.

It is usually granted that in citing the function or role of something, we are setting certain standards which it must measure up to in order to be called good. If we are suspicious of teleology, the quarrel is not with the fact that a use of "good" is generated by defining things in terms of function; the quarrel concerns what sort of "good" we are talking about. Are the standards referred to in maintaining that a good "X" is one that functions well moral standards or simply standards of efficiency? They are at least the latter; the worry is they are perhaps only that. When we say a good lawnmower is one that cuts grass well, we clearly mean good in the sense of efficient or effective. If, to take another example, we define poison in terms of its function, good poison is that which does an effective, that is, quick and fatal, job. The good referred to is clearly not moral good. However, this does not suggest that it never could be; we are not saying that a teleological use of good, because it is an instrumental use, can never be a moral one.

There may be cases where the word "good" serves both functions. For example, when Lon Fuller, a Professor of Jurisprudence at Harvard Law School, defines good law as laws that are clear, public, consistent, he is claiming that such standards are necessary for moral, that is fair, laws as well as effective ones. Laws that are unclear, secret, and inconsistent are not only ineffective, but unjust. Although some jurisprudential scholars have argued against Fuller by maintaining that an instrumental use of good cannot be a moral use, there seems to be no a priori reason why a word cannot function simultaneously in more than one way. Granting this, the criticism of teleology is not as dramatic as some would have it. We cannot scrap Plato's morality merely because we claim to have discovered that the teleological use of good is not a moral use but simply means that things are efficient. However, we must always be on guard to discover from context which use is intended since we can no longer assume that fulfilling a function or role is necessarily good in any moral sense.

For example, even if it is accepted that a good woman is one who fulfills her role, it may well be that "good" means nothing more than contributing to efficiency. Morton Hunt, in the May, 1970, issue of *Playboy*, argues against husband and wife sharing equally in all tasks (career and home) on the grounds that "when there is no specialization of function, there is inefficient performance. . . ."[2] Although specialization is supposedly one essential aspect of all successful human groups (the other being a system of leadership), it is quite conceivable that a group of two (as opposed to a large corporation) might not prize efficiency as its highest value.

Much depends upon what is meant by "success." Liberty or freedom of role choice may not be very "successful" if success is measured in terms of efficiency. Freedom has never been known for its efficiency; it is always getting in the way of the smooth operations of orderly systems. The conflict between freedom and efficiency can be illustrated by marriage, but is hardly confined to it. It may be inefficient for any one person (married, single, or living in a commune) to teach in a university, write articles, buy groceries, do karate, and demonstrate for political rights, but if a choice must be made between the freedom to do all these things and efficiency, the choice should at least be portrayed as a legitimate one.

Hunt argues not only that specific roles contribute to efficiency, but that they are (as opposed to unisex) attractive. "It feels good, and is productive of well-being, for man and woman to look different, smell different, act somewhat different."[3] He quotes Dr. Benjamin Spock to the effect that the sexes are "more valuable and more pleasing" to one another if they have "specialized traits and . . . roles to play for each other's benefit—gifts of function, so to speak, that they can give to each other."[4] We cannot argue against the claim that specialization of function or role yields efficiency. We can, however, question the importance of efficiency; we can also ask, as we shall see later, efficient for whom? We cannot deny that many men and women find complementarity of role attractive. Some people even find inferiority attractive. Note once again the remarks of Mary Hemingway: "Equality! I didn't want to be Ernest's equal. I wanted him to be the master, to be the stronger and cleverer than I, to remember constantly how big he was and how small I was."[5] However, arguing that specific roles are efficient and attractive does not in and of itself determine who is to do what. Telling us in advance what woman's gift of function is going to be makes Hunt's argument not only interesting, but typical of anti-women's liberation arguments that are couched in the language of role.

The *essential* content of woman's role is probably best characterized by the concept of "support"—a concept that usually does not get, but certainly deserves, much analysis. What do people mean by the "supportive role"? Why do they think it belongs to women? Hunt, after characterizing the roles of husband and wife as analogous to those of President and Speaker of the House respectively, concedes that "although the man is the head, he owes much to his wife's managerial support."[6] To prove the value of support, he appeals to a remark once made by Senator Maurine Neuberger that her greatest single need as a

senator was for a good "wife." Neuberger's comment
certainly proves that the supportive role aids efficiency; it
is undeniably easier to be a senator if one has someone to
shake hands, smile with you on campaign posters, repeat
your ideas to groups you haven't time for, and answer
your dinner invitations. That playing the supportive role
aids efficiency cannot be questioned; however, the question
remains efficient for whom? It must be remembered that
efficiency only requires that *someone* play the supportive
role, belong to the maintenance class, devote their lives
psychologically and physically to making sure that other
people get done whatever they want done. As long as
women as a class play supportive roles, they contribute to
the efficiency of a power structure that keeps freedom of
role choice for itself.

For Hunt, women's role is to some extent "naturally
based" since he feels that women are neurologically more
sensitive to infants than men and, on that account, should
be concerned with child care for "a while" after birth.
Even if one accepts this (and he does not offer much
evidence except an interesting study showing this to be the
case for virgin female rats), the leap from here to a
"supportive" role, including all the ramifications implicit in
Neuberger's comment, is not obvious. How does it follow
from this "sensitivity" that the role of men should be
characterized as "President" and "head"?

Carried to the logical extreme, slaves played a very
important supportive role for their masters; from the
master's point of view, society was the more efficient and
hence more desirable for it. At the other extreme, playing
the supportive role can mean as little as the truism that
everyone likes to be fussed over. What Hunt has in mind
is something between the two, something evidently closer
to the former, however, since he points to the current
system as admittedly unfair, but more workable and satisfying than any other alternatives. Part of what he means
by "supportive" can be gleaned from the fact that for the
most part he is thinking in terms of cases involving children (although not all of his illustrations bear this out—
for example, Neuberger). His perspective, then, centers
around the social alternatives of the married woman. They
are: the state may take care of the children, hired help
may take care of the children, or we can introduce some
notion of equality between men and women with regard

to whatever tasks confront them, but this, as we have seen, will be inefficient.

Being an essentially pragmatic society, we often buy without question the latter half of the teleological framework: that good things are those that function well; we fail to scrutinize what we mean by "good." Like Plato, we have a propensity to define the natures of things in terms of function, purpose, or role. In defining women as childbearers, we have corrupted the Platonic enterprise insofar as reproduction is not a function peculiar to human beings; however, we have in our own way fulfilled the Platonic requirement by citing a natural function that is distinctive of the "class" we have in mind.

We have overlooked, however, that possession of a function, even a natural one, does not entail its constant use. In speaking of the distinctive end of man, Plato referred to the possession, not the exercise, of reason. The fact that men or women may have made little use of their distinctive capacity in no way defeats Plato's definition of the natural. Nor does having a function, even a natural one, entail that those having it *ought* to use it. As we have seen, to use "X" when "X" is defined as functional is to have a good "X" in some sense of the word. We can explain what poison is by citing its function, but it does not necessarily follow that it ought (in any moral sense) to function. Having children is also a natural function; whether it is good to make use of this function is a separate issue. Given our current population problems, we might well decide that childbearing is not good in either the moral or efficient use of that word.

One might, at this point, legitimately object that the well-being of human beings is more complicated than that of lawnmowers (and poisons). If a lawnmower does not function well or is never used to cut grass, the lawnmower is not worse off for it. However, one might say, indeed Freudian conservatives have said, that the human being's biological potential is so integrated that when it is not realized, some kind of "maladjustment" or "unhappiness" results. Of course, some maintain that no such frustration ensues; obviously, to the extent that this is correct, there is no problem, and, for example, people can decide whether or not to have children on the basis of values already discussed (efficiency, morality) since their "happiness" or "adjustment" is not at stake.

However, if we accept the Freudian conservatives'

view, we must apply it consistently. Freudians have also taught us that suppression of sexual and aggressive impulses was necessary for the development of civilization. Even though suppression may result in frustration, we are told that in some cases this is the price that must be paid to purchase other goals. It is certainly not a new observation that one pays in some way for everything that one gets. Certainly, modern man in general has paid in increased anxiety, frustration, and, most probably, neurosis for his advanced technological society. Freudians must allow the same perspective on the question of childbearing as on the questions of sexuality and aggressiveness. In the latter case, we realize that some sort of suppression, probably resulting in some unhappiness, is required for civilization and/or technology. Some women's deliberate suppression of their biological potential should be regarded as an enhancement of the civilized and rational aspects of experience. If there is some biological or psychological frustration involved in the suppression of biological potential, only the individual woman should decide how she wishes to balance her desire for biological "completion" and her desire to experience the world as an independent human being. To recognize the possibility of such unhappiness is not to condone social arrangements which intensify the either/or character of this choice, but to elucidate once again the importance of liberty, and to complicate values (liberty, morality, efficiency) by which we decide which units capable of functioning ought to function.

In the conclusion of his article, Hunt once more calls upon natural law, assuring us that we need not fear the eradication of all sex-role differences because "nothing as joyless and contrary to our instincts is likely to become the pattern of the majority."[7] The language of "instinct," a somewhat modern way to refer to those things that we want to call "natural," is usually attached to some variation of philosophical determinism. "Instincts" are not considered to be matters of value choice, but a small class of desires that are somehow given. Some uses of "natural" lose their force without this built-in determinism; for example, excusing an action on the grounds that one was jealous, and "jealousy is only natural," will work only if the people listening accept the reasoning, "I couldn't help myself." If we do not buy the determinism, we do not buy the excuse.

If we really believe these instincts to exist, we can guarantee much more than that their obliteration will not become "the pattern of the majority." As John Stuart Mill argued a hundred years ago in *The Subjection of Women*, if the "proper sphere" of women is naturally determined, there will be no need for social and legal coercion to insure that women stay in that sphere. We need not fear that women will do what they cannot do. If natural inclination means determined inclination, recommendations are automatically out of place. Strictly speaking, if something is determined, it *must* happen; there is no point in recommending that people desire what they must desire anyway. If jealousy, heterosexuality, motherhood, and supportive sex roles are not value choices, but instincts, in the sense that we all (not quite all, as some of the above are for women, some for men, some for both) have them and cannot help it, it is unnecessary to urge people to aspire to them. Insofar as we recommend any of them, we recognize them to be at least to some extent, or for some people, items of choice. Probably none of us would accept a complete determinism; carried to its logical extreme, it is self-defeating. If no one can in any sense help being what they are, then the person telling us this truth cannot help telling us this, nor can he resist his impulse to believe in determinism.

The extent to which a theory of instincts involves belief in some form of determinism is an intricate philosophical problem. To deal with it adequately would require a full-scale analysis of the sense of talking about "unconscious motivation." Although we cannot accomplish that here, we can raise some important questions about the ordinary meanings of "instinct" that are used against women.

Freud, in his *New Introductory Lectures on Psycho-Analysis*, defined the unconscious, ". . . we call a psychical process unconscious whose existence we are obliged to assume—for some such reason as that we infer it from its effects—but of which we know nothing."[8] In other words, the unconscious is not a thing, not some kind of container filled with desires that "drive" us to do this or that, but rather an explanatory device, not itself empirically evident, but *needed* to explain certain behavior which is. "Needed," that is, in the sense that there are certain "effects" that defy explanation, that simply cannot be accounted for unless we posit an unconscious. For example, if people say they desire one thing, but act as if they desired the contrary, and we know they are not lying, we may be tempted to say that they are somehow unaware of what their "real" motivation is.

If Susan says she wants a career more than anything in the world, but she does nothing all day except stay home and put on make-up, we are puzzled and desire an explanation. If she is not lying or frivolous, we still lack an explanation; anything, including childhood and gene structure, is fair game as far as possible explanations go. But if Leslie has spent eight years preparing for a career and assures a prospective employer that she is serious about it, she does not deserve as an answer: "I would like to believe you, my dear, but all women really desire to devote their lives to men and children . . ." Such a remark is unwarranted because there are no "effects" in this case that need to be explained. (Of course, external evidences of competence, such as Ph.D.'s and M.D.'s do help when one wants to be taken seriously. The undergraduate argument, "she only went to college to find a husband," does not seem so plausible when applied to Ph.D's. There simply has to be an easier way to get a husband!)

Lying, frivolity, insufficient awareness of one's personality and values (whether we explain these in terms of an unconscious or not) are all human problems; all serve as "explanations" of certain human behavior. If employers cannot afford any of these qualities in their employees, there are surely strategic moves open to them (for example, contracts) to cut their risk. Such measures should be applied to men and women alike without any philosophical pronouncements on "what all women really want" that are empirically false, psychologically naive, intolerant of human differences and human liberty, and might even be un-Freudian.

Another contemporary effort to suggest a concept of the "natural" is Lionel Tiger's *Men in Groups,* which receives its impetus from an attempted combination of social science and biology. His thesis, insofar as it can be ascertained, is that a male biological propensity to bond with other males may account for male domination of the political-religious-business scene. This "genetically programmed behavioral propensity" became so programmed

by continual participation in hunting, which requires cooperation, aggression, and organizational ability, all characteristics of a bond.

A cursory look at the reviews of Tiger's book indicate
that the thesis is received as antifeminist; however, it is
not clear from the text whether such an assessment is
correct or not. In his review, Melvin Maddocks points to
what he calls Tiger's "ultimate shocker," namely that
"ancient occupational differences between males and females have produced 'brain-process differences' which no
amount of militant feminism can change."[9] However,
even if we grant Tiger's thesis and agree that male political advantage accrues from a biological propensity, it does
not follow either that women cannot engage in politics, or
that they should not; it simply indicates that their struggle
for power will be more difficult.

Strategically speaking, men are clearly in "better
shape"; they have the advantages of power, confidence,
aggressiveness, all of which result from bonding. One
could say that through bonding (and also secret societies)
men "accidentally" hit on the strategy of dominance essential to maintaining political control. Perhaps staying home
to sweep the cave was a profound strategic error on the
part of women, but it was one which, according to Tiger
himself, can be corrected.

Tiger insists that his personal political bias is "toward a
rapid and meaningful expansion of women's participation
in and effect on politics."[10] But, he continues, "my
sociological work suggests the difficulty of achieving this
because more than just routine education and emancipation may be involved."[11] He further suggests that a
radical restructuring of political society may be necessary
before "what may be a deep predisposition can be overcome in the name of equity."[12] It is doubtful, however,
that anyone who has ever entertained the thought of
equality between the sexes would believe that anything
short of a major restructuring could realize this end.

It is understandable, however, that reviewers or anyone
else might interpret Tiger as antifeminist, for he also says
things like "during this study I have become increasingly
aware that it is very possible that certain actions I think
desirable are better done by all-male groups than by
heterosexual ones."[13] Unfortunately, this statement is
not followed by any specification of either the actions or
what is meant by "better." Nor does the statement's con-

text provide any clue; it appears in the introductory re-marks of a chapter on secret societies. Such a statement could be made into the "efficiency argument." If such an argument were constructed, we might agree that in pol-itics, efficiency, or the capacity to perform a task "bet-ter" than someone else, is more important than allowing people freedom to do whatever they want, even if they are inefficient.

Obviously, we do not know if high percentages of women in high-status positions would improve matters. Surely, however, Tiger cannot be saying that the male's propensity for bonding makes *him better* at political man-agement. If the contemporary political scene is the result of our allowing unchecked biological propensities to assert themselves, perhaps what is needed is a more cerebral approach, more distant from the "biological flow" of things. Perhaps women are needed to rescue men from being caught up in their anatomical destiny.

Although Tiger's recommendations are ambiguous, the absence of a hard determinism at least allows us to argue whether "natural" values are good values.

Our primary concern has been with whether references to the "natural" ever entail or support recommendations. Tiger's thesis, however, if adequately considered, would also have to be appraised for its explanatory power. Pre-sumably, at least part of the value of explanation for Tiger is ability to predict. After all, how can social science be real science unless it formulates general or "natural" laws from which we can predict and subsequently control behavior? A number of Tiger's claims include the word "prediction" as an essential feature of that claim. For example, "The logic of my argument then is males are prone to bond, male bonds are prone to aggress, there-fore, aggression is a predictable feature of human groups of males."[14] Other logical problems aside, the success of this prediction does not depend on explaining the cause of the proneness to bond, which could be either biological or cultural, but simply upon our establishing the fact of bonding. The questions, "Why do men bond?" "Why do men assume power?" are not being discussed as empirical questions, nor do the answers we are given yield predic-tions. (Perhaps this accounts for Tiger's perpetual tenta-tiveness in stating his conclusion.) It may be that men do assume power because of their history as hunters. One cannot discount the possibility; on the other hand, one cannot empirically verify it.

The nonempirical character of Tiger's thesis is most clearly seen in his approval of Golding. He sees Golding's *Lord of the Flies* as illustrative of the species-specific pattern of "coalition, aggression, violence, and the savor of blood." Although Golding suggests the above is inevitable, Tiger maintains that from the point of view of social reality this is obviously not the case. Golding, however, is exempt from criticism because his intention is not "the definition of sociological reality but the extrapolation from this reality of an absolute possibility of human life."[15] Apparently, an "absolute possibility" means that certain kinds of behavior (in this case, violence, aggression, and the like) are always possible. In other words, violence, for example, is not necessarily a part of social reality, but it somehow always exists "behind the scenes," a permanent natural theme which may manifest itself in many social variations.

We must ask how many natural themes or absolute possibilities there are. Is Tiger citing another one when he says, "The nature of man could be that he is constitutional not predatory. . . . Just as the boys can become savages, so can they become parliamentarians"?[16] If the urge to be a parliamentarian has a natural basis, and the urge away from social order is also natural, the "natural" has lost its explanatory power (either to predict or to say anything at all); it has become a vacuous "explanation." To say that men have a tendency with regard to social orders to construct them and to wreck them is to approach a level of generality too vague to be informative.

We have tried to show some of the muddles that language of the "natural" gets us into. Except in cases where the natural is defined in terms of purpose or function, it carries no automatic value tag. After finding out what a person means by "natural," we then have to decide on independent grounds whether what is meant is in any sense good. For example, why is it good to do what animals do, or to avoid invented devices which interrupt what ordinarily happens? Why is what ordinarily happens considered to be a good thing? What is so good about order? Teleological uses of "natural" automatically set up an evaluative context; knowing the function of "X" makes it possible for us to evaluate "X" on grounds of functioning well. But as we have seen, teleological uses have to be evaluated: a good bomb is one that goes off, but is a good bomb good?

There is no reason to assume that the problem of evaluation would change because some functional units are manmade and others are not. Many people, for example, argue that nature is good because God made it. This, of course, precipitates the old problem of evil. How can earthquakes and birth defects be good? The answer does not abandon the language of purpose, but rather tells us in Platonic fashion that all of "creation" functions for some good end; however, man is incapable of knowing this end or purpose. Indeed, part of what it means to have faith is to believe that all natural, that is, created, purposes (in humans or otherwise) are good purposes, and work together toward some larger purpose. Since man cannot know this larger end, there is no way that he can evaluate it. This, however, does not eliminate the problem of evaluation. It does not eliminate the question. "In what sense are things that function well good?" It simply tells us that there is no cognitive answer, or more precisely, that only the faithful, after they have been faithful in believing the acceptability of God's answer, will receive an answer. The position comes to this: because we believe in God, we should believe that nature is good in some good sense.

Theological positions, however, in no way exempt us from either defining what we mean by "natural" or appraising it. Indeed, even if the ultimate evaluation is said to be a matter of faith, the task that Thomas Aquinas referred to as natural or rational theology (in this case, the "calling off," so to speak, of the ends of things that are imprinted on the natures of things) is something that human beings must be prepared to perform without divine assistance. This task brings us right back to the beginning of our inquiry, namely, what in the world do people mean when they say that " 'X' is natural"?

NOTES

1. Mary Hemingway, Look, September 6, 1966, p. 66.
2. Morton Hunt, "Up against the Wall, Male Chauvinist Pig," Playboy, May 1970, p. 209.
3. Ibid., p. 207.
4. Ibid.
5. Hemingway, op. cit., p. 66.
6. Hunt, op. cit., p. 209.

7. *Ibid.*
8. Sigmund Freud, *New Introductory Lectures on Psycho-Analysis* (1933), reprinted in E. Kuykendall, *Philosophy in the Age of Crisis*, (New York: Harper & Row, 1970), p. 122. To philosophers the above sounds like the kind of move John Locke made when he posited the existence of material substance as an explanatory account for why collections of qualities regularly occur together. To the extent that the move is similar to Locke's, it is, of course, subject to the same types of criticisms.
9. Melvin Maddocks, *Christian Science Monitor*, July 10, 1969, p. 11.
10. Lionel Tiger, *Men in Groups* (New York: Random House, 1969), p. 103.
11. *Ibid.*
12. *Ibid.*, p. 112. The same point is reiterated in the following passage: ". . . I am proposing that 'human nature' is such that it is 'unnatural' for females to engage in defense, police, and by implication, high politics. For human females to do so requires explicit self-conscious provision of special facilities by a concerned, sensitive and willing community."
13. *Ibid.*, p. 162.
14. *Ibid.*, p. 241.
15. *Ibid.*, p. 207.
16. *Ibid.*

11

BEING AND DOING: A Cross-Cultural Examination of the Socialization of Males and Females

Nancy Chodorow

There are two crucial issues that people concerned about the liberation of women and men from rigid and limiting sex roles must consider. One is whether there is any basis to the claim that there are biologically derived (and therefore inescapable) psychological or personality characteristics which universally differentiate men and women. The other is to understand why it is that in almost every society women are physically, politically, and/or economically dominated by men and are thought to be (and think themselves to be) inferior to men. This essay refutes the claim for universal and necessary differentiation, and provides an explanation based on a comparison of cultures and socialization practices to account for such differences where and when they occur. It then examines the development of identity in males and females and shows how this development, and in particular the socialization and development of males, leads to and perpetuates the devaluation and oppression of women.

CROSS-CULTURAL RESEARCH

Cultural Personality

Cross-cultural research[1] suggests that there are no absolute personality differences between men and women, that many of the characteristics we normally classify as masculine or feminine tend to differentiate *both* the males and females in one culture from those in another, and in still other cultures to be the reverse of our expectations.

Margaret Mead's studies describe societies in which both men and women are gentle and unaggressive (the Arapesh); in which women dislike childbearing and children and both sexes are angry and aggressive (the Mundugumor); in which women are unadorned, brisk and efficient, whether in childrearing, fishing, or marketing, while men are decorated and vain, interested in art, theater, and petty gossip (the Tchambuli); in which adult sex roles follow conventional expectations, but both boys and girls are initially raised alike—to be alternately gentle and nurturant or assertive—following which boys undergo severe initiation ceremonies and "and claim to forget" any feminine-type experiences or reactions (the Iatmul).[2] Mead's suggestion, typifying the approach of culture and personality theorists, is that cultures emphasize and reinforce behavior according to many sorts of criteria. Although one culture may have different expectations for male and female behavior, the criteria of differentiation may bear no relation to the criteria of differentiation in other cultures. Male and female personality in one culture may be poles along one continuum of behavior, which is itself differentiated from the continua of behavior of other cultures.

Herbert Barry, Irvin Child, and Margaret Bacon[3] and Beatrice and John Whiting[4] have also compiled data indicating that children's behavior and socialization tend to differ between cultures along dimensions normally thought to differentiate male from female behavior and socialization.[5] According to Barry, Child, and Bacon, societies with economies relying on "high" or "intermediate high" accumulation of resources ("high" being societies in which the subsistence economy is either pastoral or agricultural with animal husbandry also important; "intermediate high" being agricultural societies without animal husbandry) train *all* children to be more "compliant," that is, to be responsible and obedient (typically feminine). In contrast, societies with economies relying on "low" or "intermediate low" accumulation ("low" being societies with hunting and fishing; "intermediate low" being agricultural societies without animal husbandry but with hunting and fishing) train their children to be more "assertive," that is, to be independent, self-reliant, and oriented toward achievement (typically masculine).

The Whitings (whose data are probably more reliable than those of Barry, Child, and Bacon, since they were gathered according to uniform and fairly extensive criteria) have compared "egoistic" ("seeks attention," "seeks dominance," "seeks help,"—typically masculine) and "altruistic" ("offers support," "offers help," "suggests responsibly"—typically feminine) behavior among children of six cultures. Although the amount of "egoistic" and "altruistic" behavior observed was about equal (20.4 percent and 20.5 percent of the total behavior observed, respectively), a comparison of the two kinds of behavior within each society reveals that in three societies, children's behavior is much more "altruistic" (93 percent, 82 percent and 79 percent, respectively, of all egoistic and altruistic behavior in each society is "altruistic") and that in the other three children are clearly "egoistic" (96 percent, 79 percent and 67 percent, respectively, of all egoistic and altruistic behavior in each society is "egotistic").[6] Thus, "masculine" behavior seems to characterize certain societies, and "feminine" behavior others.

Sex Differences within Cultures

This is not to claim that within most cultures, male and female differences do not generally conform to our traditional expectations. George Murdock's[7] and Roy D'Andrade's[8] data on the division of labor by sex indicate that most work is divided regularly between men and women, along conventional lines. Men's work, for instance, is "strenuous, cooperative, and . . . may require long periods of travel";[9] women's work is mainly associated with food gathering and preparation, crafts, clothing manufacture, child care, and so forth.

The extent of these differences between the sexes may be large or small. Although in American society we can

recognize clear differences between boys' and girls' socialization and between adult sex roles, these differences are
relatively small in comparison to many other societies.
The Whitings found that the boys and girls in their New
England community showed no statistically significant differences in any of the twelve types of behavior that they
were measuring, whereas boys and girls in each of the
other cultures differed significantly on at least three of the
twelve types.[10]

Barry, Bacon, and Child show that within cultures
where sex differences in pressure toward certain kinds of
behavior occur, the socialization of boys tends to be overwhelmingly more achievement-oriented and self-reliance
oriented, while the socialization of girls tends to be overwhelmingly more nurturance-oriented.[11] Although girls
are also socialized to be more responsible and more obedient than boys, there is more variation between boys and
girls in the socialization of responsibility, and a majority
of societies were rated as without sex differences in the
socialization of obedience (see Table 11-1). This seems
consistent with their findings on societies differentiated
according to type of subsistence economy, in which, for
instance, boys in societies emphasizing assertive behavior
are "more" assertive than girls in this same type of society
and girls are "more" compliant than boys. The same is
true in societies emphasizing "compliant" behavior.[12]

TABLE 11-1   *Percentage of Cultures with Evidence of Sex
Difference in Childhood Socialization Pressures:*

DIRECTION OF PRESSURE	GIRLS	BOYS	NEITHER
Nurturance	82	0	18
Obedience	35	3	62
Responsibility	61	11	28
Achievement	3	87	10
Self-reliance	0	85	15

SOURCE: Herbert Barry III, Margaret K. Bacon, and Irvin L. Child,
"A Cross-Cultural Survey of Some Sex Differences in Socialization,"
Journal of Abnormal Psychology 55 (November 1957): 328.

The Whitings compare girls and boys within each culture and find that in five of the six cultures, boys are more
"egoistic" than girls, and girls more "altruistic" than boys.
(In the sixth, Okinawa, girls are listed as both more
"egoistic" and more "altruistic" than boys. This may be an

error in the manuscript, or an indication that in this culture boys were more often observed to exhibit behavior that was classified as neither "egoistic" nor "altruistic." What seems most likely from the data presented, however, is that one component of "egoism"—"seeks help"—was high enough in girls to outweigh male predominance in the other two components.)

Specifically, tendencies towards "egoism" and "altruism" change with age. Young girls, three to six, "seek help" and "suggest responsibly" more than young boys, while young boys "seek dominance" more than young girls. All these differences disappear with age. However, while there is no difference in the other three behavior types between young boys and girls, older boys, seven to eleven, "seek attention" more than older girls, while older girls "offer help" and "support" more than older boys. These changes make sense: young girls, used to relying on older siblings and adults ("seeking help"), soon give this help ("offer help and support") to younger children. Their not necessarily successful attempts to "suggest responsibility" to other children turn into actual instances of aid and direction. On the other hand, boys, who are allowed as very young children to be demanding ("seek dominance") to adults (especially women) and older children socializers, often lose this privilege as they get older, without receiving instead a well-defined role in the economy or division of labor. The still growing boy is then reduced to more "illegitimate" demands (to "seeking attention") that are often ignored by the people performing their work around him—people unlikely to be aware of his "roleless" status and therefore unsympathetic to his bothering them.[13] In sum, the Whitings find that while there is no statistically significant difference in "egoism" or "altruism" between boys and girls of three to six years old, boys from seven to eleven years old are significantly more "egoistic" than girls, and girls significantly more "altruistic" than boys.[14]

Explanations of Cultural and Sexual Differences: Nature or Culture?

These behavioral tendencies should not be taken to reflect "biological" (hence, "necessary") bases of sex roles and the sexual division of labor. The fact that in The Six Cultures Study (where an equal number of children of each sex were observed for equal amounts of time in each culture, and where the total amount of each type of behavior is almost exactly equivalent), 96 percent of egoistic-altruistic behavior in one society was "egoistic," while in another 93 percent was "altruistic," and that similarly extreme tendencies characterize the other four societies, proves that sex differences could not be responsible. An examination of the explanations offered for these cultural differences and for sexual differences of behavior substantiates the claim that personality and behavior are culturally determined and learned and provides insight into the apparent parallels between cultural and sexual differences.

I have already mentioned one indication that sex roles are learned and related to adult values and work: the Whitings find that young boys and girls exhibit less differentiated behavior than older children, that children, as they *learn* the actual work expected of them (or are unable to learn this work, and thus temporarily not integrated meaningfully in the culture), also learn the more general personality and behavioral characteristics which facilitate this work (or which fill time for those without work).[15]

Barry, Child, and Bacon rely for explanation of cultural differences on differences in subsistence economy.[16] This explanation is similar to the Whitings'. In societies that depend on constant care of animals, or on regular tending of crops, it is necessary to teach children to be obedient and responsible, since disobedience or irresponsibility can endanger or eliminate a food supply for a long period to come. Similarly, experimentation and individual achievement cannot be risked because of the great potential cost. On the other hand, in societies that rely totally or partially on hunting and fishing, disobedience or lack of responsibility is not so crucial; it means missing one day's catch, perhaps, but not a food supply for months to come. In this kind of economy it is worthwhile to be daring, to try new ways of doing things, since success may bring great reward and failure only temporary loss, and perhaps no greater loss than otherwise.

It is clear, however, that those qualities required by the economy in a "high accumulation" society are similar, and for the same reasons, to those normally required by woman's work, especially the requirements of child care, but also those of feeding and clothing a family.[17] Because of these more or less constant requirements, girls' socialization in societies of "low accumulation" cannot be too variable. Although girls are pressured to act "assertively" as are boys, it is noticeable that in those societies exhibiting pressures toward "masculine" behavior, ranked differences in the strength of socialization of the different kinds of behavior for girls is quite small, whereas the difference for boys between pressure toward "assertion" and pressure toward "compliance" is relatively large. The reverse is also true: in those societies which require "feminine" ("compliant") behavior, girls' socialization tends to diverge more widely among different kinds of behavior than boys', although the difference is not so extreme.[18]

These differences are accounted for by the fact that men's and boys' work in the two kinds of society can be more radically different than women's and girls' work. Men may *either* hunt, or fish, or farm, or herd. For instance, in societies with animal husbandry, it is often boys who tend livestock, and who thus from an early age must learn to be responsible in the same way that potential childrearers must learn responsibility.[19] But in societies with hunting and fishing, although women may fish, they still have to take care of children and cook food. Although reliance on gathering and general uncertainty about food supply, along with irregularity of meals and instability of living place, may contribute to differences in female behavior, these regularities remain.

Unfortunately, it is not clear from Barry, Child, and Bacon's presentation who does what in these societies. I can try to elucidate this from general ethnographic knowledge. As far as I know, men are the only hunters of large animals in any society; they also generally tend large domestic animals and pastoral herds. Both women and men, on the other hand, may fish and participate in various agricultural activities. Barry, Bacon, and Child find that in societies with hunting, herding, and animal husbandry with large animals and without fishing, the largest sex differences in socialization are found.[20] What seems characteristic of this type of society is not so much that there is specific men's work, but that this work tends to take the men away from the women and children. I would hypothesize that not only is sex-role training most different in these societies, but that they are the ones most characterized by boys' lacking continuous and regular development toward a clearly defined role.

This suggests a possible problem in studies of the relation between socialization and adult economy or culture. While girls are probably consistently and regularly trained to perform a woman's role, much of (what is viewed as) the training that boys receive in nurturant behavior particularly, but also in other "feminine" behavior, may not be indicative of or preparatory to an adult role at all, but a reflection of the fact that the normal societal organization groups women, girls, and boys in opposition to adult men; since boys are not taught actual woman's work, a natural lot that falls to them is sibling care. This difference may also be true of the Whitings' findings on "egoism" and "altruism"; while "altruistic" behavior in girls is preparatory to adult role, in boys it may either be this (as, for example, in herding societies) or a time filler where training for an adult male role is unavailable. Egoistic behavior in both sexes may also simply be an indication that these children have little "real" place in the surrounding adult world.

In the preceding consideration of the effect of economy on cultural personality and sex-role distinctions, I was often led to "explanations" of correlations in terms of the "logical" division of labor, or of familial organization and socialization patterns which a particular economy would entail. It is useful to look at these variables by themselves. The Whitings attempt to explain differences between cultures where children behave "egotistically" and those where they behave "altruistically."[21] They find that with one exception (New England), cultures with "altruistic" children have either nuclear or mother-child households, while cultures with "egoistic" children tend to have households and courtyards inhabited by extended families. Barry, Bacon, and Child find that similar societal characteristics relate to sex differences.[22] Large sex differences in socialization are correlated with large family groups with cooperative interaction—either extended families or polygynous families in which cowives help each other. The Whitings find further that more complex societies (societies with occupational specialization, a centralized political system, class or caste differentiation, and a complex settlement and land-use pattern) tend to produce "egoistic" children.

Both household structure and complexity of society would seem to entail similar tendencies in child training. In households with few adults, it is likely that more contributions are required from children, both regularly and as temporary substitutes for the mother, than in extended households in which adult substitutes are much more available. In such households as well, it is likely that a man and a woman must be prepared to take each other's role when the other is sick or away; therefore, there cannot be a very large difference in the socialization of sex roles.

Similarly, in less complex societies, children from a very young age can be and are trained toward their already known adult roles; they are usually functioning members of the economy. Whatever work they do is a necessary and expected contribution. Furthermore, children in this situation can usually understand the reasons for what they are learning and see tangible results of their work—that they took part in producing the meal which they eat. In these societies it is also more likely that women participate in the producing economy, making it necessary for children to take care of younger children and to do things at home while their mother is out working. On the other hand, in more complex societies, children cannot be as certain of their future role in the division of labor, nor can "work" for them seem as immediately contributory to family welfare as in simpler societies. Crucially, however, these characteristics would probably apply even more to boys than to girls, for whom there is always some basic household and child-care work that they can understand and expect to do, and whose relevance is immediately perceptible.

Differences in the Genesis and Meaning of Masculine and Feminine Behaviors

Similar sex-role socialization and less sex differentiation in adult work are primarily a reflection of the extent to which boys are socialized to perform more (traditionally) feminine behavior and work, although the reverse may sometimes be true (for example, according to Barry, Child, and Bacon, boys in societies stressing "compliance" are much more "compliant" according to their ratings than are girls "assertive" in societies stressing "assertion"). This is partially a result of the fact that variations in "economy" still leave women with one element of their "economic" role certain, thus one aspect of their training assured.

There seem to be differences in how compliant and assertive behavior are learned. All children have the basic experience of being raised primarily by women. In societies that stress masculine behavior, women, however resentful, must perform tasks that require reliability, responsibility, and nurturance. And if both children learn to be more independent, assertive, and achievement-oriented, girls still learn this from women, whereas it is likely that boys learn much of this behavior from men. There is a lack of symmetry in the childrearing situations of the two kinds of society. Both boys and girls learn "compliant," "altruistic" behavior from women, but while boys may learn "assertive" behavior from men, girls still learn it from women.

There also seem to be different situational and cultural reasons for pressure toward "assertion" and actual "egoistic" behavior than for pressure toward "compliance" and actual "altruistic" behavior. In the latter case, "altruistic" behavior seems to relate to actual learning of role ("offering help," "offering support," and so forth) and is thus directly supported by pressure toward "compliant" behavior, toward responsibility and obedience. Boys and girls who exhibit these behavioral characteristics are actually doing things—are taking care of siblings, being responsible for livestock, perhaps helping in agricultural work.

"Egoistic" behavior, as pointed out, is likely to be a time filler for someone who does not have a definite role. There is no necessary relation between "egoistic" behavior and adult role, although "egoism" may be an adult personality characteristic. Similarly, it would seem that in societies with pressure toward "assertive behavior, the usefulness of this behavior is greater in activities which only older people can do well—hunting, warring, successfully competing in business, and the like—and cannot seem immediately relevant to a child, nor so tied to successful fulfillment of work role for children. Pressure toward "assertion" and "egoistic" behavior seems to exist in societies where there is no "obvious" and simple relation between children's role and adult role, societies in which "characters are formed" rather than "roles learned." This seems to be *the* major characteristic of what it means to be trained to be "masculine," to perform a (typically) "male" role.

In most societies, to the extent that an economy or household structure requires that children learn real work as children, they learn what are normally thought of as female patterns of behavior. To the extent that there is no obvious continuity between childhood and adulthood, children learn what are normally male behaviors. Societies in which sex differences in socialization are small might be simple societies in which all children learn early to be responsible, obedient, and nurturant in the performance of real work, or they may be complex societies, such as ours, in which the socialization of both sexes is not perceptibly and immediately contributory to the society's economy and social organization. The extent to which sex-role socialization differs in ways we would expect, whether differentiation is great or small, reflects the difference in the extent to which boys wait, while girls do not, to be integrated into the adult world of work.

What accounts for "feminine nature," then, is that a certain part of woman's work in all societies requires feminine kinds of behavior, even when the attitude to this behavior is only disdain: women who hate childbearing must bear children and nurse them regularly in nontechnological societies where there are no contraceptives nor bottles. Men's work, on the other hand, varies across cultures both in actual type and in the kinds of personality characteristics it requires. What is "biological necessity" is biological necessity: women bear and in most societies must nurse children. However, it is clear that all those characteristics that constitute this "feminine" nature may also characterize men where other sorts of work or role expectations require them. Beyond this biological minimum, for which even girls can be socialized more or less "appropriately," girls' socialization can produce women whose adult personality can range among all those characteristics which we consider "male" and "female." It is easy to confuse statistical predominance with norm, and to explain norms as being "only natural." This is inaccurate and unnecessary; a convincing explanation considers specific facts, not normative generalizations or desires. This consideration of specific facts provides a logically consistent and empirically complete accounting for sexual and cultural differences which does not need to rely on a universal and therefore in some sense nonexplanatory truth.

IDENTITY AND SEX ROLE

Female and Male Identity: *Being and Doing*

There are many ways of characterizing the differences in the processes and goals of female and male socialization. Without trying to evaluate the exactness of these sorts of characterizations, I will describe them briefly. Distinctions can be drawn both between the degree of immediacy of (sex) roles for the child in primitive as opposed to Western societies and between boys and girls in each.

Anthropologists contrast the continuity and clarity of socialization in most primitive societies with modern society. In simpler societies the economic system is relatively understandable to a child. Work training constitutes gradual initiation into different kinds of work that will be expected of the child as an adult. Mothers' work is usually performed near children, and fathers' work, even if it is away, is liable to be a concretely describable, if not observable task—hunting game or planting and harvesting corn in the lowlands—rather than abstract thinking or assembly-line work to understand which involves understanding the whole process of production in a factory or bureaucratic paper work. In addition, in societies that are less complex, more parents (especially fathers) do the same kind of work. For an American child, even if his or her father does something concrete and complete, like running a small grocery store or farming, a comparison with other fathers indicates immediately that this particular work cannot be easily equated with *the* "male" role.

Biological differences too are less apparent. In modern society children's sexuality is played down ("the child must be sexless as far as his family is concerned"),[23] and adult sex and childbearing are hidden. Clothes do their best to hide bodies and bodily differences. Primitive societies often approach bodies and sex differently: children and often adults wear much less clothing; families may all sleep in the same room; and childbirth takes place in the home. Children's sexual behavior may be either ignored or encouraged rather than actively repressed.

While these distinctions mean that the learning of adult sex roles is easier for children in less complex societies, it is also probably true that within each of these types of society, similar distinctions insure that a girl's development into a woman is more continuous and understandable than a boy's development into a man. In some sense "feminine identity" is more easily and surely attainable than "masculine identity." Margaret Mead claims that from the time of birth, girls can begin to take on feminine identity through identification with their mothers, while for little boys, masculine identification comes through a process of differentiation, because what would be his "natural" identification—identification with the person he is closest to and most dependent upon—is according to cultural values "unnatural," this works against his attainment of stable masculine identity. The boy's "earliest experience of self is one in which he is forced, in the relationship to his mother, to realize himself as different, as a creature unlike the mother, as a creature unlike the human beings who make babies in a direct, intelligible way by using their own bodies to make them."[24] This seems to be the paradigmatic situation which describes many of the more general sex-role problems considered below.

I have already described how in many non-Western societies, a girl's development and learning of her adult female role is more regular and continuous than a boy's development. Although the case is not so clear in our society (especially because there are more cross-pressures on the girl), it would seem that here also, pressure on girls, and the development of "feminine" identity, is not as difficult for the girl to understand. Talcott Parsons claims that it is "possible from an early age to initiate girls directly into many important aspects of the adult feminine role."[25] At least part of their mothers' work is around the home, and the meaning of this activity is tangible and easily understandable to the child. Children can also participate in this work or imitate it. For a girl this is direct training in her adult role; for a boy it is often that part of his socialization which most complicates his development.

In contrast, an urban child's father works away from his home, where his son cannot participate in or observe his work. In addition, masculine functions are "of a relatively abstract and intangible character such that their meaning must remain almost wholly inaccessible to a child."[26] Thus, boys are deprived of the possibility of modeling themselves meaningfully after tangible adult male roles or of being initiated gradually into adult work.

Parsons wonders about boys in rural areas, whose fathers' work is closer to home and more available to children, and suggests that these boys tend to be "good" in a sense not typical of urban boys (and like boys in societies where children of both sexes can be gradually integrated into the economy).

This suggests that in both primitive and advanced societies, girls seem to have an easier time learning their adult role: their socialization is less conflicted, less irregular, more continuous, than the socialization of boys. However, socialization for both sexes is more continuous, and thus identity more stable, in primitive than in complex societies.

A distinction reiterated in many different sources which both characterizes and explains this difference in the relative difficulty of girls' and boys' attainment of sex-role identity is that girls and women "are," while boys and men "do": feminine identity is "ascribed," masculine identity "achieved." Karen Horney points out that even biological differences reflect this distinction: "the man is actually obliged to go on proving his manhood to the woman. There is no analogous necessity for her: even if she is frigid, she can engage in a sexual intercourse and conceive and bear a child. She performs her part by merely *being,* without any *doing.* . . . The man on the other hand has to *do* something in order to fulfill himself."[27] Mead claims that the little boy's period of "simple sureness" about his sexuality is short—the period during childhood when he knows he has a penis, the potential to be manly, like other "men," but before he finds out that he will not be big or strong enough for a number of years to act like a man.[28] This period is the little girl's only period of doubt about her sexuality; on either end is sureness about this identity, first through identification with her mother and then because she herself has borne a child.

Culturally, too, "maleness . . . is not absolutely defined, it has to be kept and re-earned every day."[29] Parsons suggests that women have an attainable goal—to marry and have children—and that how well they do this may bear on how people judge them, but not on their fundamental female status.[30] He contrasts this with male status, which is constantly dependent in a basic way on a man's success at work, at getting promotions, and as a provider.

The need to differentiate himself continues throughout the boy's childhood. Mead points out that the boy "is trained by women to be a male, which involves no identification of the self with the mother-teacher (and when it does, I would add, this identification is harmful to his attainment of identity). He is to be a boy by doing the things Mother says but doing them in a manly way."[31] His upbringing, and the attainment of any kind of success, is characterized by its conditional nature: success is always temporary—a failure wipes it out—and love and approval are dependent upon success.

Simone de Beauvoir sees positive rather than negative effects on boys (from this differentiation).[32] She describes girls' upbringing and contrasts it with boys', rather than attempting to explain how these contrasts have arisen. For her, boys' "doing" becomes men's transcendence: men are artists, creators, risk their lives, have projects. Women, on the other hand, are carefully trained to "be." A girl's natural inclination would also be to "do," but she learns to make herself into an object, to restrict herself to the sphere of immanence. Female destiny is foreordained and repetitive; men can choose their destiny:

> The young boy, be he ambitious, thoughtless, or timid, looks toward an open future; he will be a seaman or an engineer, he will stay on the farm or go away to the city, he will see the world, he will get rich; he feels free, confronting a future in which the unexpected awaits him. The young girl will be a wife, grandmother; she will keep house just as her mother did, she will give her children the same care she herself received when young—she is twelve years old and already her story is written in the heavens. She will discover it day after day without ever making it.[33]

The Cultural Universal: Socialization by Females

The common fact in all socialization situations I have mentioned is that women are the primary socializers. Men may also help in child care, but their "work" is elsewhere; for women it is the reverse. I have indicated certain effects that this seems to have on children's development in terms of primary identity, and on the differences between the development of identity in boys and girls. One result for children of both sexes is that, since "it is the mother's and not the father's voice that gives the principal early approval and disapproval, the nagging voice of conscience is feminine in both sexes."[34] Thus, as children of either sex attempt to gain independence, to make decisions on their own, different from their upbringing, they must do this by consciously or unconsciously rejecting their mother (and people like her) and the things she is associated with. This fact, and the cultural institutions and emphases that it seems to entail, has different consequences for boys and for girls.

Effects on Boys: the Dread of Women

One consequence of the fact that women are primary socializers for boys (who later become men) is what Horney calls the "dread of women."[35] This has both psychological and cultural aspects. Psychologically, Horney believes that fear of the mother (women) in men is even greater and more repressed than fear of the father (men). The mother initially has complete power over the child's satisfaction of needs and first forbids instinctual activities and therefore encourages the child's first sadistic impulses to be directed against her and her body. This creates enormous anxiety in the child. Fear of the father, on the other hand, is not so threatening. For one thing, it develops later in life, as a result of specific processes which the child is more "aware" that he is experiencing, and not in reaction to the father's total and incomprehensible control over the child's livelihood: "dread of the father is more actual and tangible, less uncanny in quality."[36] For another, it does not entail a boy's admitting fear of a different sort of being and "masculine self-regard suffers less in this way."[37] Because all men have mothers, these results are to a greater or lesser degree universal: "the anxiety connected with his self-respect leaves more or less distinct traces in every man and gives to his general attitude to women a particular stamp which either does not exist in women's attitude to men, or, if it does, is acquired secondarily. In other words, it is no integral part of their feminine nature."[38]

Individual creations, as well as folk legends and beliefs, are often attempts to cope with this dread. For instance, there are poems and ballads that talk about fears of engulfment by whirlpools, allurement by sirens who entice the unwary and kill whom they catch. Women and symbols of women in these creations and fantasies are for grown men what the all-powerful mother is for the child. But if this power can be named and externalized, it can possibly be conquered. Another way of coping with dread is to glorify and adore women—"There is no need for me to dread a being so wonderful, so beautiful, nay, so saintly"—or to debase and disparage them—"It would be too ridiculous to dread a creature who, if you take her all round, is such a poor thing."[39]

Culturally, this means that in general it is important for men to gain power and to insure that the attributes of power and prestige are masculine, or, more precisely, that whatever cultural role accrues to the male is then accorded power and prestige: "If such activities [like cooking and weaving] are appropriate occupations of men, then the whole society, men and women alike, votes them as important. When the same occupations are performed by women, they are regarded as less important."[40] It also becomes necessary to reserve many of these activities for men, to believe that women are unable to do many of the "important" things that contribute to society—to exercise political power, to be artistic or creative, to play an equal role in the economy—and at the same time to devalue whatever it is that women do—whether they are housewives, teachers, or social workers. In fact, "cultures frequently phrase achievement as something that women do not or cannot do, rather than directly as something which men do well."[41]

Melford Spiro's work on the kibbutz indicates that this "causal" argument is valid.[42] He makes it clear that this happens even in a community that is specifically trying to eliminate sexual inequalities, but in which women continue to be the main socializers of children.[43] On the kibbutz where Spiro lived, it seems clear that women's work is not as prestigious as men's work. This is particularly evident in the socialization institutions most affecting children. Until children are twelve or thirteen, all their nurses and teachers are women; when they reach thirteen and begin high school—are more clearly doing "serious work" and not just being brought up—their teachers and supervisors are all men. "Nurses" in the high school perform mainly menial functions—clean buildings and bathrooms, clean and repair clothing—and take care of children only when they are sick. Serving "as an important transitional buffer from an all-female to an all-male [sic! These children are boys *and* girls, growing into a male *and* female world] adult environment,"[44] nurses, from being the most important adults in the child's world (parents are visited several hours a day and are loving and warm, but are not really the child's "socializers"), cede this status to men and become maids, for some reason incapable of continuing to play an important socializing role in the child's life.

Around this time, girls (for reasons not apparent to, or at least not mentioned by, Spiro) cease to be moral leaders of the students and become less intellectual and artistic than boys, when before they had been more so. Boys become more interested in their work and more politically interested. Among the adult kibbutz members, women do not serve on important committees, rarely speak up at meetings—and when they do, are not listened to with the same seriousness as men—and do not participate in the economic administration or intellectual life of the kibbutz. Although they work harder and longer than most men in order to "prove" themselves and their worth, the men continue to find it necessary not to recognize the value of this work or to accord women equal status.[45]

Dread and Bisexuality

Thus, institutionally and culturally, men have often managed to overcome this "dread" of women through a devaluation of whatever women do and are. But the dread continues within the men themselves, a perfectly understandable, if errant, product of socialization by women: a retention of feminine qualities, partial identification with women, desire to be a woman like one's mother. Freud calls this bisexuality and considers that all people, both men and women, contain traits of both sexes. Without pursuing what these "traits" as universal "constituents" could mean, we can deal with the same concept by examining the fact that all people within a culture contain within themselves both what are considered (and tend to be) masculine and what are considered feminine characteristics in that culture. I would suggest that in most cultures, the earliest identity for any child is "feminine," because women are around him and provide (and do not provide) him with the necessities of life. This identification is probably more threatening to the boy, because more basic, than the elements of masculine identification that a little girl acquires. Several kinds of evidence attest to the existence (and repression) of "bisexual" or "feminine" elements in boys and men.

An indication of the continuing threat of "femininity" to

males in our culture is the strength of both external and internal pressure on little boys to conform to masculine ideals, to reject identification with or participation in anything that seems "feminine." Initially, this pressure is generated by socializers of both sexes, but it is soon rigidly internalized by young boys, who hold both themselves and their peers to account over it.

The narrowness and severity of this training is far greater than comparable "training" for femininity in girls. Girls can be tomboys, wear jeans and other men's clothing, fight, climb trees, play sports, ride bikes. Their mothers may become somewhat anxious about them, but this behavior will not be cause for great alarm, nor will it be forbidden or cruelly ridiculed. Similarly, they will be considered "strange" or "unfeminine" if they continue to be active, to succeed academically or professionally; however, many women do so nonetheless, without feeling a fundamental challenge to their identity. The training and subsequent behavior of boys is not so flexible. It would be unheard of for boys to wear dresses; if they want to cook or play with dolls, do not like sports, or are afraid to fight, this is cause for panic by parents, educators, and psychologists. And in fact, boys do conform closely to the male goals and behavior required of them. They learn early not to exhibit feminine personality traits—to hide emotions and pretend even to themselves that they do not have them, to be independent participants in activities rather than personally involved with friends. Later, as men, they are careful never to choose women's careers unless they are prepared to bear enormous stigma.

The extent and strength of boys' training not to have or admit "feminine" traits is indicated by Daniel Brown's studies on sex-role preference in children.[46] From kindergarten age, boys are much less likely to claim a preference for anything feminine than girls to prefer masculine roles or objects. The extent of this difference is demonstrated by some of Brown's data: of girls 3½ to 5½, about half tend to prefer "feminine" and half to prefer "masculine" toys, roles, and activities; at this age, 70 percent to 80 percent of boys express "masculine" preferences. The differences increase as children get older. From six to nine years old, boys become even more strongly masculine in their preferences, and girls' preferences become *less* feminine, that is, more girls from six to nine make "masculine" choices than "feminine" choices.

The extent of boys' masculine "preferences," particularly in contrast to the willingness of girls to claim cross-sexual preferences, is striking. Clearly, part of the reason may be that it is apparent to both boys and girls, and becomes more apparent as they grow older, that in our society "male" roles and activities are more prestigious and privileged than "female" roles and activities. However, another interpretation is that the extreme unwillingness of boys to make cross-sex choices indicates that they have been taught very early, and have accepted more or less completely, that it is right for them to prefer masculine things; therefore, they are extremely reluctant to make feminine choices. More important, it would seem that these boys, in contrast to the girls, believe that making such choices helps to insure their masculinity, and, alternatively, that different choices would not just be different choices among a number of possible alternatives, but rather threatening in the deepest sense.

This latter explanation, in terms of fear and attempts to insure masculinity, seems to account better for the regularity with which even very young boys—boys who spend most of their time in a world of female privilege with their mother or female teachers, and who play with children of both sexes—refuse to choose those things that are associated with females and that thus might give them some of the feminine attributes of power. Studies of parental orientation in young boys also support such an interpretation. At ages when boys are already making strongly "masculine" choices of objects and playmates, they still do not identify with their fathers or male figures as strongly as girls, who are not making "feminine" choices, identify with their mothers.[47]

Fear of the feminine may not be so well absorbed and repressed: according to some interpreters, certain cultural or subcultural phenomena attest to direct jealousy of women and attempt to appropriate female roles. In Plains Indian cultures, for example, which stressed extreme bravery and daring for men, transvestism was an institutionalized solution for those men who did not feel able to take on the extremely masculine life required of them. A more important example are cultures in which *all* men perform certain rituals identifying with women. The most obvious of these rituals is the *couvade*. Roger Burton and John Whiting hypothesize that in cultures with both early mother-child sleeping arrangements and matrilocal residence—

that is, a world controlled by the child's mother and other female relatives[48]—a boy child will have both primary and secondary feminine optative identity ("those statuses a person wishes he could occupy but from which he is disbarred").[49] In this situation, "the society should provide him some means to act out, symbolically at least, the female role."[50] Their data suggest that an institution that serves this purpose in a large number of societies of this type is the *couvade*.

Initiation rites have been variously interpreted as attempts to appropriate or incorporate the feminine role, or, on the other hand, to exorcise it. On the basis of both anthropological and psychological evidence, Bettelheim claims that male initiation rites, which often involve subincision, and in general include some kind of cutting or wounding of the genitals, are means for symbolically acquiring a vagina, "to assert that men, too, can bear children."[51] At the same time, circumcision and other tests of endurance, strength, and knowledge are ways of proving masculine sexual maturity, of asserting and defining maleness.[52]

Burton and Whiting's cross-cultural evidence provides the explanation of this jealousy that we are looking for, in terms of the maternal role in socialization.[53] In certain ("father-absent") societies, children sleep exclusively with their mother during their first two years, and there is a long postpartum sex taboo. All children in such societies develop a "primary feminine optative identity." These societies contrast with ones in which the father and mother continue to sleep together and in which both parents give and withhold resources to some extent; in such societies children's primary optative identity is "adult."[54] Further, among "father-absent" societies, there is a contrast between matrilocal and patrilocal societies. In the latter, a boy's secondary identity—which develops when he becomes a "yard child" and observes that in the society at large, it is males who have higher status and power—is masculine; boys thus develop a "cross-sex identity." Burton and Whiting demonstrate that initiation ceremonies tend to occur in societies whose sleeping arrangements and residence patterns produce cross-sex identity in boys; the function of these ceremonies is "to brainwash the primary feminine identity and to establish firmly the secondary male identity."[55] In many societies with male initiation rites, sex-identity terms, rather than being the equivalent

of "male" and "female" in our society, are instead differentiated so that one term refers to women, girls, and
uninitiated boys, while the other refers only to men who
have already been initiated.

Evidence from more advanced societies also suggests
that "father-absence" or "low father-salience" in childhood
may lead to "compulsively masculine" behavior which
entails the same rejection, although not in a ritual context,
of the female world and feminine behavior. Gang and
delinquent behavior among American lower-class men often includes compulsive, and strong denial of anything
feminine with corresponding emphasis on masculinity—
risk and daring, sexual prowess, rejection of home life,
physical violence—as well as severe "tests" (which might
be seen as forms of "initiation rites") as requirements of
gang membership. Similar behavior also seems characteristic of Caribbean men raised in "father-absent" households.[56]

Beatrice Whiting shows that criminal and other violent
behavior occurs more frequently in those two out of the
six cultures in which husband and wife may neither sleep
nor eat together and seldom work or play together. Sex-
identity conflict seems to develop differently in the two
societies, however. One is an Indian Rajput caste community, in which children of both sexes score high in "egoistic" behavior. Boys are around women, perhaps desire
their role, and have no role of their own until they grow
up. Children in the other community, Nyansongo, Kenya,
score highest in "altruistic" behavior. Here, boys from a
quite young age are herders. Since they are being taught
"feminine" behavior of responsibility and nurturance, and
eat and sleep only with women, it is probable that their
identity is even more strongly "feminine" than that of the
Rajput boys. Like violent behavior, male narcissism, pride,
and phobia toward mature women—other indications of
compulsive assertion of masculinity—seem to be prevalent
in societies in which boys spend their earlier years exclusively or predominantly with women, and in which the
"degree of physical or emotional distance between mother
and father as compared with that between mother and
child" is great.[57]

All this evidence—of cultural institutions that exercise
or attempt to gain control of feminine powers for men; of
institutions that provide for the assertion of compulsively
masculine behavior; of the threats of bisexuality or femi-

ninity to boys and men—suggests that it is not sufficient to attribute the devaluation of female work roles and personality to external and conscious "dread of women," to known fear of woman's power. Rather, it must be attributed to fear of that womanly power which has remained *within* men—the bisexual components of any man's personality. This is so threatening because in some sense, there is no sure definition of masculinity, no way for the little boy to know if he has really made it, except insofar as he manages to differentiate himself from what he somehow vaguely defines as femininity. "For maleness in America [and, I would suggest, elsewhere] is not absolutely defined, it has to be kept and re-earned every day, and one essential element in the definition is beating women in every game that both sexes play, in every activity in which both sexes engage."[58]

Although the reasons for the difficulty in defining male identity are very complicated, I have tried to indicate one direction which may provide some answers. This direction is based on an examination of how children attain sureness of themselves, of an "identity" which is theirs, and of what it means for one sex that there are no people "like me" who are there—and as important as people "not like me"—from earliest infancy, as nurturers, as models, as providers and deniers of resources. What it means, according to Mead, is that "the recurrent problem of civilization is to define the male role satisfactorily enough,"[59] both for societies and for individuals who must live up to these undefined roles.

Feminine Development: Identity Versus Preference

In this section I will examine comparatively the development of "feminine identity" in girls, studying especially how the problems of male socialization seem to affect this development and sex-role preference in girls and women.

Most of the evidence presented so far indicates that girls should have an easier time than boys developing a stable sexual identity: they are brought up primarily by women; their socialization is fairly gradual and continuous in most societies; the female role is more accessible and understandable to the child. I will not be able to evaluate or examine cross-cultural evidence about feminine identity and about how women or girls in other (non-Western) cultures view their feminine role. For the purposes of this or any specific investigation about the psychological effects of female socialization, evidence on conflict about the feminine role and its causes, comparable to that on cross-sex identity in males, is so scanty that even hypothesizing about what must "logically" be the case seems unacceptable. I will be primarily concerned with the different forms (and "secondary" psychological importance) which female envy of males seems to take in Western society.

In contrast to non-Western societies, Western female socialization is not so clear or unambiguous, just as the adult feminine role is not so clearly an essential or important part of the society. The universal, and not just sexually defined, "superiority" of men and masculinity in the "important" realms of the culture means that women get trained partially for traditionally feminine roles (child-rearing, housekeeping) and personality (passivity, compliance, "goodness"); at the same time in school they are taught goals of achievement and success, and it is made clear to them that their other (feminine) role and its values are less desirable, less highly valued, in the progress of humanity and the world.

This situation is comparable to the problem of cross-sex identity for boys. Girls are initially brought up in a feminine world, with mothers all-powerful and all-prestigious, where it is desirable to acquire a feminine identity. They later go into a world where male power is clearly important (even if, as in school, its values are transmitted by women), where males dominate society and its important resources. Beauvoir (in a somewhat culturally limited and dated, but still suggestive, way) describes this situation:

> If the little girl at first accepts her feminine vocation, it is not because she intends to abdicate; it is, on the contrary, in order to rule; she wants to be a matron because the matrons' group seems privileged; but, when her company, her studies, her games, her reading, take her out of the maternal circle, she sees that it is not the women but the men who control the world. It is this revelation—much more than the discovery of the penis—that irresistibly alters her conception of herself.[60]

However, this does not seem to present the same challenge to fundamental identity as a shift from a female to a male world presents for boys, because in the little girl's case, her primary identity is feminine.

It is apparently the case as well that just that kind of maternal behavior most conducive to greater sex conflict in boys, to less easy attainment of a sense of masculinity—for example, general nonpermissiveness, pressures toward inhibition and nonaggression, use of physical punishment and ridicule, high sex anxiety, and severity of toilet training—is also (not surprisingly) that behavior which encourages the development of "feminine" qualities and femininity in girls.[61] This maternal behavior, according to Slater, develops especially in those kinds of societies or subcultures where the marriage relationship is "distant" and where family patterns usually entail most extreme masculine insecurity and compulsive masculine behavior.[62] I have suggested, however, that these tendencies are probably present to some extent in all childrearing situations; the mother has major responsibility for children, and this situation, in which a mother's whole life and sense of self depends on rearing "good" or "successful" children, always produces anxiety over performance and overidentification with children.[63]

This perpetuates a childrearing cycle. As long as these "feminine" qualities are produced in a socialization situation in which mothers are anxious and conflicted—as they must be in Western society—they must necessarily involve girls' resentment and conflicts over their acceptance, and thus anxious and resentful behavior toward children in the next generation. It should be emphasized, however, that these "conflicts" do not seem to be a reflection of a girl's uncertainty about whether she has attained a "feminine" identity; childhood environment and pressures on both sexes toward "feminine" compliance probably ensure that she has. Her conflicts, rather, are about whether or not she wants this identity that relies on her own ability to inhibit herself and to respond to the demands of others, eventually leading her to an adult fate where her role and her dependence upon it doom her to bring up sons and daughters resentful of her and the "femininity"" she represents.

It seems clear to the whole society, and especially to the little girl, that this identity and its future leave much to be desired. Brown's findings indicate that not only do small girls "prefer" a masculine role with much more frequency than small boys "prefer" a feminine role, but that this preference for a masculine role increases with age from kindergarten to fourth grade: after the age of five, more girls prefer a masculine role than prefer a feminine role. Lawrence Kohlberg claims that one reason for the huge discrepancy in male and female same-sex and opposite-sex choices and the huge increase in female opposite-sex choices is that, in fact, Brown's "it" figure is more masculine than feminine, and that girls become with age less self-projective and increasingly oriented to this reality aspect of the test.[64] A finding of Brown's that would seem to mitigate this criticism is that in his fifth-grade sample, girls show a strong reversal from their previous masculine choices and a strong preference for feminine role choices.

Kohlberg, however, also presents data from several other preference studies of activities, toys, and peer choices which, although they do not show the extreme differences that Brown found between boys and girls, or extreme masculine preferences in girls, do show that for boys, masculine preferences of activities and peers either begin and remain very high, or begin relatively high and increase with age. In contrast, girls' same-sex preferences are never so high as boys and tend to be more erratic—to show no consistent or increasing pattern of preference for feminine activities and peers.[65] He also mentions studies which indicate that not only are girls' sex-typed preferences of activities and playmates lower than boys', but also that "girls make fewer judgments than boys that their own sex is better . . . and girls' preferential evaluations of their own sex decrease with age."[66] Girls also tend to make more "feminine" judgments, or preferences when they are asked directly "which do you like?" than they do when asked "which do girls like?"[67] My guess is that the former question puts girls more on the line—they are afraid of not being "good"—whereas the latter is a way for them to express their real preferences and judgments of value, without indicating to the interviewer that they do not know or believe in what they really "ought" to like or do.

All of these preferences seem to reflect the clear cultural evaluation of masculine pursuits and characteristics as superior, an evaluation that is probably made more evident to the girl as she grows up and learns more about the world around her. Karen Horney calls this the development of the girl's "flight from womanhood." "In actual fact a girl is exposed from birth onwards to the suggestion—inevitable, whether conveyed brutally or delicately—of her inferiority, an experience which must constantly stimulate her masculinity complex."[68] Horney attributes this both to unconscious psychological motives and to cognitive assessment of the world around her. The girl's unconscious motives stem from an attempt to deny an oedipal attachment to her father by recoiling from femininity and therefore these feminine desires. This is in contrast to the boy, whose fear of his attachment to his mother leads to increased compensatory masculinity. Importantly, these unconscious motives "are reinforced and supported by the actual disadvantage under which women labour in social life."[69] Horney, writing from within the psychoanalytic tradition, seems more defensive about emphasizing the cultural components of the "flight" than we would be today; however, she still describes those components accurately. While these latter reasons may be partially a form of "rationalization" for less acceptable unconscious motives, "we must not forget that this disadvantage is actually a piece of reality," that there is an "actual social subordination of women."[70] This "flight" is not from an unsureness of feminine identity, but from a knowledge of it and its implications.

Partially because of this social subordination of women and cultural devaluation of feminine qualities, girls are allowed and feel themselves free to express masculine preferences and to have much greater freedom than boys—to play boys' games, dress like boys and so forth. For this reason, they are encouraged to achieve in school, and it is considered "only natural" that they would want to do so. In neither case does the girl or her socializers doubt that her feminine identity is firm, that she will eventually resign herself to her feminine adult role, and that at this time, this role will come naturally to her.

As she gets older, however, her peers and the adults around her cease such tolerance of this envy of males and of these attempts to engage in male activities or to achieve like men: "any self-assertion will diminish her femininity and her attractiveness."[71] She is supposed to begin to be passive and docile, to become interested in her appearance, to cultivate her abilities to charm men, to mold herself to their wants. This is not a one-sided requirement, however. At the same time she is supposed to continue to do well in school, but must expect to be stigmatized or reproved if she does. In American society she continues in school to be instilled with "American" (masculine) goals—success, achievement, competition. She fails as a good citizen, as a successful human being, if she does not succeed, and as a woman if she does. Mead sums up the girl's position:

> We end up with the contradictory picture of a society that appears to throw its doors wide open to women, but translates her every step towards success as having been damaging—to her own chances of marriage, and to the men whom she passes on the road [whom she must pass, in a society where success is defined only by beating other people].[72]

And it does seem that the society succeeds in imposing its demands. We can recall Brown's finding that fifth-grade (prepubertal and pubertal) girls make a dramatic switch and all of a sudden develop strong "preferences" for feminine activities and objects; we remember the "unexplainable" fact that girls on the kibbutz, formerly creative and interested in their work, moral and social leaders and organizers in their children's group, suddenly in high school become uninterested in intellectual activities, unconcerned about politics, uncreative and unartistic. We know that in general, as children grow up, girls become less successful in school and drop out of the role of equal participant in activities that they once held.

Conclusion

Sex-role ideology and socialization for these roles seem to ensure that neither boys nor girls can attain both stable identity and meaningful roles. The tragedy of woman's socialization is not that she is left unclear, as is the man, about her basic sexual identity. This identity is ascribed to her, and she does not need to prove to herself or to society that she has earned it or continues to have it. Her problem is that this identity is clearly devalued in the society in which she lives. This does not mean that women too should be required to compete for identity, to be assertive and to need to achieve—to "do" like men. Nor does it suggest that it is not crucial for everyone, men and women alike, to have a stable sexual identity. But until male "identity" does not depend on men's proving themselves, their "doing" will be a reaction to insecurity, not a creative exercise of their humanity, and woman's "being," far from being an easy and positive acceptance of self, will be a resignation to inferiority. And as long as women must live through their children, and men do not genuinely contribute to socialization and provide easily accessible role models, women will continue to bring up sons whose sexual identity depends on devaluing femininity inside and outside themselves, and daughters who must accept this devalued position and resign themselves to producing more men who will perpetuate the system that devalues them.

NOTES

NOTE: I am grateful to Susan Contratto Weisskopf for first suggesting to me certain severe problems in male-identity development which led me to the particular comparative approach taken in this essay.

1. I am aware of many potential drawbacks in "cross-cultural" studies: their dubious reliability; in many cases, the relatively incomparable nature of much of the data used for cross-cultural comparisons, particularly those comparisons based on material from the Human Relations Area Files or other large-scale comparisons in which the original gathering of data was not under the control of the person using this data; the difficulty of rating cultures according to nonculturally defined variables; and the tenuous nature of causal explanations based on statistical correlation or comparison. Although it is beyond the scope of this essay to offer a specific criticism of such studies and beyond the scope of my abilities to evaluate statistical methods and results, I have attempted to avoid reliance on minute statistical differences for proof, and to attribute adequacy to explanations according to their logical and experiential plausibility, rather than their statistical reliability.
2. Margaret Mead, *Male and Female* (New York: William Morrow, 1949).
3. Herbert Barry III, Margaret K. Bacon, and Irvin L. Child, "Relation of Child Training to Subsistence Economy," *American Anthropologist* 61 (1959): 51-63.
4. Beatrice B. and John W. M. Whiting, "Task Assignment and Personality: A Consideration of the Effect of Herding on Boys," paper presented at the Social Science Conference, University of East Africa, Dar-es-Salaam, 1968; "Egoism and Altruism," *Children of Six Cultures, Part 1: Egoism vs. Altruism* (forthcoming).
5. They are measuring slightly different things. Barry, Child, and Bacon, in both this study and one mentioned later, are talking about *pressure toward* certain kinds of behavior in children, while the Whitings are talking about *observed* behavior.
6. For the record: children's behavior is 96 percent "egoistic" in a New England village, the only Western "society" in their sample.
7. George P. Murdock, "Comparative Data on the Division of Labor by Sex," *Social Forces* 15 (1937): 551-553.
8. Roy D'Andrade, "Sex Differences and Cultural Institutions," in

E. Maccoby, ed., *The Development of Sex Differences* (Stanford: Stanford University Press, 1966).

9. *Ibid.*, p. 176.
10. Whiting and Whiting, "Egoism and Altruism," p. 32.
11. Herbert Barry III, Margaret K. Bacon, and Irvin L. Child, "A Cross-Cultural Survey of Some Sex Differences in Socialization," *Journal of Abnormal Psychology* 55 (1957): 327-332.
12. This last claim is not stated explicitly but seems to be derivable from the data which they present on comparison within sexes for each type of society.
13. Zinacantan, a highland Indian community in Mexico where I did field work, perfectly exemplifies this hypothetical description. Men's agricultural work is done in the lowlands, away from the community, and boys, depending on whether or not they are in school, do not work with their fathers until they are nine to eleven. They perform a certain amount of "helping" work when they are young—fetching things, and so forth—but this is not seen as "real" work for them. They remain without real work training from their mothers, while their sisters as they grow up learn progressively how to tend fires, cook, and weave. As the boy's role in his house seems to become less and less relevant, and he is less and less able to fill his time meaningfully, he turns increasingly to antics to get attention from his all-too-busy mother and sisters.
14. Whiting and Whiting, "Egoism and Altruism," p. 35.
15. *Ibid.*
16. Barry, Bacon, and Child, "Relation of Child Training to Subsistence Economy."
17. Beatrice Whiting told me in a conversation that their data indicate that girl children stay closer to their mothers, receive more numerous and frequent commands than boys. She suggests that this is training specifically useful for childrearing and household work, in which a woman has to expect to be interrupted irregularly in whatever tasks she is doing, and cannot detach herself from her surrounding situation nor try many new ways to work. This seems to relate to typical "feminine" intellectual characteristics—nonabstract thinking, field dependence, etc.—and also to be closer to the kind of training boys would get in economies where they are gradually trained and given specific work to do.
18. Barry, Bacon, and Child, "Relation of Child Training to Subsistence Economy," p. 56.
19. Whiting and Whiting, "Task Assignment and Personality."
20. Barry, Bacon, and Child, "Cross-Cultural Survey of Some Sex Differences in Socialization," p. 330.
21. Whiting and Whiting, "Egoism and Altruism."
22. Barry, Bacon, and Child, "Cross-Cultural Survey of Some Sex Differences in Socialization."
23. Ruth Benedict, "Continuities and Discontinuities in Cultural Condition," in Margaret Mead and Martha Wolfenstein, eds., *Childhood in Contemporary Cultures* (Chicago: University of Chicago Press, 1955), p. 22.
24. Mead, *op. cit.*, p. 167.
25. Talcott Parsons, "Age and Sex in the Social Structure of the United States," *American Sociological Review* 7 (1942): 604-616. I would like to note here that the fact that these are "important aspects" does not necessarily mean that they are im-

portant in actual economic or social fact or in a society's, or
the little girl's, evaluation of them. I will go into the implications of this fact for female development below.

26. *Ibid.*
27. Karen Horney, "The Dread of Women," *International Journal
    of Psychoanalysis* 13 (1932): 359.
28. Mead, *op. cit.*, p. 167.
29. *Ibid.*, p. 303.
30. Parsons, *op. cit.*
31. Mead, *op. cit.*, p. 295.
32. Simone de Beauvoir, *The Second Sex* (New York: Bantam
    Books, 1968).
33. *Ibid.*, p. 278.
34. Mead, *op. cit.*, p. 298.
35. Horney, *op. cit.*
36. *Ibid.*, p. 351.
37. *Ibid.*
38. *Ibid.*, p. 357.
39. *Ibid.*, p. 351.
40. Mead, *op. cit.*, p. 168.
41. *Ibid.*
42. Melford E. Spiro, *Children of the Kibbutz: A Study in Child
    Training and Personality* (New York: Schocken Books, 1965).
43. The following interpretation was not made by Spiro, but seemed
    to me to explain fairly clearly many differences between men
    and women which Spiro did not seem to understand.
44. Spiro, *op. cit.*, p. 291.
45. *Ibid.*, p. 352.
46. Daniel G. Brown, "Sex-Role Preference in Young Children,"
    Psychological Monographs 70 (1956): 1-19; "Masculinity-Fem-
    ininity Development in Children," *Journal of Consulting Psy-
    chology* 21 (1957): 197-202; "Sex Role Development in a
    Changing Culture," *Psychological Bulletin* 55 (1958): 232-242.
47. Brown, "Sex Role Development in a Changing Culture," pp.
    237-238; Lawrence Kohlberg, "A Cognitive-Developmental
    Analysis of Children's Sex Role Concepts and Attitudes," in
    Maccoby, *op. cit.*
48. The dynamics of this are not as clear as Burton and Whiting
    suggest. In most "matrilocal" societies (usually also matrilineal),
    "control" or "power" still rests in the hands of men, although
    these men are now "mother's brothers" or "mother's maternal
    uncles" rather than fathers and grandfathers (see David
    Schneider and Kathleen Gough, eds., *Matrilineal Kinship*
    [Berkeley: University of California Press, 1967], for the most
    extensive treatment of matrilineal societies). Although these
    men may spend a lot of time with their own wives, thus away
    from the maternal residence, it is not clear how the exercise of
    power is then distributed: whether it is given to the women of
    the lineage, exercised only on special occasions by men of the
    lineage, or entrusted to in-marrying men. In-marrying men may
    control the day-to-day operation of the economy, even though
    they are not owners of the lands or their produce. I do not wish
    to discount Burton and Whiting's theory, but simply to point
    out that to understand it, the relation between matrilocal resi-
    dence and the operation of control and power both in lineage
    theory and in everyday life (perhaps the instability of what men
    control what and are around when) would have to be examined

more closely than their initial hypothesis would lead us to believe.

49. Roger V. Burton and John W. M. Whiting, "The Absent Father and Cross-Sex Identity," *Merrill-Palmer Quarterly* 7 (1961): 85-95. It is not within the scope of this essay to evaluate Whiting's status-envy hypothesis as a learning theory, although clearly, the extent to which we would want to accept his conclusions depends largely on this evaluation.

50. *Ibid.*, p. 91.

51. Bruno Bettelheim, *Symbolic Wounds: Puberty Rites and the Envious Male* (Glencoe: The Free Press, 1954), p. 45.

52. Bettelheim does not restrict this interpretation to male initiation rites only, but claims that female initiation rites may equally be expressions of envy for the masculine role. He emphasizes male initiation and envy of the female because he feels that female envy of male sex functions—penis envy—has been overemphasized at the expense of the other. He suggests that this is because "in any society, envy of the dominant sex is the more easily observed [and] more readily admitted, more openly expressed and more easily recognized." (Bettelheim, *op. cit.*, p. 56.) It is also true that female initiation rites are not nearly so widespread nor so complex as male rites. Bettelheim suggests, rightly, I think, that this is because while women can express their jealousy of men openly in most societies and it is considered only natural that they should be jealous—"the consensus is that it is desirable to be a man" (*ibid.*)—men's jealousy is not so admissible and "can be expressed only in ritual" (*ibid.*). This is in accordance with reasons for differences in the strictness of male and female socialization which I discussed earlier.

53. Burton and Whiting, *op. cit.*

54. I would maintain that even in these societies, mothers have more control of resources and spend more time with children, so that boys would still have a harder time than girls in developing a sex-role identity.

55. Burton and Whiting, *op. cit.*, p. 90.

56. *Ibid.*; Beatrice B. Whiting, "Sex Identity Conflict and Physical Violence: A Comparative Study," unpublished paper.

57. Philip and Dori I. Slater, "Maternal Ambivalence and Narcissism: A Cross-Cultural Study," *Merrill-Palmer Quarterly* 2 (1965): 241-259. Both B. Whiting and Slater suggest that the personality structure of women in societies where husbands are absent or where the marriage relationship is distant may also be affected. Slater suggests that women may be resentful of their subordinate and isolated role in the society at large and compensate for this by exercising arbitrary and great power in the household, particularly over male children. The crux of this behavior is that it is not simply an expression of the mother's need to denigrate sons in order to get back at older men for denigrating her, but that it expresses a need both to build up and to deflate sons, to push achievement and punish for success—thus, to insure that her son's sense of self is dependent on her arbitrary whim. Whiting suggests also that women raised in mother-child households and mothers in these households tend to be more assertive and dominant than women reared in nuclear households. This would combine with the actual fact of their sole power in the household and over

children to create greater difficulty for boys to assert themselves or to feel capable of achieving a different male identity.

58. Mead, *op. cit.*, p. 303.
59. *Ibid.*, p. 168.
60. Beauvoir, *op. cit.*, p. 267.
61. Kohlberg, *op. cit.*, p. 162.
62. Slater and Slater, *op. cit.*, pp. 249-250.
63. Beauvoir, *op. cit.*, pp. 249-497; Betty Friedan, *The Feminine Mystique* (New York: Dell Publishing Co., 1963).
64. Kohlberg, *op. cit.*, p. 117.
65. *Ibid.*, pp. 118-119.
66. *Ibid.*, p. 120. Further evidence that these changes of preference do not reflect identity confusion but rather identity disenchantment is provided by the existence of parallel changes with age of preferences in mildly disadvantaged racial groups. Kohlberg cites a study (Doris V. Springer, "Awareness of Racial Differences by Preschool Children in Hawaii," 1950) which shows that same-race preferences among Oriental children in Hawaii show a similar decline with age as same-sex preferences in girls. It seems inconceivable that this could indicate that these children were becoming less sure of their racial identity as they grew older, just as it seems inconceivable that girls should become less sure of their feminine identity.
67. *Ibid.*, p. 121.
68. Karen Horney, "The Flight from Womanhood: The Masculinity Complex in Women, as Viewed by Men and by Women," *International Journal of Psychoanalysis* 7 (1926): 324-339.
69. *Ibid.*, p. 337.
70. *Ibid.*, p. 338.
71. Beauvoir, *op. cit.*, p. 314.
72. *Ibid.*, p. 301.

12

ORGANS AND ORGASMS

Alix Shulman

This essay is not about love-making, a subject comprising emotional as well as anatomical considerations. Rather, it is about genital relations, and how they have adversely affected the lives of women. The myths and lies about female genital anatomy are so widespread and so harmful to women that the subject deserves an altogether separate consideration, even though it is only half the story.

Almost from the very beginning of our lives, we are all taught that the primary male sex organ is the penis, and the primary female sex organ is the vagina. These organs are supposed to define the sexes, to be the difference between boys and girls. We are taught that the reason for the differences, and the use to which the sex organs are put, has to do with making babies.

This is a lie. In our society only occasionally are those organs used to make babies. Much more often they are used to produce sexual pleasure for men, pleasure which culminates in ejaculation. The penis and the vagina together can make either babies or male orgasms; very rarely do the two together make female orgasms. Men, who have benefited greatly from both orgasms and babies, have had no reason to question the traditional definition of penis and vagina as true genital counterparts.

Women, on the other hand, have. Woman's sexual pleasure is often left out in these definitions. If people considered that the purpose of the female sex organs is to bring pleasure to *women*, then female sex would be defined by, and focused on, a different organ. Everyone would be taught from infancy that, as the primary male sex organ is the penis, so the primary female sex organ is the clitoris.

Men could never plead ignorance, as they now commonly do, if from the beginning, their sex education went something like this:

BOY: What's the difference between boys and girls?
MOTHER: Mainly their sex organs. A boy has a penis and a girl has a clitoris.
BOY: What's a clitoris?
MOTHER: It's a tiny sensitive organ on a girl's body about where a penis is on a boy's body. It feels good to touch; like your penis.
BOY: Do girls pee through their clitorises?
MOTHER: No.
BOY: What's it for?
MOTHER: For making love, for pleasure. When people love each other, one of the ways they show it is by caressing one another's bodies, including their sex organs.
BOY: How do girls pee?
MOTHER: There's an opening below the clitoris for peeing. A man uses his penis for peeing, for making love, and for starting babies. Women have three separate places for these. For peeing they have an opening into the urethra; for making love they have a clitoris; and for the first step in making babies they have a separate opening into the vagina. A lot of other organs in women and men are used in making babies too.
BOY: How are babies made? (And so on . . .)

ORGANS

It has long been known that the clitoris is endlessly more sensitive than the vagina, more sensitive than the penis too, if one judges by the number of nerve endings in the organs. In fact, anatomically, the clitoris and the penis have many similarities since they develop from the same cells in the female or male fetus. Yet, as Ruth Herschberger pointed out in her brilliant 1948 book on female sexuality, *Adam's Rib*, society refuses to acknowledge it: "It was quite a feat of nature to grant the small clitoris the same number of nerves as the penis. It was an even more incredible feat that society should actually have convinced the possessors of this organ that it was sexually inferior to the penis."[1] The vagina, on the other hand, is for the most part so little sensitive that women commonly wear a diaphragm or tampon in it, and even undergo surgery on it, without feeling any sensation at all.

Despite the known anatomical facts and the experiences of many, many women, men usually insist that the vagina *is* the organ of female pleasure. Most of them insist, and probably believe, that women, like men, achieve orgasm by means of the movement of the penis back and forth into the vagina. While perpetuating this myth of vaginal primacy, from which they so readily benefit, the male "experts" make a small concession to the puzzling discrepancies in the "facts." Taking their cue from Freud, they claim that there are *two* kinds of orgasm: vaginal and clitoral. But of the two, they argue, only the vaginal kind, which is adapted to the male anatomy and suits male pleasure, is necessary, is valuable; the clitoral kind is not. Here is Freud himself:

> In the phallic phase of the girl, the clitoris is the dominant erotogenic zone. But it is not destined to remain so; with the change to femininity, the clitoris must give up to the vagina its sensitivity, and, with it, its importance, either wholly or in part. This is one of the two tasks which have to be performed in the course of the woman's development; the more fortunate man has only to continue at the time of his sexual maturity what he has already practiced during the period of early sexual expansion.[2]

A woman who fails to transfer her sexual sensitivity from the clitoris to the vagina at puberty is, according to Freud, regressive, infantile, neurotic, hysteric, and frigid. The vaginal orgasm is supposedly mature, beautiful and good, while the clitoral orgasm is infantile, perverse, bad. A woman is frigid according to many of Freud's followers even today, if she does not have vaginal orgasms even though she may have frequent clitoral orgasms.

In their jokes and in their pornography, in their theories and in their marriage manuals, men treat the clitoris as simply one more erogenous zone like the breasts, underarms, or ears, to be used to arouse a woman sexually so that she will permit intercourse. They may remember the clitoris in foreplay, but for real sex, back to the vagina! The true center of female sexuality, the clitoris, is never identified for little girls who, when they accidentally discover they have one, often think themselves freaks to have on their bodies such a sensitive, unnamed thing. Most girls are not even told about the clitoris at puberty, when they may be instructed in the rites of feminine hygiene and intercourse. The diagrams of female genital anatomy that accompany most tampons and birth control devices usually illustrate the urinary bladder and the ovaries, but hardly ever the clitoris.

ORGASMS

Women know from personal experience that there is only one kind of orgasm, no matter what name it is given, vaginal, clitoral, psychological. It is a sexual orgasm. Women know there is only one set of responses, one group of things that happen in their bodies during orgasm. It may vary in intensity from one experience to another, but for any woman who has ever masturbated, orgasm is unmistakable and certainly cannot be confused with anything else. No woman masturbating ever wonders whether or not orgasm has occurred. She has no doubts about that. When it happens, she knows it.

The recent laboratory research on female sexuality conducted by Virginia Johnson and William E. Masters confirms clinically what women know to be true from their own experience. If a woman experiences orgasm during intercourse, it is not a special kind of orgasm with a special set of physiological responses; it is like any other orgasm. Without exception, the Masters-Johnson data show that all orgasms, *no matter what kind of stimulation produces them,* result in almost identical bodily changes for all women—vaginal contractions, increase in body temperature, increase in pulse and respiration rate, and so forth. Though it is produced through the clitoris, the orgasm occurs as well in the vagina, the anus, the heart, the lungs, the skin, the head.

Given this clarity about what an orgasm feels like, why then does a woman occasionally confess she "doesn't know" whether or not she has had orgasm during intercourse? If orgasm had occurred, she would know it. Since she does not know it, it cannot have occurred. Nevertheless, since she has been taught to expect some special kind of orgasm called vaginal orgasm which can occur only during intercourse, she wonders. She can not know what such an orgasm is supposed to feel like because *there is no such thing.* The sensations of a penis in a vagina are indeed different from other sensations; accompanied by the right emotions they may be so pleasurable as to tempt a woman to hope that they can somehow qualify for that mysterious, desirable thing that has been touted as vaginal orgasm, even though they may not at all resemble the sensations she knows as orgasm. If she does not take advantage of the mystery and confusion surrounding the term to believe that perhaps she has indeed had a vaginal orgasm, she may feel compelled at least to pretend that she has. If not, she must submit to being called frigid or infantile by professional name-calling psychologists, doctors, and all who listen to them, and she must risk the displeasure and reprisal of her mate.

The truth is, there is only *one* kind of orgasm, one set of physiological responses constituting orgasm, all those Freudians to the contrary. The term "vaginal orgasm" must go. It signifies orgasm achieved by means of intercourse alone (for which no special term is necessary), or it signifies nothing at all. Some women testify to having experienced orgasm at some time in their lives through intercourse alone; some women say they have experienced orgasm through stimulation of the breasts alone, or through stimulation of the mind alone, or during dreams. Apparently orgasm can be achieved by various routes. However, the Masters-Johnson research shows, the most reliable way of regularly reaching orgasm for most women is by stimulation of the clitoris.

The clitoris may be stimulated to climax by a hand, by a tongue, or, particularly if the woman is free to move or to control the man's movements, by intercourse. No one way or combination of ways is "better" than any other, though women often prefer one way or another, finding that one way is rather more effective than another. Evidently for most women, intercourse by itself rarely results in orgasm, though vaginal stimulation may certainly make enjoyable foreplay or even afterplay. Masters and Johnson observe that the clitoris is automatically "stimulated" in intercourse since the hood covering the clitoris is pulled over the clitoris with each thrust of the penis in the vagina—much, I suppose, as a penis is automatically "stimulated" by a man's underwear whenever he takes a step. I wonder, however, if either is erotically stimulating by itself.

REACTIONS

The word about the clitoris has been out for a long time, and still, for political reasons, society goes on believing the old myths and enforcing a double standard of sexuality. Some societies have dealt with the facts by performing clitoridectomies—cutting off clitorises. More commonly, the facts about female sexuality are simply suppressed, ignored, or explained away. A century before Freud, for example, the learned Diderot cited women's lack of control over her senses[3] to explain the infrequency of her orgasm during intercourse:

> There are some women who will die without ever having experienced the climax of sensual pleasures. . . . Since [women] have much less control over their senses than we, the rewards they receive from them are less certain and less prompt. Their expectations are being continually belied. With a physical structure so much the opposite of our own, the cue that sets their sensuality in play is so delicate and its source so far removed that we cannot be surprised at its not reaching fulfillment or becoming lost on the way.[4]

Freud's ingenious formulation, though widely believed, is only one of many.

Since the Kinsey Report and the Masters-Johnson studies, it has become increasingly embarrassing to certain experts and self-styled lovers to go on ignoring the clinical facts and the testimony of women. In 1966 in an analysis of the Masters-Johnson research, Ruth and Edward Brecher listed three myths now recognized to have been disproved by the sex research, among them the myth that women have two kinds of orgasm, one clitoral, the other vaginal. The Brechers' conclusion was that "women concerned with their failure to reach 'vaginal orgasm' can thus be reassured."[5] But that is surely the wrong conclusion. It is not women who have been "failing" and must be "reassured." It is the male-dominated society that has been failing and must be changed. Many studies of female sexuality (95 percent of which, Masters and Johnson point out, are undertaken by men "either from the defensive point of view of personal masculine bias, or from a well-intentioned and often significant scientific position, but, because of cultural bias, without opportunity to obtain unprejudiced material")[6] remark on the spectacularly high degree of frigidity among women. Almost all of them interpret it as a failing of women, not of men or of society, despite the intrusive fact that, as Masters and Johnson observe, "women's ... physiological capacity for sexual response infinitely surpasses that of man."

Although Masters and Johnson share the assumptions of our male culture that woman's goal must be to reach orgasm during intercourse—even though this usually requires getting to the brink of orgasm outside intercourse—in their newest report, *Human Sexual Inadequacy*, they examine the causes of "female sexual dysfunction" more honestly than their predecessors.

Sociocultural influence more often than not places woman in a position in which she must adapt, sublimate, inhibit, or even distort her natural capacity to function sexually in order to fulfill her genetically assigned role [i.e., breeding]. *Herein lies a major source of woman's sexual dysfunction.*[7]

Probably hundreds of thousands of men never gain sufficient ejaculatory control to satisfy their wives sexually regardless of the duration of marriage or the frequency of natural sexual exposure.[8]

Another salient feature in the human female's disadvantaged role in coital connection is the centuries-old concept that it is woman's duty to satisfy her sexual partner. When the age-old demand for accommodation during coital connection dominates any woman's responsivity, her own opportunites for orgasmic expression are lessened proportionately. . . . The heedless male driving for orgasm can carry along the woman already lost in high levels of sexual demand, but his chances of elevating to orgasm the woman who is trying to accommodate to the rhythm, depth, and power of his demanding pelvic thrusting are indeed poor.[9]

The most unfortunate misconception our culture has assigned to sexual functioning is the assumption, by both men and women, that men by divine guidance and infallible instinct are able to discern exactly what a woman wants sexually and when she wants it. Probably this fallacy has interfered with natural sexual interaction as much as any other single factor.[10]

The husband must not presume his wife's desire for a particular stimulative approach, nor must he introduce his own choice of stimuli.[11]

But of the experts, Masters and Johnson are almost alone in not blaming women for the terrible betrayal of their sex lives.

Why? Clearly, this state of ignorance is not a result of simple unavailability of the facts. It is a manifestation of political and social choices. For, as Ann Koedt pointed out in "The Myth of the Vaginal Orgasm," "Today, with extensive knowledge of anatomy . . . there is no ignorance on the subject. There are, however, social reasons why this knowledge has not been popularized. We are living in a male society which has not sought change in women's role."[12] No, given our male-dominated society, the mere facts about female sexuality are not enough. The medical experts to this day find it easy to acknowledge the research evidence about the primacy of the clitoris—and *then* to dismiss its obvious meaning. Dr. Leslie H. Farber, for example, upon learning that the female orgasm is not produced by the vagina, simply throws out the importance of female orgasm. In a celebrated essay lamenting the Masters and Johnson research, Dr. Farber announced:

As far as I know little attention was paid to female orgasm before the era of sexology. Where did the sexologists find it? Did they discover or invent it? Or both? . . . My guess, which is not subject to laboratory proof, is that the female orgasm was always an occasional, though not essential, part of woman's whole sexual experience. I also suspect that it appeared with regularity or predictability only during masturbation. . . . *She was content with the mystery and variety of her difference from man, and in fact would not have had it otherwise.*[13]

But surely, some attention was paid to female orgasm before the era of sexology, or else how could it have appeared "with regularity . . . during masturbation"? What Dr. Farber apparently means to say is that before Kinsey little attention was paid to female orgasm *by men*. Too true. Why does Dr. Farber lament the findings of the sexologists? Because look what the findings do to a man's sex life. Nowadays, while ejaculating a man must "learn to take his moment in stride, so to speak, omitting the deference these moments usually call forth and then with-

out breaking stride get to his self-appointed and often
fatiguing task of tinkering with his mate—always hopeful
that his ministrations will have the appearance of affection."[14] If a woman had to endure that attitude to reach
orgasm outside of masturbation, no wonder she preferred
to accept her "difference from man." As Masters and
Johnson observe "epaculation . . . may provide welcome
relief for the woman accepting and fulfilling a role as a
sexual object."[15]

Donald W. Hastings, reviewing medical literature
dealing with masturbation, observes a double standard of
sexuality (and likely its cause) which in less sensational
form persists to this day.

> Articles in the older literature even went so far as to
> advocate the following procedures for correcting female
> masturbation: amputation or cautery of the clitoris, . . .
> miniature chasity belts, sewing the vaginal lips together to
> put the clitoris out of reach, and even castration by
> surgical removal of the ovaries. [But, continues Dr.
> Hastings in a footnote,] there are no references in the
> medical literature to surgical removal of testicles or ampu-
> tation of the penis to stop masturbation. One wonders
> what heroic measures might have been proposed for boys
> if women instead of men had composed the medical
> profession of the time.[16]

Yes, one wonders. And one wonders what might have
been defined as the major male and female sex organs, the
standard sexual position, the psychic "tasks of development" as Freud called them, and in fact, masculinity and
femininity themselves, if women instead of men had composed not only the medical profession, but the dominant
caste in society as well.

Men do not easily give up the myths about female
sexuality because, whether they are aware of it or not, men
benefit from believing them. Believing in the primacy of
the vagina allows them to use women for their own sexual
pleasure, commandeering vaginas without considering
themselves rapists. Believing in vaginal orgasm frees them
of responsibility for a woman's sexual pleasure; if a woman does not reach orgasm through intercourse, it is her
own psychological failing. If they give pleasure to a woman another way, they are doing her a favor. It does not
occur to them that, as Ann Koedt says, "if certain sexual
positions now defined as 'standard' are not mutually con-

ducive to orgasm, they [must] no longer be defined as standard."[17] They do not admit that, as Ti-Grace Atkinson observes in "The Institution of Sexual Intercourse," "the whole point of vaginal orgasm is that it supports the view that vaginal penetration [by a penis] is a good in and for itself."[18] By perpetuating these myths society perpetuates the notion that women must be dependent solely on men for their sexual satisfaction and subordinate to the male interpretation of female pleasure.

THE DISCOVERY

For thousands of years men have—perhaps unconsciously—benefited from these myths and have therefore believed them, nourishing them through all the various channels of culture, despite all the evidence to the contrary. But why have women, who know from experience that the vagina is *not* the source of their sexual pleasure, and who know only one kind of orgasm, believed in these myths?

Kept apart for so long, women until recently have been under great pressure not to discuss their sexual experiences with other women, just as Masters and Johnson were under great pressure not to study sex in the laboratory. Without information many women have, from childhood on, considered their own sexual experience exceptional and themselves inadequate, if not neurotic, infantile, frigid, or simply freaks. Though each one recognized that the sex myths did not describe *her own* experience, she assumed that they did describe the experience of *other* women, about whom she had no real information. And many women secretly hoped that their own experience would some day follow suit. Now that women, the only real experts on female sexuality, are beginning to talk together and compare notes, they are discovering that their experiences are remarkably similar and that they are not freaks. In the process of exposing the myths and lies, women are discovering that it is not they who have individual sex problems; it is society that has one great big political problem.

There are actually laws on the books in most states that define as "unnatural" and therefore criminal any (sexual) position other than that of the woman on the bottom and the man on the top; laws that make oral sex a crime though for many women it is the only way of achieving orgasm with another person; laws that make homosexuality a crime, though for some people it is the only acceptable way of loving.

The pressures that have long made so many women forego orgasm during love-making and fake orgasm during intercourse are real social pressures. The explanation that it is all simply a result of ignorance, men's and women's, will not do. Hopelessly isolated from each other in their cells in a male-dominated society, even with the facts around, women have still had to fake orgasm to keep their men, to hide their imagined or imputed inadequacy, to demonstrate "love," to gain a man's approval, to boost a man's ego, or, with orgasm nowhere in sight, to get the man please to stop. But with women getting together, the day may soon be approaching when they will exert enough counterpressure to define female sexuality in their own way, and to insist that, just as male sexuality is centered not in the scrotum but in the penis, female sexuality is centered not in the vagina but in the clitoris. When that happens, perhaps it will seem as perverse for a man to ejaculate without stimulating a woman to orgasm as it is now for a woman to reach climax outside intercourse.

Think clitoris.

NOTES

1. Ruth Herschberger, *Adam's Rib* (New York: Pellegrini & Cudahy, 1948), p. 31.
2. Sigmund Freud, *New Introductory Lectures on Psycho-Analysis* (London: Hogarth Press, 1946), pp. 151-152.
3. It is not their senses, but their bodies, over which women have less control than men: men control them.
4. Denis Diderot, "On Women" (1772), in Lester Crocker ed., *Selected Writings*, tr. Derek Coltman (New York: Macmillan, 1966), p. 310.
5. Ruth and Edward Brecher, *An Analysis of Human Sexual Response* (New York: Signet, 1966), p. 84.
6. William H. Masters and Virginia E. Johnson, *Human Sexual Inadequacy* (Boston: Little Brown, 1970), p. 214. See also the earlier study by the same authors, *Human Sexual Response* (Boston: Little Brown, 1966).
7. Masters and Johnson, *Human Sexual Inadequacy*, p. 218.
8. *Ibid.*, p. 96.
9. *Ibid.*, p. 229.
10. *Ibid.*, p. 87.
11. *Ibid.*, p. 301.

12. Ann Koedt, "The Myth of the Vaginal Orgasm," in Shulamith Firestone and Ann Koedt, eds., *Notes from the Second Year: Women's Liberation* (New York, 1970), p. 39.
13. Leslie H. Farber, "I'm Sorry, Dear," in Brecher and Brecher, *op. cit.*, p. 310. Italics added.
14. *Ibid.*
15. Masters and Johnson, *Human Sexual Inadequacy*, p. 93.
16. Donald W. Hastings, "Can Specific Training Procedures Overcome Sexual Inadequacy?" in Brecher and Brecher, *op. cit.*, p. 232.
17. Koedt, *op. cit.*, p. 38.
18. Ti-Grace Atkinson, "The Institution of Sexual Intercourse," in Firestone and Koedt, *op. cit.*, p. 44.

13

THE IMAGE OF WOMAN IN ADVERTISING

Lucy Komisar

Look in a mirror. If you are a woman, what do you see? A woman waxing a floor? Feeding children? Spraying her hair? Scribbling on a steno pad? Gazing at a man with mixed reverence and awe? The simple mirrors that hang over bureaus and on the backs of closet doors only tell us superficial physical things about ourselves. The real-life mirrors are the media, and for women the most invidious mirror of all is advertising.

There once was some concern over the danger of subliminal advertising that would force people to make subconscious decisions about products or politics. Advertising today is not subliminal, but its subtle psychological effect is as devastating as any secret message flashed at high speeds to unsuspecting viewers. Advertising exploits and reinforces the myths of woman's place with messages of such infinite variety and number that one might as easily deny that the earth revolves around the sun as entirely reject their influence. Advertising is an insidious propaganda machine for a male supremacist society. It spews out images of women as sex mates, housekeepers, mothers and menial workers—images that perhaps reflect the true status of most women in society, but which also make it increasingly difficult for women to break out of the sexist stereotypes that imprison them.

Ironically, one hope remains: that the constant humiliating image of the role women are expected to play will draw their degradation in lines too bold and clear to ignore, and that women finally will arise in disgust and outrage to destroy the distortions reflected by that real-life mirror and to challenge the existence of sexism itself.

In December 1969, outside Macy's department store in New York City, a group of women staged what may have been the first protest demonstration against the image of women presented by advertising. Mattel Toys, the target of the protest, had run an ad in *Life* magazine to promote its line for the Christmas trade.

> Because girls dream about being a ballerina, Mattel makes Dancerina . . . a pink confection in a silken blouse and ruffled tutu. . . . Wishing you were older is part of growing up . . . Barbie, a young fashion model, and her friends do the "in" things girls should do—talk about new places to visit, new clothes to wear and new friends to meet,

said one part of the ad. The other half declared:

> Because boys were born to build and learn, Mattell makes Tog'l [a set of building blocks for creative play].

The illustration showed a boy playing with

> . . . imaginative and fantastic creatures that challenge young minds to think as they build. . . . Because boys are curious about things big and small, Mattel makes Super-Eyes, a telescope that boys can have in one ingenious set of optically engineered lenses and scopes . . . that . . . create dozens of viewing devices—all for science or all for fun.

"Mattel Limits Little Girls' Dreams" and "Girls Were Also Born to Build and Learn" charged the signs strung out in front of Macy's that day. Passersby were curious. Some stopped to read the leaflets; some nodded their agreement as the sidewalk traffic nudged them on. Media Women, sponsor of the demonstration, wrote a letter to Mattel, but there was no reply.

Advertising begins stereotyping male and female very early in life: the little girl who was taught to want to be a model or a ballerina and imbued with the importance of how she looks and what she wears grows up to be a thirty-year-old Barbie Doll with advertising still providing the cues.

Madison Avenue Woman is a combination sex object and wife and mother who achieves fulfillment by looking beautiful and alluring for boy friends and lovers and cooking, cleaning, washing, or polishing for her husband and family. She is not very bright; she is submissive and subservient to men; if she has a job, it is probably that of a secretary or an airline hostess. What she does is not very important anyway since the chief interest in her life is the "male reward" advertisers dangle enticingly in front of her. ("Male reward" is, in fact, the argot used in the trade.)

Behold the compleat woman constructed by American advertising. In adolescence she has passed the stage of playing with dolls, but her life goals and interests have not advanced appreciably, as witnessed by this ad from Parker Pens:

> You might as well give her a gorgeous pen to keep her checkbook unbalanced with. A sleek and shining pen will make her feel prettier. Which is more important to any girl than solving mathematical mysteries.

Later, the Quest for the Holy Male becomes more serious business, with toothpaste, hair color, brassiere, cosmetic, and mouthwash companies all competing to help land the man who is, after all, the prize a young woman has striven for since prepubescence. Ultra Brite toothpaste "gives your mouth sex appeal"; Colgate mouthwash is "the mouthwash for lovers." An ad for bath oil shows a man embracing a woman while the copy blazes away: "Sardo. When you live with a man."

Nearly half the women in the country work, but you wouldn't think so to look at American advertising. A woman's place is not only in the home, according to most copywriters and art directors, it is in the kitchen or the laundryroom. An ad for IBM declares, "Your wife's office is probably better equipped than yours" and pictures a youthful housewife surrounded by the shining implements of her trade: wall oven, electric stove with grease hood, blender, rotisserie, four-slice toaster, and electric coffee pot.

If television commercials are to be believed, most American women go into uncontrollable ecstasies at the sight and smell of tables and cabinets that have been lovingly caressed with long-lasting, satin-finish, lemon-scented, spray-on furniture polish. Or they glow with rap-

ture at the blinding whiteness of their wash—and the
green-eyed envy of their neighbors. The housewife in the
Johnson's Wax commercial hugs the dining room table
because the shine is so wonderful; then she polishes herself
into a corner and has to jump over the furniture to get
out. Bold detergent shows one woman in deep depression
because her wash is not as bright as her neighbor's.

In a country where the low status of maids probably
cannot be matched, where the more than one and a half
million household workers (98 percent female, nearly
two-thirds black) have median year-round, full-time wages
of $1,523—they are excluded from the federal minimum
wage laws—it is an amazing feat of hocus pocus worthy
of Tom Sawyer and Phineas T. Barnum to lovingly declare that domestic labor is the true vocation of women
wearing wedding bands.

There is a special irony in the fact that women, who
presumably spend most of their waking hours in the kitch-
en or laundryroom, receive instructions about how to do
their housework from men: Arthur Godfrey, who probably never put his hands into soapsuds, tells women across
the country why they ought to add still another step to
their washing routine with Axion Pre-Soak. Joseph Daley,
president of Grey Advertising, says that men are used
because the male voice is the voice of authority. Others
add that while the execution of housework is only menial,
thus female, the development of detergents and polishes is
scientific, therefore male.

One of some half-dozen female advertising agency pres-
idents, Franchellie Cadwell (Cadwell-Davis), adds another
wrinkle to the interpretation of the strategy behind household cleaning product commercials. She thinks the White
Knight and Giant-in-the-Washing-Machine images are sex
symbols that help housewives assuage their own guilts and
imagined inadequacies by acting out a cleanliness neurosis
(or fetish!). In any event there is an obvious attempt to
promote sexual fantasies with soap advertising. One Lever
Brothers commercial tried to project a virtual love affair
between housewife and soap-suds. The product, called
"Hero," was to be terribly male; women were to be able
to have a liason with the detergent while their husbands
were at the office. "Hero" was an animated Greek God,
and hundreds of women bearing baskets of laundry were
shown worshipping at his feet. The commercial was run in
test markets but was withdrawn because of objections

from the public—not from women, but from people who protested on religious grounds, saying it was blasphemous! In a commercial for Chiffon dishwashing liquid, a woman is dreamily doing the dishes when a handsome stranger à la Marcello Mastroianni slips in through the back door, kisses her hand, and gets soap on his lip. End of fantasy.

The mother role is expressed more by cooking than cleaning. "Nothin' says lovin' like something from the oven. . . ." Pillsbury did a study of the American housewife which came up with the not unexpected conclusion that motherhood is her primary drive,—and obviously she loves to stay home and cook. In fact, advertisers appear to believe that women feel *guilty* when they don't spend enough time preparing meals for their families. One marketing consultant declared that Kellogg's corn flakes with freeze-dried bananas failed, because Kellogg "violated woman's sacred prerogative, that of participating in the preparation of at least a portion of a meal for her family. She wants convenience foods, but she doesn't want to feel guilty or foolish because everything has been done for her." The consultant did not consider the possibility that dried-up bananas might be unappetizing.

Like the "soaps," ads that involve cooking or child care assume that only women can do these jobs—or ought to—except for backyard barbecuing, which was somehow certified as "male." Even advertisers for other products seem to think that women have a cooking fixation. Buick ran an ad with a picture and recipe for seafood mousse on the apparent assumption that there wasn't anything it could say about cars to interest women readers.

It is recognized that women do work outside the home, but the only work they appear to do in advertising is the kind that allows them to assist, or make life more pleasant for, men. Some of the ads seem to be selling flesh on the hoof. Like this one for Iberia Airlines: "This nice little blonde from Barcelona will romance you all the way to Spain. And England. And France. And Germany. And . . ." Iberia leaves the rest to your imagination. New York Chemical Bank's ad about its new "hostesses" boasts that "We have a pretty girl who won't let you get in the wrong line."

IBM talks about the businessman, obviously male, and his secretary: "If she makes a mistake, she types right over it. If her boss makes a revision, she types just the revision." Somehow, secretaries, who are always women, make mistakes; bosses, who are always men, make "revisions."

Dictaphone Corporation adds a new insult to the men-are-bosses-women-are-secretaries routine. A pretty blonde woman in a micro-mini skirt sits at her desk polishing her nails as four worried men try to arouse her interest in some calculating machines. Says the copy: "Our new line of calculators goes through its final ordeal. The dumb blonde test."

Often the image of woman as sex object is not cluttered up with the extraneous idea that women hold jobs, even if they are jobs as helpers to men. In the "pure sex object" category, women are exploited outrightly for the titillation and amusement, sometimes even the sadistic fascination, of men.

Myra Janco Daniels, president of Draper Daniels, Inc., in Chicago, sees a "feudal concept of women as property" in some cigarette commercials: "One gets the impression that the girls are given away as premiums although these brands aren't featuring coupons at present." Silva Thins is the epitome of the genre. The handsome, unsmiling man in dark glasses punishes any woman who presumes to take his cigarettes. With cool deliberation, he deserts them on highways, ocean liners, cable cars, and mountain tops. Another variation in the campaign proclaims: "Cigarettes are like women—the best ones are rich and thin."

A male columnist in the trade publication *Ad Age* admits that the commercials have "silent masochistic overtones," meaning that the ad relies on the culturally submissive female response. Women, the columnist says, "seem to feel right at home with the situations. They quite willingly put themselves in the place of the suffering heroine." He concludes, "The makers of this campaign demonstrate a shrewd insight into the emotional make-up of today's woman." The hero "summarily puts his girl-friend in her place, exactly where so many women would unconsciously like to be."

Like the Silva Thins commercial, woman-as-sex-object ads generally seek to fulfill male fantasies about seducing or wielding power over women. For example, "Tonight offer her a daiquiri made with Ronrico, Puerto Rico's tasteful rum. Then watch her slip into something light and comfortable." A promotion for *Newsweek* magazine, featuring scantily dressed harem girls lounging voluptuously around a grinning, rotund Arab shiek, reads: "Compound

your interest. Quote *Newsweek....*" An ad for Thane
Mills, a company that manufactures cotton, pictures a
supercilious-looking man standing over a woman, her eyes
cast downward. "The Thane of Scarsdale," trumpets the
ad. "In blue-chip suburbs like Scarsdale, or anywhere else,
it gives you that special look of authority. . . . For the man
who's in control."

Automobiles are this country's phallic power symbol,
and cars are used to prove a man's masculinity. Obviously,
women are the logical props for such symbolism. Myra
Janco Daniels calls automobile advertisements "the first
fully Americanized fertility rites," wondering wryly whether the final act of love will be between boy and auto, girl
and auto, or attain the ultimate in some kind of intercourse
among the three.

The image of woman in advertising is as much defined
by the ads that omit her as those that exploit her. Business
executives and doctors, for example, are always men. Even
the language is male-oriented, like General Electric's
"Men Helping Man" on an ad that discusses the development of nuclear power plants.

Advertising did not create these images about women,
but it is a powerful force for their reinforcement. It legiti-
mizes the idealized, sterotyped roles of woman as temptress,
wife, mother, and sex object, and portrays women as less
intelligent and more dependent than men. It makes wom-
en believe that their chief role is to please men and that
their fulfillment will be as wives, mothers, and homemak-
ers. It makes women feel unfeminine if they are not pretty
enough and guilty if they do not spend most of their time
in desperate attempts to imitate gourmet cooks and
eighteenth-century scullery maids. It makes women believe
that their own lives, talents, and interests ought to be
secondary to the needs of their husbands, and families and
that they are almost totally defined by these relationships.

It creates false, unreal images of women that reflect
male fantasies rather than flesh and blood human beings.
And the idealization of women is not much healthier than
their derogation; goddesses are easily pulled off their
pedestals and turned into temptresses and whores.

Advertising also reinforces men's concepts about wom-
en's place and women's role—and about their own roles.
It makes masculine dominance legitimate—and conversely
questions the manhood of men who do not want to go
along with the stereotypes. Why is it masculine for men to

wash cars, but a sign of "henpecking" for them to wash dishes? Why is it a man's job to be the breadwinner and a woman's to be the homemaker? Why do some men feel guilty when their wives work—as if it were a reflection on their own inadequacies? Advertising prolongs the myths of male supremacy, painting pictures of men who are superior to women and etching those images in the eyes of men who use these "eternal verities" as the excuse for forcing women's continued subjugation.

Male reactions to charges of sexism in advertising vary from defensive, "We didn't think that was degrading. . . . It's a woman's role to care for the home," to the coldly, consciously contemptuous, "all women are masochists." "Insulting?" inquired William Judd, creative services manager for Parker Pen. "No, I would have to say that I don't recall that question coming up." He did get about ten letters complaining about the "Give her a gorgeous pen" ad; he noted parenthetically that the ad was aimed at men. "It was a surprise to us that anyone felt that strongly about it. We still don't feel that this ad in any way was degrading at all. You'd have to have a pretty thin skin to go away with that attitude." The reaction from Dictaphone ("the dumb blonde test") was the same: "It's just an expression—everybody took it in good fun." They did get a few protesting calls and letters.

Not a surprising response when one considers what businessmen seem to think about the American woman's intelligence. Here is the conclusion of a survey of the average housewife done by Haug Associates, Los Angeles, California and printed in *Ad Age:*

> She likes to watch television and she does not enjoy reading a great deal. She is most easily reached through television and the simple, down-to-earth magazines. She finds her satisfaction within a rather small world and the center of this world is her home.

> She has little interest or skill to explore, to probe into things for herself. Her energy is largely consumed in day-to-day living. She is very much open to suggestion and amenable to guidance that is presented in terms that fit in with her needs and with her view of the world.

> She tends to have a negative or anti-conceptual way of thinking. Mental activity is arduous for her. Her ability for inference particularly in unfamiliar areas is limited. And she tends to experience discomfort and confusion

when faced with ambiguity or too many alternatives. . . .
She is a person who wants to have things she can believe
in with certainty, rather than things she has to think about.

Needless to say, this somewhat moronic average American
housewife trusts securely in name brands that are widely
advertised.

Most of the people who make decisions about advertising are men. The satirical interview with the mythical
"sixteen-year-old president of J. Walter Thompson," written by Gordon Webber, vice-president of Benton & Bowles,
probably is more fact than fancy when it comes to describing those men's attitudes toward women.

Q: What do you think about women's role during the last
  decade?
A: Women are irrelevant—except, of course, my mother.
Q: But don't you think women have grown in prestige and
  power during the 70's?
A: Yes, I guess you might say that. Mary Wells has her own
  agency, Golda Meir has her own country. And my mother
  has me.

Enough said.

Women in advertising generally agree on the genesis of
sexist advertising. According to Frankie Cadwell.

Most men in advertising think of women as having low intelligence. They believe that across the country, women are
really children. You can't say anything too fancy to them.
Conversations with doves in kitchens, giants coming out of
washing machines, crowns magically appearing on heads
when a certain margarine is used. Even the caliber of
daytime television soap operas doesn't approach the idiocy
of commercials. I think it's a security thing—they want to
think of woman as having very few interests—that her life
really does begin and end with clean floors. You could
substitute women for mentally-retarded, and they say, "It
sells, doesn't it?" That is their principal argument. That
this low level fantasy sells. They always show a woman in
the kitchen so they always show a woman in the kitchen.
They want that same old stuff because it worked the last
time.

Diana Gartner, vice president for research at Daniel &
Charles, concurs, "Why do they do it? Because it works."
But she says advertising men avoid the notion that the

current images may be stereotyping and demeaning and that other approaches would work as well or better:

> Caroline Bird spoke on the marketing implications of women's changing role at the International Congress of the American Marketing Association in April 1970. The resistance was tremendous—the men, who represented manufacturers, ad agencies and marketing research houses, made fun of what she was talking about; they said it was all ridiculous.
>
> Now it's a matter of opinion, because we don't have the data. They say this is what turns Mrs. America on. They are so convinced that they're right, they don't see any point in investing money to do research on how women react to the stereotypes. I suggested to my boss that we hold a conference in New York on women's liberation and its implications for marketing. It was set up—then the Board of Directors of the A.M.A. chapter here vetoed the program. That's not objective; that's emotional.

Marketing research is based on testing advertisements through methods like surveys, group interviews (called "focus" groups), and trial runs in selected cities. But Diana Gartner says copy-testing techniques have bias built into them. "They assume that anything showing a woman getting a man's praise or attention is automatically motivating. It's a firmly established principle." The same motivation and reward exists for the housewife, Mrs. Gartner notes:

> I recently had some focus group sessions and it was clear that the women wanted to say that they wanted products that would save time and energy. There was only a mention of doing something creative, but the man who conducted the session played on this theme more than the other. Instead of giving them conveniences to save time, they try to funnel the creative urge back into the household scene. The motivation is, "You can fulfill your duties and responsibilities to your family." They won't play on a woman's own needs, they play on her guilt. And there's a lot of guilt around. After all, a woman's husband is doing the important work, bringing home the money and winning recognition from the world outside. She is merely housecleaning, cooking, and sending the kids off to school— work which commands so little regard that she is not paid a salary for it or recognized as more than "just a housewife." She knows her husband is making the most valuable contribution to the family—the least she can do is perform

her meager tasks adequately by whipping up gourmet meals and ironing her husband's socks and underwear.

Mrs. Gartner recalled another focus group that centered on a completely prepackaged meal. In answer to prodding from the questioner, one woman finally laughed and said, "Maybe I *should* feel guilty." "When men do the interviews," says Mrs. Gartner, "they are more likely to want women to live up to these expectations. And it's such an emotional area, a woman's identity is so tied up with this, that women are almost afraid to admit to themselves, much less to an interviewer, that the sex role stereotypes bother them."

THIS AD INSULTS WOMEN
THIS EXPLOITS WOMEN

Stickers with those messages are proclaiming the feminist protest against degrading advertising on buses, subways, and wall posters throughout the country. The National Organization for Women has devised "The Barefoot and Pregnant Award of the Week for Advertising Degrading to Women." At the national convention in March, 1970, the organization vowed to take action against companies who refused to eliminate objectionable ads. Throughout the movement, feminist magazines and newspapers are focusing on sexist advertising and urging others to boycott products where commercials demean or exploit.

Feminists are sensitive to sexist advertising because of their increased consciousness about the stereotyped role of women in society. And the humiliating images of women in the ads work to increase feminist consciousness and resentment of their status. However, protest is not limited to the adherents of women's liberation. Advertising professionals are also speaking out to their colleagues and to the industry.

"The Lady of the House is dead," proclaimed a full page in *Ad Age*. Frankie Cadwell placed that ad to serve notice on Madison Avenue that:

The notion that women are hysterical creatures with inferior intellects that respond best to tales of Aladdin-like giants and magical clowns is horrendously insulting. When over 55% of the women in the country are high school graduates and 25% have attended colleges . . . aren't they beyond "house-i-tosis"? At the very least women deserve recognition as being in full possession of their faculties.

"The Revolution is ready," she warned them, "and one of women's first targets will be to rebel against moronic, insulting advertising." She predicted that consumer boycotts might be the result, and she offered copies of a list of the "Ten Brands Whose Advertising Women Hate Most" gleaned from the Disneyland survey she conducted. The research team interviewed some 600 women age eighteen and over from all parts of the country. The vote was limited to television advertising, with cigarettes excluded because of the possible negative effects of antismoking campaigns. Right Guard Deodorant had the distinction of being disliked by over fifty participants. The others in the top ten were: Axion Pre-Soak, Ultra Brite Toothpaste, Crest Toothpaste, Bold Detergent, Dove Dishwashing Liquid, Colgate 100 Mouthwash, Punch Detergent, Ajax Liquid Cleaner, and Scope Mouthwash.

Jane Trahey, president of Trahey-Wolf, turned around traditional advertising patterns. One copywriter assigned to do a watch advertisement proposed showing a man waiting outside a phone booth and tapping impatiently on his watch as the stereotyped "talkative woman" engaged in protracted conversation inside. "I'm making him do it the other way around," she grinned. She points out the most ludicrous lapses of the creative imagination in an occasional column for *Ad Age*. One focused on a TV spot about Mr. Clean that

> . . . shows a woman who has gone quite bonkers over her dining room table waxing job. She sits at one end of the table and rubs it lovingly. If her husband found her this way, he most certainly would either return her to her mother or, if he were kind, suggest a shrink.

Ad Age's letters to the editor sporadically present protests from others in the trade, even men, like one from Alfred McCrea, president of his own Philadelphia agency. He protests the "bitchy" image of women in soap and detergent commercials:

> It seems that all of them depict the average housewife as a nasty, sneering individual making caustic remarks to or about her neighbor just because she doesn't use a certain brand of soap. Maybe the product could be put to better use washing out the mouths of some of these people.

Another male-run agency decided to explore the feminist viewpoint on advertising in a project proposed by two women in its research department. Batten, Barton, Durstine & Osborne—the agency that created the Silva Thins commercial—invited eleven women to participate in a focus group about what they considered degrading to women in advertising. I was a member of the group. The session was videotaped and shown to agency executives. "It blew their minds," says Diane Daley, who organized the project with Ellen Levy. They ran another group to expand their findings. Daley's report to BBD&O summed up everything feminists there and elsewhere have been saying: women do not like ads that either blatantly exploit and insult them or reinforce the sex-role stereotypes.

I made a few suggestions that I hope the BBD&O executives and others will take up. For example, why not an ad showing men and women rushing out to work after leaving the dishes soaking in some wonderful pink liquid that eats away the grease while they are poring over their accounts? Or stumbling home wearily from the office, throwing their briefcases on the table, and exuding praise for some jiffy convenience food that lets them eat without an hour's preparation?

Or this for an anti-discrimination public service spot: a woman sits behind an executive desk with a man beside her taking dictation. The underline: "What is wrong with this picture?" The answer: "Absolutely nothing!"

There are some companies that already see women outside the stereotyped roles. National Life Insurance of Vermont has an ad showing a woman sitting before a microscope. "She's working to make your life better," says the ad. "She's a biochemist. . . . The same motivation drives our agents in serving your life insurance needs."

And Sanitone Drycleaners ran a series showing successful women—a sales vice president, a lawyer, an advertising manager and the like. Yet half the people in that series were executive secretaries and assistants, a trenchant comment on the relative status of even "successful" women.

How can women get other companies to change? "Boycotts," answer the ad women in unison. Women are 85 percent of the retail market; they could end degrading advertising tomorrow if they refused to buy products that use such methods. Even written complaints to companies would have an effect.

No matter what method is used to accomplish it, changing sexist advertising is prominent on the feminist agenda.

However, the new feminist attacks on advertising have revealed a curious phenomenon. I have said that advertising does not create sex-role stereotypes, it only reflects them; it acts on how people consciously perceive their roles so that it can win identification with its message. It exploits existing insecurities and guilts. As feminist consciousness increases, the advertising that crystallizes and mirrors the sex-role stereotypes makes those stereotypes and attitudes more blatant and odious and helps women see them more clearly. Advertising reflects and magnifies the prevalent image of women and makes it clear how limiting and oppressive their accepted roles are. (Even masochistic Silva Thins commercials may have some therapeutic value.) And advertising presents a focus and a target for the destruction of those images. For women who are made aware of the stereotypes, advertising is a permanent consciousness-raising mechanism, constantly reminding them of their position in American life, constantly dredging up insulting and demeaning images that anger them and make them reflect upon the condition of all women today.

When women claim that they are insulted by ads that portray women as housekeepers or sex objects, they are protesting the fact that *society* views women as such and that most women are condemned to exist within the confines of those roles. When women reject ads that give beautiful women "male rewards," they are protesting the culture that requires women to be beautiful and that sets up a man as the ultimate prize. When women resent ads that show them only as stewardesses or secretaries, they are showing their anger at the system that countenances rampant discrimination against women in virtually all areas of employment and at the unspoken assumption that they lack the talents or intelligence to do the jobs men control.

Ironically, it may be the ludicrous and humiliating exaggerations of advertising itself that force some women to confront the reality of their subservient position and lead them to demand the changes that will bring them a new humanity and liberation.

14

THE IMAGE OF WOMAN IN TEXTBOOKS

Marjorie B. U'Ren

Males and females do not receive equal educations under our present coeducational system. Their educations reflect the roles that society intends them ultimately to occupy. In our society the male, rather than the female, is taught to achieve, to advance, to create. This deference to the male is particularly evident in the textbooks used by children in primary grades.

In recent years these books have gained much in fine appearance and in social interest. Illustrations are usually excellent; the stories are varied; and the racial and social backgrounds reflected have begun to expand beyond the white middle-class suburban family unit. The child of a minority race can now expect to find successful representatives of his own people in the more up-to-date textbooks, and thus he is taught that ability does not depend upon skin color. Unfortunately, whereas racial biases are disappearing, sexual biases are not. In the most recent textbooks adopted or recommended for second-through sixth-grade use in California, at least 75 percent of the stories' main characters are male. This figure itself does not offer a full picture of the preference given to masculine characters. Accounts of adult females are almost nonexistent, though adult males appear frequently; stories about females are not as long as those about males. As a result, in page by page calculation, the average book devotes less than 20 percent of its story space to the female sex. Furthermore, many of the stories centered around a male figure include no female characters; while the female-centered stories, in nearly every instance, include several males with whom the lead females interact. Apparently the male world is more readily taken as complete in itself, while the female world is dependent upon male support and interest.

Most stories about girls are not only far shorter than stories about boys, but are considerably less interesting as well. Those based on what are thought to be female interests will typically be restricted to domestic settings. Girls rarely leave the confines of the family and rarely receive community recognition for their achievements; boys, on the other hand, are allowed great freedom of movement and choice. Moreover, the adventures that boys encounter often stretch the limits of probability and place the boys in situations demanding a freedom few parents would be willing to grant to children of either sex.

A close look at one third-grade text entitled *Winging through Lights and Shadows* will illustrate these points. Seven out of the eight stories in the book have main characters who are male. The one tale centered around a girl, "A Story of Numbers Long Ago," is ten pages long, while the stories about boys range from twenty-five to sixty pages. "A Story of Numbers Long Ago" tells about Nom, a girl living in the stone age, who "has many tasks to do. She helps her mother and her brother find food for the family to eat." In addition, Nom helps clean hides while her brother fishes. What is both typical and noteworthy in this account is the way it immediately defines Nom in relationship to her brother and places her in subordination to him as well as to her mother. Admittedly, there are accounts of boys helping with adult chores, but more often boys work at independent tasks, and they are never under the direction of a female sibling. This subordination of the sister to her brother is so common a stereotype in textbooks that it is rare to find a story where a female is the older and therefore potentially more dominant sibling.

Nom's story is based on her interest in a male activity. As the men in her tribe return from hunting, Nom begins to record the number of deer brought back to the cave. She scoops a shallow hole in the cave floor and places in it one pebble to represent each deer; when the number of pebbles reaches seven, she scoops out a new hole in which she places one pebble representing collectively the seven pebbles from the first hole. Nom has discovered a method of counting in sets of sevens, but there the tale ends. She is never recognized for her achievement; she has never once left the cave. There has been no activity, no excitement. "A Story of Numbers Long Ago" is, in fact, a very dull little story, as the illustrations help to demonstrate. All the pictures are of the cave. We see Nom peering out at the returning hunters, and working at a domestic task, but most of the illustrations show nothing more than the process of scooping out a hole, followed by repeated drawings of the hole itself with various numbers of pebbles.

It is hard to see how present-day schoolgirls could find much to identify with in this short, uneventful story. Although a tale of real adventure in the stone age would make excellent reading for any child, what could be more removed from modern experience and less inspiring than counting in sets of sevens in the confines of a prehistoric cave?

This same book is full of long, exciting tales where men and young boys, in a more modern world, solve complex problems that earn them considerable social recognition. "Black Gold," a sixty-page account of a young boy's adventure at the turn of the century, deserves special attention since it seems to be the male counterpart of the "female interest" story about Nom. The hero of "Black Gold" is a boy perhaps ten or eleven years old who earns his pocket money by dipping an old blanket into a pond that contains a mixture of water and oil; by wringing out the water from the blanket, he is able to collect small amounts of oil which he then sells. One day the boy, who is already established as enterprising and industrious, is approached by a gentleman who has been observing him at work. He asks the boy if he would care to join a team of two adults in drilling for oil. The boy is happy to accept and leaves to help the two men with their project. He does this without parental approval; in fact, we never see any member of his family, though the reader is made aware that he belongs to a respectable and reasonably well-off household.

Three difficulties confront the workers over the following weeks. When water gets in the way of the drilling operation, the boy suggests a pump. The pump is successful until mud becomes a problem; the boy proposes holding off the mud by drilling through a pipe. But how are they to get a pipe through the mud? The boy's suggestion of using a log as a pile driver works. Oil is struck, and the heretofore doubting townspeople are forced to admit that there is much to be said for this new method of drilling for oil. The venture makes newspaper headlines; the boy becomes a public hero; and the final illustration shows the original hill covered with oil derricks. The implication of financial success is strong.

There are striking contrasts between this story and the story about Nom. Most obviously, "Black Gold" is six times as long as "A Story of Numbers Long Ago." The characters in the one are all male, and in the other, though the main character is female, events are centered around male activity. The boy in "Black Gold" is extremely independent; Nom is extremely restricted. The boy receives considerable social recognition for his work; the girl's somewhat dubious achievement goes undetected. The boy becomes a leader of men and deals successfully with original and difficult situations; the girl remains her mother's and brother's assistant in routine tasks that lead to no specific goal.

Some have raised the argument that girls face a more domestic and routine adulthood than their male counterparts, and that it is therefore appropriate to present girls with stories about what is likely to be their future experience. Yet stories for boys are not restricted by this same "reality" concern. There are no stories which treat of or anticipate an office job, none which touch on the reality of the factory line or glorify the role of the salesman. Boys, on the contrary, are encouraged to aim for those levels of achievement that our society most values, though in fact most males will have routine adulthoods, devoid of the high adventure they have been taught to dream of.

"Black Gold" is followed by "Burning Up the Track," a forty-page account of how a young boy persuades his elders to accept a novel idea in car racing. As a result of the boy's plan, an elder brother is able to win first prize in the final race: "It was Hugh's advice that helped his brother Lou to win the most important race of his life." Once again the boy is independent and enterprising in an all-male world; his success is recognized and lauded; the plot is far from lacking action. The opening sentence asks, "Does a race excite you?" "A story of Numbers Long Ago" can hardly compete on that level.

In crowd scenes females are rarely named; a female is "the little girl in red" or "the girl sitting next to Tom." Nor do girls stand up against the press of opinion; nearly always they go along with the popular position. The first story in *Winging through Lights and Shadows* deals, on a child's level, with the questions of mob rule and false accusation. The main character again is male, he is granted a forcefulness and versatility never allowed to females. Even his name emphasizes this stereotype. "Bob Quick was bigger than the other children and a little bit older. He was like a leader to the rest of the children. When he came into the park, he was carrying his baseball mitt in one hand and a banjo in the other hand." When Bob's banjo disappears, all the children, except one boy named Tom Sanchez, accuse an absent boy, Sam Kaplan, of the theft. All the females in the group, none of whom are named, proclaim Sam to be guilty. Only the arrival of a policeman, Officer Woods, who, incidentally, is black, settles the issue; he applies skill and understanding to teaching the children a kindly lesson in the errors of hasty judgment and proves the innocence of Sam Kaplan.

Officer Woods appears in another story in the same third-grade reader. As a character he serves particularly well to demonstrate the textbook adult stereotypes. In "The Glass Bank" Officer Woods solves the problem of his son's difficulty in comprehending numbers. Howard has fallen behind in arithmetic, though his sister does well in the subject. While this sister does contribute to the dialogue, she serves mainly as a support character to the father and son; it is not her story. Nor is it her mother's. In the thirty newly issued textbooks read for this study not one presented a family crisis wherein the mother so much as suggested a solution; in every case father came home and took over. In "The Glass Bank" when the family has finished eating dinner, "Mrs. Woods went to work washing dirty dishes, and Officer Woods set about his plan."

Invariably the father solves problems in the world as well as within the family; he is presented as the builder, the controller, and the creator and executor of ideas. This produces a striking contradiction with reality. Most of our elementary teachers are female, but all of our primary texts bear the message that it is men rather than women who work with ideas and who seek, gain, and dispense knowledge. Even the illustrated cartoon figures used to indicate and enliven points of grammar are male.

Primary texts present the mother figure as a pleasant, hardworking, but basically uninteresting, individual; her life offers little excitement; she has no effect upon the world beyond her family, and even within the family her contribution is limited to housekeeping and cooking. Often she is merely a propman for the story; she enters a scene only to place a cake on the table and then disappears, or she plays foil to her husband by setting him up for his line. It is mother who asks what can be done and invites a speech from father.

The three remaining stories in *Winging through Lights and Shadows* are about adults; they fit the stereotypes presented in the other sections of the book. In one chapter photographer of wild animals, Commander Headly, relates the close calls he experienced while hunting for game in Africa. Set in a Mexican village, another story recounts the struggles of an old man who, alone with his pet female wolf, captures the killer wolf of the valley and earns a belated respect from the villagers. But only "Safety-Pin Stew," an inane tale about a hobo who wants to marry the best cook in the world, contains anything like an adult female main character. The woman he chooses is a plump, generous, simple-minded widow who is all too happy to cook for free and to marry the hobo, who can hardly be said to have earned such a comfortable setup.

In the thirty textbooks studied, only one adult female character was allowed ambition for herself. This exception was a short, factual biography of a woman athlete; it fit easily and naturally into the text without appearing forced or inappropriate. But far more often the adult female (found in only about 4 percent of those stories with an adult main character) is pictured in the role of assistant.

In one account of Madame Curie she appears to be little more than a helpmate for her husband's projects. The illustration that accompanies this section even portrays Madame Curie peering mildly from behind her husband's shoulder while he and another distinguished gentleman loom in the foreground, engaged in a serious dialogue. Certainly the male sex provides more historical figures than the female sex, but even famous women in history rarely appear in textbooks or, as in the case of Madame Curie, are unjustly played down.

Most stories about adult males do not concern specific, historical figures; rather, the greater number of such stories are fictional attempts to describe the lives of imaginary heroes and typical modern professionals. As a result, there are chapters on "the explorer," "the scientist," or "the architect," the latter being described in one text simply as "the man who shapes the plan."

Only one working female appeared in all the various descriptions of present-day professionals; this was a woman scientist who is described in a chapter on scientific achievement. The three other scientists mentioned are males who are depicted working alone on projects that demand originality and exacting mental effort, but it is repeatedly mentioned that the female scientist is not independent. An illustration shows her at work, and beneath the illustration is the following explanation: "The project the young woman is working on is not her own idea. She was assigned to work on it. And she has been using her scientific knowledge to help develop a useful, safe drug which her company can then produce and sell. As an employee working on someone else's idea, she is typical of thousands of scientists working in industry today."

The textbook writers are apparently uncomfortable with the idea of a female succeeding in her own right. If she does make use of a talent, it must be for the benefit of others, under the direction of others; any contribution she makes to her field of knowledge should preferably be made quietly, without fanfare or public recognition. Thus, Madame Curie is reduced to a laboratory assistant, and few girls receive any community publicity for contributions they have made, though they may be praised by members of their immediate family for work done in the house or at school. In thirty textbooks only two girls receive public acclaim.

The belief that females do not need or perhaps should not receive public recognition is paralleled by the attitude that women should not be interested in financial success for its own sake. The hero of "Black Gold" was lauded for working hard and making money, though the money he earned was apparently intended for his own use, not for anyone else's. On the other hand, it is only a virtue for a girl to earn money for others' use. It is therefore possible to find one story about a girl who has great success selling tickets to a benefit gathering; yet a girl who seeks material gain for its own sake, however honestly, appears in stories only as a negative example. This is not to say that the world would benefit if more women were encouraged to strike it rich, but an obvious double standard is revealed when an ability considered praiseworthy in one sex is deplorable in another.

In 1946 Irvin Child, Elmer Potter, and Estelle Levine discovered that elementary textbooks show females using undesirable means of acquisition far more frequently than males.[1] While girls are often depicted as helpful and less likely to bring harm to themselves, these same characteristics render them dependent and unoriginal. Girls risk little and gain little. But more strikingly this emphasis on dependency seems to make female characters more manipulative. A girl in a textbook story is less likely to strike out directly after a goal; by being indirect she is not always perfectly honest. Furthermore, the passivity ascribed textbook females causes them to be portrayed as lazy far more often than males.

The emphasis on masculine strength extends beyond physical qualities. Males of all ages are pictured as having greater mental perseverance and moral strength than females. Not only are females more often described as lazy and incapable of independent thinking or direct action but they are also shown as giving up more easily. They collapse into tears, they betray secrets; they are more likely to act upon petty or selfish motives. This last somewhat contradicts girls' typical representation as helpmates both to adults and to males of their own age.

In nearly every story intended to be humorous, the butt of the joke is a female. In one story a fat, selfish queen keeps all the ice cream in the kingdom to herself, even denying any to her undersized husband, the king. When at last the queen is reformed, she loses weight, becomes pretty, and gives away ice cream to all. This particular story opens with the following: "You expect a kingdom to be run by a king, but this one was run by a queen." As a finale to a play, the shrill, nagging wife of a kindly inventor is dumped into a trash can by one of the inventor's own robots—a robot, it should be mentioned, created specifically for the job of trash collecting. In still another story a man who finds it accidentally lucrative to have killed his wife (albeit unintentionally) inspires the other men of the town to "bump off their old wives," too.

The fact that such textbook stories are quite frequently written by females suggests the low opinion many women have of their own sex. This is not surprising; individuals generally adopt the attitudes of their culture even when these attitudes are directed against their own kind. Experiments show that preschool children learn very early to discriminate against themselves. Given a choice of white and black dolls, for example, and asked to pick out the prettiest, both black and white children in our culture choose the white doll.

Females fare even worse in the illustrations than in the stories. Many books devote only 15 percent of their illustrations to girls or women. In all but a few group scenes, females appear only as background figures. The most important illustrations, those on the book covers or at the heads of chapters, are invariably male-dominated. Moreover, a photograph of an everyday street scene will yield a normal mixture of the sexes, but a drawing of a street scene will show far more males. The significance of this imbalance is obvious. We tend to forget the simple fact that the female sex is half the species, that women are not merely a ladies' auxiliary to the human race.

In one long beautifully illustrated book, each of six main sections had a two-page drawing on the appropriate theme. A large male figure dominated each of these illustrations; below were ten to twenty smaller figures. Only two of the drawings had any female characters; both times these were small background figures, partly covered by one or more males in the foreground. It is perhaps not surprising that the textbook illustrators drew no females for the section on "Striking It Rich," but no women were represented in another section entitled "Fair Play." Whether one takes "fair play" to mean nothing more than athletics or sees in it the broader themes of honesty and fair dealings, it is still an area that should encompass both sexes. However, neither the illustrations nor the text gave any indication that fair play is expected of the female sex.

Certainly none of this is intentional. The textbook writers are not consciously conspiring to keep females out of their books, but stereotypes get in the way. Perhaps we are too eager to offer children a "normal" world in their reading; in doing so we confuse what is actually normal with what is simply most apparent. We like to imagine that each child lives in a two-parent household; and by taking this as a norm, we forget it often is not so. It is an everyday event to see a mother in the kitchen, but that is not necessarily the only feature of a mother's existence. We like to imagine that each child has two parents, who are also separate human beings, but by presenting women only as mothers we create a norm contrary to this view.

Perhaps because mother is usually a youngster's main source of security, textbook writers present women only in the role of mother; yet many women work, by choice or necessity, and are nevertheless mothers. Perhaps the worst transgression is that any women who do not marry are destined to be seen by children as women-manqué since no other female existence is acknowledged in our texts.

In trying for what we consider a normal standard, we often fail to present what is true since cultural stereotypes are not always based on what is factual or even desirable. For example, it is a common sight to see women driving cars, and yet textbooks only occasionally show women doing so. There are women in medicine, law, and business; yet when describing the professions, textbook writers reserve these fields solely for men. Furthermore, mothers are individuals with individual projects, interests, and talents. It is not unusual to find a mother who does the repairs, the yard work, and even the carpentry for her family; still we continue to see these as male activities. Textbook writers seem to have reduced all women to a common denominator of cook, cleaner, and seamstress. And when a story mother is needed, this cardboard woman is picked off the shelf and put, as is, on the page.

It would be far better if young girls could look to the role of mother and housewife as something they might *choose* to be and could see this role as only one of a number of possibilities in life. In the word "choose" lies the key. Beyond the occasional mother figure the textbooks give the young female little to model herself after. The message is that nothing happens to women, that women tend to the routine needs of others, but accomplish nothing unique themselves. It is important to present children with stories about girls who endeavor and women who succeed on all levels.

Quite simply, education should direct and inspire the individual to make the highest use of his or her particular abilities. Yet in the case of women, we seem to forget this obvious fact. No one becomes a professional without encouragement; in a world that encourages few women to use their talents, it is inevitable that few women do so. Girls are not so much told that they cannot do something as *not* told that they can. And, if in spite of all, a girl does decide to tackle a traditionally male profession, others are more likely to discourage her than to offer support.

Oddly enough, textbooks written for coeducation early

in this century present a much more favorable picture of the female sex than do textbooks written from 1930 on. Mothers in these stories sit down with their children, instruct them, help them, and participate in their activities. There are stories of girls who handle physical dangers or stand up against popular and false opinion. Women are given a greater place in history, and frequently there are biographies of the women writers whose selections appear in the books.

These older textbooks—written under the nineteenth-century tradition of rough frontier equality—prove that stories about girls need not be dull, and that women may be active and talented without in any way being harsh and unsympathetic. No one asks that stories be artificially measured out part by part to assure an absolute equality of material. What is asked is distribution of stories that inspire all peoples and both sexes to aim high and achieve their best, and an end to a textbook world where male figures outnumber and dominate, and female characters lack spirit, curiosity and originality.

NOTE

1. Irvin L. Child, Elmer H. Potter, and Estelle M. Levine, "Children's Textbooks and Personality Development: An Exploration in the Social Psychology of Education," in Judy F. Rosenblith and Wesley Allinsmith, eds., *Causes of Behavior Readings in Child Development and Educational Psychology* (Rockleigh, N.J.: Allyn, 1960).

15

SEDUCED AND ABANDONED IN THE NEW WORLD: The Image of Woman in American Fiction

Wendy Martin

> And the Lord God said unto the woman, What is this that thou has done? And the woman said, the serpent beguiled me, and I did eat.
> —GENESIS 3:13

> Unto the woman he said, I will greatly multiply thy sorrow and thy conception; in sorrow thou shalt bring forth children; and thy desire shall be to thy husband, and he shall rule over thee.—GENESIS 3:16

Ever since Susanna Rowson's *Charlotte Temple* (1794)— the first American best-seller—heroines of America fiction have reenacted Eve's fall from grace and thereby inherited the legacy of Eden. As daughters of Eve, American heroines are destined to dependency and servitude as well as to painful and sorrowful childbirth because, like their predecessor, they have dared to disregard authority or tradition in the search for wisdom or happiness; like Eve, they are fallen women, eternally cursed for eating the apple of experience. *Charlotte Temple,* a Richardsonian tale of passion and its penalties, narrates the story of a naive young woman whose lover, Montraville, persuades her to accompany him on a military mission to the United States. Shortly after arriving in New York, he abandons her for a wealthy socialite, whereupon grief-stricken, guilt-ridden Charlotte dies after giving birth to an illegitimate daughter. The American novel has never outgrown the sentimental and sensational plot of its first best-seller; heroines from Hester Prynne to Catherine Barkley have been condemned to variations upon Charlotte's fate.

Since the concept of the fallen woman is central to Christianity, it is not surprising that the fiction of a nation founded by Puritans, who were obsessed with salvation and the scriptures, should reflect this bias. The American novel has inherited the Puritan conviction that life is a continual moral struggle and that man, and especially woman, is a frail creature. Like the Puritan sermon, the eighteenth-century novel attempted to instruct by example, exhorting readers to lead virtuous lives: sermons relied on homily and plain style to bring the message home; the sentimental novel used example and emotion to achieve the same result. The guilt and anguish that Charlotte experiences as a result of her transgressions are the same emotions evoked by Jonathan Edwards' sermon, "Sinners in the Hands of an Angry God." In American fiction women are perceived as morally inferior creatures who, beguiled by their own passions, are destined to tragic lives if they deviate from the laws of God and man.

In addition to reinforcing Puritan morality, American fiction conditions its readers to accept bourgeois economic values (demonstrably an outgrowth of Puritan morality); women are encouraged to be virtuous so that they can make a good—that is, a financially respectable—marriage. As Ian Watt argues in *The Rise of the Novel*,[1] the novel's moral values reinforce bourgeois economic reality in which women are totally dependent on marriage for economic survival (a woman's wage in the late eighteenth century was approximately a quarter of a man's wage, and a woman's property automatically became her husband's upon marriage). In this economic system, virtue is a commodity to be sold to the highest bidder, and virginity relinquished before marriage inevitably means that a woman is less marketable, and therefore less likely to survive economically. The virtuous Pamela was rewarded with financial security in marriage; Charlotte Temple would have died of starvation had she not first died in childbirth.

The polarization of economic roles that occurred on a widespread scale in the eighteenth century was accompanied by a polarization of psychological roles, requiring women to be emotionally passive and weak as well as economically dependent. (The principle that man is the breadwinner and woman the helpmate and homemaker has biblical antecedents.) The myth provides a basis for the economic and social system of industrial society, which requires that men be strong in order to face the harsh world of the competitive marketplace, to be captains of industry, to steer the ship of state, and that woman, the weaker sex, withdraw from the rough world for which she is not suited in order to nurture children and preserve culture within the home. The novel reflects this social definition of woman as a private creature, reinforcing purity, piety, and submissiveness as the proper feminine virtues and punishing those women who fail to comply with a behavior code that is economically viable in addition to being Christian.

An analysis of the numerous ways in which many of the most important American novels from *Charlotte Temple* to *Farewell to Arms* perpetuate the archetype of the fallen woman, thereby conditioning women to accept their inferior status, reveals the extent to which a myth can influence behavior long after widespread belief in the formal religious or economic mythology that gave rise to it has ceased to exist. It also indicates that fiction not only reflects and expresses social values but transmits them to future generations. A thorough understanding of the conditioning process occurring in the American novel—which in turn represents an aspect of larger cultural conditioning—is necessary in order to sensitize readers to the often subtle but pervasive negative influence of destructive archetypes.

Hester Prynne in Nathaniel Hawthorne's *Scarlet Letter* (1850)[2] is one of the better known heiresses of Eve's legacy. She is doomed to wear the scarlet A—the sign of adultery—and her fall from grace is underscored by her apparent loss of beauty: "All the light and graceful foliage of her character had been withered up by this red hot brand, and had long ago fallen away, leaving a bare and harsh outline which might have been repulsive, had she possessed friends or companions to be repelled by it" (pp. 157–158). Her diminished beauty is a source of yet greater pain when it is finally revealed as existing, stifled, beneath the burden of her cruel public punishment. Flinging away the scarlet letter, she is suddenly free:

> The stigma gone, Hester heaved a long, deep sigh, in which the burden of shame and anguish departed from her spirit. O exquisite relief! She had not known the weight until she felt the freedom! By another impulse, she took off the formal cap that confined her hair; and down it fell upon her shoulders, dark and rich, with at once a shadow and a light in its abundance, and imparting the charm of softness to her features. There played around her mouth and beamed out of her eyes a radiant and tender smile, that seemed gushing from the very heart of womanhood. A crimson flush was glowing on her cheek, that had been long so pale. Her sex, her youth, and the whole richness of her beauty, came back from what men call the irrevocable past, and clustered themselves, with her maiden hope and a happiness before unknown, within the magic circle of this hour. [P. 192]

However, her efforts to free herself were useless and she was forced to forfeit her sexuality; she had to gather up "the heavy tresses of her hair, confined them beneath her cap . . . her beauty, the warmth and richness of her womanhood departed" (p. 200).

Hawthorne reminds his readers that independent thought and emotion, that is, self-reliance, can be dangerous for women. The scarlet letter had been Hester's "passport into regions where other women dared not tread: Shame, Despair, Solitude! These had been her teachers—stern and wild ones—and they had made her strong, but taught her much amiss" (p. 190). This is ironic since self-reliance is an American virtue, and male protagonists in American fiction are praised for their courage in breaking out of the confines of traditional society. Hester, however, does harsh penance for her moment of passion and demonstrates her piety by spending the rest of her days counselling women "in the continuing trials of wounded, wronged, misplaced or erring and sinful passion" (pp. 245–246). Hawthorne further undermines Hester's position by concluding that "no mission of divine and mysterious truth should be confided to a woman stained with sin, bowed down with shame, or even burdened with lifelong sorrow. The angel and apostle of the coming revelation must be a woman, indeed, but lofty, pure, and beautiful; and wise, moreover, not through dusky grief, but the ethereal medium of joy" (p. 246). Yet, the questioning reader remembers the dramatic scene in the woods in which Hester flings the scarlet letter away and lets down her hair and cannot help wondering what authorial perversity prevents Hester from being the prophetess of "a whole relation between man and woman on a surer ground of mutual happiness" (p. 246), why she must bear the burden of such a complicated set of spiritual values that she is ultimately denied her human portion of understanding and generosity.

The Blithedale Romance[3] is Hawthorne's secular version of The Scarlet Letter. A study of the activities of a commune similar to Brook Farm, the novel portrays two women, Zenobia and Priscilla, who represent passion and piety respectively. Zenobia, named after a queen who ruled Palmyra in 267–273 A.D., is stately and commanding; Priscilla, passive and pristine as her name suggests, is a "delicate instrument" with nerves like "fragile harp strings." Many critics think Zenobia is based on Margaret Fuller, who was associated with Brook Farm and who knew Hawthorne. Like Margaret Fuller, Zenobia is a champion of women's right. She asks the narrator Coverdale:

Did you ever see a happy woman in your life? Of course, I do not mean a girl, like Priscilla, and a thousand others,—for they are all alike, while on the sunny side of experience,—but a grown woman. How can she be happy, after discovering that fate has assigned her but one single event, which she must contrive to make the substance of her whole life? A man has his choice of innumerable events. [P. 82]

Hawthorne's descriptions of Zenobia's opulent beauty resemble his description of Hester in the woods—like Hester, Zenobia is depicted as being warm, generous, and above all passionate:

Zenobia had a rich, though varying color. It was, most of the while, a flame, and anon a sudden paleness. Her eyes glowed, so that their light sometimes flashed upward to me, as when the sun throws a dazzle from some bright object on the ground. Her gestures were free and strikingly impressive. The whole woman was alive with a passionate intensity, which I now perceived to be the phase in which her beauty culminated. Any passion would have become her well; and passionate love, perhaps, the best of all. [P. 121]

... her beauty was set off by all that dress and ornament could do for it. And they did much. Not, indeed, that they created or added anything to what Nature had lavishly done for Zenobia. But, those costly robes which she had on, those flaming jewels around her neck, served as lamps to display the personal advantages which required nothing less than such an illumination to be fully seen. [P. 176]

Ironically, instead of recognizing her own strength and beauty, Zenobia submits to Hollingsworth's egotism and capitulates to his very traditional definition of woman as man's subordinate:

She is the most admirable handiwork of God, in her true place and character. Her place is at man's side. Her office, that of sympathizer, the unreserved, unquestioning believer; the recognition, withheld in every other manner, but given, in pity, through woman's heart, lest man should utterly lose faith in himself. . . . All the separate action of woman is, and ever has been, and always shall be, false, foolish, vain, destructive of her own best and holiest qualities, void of every good effect, and productive of intolerable mischiefs! Man is a wretch without woman; but woman is a monster—thank Heaven, an almost impossible and hitherto imaginary monster—without man as her acknowledged principal! . . . if there were a chance of their attaining the end which these petticoated monstrosities have in view, I would call upon my own sex to use its Physical force, the unmistakable evidence of sovereignty, to scourge them back within their proper bounds! But it will not be needful. The heart of true womanhood knows where its own sphere is, and never seeks to stray beyond it. [Pp. 139–140]

Coverdale observes that women always acquiesce to man's definition of them and wonders, somewhat patronizingly, if women are innately frail: "Women almost invariably behave thus . . . what does the fact mean? Is it their nature? or is it, at last, the result of ages of compelled degradation? And, in either case, will it be possible to redeem them?" (p. 141). Although Zenobia struggles against Hollingsworth's edict of women's dependency, denouncing his egotism—"It's all self! Nothing else; nothing but self, self, self" (p. 224)—she confides her despair and defeat to Coverdale: "In the battlefield of life, the downright stroke, that would only fall on a man's steel head-piece, is sure to light on a woman's heart, over which she wears no breastplate, and whose wisdom it is, therefore, to keep out of the conflict . . . the woman who swerves one's hair's breadth, . . . that, with that one hair's breadth, she goes all astray, and never sees the world in its true aspect afterwards" (p. 229).

In a moment of self-abasement, Zenobia drowns herself, and Coverdale mourns, "It was a woeful thought, that a woman of Zenobia's diversified capacity should have fancied herself irretrievably defeated on the broad battlefield of life, and with no refuge, save to fall on her own sword, merely because Love had gone against her" (p. 245). Yet, in spite of his railing against male egotism which confines women to the sphere of emotions defining them as failures if they are not loved, Coverdale reveals his own chauvinism in the concluding sentence of the novel: "I—I myself— was in love—with *Priscilla*" (p. 259)—Priscilla, whom he had described earlier as a "gentle parasite, the soft reflection of a more powerful existence" (p. 140), who sat at Hollingsworth's feet in mute adoration while Zenobia struggled against him for her womanhood and recognition as a human being. In revealing his own preference for the "gentle parasite," Priscilla, Coverdale was perhaps echoing Hawthorne himself, who had strong antifeminist predilections as revealed by his statement in 1855 that "America is now wholly given over to a damn mob of scribbling women, and I should have no chance of success while the public taste is occupied with their trash."

Perhaps the "scribbling women" Hawthorne was referring to were women like Verena Tarrant and Olive Chancellor, the feminist heroines of Henry James' *The Bostonians*[4] (1886). Verena, an articulate and passionate public speaker for woman's rights, and Olive, a theoretician of the movement, both vow "to become great not to be obscure, and powerful, in order not to be useless" (p. 159). Convinced that "it is women in the end who had paid for everything" (p. 185), Olive, who is politically more sophisticated than Verena, rejects men as a class; but Verena takes a vow of celibacy simply to please Olive. It is suggested that Olive has a sexual interest in Verena, but Verena is sexually attracted to Basil Ransom, who insists that "the use of a truly amiable woman is to make some honest man happy" (p. 244); he despises feminists and paternalistically asserts that they are ineffectual in public life. His statements to Verena reveal his immense hostility to her values:

> The whole generation is womanized; the masculine tone is passing out of the world; it's a feminine, a nervous, hysterical, chattering, canting age, an age of hollow phrases and false delicacy and exaggerated solicitudes and coddled sensibilities, which, if we don't look out will usher in a reign of mediocrity, of the feeblest, flattest and most pretentious that has ever been. The masculine character, the ability to dare and endure, to know and yet not fear reality, to look the world in the face and take it for what it is—a very queer and partly very base mixture—that is what I want to preserve, or rather, as I may say, to recover; and I must tell you that I don't in the least care what becomes of you ladies while I make the attempt. [P. 343]

The novel's crisis occurs when Ransom attempts to convince Verena to give herself to a man rather than a movement, assuring her that "the dining-table itself shall be our platform" (p. 401). Olive entreats Verena to live her own life, devoting herself to the cause of women's rights rather than sitting at the feet of Ransom and thereby providing their adversaries "with consummate proof of the fickleness, the futility, the predestined servility of women" (p. 391). Verena despises Ransom's philosophy but confesses with anguish to Olive that she is irresistibly drawn to him: "I like him—I can't help it—I do like him. I don't want to marry him, I don't want to embrace his ideas, which are unspeakably false and horrible; but I like him better than any gentleman I have seen" (pp. 386–387).

In the tug of war between Olive Chancellor and Basil Ransom for Verena's allegiance, Ransom gets the upper hand, forcing the issue minutes before Verena is scheduled to speak on women's rights to a huge Boston audience. Paralyzed and unable to bring herself to address the crowd without Ransom's permission, Verena allows herself to be "wrenched away" by "muscular force" in a scene very much like the one in which Montraville abducts Charlotte Temple (it is interesting to note the frequent occurrence in fiction of women who faint at the crucial moment, thereby relinquishing conscious choice or, if they fail to cooperate by swooning, have men assert their physical strength over them). James reveals his own misgivings about Verena's fate by confiding that Ransom cannot redeem Verena: "He presently discovered that with the union, so far from brilliant, into which she was about to enter, those were not the last (tears) she was destined to shed" (p. 464). The conclusion of the novel reveals James' essential sympathy for Verena. Yet she is placed in a double bind, an either/or situation no man would ever really face: Because she has to make a choice between a husband and her ideals, Verena is damned if she does and damned if she doesn't; in order to cut the Gordian knot, she must sacrifice an important part of herself, giving up her ability to function effectively in the world in order to play a supporting role in Ransom's domestic drama.

Isabel Archer in Henry James' *Portrait of a Lady* (1881)[5] is a much stronger person than Verena and one of the most interesting and engaging American heroines. Attractive, articulate, and intelligent, Isabel reveals her capacity for existential consciousness in her wish to actively shape her life:

> She was intelligent and generous; it was a fine free nature; but what was she going to do with herself? This question was irregular, for with most women one had no occasion to ask it. Most women did with themselves nothing at all; they waited in attitudes more or less gracefully passive, for a man to come their way and furnish them with a destiny. Isabel's originality was that she gave one an impression of having intentions of her own. [P. 59]

Because she wants to see life for herself, she declines to marry her two most ardent suitors—Lord Warburton, a kind and gentle British aristocrat, and Casper Goodwood, a sturdy American industrialist. Although Isabel insists that she "doesn't want to begin life by marrying" (p. 139), she admits to herself that she likes Warburton "too much to marry him, that was the point, something told her that she should not be satisfied, and to inflict upon a man who offered so much, a tendency to criticize would be a particularly discreditable act" (p. 103). The reader is told that Isabel is really "frightened of herself" (p. 103); yet it is difficult to imagine the cause of this fear unless she has internalized the conventional definition of wife and worries that her ego is too assertive to permit her to be pious, passive, and supportive. On the one hand, Isabel wishes to choose her fate, to know "something of human affairs beyond what other people think it compatible with propriety to tell me" (p. 149) but, on the other hand, she is afraid of not being able to meet social expectations, and her newly inherited fortune simply compounds her fear and guilt: "I try to care more about the world than about myself—but I always come back to myself. It is because I am afraid.... A large fortune means freedom, and I am afraid of that. It's such a fine thing, and one should make such good use of it. If one shouldn't, one would be ashamed" (p. 206).

Encouraged and manipulated by Madam Merle, Isabel ignores the advice of her cousin Ralph and marries Gilbert Osmond, a sterile dilettante whom Isabel mistakes for a man of sensitivity. Isabel had hoped that her fortune could expand Osmond's life, but a year after her marriage, she admits to herself that "she had not read him right" (p. 393). Although her life as Mrs. Osmond is one in which "suffering is an active condition" (p. 390), she is committed to her marriage vow and remains with her husband in order to care for his daughter Pansy, whom she genuinely loves. Isabel is unwilling or afraid to act for her own happiness and becomes a martyr in marriage. Ironically, she too is imprisoned by her own sense of duty and—like many a woman before and after her—no longer dares to live her own life.

A decade later, Edna Pontellier in Kate Chopin's *The Awakening*,[6] unlike Isabel, worries less about social convention and more about her own fulfillment. *The Awakening* is the first American novel to focus on the perceptions and experience of a woman who finds that her marriage damages her sense of self—Edna Pontellier's story begins where Isabel's left off. At twenty-eight she has been married for six years to a New Orleans financier and is the mother of two children; in the course of the novel, she is gradually awakened to her "position in the universe as a human being, and to recognize her relations as an individual to the world within her and without her" (p. 214). From her youth, Edna has understood "the dual life—that outward existence which conforms, the inward life which questions" (p. 215); although she loves her husband and children, nevertheless an "indescribable oppression, which seemed to generate in some unfamiliar part of her consciousness, filled her being with anguish" (pp. 205–206). from a stereotyped perception of herself as wife and mother to that of a knowing, feeling, self-aware person. The novel captures the flux of Edna's moods as she moves

As she becomes less and less repressed, her will asserts itself more strongly. Her first act of freedom is minor—she defiantly refuses to comply with her husband's request to come indoors at bedtime—then she fails to meet her social obligations to the wives of her husband's business associates; later, she begins to keep her own hours; finally, she moves into a small house of her own. Edna's yearning for independence confuses and frightens her at first, but as the novel progresses, she becomes more and more sure of her need for solitude—reflected by the increasingly more frequent appearance of bird and sea imagery—and her stature heightens.

Like Zenobia, Edna is characterized by her queenlike magnificence:

> The golden shimmer of Edna's satin gown spread in rich folds on either side of her. There was a soft fall of lace encircling her shoulders. It was the color of her skin, without the glow, the myriad living tints that one may sometimes discover in vibrant flesh. There was something in her attitude, in her whole appearance when she leaned her head against the high-backed chair and spread her arms, which suggested the regal woman, the one who rules, who looks on, who stands alone. [P. 308]

Edna's appearance is in direct contrast to the madonnalike Madame Ratingnole with hair like "spun gold" and eyes "like nothing but sapphires; two lips that pouted, that were so red that one could only think of cherries or some other delicious fruit in looking at them. ... Never were hands more exquisite than hers, and it was a joy to look at them when she threaded her needle or sewed away on little night drawers or fashioned a bodice or a bib" (p. 208).

Although Edna feels affection for her children, she asserts, "I would give my life for my children, but I wouldn't give myself" (p. 257). She resents being a victim of nature's "torture" (p. 334) and feels dread while witnessing Madame Ratingnole's labor pains. In spite of Edna's efforts to divest herself of the illusions that nature provides in order to "secure mothers for the race" (p. 335), she feels enmeshed by social pressures to meet her obligations as wife and mother. Madame Reiz had told her that "the bird that would soar above the level plain of tradition must have strong wings. It is a sad spectacle to see the weaklings, bruised, exhausted, fluttering back to earth," (p. 301). However, in spite of Edna's yearning for the unconventional life, her wings are really not strong enough for the flight.

Like so many heroines in American fiction, she is not able to bear the rejection of the man she loves: "despondency had come upon her there in the wakeful night, and had never lifted. There was no one thing in the world that she desired. There was no human being whom she wanted near her except Robert; and she even realized that the day would come when he, too, and the thought of him would melt out of her existence, leaving her alone. The children appeared before her like antagonists who had overcome her, who had overpowered and sought to drag her into the soul's slavery for the rest of her days" (p. 339). Just before Edna drowns herself, she sees a bird with a "broken wing beating the air above, reeling, fluttering, circling disabled down, down to the water" (p. 340). Perhaps Edna is foolish to look for freedom in solitude, but, after all, solitude is the essential basis for the profoundly American belief in self-reliance. In any case, the novel's significance lies in its depiction of Edna's desire to free herself from biological determinants—a necessary prerequisite to becoming a whole person rather than an extension of nature.

Edith Wharton's *Age of Innocence* (1920)[7] has both a dark and a fair heroine, but this time the protagonist Newland Archer prefers the exotic Ellen Olenska to his compliant, fair wife May. May is described as having the "vacant serenity of a young marble athlete" (p. 119), while Ellen looks very much like Zenobia or Edna Pontellier: "(she) sat half-reclined, her head propped on a hand and her wide sleeve leaving the arm bare to the elbow . . . heedless of tradition, (she) was attired in a long robe of red velvet bordered about the chin and down the front with glossy black fur" (p. 91).

Although his marriage to May is proclaimed "the most brilliant of the year" (p. 153), Archer feels himself sinking into a black abyss; he feels claustrophobic, "as though he were being buried alive by the future" (pp. 117–118). Because he knows that May will never surprise him "by an unexpected mood, by a weakness, a cruelty, or an emotion" (p. 235), he cannot avoid feeling that he has missed "the flower of life" (p. 275). However, like Isabel Archer, he resigns himself to honoring his marriage commitment: "it did not matter so much if marriage was a dull duty:

lapsing from that, it became a battle of ugly appetites" (p. 275). Interestingly, Newland Archer, one of the few male protagonists in American fiction who appreciates women who are people rather than extensions of his ego, is a creation of a woman novelist; although Archer is a somewhat atypical protagonist, his appreciation and concern for Ellen Olenska reveal other possible dimensions in human relationships than those designated by the breadwinner-homemaker recipe.

While it is obvious that human relationships are complex, and that, as Edith Wharton's novel reveals, men as well as women suffer thwarted love, the happiness of American heroines is sacrificed more readily than that of their male counterparts. In order to meet the demands of a conventional marriage, most women must submerge their individual identities: Newland Archer may feel that he has "missed the flower of life," but he has not lost his sense of self—his ego survives and his place in society is not questioned. Ellen Olenska, however, has a very uncertain future; she depends on family and friends for support, and it is clear that she will never have the financial, social, or professional freedom that Newland Archer has.

In Willa Cather's *My Mortal Enemy* (1925),[8] Myra Henshawe gives up an inheritance in order to marry for love. Myra is as dramatically beautiful as the women who precede her in the gallery of dark American heroines:

> Her deep-set, flashing grey eyes seemed to be taking me in altogether—estimating me. For all that, she was no taller than I, I felt quite overpowered by her—and stupid, hopelessly clumsy and stupid. Her black hair was done high on her head, alla Pompadour, and there were curious zigzag, curly streaks of glistening white in it, which made it look like the fleece of a Persian goat or some animal that bore silky fur. I could not meet the playful curiosity of her eyes at all, so I fastened my gaze upon a necklace of carved amethysts she wore inside the square-cut neck of her dress. [P. 6]

In spite of her romantic disposition, Myra confides to the narrator Nellie that her marriage has not really been satisfying, that she has had to relinquish many of her own needs—a sacrifice she has bitterly regretted:

> People can be lovers and enemies at the same time, you know. We were ... A man and a woman draw apart from

that long embrace, and see what they have done to each other. Perhaps I can't forgive him for the harm I did him. Perhaps that's it. When there are children, that feeling goes through natural changes. But when it remains so personal . . . something gives way in one. In age we lose everything, even the power to love. [Pp. 88–89]

Convinced that she has permitted her romantic illusions to rob her of selfhood, Myra cries, "Why must I die like this, alone with my mortal enemy?" (p. 95). Her cry is sufficiently ambiguous so that the reader does not know if she considers her mortal enemy to be her husband or herself. The ambiguity is interesting because she made the decision to marry and therefore is responsible for the erosion of self she has experienced in marriage. Myra Henshawe is very much like Edna Pontellier—dissatisfied with the limitations of her married life but without sufficient conviction and strength to create an alternative life for herself.

In *Love and Death in the American Novel*, Leslie Fiedler observes that the American heroine is bifurcated into "Fair Virgin and Dark Lady"; that is, into the good blonde girl and the evil dark woman. According to Fiedler, the male protagonist in American fiction is essentially antisexual; the dark heroines in American fiction represent the authors' masturbatory fantasies and must be destroyed because they are too threatening. The Priscilla-Zenobia, Olive-Verena, Edna Pontellier-Madame Ratingnole, Ellen Olenska-May Welland rivalries certainly corroborate Fiedler's perception of the schizophrenic split between good and evil or passion and frigidity that pervades American literature. As this essay argues, this duality also reveals the Puritan bias in our literature, characterized by the need to *punish* women for original sin as well as the imperative to reward those women who are content to be subservient to men's needs. This need indicates that the dual image of goddess and temptress manifests man's terrible fear of his own sexuality—in the shadow of this image most women have lived out their lives.

Twentieth-century novels such as *Farewell to Arms* and *An American Dream* reveal that the stigma of original sin still taints American heroines. *Farewell to Arms* (1929)[10] is a contemporary reenactment of Eden. Catherine Barkley is the subservient, compliant companion par excellence: as nurse-mistress to Frederic Henry, she is passive femininity incarnate. When they make love, she obsessively asks, "I'm good. Aren't I good ... I do what you want" (p. 106). Henry feels that the relationship is blissful, and it should be for him because there is only one ego—his. "Oh, Darling, I want you so much I want to be you too," Catherine says. "You are," Henry responds, "We're the same one" (p. 299). Although Catherine cleaves to Frederic, ironically, she cannot still escape pain and destruction: she experiences intense agony in labor and, like Charlotte Temple, dies of childbirth complications. The labor-room scene could be right out of a Puritan sermon, depicting the consequences of God's wrath on adulteresses. Catherine's pain is horrifying, and the pitiful moralizing of Frederic Henry does not diminish its terror: "Poor, poor dear Cat. And this was the price you paid for sleeping together" (p. 320). While Henry mouths platitudes, Catherine screams in agony because the gas is no longer sufficient to subdue the pain:

> I'm just a fool, darling, Catherine said. But it (the gas) doesn't work anymore. She began to cry. Oh, I wanted so much to have this baby and not make trouble, and now I'm all done and gone to pieces and it doesn't work. Oh, darling, it doesn't work at all. I don't care if only it will stop. There it comes. Oh Oh Oh! She breathed sobbingly into the mask. It doesn't work. It doesn't work. It doesn't work. Don't mind me darling. [P. 322]

Catherine dies, thereby expiating their sin, and Henry, keeping a stiff upper lip, leaves the hospital and walks back into the hotel in the rain.

In Norman Mailer's *An American Dream* (1965)[11] Stephen Richards Rojack echoes Frederic Henry's manly fortitude: "if one wished to be a lover, one could not find one's sanity in another, that was the iron law of romance: one took the vow to be brave" (p. 191). Obviously, this is one lesson American heroines have never learned. However, it appears that Rojack has not really learned it either because he makes such statements as "women must murder us unless we possess them altogether" (p. 16), and then proceeds to murder his wife because he feels possessed by her. Sex is a battle for Rojack in which wills meet "locked in an exchange of stares which goes on and on" (p. 122). Rojack decides he loves the night-club singer Cherry and prays for a romantic idyll much like

Catherine and Frederic's: "let me love that girl, and become a father and try to be a good man" (p. 153), but because his courage fails him, she is killed as retribution for his cowardice and egotism. Again, the grief-stricken hero leaves, but this time he valiantly heads for Yucatan instead of resolutely returning to the hotel.

Perhaps the woman who comes closest to taking Rojack's vow of courage is the narrator of Mary McCarthy's *The Company She Keeps* (1942)[12]—a brilliant novel that has received little critical attention to date. This novel chronicles a twentieth-century woman's attempts to resist biblical strictures and to attain selfhood on her own terms. It begins with her divorce which she regards ironically and self-deprecatingly but which does permit her to begin to take responsibility for her own life. To prove her social emancipation, she becomes sexually aggressive but nevertheless worries about becoming a spinster; she experiences a strange combination of timidity and defiance and is alternately predatory and victimized. Her favorite quotation is from Chaucer's Criseyde "I am my owene woman, wel at ese", but although she is sexually liberated, she continues to be psychologically enslaved because she persists in looking for her identity in a man. She remarries, this time to a successful architect, but the marriage does not create selfhood. Finally, with an analyst's help, she begins to make the transition from dependency to selfhood, realizing that *she* is her greatest enemy and that her failures are due to insufficient self-love to which both her childhood and cultural conditioning contribute:

> Now for the first time she saw her own extremity, saw that it was some failure in self-love that obliged her to snatch blindly at the love of others, hoping to love herself through them, borrowing their feelings, as the moon borrowed light. She herself was a dead planet. [P. 303]

Yet, this new knowledge frightens her (her fear is not surprising considering this is the first perception of its kind to be made by a woman in American fiction); she wonders and perhaps even hopes that it is a therapeutic lie: "There was no use talking. *She knew*. Only a man ... she was under a terrible enchantment, like the beleagured princesses in the fairy tales" (p. 302). In spite of the emotional red herring with which she tries to distract herself, she realizes that no man can ever create self-love;

she must do that for herself. The novel concludes ironically: her prayer for continued insight, *"O dei reddite me hoc pro pietate mea"* (p. 304), is belied by her unbelief in God.

The novel reveals how badly our culture needs a new mythology for women. Although psychoanalysis often confines women as much as Christianity, at least it has made us aware of the extent of psychic damage resulting from a failure of self-love. However, insufficient self-love continues to be the norm by which our culture measures adjustment for women, and self-abnegation is considered to be a form of feminine maturity.

The problem of self-doubt still plagues the American heroine, and unfortunately, not much progress has been made since *The Company She Keeps*. As has been pointed out, major social and economic change will have to take place before improvements in the female psyche can occur. However, fiction can contribute to changing female consciousness and men's concept of women by providing a vision of a new Eve, of a woman who is self-actualizing, strong, risk-taking, independent, but also capable of loving and being loved. Women like this have existed in real life—consider Anne Bradstreet, Elizabeth Cady Stanton, Margaret Fuller, Frances Wright, Frances Bloomer, Amelia Earhart. Why have our novelists persisted in ignoring these examples of strong women, reinforcing instead the image of women as forlorn, helpless creatures, who are certain to be destroyed or hopelessly embittered unless they devote themselves exclusively to their domestic lives and duties as wives and mothers? Why have novelists persisted (consciously or unconsciously) in perpetuating the tradition of the fallen woman consistently punished for her frailty? Why have novelists insisted that heroines can redeem themselves only if they forego sexuality? Furthermore, why have women internalized cultural concepts of themselves defining them as inferior or potentially evil creatures when their own experience often tells them otherwise? These are not easy questions to answer, but it is time to attempt to reverse the effects of centuries of conditioning which have reinforced the biblical perception of women as fallen creatures who must do penance for original sin. Unfortunately, most women as well as most men unquestioningly accept this myth which renders one-half of the race less than human. Sacrificing the humanity of slightly more than 50 percent of the species is a pretty high price to pay for eating an apple—and it was probably a rotten apple at that.

NOTES

1. Ian Watt, *The Rise of the Novel: Studies in De Foe, Richardson, and Fielding* (Berkeley: University of California Press, 1959).
2. Nathaniel Hawthorne, *The Scarlet Letter* (New York: New American Library, 1959). All other references to the novel will be made by page number only; this citation procedure will be followed throughout the chapter for all novels.
3. Nathaniel Hawthorne, *The Blithedale Romance* (New York: William Norton, 1958).
4. Henry James, *The Bostonians* (New York: Modern Library, 1956).
5. Henry James, *The Portrait of a Lady* (New York: New American Library, 1963).
6. Kate Chopin, *The Awakening and Other Stories* (New York: Holt, Rinehart and Winston, 1970).
7. Edith Wharton, *The Age of Innocence* (New York: New American Library, 1962).
8. Willa Cather, *My Mortal Enemy* (New York: Random House, 1956).
9. Leslie A. Fiedler, *Love and Death in the American Novel* (New York: Dell Publishing Company, 1966).
10. Ernest Hemingway, *A Farewell to Arms* (New York: Charles Scribner's Sons, 1957).
11. Norman Mailer, *An American Dream* (New York: Dell Publishing Company, 1965).
12. Mary McCarthy, *The Company She Keeps* (New York: Harcourt, Brace, and Company, 1942).

16

OUR SEXIST LANGUAGE

Ethel Strainchamps

Few people would care to take the negative side of the proposition that the women of the world are oppressed and scorned. Statistics are against them. What has not been made so clear, however, is that the women of America, the world's most highly advanced (that is, technological) society, may be among the most oppressed and scorned of all.

Various data suggest the conclusion. Compared to other advanced nations, we have had fewer women in high government offices and fewer women in the professions. America men are more attracted by the primal aggressive activities of hunting and fishing than are men of other nations. More of them are seduced by the atavistic appeal of all-male organizations—reminiscent of the male-bonding propensities of the apes—from the Knights of Columbus to the Rotary Club. Our culture heroes are not benevolent rulers or noble wise men, in spite of the schools' efforts on behalf of Washington, Jefferson, and Lincoln, but aggressive men of action: cowboys, aviators, baseball players, outlaws, military men. All *muy macho*.

It may be argued, of course, that these facts only confirm what we all know (men and women are different) and that they do not prove that the women in our society are held in particularly low esteem; merely because a rampant male person is the national ideal does not necessarily prove that feminine qualities are not accorded due respect in their proper place. But it is impossible to despise certain traits to the extent that you suppress them in yourself without feeling superior to people who do not suppress them, especially people you live with. Females serve as ever-present reminders to developing males of what they must not become. The deleterious effect this has on the status of women is shown most unarguably in our national language, the most masculine branch of English, itself the most masculine of languages.

Early in this century, anthropologists made a discovery that transformed the nature of their own discipline and of several related ones—linguistics most of all. They found that by painstakingly examining a language they could learn more about the culture of the people who spoke the language than any number of its native speakers, however willing, could tell them. Without any particular interest in learning to converse in a given language, the anthropologists could phonetically record large samples of it and learn things about its speakers that the speakers themselves did not know and might deny if they were asked—things about their concepts of time and space, about their taboos, about their social and family hierarchies.

Using such methods, an anthropologist from another planet visiting the earth could soon learn from examining human language that the half of the human race bearing offspring is scorned and oppressed by the half doing the impregnating. He would no doubt be puzzled unless he used his imagination to recapitulate the social history of the race. Ah! Of course! Pregnancies and child nurture incapacitate females for all their adult lives, so the males have to go out and fight to defend the nest and hunt to bring in the food. To prerational creatures greater physical strength and mobility would naturally spell superiority. But how amazing that these archaic attitudes persist in a society where the socially valuable potentials of the two sexes are so little differentiated—where brute strength is about as useful to those who aspire to the seats of power as the caudal appendage.

Nevertheless, the anthropologist could discover that English, one of the most highly evolved of the world's hundreds of languages and the one spoken in the most thoroughly technological society, retains more vestiges of the archaic sexual attitudes than any other civilized tongue. It would take some time to document this assertion. Several of our distinguished linguists—all male—have examined dozens of languages to see how their speakers' minds worked, but it has never occurred to any of them to compare the languages from the standpoint of their sexist quotient.

Some of them, however, have been struck by the unique dominance of the masculine viewpoint in the development of English, though they all regard this as to the great advantage of the language. One of the most eloquent advocates of this view is Otto Jespersen, a multilingual Dane. Because Jespersen could look at English from the viewpoint of a nonnative speaker, and because the remainder of his analysis of the language is so nearly flawless, his opinions on its masculinity deserves special credence. The entire whole first chapter of his most popular book, *The Growth and Structure of the English Language,* is devoted to proving his thesis that English is "the most positively and expressly masculine" of all the languages he knew. It is, he said, "the language of a grown-up man, with very little childish or feminine about it."[1]

To accept Jespersen's major thesis, you do not have to accept his belief that the most admirable qualities of English—its terseness, logicality, freedom from pedantry, openness to innovation, and emotional restraint—are strictly masculine characteristics, or his argument that the effusiveness, long-windedness, ebullience, and adherence to the status quo distinguishing the languages he contrasts with it are "childish and feminine" or "childlike and effeminate." (He used the two sets of adjectives interchangeably.) Jespersen's notion that women and children are practically identical temperamentally and cognitively is universally shared. Stoicism, efficiency, logic, and aggressiveness are masculine; their opposites are feminine (or childlike). It has even been suggested that the countless millennia during which women's role was chiefly maternal, forcing them to be more closely attuned to their young, have resulted in a sex-connected genetic change. But psychologists attribute the apparent child-woman similarity to the cultural conditioning of females. Women, like children, are weaker than males and are therefore subjugated by them. To get along, they learn to be obedient and complaisant; this does not exactly make for boldness and inventiveness in language or anything else. Nobody knows what direction language would take in a society where men and women were equal; no such society has ever been known to exist. But, with things as they are, we may accept Jespersen's thesis as valid. The unique characteristics of English that make it, in his view, superior to other languages *are* masculine.

Americans will be encouraged—or discouraged, depending on their sex—to learn that, using Jespersen's criteria, it can be demonstrated that the masculinity of English has been enhanced on this side of the Atlantic. Jespersen applauds, for example, the distinct pronunciation of the consonants in English, lamenting the neglect of *r* when it is not followed by a vowel. But in most of America, *r* is pronounced distinctly. He believes that the use of superlatives, to which the Latins—and even the Germans—are more prone than the British, is effeminate. But to Americans, even the British overdo hyperbole—hence the "frightfully's" and "delightfully's" of the staid Englishman. Jespersen thinks that clusters of strong consonants are masculine and that diminutive endings are feminine: compare lists of related British and American words (British: *hotchpotch, rumbustious, telly;* American: *hodgepodge, rambunctious, TV*). As for freedom from pedantry and openness to innovation, Americans, including women, disregard rules and coin new words so freely that they drive even the British wild. A British reviewer of Rachel Carson's *Silent Spring* moaned that he was at first put off "by the trans-Atlantic vigour of her style."

But more objective evidence of the male dominance of the language lies in our lexicon of sexual words and words denoting gender. The word *man* originally meant human being, but males appropriated it; later they came up with the word *wif-man* (now *woman*) for the other half of the race. *He,* with different endings to show gender, was once the pronoun for all third persons, but men took over the root word; *she* was an afterthought. *Female* came into Middle English as Old French *femelle,* a diminutive of *femina,* but was soon corrupted into its present form through the process of (male) folk etymology. (Phonetic symbolism, which I will discuss later, must have contributed to the lodging of this word in our lexicon, just as it has helped to change the meaning of *effete* in our own time. Even *she* looks suspicious.)

Many words that were nonemotive when they referred to either gender became contemptuous after they came to apply to women alone; some that were pejorative lost that sense when they acquired an exclusively masculine reference. The *shrewd-shrewish* pair exemplifies both tendencies: in the sixteenth century, both words meant wicked and were equally pejorative; when they became gender-specific, their connotation diverged sharply. *Virago* originally meant *heroic woman;* being a complimentary word, it was sometimes applied to men. In Chaucer's time, *harlot* meant nothing worse than what *rogue* means now. However, when *rogue* entered the language a couple of centuries later, it meant *shiftless vagrant* and was used as a term of abuse to servants of both sexes; it acquired its romantic aura only after it was masculinized.

According to the *Oxford English Dictionary*, the noun *female* had already become "only contemptuous"; when its entry was written (late nineteenth century), the dictionary cites an author of the period who noted that *female* was a "term of opprobrium." By the twentieth century, the noun no longer was used in print and "polite conversation," as the dictionaries used to call speech fit for public ears. (The recent attempts by women liberationists to restore it are misguided.)

The history of *female* offers such a clear-cut example of the linguistic effects of male supremacism that the process at work should be obvious even to the layman. But the experts in the field (all male, of course), far from acknowledging male guilt, blame women not only for the decline in status of the word but for the inconvenience caused by denying to the language the logical counterpart of *male*.

H. W. Fowler, whose *Modern English Usage* (1926) remains the American editors' bible (so much for Jespersen's idea that openness to innovation is a masculine trait), was so convinced that oversensitive women were responsible for the demise of words disclosing their sex that he called his article on "feminine designations" a "counterprotest." He admitted that using the noun *female* to refer to women was "impolite" and "reasonably resented" because the word may apply to "nonhuman as well as to human female creatures."[2] But he held out for the adjective. When *female* is used before words like *suffrage* and *education*, he pointed out with unassailable logic, it describes, "of course, human f. creatures, i. e. women." Who ever heard of a female of another species getting the vote or going to college? He hoped that when the voting of women became a topic of general discussion, it would be called the female vote and not the woman vote, just as its counterpart would certainly be called the male vote and not the man vote. "To turn *woman* into an adjective with *female* ready made," he concluded, "is mere perversity."

Of course, it did not occur to the usually astute grammarian to ponder the implications of the odd fact that the noun *male*, which has the same dual reference, is not "impolite" and "reasonably resented." If it had, we would have been spared the perpetuation of some further nonsense.

After setting us straight on *female*, he goes on to castigate women for protesting against feminine endings for nouns, accusing them of putting their "sectional claims" above "general convenience and the needs of the King's English." He holds actresses up to us as an admirable example, pointing out that they "are not known to resent the indication of *their* sex." The proof of real equality," he concludes ringingly, "will be not the banishment of *authoress* as a degrading title, but its establishment on a level with *author*." He cites a long list of other "feminine designations" that have survived the irate female onslaughts, among them adulteress, adventuress, enchantress, goddess, hostess, Jewess, stewardess, and waitress. He failed to note that all of these terms, like actress, refer to women who are either generally conceded to be just as good at what they do as men are, or who are too low in the social scale for men to worry about their reasonable resentment at having their gender made known.

As Fowler should have realized, neither protests nor counterprotests have ever altered the course of one English word. Emotive words acquire their connotations by reflecting the sentiments of the dominant group in a society—in our case white Anglo-Saxon males (WASMs)—and to ask women to remove the stigma from words applying to them by trying harder is like asking Jews or Negroes to do the same thing. On the other hand, it is impossible to conceive of a generic term for WASMs that would not be flattering once its referent became generally understood. With *honkie*, which is just a Southern pronunciation of *hunkie*, the militant blacks succeeded only in doing an inadvertent good turn for Central-European immigrant laborers. (They could have benefited a much larger group and riled their adversaries much more effectively if they had thought of calling them *females*. But there seems to be a fraternal bond among males that cuts across even class and race lines; this would have been too low a blow.) When certain racial and sexual epithets have, like *female*, generally disappeared from print in "polite conversation," it has been due not to protests from the maligned but to a recognition by the WASMs that they had reached the point of overkill. In any case, the true viability of a word cannot be judged by its life within the public media, as the longevity of our Anglo-Saxon obscenities so vividly illustrates.

These words are recorded in the earliest word lists and dictionaries of modern English. Nathaniel Bailey's dictionary (1721) included *fuck*, but Samuel Johnson's (1755) omitted it, as did all succeeding general dictionaries of the language until 1969. It was taken as a matter of course that the sight of certain words in print could lead to moral depravity. To understand this bizarre taboo against setting down on paper certain words that everybody knows, we must try to attune ourselves to that weird repository of myths, the male mind. As James Lincoln Collier has pointed out in *Language in America*,[3] the concepts of obscenity and pornography, with censorship following naturally in their wake, developed as a result of the class war that began with the Industrial Revolution, the period that saw the world's first experiments in mass education. In ancient Greece, where everybody who could read was a member of the elite, obscenity was not possible; anything that could be thought or spoken could be written. But, as Collier points out, the victors in a war claim the spoils, including the nubile women. The WASM victors, still naively confusing the word with the thing, felt that the vanquished lower-class males should not be permitted to feast their eyes on the common words for the female genitals and the sex act. They regarded the sight of these words as sufficiently inflammatory to set off any uncultured male on a round of seduction and rape, with a resulting loss in the number of virgins available to their own class. Within this elite class, the writing, printing, and circulating of pornography—by and for the delectation of upper-class males—reached the dimensions of a minor industry during the Victorian period.

From years of working as an editor and writer for men's magazines that had to push at the edges of public tolerance without overstepping the bounds, Collier devised a neat formula for would-be pornographers. It was concerned not with the *content* of a printed medium, but with the page size, binding, quality of paper and printing, the professionalism of the art, and—most importantly—the price, the true class divider. The middle-class male guardians of our literary morals—the customs officials, policemen, sheriffs, judges—seem to have tacitly agreed that a book that costs fifteen dollars or more is not pornography but art. In other words, it will not fall into the wrong hands.

A study of the last three and a half centuries of our language's history will disclose to any woman that it is a history compiled by male chauvinists. Philologists inform us confidently, for instance, that *fuck* and *cunt* are the two most "sexually energizing" words in the language, an opinion that surely disregards women's sexual response, if any, to these words. However, the learned male spokesmen have more than their individual reactions to go on. Those two words and *twot* (or twat), a synonym for *cunt*, were the only ones with such an ancient lineage that the editors of the *Oxford English Dictionary* felt conscience-bound to omit. Their male bias is indicated by their feeling no such compunction about including the vulgar words for *penis*. In these words we see English sexism rampant: *penis* (Latin) means tail; *phallus* (Greek) means something round; *prick* (English) first referred to a goad for oxen.

Etymologists also believe that the word *fuck* (and its postulated forerunners, probably *vüchen* to *fücken*) has always had a unique power to turn men on; it was not one of the words our ancestors went around carving on runic stones. In fact, its etymology is uncertain because so far as is now known, it was never inscribed anywhere in any of its earlier forms. Unfortunately, the Victorian WASM mentality of the Oxford English Dictionary editors, who had legions of brilliant men combing old records for decades, has deprived us forever of the benefit of anything they may have learned about that word.

We are not much better informed about *cunt* and *twot*, though these words were apparently invested with their galvanizing charisma somewhat later. Chaucer used the word *cunt* (spelled *queinte* or *queynte*); Shakespeare ventured a little word play on it; and there was an entry for it, minus the two middle letters (it was against the law in England to publish the word from 1700 to 1960) in a dictionary published in 1788. The definition was "a nasty name for a nasty thing." The lexicographers' dereliction in regard to *twot* occasioned one of the greatest bloopers in literary history. Browning, misled by the apparent sense of

the word as it was used in an old rhyme, employed it thus
in *Pippa Passes:*

> Then, owls and bats,
> Cowls and twats,
> Monks and nuns, in a cloister's moods,
> Adjourn to the oak-stump pantry.

Webster's Second New International Dictionary (1934),
which was very conscientious about including words you
might run across in literature, had the mandatory entry
for this one, but defined it disingenuously as "some part of
a nun's garb. Erroneous. Browning." It could thereby have
perpetuated an error forever, except that nobody learns
the *meanings* of Anglo-Saxon words from dictionaries and
that there have been few such innocents as Browning who
ever undertook to write anything.

As a matter of fact, men become so certain of their
sexual omniscience after they have achieved a few orgasms that they feel no necessity for consulting dictionaries even on technical terms. The Victorian experts on
love were sure that women ejaculated during orgasm, and
the playboys of 1970, if Gore Vidal can be taken as an
example, believe that women urinate through the vaginal
canal.[4] It was partly the fault of the lexicographers,
though, that the existence of Bartholin's glands, an essential part of the female sexual anatomy, came as such a
surprise to everybody when Masters and Johnson revealed
it a few years ago. Actually the glands had been discovered and described by a Danish physician more than 200
years previously—rather late in the day, even then. The
term can be found in *Webster's Unabridged* after some
searching—you have to look under *glands*—but it is not in
the two self-styled unabridged dictionaries that came out
after the Masters-Johnson revelation.

Dr. Bartholin's name and an account of his chief discovery have been preserved for us by the medical historians. But another benefactor of womankind who is believed to have been working away in his laboratory at
about the same time has been neglected by the anatomists
as well as the lexicographers. As a result, the etymology of
a common English noun that probably came into the
language as late as the eighteenth century remains as
shrouded in mystery as some of the early Indo-European
stumpers. We are not even sure of the spelling and

pronunciation. Is it *condom* or *cundum?* The consensus soon evolved concerning the device, that it was deleterious to the penis and detracted from male enjoyment of sexual intercourse, was enough to bring on selective lexicographical amnesia. In our own more scientific age, therefore, there is still uncertainty about whether the device is named for an Englishman called Condom, Conton, or Cundum, whether he was a colonel or a doctor, or whether the whole thing is not one of those old word-myths concocted to give the British credit for a popular French import shipped from the village of Condom. All that is really known is that the word—if not the device—was familiar to the grandfathers of the first generation that was permitted the great privilege of looking it up in a dictionary. The Third Edition of *Webster's Unabridged* (1961) is the first one to consider it fit to print.

Curiously, *condom*—and also *diaphragm* in the related sense—was omitted from *Webster's Seventh Collegiate Dictionary,* an abridgement of the *Third* for college students, though, as the editor once boasted in a letter to *Playboy,* it does include *fellatio, cunnilingus,* and *soixante-neuf.* The choice of entries was obviously the result of masculine decision-making; males may find graphic descriptions of exotic forms of sexual connection more fun to write (and read) but females—the childbearers—would give priority to informing college students about more practical methods of contraception, just in case some atavistic impulse should lead a couple to fall into the old Adam-and-Eve trap, with possible dire consequences for the girl.

In their eternal—and foredoomed—quest for the origins of language, philologists have naturally surmised that the exchange of meaningful vocal sounds began among males. It was men working, fighting, or hunting together, they assume, who first discovered the value of exchanging complicated vocal signals. From this assumption, they have gone on to present us with such fanciful theories of language origin as the "bowwow" and the "yo-heave-ho." (It might have occurred to a woman that a "no-no" theory was more likely, considering the importance to racial survival of the mother-child communication, with the prevalence of open fires, poisonous reptiles, and other hazards). But some philologists have speculated that the first sounds that could be called words were those addressed by males to females for sexual purposes—formalized mating calls—summoning them to the act that was truly essential to species survival.

It is possible that the two utterances that modern English-speaking men find so galvanizing originated then, of course. In spite of assiduous scholarly efforts, which, until recently, had to be carried on secretly in defiance of customs and postal laws, etymologists have not been able to establish any kinship between *fuck* and *cunt* and words even remotely related in other Indo-European languages. The seeming cousinship between *fuck* and the Latin *futuere* (whence French *foutre*) is illusory; Grimm's Law of sound changes rules it out. A kinship with Latin *pungere* (whence *puncture*) is more likely but not proved.

My own theory, similarly unprovable, is that the Anglo-Saxon word originated as an expression of disgust. If that is true, it would be as fruitless to look for its kinship with words in other languages as it would be to try to establish such a base for *fooey, eckhh,* or *ugh,* sounds that no English-speaking person needs to have defined, regardless of how they are represented in print, and of which, after all, *fuck* is only a blend. Besides, so far as is known, the word may have been used longer—as it is certainly now used more often—as an expletive than as a transitive verb.

Such communication of meaning through what amounts to oral gestures is called phonetic symbolism, a phenomenon that is only peripherally related to onomatopoeia. The consonants in *splash* are onomatopoeic; the vowels that make the difference in the meanings of *splish, splash,* and *splosh* are phonetically symbolic. The widening of the vowels is understood to correspond to the widening of the space between the hands in gestures indicating an increase in size or intensity. The consonants in *flash* are phonetically symbolic; light makes no sound to be imitated. Nevertheless, in the semantic code to which native speakers of English are privy, one of the meanings of *fl* is "moving light" (flare, flash, flame, flicker). The initial sounds of Anglo-Saxon taboo words similarly have semantic content. They all begin with the blowing or ejective sounds—*p, f, sh,* or *k*—instinctive oral gestures of disgust. (If other peoples have not formalized these gestures into words, so much the worse for the expressiveness of their languages.)

Women who object to the use of the taboo words in love-making do so not from a fear of them as insidious aphrodisiacs but from a linguistic perception that seems to

be shared by everybody except a few adult males. Say
"Fuck off" to a six-year-old child who has never heard the
word before—in the unlikely event that one can be found—
and he will resent it; he will resent it more than if you had
said "Run along" in the same tone of voice. There is no
sexual content in the word as it appears in that phrase, or
in most of its other uses, and perhaps there never was.
The *American Heritage Dictionary*, the first dictionary to
include the word for 250 years and the first one ever to
offer a full range of definitions based on actual usage,
gives two nonsexual definitions of the verb and has a
separate entry for *fucking* as an intensive. The second
definition of the transitive verb is "to deal with in an
aggressive, unjust, or spiteful manner."

There is an interesting, but unanswerable, question as to
which meaning came first. All the older Anglo-Saxon
synonyms for *fuck* range from mildly aggressive to sadistic: swive, plow, cut, take, bang, shaft, score, screw; all of
them, as transitive verbs, have a male subject and a
female object. So does *fuck* in its sexual sense; on this,
their number-one definition, the *American Heritage* lexicographers made the customary lexicographical error.
Their definition reads simply "to have sexual intercourse
with." But actually fucking is exclusively something that a
male human being can do to another object, animate or
inanimate. Young Alex Portnoy, you will recall, his imagination fired by a chunk of liver he spied in the refrigera-
tor, fucked his family's dinner (to use his words). Some
small progress toward the civilization of males is shown by
the fact that *lay*, the least aggressive of the currently
popular synonyms, is used by below-forty men in either
the active or the passive voice—they can lay or get laid.

For speakers of English the Latinate synonyms lack the
phonetic symbolism of the Anglo-Saxon ones, and therefore their provocativeness. Copulation and coition can be
spoken of on TV and in the classroom. They also lack the
sense of the male's being the sole operator. The one Latin
sexual word that did become obscene—too obscene to be
used in any sense for all of the seventeenth and most of
the eighteenth century—was *occupy*, defined by the *Oxford English Dictionary*, with palpable inaccuracy, as to
deal with sexually. (Could a woman occupy a man?) It is
to the men's credit that they have always been more or
less embarrassed about the use of transitive verbs for the
sex act that imply that the subject is singular, masc.; so

embarrassed, in fact, that they sacrifice accuracy in definitions to avoid shameful admissions.

Lacking the galvanic response of males to Anglo-Saxon sex words, women are less subject to the force of the taboo against them. Three of the first authors of international standing to use the word *fuck* in their books after the courts made it legally permissible were women: Iris Murdoch, Doris Lessing, and Carson McCullers. Many more probably had it edited out of their manuscripts by timorous male editors. In Sybille Bedford's report of the *Lady Chatterley* obscenity trial, where the taboo words were discussed in detail, *Esquire* "the magazine for men," let all the other words stand but substituted "that word" for *fuck*. *Playboy*, more aggressively all-male used an *f* and three dashes to represent the word as it was spoken by Helen Gurley Brown in an interview. Mrs. Brown had been asked if she had had any difficulty with editors in getting *Sex and the Single Girl* into print as she wrote it. She replied that the only serious contretemps occurred when she discovered in the galleys that *Frig you!* had been substituted for *Fuck you!* as the proper retort by a young woman to neighbors who criticized her for sleeping with a man she was not married to. Mrs. Brown said she was outraged and told the editor, "No lady would ever say that word!"

But if anything is more intense than the *frisson* men feel at seeing an unattributed *fuck* in print, it is their numb shock at seeing it in something written by a woman. A few years ago I got together some usage data I had compiled as a reader for a dictionary and wrote a report on the effect that the loosening of the obscenity laws was having on family newspapers and magazines. Before I started writing the piece, a *Harper's* editor told me he was interested, but he returned it with the excuse that the magazine had run a piece on pornography a few months before. Then I sent it to *Playboy*, and they said it was too scholarly. I sent it to *American Scholar*, and they said it was too journalistic. I sent it to *Yale Review*, admitting the previous rejections and offering to alter the piece if the information in it seemed to make it worth the trouble. I got a letter back from Editor-in-Chief Paul Pickrel. It began, "At last you have found an honest editor." He said that none of the excuses I had been given had anything to do with the reason the piece had not been published and that the criticisms were not valid. The real trouble, he said, "is that you are a woman writing on a subject which, according to contemporary mores, women do not write on."

The comparatively sane and rational attitude that women have toward taboo words can serve as a model for the whole society as it recovers from its Victorian sexual hangups. As is often true in master-slave relationships, the benign neglect of certain aspects of life in the female subculture has allowed them to develop in a more natural way. The English language itself made its most important advances when it was the language mainly of the lower classes and not considered worthy of the restricting and regulating attention of the ruling class.

The laws aimed at controlling sexual conduct have all been devised by men who considered the sexual drives of women as too unimportant to require regulation. So long as a woman does not threaten male property rights—specifically by adultery—she may indulge any of her natural sexual bents without fear of serious penalties. The Victorian tracts on the evils of masturbation were never directed at girls. Either it was not known that girls practiced it—which seems most likely at the height of the masturbation phobia—or female orgasms were not considered cataclysmic enough to bring on the bad complexions, falling hair, weakening of the muscle tone, and infertility that threatened boys.

Female homosexuality is looked upon as nothing more than an odd bent that isolates those so afflicted from normal social life and denies them the blessing of housewifery. The linguistically significant result of this less censorious attitude toward them is that *homosexual* is now understood to refer only to the nominally male. The common practice now is to speak of homosexuals *and* lesbians.

The same sort of thing has occurred with words for other sexual deviations. A sexual *voyeur* or *exhibitionist* is assumed to be male because it is against males that the legal sanctions are invoked. If a man watches a woman undressing before a window, he can be arrested as a Peeping Tom. If a woman watches a man undressing before a window, the man can be arrested for indecent exposure. The penalties for statutory rape have probably never been invoked against a woman; the Mrs. Robinsons are given points for initiating inexperienced males, while the Humbert Humberts are ostracized as dirty old men. The contrast in the sex-offense penalties meted out to the two sexes should instruct men on the vindictive, envious, and spiteful nature of the laws they now have on the books.

Laws are sometimes changed in advance of the public consensus. Language never is. The English language will continue to imply that women are inferior creatures until Anglo-American men can be persuaded that they are not.

NOTES

1. Otto Jespersen, *The Growth and Structure of the English Language* (New York: D. Appleton, 1923) pp. 1 ff.
2. H. W. Fowler, *Modern English Usage* (New York: Oxford University Press, 1926) pp. 174-175.
3. James Lincoln Collier, *Language in America* (New York: Pegasus, 1969) pp. 57-70.
4. Gore Vidal, "Number One," *New York Review of Books*, June 4, 1970.

17

PATIENT AND PATRIARCH: Women in the Psychotherapeutic Relationship

Phyllis Chesler

Like all sciences and valuations, the psychology of women has hitherto been considered only from the point of view of men. It is inevitable that the man's position of advantage should cause objective validity to be attributed to his subjective, affective relations to women . . . the question then is how far analytical psychology also, when its researches have women for their object, is under the spell of this way of thinking.[1]

—KAREN HORNEY

Although Karen Horney wrote this in 1926, very few psychiatrists and psychologists seem to have agreed with and been guided by her words. Female psychology is still being viewed from a masculine point of view. Contemporary psychiatric and psychological theories and practices both reflect and influence our culture's politically naive understanding and emotionally brutal treatment of wom-

A paper presented at the annual convention of the American Psychological Association, September 1970, Miami Beach, Florida.

en. Female unhappiness is viewed and "treated" as a problem of individual pathology, no matter how many other female patients (or nonpatients) are similarly unhappy—and this by men who have studiously bypassed the objective fact of female oppression. Woman's inability to adjust to or to be contented by feminine roles has been considered as a deviation from "natural" female psychology rather than as a criticism of such roles.

I do not wish to imply that female unhappiness is a myth conjured up by men; it is very real. One of the ways white, middle-class women in America attempt to handle this unhappiness is through psychotherapy. They enter private therapy just as they enter marriage—with a sense of urgency and desperation. Also, black and white women of all classes, particularly unmarried women, comprise the largest group of psychiatrically hospitalized and "treated" Americans. This paper will present the following analysis:

1. that for a number of reasons, women "go crazy" more often and more easily than men do; that their "craziness" is mainly self-destructive; and that they are punished for their self-destructive behavior, either by the brutal and impersonal custodial care given them in mental asylums, or by the relationships they have with most (but not all) clinicians, who implicitly encourage them to blame themselves or to take responsibility for their unhappiness in order to be "cured."

2. that both psychotherapy and marriage, the two major socially approved institutions for white, middle-class women, function similarly, i.e., as vehicles for personal "salvation" through the presence of an understanding and benevolent (male) authority. In female culture, not being married, or being unhappily married, is experienced as an "illness" which psychotherapy can, hopefully, cure.

This paper will discuss the following questions: What are some of the facts about women as psychiatric or psychotherapy patients in America? What "symptoms" do they present? Why are more women involved, either voluntarily or involuntarily with mental health professionals than are men? Who are the psychotherapists in America and what are their views about women? What practical implications does this discussion have for women who are in a psychotherapeutic relationship?

GENERAL STATISTICS

A study published in 1970 by the U.S. Department of Health, Education, and Welfare[2] indicated that in both the black and white populations significantly more women than men reported having suffered nervous breakdowns, having felt impending nervous breakdowns,* phychological inertia* and dizziness. Both black and white women also reported higher rates than men for the following symptoms: nervousness,* insomnia, trembling hands,* nightmares,* fainting,*[3] and headaches* (See Table 17–1). White women who were never married reported fewer symptoms than white married or separated women. These findings are essentially in agreement with an earlier study published in 1960, by the Joint Commission on Mental Health and Illness.[4] The Commission reported the following information for nonhospitalized American adults: (1) Greater distress and symptoms are reported by women than by men in all adjustment areas. They report more disturbances in general adjustment, in their self-perception, and in their marital and parental functioning. This sex difference is most marked at the younger age intervals. (2) A feeling of impending breakdown is reported more frequently by divorced and separated females than by any other groups of either sex. (3) The unmarried (whether single, separated, divorced or widowed) have a greater potential for psychological distress than do the married. (4) While the sexes did not differ in the *frequency* with which they reported "unhappiness," the women reported more worry, fear of breakdown, and need for help.

What such studies do not make clear, is how many of these "psychologically distressed" women are involved in any form of psychiatric or psychological treatment. Other studies have attempted to do this. William Schofield[5] found that the average psychiatrist sees significantly more female than male patients. A study published in 1965 reported that women patients outnumbered men patients 3 to 2 in private psychiatric treatment.[6] Statistics for public and private psychiatric hospitalization in America do exist and of course, are controversial. However, statistical studies have indicated certain trends. The National

* at all age levels

Institute of Mental Health has reported that from 1965–
1967 there were 102,241 more women than men involved in the following psychiatric treatment facilities:
private psychiatric hospitals, state and county psychiatric
hospitals, inpatient psychiatric wards in General and Veterans' Administration hospitals, and General and Veterans'
Administration outpatient psychiatric facilities. This figure
excludes the number of Americans involved in various
forms of private treatment. Earlier studies have reported
that admission rates to both public and private psychiatric
hospitals are significantly higher for women than for men.[8]
Unmarried people (single, divorced or widowed) of both
sexes are disproportionately represented among the psychiatrically hospitalized.[9] Thus, while according to the 1970
HEW report, single, white women in the general population report less psychological distress than married or
separated white women,[10] women, (as well as men) who
are psychiatrically *hospitalized* tend to be unmarried.

Private psychotherapy, like marriage, is an integral part
of middle-class female culture. Patients entering private
therapy betray significantly different attitudes toward men
and women therapists. A number of them indicate that
they feel sex is important in the therapeutic relationship
by voluntarily requesting a therapist of a particular sex.

I have recently completed a study of 1,001 middle-
income clinic outpatients (538 women and 463 men) who
sought therapeutic treatment in New York City from
1965 to 1969. Patient variables, such as sex, marital
status, age, religion, occupation, and so forth, were related
to patient requests for a male or a female therapist at the
time of the initial interview. These findings are based on a
sample of 258 people (159 women and 99 men) who
voluntarily requested either a male or a female therapist
or who voluntarily stated that they had no sex-of-therapist
preference. Twenty-four percent of the 538 women and
14 percent of the 463 men requested a therapist specifically by sex. The findings were as follows:

1. The majority of patients were single (66 percent)
and under thirty (72 percent). Whether male or female,
they overwhelmingly requested a male rather than a female therapist. This preference was significantly related to
marital status in women but not in men (Tables 17–2 and
17–3). This suggests that a woman may be seeking therapy
for very different reasons than a man; and that these
reasons are generally related to or strictly determined by

TABLE 17-1 Symptom Rates by Sex, Sex and Age, and Sex and Race (per 100)

SYMPTOM AND SEX	TOTAL, 18-79 YEARS	AGE							RACE	
		18-24 YEARS	25-34 YEARS	35-44 YEARS	45-54 YEARS	55-64 YEARS	65-74 YEARS	75-79 YEARS	WHITE	NEGRO
Nervous breakdown										
Male	3.2	1.3	1.8	3.5	3.0	5.4	5.4	1.5	3.2	2.8
Female	6.4	1.0	3.6	5.0	7.3	12.7	10.7	13.1	6.0	10.4
Felt impending										
Nervous breakdown										
Male	7.7	6.9	7.4	8.6	11.7	6.4	3.1	2.2	7.7	8.2
Female	17.5	14.6	21.6	19.3	18.8	14.5	13.8	10.2	17.8	16.1
Nervousness										
Male	45.1	43.5	47.5	51.9	48.1	37.7	36.6	30.2	47.2	31.3
Female	70.6	61.4	74.4	75.0	72.5	72.6	62.9	65.6	73.2	55.2
Inertia										
Male	16.8	17.2	16.1	17.6	16.3	16.9	18.2	12.1	16.9	17.1
Female	32.5	31.0	34.0	35.2	31.1	29.7	31.9	35.6	33.1	29.5
Insomnia										
Male	23.5	20.4	16.7	20.8	26.8	27.0	35.9	26.5	24.1	20.4
Female	40.4	28.0	33.5	33.7	42.8	53.8	59.0	51.0	40.9	38.9
Trembling hands										
Male	7.0	7.6	6.5	5.4	5.7	8.8	10.0	8.5	6.9	7.1
Female	10.9	10.4	12.2	12.1	10.6	9.3	9.2	13.0	10.6	12.3
Nightmares										
Male	7.6	5.7	9.4	7.7	7.7	8.2	5.8	6.5	6.9	13.0
Female	12.4	12.8	15.8	14.7	9.9	7.5	11.6	11.8	12.3	14.3

TABLE 17-1 Symptom Rates by Sex, Sex and Age, and Sex and Race (per 100) (continued)

| SYMPTOM AND SEX | TOTAL, 18-79 YEARS | AGE | | | | | | | RACE | |
		18-24 YEARS	25-34 YEARS	35-44 YEARS	45-54 YEARS	55-64 YEARS	65-74 YEARS	75-79 YEARS	WHITE	NEGRO
Perspiring hands										
Male	17.0	23.2	24.9	17.7	14.7	11.0	7.9	3.0	17.0	16.8
Female	21.4	28.6	27.7	24.2	19.6	15.0	9.2	5.9	22.2	16.0
Fainting										
Male	16.9	17.6	15.7	15.7	18.1	17.3	17.8	17.2	17.5	13.8
Female	29.1	28.5	33.2	29.9	27.0	26.2	29.7	24.8	30.4	20.5
Headaches										
Male	13.7	13.0	12.8	13.8	15.2	15.6	11.3	10.0	13.8	11.9
Female	27.8	24.0	31.6	29.6	29.5	25.9	24.2	19.3	27.5	30.9
Dizziness										
Male	7.1	6.3	3.0	5.0	7.6	10.7	12.8	14.3	6.9	9.2
Female	10.9	8.4	9.5	8.5	10.1	14.3	16.9	16.6	10.3	15.7
Heart palpitations										
Male	3.7	3.3	2.0	2.1	3.9	7.2	6.4	1.5	3.6	4.8
Female	5.8	1.7	3.1	4.7	6.2	9.7	10.4	14.8	5.7	6.4
SCALE MEAN VALUE[1]										
Male										
White	1.70	1.72	1.70	1.72	1.78	1.69	1.66	1.19	1.70	...
Negro	1.55	1.25	1.03	1.37	1.79	1.87	2.23	2.99	...	1.55
Female										
White	2.88	2.61	3.07	2.93	2.89	2.86	2.82	2.80	2.88	...
Negro	2.65	1.91	2.61	2.60	2.52	3.27	3.79	2.62	...	2.65

[1] Scale is from 0 to 11.
SOURCE: Study by the U.S. Department of Health, Education, and Welfare. 1970.

her relationship (or lack of one) to a man. The number of requests for female therapists was approximately equal to the number of "no preference" requests for both men and women.

TABLE 17-2 *Percentage Distribution of Patient Therapist Preference, Marital Status, Age, and Religion*

	WOMEN (n=159)	MEN (n=99)	TOTAL
Therapist preference			
Male	49% (n=77)	40% (n=40)	45% (n=117)
Female	31% (n=49)	25% (n=26)	23% (n=75)
None	20% (n=33)	35% (n=33)	27% (n=66)
Marital Status			
Single	69% (n=109)	63% (n=62)	
Married/ living with someone	17% (n=27)	24% (n=24)	
Divorced/ separated	14% (n=23)	13% (n=13)	
Age			
Under 30	75%	69%	
Over 30	25%	31%	

Religion	Jewish	Cath.	Prot.	None	Jewish	Cath.	Prot.	None
	40%	19%	16%	25%	41%	22%	14%	23%

TABLE 17-3 *The Relationship between Therapist Preference and Patient Marital Status*

	FEMALE			MALE		
Marital Status	Preference			Preference		
	Male	Female	None	Male	Female	None
Single	54%	30%	16%	44%	28%	29%
Married/living with someone	41%	37%	22%	25%	25%	50%
Divorced	35%	26%	39%	53%	23%	23%

2. Single women, under or over thirty, of any religion, requested male therapists more often than married or divorced women did. Married women requested female therapists more often than any of the other sample groups.

3. While all of the male patients regardless of their marital status, requested male therapists rather than fe-

male therapists, some differential trends did exist. A higher percentage of divorced men requested male therapists, as compared with either divorced women (53 percent vs. 35 percent), married women (53 percent vs. 41 percent) married men (53 percent vs. 25 percent), or single men (53 percent vs. 44 percent). There was a significant relation between a male patient's request for a male therapist and his age (under thirty) and his religion: specifically, 63 percent of the Jewish male patients (who composed 40 percent of the entire male sample and 73 percent of whom were under thirty) requested male therapists—a higher percentage than in any other group.

4. Some of the most frequent reasons given by male patients for requesting male therapists were: greater respect for a man's mind; general discomfort with and mistrust of women; and specific embarrassment about "cursing" or discussing sexual matters, such as impotence, with a woman.[11] Some of the most common reasons given by female patients for requesting male therapists were: greater respect for and confidence in a man's competence and authority; feeling generally more comfortable with and relating better to men than to women; and specific fear and mistrust of women as authorities and as people, a reason sometimes combined with statements about dislike of the patients' own mothers.[12] In general, both men and women stated that they trusted and respected men—as people and as authorities—more than they did women, whom they generally mistrusted or feared.

Patients who requested a female therapist generally gave fewer reasons for their preference; one over-thirty woman stated that "only a female would understand another female's problems"; another woman stated that she sees "all males as someone to conquer" and is "less open to being honest with them." Almost all of the male patients who *gave reasons* for requesting a female therapist were homosexual.[13] Their main reasons involved expectations of being "sexually attracted" to a male therapist, which they thought would distract or upset them. One nonhomosexual patient felt he would be too "competitive" with a male therapist.

5. Thirty-six percent of the male and 37 percent of the female patients reported generally unclassifiable symptoms during the initial clinic interview. Thirty-one percent of the female and 15 percent of the male patients reported depression as their reason for seeking therapy; 25 percent

of the male and 7 percent of the female patients reported active homosexuality; 15 percent of the female and 14 percent of the male patients reported anxiety; 8 percent of the female and 7 percent of the male patients reported sexual impotence; 4 percent of the male and 3 percent of the female patients reported drug or alcoholic addiction. The fact that twice as many female as male patients report depression, and almost four times as many male as female patients report homosexuality accords with previous findings.

6. Male and female patients remained in therapy for approximately equal lengths of time (an average of thirty-one weeks for males and twenty-eight weeks for females). However, men requesting male therapists remained in therapy longer than other patient groups, an average of forty-two weeks) compared to an average of thirty weeks for females requesting a male therapist; an average of thirty-four weeks for male and thirty-one weeks for female patients requesting a female therapist; an average of twelve weeks for male and seventeen weeks for female patients with a stated "no preference."[14]

In other words, male patients who requested (and who generally received) a male therapist remained in treatment longer than their female counterparts. Perhaps one of the reasons for this is that women often get married and then turn to their husbands (or boy friends) as authorities or protectors, whereas men generally do not turn to their wives or girl friends as authorities, but rather as nurturing mother-surrogates, domestics, sex objects, and perhaps, friends. They usually do not turn to women for expert advice; hence, when they decide they need this kind of help, they tend to remain in therapy with a male therapist. Female patients can transfer their needs for protection or salvation from one man to another. Ultimately, a female patient or wife will be disappointed in her husband's or therapist's mothering or saving capacities and will continue the search for salvation *through a man* elsewhere.

PRESENTING SYMPTOMS

From clinical case histories, psychological studies, novels, mass magazines, and from our own lives, we know that women are often chronically fatigued and/or depressed; they are frigid, hysterical, and paranoid; and they suffer from headaches and feelings of inadequacy.

Studies of childhood behavior problems have indicated that boys are most often referred to child guidance clinics for aggressive, destructive (antisocial), and competitive behavior; girls are referred for personality problems, such as excessive fears and worries, shyness, timidity, lack of self-confidence, and feelings of inferiority.[15] This should be compared with adult male and female psychiatric symptomatology: "the symptoms of men are also much more likely to reflect a destructive hostility toward others,"[16] as well as a pathological self-indulgence. . . . Women's symptoms, on the other hand, express a harsh, self-critical, self-depriving and often self-destructive set of attitudes.[17] A study by E. Zigler and L. Phillips, comparing the symptoms of male and female mental hospital patients, found male patients significantly more assaultive than females and more prone to indulge their impulses in socially deviant ways like robbery, rape, drinking, and homosexuality.[18] Female patients were more often found to be self-deprecatory, depressed, perplexed, suffering from suicidal thoughts, or making actual suicidal attempts.[19]

According to T. Szasz, symptoms such as these are "indirect forms of communication" and usually indicate a "slave psychology":

> Social oppression in any form, and its manifestations are varied, among them being ... poverty ... racial, religious, or sexual discrimination ... must therefore be regarded as prime determinants of indirect communication of all kinds (e.g. hysteria).[20]*

At one point in *The Myth of Mental Illness*, Szasz refers to the "dread of happiness" that seems to afflict all people involved in the "Judaeo-Christian ethic." Although he is not talking about women particularly, his analysis seems especially relevant to our discussion of female psychiatric symptomatology:

> In general, the open acknowledgment of satisfaction is feared only in situations of relative oppression (e.g. all-suffering wife vis-à-vis domineering husband). The experiences of satis-

* *The Myth of Mental Illness*, Thomas S. Szasz, excerpts from pp. 213, 194-195, 263-264. Copyright © 1961 by Hoeber Medical Division of Harper & Row, Publishers, Inc. Reprinted by permission of the publishers.

faction (joy, contentment) are inhibited lest they lead to an augmentation of one's burden. ... *the fear of acknowledging satisfaction is a characteristic feature of slave psychology.*

The "properly exploited" slave is forced to labor until he shows signs of fatigue or exhaustion. Completion of his task does not signify that his work is finished and that he may rest. At the same time, even though his task is unfinished, he may be able to influence his master to stop driving him—and to let him rest—if he exhibits signs of imminent collapse. Such signs may be genuine or contrived. Exhibiting signs of fatigue or exhaustion—irrespective of whether they are genuine or contrived (e.g., "being on strike" against one's boss)—is likely to induce a feeling of fatigue or exhaustion in the actor. I believe that this is the mechanism responsible for the great majority of so-called chronic fatigue states. Most of these were formerly called "neurasthenia," a term rarely used nowadays. Chronic fatigue or a feeling of lifelessness and exhaustion are still frequently encountered in clinical practice.

Psychoanalytically, they are considered "character symptoms." Many of these patients are unconsciously "on strike" against persons (actual or internal) to whom they relate with subservience and against whom they wage an unending and unsuccessful covert rebellion.[21]*

The analogy between "slave" and "woman" is by no means a perfect one. Women are probably the prototypes for slaves;[22] they were probably the first group of human beings to be enslaved by another group. In a sense, a woman's "work" is in exhibiting the signs and "symptoms" of slavery—as well as, or instead of, doing slave labor in the kitchen, the nursery, and the factory.[23]

WHY ARE THERE MORE FEMALE PATIENTS?

Psychiatrists and psychologists have traditionally described the signs and symptoms of various kinds of real and felt oppression as mental illness. Women often manifest these signs, not only because they are oppressed in an objective sense, but also because the sex role (stereotype) to which they are conditioned is composed of just such signs. For example, Phillips and Segal report that when the number of physical and psychiatric illnesses were

* *The Myth of Mental Illness*, Thomas S. Szasz, excerpts from pp. 213, 194-195, 263-264. Copyright © 1961 by Hoeber Medical Division of Harper & Row, Publishers, Inc. Reprinted by permission of the publishers.

held constant for a group of New England women and men, the women were more likely to seek medical and psychiatric care. They suggest that women seek psychiatric help because the social role of women allows them to display emotional and physical distress more easily than men. "Sensitive or emotional behavior is more tolerated in women, to the point of aberration, while self-assertive, aggressive, vigorous physical demonstrations are more tolerated among men."[24]

It may be that more women than men are involved in psychotherapy[25] because it—along with marriage—is one of the only two socially approved institutions for middle-class women. That these two institutions bear a strong similarity to each other is highly significant. For most women the psychotherapeutic encounter is just one more instance of an unequal relationship, just one more opportunity to be rewarded for expressing distress and to be "helped" by being (expertly) dominated. Both psychotherapy and marriage isolate women from each other; both emphasize individual rather than collective solutions to woman's unhappiness; both are based on a woman's helplessness and dependence on a stronger male authority figure; both may, in fact, be viewed as reenactments of a little girl's relation to her father in a patriarchal society;[26] both control and oppress women similarly—yet, at the same time, are the two safest havens for women in a society that offers them no others.

Both psychotherapy and marriage enable women to safely express and defuse their anger by experiencing it as a form of emotional illness, by translating it into hysterical symptoms: frigidity, chronic depression, phobias, and the like. Each woman as patient thinks these symptoms are unique and are her own fault. She is neurotic, rather than oppressed. She wants from a psychotherapist what she wants—and often cannot get—from a husband: attention, understanding, merciful relief, a *personal solution*—in the arms of the right husband, on the couch of the right therapist.[27] The institutions of therapy and marriage not only mirror each other, they support each other. This is probably not a coincidence, but is rather an expression of the American economic system's need for geographic and psychological mobility, i.e., for young, upwardly mobile "couples" to "survive," to remain more or less intact in a succession of alien and anonymous urban locations, while they carry out the function of socializing children.

The institution of psychotherapy may be used by many women as a way of keeping a bad marriage together, or as a way of terminating it in order to form a good marriage. Some women, especially young and single women, may use psychotherapy as a way of learning how to catch a husband by practicing with a male therapist. Women probably spend more time during a therapy session talking about their husbands or boy friends—or lack of them—than they do talking about their lack of an independent identity or their relations to other women.

The institutions of psychotherapy and marriage both encourage women to talk—often endlessly—rather than to act (except in their socially prearranged roles as passive women or patients). In marriage the talking is usually of an indirect and rather inarticulate nature. Open expressions of rage are too dangerous, and too ineffective for the isolated and economically dependent women. Most often, such "kitchen" declarations end in tears, self-blame, and in the husband graciously agreeing with his wife that she was "not herself." Even control of a simple—but serious— conversation is usually impossible for most wives when several men, including their husbands, are present. The wife-women talk to each other, or they listen silently while the men talk. Very rarely, if ever, do men listen silently to a group of women talking; even if there are a number of women talking and only one man present, the man will question the women, perhaps patiently, perhaps not, but always in order to ultimately control the conversation from a superior position.

In psychotherapy the patient-woman is encouraged—in fact directed—to talk, by a therapist who is at least expected to be, or is perceived as, superior or objective. The traditional therapist may be viewed as ultimately controlling what the patient says through a subtle system of rewards (attention, interpretations, and so forth) or rewards withheld—but, most ultimately, controlling in the sense that he is attempting to bring his patient to terms with the female role, i.e., to an admission and acceptance of dependency. Traditionally, the psychotherapist, has ignored the objective facts of female oppression. Thus, in every sense, the female patient is still not having a "real" conversation—either with her husband or her therapist But how is it possible to have a "real" conversation with those who directly profit from her oppression? She would be laughed at, viewed as silly or crazy, and if she per-

sisted, removed from her job—as secretary or wife, perhaps even as patient.

Psychotherapeutic talking is indirect in the sense that it
does not immediately or even ultimately involve the woman in any reality-based confrontations with the self. It is
also indirect in that words—*any* words—are permitted, so
long as certain actions of consequence are totally avoided.
(Such is not paying one's bills.)

WHO ARE THE PSYCHOTHERAPISTS AND
WHAT ARE THEIR VIEWS ABOUT WOMEN?

Contemporary psychotherapists, like ghetto schoolteach-
ers, do not study themselves or question their own motives
or values as easily or as frequently as they do those of
their neurotic patients or their culturally deprived pupils.
However, in a 1960 study Schofield found that 90 percent
of psychiatrists were male; that psychologists were predominantly males, in a ratio of two to one; and that social
workers (the least prestigious and least well-paying of the
three professional categories) were predominantly females, in a ratio of two to one. The psychologists and
psychiatrists were about the same age, an average of
forty-four years; the social workers' average age was thir-
ty-eight. Less than 5 percent of the psychiatrists were
single; 10 precent of the psychologists, 6 percent of the
social workers, and 1 percent of the psychiatrists were
divorced. In other words, the majority of psychiatrists and
psychologists are middle-aged married men, probably
white, whose personal backgrounds were seen by Schofield
as containing "pressure toward upward social mobility."[28] In 1960 the American Psychiatric Association
totaled 10,000 male and 983 female members.

What must further be realized is that these predominantly male clinicians are involved in (a) a political institution that (b) has taken a certain traditional view of
women. A great deal has been written about the covertly
or overtly patriarchal, autocratic, and coercive values and
techniques of psychotherapy.[29] Freud believed that the
psychoanalyst-patient relationship must be that of "a superior and a subordinate."[30] The psychotherapist has been
seen—by his critics as well as by his patients—as a surrogate parent (father or mother), savior, lover, expert, and
teacher—all roles that foster "submission, dependency,

and infantilism" in the patient: roles that imply the therapist's omniscient and benevolent superiority and the patient's inferiority.[31] (Szasz has remarked on the dubious value of such a role for the patient and the "undeniable' value of such a role for the "helper.") Practicing psychotherapists have been criticized for treating unhappiness as a disease (whenever it is accompanied by an appropriately high verbal and financial output); for behaving as if the psychotherapeutic philosophy or method can cure ethical and political problems; for teaching people that their unhappiness (or neurosis) can be alleviated through individual rather than collective efforts; for encouraging and legitimizing the urban middle-class tendency toward moral irresponsibility and passivity; for discouraging emotionally deprived persons from seeking "acceptance, dependence and security in the more normal and accessible channels of friendship."[32] Finally, the institution of psychotherapy has been viewed as a form of social and political control that offers those who can pay for it temporary relief, the illusion of control, and a self-indulgent form of self-knowledge; and that punishes those who cannot pay by labeling their unhappiness as psychotic or dangerous, thereby helping society consign them to asylums where custodial care (rather than therapeutic illusions) is provided.

These criticisms, of course, apply to both male and female therapy patients. However, the institution of psychotherapy differentially and adversely affects women to the extent to which it is similar to marriage, and insofar as it takes its powerfully socialized cues from Freud and his male and female disciples (Helene Deutsch, Marie Bonaparte, Marynia Farnham, Bruno Bettelheim, Erik Erikson, Joseph Rheingold), viewing woman as essentially "breeders and bearers," as potentially warm-hearted creatures, but more often as simply cranky children with uteruses, forever mourning the loss of male organs and male identity. Woman's fulfillment has been couched—inevitably and eternally—in terms of marriage, children, and the vaginal orgasm.[33]

In her 1926 essay entitled "The Flight from Womanhood," Karen Horney says:

The present analytical picture of feminine development (whether that picture be correct or not) differs in no case by a hair's breadth from the typical ideas that the boy has of the girl.

We are familiar with the ideas that the boy entertains. I will therefore only sketch them in a few succinct phrases, and for the sake of comparison will place in a parallel column our ideas of the development of women.

THE BOY' IDEAS	OUR PSYCHOANALYTIC IDEAS OF FEMININE DEVELOPMENT
Naïve assumption that girls as well as boys possess a penis	For both sexes it is only the male genital which plays any part
Realization of the absence of the penis	Sad discovery of the absence of the penis
Idea that the girl is a castrated, mutilated boy	Belief of the girl that she once possessed a penis and lost it by castration
Belief that the girl has suffered punishment that also threatens him	Castration is conceived of as the infliction of punishment
The girl is regarded as inferior	The girl regards herself as inferior. Penis envy
The boy is unable to imagine how the girl can ever get over this loss or envy	The girl never gets over the sense of deficiency and inferiority and has constantly to master afresh her desire to be a man.
The boy dreads her envy	The girl desires throughout life to avenge herself on the man for possessing something which she lacks[34]

The subject of women seems to elicit the most extraordinary and yet authoritative pronouncements from many "sensitive" psychoanalysts:

SIGMUND FREUD:
(Women) refuse to accept the fact of being castrated and have the hope of someday obtaining a penis in spite o everything. . . . I cannot escape the notion (though hesitate to give it expression) that for woman the level of what is ethically normal is different from what it is in man. We must not allow ourselves to be deflected from such conclusions by the denials of the feminists who are anxious to force us to regard the two sexes as completely equal in position and worth.[35]

We say also of women that their social interests are weaker than those of men and that their capacity for the sublimation of their interests is less . . . the difficult development which leads to femininity [seems to] exhaust all the possibilities of the individual.[36]

ERIK ERIKSON:
For the student of development and practitioner of psycho-analysis, the stage of life crucial for the understanding of womanhood is the step from youth to maturity, the state when the young woman relinquishes the care received from the parental family and the extended care of institutions of education, in order to commit herself to the love of a stranger and to the care to be given to his or her offspring. . . . young women often ask, whether they can "have an identity" before they know whom they will marry and for whom they will make a home. Granted that something in the young women's identity must keep itself open for the peculiarities of the man to be joined and of the children to be brought up, I think that much of a young woman's identity is already defined in her kind of attractiveness and in the selectivity of her search for the man (or men) by whom she wishes to be sought.[37]

BRUNO BETTELHEIM:
. . . as much as women want to be good scientists and engineers, they want first and foremost to be womanly companions of men and to be mothers.[38]

JOSEPH RHEINGOLD:
. . . woman is nurturance . . . anatomy decrees the life of a woman. . . . When women grow up without dread of their biological functions and without subversion by feminist doctrines and therefore enter upon motherhood with a sense of fulfillment and altruistic sentiment we shall attain the goal of a good life and a secure world in which to live.[39]

These are all familiar views of women. But their affirmation by experts indirecly strengthened such views among men and *directly* tyrannized women, particularly American middle-class women, through the institution of psychotherapy and the tyranny of published "expert" opinion, stressing the importance of the mother for healthy child development. In their view, lack of—or superabundance of—mother love causes neurotic, criminal, psychiatric, and psychopathic children! The blame is rarely placed on the absence of a father or on the intolerable power struggle at the heart of most nuclear monogamous families—between child and parent, between wife and husband, between the whole economic unit and the struggle to survive in an urban capitalist environment.

Most child development research, like most birth control research, has centered around women, not men: for this is "women's work," for which she is totally responsible, which is "never done," and for which, in a wage-labor economy, she is never directly paid. She does it for love and is amply rewarded—in the writings of Freud et al.

The headaches, fatigue, chronic depression, frigidity, "paranoia," and overwhelming sense of inferiority that therapists have recorded about their female patients have not been analyzed in any remotely accurate terms. The real oppression (and sexual repression) of women remains unknown to the analysts, for the most part. Such symptoms have not been viewed by most therapists as "indirect communications" that reflect a "slave psychology." Instead, such symptoms have been viewed as hysterical and neurotic productions, as underhanded domestic tyrannies manufactured by spiteful, self-pitying, and generally unpleasant women whose *inability to be happy as women* probably stems from unresolved penis envy, an unresolved Electra (or female Oedipal) complex, or from general, intractable female stubbornness.

In a rereading of some of Freud's early case histories of female "hysterics," particularly his *Case of Dora*, what is remarkable is not his brilliance or his relative sympathy for the female "hysterics";[40] rather, it is his tone: cold, intellectual, detective-like,[41] controlling, sexually Victorian. He really does not like his "intelligent" eighteen-year-old patient. For example, he says: "For several days on end she identified herself with her mother by means of slight symptoms and peculiarities of manner, which gave her an opportunity for some really remarkable achievements in the direction of intolerable behavior." The mother has been diagnosed, unseen, by Freud, as having "housewife's psychosis."[42]

L. Simon reviews the plight of Dora:

. . . she had been brought to Freud by her father for treatment of ". . . tussis nervosa, aphonia, depression, and taedium vitae." Despite the ominous sound of these Latinisms it should be noted that Dora was not in the midst of a symptom crisis at the time she was brought to Freud, and there is at least room for argument as to whether these could be legitimately described as symptoms at all. If there was a crisis, it was clearly the father's. Nevertheless, Freud related the development of these "symptoms" to two traumatic sexual experiences Dora had had with Mr. K., a friend of the family. Freud eventually came to explain the symptoms as expressions of her disguised sexual desire for Mr. K., which he saw, in turn, as derived from feelings she held toward her father. Freud attempted, via his interpretations, to put Dora in closer touch with her own unconscious impulses.

. . . Indeed, the case study could still stand as an exemplary effort were it not for a single, but major, problem having to do with the realities of Dora's life. For throughout his therapeutic examination of Dora's unconscious Freud also knew that she was the bait in a monstrous sexual bargain her father had concocted. This man, who during an earlier period in his life had contracted syphilis and apparently infected his wife . . . was now involved in an affair with the wife of Mr. K. There is clear evidence that her father was using Dora to appease Mr. K., and that Freud was fully aware of this. . . . At one point Freud states: "Her father was himself partly responsible for her present danger for he had handed her over to this strange man in the interests of his own love-affair." But despite this reality, despite his full knowledge of her father's predilections, Freud insisted on examining Dora's difficulties from a strictly intrapsychic point of view, ignoring the manner in which her father was using her, and denying that her accurate perception of the situation was germane.

. . . Freud appears to accept fully the willingness of these men to sexually exploit the women around them. One even finds the imagery of capitalism creeping into his metapsychology. Freud's work with Dora may be viewed as an attempt to deal with the exploitation of women that characterized that historical period without even an admission of the fact of its existence. We may conclude that Freud's failure with Dora was a function of his inappropriate level of conceptualization and intervention. He saw that she was suffering, but instead of attempting to deal with the conditions of her life he chose—because he shared in her exploitation—to work within the confines of her ego.[43]

Although Freud eventually conceded (but not to Dora) that her insights into her family situation were correct, he still concluded that these insights would not make her "happy." Freud's own insights—based on self-reproach, rather than on Dora's reproaching of those around her— would hopefully help her discover her own penis envy and Electra complex; somehow this would magically help her to adjust to, or at least to accept, her only alternative in life: housewife's psychosis. If Dora had not left treatment (which Freud views as an act of revenge), her cure presumably would have involved her regaining (through desperation and self-hypnosis) a grateful respect for her patriarch-father; loving and perhaps serving him for years to come; or getting married and performing these functions for a husband or surrogate-patriarch.

Szasz comments on the "hysterical" symptoms of another of Freud's female patients, Anna O., who fell "ill" while nursing her father.

Anna O. thus started to play the hysterical game from a position of distasteful submission: she functioned as an oppressed, unpaid, sick-nurse, who was coerced to be helpful by the very helplessness of a (bodily) sick patient. The women in Anna O.'s position were—as are their counterparts today, who feel similarity entrapped by their small children—insufficiently aware of what they valued in life and of how their own ideas of what they valued affected their conduct. For example, young middle-class women in Freud's day considered it their duty to take care of their sick fathers. They treasured the value that it was their role to take care of father when he was sick. Hiring a professional servant or nurse for this job would have created a conflict for them, because it would have symbolized to them as well as to others that they did not love ("care for") their fathers. Notice how similar this is to the dilemma in which many contemporary women find themselves, not, however, in relation to their fathers, but rather in relation to their young children. Today, married women are generally expected to take care of their children; they are not supposed to delegate this task to others. The "old folks" can be placed in a home; it is all right to delegate their care to hired help. This is an exact reversal of the social situation which prevailed in upper middle-class European circles until the First World War and even after it. Then, children were often cared for by hired help, while parents were taken care of by their children, now fully grown.[44]*

To Freud, it was to Anna's "great sorrow" that she was no longer "allowed to continue nursing the patient."

We may wonder to what extent contemporary psychotherapists[45] still view women as Freud did, either because they believe his theories, or/and because they are men first and so-called objective professionals second: it

* *The Myth of Mental Illness*, Thomas S. Szasz, excerpts from pp. 213, 194-195, 263-264. Copyright © 1961 by Hoeber Medical Division of Harper & Row, Publishers, Inc. Reprinted by permission of the publishers.

may still be in their personal and class interest to (quite unmaliciously) remain "Freudian" in their treatment of women. Two studies relate to this question.

As part of Schofield's 1960 study, each of the psychotherapists were asked to indicate the characteristics of his "ideal" patient, "that is, the kind of patient with whom you feel you are efficient and effective in your therapy." Schofield reports that "for those psychotherapists who did express a sex preference, a preference for females was predominant in all three professional groups." The margin of preference for female patients was largest in the sample of psychiatrists, nearly two-thirds of this group claiming the female patients as "ideal."[46] From 60 to 70 percent of each of the therapist groups place the ideal patient's age in the twenty to forty year range. Very rarely do representatives of any of the three disciplines express a preference for a patient with a graduate degree (M.A., M.D., Ph.D.).

Summarizing his findings, Schofield suggests that the efforts of most clinical practitioners are "restricted" to those clients who present the Yavis syndrome—youthful, attractive, verbal, intelligent, and successful. And, we may add, hopefully female.[47]

A recent study by Broverman et al. supports the hypothesis that most clinicians still view their female patients as Freud viewed his.[48] Seventy-nine clinicians (forty-six male and thirty-three female psychiatrists, psychologists, and social workers) completed a sex-role stereotype questionnaire. The questionnaire consists of 122 bipolar items, each of which describes a particular behavior or trait. For example:

> very subjective ——————— very objective
> not at all aggressive ——— very aggressive

The clinicians were instructed to check off those traits that represent healthy male, healthy female, or healthy adult (sex unspecified) behavior. The results were as follows:

1. There was high agreement among clinicians as to the attributes characterizing healthy adult men, healthy adult women, and healthy adults, sex unspecified.
2. There were no differences among men and women clinicians.
3. Clinicians have different standards of health for men

and women. Their concepts of healthy mature men do not differ significantly from their concepts of healthy mature adults, but their concepts of healthy mature women do differ significantly from those for men or for adults. Clinicians are likely to suggest that women differ from healthy men by being: more submissive, less independent, less adventurous, more easily influenced, less aggressive, less competitive, more excitable in minor crises, more easily hurt, more emotional, more conceited about their appearance, less objective, and less interested in math and science.

Finally, what is judged healthy for adults, sex unspecified, and for adult males, is in general highly correlated with previous studies of social desirability as perceived by nonprofessional subjects.

It is clear that for a woman to be healthy she must "adjust" to and accept the behavioral norms for her sex even though these kinds of behavior are generally regarded as less socially desirable. As the authors themselves remark, "This constellation seems a most unusual way of describing any mature, healthy individual."

Obviously, the ethic of mental health is masculine in our culture. Women are perceived as childlike or childish, as *alien* to most male therapists. It is therefore especially interesting that some clinicians, especially psychiatrists prefer female patients. Perhaps their preference makes good sense; a male therapist may receive a real psychological "service" from his female patient: namely, the experience of controlling and feeling superior to a female being upon whom he has projected many of his own forbidden longings for dependency, emotionality, and subjectivity and from whom, as a superior expert, as a doctor, he is protected as he cannot be from his mother, wife, or girl friend. And he earns money to boot!

Private psychoanalysis or psychotherapy is a commodity available to those women who can buy it, that is, to women whose fathers, husbands, or boy friends can help them pay for it.[49] Like the Calvinist elect, those women who can *afford* treatment are already "saved." Even if they are never happy, never free, they will be slow to rebel against their psychological and economic dependence on men. One look at their less-privileged (poor, black, and/or unmarried) sisters' position is enough to keep them silent and more or less gratefully in line. The less-privileged women have no real or psychological silks to smooth down over, to disguise their unhappiness; they have no class to be "better than." As they sit facing the walls, in factories, offices, whorehouses, ghetto apartments, and mental asylums, at least *one* thing they must conclude is that "happiness" is on sale in America—but not at a price they can afford. They are poor. They do not have to be bought off with illusions; they only have to be controlled.

Lower-class and unmarried middle-class women do have access to free or sliding-scale clinics, where, as a rule, they will meet once a week with minimally experienced psychotherapists. I am not suggesting that *maximally* experienced psychotherapists have acquired any expertise in salvation that will benefit the poor and/or unmarried woman. I am merely pointing out that the poor woman receives what is generally considered to be "lesser" treatment.

Given these facts—that psychotherapy is a commodity purchasable by the rich and inflicted on the poor; that as an institution, it socially controls the minds and bodies of middle-class women via the adjustment-to-marriage ideal and the minds and bodies of poor and single women via psychiatric incarceration; and that most clinicians, like most people in a patriarchal society, have deeply antifemale biases—it is difficult for me to make practical suggestions about "improving" therapeutic treatment. If marriage in a patriarchal society is analyzed as the major institution of female oppression, it is logically bizarre[50] to present husbands with helpful hints on how to make their wives "happier." Nevertheless, wives, private patients, and the inmates of mental asylums already exist in large numbers. Therefore, I will make several helpful suggestions regarding women, "mental illness," and psychotherapy.

Male psychologists, psychiatrists, and social workers must realize that as scientists they know nothing about women; their expertise, their diagnoses, even their sympathy is damaging and oppressive to women. Male clinicians should stop treating women altogether, however much this may hurt their wallets and/or sense of benevolent authority. For most women the psychotherapeutic encounter is just one more power relationship in which they submit to a dominant authority figure. I wonder how well such a structure can encourage independence—or healthy dependence—in a woman. I wonder what a woman can learn from a male therapist (however well-intentioned) whose own values are sexist? How free from the dictates of a sexist society can a female as patient be with a male therapist? How much can a male therapist empathize with a female patient? In *Human Sexual Inadequacy* Masters and Johnson state that their research supported unequivocally the "premise that no man will ever fully understand a woman's sexual function or dysfunction . . . (and the same is true for women). . . . it helps immeasurably for a distressed, relatively inarticulate or emotionally unstable wife to have available a female co-therapist to interpret what she is saying and even what she is attempting unsuccessfully to express to the uncomprehending husband and often to the male co-therapist as well." I would go one step further here and ask: what if the female co-therapist is male-oriented, as much of a sexist as her male counterpart? What if the female therapist has never realized that she is oppressed as a woman? What if the female therapist views marriage and children as sufficient fulfillment for women—except herself?

All women—clinicians as well as their patients—must participate in and/or think seriously and deeply about the woman's liberation movement. Women patients should see female clinicians who are feminists. Female clinicians, together with all women, should create a new or first psychology of women, and as a group, act on it. This might include politically educating and supporting females in mental asylums and in other ghettos of the mind. Perhaps all-female therapeutic communities can be tried as a necessary, interim alternative to female economic and psychological dependence on patriarchal structures such as marriage, psychotherapy, and mental asylums. In such a communal setting, it is not unlikely that friendship, understanding, or objectivity may be desired on a private basis, and that such an interchange might resemble or draw upon psychoanalytic or psychotherapeutic "knowledge" or practice. Who will be—or whether there will be— "experts" of understanding is unknown; who will be—or whether anyone will be—considered "mentally ill" and treated by isolation and ostracism is unknown.

NOTES

1. Karen Horney, "The Flight from Womanhood" (1926), in

Feminine Psychology, ed. Harold Kelman (New York: W. W. Norton, 1967).

2. "Selected Symptoms of Psychological Distress," U.S. Department of Health, Education and Welfare. Public Health Services, Health Services, and Mental Health Administration. This study is based on data collected in 1960-1962 from a probability sample of 7,710 persons selected to represent the 111 million adults in the U.S. noninstitutional population, aged 18-79.

3. A fascinating and predictable finding in this study was that men with low incomes and females with high incomes reported the highest rate of fainting.

4. G. Gurin, J. Veroff, and S. Feld, *Americans View Their Mental Health* (New York: Basic Books, 1960).

5. William Schofield, *Psychotherapy: The Purchase of Friendship* (Englewood Cliffs, N.J.: Prentice-Hall, 1963).

6. A. K. Bahn, M. Conwell, and P. Hurley, "Survey of Psychiatric Practice," *Archives of General Psychiatry,* vol. 12 (1965). This data was collected in New York, Washington, D.C., Wisconsin, Kentucky, and California.

7. "Reference Table on Patients in Mental Health Facilities, Age Sex and Diagnosis," U.S. Department of Health, Education, and Welfare. Health Services and Mental Health Administration, United States, 1965, 1966, 1967. National statistics on "mental illness" are exceedingly troublesome. The data shown for the predominately male, VA psychiatric hospital represent a 100 percent projection based on a 30 percent random sampling of VA hospitals, whereas the data shown for all of the other facilities are raw data, based on the number of hospitals reporting for a given year. From 1965-1967, 1,627 of the *known* psychiatric out-patient facilities, 115 of the known state and county hospitals, 121 of the known private hospitals, and 959 of the known General hospitals did *not* report any patient statistics. Although there are more female than male patients in each of the reporting hospitals, particularly in the private, general and out-patient facilities, there is no way of checking the sex-ratios in the non-reporting hospitals. Further difficulties involved the fact that the criteria for certain of the statistics, such as "first admissions" or "residents at year's end" may (1) count the same patient twice in a given year; (2) may exclude some patients altogether (the "invisible" housewife alcoholic or prostitute-drug addict); (3) may not adequately reflect the phenomena of frequent short- or long-term readmissions and long-term stays that often characterize female patients; (4) are not based on the sex-ratio in the American population at large for the given year; or, more important, (5) are not based on the "real" population the particular patient derived from, e.g., the "population" of white divorced working women with children, or of foreign or native-born migrants, etc. In other words, relevant demographic characteristics such as age, race, marital status, birthplace, social class, education, etc. are not taken into account where they do present a breakdown by "per 100,000" population. (Except in smaller studies which attempt to do just this.) Without such demographic variables we cannot answer such questions as "What is the probability of a black working mother's admission to a psychiatric facility compared with a black working

father's, or a white non-working mother's, or with a black non-working father's?"

8. Benjamin Maltzberg, "Important Statistical Data about Mental Illness," *American Handbook of Psychiatry*, Vol. I, ed. Silvano Arieti (New York: Basic Books, 1959).

9. M. A. Dayton, *New Facts on Mental Disorders* (Springfield, Ill.: Charles C. Thomas, 1940); E. Zigler and L. Phillips, "Social Effectiveness and Symptomatic Behaviors," *Journal of Abnormal and Social Psychology* (1960), pp. 231-238; Maltzberg., *op. cit.*; Srole, et al, *Mental Health in the Metropolis: Midtown Manhattan Study* (New York: McGraw-Hill, 1962).

10. A study on the psychiatric "health" of the Manhattan Community conducted by Srole et al., 1962, found higher psychiatric "impairment" among single men when compared with married men, than among single women when compared with married women. Among married people the sexes did not differ in the proportions rated psychiatrically "impaired."

11. One wonders why women are not equally "embarrassed" about discussing their impotence (frigidity) with male therapists.

12. This, as well as the significantly greater female preference for a male therapist, supports Goldberg's 1968 findings of female antifemale prejudice. See P. Goldberg, "Are Women Prejudiced against Women," *Trans-Action*, April 1968, pp. 28-30.

13. There is a definite but not significant tendency toward homosexuality (both active and latent) in the group of men who requested female therapists. This almost suggests that preference for a female—either as an authority figure or as an expert mother figure—requires some break with the dominant sex-role stereotypes of our society.

14. Approximately 80 percent of the male and 76 percent of the female patients who stated a sex preference in requesting a therapist were assigned to therapists of the preferred sex.

15. Jean MacFarlane et al., *A Developmental Study of the Behavior Problems of Normal Children between Twenty-One Months and Thirteen Years* (Berkeley: University of California Press, 1954); L. Phillips, "Cultural versus Intrapsychic Factors in Childhood Behavior Problem Referrals," *Journal of Clinical Psychology* 12 (1956): 400-401; G. M. Gilbert, "A Survey of Referral Problems in Metropolitan Child Guidance Centers," *Journal of Clinical Psychology* 13 (1957): 37-42; D. R. Petersen, "Behavior Problems of Middle Childhood," *Journal of Consulting Psychology* 25 (1961): 205-209; L. M. Terman and Leona E. Tyler, "Psychological Sex Differences," in L. Carmichael, ed., *Manual of Child Psychology* (New York: John Wiley & Sons, 1954).

16. We may note that nearly five million crimes are reported in the United States each year, of which 87 percent are property crimes and the remainder are violent crimes. American adult males have significantly higher rates of arrests for criminal activity; they outnumber women by more than 6:1.

17. Leslie Phillips, "A Social View of Psychopathology," in P. London and D. Rosenhan, eds., *Abnormal Psychology* (New York: Holt, Rinehart & Winston, 1969).

18. Zigler and Phillips, *op. cit.*

19. A government pamphlet entitled *Suicide among Youth* (1970) notes that attempted suicide is far more frequent among girls in the student age bracket than among boys. The boys attempt

fewer suicides but complete more than the girls. Nonwhite males between fifteen and twenty-five have the highest successful suicide rate. Although it is fruitless and irrelevant to attempt to decide whether racism, class conflict, or sexism takes the heaviest toll of physical and psychological life in America, we may, parenthetically (and nevertheless) wonder whether there are more poor and black men in jail and in mental asylums for criminal activity (one measure of racism and class conflict) than there are poor, middle- and upper-class women in mental asylums and in private psychotherapeutic treatment (one measure of sexism). In many ways (physical, economic, and psychological), mental and ex-mental patients suffer more than jailed criminals or ex-convicts. (E. Goffman, *Asylums* [New York: Doubleday-Anchor, 1961.] For this reason alone—namely, the greater punishment involved in being labeled mentally ill—without looking at any statistics I would personally suspect that more women than men receive the mentally ill rather than the criminal label. And that the kinds of behaviors considered criminal and mentally ill are sex-typed, each sex being conditioned accordingly. Further, that what we consider "madness"—whether it appears in women or men is either (a) the acting out of the female experience or (b) the rejection of one's sex-role stereotype.

20. T. T. Szasz, *The Myth of Mental Illness* (New York: Harper & Row, 1961).

21. *Ibid.* My italics.

22. Frederick Engels, *The Origins of Family, Private Property, and the State* (New York: International Publishers, 1942).

23. Konrad Lorenz, a noted student of animal behavior, has recently been quoted as saying that "there's only one kind of people at a social disadvantage nowadays—a whole class of people who are treated as slaves and who are exploited shamelessly—and that's the young wives. They are educated as well as the men. And the moment they give birth to a baby, they are slaves. They have a 22-hour working day and no holidays and they can't even be ill." *New York Times* interview, July 5, 1970.

24. D. L. Phillips and B. E. Segal, "Sexual Status and Psychiatric Symptoms," *American Sociological Review* (1969): vol. 34.

25. Either actively and voluntarily or when they are involuntarily psychiatrically hospitalized.

26. M. Foucault, in *Madness and Civilization* (New York: Mentor Books, 1967), a brilliant essay on the history of madness in the western world characterizes the organization of mental asylums: "The entire existence of madness, in the world now being prepared for it, was enveloped in what we may call, in anticipation, a 'parental complex.' The prestige of patriarchy is revived around madness. . . . henceforth . . . the discourse of unreason will be linked with . . . the dialectic of the Family. . . . the madman remains a minor and for a long time reason will retain for him the aspect of the Father. . . . He (Tuke, a psychiatrist) isolated the social structure of the bourgeois family, reconstituted it symbolically in the (mental) asylum, and set it adrift in history." Also Freud, in his 1931 essay entitled "Female Sexuality," in *International Journal of Psychoanalysis* 13 (1932), noted how difficult it was for him to "revive the female patient's attachment to the mother . . . but possibly I have received this impression because when I have analyzed women, they have been

able to cling to that very father-attachment in which they took refuge from the early phase (of mother-attachment)."

27. Gloria Steinem, "Laboratory for Love Styles," *New York Magazine*, February 1970, quotes one middle-class discussion of psychoanalysts:

> Psychiatrists are the male geishas of our time. I mean, the women who go to analysts usually have empty days on their hands, right? And Freud was too male-chauvinist to figure out we needed professions as well as sex, right? So these analysts get a lot of attractive women in their offices and encourage them to talk about their sex lives and, well, one thing leads to another. Those poor bastards are usually stuck with the wives who put them through medical school anyway, if you see what I mean.
>
> Now, the beautiful part of all this is it's perfect for the woman. She gets sex and someone to listen to her with a little sympathy—the two things she's probably missing in her marriage. Intelligent companionship in the daytime. What husband could object to his wife's appointments with her doctor?

28. Schofield sent basic information questionnaires to randomly selected practitioner members of the American Psychiatric Association, the American Psychological Association, and the National Association of Social Workers. Complete returns were obtained from 140 psychiatrists, 149 psychiatric social workers, and 88 clinical psychologists.

29. Goffman, *op. cit.*; Szasz, *op. cit.*; Schofield, *op. cit.*; Foucault, *op. cit.*; T. J. Scheff, *Being Mentally Ill: A Sociological Theory* (Chicago: Aldine, 1966).

30. Sigmund Freud, "On the History of the Psycho-analytic Movement" (1914), in *Collected Papers of Sigmund Freud*, Vol. I (New York: Basic Books, 1959).

31. Szasz, *op. cit.*

32. Schofield, *op. cit.*

33. The traditional psychoanalytic theories about women, especially Freud's, have been well and fully criticized by Karen Horney, Simone de Beauvoir, Clara Thompson, Natalie Shainess, Betty Friedan, Albert Adler, Thomas Szasz, and Harry Stack Sullivan.

34. Karen Horney, "The Flight from Womanhood," in *Feminine Psychology*, ed. by Harold Kelman (New York: W. W. Norton, 1967). Freud's indirect rejoinder, made in his 1931 essay entitled "Female Sexuality," is as follows:

> It is to be anticipated that male analysts with feminist sympathies, and our women analysts also, will disagree with what I have said here. They will hardly fail to object that such notions have their origin in the man's "masculinity complex," and are meant to justify theoretically his innate propensity to disparage and suppress women. But this sort of psychoanalytic argument reminds us here, as it so often does, of Dostoevsky's famous "knife that cuts both ways." The opponents of those who reason thus will for their part think it quite comprehensible that members of the female sex should refuse to accept a notion that appears to gainsay their eagerly coveted equality with men. The use of analysis as a weapon of controversy obviously leads to no decision.

35. Sigmund Freud, "Some Psychological Consequences of the Anatomical Distinction Between Sexes," *Collected Papers*, Vol. V (London: Hogarth Press, 1956), pp. 196-197.

36. Sigmund Freud, *New Introductory Lectures in Psychoanalysis* (New York: W. W. Norton, 1933).

37. E. H. Erikson, "Inner and Outer Space: Reflections on Womanhood," *Daedalus* 93 (1964):582-606.

38. B. Bettelheim, "The Commitment Required of a Woman Entering a Scientific Profession in Present Day American Society," in *Woman and the Scientific Professions*, an MIT symposium on American Women in Science and Engineering (Cambridge, Mass., 1965).

39. J. Rheingold, *The Fear of Being a Woman* (New York: Grune & Stratton, 1964).

40. S. Freud, *Case of Dora: An Analysis of a Case of Hysteria* (New York: W. W. Notron, 1952). Early in this case history he says: "The demands hysteria make on a physician can be met only by the most sympathetic spirit of inquiry and not by an attitude of superiority and contempt." Unfortunately, Freud does not always maintain this spirit.

41. Like Sherlock Holmes, when Freud has a fact "he doesn't neglect to use it against Dora." He says: "When I set myself the task of bringing to light what human beings keep hidden within them, not by the compelling power of hypnosis, but by observing what they say and what they show . . . no mortal can keep a secret. If his lips are silent, he chatters with his fingertips; betrayal oozes out of him at every pore."

42. Freud was not the only one who disliked Dora. Twenty-four years later, as a forty-two-year-old married woman, Dora was referred to another psychiatrist, Felix Deutsch, for "hysterical" symptoms. Let me quote his description of her:

The patient then started a tirade about her husband's indifference toward her offerings and how unfortunate her marital life had been. . . . this led her to talk about her own frustrated love life and her frigidity. . . . resentfully she expressed her conviction that her husband had been unfaithful to her . . . tearfully she denounced men in general as selfish, demanding, and ungiving. . . . (she recalled that) her father had been unfaithful even to her mother . . . she talked mainly about her relationship to her mother, of her unhappy childhood because of her mother's exaggerated cleanliness . . . and her lack of affection for her. . . . she finally spoke with pride about her *brother's* career, but she had little hope that her *son* would follow in his footsteps. . . . more than 30 years have elapsed since my visit at Dora's sickbed . . . from (an) informant I learned the additional pertinent facts about the fate of Dora. . . . she clung to (her son) with the same reproachful demands she made on her husband, who had died of a coronary disease—*slighted and tortured by her almost paranoid behavior, strangely enough, he had preferred to die . . . rather than divorce her. Without question, only a man of this type could have been chosen by Dora for a husband.* At the time of her analytic treatment she had stated unequivocally *"men are all so detestable that I would rather not marry. This is my revenge!"* Thus, her marriage had served only to cover up her distaste of men. . . . (Dora's) death from *a cancer of the colon, which was diagnosed too late for a successful operation, seemed a blessing to those who were close to her. She had been, as my informant phrased it, "one of the most repulsive hysterics" he had ever met. [My italics.]* Felix Deutsch, "A Footnote to Freud's 'Fragment of an Analysis of a Case of Hysteria'," *The Psychoanalytic Quarterly* 26 (1957).

43. L. J. Simon, "The Political Unconscious of Psychology: Clinical Psychology and Social Change," unpublished manuscript, 1970.
44. Szasz, *op. cit.*
45. The majority of whom, unlike Erikson or Bettelheim (quoted earlier) are practitioners and not published theorists.
46. Less than one-third of the psychiatrists and one-fourth of the psychologists expressed a preferred sex in their ideal patient.
47. *Ibid.*
48. I. K. Broverman et al., "Sex Role Stereotypes and Clinical Judgments of Mental Health," *Journal of Consulting and Clinical Psychology* 34 (1970): 1-7. This summary of this study was done by Jo-Ann Gardner, *The Face across the Breakfast Table* (Pittsburgh: Know, Inc., 1970).
49. There are many women who spend most of their salary on their "shrink," and who live with men or with their parents, usually under infantilizing conditions, in order to do so. One wonders who exactly, and how many at that, can pay for private psychoanalytic or psychotherapeutic treatment—treatment that costs anywhere from fifteen to fifty dollars per session, two to five times a week, for anywhere from two to five years. None but a small urban minority can afford such treatment at its supposed "best."
50. But very human—especially when people are clamoring to be helped and "helpers" need to survive economically.

FOR FURTHER READING

Adler, A. *Individual Psychology.* Paterson, N.J.: Littlefield Adams & Co., 1963.
Bart, P. B. "Social Structure and Vocabularies of Discomfort: What Happened to Female Hysteria." *Journal of Health and Social Behavior* 9 (1968).
Brecher, Ruth and Edward. *An Analysis of Human Sexual Response.* New York: Signet Books, 1966.
Clarke, A. R. "Conformity Behavior of Schizophrenic Subjects with Maternal Figures." *Journal of Abnormal Social Psychology* 68 (1964): 45-53.
De Beauvoir, Simone. *The Second Sex.* New York: Alfred A. Knopf, 1953.
Dunham, R. M. "Sensitivity of Schizophrenics to Parental Censure." Unpublished doctoral diss., Duke University, 1959.
Dunn, W. L., Jr. "Visual Discrimination of Schizophrenic Subjects as a Function of Stimulus Meaning." *Journal of Personality* 23 (1954): 48-64.
Erikson, E. H. "Reality and Actuality." *Journal of the American Psychoanalytic Association* 10 (1962).
———. *Insight and Responsibility.* New York. W. W. Norton, 1964.

Facts about Mental Illness. Washington, D.C.: National Association for Mental Health, January 1956.

Fifteen Indices. Washington, D.C.: Joint Information Service of the American Psychiatric Association and the National Association for Mental Health, 1964.

Flexner, Eleanor. *Century of Struggle.* New York: Atheneum, 1968.

Freud, S. "On the History of the Psycho-Analytic Movement." In *Collected Papers.* London: Hogarth Press, 1948. I:287-359.

————. "Some Psychological Consequences of the Anatomical Distinction between the Sexes" (1925). In *Collected Papers.* London: Hogarth Press, 1956. Vol. 5.

———— and Breuer, J. *Studies on Hysteria, 1893-1895.* New York: Avon Books, 1966.

Goodman, D. "Performance of Good and Poor Premorbid Male Schizophrenics as a Function of Paternal versus Maternal Censure." *Journal of Abnormal Social Psychology* 69 (1964):550-555.

Health-Pac. Health Policy Advisory Center, 17 Murray St., New York, New York 10007.

Hinton, William. *Fanshen: A Documentary of Revolution in a Chinese Village.* New York: Random House, 1966.

Hollingshead, A. B. and Redlick, F. C. *Social Class and Mental Illness.* New York: Basic Books, 1958.

Hospitals. August 1, 1963, guide issue.

Jeffery, C. R. *Criminal Responsibility and Mental Disease.* Springfield, Ill.: Charles C. Thomas, 1967.

Lederer, W. *The Fear of Women.* New York: Grune & Stratton, 1968.

Masters, William H. and Johnson, Virginia E. *Human Sexual Inadequacy.* Boston, Little Brown, 1970.

Nicole. "The Shrink and the Shriek." *It Ain't Me, Babe,* May 21, June 10, 1970.

Patients in Mental Institutions. Part II. Bethesda, Md.: Biometrics Branch, National Institute of Mental Health, 1960.

Phillips, L. "Cultural versus Intrapsychic Factors in Childhood Behavior Problem Referrals," *Journal of Clinical Psychology* 12 (1956):400-401.

"Reference Table on Patients in Mental Health Facilities, Age, Sex, and Diagnosis: United States, 1968." U.S. Department of Health, Education, and Welfare, Health Services and Mental Health Administration.

Ruitenbeck, H. M., ed. *Psychoanalysis and Female Sexuality.* New Haven: Yale University Press, 1966.

Scheff, T. J. ed. *Mental Illness and Social Processes.* New York: Harper & Row, 1967.

"Selected Symptoms of Psychological Distress, United States." U.S. Department of Health, Education, and Welfare, Public Health Service, Health Service and Mental Health Administration. August 1970.

Shainess, N. "Images of Woman Past and Present, Overt and Obscured." *American Journal of Psychotherapy* 13(1969):77-97.

Stoller, R. J. "The Sense of Femaleness." *Psychoanalytic Quarterly* 37 (1968):42-55.

Szasz, T. T. *Law, Liberty and Psychiatry.* New York: Macmillan, 1963.

What Are the Facts about Mental Illness in the United States? Washington, D.C.: National Committee against Mental Illness, 1964.

18

WOMEN IN OTHER CULTURES

Ruby R. Leavitt

According to a popular myth in the patriarchal cultures of the West, the biological act of giving birth to a child has always limited woman's activities, and thus, because of either this limitation or her innate inferiority, woman has contributed little or nothing to the development of human society. Another widely circulated myth is that women have achieved their highest status in the Western industrialized world. But when we go back to our human beginnings and then look at the role and status of woman in some non-Western societies, we find that neither myth has any substance.

For about two million years human beings lived by hunting and gathering their food. Males hunted the wild animals, and females gathered the wild plants. Then, about 10,000 years ago, at the beginning of the Neolithic or New Stone Age, man began to domesticate the animals he hunted, and woman began to cultivate the plants she gathered.

It is generally accepted that owing to her ancient role as the gatherer of vegetable foods, woman was responsible for the invention and development of agriculture. Modern analogies indicate that so long as the ground was prepared by hoeing and not by ploughing woman remained the cultivator.[1]

The invention of agriculture was a revolution of the greatest significance because it radically altered the way

393

human beings had lived since they were proto-men. Now for the first time there was the need and the leisure to develop textiles and pottery. These were also invented by woman, who planted the flax that she spun and made into clothes for the family, and who fashioned the containers for the grains she collected, reaped, stored, and cooked. "It has never been doubted that . . . pottery was both shaped and decorated by women."[2]

Only when plants were cultivated and surplus food was available could nonfarming specialists improve tools and invent writing and all the arts and sciences that were the prerequisites for civilization. No wonder then that with the invention of agriculture woman enjoyed greater esteem. Probably "the earliest Neolithic societies throughout their range in time and space gave woman the highest status she has ever known."[3] The widespread remains of the shrines and the clay figurines of the Mother Goddess indicate that woman was venerated "in nearly all Neolithic peasant settlements from Southwest Asia to Britain"[4] and testify to her primary economic and religious importance. The woman with the hoe was linked with the fecundity of the earth not only because she herself bore children, but because she also caused the earth to bear fruit. "Clearly the divinity so universally honored by the early Neolithic farming communities was identified with the earth where the dead seed is buried and lives again."[5] The basic contributions of woman to the development of civilization are curiously overlooked by the anthropologist Ashley Montagu, when he enumerates the activities that account for the creativity of prehistoric man and the limitations of prehistoric woman.[6]

But in the very civilizations that she played so essential a part in producing, the status of woman changed drastically with the emergence of male rulers and priests, urban life and military conquests.[7] The earliest written records from the Middle East and from ancient Egypt, Babylonia, Greece, and Rome all show that these civilizations, the fountainheads of Western culture, were patriarchal. In these patriarchal civilizations men dominated women, treated them as property, and valued them only for their childbearing function, which at the same time they regarded as a handicapping weakness.

In many non-Western cultures the status of woman remained high, but these cultures came to the attention of the Western word only a little more than a century ago, when anthropology was born. The anthropologists of this period were extremely interested in the position of woman and the relations between the sexes in the various cultures; in fact, their interest in these subjects was singular in view of the sexual puritanism that prevailed at the time.[8] Their initial sources were the reports of travelers, explorers, and missionaries, who were ethnocentric and prejudiced to an extreme and provided more insight into the views of their own society than into the primitive cultures little better than that of animals or slaves, bought and sold by their husbands and masters.[9]

they discussed. From the vantage point of Victorian culture the status of women in the "primitive" societies was

However, when the anthropologists emerged from the libraries and went into the field, they found a vast array of cultures, in which the status of women varied widely. In some of the more highly developed societies, women were indeed little more than chattels, but among the Australian aborigines, technologically the most primitive of peoples, men and women were in the fullest sense partners. Thus, ethnographic data that were collected scientifically showed very clearly that the status of woman was not an index of technological advance. The notion that woman's status was directly correlated with the technological and cultural level of a society was very popular among some eminent Victorian social scientists. Herbert Spencer, for one, claimed that "perhaps in no way is the moral progress of mankind more clearly shown than by contrasting the position of women among savages with their position among the most advanced of the civilized."[10] Influenced by the Darwinian theory of biological evolution, the early anthropologists set up various cultural evolutionary schema which related the status of woman to the stages of family development. They represented the earliest peoples as living in promiscuous sexual hordes, which later developed into matriarchal societies where the fathers of children were unknown, and finally culminated in the monogamous patriarchal family. This family, characteristic of Europe, was, of course, depicted as the highest stage achieved by civilization thus far, and in this family woman had reached the ultimate status. With little data available to them, the anthropologists had no way of knowing that the position of women in Europe and America as recently as the late nineteenth century differed in only minor details from that

of the Near Eastern women of four or five thousand years
earlier.

> It is significant that, dissatisfied as European man was
> with most aspects of his cultural patrimony, he found
> nothing to be changed or improved in connection with the
> traditional status of women. Consequently, while he de-
> voted prodigious energy to introducing successive improve-
> ments into practically all of the cultural realms bequeathed
> to him by preceding generations ... he left untouched the
> ancient rules that governed the position of women and the rela-
> tionship between women and men. . . . Even after the aboli-
> tion of serfdom and slavery, men felt no shame at keeping
> women in a state of subjugation.[11]

It is now clearly recognized that the status of woman in
any society, preliterate or literate, reflects and is integrated with all of its values and institutions. The most important clue to woman's status anywhere is her degree of
participation in economic life and her control over property and the products she produces, both of which factors
appear to be related to the kinship system of a society.
The basic types of kinship systems are bilateral, patrilineal, and matrilineal. In the bilateral community children of
both sexes inherit the name and property of either or both
parents and form a new family upon marriage, separate
from either set of parents. In the patrilineal community
descent and property are inherited through males. Patrilineal societies are also usually patriarchal and patrilocal; that is, men do the governing, and women go to live
with or near the husband's family, or go with the husband
wherever he chooses or needs to live. Matrilineal societies
are also generally matrilocal, for the husbands go to live
with or near the wife's family. But matrilineal societies
are not now truly matriarchal, for even when descent and
property are inherited through the female line, the political and religious powers are rarely in the hands of women.
Thus, it is nonsense to call the United States a matriarchy,
as has so often been done in recent years.

> In the United States women take their husbands' names
> and the children bear their fathers' names. Women are
> expected to live where their husbands elect to live, and
> refusal to do so is tantamount to desertion. Men are liable
> for the support of their wives and children, and women are
> not liable for the support of their husbands. . . . The basic
> legal assumption is that a woman as a minor is dependent

upon her father, and thereafter upon her husband. In our legal forms we are a patrinominal, patrilineal, patrilocal and . . . for the most part, a patriarchal society.[12]

There are now many fewer matrilineal than patrilineal societies in the world, but "there is much to show that formerly matrilineal descent and matrilineal marriage were general."[13] And "there is every reason to suppose that under the conditions of the primary Neolithic way of life mother-right and the clan system were still dominant and land would generally have ascended through the female line."[14]

According to British anthropologist E. E. Evans-Pritchard, "matrilineal societies . . . are not found among any of the great civilizations of the world, which have all been patriarchal."[15] But Jacquetta Hawkes and Sir Leonard Woolley, also British anthropologists, find evidence of matrilineal descent in the great civilizations "in the background of Egyptian and Homeric society, while among the Cretans the position of women seems to have remained exceptionally high."[16] Many matrilineal societies reached high levels of social and political development, and typically they are far from primitive.[17]

Matrilineal societies also appear to be more peace-loving and cooperative, less competitive and militaristic than the patrilineal societies, and "there are facts pointing definitely to the close connection between communal ownership and mother-right, on the one hand, and individual ownership and father-right, on the other hand."[18] Certainly the status of woman is higher in the matrilineal than in the patrilineal societies. Where women own property and pass it to their daughters or sisters, they are far more influential and secure. Where their economic role is important and well defined, as it generally is in the matrilineal societies, they are not nearly so subject to male domination, and they have much more freedom of movement and of action.

Matrilineal descent and marriage still prevail "among many societies in North America and Africa and among the Dravidians of India; relics . . . persist in Melanesia, Micronesia and Indonesia."[19] The position of woman in some of these cultures illustrates the vast difference between woman's status in the matrilineal and patrilineal societies, as well as the impact of the patriarchal religions and conquering peoples upon matrilineal institutions.

PUEBLO INDIANS

Among the many matrilineal cultures in North America the Pueblo Indians are outstanding for the value they place upon peace and cooperation. These Indians are the descendants of seed-gathering peoples who established a desert culture about 11,000 years ago in the Southwest, and the culture of their direct farming ancestors dates back about 4,000 years.

In Arizona the Hopi (a word which means "people of peace"), one of the better-known Pueblo peoples, "appear to represent human society . . . as it seems to have been during the New Stone Age."[20] In the face of intense and continuous environmental pressures, such as a precarious water supply, drought, sand storms, floods, and frost, the Hopi not only solved the problem of group survival, but "evolved a marvellously well adjusted social system."[21] They are "the most fully developed and integrated individuals existing anywhere on this planet," and "more than any other native group in the Western hemisphere," they have "resisted the disintegrative pressures of coercive officials and proselytizing priests of an alien white civilization."[22]

The social unit is the clan, consisting of groups of families headed by older active women and including their sisters, and all their descendants, their brothers and all the male descendants, but excluding relatives by marriage. The group is a democratic unit resembling the ancient Greek city state, independent and self-sufficient. Leaders and people are closely associated, public opinion is very powerful, and decisions usually result from unanimous consent. Privilege does not exist; every individual is responsible for the welfare of the whole, and functions both independently and cooperatively within the society, which is "directed from within and not by outside coercions."[23]

The clan collectively owns the springs, gardens, and farm land, but the children, the house, the food, and furnishings belong to the group of women within the clan. Thus, the Hopi women own everything of any value except livestock, "and a Hopi woman has social and economic security independent of her marital status." The system gives priority and responsibility to women for the goals of "health and life, with no room for thoughts of war and death." "Each sex has its place in a well balanced society."[24] The men farm, herd, hunt, and collect fuel, and contribute the products of their labor to the female households to which they belong, but their primary and most cherished activity is ceremonial preparation and the enactment of ritual. While a woman is the head of the clan, her brother is the ceremonial head, and he joins with other male members of secret religious societies to perform rituals connected with communal welfare and their view of nature. Hopi pottery, baskets, ceremonial garments and masks are "strikingly beautiful" and express their religious feeling, which is dramatized in song, dance, poetry, and mythology.[25]

> We see here expressed in actual practice much of the old accumulated understanding of human values that early man acquired over a long period of time, retained by the Hopi in an almost unsullied form but over-ridden elsewhere by intrusive forces.[26]

Children are benevolently guided by their parents, siblings, and their many aunts and uncles. They develop personalities which are "quietly poised, serenely content, inwardly intense and intellectually adept at problem-solving." On intelligence tests the average Hopi child is "very intelligent, highly observant, and capable of complex, abstract thinking."[27]

Aside from environmental pressures, Hopi survival is most threatened by the evangelical missionary, especially "the Mennonite, in his most uncompromising and destructive form." To the extent that he is successful, the Hopi world is scarred by the familiar stigmata of the outside world, "anxiety, personality disturbance, and a tendency to social disruption." "The missions teach above all the doctrine of original sin and the threat of deferred punishment, of subordination of the spirit and mind of man to an unwarranted feeling of guilt."[28]

The culture has been able to withstand the assaults upon it with remarkable strength, but in the long run "the Hopi as such have about as much chance of survival under modern pressures as the Whooping Cranes and Trumpeter Swans."[29] The communal ownership of land among all the Indian peoples was alien to the individualistic European settlers and their American descendants, but they were particularly confused and irritated when they found that the women in the matrilineal cultures owned and worked the soil, and they have done everything in their power to destroy or "civilize" the Indians. "To be outstandingly different, particularly if beautiful and defenseless, is to invite destruction in these days of advanced and intolerant civilizations, and the Hopi have been as much under fire as any other rare and beautiful creation."[30]

INDONESIA

On the other side of the world, women generally have low status in the patriarchal civilizations of India, China, and Japan and in the Islamic cultures. But in parts of Southeast Asia, in Burma, Indonesia, and Sub-Saharan Africa, women have had more freedom and equality than in many regions of Europe and Asia.

> These cultures have traditionally included freedoms which, in other parts of the world, women have only recently begun to enjoy or aspire to. Outstanding among these is the sexual liberty of women in certain African societies, and the important roles women play in commercial activities in both Africa and Southeast Asia.[31]

In these cultures the military power and the ideologies of the conquering peoples and their patriarchal world religions had a great impact on the position of women. In each culture, however, the foreign influences were variously assimilated by the different local traditions. Whereas in India the status of women degenerated under Hinduism, it flourished under the same religion in many parts of the Indonesian archipelago. Women often ruled over Java, for centuries the center of a mighty Hindu empire, as well as over Sumatra and the Celebes Islands, and married women played an important part in the religious, family, and village councils. The Indonesian islands had long since developed distinctive regional cultures with different kinship systems, but whether in patrilineal, matrilineal, or bilateral communities, women acquired property, retained their claim to it in marriage, and were sure of some legal redress in case of marital injustice.[32]

The traditional high status of the Indonesian woman was also affected by Islam, Christianity, and a European colonial government. Islam was introduced into the islands via trade routes leading to Java in the thirteenth century.

When the Portuguese and the Dutch began to trade with the archipelago in the sixteenth century they tried to introduce Christianity by force of arms. But most of the people had already accepted Islam, which was now embraced by the native rulers as they attempted to unify their subjects in resistance to the Europeans.

Because of their important and active participation in the economy, the Indonesian women could not be veiled or segregated, as in other Muslim countries, but Islam did introduce polygamy and divorce by means of repudiation. Since a Muslim man may contract polygamous marriage only if he is able to provide equal support for each wife and her children, polygamy is generally a luxury of the wealthy upper classes in Islamic cultures. But in Indonesia the lower-class man modified polygamy into a kind of serial monogamy by using repudiation to rid himself of a wife and to marry again and again. However, the effect of polygamy and repudiation on women depended on the kinship system of the respective communities.

Most of the sedentary Indonesians are rice-growing farmers, with "mixed" or kitchen gardens associated with the matrilineal and the bilateral communities. Where the chief occupation is pastoral cattle breeding, from which women everywhere are excluded, a patrilineal system prevails and the mixed gardens are absent. In these communities the bridegroom's family pays a substantial bride price to the bride's family, which also provides the bride with a dowry of equal value when she goes to live with her husband's family. Because the bride price would be totally lost if the wife were divorced and sent back to her family, and the dowry would return with her, the divorce rate in the patrilineal communities is the lowest in Indonesia.[33]

In the matrilineal communities the husband lives with his wife's family. Since her services are still available to her family and she is still entitled to her share of the family estate, which is owned jointly by the women, neither a bride price nor a dowry is paid. The wife's eldest brother is responsible for her children's education, and her husband protects his own sister's children. In case of divorce the woman in the matrilineal community is physically and economically secure, for she continues to live with her own family, retains her property rights, and is also entitled to her share of the goods acquired by common effort during the marriage.

In the bilateral community each married couple forms a

new nuclear family which is separated from both the wife's and the husband's families, and the divorced woman does not have an extended family to which she can return. However, she may inherit cultivatable land, including the mixed gardens, and she retains the personal property she owned when she was married or that she acquired after marriage. Also, the belief prevails that "by running the home, a wife helps her husband to earn his living and is consequently entitled to her share of the family income."[34]

In both the matrilineal and bilateral communities, the divorce rate is very high, sometimes as high as 50 percent.[35] This is blamed on polygamy and repudiation, but in the Muslim Middle East, where women are much more subordinate and restricted than in Indonesia, as well as in the Indonesian patrilineal communities, the divorce rate is considerably lower.

In all three kinship systems in Indonesia, the woman owns property which provides her with a personal income and a measure of economic independence. In the matrilineal and bilateral communities the woman cultivates her mixed gardens and markets the surplus fruit and vegetables. In the patrilineal communities, the woman's dowry may consist of a plot of land which she may not sell but may use to grow products for the market. She also sells the textiles and pottery she makes and retains the money she earns for her own personal use. In Indonesia the markets are full of women traders.

The ninety-six million Indonesians are mainly Muslim, but about four and a half million are Christian; in the Christian communities, where bilateral kinship and the monogamous family prevail, the women were emancipated at an early period and have equal rights with the men.

Under the Dutch colonial administration population increased rapidly, land became scarce, and many of the traditional communities were disrupted. They were further disorganized by the Japanese occupation and the revolution for independence, in which Indonesian women fought beside the men in Java and Sumatra. (The Christian women had their own battalion.) In 1941 the Dutch granted women the right to vote and to hold elective office, and more girls were educated. After independence the women were even more active economically in the cities; "25 percent of adult urban women have jobs, a unique figure for a Moslem country."[36] But while the

Indonesian woman has full civil rights and with increasing education is entering the professions, "masculine opinion has proved reluctant to admit her right to equal treatment in the matter of marriage."[37] Repudiation is blamed for the insecurity of married women, growing disintegration of the family, and neglect of the children, especially in the cities.

The major goals of the Indonesian women's movement are the abolition of polygamy and increased vocational training to secure the economic independence of all women. In both rural and urban areas the women's movement has organized very successful economic enterprises, including savings banks run by and for women. In Indonesian society the woman is pivotal. "It is she and not the man who is the permanent and essential element."[38]

BURMA

A women's movement exists in most countries that discriminate against women, but in Burma there is no nationwide organization of women as such, and no movement to improve their status, for Burmese women retain their traditional full equality with men. In Burma rights for women are an integral part of traditional Buddhism and can be understood only in the context of the values and institutions of the culture both before and after the changes imposed by the West.

Burma has been called "a community of equals,"[39] and equality was an integral component of all its institutions. The king and his officials held certain traditional powers, but they were arbitrators, not judges, and they referred to the law books only for guidance. They did not interfere with the daily lives of the people, who lived predominantly in rural villages under a hereditary headman. The authority of the headman, like that of the king, rested on his ability to guide and arbitrate, not to coerce. With very little crime and few quarrels or litigations, there was, in fact, no need to coerce. And there were few means of coercion, for Burma had no army, no regular police, and very few prisons.

Buddhist civilization, which is very sophisticated in religious and social matters, does not value technological advance, and technologically Burma was simple. Neither very poor nor very rich, the people were civilized, literate, artistic, and gay. The land belonged to the family as a whole and could not be mortgaged, nor could any part of it be alienated by a family member. If it was sold the family had the right to redeem it. The land was very fertile, and the Burmese enjoyed cultivating it.

Village life was focused on the monastery, and the monks were very powerful, respected even by the king. Traditionally the education of all males was in their hands; this education, egalitarian by precept and example, included literacy, discipline, and principles of morality and interperson relations. The central religious principle was to increase in merit so as to be reincarnated at a higher stage and finally to be liberated entirely from the flesh, from the necessity to be born again. Merit was accumulated by giving, by doing good deeds. The best way of spending money was to give to charity as an act of merit. Thus, religion redistributed the wealth and prevented hoarding, which the Burmese detested. The individual was responsible for his own state or fate, since everyone was capable of deeds of merit and therefore could rise in status along a known path. Thus, Buddhism strengthened and advanced the individual. The Burmese were very independent, believing strongly in the inviolability of the individual, in personal worth and integrity. But this type of individual responsibility precluded concern for the welfare of others, and the Burmese did not try to proselytize their religion or way of life.

Work was performed voluntarily and without anxiety and was a virtue only when done deliberately as an act of merit. Work in itself was not valued; neither was living off the labor of others. Making money in order to gain material wealth was not an important part of life, since only accumulated personal merits helped one to reach a higher stage of reincarnation.

No one needed save against illness or old age because all had security through the family and the village. Parents took care of their children, and children supported parents in their old age as a matter of course. The Burmese enjoyed family life; everyone wanted children, but not in order to continue the family name, for only the individual was reincarnated. Traditionally family names did not exist; only personal names were important. Thus, Burma was neither a matrinominal nor a patrinominal society.

The patterns of equality that characterized the political and religious life of Burma were also basic to the position of women. Although theoretically they had some-what less status than men, in practice they were fully equal and did not depend on men except as all members of a family were interdependent. The women did much of the farming and made up half the trading labor force of Burma. Almost every house had a little shop, which was also a place in which to socialize, and each house had its own loom on which both men and women wove beautiful fabrics. The houses were small and sparsely furnished and housework—which the women did—was light.

The men paid a bride price to the wife's family, which is a customary compensation wherever women do most of the farming. However, men and women had the same legal rights in marriage and divorce. Wives kept their own names and wore no sign of their married status. Husbands had no power over their wives' property, whether brought as a dowry, inherited, or earned. The women acted on their own behalf, handled their own property, and partici-pated in family affairs. When the husband was absent, his wife acted for him and would sell an entire rice crop to an English agent. "Men consulted their wives and women deferred to their husbands."[40]

When, in the nineteenth century, the British brought a money economy and Western political and educational values into Burma, the Burmese were forced to change their traditional life patterns. The expansion of commerce led to the demand for more labor, which the Burmese were unwilling to provide. The British encouraged Indians and Chinese to immigrate, and by 1942 there were two million immigrants in the large urban centers.[41]

With the opening of the Suez Canal the British strongly pressured the Burmese to grow more rice, and the Indian moneylenders made loans available for the purchase of more land. New villages were established without a monastery and traditional law, and peasants were no long-er protected against the loss of their land. When they got into debt, they lost their land and became tenants on land concentrated in the hands of rich absentee landlords. Indi-vidual ownership of land was substituted for family own-ership. Individuals began to take up the common land of the village which had been used for festivities, common grazing, and fuel, depriving the village of a place for social gatherings, bullock races, dances and theatrical per-formances. However, the people now had little time for such activities. The British urged the Burmese to abandon their elaborate time-consuming festivals, the weaving and embroidering of fabrics, the carving of cargo boats, the making of lacquered pottery, and encouraged them instead to work for wages and to buy shoddy machine-made articles.

The British changed the village headmen into salaried government officials, imposed new duties on them and on the villagers, and imposed heavy penalties for noncompliance. The village was changed from a social and residential unit into an administrative unit; this destroyed the traditional principles of law and orderly social conduct based on an accepted way of life. With the decline of interpersonal relations crime increased tremendously. Because self-government had been replaced by "a foreign legal system unable to control the anti-social forces it liberated,"[42] a village police force and Western-style courts had to be established.

The British introduced vernacular schools in the villages, but in the large urban centers English was taught from the fourth grade on and high school classes were conducted in English. The village boys generally continued at the monastic schools; mainly the girls went to the new schools, where they were taught to read and to do arithmetic to help them with their trading accounts. The urban schools stressed success in examinations above everything else, and "in 1932 the Director of Education noted that districts with the best record for education had the worst record for crime."[43] The foreign schools substituted an economic goal for the social and moral goals of the monastery, but relatively few children attended long enough to gain economic advantages through education. The missionary schools taught respect for Western values, and children were sometimes alienated from their own parents and culture.

In the past children did not need to leave their villages to attend school, and education was free and egalitarian. Now mainly urban people could afford to educate their children in the Western schools. Thus, the advent of Western education created divisions between the educated and the uneducated, the well-to-do and the poor, the village and the city, Burmese culture and a foreign culture. Higher education did not dispel problems of racial discrimination, for Burmese graduates of professional schools were treated with less respect than Europeans.

The British disregarded the self-dependent role of the

Burmese women and their greater freedom than most European and Asiatic women. The West brought scouting for boys, needlework for girls, special hospitals for women, public toilets separated by sex, and adversely affected the position of women by making sharper distinctions between the sexes than had traditionally existed.[44] But since the Burmese woman had for so long been active and important in economic matters, she has had no difficulty adjusting to change both in the villages and in the towns. In the towns she adds new occupations to the traditional ones. She sells gems, knits sweaters on a knitting machine, makes pickles and preserves for local schools, sells flowers and ice cream from her home, builds a smithy beside her house and finances goldsmiths, sells woven cloth sent by her country cousin, and has a thriving timber or cheroot-rolling business in the basement.[45] She occupies high positions in all walks of life, in politics, journalism, the armed forces, the universities, and corporation administration. Recently the "joint venture" corporation "which made the highest profit was the one with an all-woman Board of Directors."[46] When Burma became independent, women's traditional equality with men was formally incorporated into the constitution: "All citizens, irrespective of birth, religion, sex or race, are equal before the law. . . . Women shall be entitled to the same pay as that received by men in respect to similar work."[47]

AFRICA

In view of the important role of women throughout Southeast Asia in producing essential staple foods, it is surprising to find a statement by so distinguished an anthropologist as Margaret Mead to the effect that men everywhere are the primary food producers.

> The home shared by a man or men and female partners, into which men bring the food and women prepare it, is the basic common picture the world over. But this picture can be modified, and the modifications provide proof that the pattern itself is not something deeply biological.[48]

While women have been given a monopoly over the preparation of food, and hunting is done almost exclusively by men, when it comes to farming, especially subsistence farming, it is a moot point as to whether men or women predominate. At any rate, there is no question that in Africa virtually all rural women do farm work "and the agricultural force is predominantly female."[49] In Africa, especially south of the Sahara, where shifting cultivation is practiced, men usually fell the trees to clear the land, but women remove and burn the trees, sow and plant in the ashes, weed the crops, and harvest and store them.

Before European colonization the chief occupations of the African male were warfare, hunting, and felling trees. When Europeans abolished intertribal warfare, the men seemed to be idle most of the time and the Europeans stigmatized them as lazy. The European settlers, colonial administrators, technical advisers, and extension services wanted the Africans to produce commercial crops; they used various devices, like placing a poll tax on households, to force them to farm. They also taught the men modern farming techniques, but ignored the female farmers who played such an important role in traditional agriculture. To the Europeans, "cultivation is naturally a job for men," and African "men could become far better farmers than women, if only they would abandon their customary 'laziness.' "[50] This attitude was shared by men from other patriarchal cultures, such as Americans and Chinese.

In Senegal, West Africa, Chinese instructors (from Taiwan) failed in their efforts to introduce better techniques in paddy production because they taught only the men, who took no notice since their wives were the cultivators and the wives being untaught, continued, of course, in the old way, subdividing the carefully improved fields into small traditional plots.[51]

Whenever there is enough land for shifting cultivation, and proteins can be obtained from hunting, fishing, and cattle in distant grazings, villages refuse to change to plow cultivation, which is associated with modern farming techniques, even when agricultural experts demonstrate how much more the land will yield. For when the changeover to plow farming takes place, it is the men who do the plowing and their work load increases greatly while that of the women diminishes. "The more the work of hoeing is done by women, the less likely will men be willing to change from hoeing to ploughing."[52] Agricultural change in developing countries with increasing populations is often retarded because men or women refuse to do more than the usual amount of work, or work that has traditionally been done by the other sex.

The Europeans had recruited the men to do work, either voluntary or forced, in road building, heavy construction, mines, and plantations, and when the men were absent the work load of the women in the villages increased. The recent rapid population increase in many parts of Africa has also forced the men to migrate to the towns in search of wage labor. The African woman's primary role in agriculture, in the present as in the past, is due to the migration of the young unmarried men; in addition, many old widows must fend for themselves, the older men leave farming to their younger wives and children, and more boys attend school than girls.

With population pressures more land must be used continuously and cultivated intensively. As the forests contract, shifting agriculture with the hoe becomes inadequate and is replaced by plow farming. Since it is the man who is taught modern farming techniques, the men who remain in the villages use the plow and become the primary cultivators. This entails "a radical shift in sex roles in agriculture," which undoubtedly explains woman's deteriorated status after the plow was invented in the Middle East about 5,000 years ago. As Boserup observes. "The adoption of a farming system where the main farming equipment is operated only by men entails a tremendous change in the economic and social relationship between the sexes."[53]

When the male farmer uses the plow, he usually grows cash crops while the woman continues to grow food crops for family consumption. Using scientific techniques the man expends much less energy and increases his productivity, while the woman's work with the hoe is exhausting, boring, and relatively less productive. The government also does research to improve cash crops, but food crops are not supported. The man can use the income from his crops to improve production further, but the woman receives little income from the food crops. Because he uses scientific farming methods the man becomes the decision-maker in the family, and the role of the woman changes from that of primary food producer to family aid. The man's prestige is enormously enhanced and the woman's relative status declines.

It is the men who do the modern jobs. They handle industrial inputs while women perform the degrading manual jobs; men often have the task of spreading fertilizer in the fields, while women spread manure; men ride the bicycle and drive the lorry, while women carry headloads, as did their grandmothers. In short, men represent modern farming in the village, women represent the old drudgery.[54]

The spread of primary education under the Europeans also helped to create technical and cultural gaps between the sexes in Africa. Everywhere, many more boys were sent to school. The boys started at a yonger age than the girls, and stayed longer. Boys were given vocational training, while girls only learned reading, better child care, nutrition, and sewing. When boys learn scientific techniques and girls mainly traditional beliefs from illiterate mothers, "it is more effective to teach modern agricultural methods to male than to female farmers."

In short, by their discriminatory policy in education and training the Europeans created a productivity gap between male and female farmers, and subsequently this gap seemed to justify their prejudice against female farmers.[55]

Under tribal land tenure, land ownership is vested in the chiefs, tribal land is rarely sold, and those who work the land own the crops and the acreage on which they are grown. Fortified by the European value of male ownership of land, some of the patrilineal African tribes, when land became scarce, began to claim that the men owned the land and that only the crops belonged to the female subsistence farmers. Again, as land for new fields ran short, farmers took over the old fallow land as *de facto* private property, prevented others from using it, and began to rent or sell it. But since only the men worked for wages in the towns or grew cash crops, only the men had the money to buy land. Thus, land ownership began to pass from women to men, even in matrilineal tribes. The woman who grew food crops on land belonging to her husband was no longer an independent cultivator with her own farming rights. While she might still be permitted to sell surplus food crops and keep the proceeds, at the next stage she might become an unpaid helper on her husband's farm.[56]

The land reforms introduced by European administrations also resulted in the loss of women's rights to land.

"The Europeans everywhere seem to have objected to the peculiar position of African women, which was so different from anything the Europeans were accustomed to."[57] In one region in the Congo, with 38,000 female and only 18,000 male cultivators, there was "always very strong propaganda coming from the Missions and the Government against matrilineal custom. Emphasis was laid upon the teachings of the Bible where all authority comes from God through the father."[58] In the Congo only the Belgians recognized women as cultivators in modern farming, but in other parts of Africa where female farming predominated and women were independent cultivators, "women were eliminated by European-styled land reforms, and the land was given to their husbands."[59]

In the Bikita Reserve in Rhodesia, a female farming area, land reform in 1957 allocated land to men and widows, but not to married women; 23 percent of those receiving land were men working for wages off the reserve. These men often divorced their wives on the reserve and married other women, depriving their former wives of the land they farmed. When land was irrigated in the Taung Reserve in the Union of South Africa, the fields were allocated to the men, who alone were taught irrigation techniques, although the main cultivators were women. In the Transkei, where each wife in a polygamous marriage had owned her own plot, the land as a whole was transferred to the husband; the women had to cultivate the common land and lost it to male heirs when the husband died. The people in the Transkei wanted to restore to the women their former rights in the land, "but all attempts to bring about the change have failed to persuade an inflexible bureaucracy which is not responsible to the people."[60]

The African women held the Europeans mainly responsible for these injustices and frequently refused to submit to them. Women refused to help their husbands produce cash crops or perform household chores unless they were paid for their work. In 1923 the Ibo women instigated riots in Aba, eastern Nigeria, because of a rumor that the government intended to tax female farmers. A group of 10,000 women looted European shops and released prisoners from the jail in Aba. The unrest spread to the Calabar region, where fifty people were killed and another fifty wounded during two days of demonstrations. "Throughout the entire disturbance the solidarity of the women never wavered, and a subsequent inquiry revealed the vigor and conviction with which they organized their opposition".[61] In 1929 the Ibo women of Aba organized the first large-scale uprising against colonial rule in Nigeria when they rioted against a tax imposed by the British administration.[62] This revolt was initiated by the Ibo women's associations, which had come into being to solve the special problems of women and were led by women elected for their wisdom rather than their age or wealth. When official methods brought no results, "the members would resort to strikes, ridicule and cursing."[63] The group also enforced its decisions by the ridicule and ostracism of members and by the destruction of property.

The women in the Kon region of eastern Nigeria rioted because their farming status had deteriorated and they were afraid of losing the land to male farmers. About 2,000 women, led by the women's organizations in the region, passed a resolution to eliminate all foreign institutions, such as courts, and schools, and to expel from the region all foreigners, including members of other tribes and Europeans. The women marched to the neighboring town and set fire to the market. The unrest spread to nearby tribes where the women were also afraid that the introduction of new farming techniques would undermine their position as farmers.[64]

Both in Africa and Asia labor costs in the production of export crops were held down at the expense of the women. In Africa labor costs on plantations, mines, and industries are reduced when only male workers are employed, but this increases the work load of the women who support dependents in the home village. In Asia men who use the plow must remain in the village to support the family. The plantation owner must hire the whole family, but every member works in the fields. However, while the man is free when his work in the fields is over for the day, the woman not only takes care of the children when she is working in the fields, but also has the double job of housewife and full-time laborer.

In regions like Africa and Southeast Asia, where shifting agriculture and the female farmer predominate, the women work very hard and receive limited support from their husbands, but they also have some economic independence, considerable freedom of movement, and an important place in the community. In such areas polygamy and the bride price are widespread. Under farming systems using the plow, where men do most of the work, as in the Arab, Hindu, and Chinese cultures, a second wife is an economic burden, for the husband must work harder in order to support her. Parents pay a large dowry to the husband's family, and the economic burden of daughters is so great that in some north Indian communities the number of girls was at one time limited by the practice of infanticide. In a system which obligates the husband to support his wife and children, and which makes the wife economically dependent on her husband, woman's status is subordinate and inferior. The veil and seclusion are associated with plow agriculture, but are unknown in shifting agriculture.

"Women always seem to bear a large part of the work burden in the more egalitarian communities," but "they are valued both as workers and as mothers of the next generation,"[65] and men desire plural wives on both accounts. However, when rural women take little part in agriculture they are only valued as mothers.

> There is a danger in such a community that the propaganda for birth control, if successful, may further lower the status of women both in the eyes of men and in their own eyes. This risk is less in communities where women are valued because they contribute to the well-being of the family in other ways, as well as bearing sons.[66]

Margaret Mead points out that "a society that has not defined women as primarily designed to bear children has far less difficulty in letting down taboos or social barriers."[67]

In Africa and Southeast Asia a very large part of the traditional market trade is in the hands of women because it consists primarily of agricultural products that the women grow and of the handicrafts they make. Where market trade is dominated by men, as in the Arab, Hindu, and Chinese cultures, men also do most of the agricultural work. However, Moslem women are not prevented by their religion from trading in regions where women predominate in trade.

In traditional African marriages the woman is expected to support herself and her children and to feed the family, including the husband, with the food she grows. Since rural African women have few ways of earning money, nearly all the women in some communities sell their surplus products in the market. In many developing countries they can compete successfully with department stores and supermarkets because they make only a very small profit on each transaction. Trading gives rural women a measure of economic independence, and African women much prefer trading to the hard work in the fields. They also enjoy socializing with each other and with their customers.

A much higher proportion of women are in market trade and the service occupations "in those parts of West Africa where climate discouraged European settlements and where the Moslem religion failed to penetrate"[68] than in South, East, or North Africa. Also, a number of West Coast societies are matrilineal, and this "gives women a status not permitted in patrilineal systems."[69] The trading women of West Africa are famous. In Ghana women account for 80 percent of the trade labor force; in eastern Nigeria and the Yoruba region of western Nigeria they account for about half the trade.[70] Yoruba and Ghana women recently began to import goods, and they sometimes make large profits in wholesale trade. A few West African women traders earn enough money to buy buses or trucks which some of them parlay into fleets.[71]

The Yoruba girl is brought up to earn her own living and is trained to make money. She is considered fit to marry only after she has acquired a craft, such as weaving, potting or mat-making, and has learned to trade, as well as to cook and farm. "The woman without a craft or trade, who is wholly dependent on the husband is rare and often regarded with contempt."[72] Yoruba women are organized in craft guilds, and the guild leaders hold responsible positions in the governing bodies of their communities. The guilds are also represented in the state council, the highest judicial body of the chiefdom.[73]

In many areas the market women organize to safeguard their interests and to limit competition. In West Africa unions of women traders sometimes persuade the authorities to grant permits for market stalls only to members of their own organizations; in independent Africa the women traders actively try to oust immigrant traders.[74] In the Cameroons the African women expressed such violent resentment when they were denied access to the market (to force them to work longer hours in the fields) that the authorities were compelled to rescind the restrictions. In the last years of colonial rule in Kenya market women were granted only 20 percent of the hawkers' licenses, and illegal hawking accounted for most of the crimes committed by the Nairobi women.[75]

Polygamy is fully integrated with all the other institutions in rural Africa. Under the tribal system of land tenure, still in effect in much of the continent, only family size limits the amount of land that can be worked both for food and for cash crops. Thus, the size of the area cultivated by a family usually corresponds directly with the number of wives in the family. The women contribute much more to the family income than the amount of their keep since they provide not only their own labor, but that of the sons they bear. Also, the more wives a man has, the fewer wage laborers he needs to hire.[76] In fact, in Sierra Leone the wives are sometimes used to ensnare male farm workers to work without pay.[77] On the Ivory Coast husbands and fathers in 1959 still paid off their debts by sending their wives and daughters to work without pay in the fields of their creditors. And the girl's family sometimes cancelled the bride price when money was owed to a man who wished to marry her.[78] Another wife is not always used to expand cultivation but sometimes to provide the husband with more leisure to hunt which, besides being a source of valued food, is "the most cherished spare time occupation for the male members of the village population."[79]

An additional incentive for polygamy is the desire for many children, for children are not only agricultural and domestic assets, but also enhance a man's standing and dignity in the community. Three to five children out of every ten born die in infancy, and no more than half of those who survive reach adulthood.[80] The taboo on sexual relations from the onset of pregnancy until the child is weaned at the age of two is also used to justify polygamy. The wife may return to her family to wean the baby, or she may be away from home for long stretches while she is trading. Without a second wife a man would be celibate for long stretches, and he would have no one to keep house for him.

In a family system where the female farmer not only provides the food for the family but also trades, rears the children, and does the housework, a wife welcomes one or more cowives to share the burden of work. Domestic duties include the processing of food before it is cooked, for the grains must be husked, pounded, and ground. Women fetch the water and fuel sometimes over a distance of several miles; they collect wild vegetables and fruit, work on handicrafts, and help to build the house. Thus, on the Ivory Coast 85 percent of the women prefer to live in polygamous rather than monogamous marriage.[81] Many women prefer to marry Muslims because Islam requires a man to support each wife equally, and secluded women do not work in the fields.

The incentives for polygamy are so powerful in Africa that no religious or legal prohibition prevails against them. While it is declining to some extent, polygamy persists even among families that have become Christian. At the present time a fourth to a third of the men in many parts of Africa south of the Sahara have more than one wife.[82] "Thoughtful churchmen agree that the Christian concept of marriage will be accepted only when industrialization and urbanization impose supporting values on the society."[83]

Under a system of polygamy restrictions on premarital sexual relations are rare, but neither is sexual behavior completely free. Premarital relations in Africa are institutionalized in a type of trial marriage in which both boys and girls are sexually educated, but the rules set forth clear patterns of sexual behavior and premarital conception is not approved. In the polygamous marriage a wife's adultery may be permitted so that an impotent husband can have legal issue, or a woman may have a lover if he works for her husband.[84] In most of Africa a wife may leave her husband if she repays the bride price; older men therefore keep the bride price very high. The woman frequently initiates a divorce by running away, or she may provoke her husband to take the initiative by refusing to cook and clean and by quarreling with him. But even when he sends her back to her parents, the marriage is not officially terminated until the bride price is returned.[85]

Where polygamy exists many men have to postpone marriage or forego it. "Widespread prostitution or adultery is therefore likely to accompany widespread polygamy, marriage payments are likely to . . . be high for the bridegroom's family, sometimes amounting to several years' earnings of a seasonal laborer."[86] In towns with a large surplus of single males, as in the Republic of South Africa, the market women sometimes prepare meals, brew beer, and serve as prostitutes. The women traders who travel long distances from market to market often supplement their earnings by prostitution. In some tribes the women look upon prostitution as "merely a new calling like any other and they become prostitutes as reasonably and as self-righteously as they would have become typists or telephone girls."[87] In Brazzaville prostitution is not stigmatized; in fact, prostitutes who become well-to-do enjoy great prestige. In Ghana and Nigeria the prostitutes have professional associations which organize festivities and funerals and help members in trouble.

Many villagers in Africa are moving to the towns because the men need to work for wages to earn money for the bride price, because the women reject farming when plow agriculture deprives them of their status of independent cultivators, because the women want to escape the hard labor of farming or the rigors of tribal discipline. The women are particularly eager to live a life of relative leisure in the towns. A wife who migrates with her husband can do little to contribute to the family's support. She may keep a goat and try to find fodder to feed it, grow a few vegetables, beg for leftover food, collect scrap material to build a hut in the slums, and collect animal droppings for fuel. But the activities of women change radically when they move from rural to urban areas in Africa.

In countries with a tradition of female trading, like much of Southeast Asia, many women enter the modern trade sector when they move to the towns. But in Africa, with the same tradition, modern trade is virtually a male preserve. The average market woman is illiterate and cannot get work in the modern stores, but young literate girls are not hired either. As the modern shops increase, even the petty trade of women in traditional markets declines. When the man works in modern trade and industry, even as an unskilled laborer, and the woman finds little or no employment, the wide gap in the productivity and income between urban men and women lowers the woman's relative status, as in the farming areas when the plow is adopted. Also, tension usually arises between a husband and wife when he has the unaccustomed role of sole family breadwinner and she has unaccustomed leisure and idleness.

Because the men are generally unwilling to accept the doubling of their work load, they often leave their wives and children in the village when they migrate. Although colonial restrictions on female migration disappeared with independence, most towns in Sub-Saharan Africa continue to be predominantly male while the villages have a surplus of women. The excess of men in the towns, together with the limited opportunities for female employment, sometimes leads married women into prostitution: this is another reason why men leave their wives in the village where unmarried men are rare and women are controlled by older family members. The men are also afraid that if the women become prostitutes they will earn enough money to repay the bride price and leave them.

These attitudes block the emancipation of women from tribal and family authority and thwart their attempts to obtain genuine urban employment. They also perpetuate the policies of the colonial European missionaries and administrators, who prevented single African women from migrating to the towns in search of work and expelled from the towns women who were not living under male authority. In East Africa well-dressed urban girls who work in offices and the professions are often suspected of being prostitutes. African women in the Republic of South Africa are still forbidden to migrate to the towns without special permission. The European influence adversely affected the position of women in the urban as well as the rural areas of Africa.

> Missionaries, Catholic as well as Protestant, are blamed for having taught the girls little more than domestic skills and for having more or less encouraged a stay-at-home policy of the urban women on moral grounds.[88]

In European-owned industries in Africa and Asia work is divided along race and sex lines, with European men at the top and the indigenous women at the bottom. In Kenya and the Republic of South Africa the white men are the administrators, Asian men or white women perform the clerical work, and African men and women are left with unskilled manual labor. The fact that Asian men can find administrative jobs more easily than European women reveals the extent of the European prejudice against all women in the upper echelons of employment.

However, even where political power is now in the hands of the people who were formerly at the bottom of the labor market, men and women receive equal wages only for unskilled work.

> When the better jobs previously filled by women of the favored minority are now taken over by men from the

majority groups the result is, on one hand, a mitigation of racial discrimination and, on the other hand, a reinforcement of sex discrimination.[89]

Many African men object to careers for women "because it will make the urban woman economically independent and unwilling to submit to male authority."[90] But as industrialization and urbanization weaken tribal authority African men substitute Western ideas for tribal custom. "They claim authority and obedience on the grounds of women's educational deficiencies and not because of tribal rights."[91] However, they do little to equalize educational opportunities and vocational training for women. Moreover, "in cases where lack of qualified manpower causes educated African women to be employed in white collar jobs, it seems to be generally accepted that they must be employed in low grade jobs, while the men move up to the more responsible jobs."[92]

Sékou Touré, the president of Guinea, believes the emacipation of African women to be essential if the goals of the revolution and independence are to be realized.

If we question ourselves objectively about what was the hardest thing for us to bear under foreign domination, we must give pride of place to the permanent constraint, the perpetual subordination . . . the constant disrespect. . . . Can we now bring the same subordination to bear on our sisters, our wives, our daughters? Can we now treat them with the same contempt?[93]

Touré's position is public policy in almost all African nations. But while their constitutions include universal adult suffrage and the right to hold public office, few women are in high public office or in the upper echelons of industry and the professions. However, some of the African governments are establishing vocational training centers for women, and Africa is the only developing region that is beginning to provide agricultural courses for female farmers.

Most educated women resent polygamy, and it is much less usual in the cities, where change is greatest. Interviews with young urban couples reveal the extent of change.

Many young husbands not only provided their wives with a means of livelihood, but gave or lent them additional capital, bought them clothes, added pocket money to their incomes. They helped with the housework, cleaning or washing, cooking or looking after the children when their wives were busy. ... The wives, in return, helped to meet the housekeeping bills, lent money to their husbands, or even maintained them altogether when their business was going badly. In marriages like this, husbands and wives are partners.[94]

The traditional women's organizations are playing a major role in enlarging the participation of African women in public and economic life. They have succeeded in increasing the number of civil service positions for women; they help "the poor, the aged, the physically handicapped, and the mentally retarded"; they establish shelters for unmarried mothers and abandoned children, social centers for women, day nurseries for children of working mothers, and centers for family and child guidance. They also work "to overcome racial, cultural and language barriers which impede the unity of the community."[95]

Elizabeth Wheeler, who has studied the many aspects of African women, predicts that women's movements in Africa will take a different direction from those in the West.

It is unlikely that the African women will ever need to engage in emancipation movements, like those ... in the United States and Europe. The strength of social movements which embrace her may ultimately make the African woman's participation in community life more genuine, complete and influential than anything her American counterpart has yet achieved.[96]

COMPARISON BETWEEN DEVELOPING AND INDUSTRIALIZED NATIONS

Comparisons of the role of urban women in developing and industrialized countries reveal interesting similarities and contrasts. In developing countries in which women have a traditionally high status, girls form a large percentage of the few adult students, and women continue to play an important economic role, even if the countries are poor. But if the dominant attitude is indifferent or hostile to women, few girls are educated and can enter the modern economic sector even if the country is relatively advanced economically. A crucial variable, however, is the impact of a foreign power on indigenous cultures.

In Southeast Asia urban women have an unusually wide range of employment opportunities, considering the low level of economic development: they account for about half the trading labor force in Burma, Thailand, Cambodia, Laos, Vietnam, and the Philippines.[97] In the Philippines, where American control outweighed the entrenched Spanish influence, women account for 30 percent of modern-sector employment, the highest level of female participation in any colonized developing country outside the Western hemisphere.[98] In Buddhist Thailand, however, the only country in Southeast Asia that managed to remain independent of European colonization, more than 40 percent of the women are active in the towns, and the number of women medical students has been formally restricted to prevent the medical profession from becoming predominantly female.[99] Even in the Philippines, the only Asian country to educate almost as many girls as boys, most girls drop out after the age of nineteen, "when it is still possible to find husbands of a similar (or higher) educational level."[100]

In the developing countries men with a higher education generally find administrative or professional jobs, but the proportion of women in administration is always very much lower than the proportion of women students. Only in the developing countries that have been most influenced by the United States—Latin America, the Philippines, South Korea—does a larger proportion of women hold top jobs, but even in South Korea, where the proportion is highest, it reaches only 18 percent.[101] In any country where the number of male and female students is equal, only about 10 percent of the administrative personnel are women. "In effect, administrative work is a male monopoly in developing countries just as it is in nearly all industrialized countries," including the United States. In the Soviet Union only 12 percent of the top administrative jobs are held by women.[102]

In the industrialized West girls with a high school education do the clerical work, but only in those developing countries under American influence is there a high proportion of female clerks, for the modern sector overwhelmingly favors the employment of men in both clerical and administrative jobs. Since most of the women in the developing countries must therefore do unskilled work, the productivity, income, and prestige of men and women diverge. Economic progress benefits the man, while the position of women may deteriorate even further as the growing modern economy eliminates the traditional female occupations.

The division of work roles along sexual lines so dominates the developing and industrialized countries alike that both men and women tend to regard it as "natural." Yet, in family production and in home industry for a local market, work is generally distributed horizontally between the sexes and vertically only between adults and the young. As men and women become older and more experienced in their craft or trade, both are skilled supervisory workers who train young people. Thus, at simpler economic levels the division of work and responsibilities is less rigid and more predictable than in the modern economic sector.

Because of the "widespread and deeply ingrained prejudice against women's participation in industry"[103] in both the developing and the industrialized countries, only the least competent and reliable women from the poorest and most unstable social groups apply for industrial work; this type of employee perpetuates the employer's dissatisfaction with female workers. "The idea that women are by nature inferior workers is widespread in developing as well as industrial countries."[104]

In most of the Arab countries and in multiracial regions with very limited opportunities for women from groups that are designated as inferior, more than 20 percent of all women in nonagricultural work are in the professions.[105] Moreover, in all the developing countries the proportion of women students and professional women is equal. Because of the great demand for increased education and health services, at least two-thirds of all professional women are teachers and most of the rest are nurses, for in both the developing and industrial countries women extend their traditional roles of educating the young and caring for the sick. In countries where women are secluded, they reach as high a status as men in the same professions, even though many fewer women are educated and the professions are segregated by sex. In the Arab cultures women benefit from the prejudice against male teachers and physicians for girls, and in the countries influenced by Anglo-American culture women benefit from the fact that men do not become primary school teachers, traditionally a lower-status woman's job. In regard to promotions, women in the Arab cultures, who teach at all levels of education, hold all the jobs from primary schools through professional levels, whereas in the industrialized countries and in developing countries like the Philippines, the number of women teachers and administrators decreases at every educational level.

Thus, it is not very surprising that "the first two governments to be presided over by women prime ministers were not in countries with a high degree of female participation in the labor market, but in two Asian countries with highly secluded labor markets, where upper-class women are in the professions only, and men have not become accustomed to viewing the role of educated women as that of a less qualified assistant to a male supervisor."[106]

Despite their different methods of segregating women, the Asian countries with their secluded labor markets and the industrialized West are linked by their common patriarchal practice of sexual discrimination. While the East practices physical segregation, Western women are segregated occupationally, with sharp limitations on the upper range of even those occupations to which they have access. Moreover, an open expression of the deep-seated male desire to seclude Western women in the home is still by no means rare. An example is Raphael Patai's introduction to the book *Women in the Modern World*, in which he asserts that in "the most Westernized part" of the Western world, "the one which spearheads the achievements of modern Western civilization," women are returning to their traditional role "rather than competing with men on various occupational levels."[107] Making anonymous women the mouthpiece for his own wishful thinking, Patai adds that in the "societies which allow their women sufficient leeway to play ... 'women's two roles,'" women are now "saying in effect," the following:

> Now that we have won the right to take an equal place in a man's world, we prefer to return to the home, to our own places in our women's world. It is good to know that we can play both roles, that we have a right to both worlds, but we shall be satisfied with relatively brief excursions into the world of men before taking up, or after having fulfilled, the role to which nature has predestined us, of being wife, mother and homemaker.[108]

Since a basic tenet of anthropology, formulated as a result of extensive cross-cultural research, is that, except for childbearing, all female roles are culturally assigned, one blushes when a contemporary fellow anthropologist uses such a phrase as "the role to which *nature has predestined us,* of being wife, mother and homemaker." Shades of the Victorian anthropologists and their armchair speculations!

Moreover, the data submitted by the Western women who wrote the articles on women in the Western world in the book Patai edited, directly contravene his assertions. So tenaciously does he cling to his patriarchal biases that he blatantly ignores the statistics quoted by the contributors he himself selected, which show the increasing number of women, especially those with a higher education, who are working outside the home throughout the Western world. Harriet Holter, writing about Scandinavia, states:

> In Norway, the 1960 census data show that 55 per cent of the married women with a university degree work outside the home, as against 22 per cent of those with only elementary school education. The figures are somewhat higher in the other Scandinavian countries.[109]

In Britain "in 1947 roughly 18 per cent of all married women were working outside their homes, in 1951 just under 25 per cent, and in 1961 over 32 per cent."[110] And in the United States "the most important single change in the life of women is in their gainful employment outside the home. . . . The census records have year by year shown an increasing number of women thronging into occupations and activities formerly regarded as masculine. . . . In 1960 . . . full-time work by the wife was about twice as prevalent in higher-income families as in lower."[111]

In the United States, particularly in the West, woman was not always viewed as "man's little helper" or as the sexual object portrayed by the media. When the country was being settled, women participated with men in plowing the land and fending off the Indians, as well as in their traditional roles of potter, weaver, spinner, cook, teacher, and nurse; such participation helped to weaken the traditional European patriarchal values and democratize the family. Strong and determined women worked side by side with men and achieved practical equality, for the brutal frontier conditions "established a certain rough egalitarianism which challenged other, long-established concepts of propriety."[112] In 1889, when the Wyoming legislators were told to abandon woman's suffrage as the price of admission to the Union, they said: "We will remain out of the Union a hundred years rather than come in without the women."[113]

The values of the complex American culture include equality, as well as discrimination; justice, as well as entrenched privilege; cooperation, as well as competition; a sense of mission, as well as the quest for material wealth; and, above all, a belief in change, as well as in tradition. At present our fate depends on which values and institutions we choose to honor most.

> Institutions are the various forms in which the social life of a people finds expression. Some it will take for granted as a matter of custom; others it will adopt of its own choice; and yet others will be imposed upon it by an authority. Individuals are subject to the nation's institutions, but the institutions themselves exist, ultimately, for the sake of the society whose welfare they promote, . . . their distinguishing characteristic is that they all proceed, in the end, from the human will.[114]

NOTES

1. Jacquetta Hawkes and Sir Leonard Woolley, *Prehistory and the Beginning of Civilization* (New York: Harper & Row, 1963), p. 265.
2. *Ibid.*, p. 331.
3. *Ibid.*, p. 264.
4. *Ibid.*, p. 227.
5. *Ibid.*, p. 340.
6. Ashley Montagu, *The Natural Superiority of Women*, rev. ed. (New York: Macmillan, 1968), pp. 12-14.
7. Hawkes and Woolley, *op. cit.*, p. 343.
8. E. E. Evans-Pritchard, *The Position of Women in Primitive Societies* (New York: The Free Press, 1965), p. 39.
9. *Ibid.*, p. 41.
10. *Ibid.*, p. 37.
11. Raphael Patai, ed., *Women in the Modern World* (New York: The Free Press, 1967), p. 3.
12. Margaret Mead, *Male and Female* (New York: William Morrow, 1949), pp. 301-302. Reprinted by permission of William Morrow and Co., Inc. Copyright © 1949, by Margaret Mead.
13. Hawkes and Woolley, *op. cit.*, p. 122.
14. *Ibid.*, p. 264.
15. Evans-Pritchard, *op. cit.*, pp. 50-51.
16. Hawkes and Woolley, *op. cit.*, p. 122.
17. Evans-Pritchard, *op. cit.*, pp. 50-51.
18. Hawkes and Woolley, *op. cit.*, p. 264.
19. *Ibid.*, p. 122.
20. N. J. Berrill, *Man's Emerging Mind* (London: Dennis Dobson, 1958), p. 170.

21. *Ibid.*, p. 159.
22. *Ibid.*
23. *Ibid.*, p. 169.
24. *Ibid.*, p. 168.
25. Robert F. Spencer, Jesse D. Jennings et al., *The Native Americans* (New York: Harper & Row, 1965), p. 298.
26. Berrill, *op. cit.*, p. 168.
27. *Ibid.*, p. 169.
28. *Ibid.*, p. 170.
29. *Ibid.*, p. 167.
30. *Ibid.*
31. Patai, *op. cit.*, p. 315.
32. Mi Mi Khaing, "Burma and South-East Asia," in Raphael Patai, *Women in the Modern World* (New York: The Free Press, 1967), p. 346.
33. Cora Vreede-de Stuers, "Indonesia," in Patai, *op. cit.*, p. 365.
34. *Ibid.*
35. *Ibid.*, p. 378.
36. Ester Boserup, *Woman's Role in Economic Development* (London: George Allen and Unwin Ltd., 1970), p. 189.
37. Vreede-de Stuers, *op. cit.*, p. 382.
38. *Ibid.*, p. 366.
39. Margaret Mead, ed., *Cultural Patterns and Technical Change* (New York: Mentor Books, 1955), p. 30.
40. *Ibid.*, p. 42.
41. *Ibid.*, p. 25.
42. *Ibid.*, p. 34.
43. *Ibid.*, p. 50.
44. Boserup, *op. cit.*, p. 219.
45. Khaing, *op. cit.*, pp. 356-357.
46. *Ibid.*, p. 357.
47. *Ibid.*, p. 347.
48. Mead, *Male and Female*, p. 190.
49. Boserup, *op. cit.*, p. 25.
50. *Ibid.*, p. 54.
51. *Ibid.*, p. 55.
52. *Ibid.*, p. 33.
53. *Ibid.*
54. *Ibid.*, p. 56.
55. *Ibid.*, p. 57.
56. Phyllis M. Kaberry, *Women of the Grasslands* (London: Colonial Office Research Publication No. 14, 1952), p. 148.
57. Boserup, *op. cit.*, p. 60.
58. *Ibid.*
59. *Ibid.*
60. H. J. Simons, *African Women: Their Legal Status in South Africa* (Evanston, Ill.: Northwestern University Press, 1968), p. 266.
61. Elizabeth Hunting Wheeler, "Sub-Saharan Africa," in Patai, *op. cit.*, p. 340. Reprinted with permission of the Macmillan Co. Copyright © 1967 by The Free Press, a division of the Macmillan Company.
62. Sylvia Leith-Ross, *African Women: A Study of the Ibo of Nigeria* (London: Faber & Faber, 1939), pp. 23-29.
63. *Ibid.*
64. Robert E. Ritzenthaler, "Anlu: A Women's Uprising in the British Cameroons," *African Studies* 1 (1960): 151-156.

65. Boserup, *op. cit.*, p. 51.
66. *Ibid.*
67. Mead, *Male and Female*, p. 229.
68. Boserup, *op. cit.*, pp. 182-183.
69. Wheeler, *op. cit.*, p. 320.
70. Boserup, *op. cit.*, pp. 87-89.
71. Wheeler, *op. cit.*, p. 336.
72. *Ibid.*, p. 334.
73. *Ibid.*, p. 340.
74. *Ibid.*
75. *Ibid.*
76. *Ibid.*, p. 38.
77. K. L. Little, *The Mende of Sierra Leone: A West African People* (London: Routledge & Kegan Paul Ltd., 1951), p. 141.
78. Boserup, *op. cit.*, p. 46.
79. *Ibid.*, p. 41.
80. Wheeler, *op. cit.*, p. 325.
81. Boserup, *op. cit.*, p. 43.
82. Boserup, *op. cit.*, p. 48.
83. Wheeler, *op. cit.*, p. 327.
84. Wheeler, *op. cit.*, p. 325.
85. *Ibid.*, p. 326.
86. Boserup, *op. cit.*, p. 44.
87. *Ibid.*, p. 100.
88. *Ibid.*, p. 219.
89. *Ibid.*, p. 151.
90. *Ibid.*, p. 219.
91. *Ibid.*
92. *Ibid.*, p. 220.
93. Wheeler, *op. cit.*, p. 341.
94. Peter Marris, *Family and Social Change in an African City* (Evanston, Ill.: Northwestern University Press, 1960), pp. 54-55.
95. Wheeler, *op. cit.*, p. 343.
96. *Ibid.*, p. 324.
97. Boserup, *op. cit.*, p. 89.
98. *Ibid.*, p. 182.
99. *Ibid.*, p. 216.
100. *Ibid.*, p. 122.
101. *Ibid.*, p. 125.
102. *Ibid.*, p. 123.
103. *Ibid.*, p. 144.
104. *Ibid.*, p. 214.
105. *Ibid.*, p. 153.
106. *Ibid.*, p. 154.
107. Patai, *op. cit.*, p. 10.
108. *Ibid.*
109. Harriet Holter, "Scandinavia," in Patai, *op. cit.*, p. 447.
110. Viola Klein, "Great Britain," in Patai, *op. cit.*, p. 477.
111. Margaret G. Benz, "United States," in Patai, *op. cit.*, pp. 503-505.
112. Eleanor Flexner, *Century of Struggle* (New York: Atheneum, 1968), p. 9.
113. *Ibid.*, p. 178.
114. Roland de Vaux, *Ancient Israel* (New York: McGraw-Hill Book Co., 1965), I: vii.

68. *Ibid.*, pp. 47, 51.

69. Wied, *Life and remains*, p. 394.
70. Bergman, *op. cit.*, pp. 153-192.
71. Rhodes, *see* ch. 7.
72. Murdock, *op. cit.*, pp. 6-8.
73. *Ibid.*, p. 306.
74. *Ibid.*, p. 307.
75. *Ibid.*
76. *Ibid.*
77. *Ibid.*, p. 58.
78. Lichtblau, *The Mating of Sheep a New Nation* (New York: Columbia University Press, 1951), p. 141.
79. Benedict, *op. cit.*, p. 262.
70. *Ibid.*, p. 263.
80. Wheeler, *op. cit.*, p. 28.
81. Speroni, *op. cit.*, p. 42.
82. *Ibid.*, *op. cit.*, p. 45.
83. Wheeler, *op. cit.*, p. 157.
84. *Ibid.*, *op. cit.*, p. 253.
85. *Ibid.*, p. 262.
86. Benedict, *op. cit.*, p. 94.
87. *Ibid.*, p. 110.
88. *Ibid.*, p. 212.
89. *Ibid.*, p. 131.
90. *Ibid.*, p. 216.
91. *Ibid.*
92. *Ibid.*, p. 229.
93. Benedict, *op. cit.*, p. 191.
94. Peter Murray, *Family and Social Change in an Affluent Society* (Evanston, Ill.: Northwestern University Press, 1960), p.

95. Wheeler, *op. cit.*, p. 155.
96. *Ibid.*, p. 65.
97. Murray, *op. cit.*, p. 80.
98. *Ibid.*, p. 141.
99. *Ibid.*, p. 166.
100. *Ibid.*, p. 173.
101. *Ibid.*, p. 172.
102. *Ibid.*, p. 173.
103. *Ibid.*, p. 164.
104. *Ibid.*, p. 234.
105. *Ibid.*, p. 235.
106. *Ibid.*, p. 351.
107. *Ibid.*, *op. cit.*, p. 164.
108. *Ibid.*
109. Martin Roher, "Scandinavia," in *Ibid.*, *op. cit.*, p. 317.
110. Viola Klein, "Great Britain," in *Ibid.*, *op. cit.*, p. 171.
111. Margaret G. Reid, "United States," in *Ibid.*, *op. cit.*, pp. 305-306.
112. Eleanor Flexner, *Century of Struggle* (New York: Atheneum, 1959), p.
113. *Ibid.*, p. 124.
114. Rollo May, *Man's Search for Himself* (New York: New American Library Book Co., 1953), ii-vii.

III:

WOMAN AT WORK

19

WOMEN AND CREATIVITY:
The Demise of the Dancing Dog

Cynthia Ozick

> Young women, . . . you are, in my
> opinion, disgracefully ignorant. You
> have never made a discovery of any
> importance. You have never shaken
> an empire or led an army into battle.
> The plays of Shakespeare are not by
> you, and you have never introduced
> a barbarous race to the blessings of
> civilization. What is your excuse?—
> Virginia Woolf, *A Room of One's Own*

> No comradely socialist legislation on
> women's behalf could accomplish a
> millionth of what a bit more muscle
> tissue, gratuitously offered by nature,
> might do . . .—Elizabeth Hardwick,
> *A View of One's Own*

Several years ago I devoted a year to Examining the
Minds of the Young. It was a curious experience, like
going into theatre after theatre in a single night, and
catching bits of first acts only. How will the heroine's
character develop? Will the hero turn out to be captain of
his fate or only of some minor industry? I never arrived at

From *Motive* 29 (March-April 1969): 7-16.

the second act, and undoubtedly I will never be witness to
the denouement. But what I saw of all those beginnings
was extraordinary: they were all so similar. All the characters were exactly the same age, and most had equal
limitations of imagination and aspiration. Is "the individual," I wondered, a sacred certainty, and the human mind
infinitely diversified, as we are always being told? Examine for yourself the Minds of the Young and it is
possible you will begin to think the opposite. Democratic
theory is depressingly correct in declaring all men equal.
Just as every human hand is limited at birth by its five
fingers, so is every human mind stamped from a single,
equally obvious, pattern. "I have never in all my various
travels seen but two sorts of people, and those very like
one another; I mean men and women, who always have
been, and ever will be, the same," wrote Lady Mary
Wortley Montagu in the middle of the eighteenth century.
Human nature is one.

The vantage point from which I came to these not
unusual conclusions was not from reading the great philosophers, or even from reading Lady Mary—it was from
a job. I was hired by a large urban university to teach
English to freshmen: three classes of nearly a hundred
young men and young women, all seventeen, some city-
born, some suburban, some well-off, some only scraping
by, of every ethnic group and of every majority religion
but Hindu. Almost all were equipped with B high school
averages; almost all were more illiterate than not; almost
all possessed similar prejudices expressed in identical platitudes. Almost all were tall, healthy, strong-toothed, obedient, and ignorant beyond their years. They had, of course,
very few ideas—at seventeen this can hardly be called a
failing; but the ideas they had were plainly derived not
from speculation but from indoctrination. They had identical minuscule vocabularies, made identical errors of
grammar and punctuation, and were identically illogical.
They were identically uneducated, and the minds of the
uneducated young women were identical with the minds
of the uneducated young men.

Now this last observation was the least surprising of all.
Though unacquainted with the darkest underbrush of the
human mind (and here it must be emphatically decreed
that deep scrutiny, at indecently short intervals, of one
hundred freshman themes is the quickest and most scarify-
ing method of achieving intimacy with the human mind in

its rawest state), I had never doubted that the human mind was a democratic whole—that it was androgynous, epicene, asexual: call it what you will; it had always seemed axiomatic to me that the minds of men and women were indistinguishable.

My students confirmed this axiom to the last degree. You could not tell the young men's papers from the young women's papers. They thought alike (badly), they wrote alike (gracelessly), and they believed alike (docilely). And what they all believed was this: that the minds of men and women are spectacularly unlike.

They believed that men write like men, and women like women; that men think like men, and women like women; that men believe like men, and women like women. And they were all identical in this belief.

But I have said, after all, that they were alike in illiteracy, undereducation, ignorance, and prejudice.

Still, to teach at a university is not simply to teach; the teacher is a teacher among students, but he is also a teacher among teachers. He has colleagues, and to have colleagues is to have high exchanges, fruitful discourses, enlightening quarrels. Colleagues, unlike students, are not merely literate but breathtakingly literary; not merely educated but bent under the weight of multitudinous higher degrees; not merely informed but dazzlingly knowledgeable; not merely unprejudiced but brilliantly questing. And my colleagues believed exactly what my students believed.

My colleagues were, let it be noted, members of the Department of English in the prestige college of an important university. I was, let it be revealed, the only woman instructor in that department. Some years before, the college had been all male. Then the coeds were invited in, and now and then in their wake a woman was admitted, often reluctantly, to the faculty. Before my own admittance, I had been living the isolated life of a writer—my occupation for some years had consisted in reading great quantities and in writing embarrassingly tiny quantities. I was, I suppose, not in that condition generally known as "being in touch with the world." I was in touch with novels, poetry, essays, enlarging meditations; but of "the world," as it turned out, I apparently knew little.

I came to the university in search of the world. I had just finished an enormous novel, the writing of which had taken many more years than any novel ought to take, and after so long a retreat my lust for the world was prodigious. I wanted Experience, I wanted to sleep under bridges—but finding that all the bridges had thickly trafficked cloverleafs under them, I came instead to the university. I came innocently. I had believed, through all those dark and hope-sickened years of writing, that it was myself ("myself"—whatever that means for each of us) who was doing the writing. In the university, among my colleagues, I discovered two essential points: (1) that it was a "woman" who had done the writing—not a mind— and that I was a "woman writer"; and (2) that I was now not a teacher, but a "woman teacher."

I was suspect from the beginning—more so among my colleagues than among my students. My students, after all, were accustomed to the idea of a "woman teacher," having recently been taught by several in high school. But my colleagues were long out of high school, and they distrusted me. I learned that I had no genuinely valid opinions, since every view I might hold was colored by my sex. If I said I didn't like Hemingway, I could have no *critical* justification, no *literary* reason; it was only because, being a woman, I obviously could not be sympathetic toward Hemingway's "masculine" subject matter— the hunting, the fishing, the bullfighting which no woman could adequately digest. It goes without saying that among my colleagues there were other Hemingway dissenters; but their reasons for disliking Hemingway, unlike mine, were not taken to be simply ovarian.

In fact, both my students and my colleagues were equal adherents of the Ovarian Theory of Literature, or, rather, its complement, the Testicular Theory. A recent camp follower (I cannot call him a pioneer) of this explicit theory is, of course, Norman Mailer, who has attributed his own gift, and the literary gift in general, solely and directly to the possession of a specific pair of organs. One writes with these organs, Mailer has said in *Advertisements for Myself;* and I have always wondered with what shade of ink he manages to do it.

I recall my first encounter with the Ovarian Theory. My students had been assigned the reading of *Wise Blood,* the novella by Flannery O'Connor. Somewhere in the discussion I referred to the author as "she." The class stirred in astonishment; they had not imagined that "Flannery" could connote a woman, and this somehow put a different cast upon the narrative and their response to it. Now among my students there was a fine young woman, intelligent and experimental rather than conforming, one of my rare literates, herself an anomaly because she was enrolled in the overwhelmingly male College of Engineering. I knew that her mind usually sought beyond the common-place—she wrote with the askew glance of the really inquisitive. Up went her hand. "But I could *tell* she was a woman," she insisted. "Her sentences are a woman's sentences." I asked her what she meant and how she could tell. "Because they're sentimental," she said, "they're not concrete like a man's." I pointed out whole paragraphs, pages even, of unsentimental, so-called tough prose. "But she *sounds* like a woman—she has to sound that way because she is," said the future engineer, while I speculated whether her bridges and buildings would loom plainly as woman's work. Moreover, it rapidly developed that the whole class now declared that it too, even while ignorant of the author's sex, had nevertheless intuited all along that this was a woman's prose; it had to be, since Flannery was a she.

My second encounter with the idea of literature-as-physiology was odder yet. This time my interlocutor was a wonderfully gentle, deeply intellectual, young fellow teacher; he was going to *prove* what my freshmen had merely maintained. "But of course style is influenced by physical make-up," he began in his judicious graduate-assistant way. Here was his incontrovertible evidence: "Take Keats, right? Keats fighting tuberculosis at the end of his life. You don't suppose Keats's poetry was totally unaffected by his having had tuberculosis?" And he smiled with the flourish of a young man who has made an unanswerable point. "Ah, but *you* don't suppose," I put it to him cheerfully enough, "that being a woman is a *disease?*"

But comparing literary women with having a debilitating disease is the least of it. My colleague, after all, was a kindly sort, and stuck to human matters; he did not mention dogs. On the other hand, almost everyone remembers Dr. Johnson's remark upon hearing a woman preacher—she reminded him, he said, of a dog dancing on its hind legs; one marvels not at how well it is done, but that it is done at all. That was two centuries ago; wise Lady Mary was Johnson's contemporary. Two centuries, and the world of letters had not been altered by a syllable, unless you regard the switch from dogs to disease as a rudimentary advance. Perhaps it is. We have advanced so

far that the dullest as well as the best of freshmen can
scarcely be distinguished from Dr. Johnson, except by a
bark.

And our own Dr. Johnson—I leave you to guess his
name—hoping to insult a rival writer, announces that the
rival "reminds me of nothing so much as a woman
writer."

Consider, in this vein, the habits of reviewers. I think I
can say in good conscience that I have never—repeat,
never—read a review of a novel or, especially, of a
collection of poetry by a woman which did not include
somewhere in its columns a gratuitous allusion to the
writer's sex and its supposed effects. The Ovarian Theory
of Literature is the property of all society, not merely of
freshmen and poor Ph.D. lackeys: you will find it in all
the best periodicals, even the most highbrow. For example: a few years ago a critic in *The New York Review of
Books* considered five novels, three of which were by
women. And so his review begins: "Women novelists, we
have learned to assume, like to keep their focus narrow."
And from this touchstone—with no ground other than the
"we have learned to assume"—falls his praise and his censure. The touchstone, of course, is properly qualified, as
such touchstones always are, by reverent asides concerning
the breadth of George Eliot and the grasp of Jane Austen.
Ah, indispensable George and Jane! They have come into
the world, one concludes, only to serve as exceptions to
the strictures of reviewers; and they *are* exceptions. Genius always is; it is how genius is defined. But if the
exception is to be dragged into every routine review of
novelists and poets who are women, then the rule must
drop equally on all. Let every new poet, male and female,
be reviewed in the shadow of Emily Dickinson and
Coleridge. Let every unknown novelist, male and female,
be reviewed in the blaze of *Anna Karenina* and *Wuthering
Heights*. If this seems like nonsense, then reviewers must
take merit as their point of concentration, not the flap of
skirts, not the glibbest of literary canards.

Still, the canards are, in their way, great fun, being as
flexible and fragile as other toys. A collection of canards is
bound to be a gaggle of contradictions. When, for instance, my bright engineering student identified Flannery
O'Connor as "sentimental," she was squarely in one-half
of a diluvial, though bifurcated, tradition. Within this
tradition there are two hoary veins of woman. One: she is

sentimental, imprecise, irrational, overemotional, impatient, unperseveringly flighty, whimsical, impulsive, unreliable, unmechanical, not given to practicality, perilously vague, and so on. In this view she is always contrasted with man, who is, on the other hand, unsentimental, exact, rational, controlled, patient, hard-headed, mechanically gifted, a meeter of payrolls, firm of purpose, wary of impulse, anything but a dreamer. Description One accounts for why throughout her history she has been a leader neither of empires nor of trades nor of armies. But it is also declared that, her nature having failed her in the practical world, she cannot succeed in the world of invention either: she is unequipped, for example, for poetry, in that (here is Description Two) she is above all pragmatic, sensible and unsentimental, unvisionary, unadventurous, empirical, conservative, down-to-earth, unspontaneous, perseveringly patient and thus good at the minutiae of mechanical and manipulative tasks, and essentially unimaginative. In short, she will wander too much or she will wander not at all. She is either too emotional or she is not emotional enough. She is either too spontaneous or she is not spontaneous enough. She is either too sensitive (that is why she cannot be president of General Motors) or she is not sensitive enough (that is why she will never write *King Lear*).

But none of this is to imply that woman is damned, and damned from every direction. Not at all. The fact is that woman *qua* woman is more often celebrated. If she cannot hear the Muse, says Robert Graves, what does it matter? She *is* the Muse. *Man Does, Woman Is* is the title of Grave's most recent collection of poetry. If we are expected to conclude from this that woman is an It rather than a Thou (to use Martin Buber's categories), why deplore it? The Parthenon too is beautiful, passive, inspiring. Who would long to *build* it, if one can *be* it?

And even this is unfair, for it is simultaneously true that woman is frequently praised as the more "creative" sex. She does not need to make poems, it is argued; she has no drive to make poems, because she is privileged to make babies. A pregnancy is as fulfilling as, say, Yeats' *Sailing to Byzantium*. Here is an interesting idea worth examination. To begin wtih, we would have to know what it cost Yeats—I am speaking physically—to wring out a poem of genius. Perhaps we cannot know this. The writing of great and visionary literature is not a common experience and is not readily explorable. A. E. Housman—a lesser poet than Yeats, to be sure, though as pure a one—said of the genesis of a poem that it affected his flesh: that if a wisp of a line came to him while he was in the middle of shaving, for instance, he could sense the bristles standing on end. Most poets, if they speak of it at all, report extreme exhaustion accompanied by supreme exaltation. Yeats himself spoke of the poet living amid whirlwinds. Virginia Woolf, a writer of a kind of prose very near poetry in tone and aspiration, was racked in the heat of composition by seizures of profoundly tormenting headaches. Isaac Babel called himself a "galley slave." Conrad was in a frenzy for weeks on end—"I turn in this vicious circle and the work itself becomes like the work in a treadmill—a thing without joy—a punishing task. . . . I am at it day after day, and I want all day, every minute of a day, to produce a beggarly tale of words or perhaps to produce nothing at all. . . . One's will becomes a slave of hallucinations, responds only to shadowy impulses, waits on imagination alone." Dostoevski said plainly: *"I worked and was tortured."* Flaubert wrote, "You don't know what it is to stay a whole day with your head in your hands trying to squeeze your unfortunate brain so as to find a word." Tolstoy told a friend, "One ought only to write when one leaves a piece of flesh in the ink-pot each time one dips one's pen." For Isak Dinesen, the "great and difficult task" was pursued "without faith and without hope." And George Eliot said of the writing of *Romola*—it occupied two years—that she began it young, and finished it old.

That is what "creativity" is. Is a pregnancy like that? The fact is, given health (and one must never assume the abnormal, since being a woman is really *not* like having a disease), the condition of pregnancy is—in the consciousness—very nearly like the condition of nonpregnancy. It is insulting to a poet to compare his titanic and agonized strivings with the so-called "creativity" of childbearing, where—consciously—nothing happens. One does not will the development of the fetus; one can be as dull or as active, or as bored or as intense, as one pleases—anything else is mere self-absorption and daydream: the process itself is as involuntary and as unaware as the beating of one's own heart. Of course, it is a miracle that one's heart goes on beating, that the fetus goes on growing—but it is not a human miracle, it is Nature's miracle. If we want to talk about Nature, very well—but now we are talking about literature. To produce a new human being out of a pair of cells is a marvel, but it is not *our* marvel. Once we, male and female, have joined two disparate cells by our human wills, the rest is done for us, not by us. The woman's body is a vessel, thereafter, for a parasite. For the presence of the parasite she is thereafter no more responsible than she is for the presence of her intestinal tract. To call a child a poem may be a pretty metaphor, but it is a slur on the labor of art. Literature cannot be equated with physiology, and woman through her reproductive system alone is no more a creative artist than was Joyce by virtue of his kidneys alone, or James by virtue of his teeth (which, by the way, were troublesome). A poem emerges from a mind, and mind is, so far as our present knowledge takes us, an unknowable abstraction. Perhaps it is a compliment to a woman of no gifts to say of her in compensation, "Ah, well, but she has made a child." But that is a cheap and slippery mythology, and a misleading one. It induces the false value of self-inflation in mediocre women. It is scarcely our duty to compliment the mediocre for their mediocrity when we are hardly employed enough in celebrating the gifted for their gifts, wrung out by the toil of desire and imagination. It takes something away from Yeats to compare a mediocre child—and most children, like most parents, *are* mediocre—with *Sailing to Byzantium*. But it is just as irrelevant to compare a brilliant child with a brilliant poem. Biology is *there:* it does not need our praise, and if we choose to praise it, it is blasphemous to think we are praising not God but ourselves.[1]

All this is, one would think, almost stupefyingly obvious. It is embarrassing, it is humiliating, to be so obvious about the quality either of literature or of woman. She, at any rate, is not a Muse, nor is she on the strength of her womb alone an artist. She is—how stupidly obvious—a person. She can be an artist if she was born talented. She can be a Muse if she inspires a poet, but she too (if she was born talented) can find her own Muse in another person. Mme. de Sévigné's Muse was her daughter, and what male Muse it was who inspired Emily Brontë's Heathcliffe, history continues to conjecture. The Muse— *pace* Robert Graves—has no settled sex or form, and can appear in the shape of a tree (*Howard's End*) or a city (the Paris of *The Ambassadors*) or even—think of Proust—a cookie.

Yet in our culture, in our country, much is not obvious.

With respect to woman and with respect to literature (I refer you again to the reviewers), ours is among the most backward areas on earth. It is true that woman has had the vote for fifty years and has begun to enter most professions, though often without an invitation. We are far past the grievances Virginia Woolf grappled with in *A Room of One's Own* and *Three Guineas*—books which are still sneered at as "feminist." In 1929, when Virginia Woolf visited Oxford (or was it Cambridge? she is too sly to say which), she was chased off a lawn forbidden to the feet of women. By then, of course, our colleges were already full of coeds, though not so full as now. And yet the question of justification remains. Only a few months ago, in my own college, a startling debate was held— "Should a Woman Receive a College Education?" The audience was immense, but the debaters were only three: an instructor in anthropology (female), a professor of history (male), and a fiercely bearded professor of psychology (ostentatiously male). According to the unironic conventions of chivalry, the anthropologist spoke first. She spoke of opportunities and of problems. She spoke of living wholly and well. She did not ignore the necessities and difficulties of housekeeping and childrearing; she spoke of the relations of parents, children, and work-in-the-world; she talked extensively about nursery schools. She took as her premise not merely that women ought to be fully educated, but that her education should be fully used in society. She was reasoned and reasonable; she had a point of view. Perhaps it was a controversial point of view, perhaps not—her listeners never had the chance of a serious evaluation. Her point of view was never assailed or refuted. It was overlooked. She spoke—against mysterious whispered cackles in the audience—and sat. Then up rose the laughing psychologist, and cracked jokes through his beard. Then up rose the laughing historian, and cracked jokes through his field—I especially remember one about the despotism of Catherine the Great. "That's what happens when a woman gets emancipated." Laughter from all sides. Were the historian and the psychologist laughing at the absurdity of the topic the callow students' committee had selected for debate? An absurd topic—it deserves to be laughed out of court, and surely that is exactly what is happening, for here in the audience are all these coeds, censuring and contradicting by their very presence the outrageous question. Yet look again: the coeds are laughing too. Everyone is laughing the laughter of mockery. They are not laughing at the absurdly callow topic. They are laughing at the buffoonery of the historian and the psychologist, who are themselves laughing at the subject of the topic: the whole huge room, packed to the very doors and beyond with mocking boys and girls, is laughing at the futility of an educated woman. *She* is the absurdity.

The idea of an educated woman is not yet taken seriously in American universities. She is not chased off the campus, she is even welcomed there—but she is not taken seriously as a student, and she will not be welcomed if she hopes to return as a serious lifelong scholar. Nor will she be welcomed afterward in the "world." A law firm may hire her, but it will hide her in its rear research offices, away from the eyes of clients. The lower schools will receive her, as they always have, for she is their bulwark; their bulwark, but not their principal, who is a man. We have seen her crawling like Griselda through the long ordeal of medicine: she is almost always bound to be a pediatrician, for it is in her nature to "work with children."

I will not forget the appalling laughter of the two mocking debaters. But it was not so appalling as the laughter of the young men and the young women in the audience. In the laughter of the historian and the psychologist I heard the fussy cry—a cry of violated venerable decorum, no doubt—of the beadle who chased Virginia Woolf off the grass in 1929. But what of that youthful mockery? Their laughter was hideous; it showed something ugly and self-shaming about the nature of our society and the nature of our education—and by "our education" I do not mean the colleges, I mean the kindergartens, I mean the livingrooms at home, I mean the fathers and the mothers, the men and the women.

In this country the women, by and large, are at home. Let us consider that first. Most of the women are at home. Why are they at home? Well, plainly because they belong there. They are there to rear the children, and if they have a whole lot of children (in our country they have an amazing number of children, without regard to the diet of algae they are imposing on their children's children), there will usually be a helpless baby. The mother is at home to take care of the helpless baby. That is right and reasonable. Everyone agrees—Nature agrees, the father agrees, Society agrees. Society agrees? That is very interesting. That too is an idea worth examination. It is very useful for society to have the mother at home. It keeps her out of the way. If, say, she stopped at only two children (but if she stopped at only two she would be in danger of reducing the birth rate, which now rivals India's), those two might be half-grown, and safely shut up in a school building most of the day, by the time she is thirty-five. And if she were thirty-five—a young, healthy, able, educated thirty-five—with no helpless baby to keep her at home, and most of the day free, what would she do? Society shudders at the possibility: she might want to get a job. But that would never do. Why, if you counted up all the young, healthy, able, educated, free women of thirty-five, it might come to nearly half the population! And, as things stand now, there are not even enough jobs for the other half of the population, the truly breadwinning half. And what about all those three-quarters-grown persons we call adolescents? Society shudders at them too: the economy is an inn with no room for adolescents and women. But if it will not allow adolescents and women to share in its work (How can it? So much of the work is done by machines), society must at least provide something else to keep the adolescents and women occupied, if only artifically. So, out of the largesse of its infinitely adaptable lap, it gives women knitting and adolescents transistor radios to dance to. (And for the adolescents of even mediocre capacities—here there is not so much discrimination by sex—it comes up with colleges, and fraudulent debates, and more dancing.) Society provides a complete— and in essence custodial—culture for each group it is forced to keep out of the way. It is a culture of busywork and make-believe and distraction. Society is very clever and always has been. Once upon a time, before machines, women and adolescents *were* needed and used to the last degree in the economy. Women were not educated because an unautomated house requires a work horse to maintain it, and a woman who cannot read or write is somehow better at hauling water in from the pump than one who can. (Why this should be, only the experience of society can explain.) But now society—so long as we fail to renovate it —can furnish work for only a quarter of the population, and so the rest must be lured into thinking it is performing a job when it is really not doing anything beyond breathing.

That is why there are in our society separate minority cultures for adolescents and for women. Each has its own set of opinions, prejudices, tastes, values, and—do not underestimate this last—magazines. You and I are here concerned only with the culture of women. Society, remember, is above men and women; it acts *in* men and women. So you must not make the mistake of thinking that the culture of women is the conspiracy of men. Not in the least. That is an old-fashioned, bluestocking view of the matter, and it is erroneous. The culture of women is believed in by both men and women, and it is the conspiracy of neither, because it is the creature neither of men alone, nor of women alone, but of society itself—that autonomous, cunning, insensitive sibling of history.

The culture of women consists in many, many things—products as well as attitudes, but attitudes mostly. The attitudes generate the products, and the products utilize the attitudes. The most overriding attitude is summed up in a cult word: "home." (Notice that builders do not sell houses, they sell homes—a case of attitude and product coalescing.) But what does "Home" mean? It means curtains, rugs, furniture, a boiler in the cellar, magazines with dress patterns and recipes and articles full of adulterated Freud, a dog, a box of cereal bones for the dog, a kitchen floor that conscience insists must be periodically waxed, and so forth: but mostly, of course, it means "Children." And "Children" are not regarded as incomplete or new persons, as unformed destinies, as embryo participants in the society; above all, they are not regarded simply as *children:* they are a make-believe entity in themselves, a symbol of need and achievement, just as the dog biscuits (not real bones) are a make-believe entity in themselves (does the dog think they are real?). "Children" as a concept have, in their present incarnation, a definite function, which is to bolster the whole airy system of make-believe. "Children" are there to justify "Home"; and "Home" is there to justify a third phantom entity—the heroine of the fairy tale, also an invention and an abstraction, the "Homemaker."

In this sense, neither "Home" nor "Children" nor "Homemaker" has any reality at all. All are dissemblances, fables, daydreams. All are abstractions designed to give the prestige of sham significance to a fairy tale. Nothing here is in the least related to living persons or to life itself. "Home" and "Children" and "Homemaker" are fabrications in the same sense that a bank is a fabrication: we pretend we are passing something called money, but meanwhile a bookkeeper (that is, a computer) is simply balancing the columns in an account book, more on this side of the line, less on that side. If we should all insist on exchanging metal again, the bank fabrication would dissolve. And when the "Children" grow up a little, refuse to be players in the game of gauze, and insist at last on being real persons, does "Home" dissolve, does "Homemaker" dissolve? Only partially. Because now society steps in and sweeps up the remains under the heading of "Womanhood." The children go away, the dog dies, the house wears out, but "Womanhood" is eternal. Its possessor, the creature in whom "Womanhood" is immanent (divinely as it were), has her magazines to prove her reality—her reality, mind you, as a concept called "Woman," endowed with another concept called "Womanhood"; she has the benevolent chorus of society to prove it, she has the bearded psychologist and the professor of history to prove it, she has the laughing girls and boys to prove it.

They "prove" it perhaps—the Ptolemaic system was also in error, and its proofs were magnificent—but they do not justify *her*. No fabrication can be justified. Only a person can be justified. A person is justified by the quality of his life; but a daydream is not a life, no matter how many propose to declare it so.

This is our "problem"—the problem of a majority's giving its credence and its loyalty to a daydream. And it is a bigger problem than any other we know of in this country, for the plain and terrifying reason that we have not even considered it to be a problem. Whenever the cliché-question is put, "What is the number one problem in America today?" the cliché-answer comes: "Civil rights—the Black Revolution." Scarcely. The solution to that problem is there—we have only to catch up to it, with all our might. If the debate at my college had dealt with civil rights it would have been serious, passionate, and argumentative. We had a Vietnam teach-in: *it* was serious and passionate and argumentative. But until now no one has been serious and passionate, and certainly no one has been argumentative, concerning attitudes about woman. Once a problem has been articulated, the answer is implicit; the answer is already fated. But this problem was never articulated; there was no answer, because no one ever asked the question. It was a question that had not yet found its Baldwin. Its substance was, on every level, the stuff of primitive buffoonery.

Virginia Woolf is the artist-pioneer, the Margaret-Sanger-as-bard, so to speak, of this social question. Among artists she has no successor. Not until art has seized and possessed and assimilated this question will it begin to interest the scientist-humanists.

But what are the components of the question? Perhaps they can once again crudely be set out, though they are so old and so tiresome, though we have no poet to speak them forth once and for all, though we handle them with the weariness of overuse. Here they are: no great female architects, painters, playwrights, sailors, bridgebuilders, jurists, captains, composers, etc., etc. Everyone knows that list; everyone can recite it at length, now and then hesitating to allow for a Saint Joan or an empress or an influential courtesan or a salon wit. But the list of omissions is long, as long almost as history, or, to use a more telling simile, as long almost as the history of the Jews.

And here I think of a curious analogy. Say what you will about the gifted Jews, they have never, up until times so recent that they scarcely begin to count, been plastic artists. Where is the Jewish Michelangelo, the Jewish Rembrandt, the Jewish Rodin? He has never come into being. Why? Have oppression and persecution erased the possibility of his existence? Hardly. Oppression and persecution often tend to reinforce gifts; to proscribe is more effective than to prescribe. Where then *is* the Jewish Michelangelo? Is it possible that a whole people cannot produce a single painter? And not merely a single painter of note, but a single painter at all? Well, there have been artists among the Jews—artisans, we should more likely call them, decorators of trivial ceremonial objects, a wine cup here, a scroll cover there. Talented a bit, but nothing great. They never tried their hand at wood or stone or paint. "Thou shalt have no graven images"—the Second Commandment—prevented them. And it is not until a very, very little while ago, under the influence of a movement called "Emancipation" or "Enlightenment," that we begin to see creeping in a Chagall, a Modigliani, an Epstein, who have ceased to believe that art insults the Unity of God. It will be a long, long time before the Jews have their Michelangelo. Before a "David" can happen, a thousand naked Apollos must be hewn. (And Apollo *did* insult the Unity of God.) There must be a readied ground, a preparation—in short, a relevant living culture to frame the event.

The same, I think, with our problem. Gifts and brains are not transmitted, like hemophilia, from the immune sex to the susceptible sex. Genius is the property of both sexes and all nations alike. That is the humanist view. The Jews have had no artists not because they have had no genius for art, but because their image of themselves as a culture inhibited the exercise of the latent gift. And all those nonexistent female Newtons and Bachs and Leonardos and Shakespeares (all? surely they would be very few indeed, so rare is genius of that degree)—they have had no more chance of leaping from the prison of their societal fates than any Greek slave, or a nomad's child in Yemen today. The emancipation of women is spectacularly new. As with what we now call the Black Revolution, it is clear that emancipation does not instantly result in achievement. Enlightenment must follow. And the enlightenment has, for women, and especially by women, not yet occurred.

It has not yet occurred even at the most expressive point of all—in the universities. It is the function of a liberal university not to give right answers, but to ask right questions. And the ultimate humanist question, as we have seen, has not yet been expressed (my students had never in all their lives heard it put); the components of the unrealized question, as we have seen, are the experiences and needs and omissions and premises of a culture. A culture can have a seemingly unchanging premise, and then suddenly it will change; hence, among the Jews, Chagall and Modigliani and Epstein; hence, in literature, the early epistolary artists—Mme. de Sévigné and Lady Mary—and then, close on their heels, the genius novelists, Jane and George. Literature was the first to begin it, since literature could be pursued privately and at home. But here let us listen to Elizabeth Hardwick: "Who is to say that *Remembrance of Things Past* is 'better' than the marvelous *Emma? War and Peace* better than *Middlemarch? Moby Dick* superior to *La Princess de Clèves*? But everybody says so! It is only the whimsical, the cantankerous, the eccentric . . . who would say that any literary work by a woman, marvelous as these may be, is on a level with the very greatest accomplishments of men."[2] I am not sure it is whimsical, cantankerous, or eccentric not to feel the need to make such distinctions, but even if the distinctions *are* justified—perhaps they are, I cannot tell—who is to say that *Emma* and *Middlemarch* and *La Princess de Clèves* are not simply forerunners? In England Lady Mary preceded Jane. In France Mme. de Sévigné preceded George Sand. Cultivation precedes fruition. Perhaps we cannot have our great women architects, painters, playwrights, sailors, bridgebuilders, jurists, captains, composers, and so forth, until we have run-of-the-mill women in these roles, until all that is a commonplace—until in short, women enter into the central stream of mankind's activities, until woman-as-person becomes as flat and unremarked a tradition as man-as-person. Reproduction, trick it out as you will in this or that myth, is still only reproduction, a natural and necessary biological function, and biology, however fancied up with tribal significance and mystical implication, is not enough. Unless you are on the extreme verge of death, it is never enough just to keep on breathing.

Even woman's differing muscular capacity—much is made of this, unsurprisingly—is, in the age of the comprehensive machine, an obstacle to almost no pursuit. It would be difficult to insist that a woman on board the sort of ship Conrad describes in that remarkable novella *Youth* would be as efficient as most male members of the crew; but muscle is no longer an issue anywhere. Evolution has now become, in Julian Huxley's words, a "psychosocial process"—that is, man is now able consciously to contribute to his own development. He lives, Huxley writes, "not only in relation with the physicochemical and biological environment provided by nature, but with the psychosocial environment of material and mental habitats which he has himself created," and those habitats include the muscle-augmenting machine and its incalculable influences. Might a woman have written *Youth*? Who would dare to say yes? In Conrad's day—in the scope of technology a very short time ago—almost no woman and very few men could have the stamina to wrest out Conrad's incredible sea experience. Yet the machine widens experience for everyone and equalizes the physical endurance of men and women. A long journey is no longer a matter of muscle, but of jet schedules. Presumably it will become harder and harder to maintain that novelists who are women are condemned to a narrower focus than men because their lives are perforce narrower. The cult of Experience is, more and more, accessible to anyone who wishes to be lured by it: though it might well be argued that novels and poems grow out of something other than raw physical experience. "It is not suggested," Elizabeth Hardwick continues, "that muscles write books, but there is a certain sense in which, talent and experience being equal, they may be considered a bit of an advantage. In the end, it is in the matter of experience that women's disadvantage is catastrophic. It is very difficult to know how this may be extraordinarily altered."[3] Huxley's self-propelled evolutionary view is more optimistic, though perhaps both views, Hardwick's and Huxley's are at bottom equally irrelevant to the making of literature, which is, after all, as unknown a quantity as mind itself.

The question is then, I believe, a question touching at least peripherally on art. Not merely literary art, but all the human arts, including those we call science. And I have ventured that the question must be formulated as a humanistic issue, not a sectarian one, not a divisive one. Art must belong to all human beings, not alone to a traditionally privileged segment; every endeavor, every passion must be available to the susceptible adult, without the intervention of myth or canard. Woman will cease solely to be man's Muse—an It (as she is, curiously, for writers as disparate as Graves and Mailer, as she was for Freud)—and will acquire Muses of her own when she herself ceases to be bemused with gaudy daydreams and romances—with lies reinforcing lies—about her own nature. She limits—she self-limits—her aspirations and her expectations. She joins the general mockery at her possibilities. I have heard her laughing at herself as though she were a dancing dog. You have seen her regard her life as a disease to be constantly tended and pacified. She does not yet really believe that she is herself accessible to poetry or science: she whistles these into her sons, but not into her daughters. She surrounds herself with the devices and manipulations of an identity that is not an identity. Without protest she permits the intractable momentum of society to keep her from its worthiness and larger adventures, from its expressive labor. She lives among us like a docile captive; a consuming object; an accomplice; an It. She has even been successfully persuaded to work for and at her own imprisonment. No one can deny that imprisonment offers advantages, especially to the morally lazy. There have been slaves who have rejoiced in their slavery (think of the Children of Israel yearning day and night for the fleshpots of Egypt), and female infantilism is a kind of pleasurable slavishness. Dependency, the absence of decisions and responsibility, the avoidance of risk, the shutting out of the gigantic toil of art—all these are the comforts of the condoning contented subject, and when these are combined, as they are in this country, with excessive leisure, it would almost seem that woman has a vested interest in her excluded role. If one were to bow to the tempting idea that her role has come about through a conspiracy (as it could not have, for custom is no plot), it would appear as though it were a conspiracy of sluggish women, and never of excluding men. The fervor and energies of the women who are not lazy, those rare activist personalities who feel the call of a Cause, are thrown pragmatically[4] into the defense of that easy and comfortable role; the barricades of the pleasant prison are manned—no, womanned—by the inmates themselves, to prevent the rebels from breaking out.

But the rebels are few.

That is because, among us, for a long time no one rebelled, no one protested, no one wanted to renovate or liberate, no one asked any fundamental question. We have had, alas, and still have, the doubtful habit of reverence. Above all, we respect things as they are. If we want to step on the moon, it is not to explore an unknown surface or divine a new era, but to bolster ourselves at home, among the old home rivals; there is more preening than science in that venture, less boldness than bravado. We are so placid that the smallest tremor of objection to anything at all is taken as a full-scale revolution. Should any soul speak up in favor of the obvious, it is taken as a symptom of the influence of the left, the right, the pink, the black, the dangerous. An idea for its own sake—especially an obvious idea—has no respectability.

Among my students—let us come back to *them*, for they are our societal prototypes—all this was depressingly plain. That is why they could not write intelligibly—no one had ever mentioned the relevance of writing to thinking, and thinking had never been encouraged or induced in them. By "thinking" I mean, of course, not the simple ability to make equations come out right, but the devotion to speculation on that frail but obsessive distraction known as the human condition. My students—male and female— did not need to speculate on what goals are proper to the full life; male and female, they already knew their goals.

And their goals were identical. They all wanted to settle down into a perpetual and phantom coziness. They were all at heart sentimentalists—and sentimentalists, Yeats said, are persons "who believe in money, in position, in a marriage bell, and whose understanding of happiness is to be so busy whether at work or play, that all is forgotten but the momentary aim." Accordingly, they had all opted, long ago, perhaps at birth, for the domestic life, the enclosed life, the restricted life—the life, in brief, of the daydream, into which the obvious must not be permitted to thrust its scary beams.

By the "obvious" I mean, once again, the gifts and teachings and life illuminations of art. The methods of art are variegated, flexible, abstruse, and often enough mysterious. But the burden of art is obvious: here is the world, here are human beings, here is childhood, here is struggle, here is hate, here is old age, here is death. None of these is a fantasy, a romance, or a sentiment, none is an imagining; all are obvious. A culture which does not allow itself to look clearly at the obvious through the universal accessibility of art is a culture of tragic delusion, hardly viable; it will make room for a system of fantasy Offices on the one hand, and a system of fantasy Homes on the other, but it will forget that the earth lies beneath all. It will turn out role-playing stereotypes (the hideousness of the phrase is appropriate to the concept) instead of human beings. It will shut the children away from half the population. It will shut aspiration away from half the population. It will glut its colleges with young people enduringly maimed by illusions learned early and kept late. It will sup on make-believe. But a humanist society— you and I do not live in one—is one in which a voice is heard: "Come," it says, "here is a world requiring architects, painters, playwrights, sailors, bridgebuilders, jurists, captains, composers, discoverers, and a thousand things besides, all real and all obvious. Partake," it says, "live."

Is it a man's voice or a woman's voice? Students, colleagues, listen again; it is two voices. "How obvious," you will one day reply, and if you laugh, it will be at the quaint folly of obsolete custom, which once failed to harness the obvious; it will not be at a dancing dog.

NOTES

1. Sometimes the analogy is made not between poetry and childbearing proper, but between poetry and an idealized domesticity. Here is the versifier Phyllis McGinley writing in an advertisement for and in the *New York Times:* "I know a remarkable woman who is a true artist, domestic version. She creates an atmosphere in which her children and her husband can move with delight and peace, pouring out all the passion which Emily Dickinson might have spent on perfecting a stanza or—to update the comparison—as Joan Sutherland does on interpreting an aria. Her masterpiece consists of her family, her house, her community duties." But would the gifted Miss McGinley be willing to reverse the metaphor, and compare her witty verses with mopping under the bed? Or match Emily Dickinson's "I Heard a Fly Buzz when I Died" with a good nourishing family breakfast, or a morning on the telephone for the P.T.A.? Or liken rendering an aria to sitting down to an editorial in the *Times?* This sleight-of-mind does not seem to work in reverse: art will not be lessened.

    Besides, why must the obvious always be avoided with this pompous posturing, these analogues and similes? Why can't a mop be called a mop, and one who mops a mopper?
2. Elizabeth Hardwick, *A View of One's Own* (New York: Farrar, Straus & Giroux, 1966).
3. Hardwick, *op. cit.*
4. See previous footnote on Phyllis McGinley.

20

WOMEN WRITERS AND THE DOUBLE STANDARD

Elaine Showalter

Women writers in the nineteenth century were measured against a feminine, rather than a literary ideal. Even the term "woman writer," in its straightforward juxtaposition of a neutral feminine term with a neutral professional one, was a paradox for the Victorians; the associations of "woman" and the associations of "writer" were too far apart to be connected without strain. So the Victorians frequently substituted other terms—authoress, female pen, female writer, and, most characteristically, the delicately chivalrous term, lady novelist. Such terms served as constant reminders that women writers were a separate and inferior species of artist. Everyone expected that the female of the species would be weaker than the male; on the other hand, a lady novelist, if she behaved like a lady, ought not to be treated harshly or impolitely in a review, anymore than she ought to be forced to endure bad manners in a drawing room.

But the generation of women writers to which the Brontës, Mrs. Gaskell, George Eliot, Geraldine Jewsbury, and Elizabeth Barrett Browning belonged did not wish reviewers to be kind to them, to overlook their weaknesses, to flatter them on their accomplishments sim-

ply because of their sex; in this repudiation of the courtesy
ladies might exact from gentlemen, they were rebelling
against the feminine ideal and all its restrictions. As long
as ladies had to request masculine indulgence and protection, they could not expect to be considered as equals.
Victorian women writers would not cringe and plead
weakness; instead, they spoke intensely of their desire to
avoid special treatment, of their wish to achieve genuine
excellence, and of their determination to face rigorous and
impartial criticism. Most women writers felt humiliated by
the condescension of critics; by what Mrs. Browning labeled "the comparative respect which means that absolute
scorn." In *Aurora Leigh* (1856) she parodied the typical
review a woman could expect:

> What grace! What facile turns! What fluent sweeps!
> What delicate discernment . . . almost thought!
> The book does honour to the sex, we hold.
>
> Among our female authors we make room
> For this fair writer, and congratulate
> The country that produces in these times
> Such women, competent to . . . spell.

In part, this new spirit of pride and independence came
in response to the increasingly acknowledged dominance
of the novel form. Even before George Eliot had tried to
write novels herself, she felt deep interest in and respect
for the possibilities of the form, and had begun to consider the contributions women might make to it. She appealed to critics to exercise discrimination in their judgments, and not to be swayed by chivalry; severity, she
thought, was ultimately the kindest service a critic might
render the genre of the novel, and the future of women
novelists. In "Silly Novels by Lady Novelists," (1856) her
famous satiric review of several subspecies of feminine
fiction, she states her hope that

> every critic who forms a high estimate of the share women
> may ultimately take in literature, will, on principle, abstain
> from any exceptional indulgence toward the productions of
> literary women. For it must be plain to every one who
> looks impartially and extensively into feminine literature,
> that its greatest deficiencies are due hardly more to the
> want of intellectual power than to the want of those moral
> qualities that contribute to literary excellence—patient dili-

gence, a sense of the responsibility involved in publication, and an appreciation of the sacredness of the writer's art.[1]

In this article, written just ten days before she began her first work of fiction, *Amos Barton*, George Eliot was declaring some of her own artistic credos and measuring her own talents against the deficiencies of the opposition. But in addition to the personal motive, one recognizes in this essay the familiar Victorian exhortations to earnestness, duty, and self-reliance. Just as the feminists were urging women to work, to make themselves useful, to put aside needlework and sketching for charity work and teaching, so George Eliot was attempting to get the frivolity out of fiction by frightening away the incompetent. Neither was she to be softened by pleas of financial need: "Where there is one woman who writes from necessity, we believe there are three women who write for vanity; and besides, there is something so antiseptic in the mere healthy fact of working for one's bread, that the most trashy and rotten kind of feminine literature is not likely to have been produced under such circumstances."

Addressing herself directly to women, Dinah Mulock Craik, a novelist of far more modest abilities than George Eliot, expressed nonetheless the same ideals of artistic integrity and the same scorn of the dilettante. Women must not deceive themselves about their abilities; they must not confuse their feminine and their professional roles. "In any profession," Mrs. Craik wrote, "there is nothing, short of being absolutely evil, which is so injurious, so fatal, as mediocrity. . . . Therefore, let men do as they will—and truly they are often ten times vainer and more ambitious than we:—but I would advise every woman to examine herself and judge herself, morally and intellectually, by the sharpest tests of criticism, before she attempts art or literature, either from abstract fame, or as a means of livelihood."[2]

Undeniably, personal ambition and frustration throbs fiercely beneath the surface of these statements on literary women. What was the use of laborious dedication to one's art if any moralizing fool enjoyed an equal critical esteem? Why bother to achieve perfection when one's efforts would be greeted with compliments cheaply obtained by any woman who was willing to make herself an object of pity? Privately, they might be indignant at the rudeness of reviewers, or resent the demands made upon them by publishers, editors, and families; self-pity was not foreign to them. But publicly, as Mrs. Craik maintained, they agreed that "to exact consideration merely on account of her sex, is in any woman the poorest cowardice."

A striking evidence of this change in the attitudes of women writers is the use of the pseudonym. Where the eighteenth-century authoress modestly concealed her identity by publishing anonymously, or by signing only her preface, her Victorian counterpart frequently attempted to deceive the public by assuming a masculine name. Although Jane Austen, for example, never publicly acknowledged her authorship, she did not conceal her sex; the title-page of *Sense and Sensibility* (1811) showed the author to be "A Lady." Jane Austen was proud to be classed with such reputable writers as Fanny Burney and Maria Edgeworth. But the ambition of the Brontës, or of George Eliot was quite different. In the biographical notice of her sisters' lives which Charlotte Brontë wrote for the 1850 edition of *Agnes Grey* and *Wuthering Heights*, she explained their choice of pseudonyms:

> Averse to personal publicity, we veiled our own names under those of Currer, Ellis, and Acton Bell, the ambiguous choice being dictated by a sort of conscientious scruple at assuming Christian names positively masculine, while we did not like to declare ourselves women, because—without at the time suspecting that our mode of writing and thinking was not what is called "feminine"—we had a vague impression that authoresses are liable to be looked on with prejudice; we noticed how critics sometimes use for their chastisement the weapon of personality, and for their reward a flattery which is not true praise.

Although anonymity had long been a defense against unladylike publicity, and, as in the case of Sir Walter Scott, a way of protecting one's literary reputation when the novel was still a low genre, the Brontë sisters were among the first women writers in England to adopt masculine pseudonyms. Mrs. Gaskell had published three short stories under the name "Cotton Mather Mills" in 1847; *Mary Barton* (1848) was published anonymously, although a letter to her publisher shows that she was thinking of using the pen name Stephen Berwick. Why did the masculine pseudonym appear so suddenly and become so widespread? There was, of course, the example of George Sand, who was probably second only to Goethe among foreign authors influencing Victorian literature. In 1847 she would have been the most inspiring model for a woman writer of independent spirit, and Charlotte had certainly read her novels. The Brontë girls, however, were a law unto themselves, and from childhood they had been accustomed to assuming masculine roles and names in their games of imagination. Charlotte had used several masculine pseudonyms in her Angrian chronicle; Charles Thunder, Charles Townsend, and Captain Tree were some favorites.

During the latter part of the nineteenth century, the practice of anonymity on title pages and in periodical journalism lost favor and was thought cowardly; but among women writers it increased. The Brontës' example was widely imitated; although George Eliot is the only woman writer of the period who is remembered by her pseudonym, there were dozens of novelists, minor then and forgotten now, who used masculine names: "Holme Lee," "J. Masterman," "Hamilton Murray" in the 1850s and 1860s; "Lucas Malet" (the daughter of Charles Kingsley) in the 1870s and 1880s; and later still, "John Oliver Hobbes," "John Strange Winter," "Martin Ross," "George Egerton," "Vernon Lee," and "C. E. Raimond." The practice spread to the United States, where in the 1880s Mary N. Murfee, writing under the name Charles Egbert Craddock, deceived not only the public, but also her publishers, for six years. As her brother explained, "The name was assumed as well for a cloak in case of failure as to secure the advantage that a man has in literature over a woman. He obtains a quicker reading by the publishers, is better received by the public in the beginning, and altogether has an easier time of it."[3] In England women also continued to publish novels anonymously well into the latter half of the century; among them was Rhoda Broughton, who did not sign her first novel, published in 1867.

In addition to the professional risk of encountering reviewers' bias, women writers also faced the personal danger of having their fiction read as autobiography. Without anonymity or a pseudonym, they found separation of their work and their private lives impossible. Even these defenses did not preclude scandal and gossip. Because Charlotte Brontë dedicated *Jane Eyre* to Thackeray, whose wife was in a hospital for the insane, the rumor spread that Thackeray was Rochester, and that Becky Sharp was Currer Bell.

George Eliot's case was especially delicate. As Mary Ann Evans, she had acquired a reputation in literary London for political and religious liberalism which had made her some enemies; as editor of the *Westminster Review* she had offended certain factions. More seriously, by living with a married man, George Henry Lewes, she had put herself outside the boundaries of Victorian respectability, and she did not dare to sign her real name to novels that preached the message of duty and renunciation. All those most closely involved with the publication of *Adam Bede*—Lewes, the publisher John Blackwood, George Eliot's old friends—tactfully avoided the subject of her connection with Lewes. Lewes himself, writing to Blackwood, emphasized the wish to avoid critical bias: "When Jane Eyre was finally known to be a woman's book, the tone noticeably changed." When they decided to abandon the incognito, Lewes wrote proudly to George Eliot's friend, Barbara Bodichon, that "it makes me angry to think that people should say that the secret has been kept because there was any *fear* of the effect of the author's name. You may tell it openly to all who care to hear it that the object of anonymity was to get the book judged on its own merits, and not prejudged as the work of a woman, or of a particular woman. It is quite clear that people would have sniffed at it if they had known the writer to be a woman, but they can't now unsay their admiration. . . ."

Subsequent events proved that Lewes' fears about antifeminine prejudice affecting reader's responses to the books were justified. But he and George Eliot were much more frightened of possible moral outrage. The Blackwoods too were apprehensive that announcement of authorship would injure the chances of future novels by George Eliot, especially sales to families. While she was finishing *The Mill on the Floss,* George Eliot became so anxious and sensitive that she wrote to Blackwood's, asking if they wished to remain her publisher since her identity had become known. John Blackwood's reassurances were directed, albeit discreetly, to her fears of scandal: "As to the withdrawal of the incognito, you know how much I have been opposed to it all along. It may prove a disadvantage, and in the eyes of many it will, but my opinion of your genius and confidence in the truly good, honest, religious, and moral tone of all you have written or will write is such that I think you will overcome any possible detriment from the withdrawal of the mystery which has so far taken place."

To summarize, the women novelists were both fearful and defiant of the critics; they expected a certain amount of derision and hostility; they took precautions against personal attack if they could; but they had a keen sense of professional and artistic responsibilities, and where these were involved, they would not make concessions or ask for favors. Men shook their heads over female stubbornness and professed themselves mystified by the new spirit of pride and self-reliance. "We might forgive her intolerance, for it is a ladylike failing," a critic wrote of Harriet Martineau, "but she will accept of no allowance on account of sex."[4] Editors and publishers discovered, to their amazement and often chagrin, that the most gentle and feminine lady novelists could turn tough-minded and relentless when it came to business. Mrs. Gaskell's refusal to change her work to suit Dickens' preferences in *Household Words* was one such instance, showing her confidence in her own writing and her resolve to fight for her artistic freedom. Unused to such rebelliousness, Dickens made no secret of his anger. "Mrs. Gaskell—fearful—fearful. If I were Mr. G., oh, Heaven how I would beat her!"[5] It took the combined efforts of John Chapman and George Eliot to persuade Eliza Lynn to tone down the love scenes in her novel *Realities;* and neither Geraldine Jewsbury nor Rhoda Broughton was willing to surrender a word. Even Mrs. Craik, one of the most docile and conventional women novelists, demanded financial justice from her publishers and could write a sharp letter when the situation required it.

Fiction was a calling for which they might take up arms without sacrificing their own sense of feminine duty. Writing demanded freedom from the tyranny of self; so long as they had to worry about their novels' being used as evidence for or against them, they felt stifled. Charlotte Brontë wrote to Lewes that "come what will, I cannot, when I write, think always of myself and what is elegant and charming in femininity; it is not on those terms, or with such ideas, I ever took pen in hand."

But the pressures of public opinion were inescapable, and all the women writers were to feel and suffer from them. First of all, the code of feminine behavior was class-oriented. Its cruelest pretense, as Kate Millett has pointed out in *Sexual Politics,* was that all women were "ladies," members of a leisure class. The requirements of gentility were barely compatible with any professional ambition on a woman's part, although it was tacitly accepted that in the lower classes women labored in the mines as well as the mills. All Victorian women writers, in fact, came from the middle or upper class; there were no milkmaid poets or shopgirl novelists. For women of the upper classes writing was regarded as a harmless occupation so long as it remained an avocation. Literary ambition, however—the wish to publish one's writing and maybe make money from it—was not wholly respectable for women until the middle of the century. Harriet Martineau, for example, tells in her *Autobiography* that she rejoiced when her family went bankrupt: "I, who had been obliged to write before breakfast, or in some private way, had henceforth liberty to do my own work in my own way; for we had lost our gentility."

The obligations of gentility were not the only barriers to feminine ambition. From childhood, girls were taught that women were created inferior to men in body and in mind, and that God had commanded woman to submit to masculine mastery in return for economic, emotional, and spiritual protection and guidance. Most Victorians believed that women's inferior role was their punishment for Eve's crime, and rebellion against it was un-Christian. God's message to women, as recorded in Genesis 3:16, was explicit: "I will multiply thy sorrows, and thy conceptions: in sorrow shalt thou bring forth children, and thou shalt be under thy husband's power, and he shall have dominion over thee."

Women were therefore destined to find fulfillment in a sphere of life lower than men's. Yet they were told that culture, leisure, and education might produce from female nature a being of the highest stature to which such a nature could aspire. As the *Westminster Review* summarized it in 1831, the feminine ideal meant that

> Woman ... is formed to obey, and though she have an active and exclusive part to perform, still she must perform it under submission to her lord. Her duties are confined to her home, and consist in ministering to the comfort of her husband, and in educating her children during their early years. To perform these duties well, she must have a docile, patient and submissive spirit, she must

possess no elevated description of knowledge; as she is gentle in her temper, so she must be inferior in her attainments.[6]

Women were created to be dependent on men; their education and training must prepare them to find and keep husbands. Their mental qualities, therefore, should be those which would "stimulate the instincts and soothe the feelings of men": modesty, delicacy, liveliness, and sensibility. Women should be truly religious, in order to influence their husbands and children; they should be ignorant of the evils of the world, in order to preserve their purity of spirit; in short, they ought to present in every way a contrast to and an escape from the harsh intrusive realities of human vanity, greed, and sensuality. The feminine ideal combined elements of the angel and the slave.

The widespread acceptance of this impossible ideal from the eighteenth century on made life very difficult for women writers, especially if they came into open conflict with society's dictates. First, there was the question of motive; a proper woman did not seek fame. Her special virtue was modesty. Then, literature was in some degree an exposure of self, and a truly modest, delicate woman would shrink from the scrutiny of strangers. Therefore, the act of publication alone made a woman suspect.

Furthermore, the Victorians had inherited a set of negative stereotypes of women, expressing many of the qualities which women writers were likely to embody. The two most common of these were the bluestocking and the old maid; frequently they were combined. The stereotype of the woman writer, which began to develop early in the nineteenth century, drew upon these older prejudices. In contrast to the ideal woman, the bluestocking-old-maid-woman writer was seen as tough, aggressive, pedantic, vain, and ugly.

As individuals, women writers were understandably loath to class themselves with the bluestockings, or to agree that they lacked feminine charm and virtue. But individual compromises, and for that matter, individual triumphs, had little effect on the stereotyped image of the woman writer. Women writers themselves were often the first to attack the sisterhood; and, to adapt Jane Austen's query, if the authoress of one novel be not patronized by the authoress of another, from whom can she expect protection and regard? No doubt jealousy played a large part in this mutual disapproval, as well as the desire to win masculine support; by condemning the audacity of women writers en masse, they hoped to emphasize their own socially acceptable femininity. The feminine ideal, therefore, divided women writers and kept them from making a forceful, united response to the hostile stereotypes.

Because they were so susceptible to the self-doubt engendered by the ideal, most Victorian women writers also conspicuously repudiated the feminist movement, even though they were basically sympathetic to its aims. Few were willing to battle the public hostility toward feminism. Nonetheless, conservative reviewers were quick to associate an independent heroine with a concealed revolutionary doctrine; several found *Jane Eyre* to be a radical feminist document, as indeed it was. For Charlotte Brontë, however, who had demanded dignity and independence without any revolutionary intent, and who considered herself the meekest of Christian Tories, such criticism was an affront. Her bad experience served as a warning to other women writers. As a group they were so cautious in their statements about feminism that in 1851, Harriet Taylor, the future wife of John Stuart Mill, attacked them anonymously in an article on "The Enfranchisement of Women":

> The literary class of women, especially in England, are ostentatious in disdaining the desire for equality or citizenship, and proclaiming their complete satisfaction with the place which society assigns to them; exercising in this, as in many other respects, a most noxious influence over the feelings and opinions of men ... [whom they] believe hate strength, sincerity and high spirit in a woman. They are therefore anxious to earn pardon and toleration for whatever of these qualities their writings may exhibit on other subjects, by a studied display of submission on this ...[7]

Her accusations stung Charlotte Brontë, who wrote to Mrs. Gaskell that their feelings on the review were the same: the author "forgets there is such a thing as self-sacrificing love and disinterested devotion. . . . To many women affection is sweet, and power conquered indifferent, though we all like influence won."

Although both Charlotte Brontë, and Mrs. Gaskell were using their novels to protest against specific wrongs in the condition of women, neither wished to be involved in legal and political reforms. Mrs. Gaskell believed that women should be rebellious and aggressive only in the interests of others; a mother might fight for her children, but not for herself. Furthermore, she distrusted social legislation generally; what was needed, she felt, was a change of heart. Many brilliant and competent women had so completely accepted the myth of female inferiority that they had no faith in their own sex and considered themselves superior exceptions. George Eliot and Elizabeth Barrett Browning, for example approved of feminism in theory, but could not believe that Victorian women were ready to assume the responsibilities of equality. Mrs. Browning, a political liberal who wrote against American slavery and for Italian liberation, and whose verse novel *Aurora Leigh* was attacked as propaganda for women's rights, wrote, nonetheless, that she was not "a very strong partizan (sic) of the Rights-of-Women side of the argument. . . . I believe that, considering men and women in the mass, there *is* an *inequality* of intellect, and it is proved by the very state of things of which gifted women complain; and more than proved by the manner in which their complaint is received by their own sisterhood." Charlotte Yonge, Mrs. Oliphant, Mrs. Lynn Linton, Mrs. Craik, Mrs. Humphrey Ward, and Christina Rossetti were violently opposed to the movement; Mrs. Linton and Mrs. Oliphant even wrote against what the latter called the "mad notion of the franchise for women."

Although they were opposed to female emancipation, women writers supported innovations and reforms in women's education. Until 1878 women were not allowed to study at Oxford and Cambridge. Girls received one kind of secondary education; boys another; so that knowledge of Latin and Greek became a symbol of intellectual achievement for women.

Not thought, but feeling was held to be the woman's forte, and the Victorians especially distrusted women's pretensions to abstract thinking. Emotional prejudice, they believed, disqualified women from objective judgments upon such matters as history, philosophy, and government. Again and again in the journals, reviewers attacked women attempting philosophic discussions. Physical and intellectual weakness were associated, as we can observe in the following comment on Mrs. Hofland's *The Czarina* (1843): "Women have no business whatever to dabble in historical romances ... [they] are no more capable of conceiving the abstract idea of a mind which is framed for the rise and fall of empires than they are physically constituted to play a prominent part in the revolutionary drama when it opens." Similarly, affection and partiality, however charming in a wife, are repellent in a scholarly endeavor: "Ladies who assume masculine functions must learn to assume masculine gravity and impartiality."

Obviously, hearing such sermons preached from childhood would eventually affect women's estimates of their own capabilities, and thus many women writers concurred in this unfavorable opinion of their own sex. As Mrs. Gaskell put it, "I would not trust a mouse to a woman if a man's judgment could be had."

Among women writers, educational backgrounds ranged from Margaret Oliphant's simple lessons from her mother to the expensive tutoring enjoyed by Elizabeth Barrett. George Eliot studied music, drawing, French, history, arithmetic, and English composition from the Misses Franklin at Coventry. Charlotte Brontë, after her brief, disastrous experience at Cowan Bridge (the school which became the model for Lowood in *Jane Eyre*), spent happy years at Miss Wooler's School and later in Brussels studied French at the Pensionnat Heger, under the guidance of the fiery M. Heger. Young Elizabeth Barrett wrote her first poem at age four; at thirteen she spent eight hours a day at her studies which included French, Italian, Latin, and Greek; the classic she studied with her brother's tutor.

Compared to the opportunities men enjoyed, the formal education of these women was perhaps not extensive. None of them attended a university; but then, neither did Branwell Brontë or George Eliot's brother Isaac. And they read omnivorously; they taught themselves languages, subscribed to journals, and ordered books or borrowed them. Through discipline and dedication, they made use of leisure, of isolation, even of loneliness and rejection. There is Elizabeth Barrett, suddenly an invalid at fifteen, mastering, over a ten-year period, German, Spanish, and Hebrew. George Eliot, caring for her widowed father in Nuneaton, studied German, Italian, and Latin, and read theology, history, fiction, poetry, and science. Much later, she showed this same enviable ability to use periods of forced seclusion for study, instead of wasting them in nostalgia or self-pity. In the years 1855-1858, during the long

period of social ostracism, when, because of her honest
avowal of the union with Lewes, she was not invited
to dinner," she read, in Greek, the Iliad, the Odyssey,
the Ajax, the Oedipus triology, the Electra, the Philoctetes,
and the Aeschylus triology; and in Latin, Horace, Virgil,
Cicero, Persius, Livy, Tacitus, Plautus, Quintilian, and
Pliny. Her knowledge of the classics, Gordon Haight
believes, was "more solid than that Thackeray got at
Charterhouse and Cambridge, probably wider than that
Trollope got at Harrow and Winchester."[8]

It is easy enough, therefore, to see why women writers
were often thought to be bluestockings. Gentlemen meeting Mrs. Browning or George Eliot for the first time
expected them to be shrill, domineering, and masculine,
and in accounts of these meetings there is often a note of
pleased surprise that, instead, Mrs. Browning was a "quiet
little person" (Hawthorne); a "modest sensible little woman" (Coventry Patmore), who would sit with the boring
wives and let the men "discuss the universe" (D. G. Rossetti). Tennyson commented on George Eliot's "soft so-
prano voice" (he had probably expected a baritone), and
John Fiske exclaimed in astonishment, "I never saw such a
woman. There is nothing a bit masculine about her; she is
thoroughly feminine and looks and acts as if she were
made for nothing but to mother babies." These two wom-
en, however, were thought to be exceptions, and the
species of women novelists was still expected to be both
ignorant and pretentious.

Despite increased social acceptance of women writers
toward the middle of the century, working conditions
were dependent on the attitudes of an older generation
that had been brought up on the feminine ideal and had
passed it on to their daughters. The Brontës, Charlotte
Yonge, George Eliot, and, of course, Elizabeth Barrett
Browning obtained their youthful ideas about proper feminine subservience and dutifulness from their exigent fathers; Mrs. Oliphant and Harriet Martineau received the
doctrine from their domineering mothers; and these early
lessons they never unlearned completely. The attitude and
expectations confronting Charlotte Brontë at the beginning of her career are implicit in a correspondence she
had with Robert Southey, then Poet Laureate, in 1837.
She had asked his opinion of her poetry; Southey answered
that it showed talent, but he advised her to give up
thoughts of becoming a poet, "Literature cannot be the

business of a woman's life and it ought not to be. The more she is engaged in her proper duties, the less leisure will she have for it, even as an accomplishment and a recreation." Humiliated, and yet grateful for his concern, Charlotte Brontë answered him in a pathetic letter that speaks dramatically—even melodramatically—of her daily agony of renunciation of her imagination and ambitions. Explaining that she tried to curb her imagination by working with all her energy as a governess, she wrote:

> I carefully avoid any appearance of pre-occupation and eccentricity which might lead those I live amongst to suspect the nature of my pursuits. Following my father's advice—who from my childhood has counselled me just in the wise and friendly tone of your letter—I have endeavored not only attentively to observe all the duties a woman ought to fulfill, but to feel deeply interested in them. I don't always succeed, for sometimes when I'm teaching or sewing I would rather be reading or writing; but I try to deny myself, and my father's approbation amply rewarded me for the privation.[9]

No woman writer in the nineteenth century dared consider abandoning domestic responsibilities, however tedious, distasteful, and menial, for her art. The poorer ones, like the Brontës, peeled the potatoes; those with servants, like George Eliot, still kept close watch over the linen closets and the silverware.

Reconciling the parallel currents of work and female duty took great energy. Probably the exigencies of female authorship balanced its social advantages; needy women who were too dull or too timid to choose other work may well have been attracted to novel-writing, as George Eliot scornfully suggested; but a three-volume novel, even a bad one, could not have been written without some degree of concentration and endurance. Even successful professionals, like Margaret Oliphant, worked under deplorable conditions: "up to this date," she wrote in 1888, "I have never been shut up in a separate room, or hedged off with any observances. My study, all the study I have attained to, is the little 2nd drawing room where all the (feminine) life of the house goes on; and I don't think I have ever had two hours undisturbed (except at night, when everybody is in bed) during my whole literary life." A room of one's own, Virginia Woolf's symbol of artistic autonomy, was yet to be earned.

An even more insidious outgrowth of the feminine ideal
was the characteristically Victorian veneration of motherhood. In its extreme form, this doctrine proclaimed motherhood the entire purpose of a woman's life. As the
feminist pioneer Frances Power Cobbe lamented, many
Victorians believed that "the woman who has given birth
to a son has fulfilled her 'mission,' the celibate woman—be
she holy as St. Theresa, useful as Miss Nightingale, gifted
as Miss Cornwallis,—has entirely missed it."[10]

Because maternity was regarded as the highest office a
woman could attain, and because motherhood allegedly
conferred mystical gifts of wisdom and moral infallibility
upon its votaries, women writers were more respected and
admired and got better treatment from the critics if they
were also mothers. Even women who were quite revolutionary in other respects grew dewy-eyed and mealy-
mouthed when the subject of maternity came up. The
same Frances Power Cobbe who is quoted above in protest against the idealization of maternity insisted that
mothers must not dream of activity beyond the domestic
sphere until their families are grown:

> So *immense* are the claims on a mother, physical claims
> on her bodily and brain vigor, and moral claims on her
> heart and thoughts, that she cannot, I believe, meet them
> all and find any large margin beyond for other cares and
> work. She serves the community in the very best and
> highest way it is possible to do, by giving birth to healthy
> children, whose physical strength has not been defrauded,
> and to whose moral and mental nature she can give the
> whole of her thoughts.[11]

Mrs. Marsh, Mrs. Oliphant, Mrs. Gaskell, and Mrs.
Browning got on very well with conservative critics who
never tired of reminding readers that these ladies were
mothers.

Geraldine Jewsbury and Charlotte Brontë were less
fortunate. In the unkindest cut of all, Lewes criticized
Charlotte Brontë's portrayal of Mrs. Pryor in *Shirley,*
attributing the defects of the characterization to the author's childlessness. Lewes argued that no mother would
abandon her child because it resembled its detested and
depraved father. "Currer Bell!" cried Lewes, "if under
your heart had ever stirred a child, if to your bosom a
babe had been pressed,—that mysterious part of your
being, towards which all the rest of it was drawn, in which

your soul was transported and absorbed—never could you have *imagined* such a falsehood as that!"[12] No wonder Charlotte Brontë wrote to him after this review, "I can be on guard against my enemies, but God deliver me from my friends."

In the hands of a real reactionary, the maternity argument became even more absurd and repressive. In his review of Mrs. Gaskell's *Ruth*, J. M. Ludlow first noted that "the authoress of *Ruth* is a mother, and the duties of hallowed motherhood have taught her own pure soul what its blessings may be to the fallen." No admirer of "women authors as such ... certain creatures of the female sex, with ink half-way up their fingers, and dirty shawls, and frowsy hair," Ludlow suggested that for decency's sake, only married women, preferably mothers, and apparently those of middle age, should write novels:

> By this time, with family cares upon their hands, and the moral responsibilities of their now completed life upon their consciences, to write and to print will be no more temptations to their vanity, and it will be for them to judge whether they are really called upon to say something to the world—whether they have that to say which their husbands will gladly hear, which their children will never blush to read; and whether their calling be to works of fiction or to the severest exercises of thought, we are sure that the little flaxen heads at their knees will add a truth and a charm to matter and style alike, though it be only through the instinctive erasure of those hard words which Willie does so cry over in his lesson.[13]

Secure in matronhood, Mrs. Gaskell gleefully called the review "delicious," but to Charlotte Brontë and to many other lady novelists, it must have been bitter indeed.

As if this preference for motherly mediocrity were not enough, women writers also had to contend with the prejudices associating them with feminists and other political radicals. Most dangerous of these stereotyped associations was the identification of professional women with the birth control movement. In the 1840s Malthusian doctrine was almost universally regarded as diabolical. A woman who publicly supported Malthus had to expect abuse; she was, the Victorians thought, not only wicked, rebellious, and profane, but very probably perverted. Harriet Martineau's espousal of Malthusian philosophy (in the unfortunately titled *Monthly Novels*) put the *Quarterly Review* into hysterically righteous rage: "A *woman* who thinks child-bearing a *crime against society!*"[14]

Behind such outbursts was the uneasy fear that women who were given attractive alternatives to marriage and motherhood would take them, and that the proud race of Britons would wither away. This persistent anxiety explains, I think, the seemingly excessive angry response critics so often made to the books of single women that took issue with traditional social patterns. When women began questioning the structure of society, critics thought, they might end by destroying it.

In the case of women writers, the problem of family versus career seemed particularly insistent, because literary creativity seemed to rival biological creativity in the most direct way. The terminology of childbirth had been used to describe artistic creation for centuries; and the creative impulses of parenthood and authorship were familiarly spoken of as identical. Using this old joke, Thomas Moore wittily, cruelly, and anonymously attacked Harriet Martineau in a "Blue Love Song" in the *Times*:

> Come wed with me, and we will write,
> My Blue of Blues, from morn till night.
> Chas'd from our classic souls shall be
> All thoughts of vulgar progeny;
> And thou shalt walk through smiling rows
> Of chubby duodecimos,
> While I, to match thy products nearly,
> Shall lie-in of a quarto yearly.

And so on, for a dozen more lines. The obvious implication was that the bluestocking woman writer was barren and unsexed. All Harriet Martineau could do in her own defense was refuse to speak to Moore at parties.

Finally, there was the widespread belief I have already mentioned, that motherhood and authorship were essentially competitive and therefore incompatible activities. Creative energy was thought to be finite; children claimed so much of it that no good mother could have much left to spare for fiction. At any rate, she would have less than a man. The unfairness of this theory is plain; it failed entirely to allow for individual variations in personality and circumstances. But Mrs. Gaskell cited it in a letter advising a young mother not to write until her children were grown. Not only was it likely, Mrs. Gaskell thought, that a writing mother might neglect her real children for her imaginary ones, but also that a mother would be a better artist for having waited and endured and grown through the trials of maternity:

> The exercise of a talent or power *is* always a great pleasure; but one should weigh well whether this pleasure may not be obtained by the sacrifice of some duty. When I had *little* children I do not think I could have written stories, because I should have become too much absorbed in my fictitious people to attend to my *real* ones. I think you would be sorry if you began to feel that your desire to earn money, even for so laudable an object as to help your husband, made you unable to give your tender sympathy to your little ones in their small joys and sorrows; and yet, don't you know how you, how everyone who tries to write stories *must* become absorbed in them, (fictitious though they be) if they are to interest their readers in them. Besides—viewing the subject from a solely artistic point of view, a good writer of fiction must have lived an active and sympathetic life if she wishes her books to have strength and vitality in them. When you are forty, and if you have a gift for being an authoress, you will write ten times as good a novel as you could do now, *just* because you will have gone through much more of the interests of a wife and mother.[15]

Even if she had no children, a woman was expected to lag behind men because of physical problems. In particular, Victorians generally believed that menstruation was a disease that made all women invalids for much of their lives.[16] Until the twentieth century all but the most advanced medical authorities believed that during menstruation women were incapable of physical or intellectual exertion. Although convention forbade discussion of menstruation in polite journalism, it is often discussed discreetly in accounts of the problems of women's colleges, particularly in the United States. As late as 1878, the *British Medical Journal* printed a correspondence on the subject of the contamination of meat by the touch of menstruating women. Probably menstruation is one of the elements G. H. Lewes had in mind when he wrote that "for twenty of the best years of their lives—those very years in which men either rear the grand fabric or lay the solid foundations of their fame and fortune—women are mainly occupied by the cares, the duties, the enjoyments and the sufferings of maternity. During large parts of these years, too, their bodily health is generally so broken and precari-

ous as to incapacitate them for any strenuous exertion."[17]

All in all, women were told that their instincts, their
organic processes, their brains, and their religion commanded conformity to the domestic pattern. Again these
doctrines weighed most heavily on single women, who
were made to feel that their struggles to find meaningful
and profitable employment for their lives were ultimately
futile. And there was a real belief single women who
wrote were merely seeking an outlet for their pent-up
emotions and fruitless passions. Attempting to explain the
creative impetus, G. H. Lewes wrote of the lady novelist,
"if the accidents of her position make her solitary and
inactive, or if her thwarted affections shut her off somewhat from that sweet domestic and maternal sphere to
which her whole being spontaneously moves, she turns to
literature as another sphere."[18]

In short, no matter what they did, women writers were
told that they could not hope to equal the achievements of
men. If, like Mrs. Gaskell and Mrs. Oliphant, they fulfilled
their domestic responsibilities, they were at a theoretical
disadvantage with men, who could dedicate themselves
wholly to their art. If, like Charlotte Brontë and Geraldine Jewsbury, they were unmarried, their work was nonetheless interrupted by the periodic debility of menstruation. If the woman met her maternal obligations, she
would exhaust her creativity. If she devoted herself to art
instead of having children, the art would be mere compensation; it would be secondary and inferior; wish fulfillment. Thus, by 1845 critics, both male and female, came
as a matter of course to *expect* that a novel by a woman
would in all probability be inferior to that of a man.

All the confused, hostile, and repressive aspects of the
Victorian concept of femininity had their outlet in the criticism of women writers. By the late 1840s, when the
Brontës and Mrs. Gaskell, among others, were submitting
their manuscripts to publishers, an entire separate and
prejudicial critical standard for women's writing had
evolved. Through the 1850s and 1860s this criticism, both
theoretical and specific, increased in response to the large
number of important novels by women that were appearing. Hardly a journal failed to publish an essay on woman's literature; hardly a critic failed to express himself
complacently upon its innate and potential qualities.

Victorian critics agreed that if women were going to

write at all, they had best write novels. "Of all departments of literature," G. H. Lewes wrote, "fiction is one to which by nature and circumstances, women are best adapted."[19] Theories of feminine aptitude for the novel tended to be patronizing, if not insulting. According to the theory of female nature, women had a natural taste for gossip and trivia; they were sharp-eyed observers of the social scene; they enjoyed getting involved in other people's affairs. All these traits of the female character found a happy outlet in the novel. This view, as grudging toward the novel as toward women, is usually expressed in a tone of mock admiration: "Women . . . have a talent for personal discourse and familiar narrative, which, when properly controlled, is a great gift, although too frequently it degenerates into a social nuisance."[20]

In passages like this, the critic giveth and the critic taketh away; the least difficult, least demanding response to the superior woman novelist was to see the novel as the instrument that transformed feminine failings into virtues. What mattered was the channeling of these unfortunate interests and impulses. Women were dominated by sentiment and obsessed by love; well, sentiment and love were the essentials of fiction. J. M. Ludlow worked it out very carefully in his 1853 review of Mrs. Gaskell's *Ruth*:

> Now, if we consider the novel to be the picture of human life in a pathetic, or as some might prefer the expression, in a sympathetic form, that is to say, as addressed to human feeling, rather than to human taste, judgment, or reason, there seems nothing paradoxical in the view, that women are called to the mastery of this peculiar field of literature. We know, all of us, that if man is the head of humanity, woman is its heart; and as soon as education has rendered her ordinarily capable of expressing feeling in written words, why should we be surprised to find that her words come more home to us than those of men, where feeling is chiefly concerned?[21]

By eliminating from his definition of the novel all the qualities he could not bring himself to grant to women, Ludlow could accept the success of the books without having to alter in the least his feminine stereotypes. So intent is he on showing the perfect compatability of the stereotype and the real product, that he can dismiss the question of "expressing feeling in written words" as the merest trick of the literate.

"The Lady Novelists of Great Britain," a discussion in the *Gentleman's Magazine* in 1853, is another good example of the typical mid-Victorian tone, doubly offensive in this case because the reviewer so plainly believes himself to be a model of broadminded generosity: "Nothing . . . moves us from our belief that novel-writing is quite one of the legitimate occupations of women. They cannot, indeed, fetch up materials from the haunts into which a Dickens or a Bulwer may penetrate. They may in vain try to grapple with the more complicated difficulties of many a *man's* position and career; but, as far as they go—and often they can and do go far—they are admirable portrayers of character and situation." And so on, for three smug pages.

George Henry Lewes' article, "The Lady Novelists" (1852), repeats the traditional distinction that the masculine spirit is intellectual, and the feminine spirit emotional. Since fiction demands the expression of the "emotional facts of life," women are likely to succeed in it, although philosophy, history, and poetry, the more intellectual branches of literature, would exclude all but the exceptionally gifted. Lewes maintained that the sexes possess separate but equal literary abilities. Great and lasting works, such as the novels of Jane Austen and George Sand, could be produced with the materials domestic experience provided. But not even Jane Austen could have written so intellectual a work as *Vanity Fair*. The best praise Lewes could grant a woman writer he bestowed on Jane Austen (he had not met George Eliot yet); she knew her limitations, used to the fullest the distinct abilities she commanded, and never tried to invade masculine territory.

Another essay of more than ordinary interest is "Novels by the Authoress of *John Halifax*," R. H. Hutton's review of Dinah Mulock Craik's novels.[22] Hutton devoted three-fourths of his review to an analysis of "the main characteristics in which feminine fictions, as distinguished from those of men, are strong or defective." Hutton's first point concerned the narrative structure; in a woman's novel, he thought, all the narrative interest derived from the characters, whereas in men's novels the characters were placed in a broad intellectual framework and related to a general idea which dictated the composition of the narrative, such as Scott's contrast of history and the present, or Thackeray's satiric attack on his society. Hutton felt that women's novels had a special intensity which came from their strictly organized plots and invitation to identification with the characters. But this intensity was transitory, since it was intellectually limited. Accordingly, he considered Dickens a "feminine" writer: his genius "was founded on delicate powers of perception alone, though lighted up with something broader than feminine humour. There is no intellectual background to his pictures: and in this respect he resembles the numerous authoresses of modern English fiction."

Lack of imagination, rather than lack of experience, was for Hutton the major deficiency of the woman writer. When applied to character, this judgment meant that women excel at social detail, at creation of characters externally observed, but fail at depicting inner life. The exception to this rule is the central character, whose psychology is usually convincingly portrayed. Unless, in fact, the protagonist is the narrator of a pseudoautobiography, the typical woman's novel is out of proportion in Hutton's view, since only one of its characters is likely to be presented in depth. Lack of imagination also accounts for the general failure of women to portray realistic male characters. The very powers of observation that aid women in capturing the external aspects of character prevent them from reaching below the surface and discovering the truths of the hidden personality.

Although much of what Hutton says is reasonable as criticism of Mrs. Craik, his general theories are biased by his selection of examples; he bases his theories about women novelists essentially on inferior novels, whereas his ideas about the abilities of male novelists are derived from a consideration of Scott and Thackeray, among others. He cannot avoid concluding, therefore, that women novelists are inferior.

Comparisons may be odious, but they exert an undeniable fascination, and given the discursive nature of Victorian book reviewing, the many comparisons of the literary abilities of the sexes are not much more significant than comparisons of national literatures. The curious and important aspect of these essays, however, is the degree to which their generalizations were assimilated and turned into absolute standards. During the period from 1845 to 1865 especially, reviewers were virtually obsessed with finding the place of the woman writer and with putting each woman writer in her place. This obsession usually took the form of a persistent determination to expose the female authorship of a pseudonymous or anonymous work. Reviewers found the challenge of detection irresistible; and they enjoyed the pose of omniscience. The more women writers resorted to disguise to win fair treatment from the critics, the more critics focused on the question of sex.

The double standard of literary abilities overwhelmingly favored men. Like the social stereotype to which it was closely related, the literary stereotype adapted very slowly to any real evidence of feminine achievement. Women writers were supposed to have the benefit of the domestic and moral talents of the feminine character; but these talents were outbalanced by their limitations. Feminine talents included refinement, tact, and the ability to observe precisely, present female character effectively, deal knowledgeably with details of dress, housekeeping, and illness (this last a not inconsiderable element in Victorian fiction), and most important, edify the morally needy. Feminine failings were lack of originality, lack of education, inability to comprehend abstract thought, excessive emotionality, prejudice, humorlessness, and inability to portray male characters.

All the most desirable artistic qualities were assigned to men: power, breadth, distinctness, clarity, learning, understanding of history and abstraction, shrewdness, knowledge of life, and humor. Masculine faults were seen to be coarseness and passion; the latter term was used in its Victorian pejorative sense of licentiousness. This distribution of literary qualities meant that a man who approximated the stereotype could conceivably write an excellent novel, but a woman with all the qualities agreed to be essentially womanly could produce only a superfical work.

This double standard was so widely accepted that critics and readers automatically employed it in the game of literary detection. Approaching a novel as if it were a chemical to be identified, reviewers would break it down into its elements, label these masculine or feminine, and add up the total. A predominance of masculine or feminine elements determined the sex of an author. The rigidity of this method of criticism is equaled only by its unreliability. Sagas of mistaken identity are legion throughout the century; considering the odds based on chance alone, the percentage of correct guesses is not impressive. Women were no more accurate detectives than men.

The two most famous cases involving the use of male pseudonyms by female authors were the controversies attending the publication of *Jane Eyre* in 1847, and *Adam Bede* in 1859. These two works threatened the soothing stereotype of feminine incompetence with the reality of feminine genius, and they engendered a critical response extraordinary for its intensity and ambivalence.

What chiefly astounded and baffled the readers of *Jane Eyre* was the presentation of feminine independence and female passion. According to the ideal, women did not have the sexual feelings "Currer Bell" (Charlotte Brontë) described. According to the double critical standard, moreover, women writers could not attain the powers Currer Bell displayed. Therefore, as Mrs. Gaskell reports, "The whole reading world of England was in a ferment to discover the unknown author . . . every little incident mentioned in the book was turned this way and that, to answer, if possible, the much-vexed question of sex."

The critical verdicts were contradictory, to say the least. Most reviewers, judging by the book's vigor, declared the author to be a man. Others, examining circumstantial evidence of domestic life, insisted that the author must be a woman. Still other reviewers, scandalized by the accounts of passion, announced that the author must be a fallen or depraved woman, an outcast from her sex. One American reviewer solved the dilemma by imagining that *Jane Eyre* was a team effort by a brother and sister, with the brother handling plot, characters, and passion, and the sister filling in delicate detail and sensibility. Even defenses of the book were obnoxiously insistent on distinctions of sex, arguing that Currer Bell was so innocent and ladylike that she had not realized the meaning of her own words.

Most significantly, many critics bluntly admitted that they thought the book was a masterpiece if written by a man, shocking or disgusting if written by a woman. In an angry rebuttal of these reviews, written to her publisher, Charlotte Brontë eloquently defended her human and literary rights: "Jane Eyre is a woman's autobiography; by a woman it is professedly written. If it is written as no woman would write, condemn it with spirit and decision— say it is bad, but do not eulogize and then detract. . . . To such critics I would say, 'To you I am neither man nor woman—I come before you as an author only. It is the sole standard by which you have a right to judge me—the sole ground on which I accept your judgment!"

Like *Jane Eyre, Adam Bede* was an instant success, and once again, all of England was in a furor to discover the identity of the author. This time readers were virtually unanimous in supposing the author to be a man. As the *Saturday Review* later admitted, "to speak the simple truth, without affectation or politeness, it was thought too good for a woman's story." In fact, a male "George Eliot" was quickly located—a clergyman named Joseph Liggins, who lived in the town where Mary Ann Evans was born, and who was more than willing to claim credit for her books. Cheerfully, he gave interviews and accepted the homage of visitors, forcing the real George Eliot to reveal her pseudonym. Immediately the tone of the reviews changed. Where critics had previously seen the powerful mind of the male George Eliot, they now, upon second glance, discovered feminine delicacy and tact, and here and there a disturbing unladylike coarseness.

Arguments *ad feminam* in periodical reviewing were so characteritsic of the years from 1840 to 1870 that I could not begin to list them all. Many of the most talented women writers of the period were criticized for "coarseness" or a lack of ladylike refinement. Anne Brontë's second novel, *The Tenant of Wildfell Hall,* which described the suffering of a woman married to an alcoholic, scandalized James Lorimer of the *North British Review* with its "coarseness and brutality." But the reviewer for *Fraser's* found charm in what seemed to him only a feeble and innocent imitation of masculine power: "The very coarseness and vulgarity is just such as a woman, trying to write like a man, would invent—second-hand and clumsy, and not such as men do use; the more honour to the writer's heart, if not her taste." With typical Brontë spirit, Anne replied in her preface to the second edition, "All novels are or should be written for both men and women to read, and I am at a loss to conceive how a man should permit himself to write anything that would be really disgraceful to a woman, or why a woman should be censured for writing anything that would be proper and becoming for a man."

Elizabeth Barrett Browning was called by the *Edinburgh Review* "often . . . more coarsely masculine than any other woman writer." Again, the objection was to her

diction. Her verse novel *Aurora Leigh* (1857)—one of
the few works by a woman, incidentally, with a woman
writer as its heroine—was considered especially daring
and unorthodox. The *Westminster Review* commented, in
a typically personal and offensive manner, "Mrs. Browning
seems at once proud and ashamed of her womanhood. She
protests, not unjustly, against the practice of judging artists by their sex; but she takes the wrong means to prove
her manhood. In recoil from mincing fastidiousness, she
now and then becomes coarse. She will not be taxed with
squeamishness, and introduces words unnecessarily, which
are eschewed in the most familiar conversation. To escape
the imputation of over-refinement, she swears without
provocation."

Women reviewers were just as likely as men to disparage the female novelist or to draw attention to her personal qualities. George Eliot, after all, had herself written
about "Silly Novels by Lady Novelists"; the two reviews
which hurt Charlotte Brontë the most were by women:
Miss Rigby in the *Quarterly* and Anne Mosley in the
Christian Remembrancer. Mrs. Oliphant, who suffered
most of her professional life from a bitter sense of literary
inferiority, could be a harsh critic of her sister novelists.
One of the saddest aspects of prejudice is the way in
which it affects the self-image of its victims. Women
writers were all too ready to believe that they labored
under innate handicaps of mind and experience. Even the
most successful seemed to require continual reassurance.
Lewes confided to a friend that "After the publication of
'Adam Bede' Marian felt deeply the evil influences of
talking and allowing others to talk to her about her
writing ... there is a special reason in her case—it is that
excessive diffidence which prevented her writing at all for
so many years, and would prevent her now, if I were not
beside her to encourage her."

The effects of this repressive criticism were serious and
extensive. First, it denied autonomy to women writers by
insisting on treating them as a class, rather than as individual artists. This knowledge that their identity was always in danger of being subsumed to a group stereotype acted as a constant irritant. They were anxious to
detach themselves from its onus by expressing relatively
conservative views on the emancipation of women and by
stressing their domestic accomplishments. The stereotype,
however, was inescapable, and women were perpetually

frustrated when the novels they considered expressions of their own unique personalities were treated as representatives of a trend. At Mrs. Gaskell's request, Charlotte Brontë asked her publishers to delay *Villette* so that it would not appear simultaneously with *Ruth*. "... I have ever held comparisons to be odious," she wrote to Mrs. Gaskell, "and would fain that neither I nor my friends should be made subjects for the same ... I dare say, arrange as we may, we shall not be able wholly to prevent comparisons; it is the nature of some critics to be invidious; but we need not care: we shall set them at defiance; they *shall* not make us foes...." As she predicted, despite their efforts the two novels were reviewed together in many journals. Women writers were thus forced to be rivals.

More significantly, women were either implicitly or explicitly denied the freedom to explore and describe their own experience. While Victorian prudery prevented men as well as women from expressing themselves, it operated much more oppressively on women, because virtually all experience that was uniquely feminine was considered unprintable. Considering the outraged response of critics to *Jane Eyre* and *Aurora Leigh*, it is sad but not surprising that no nineteenth-century woman writer dared to describe childbirth, much less sexual passion. Men could not really write about sex, but they could write about sport, business, crime, and war, all activities from which women were barred. It is no wonder that no woman produced a novel like *War and Peace*. What is amazing is the wealth of literature, passionate, witty, and profound, written by women in this period.

NOTES

1. George Eliot, "Silly Novels by Lady Novelists," *Westminster Review*, 66 (1856): 460.
2. Dinah Mulock Craik, *A Woman's Thoughts About Women* (New York, 1858), p. 53.
3. E. F. Harkins and C. H. L. Johnston, *Little Pilgrimages Among the Women Who Have Written Famous Books* (Boston, 1892), p. 82.
4. G. S. Venables, "Miss Martineau," *Blackwood's*, 48 (1840): 181.
5. Annette B. Hopkins, *Elizabeth Gaskell: Her Life and Work* (London, 1952), p. 152.

Women Writers and the Double Standard 479

6. "The Education of Women," *Westminster Review*, 29 (1831): 71.
7. Harriet Taylor, "The Enfranchisement of Women," *Westminster Review*, 55 (1851): 310.
8. Gordon S. Haight, *George Eliot: A Biography* (New York, 1968), p. 195.
9. Elizabeth Gaskell, *Life of Charlotte Bronte* (London, 1919), p. 125.
10. Josephine E. Butler, ed., *Woman's Work and Woman's Culture* (London, 1869), p. 8.
11. Frances Power Cobbe, *The Duties of Women* (Boston, 1881), p. 190.
12. G. H. Lewes, "Currer Bell's *Shirley*," *Edinburgh Review*, 91 (1850): 165.
13. J. M. Ludlow, "Ruth," *North British Review*, 20 (1853): 90-91.
14. "Miss Martineau's Monthly Novels," *Quarterly Review*, 29 (1833): 151.
15. Letter of September 25, 1862, in *Letters of Mrs. Gaskell*, ed. J. A. V. Chapple and Arthur Pollard (Manchester, England, 1966), pp. 694-695.
16. See Elaine and English Showalter, "Victorian Women and Menstruation," *Victorian Studies*, Fall 1970.
17. Lewes, *op. cit.*, 155.
18. Lewes, "The Lady Novelists," *Westminster Review*, 57 (1852): 133.
19. *Ibid.*
20. E. S. Dallas, "Currer Bell," *Blackwood's*, 87 (1853): 19.
21. Ludlow, *op. cit.*, 90.
22. "Novels by the Authoress of *John Halifax*," *North British Review*, 29 (1858): 384-406.

21

WHY ARE THERE NO GREAT WOMEN ARTISTS?

Linda Nochlin

"Why are there no great women artists?" This question tolls reproachfully in the background of discussions of the so-called woman problem, causing men to shake their heads regretfully and women to grind their teeth in frustration. Like so many other questions involved in the red-hot feminist controversy, it falsifies the nature of the issue at the same time that it insidiously supplies its own answer: "There are no great women artists because women are incapable of greatness." The assumptions lying behind such a question are varied in range and sophistication, running anywhere from "scientifically" proven demonstrations of the inability of human beings with wombs rather than penises to create anything significant, to relatively openminded wonderment that women, despite so many years of near-equality—and after all, a lot of men have had their disadvantages too—have still not achieved anything of major sigificance in the visual arts.

The feminist's first reaction is to swallow the bait, hook, line and sinker and to attempt to answer the question as it is put: that is, to dig up examples of worthy or insufficiently appreciated women artists throughout history; to rehabilitate rather modest, if interesting and productive careers; to rediscover forgotten flower painters or David-followers and make out a case for them; to demonstrate that Berthe Morisot was really less dependent upon Manet than one had been led to think—in other words, to engage in activity not too different from that of the average scholar, man or woman, making out a case for the importance of his own neglected or minor master. Whether undertaken from a feminist point of view, such attempts, like the ambitious article on women artists which appeared in the 1858 *Westminster Review*,[1] or more recent scholarly studies and reevaluations of individual woman artists like Angelica Kauffmann or Artemisia Gentileschi,[2] are certainly well worth the effort, adding to our knowledge both of woman's achievement and of art history generally; and a great deal still remains to be done in this area. Unfortunately, such efforts, if written from an uncritically feminist viewpoint, do nothing to question the assumptions lying behind the question "Why are there no great women artists?"; on the contrary, by attempting to answer it and by doing so inadequately, they merely reinforce its negative implications.

At the same time that champions of women's equality may feel called upon to falsify the testimony of their own judgment by scraping up neglected female artistic geniuses or puffing up the endeavors of genuinely excellent but decidedly minor women painters and sculptors into major contributions, they may resort to the easily refuted ploy of accusing the questioner of using "male" standards as the criterion of greatness or excellence. This attempt to answer the question involves shifting the ground slightly; by asserting, as many contemporary feminists do, that there is actually a different kind of greatness for women's art than for men's, one tacitly assumes the existence of a distinctive and recognizable feminine style, differing in both its formal and its expressive qualities from that of male artists and positing the unique character of women's situation and experience.

This, on the surface of it, seems reasonable enough: in general, women's experience and situation in society, and hence as artists, is different from men's: certainly, the art produced by a group of consciously united and purposefully articulate women intent on bodying forth a group consciousness of feminine experience might be stylistically identifiable as feminist, if not feminine art. Unfortunately, this remains within the realm of possibility; so far, it has not occurred. While the Danube School, Caravaggio's followers, the painters gathered around Gauguin at Pont Aven, the Blue Rider, or the Cubists may be recog-

nized by certain clearly defined stylistic or expressive qualities, no such common qualities of femininity would seem
to link the styles of women artists generally, any more
than such qualities can be said to link all women writers—
a case brilliantly argued, against the most devastating, and
mutually contradictory, masculine critical clichés, by
Mary Ellmann in her *Thinking About Women*.[3] No
subtle essence of femininity would seem to link the work
of Artemisia Gentileschi, Elisabeth Vigée-Lebrun. Angelica Kauffmann, Rosa Bonheur, Berthe Morisot, Suzanne
Valadon, Käthe Kollwitz, Barbara Hepworth, Georgia
O'Keefe, Sophie Taeuber-Arp, Helen Frankenthaler,
Bridget Riley, Lee Bontecou, and Louise Nevelson, any
more than one can find some essential similarity in the
work of Sappho, Marie de France, Jane Austen, Emily
Brontë, George Sand, George Eliot, Virginia Woolf, Gertrude Stein, Anaïs Nin, Emily Dickinson, Sylvia Plath,
and Susan Sontag. In every instance women artists and
writers would seem to be closer to other artists and writers
of their own period and outlook than they are to each
other.

Women artists are more inward-looking, more delicate
and nuanced in their treatment of their medium, it may be
asserted. But which of the women artists cited above is
more inward turning than Redon, more subtle and
nuanced in the handling of pigment than Corot at his
best? Is Fragonard more or less feminine than Elisabeth
Vigée-Lebrun? Or is it not more a question of the whole
rococo style of eighteenth-century France being "feminine," if judged in terms of a two-valued scale of masculinity versus femininity? Certainly, though, if daintiness, delicacy, and preciousness are to be counted as earmarks of a
feminine style, there is nothing very fragile about Rosa
Bonheur's *Horse Fair*, or dainty and introverted about
Helen Frankenthaler's giant canvases. If women have indeed at times turned to scenes of domestic life or of
children, so did men painters like the Dutch Little Masters, Chardin, and the impressionists—Renoir and Monet
as well as Berthe Morisot and Mary Cassatt. In any case,
the mere choice of a certain realm of subject matter, or
the restriction to certain subjects, is not to be equated
with a style, much less with some sort of quintessentially
feminine style.

The problem here lies not so much with the feminists'
concept of what femininity is, but rather with their mis-

conception of what art is:[4] with the naive idea that art is the direct, personal expression of individual emotional experience, a translation of personal life into visual terms. Art is almost never that, great are certainly never. The making of art involves a self-consistent language of form, more or less dependent upon, or free from, given temporally defined conventions, schemata, or systems of notation, which have to be learned or worked out, either through teaching, apprenticeship, or a long period of individual experimentation. The language of art is, more materially, embodied in paint and line on canvas or paper, in stone or clay or plastic or metal—it is neither a sob story nor a hoarse, confidential whisper. The fact of the matter is that there have been no great women artists, as far as we know—although there have been many interesting and good ones who have not been sufficiently investigated or appreciated—or any great Lithuanian jazz pianists, or Eskimo tennis players, no matter how much we might wish there had been. That this should be the case is regrettable, but no amount of manipulating the historical or critical evidence will alter the situation; neither will accusations of male-chauvinist distortions of history and obfuscation of actual achievements of women artists (or black physicists or Lithuanian jazz musicians). The fact is that there *are* no women equivalents for Michelangelo or Rembrandt, Delacroix or Cézanne, Picasso or Matisse, or even, in very recent times, for de Kooning or Warhol, any more than there are any black American equivalents for the same. If there actually were large numbers of "hidden" great women artists, or if there really should be different standards for women's art as opposed to men's—and logically, one cannot have it both ways—then what would feminists be fighting for? If women have in fact achieved the same status as men in the arts, then the status quo is fine as it is.

But in actuality things as they are and as they have been in the arts, as in a hundred other areas, are stultifying, oppressive and discouraging to all who did not have the good fortune to be born white, preferably middle-class or above, males. The fault lies not in our stars, our hormones, our menstrual cycles, or our empty internal spaces, but in our institutions and our education—education understood to include everything that happens to us from the moment we enter, head first, into this world of meaningful symbols, signs, and signals. The miracle is, in fact, that given the overwhelming odds against women, so many have managed to achieve so much in bailiwicks of masculine prerogative like science, politics, or the arts. In some areas, indeed, women have achieved equality. While there may have been no great women composers, there have been great women singers; if no female Shakespeares, there have been Rachels, Bernhardts and Duses, to name only a few great women stage performers. Where there is a need there is a way, institutionally speaking: once the public and the authors themselves demanded more realism and range than boys in drag or piping castrati could offer, a way was found to include women in the institutional structure of the performing arts, even if in some cases they might have to do a little whoring on the side to keep their careers in order. In fact, in some of the performing arts like the ballet, women have exercised a virtual monopoly on greatness, though, it is true, they generally had to serve themselves up to Grand Dukes or aspiring bankers as an added professional obligation.

Under the institution of the British monarchy, weak women like Elizabeth I and Victoria were deemed fit to control the fate of entire nations and did so with noteworthy success. During World War II, the institutional structure of factory work found a way to transform fragile little women into stalwart Rosy the Riveters; after the war, when these jobs were needed by muscular males, the same riveters were found to be too frail to do anything more strenuous than checking out groceries at supermarkets, where they could stand on their feet lifting heavy packages all day long at much lower salaries—or housework and childcare, where they could cope with three or four children on a sixteen-hour shift at no salary at all. Wondrous are the works of man and the institutions he has established, or disestablished at his will!

When one really starts thinking about the implications of "Why are there no great women artists?" one begins to realize to what extent our very consciousness of how things are in the world has been conditioned—and too often falsified—by the way the most important questions are posed. We tend to take it for granted that there really is an East Asian problem, a poverty problem, a black problem—and a woman problem. But first we must ask ourselves who is formulating these "questions," and then, what purposes such formulations may serve; we may, of course, refresh our memories with the unspeakably sinister connotations of the Nazi's "Jewish problem." Obviously, for wolves, be they in sheep's clothing or in mufti, it is always best to refer to the lamb problem in the interests of public relations, as well as for the good of the lupine conscience. Indeed, in our time of instant communication, "problems" are rapidly formulated to rationalize the bad conscience of those with power. Thus, for example, what is in actuality the problem posed by the unwanted and unjustifiable presence of Americans in Vietnam and Cambodia is referred to by these intruding and destructive Americans as the East Asian problem, whereas East Asians may view it, more realistically, as the American problem; the so-called poverty problem might more directly and concretely be viewed as the wealth problem by the poor and hopeless denizens of urban ghettos or rural wastelands; the same not-so-foolish irony twists the white problem—what blacks are going to do to wrest their rights from a dominating, hypocritical, and often outright hostile white majority—into its opposite: a black problem; and the same inverse, but certainly not ineffective or unmotivated, logic turns up in the formulation of our own present state of affairs as the Woman Problem.

Now the woman problem, like all human problems, so-called (and the very idea of calling anything to do with human beings a problem is, of course, a fairly recent one), and unlike mathematical or scientific ones, is not amenable to solution at all, since what human problems involve is an actual reinterpretation of the nature of the situation, or even a radical alteration of stance or program of action *on the part of the problems themselves,* recourses unavailable to mathematical symbols, molecules, or microbes. In other words, the "objects" involved in the solution to human problems are at the same time *subjects,* capable of turning on that other group of human beings who has decided that their fellows are problem-objects to be solved, and capable of refusing both the solution, and, at the same time, the status of being problematic at all. Thus, women and their situation in the arts, as in other realms of endeavor, are not a problem to be viewed through the eyes of the dominant male power elite, at whose will or whose whim their demands may possibly some day be answered, at masculine convenience, of course. Women must conceive of themselves as potentially—if not actually—equal subjects, willing to look the facts of their situation as an institutional and objective problem not merely as a personal and subjective one, full in the face, without self-pity or copouts. Yet at the same time, they must view their situation with that high degree of emotional and intellectual commitment necessary to create a world in which truly equal achievement will be not only made possible, but actively encouraged by social institutions.

It is certainly not realistic to hope, as some feminists optimistically do, that a majority of men in the arts or in any other field will soon see that it is actually in their own self-interest to grant complete equality to women or to maintain that men themselves will soon realize that they are diminished by denying themselves access to traditionally feminine realms and emotional reactions. After all, there are few areas that are really denied to men, if the level of operations demanded be transcendant, responsible, or rewarding enough: men who have a need for feminine involvement with babies or children can certainly fulfill their needs adequately, and gain status and a sense of achievement to boot, in the field of pediatrics or child psychology, with a female nurse to do the more routine work; those who feel the urge for creativity at the stove may gain fame as master chefs or restaurateurs; and of course, men who yearn to fulfill themselves through what are often termed feminine artistic interests can easily find themselves as painters or sculptors, rather than as volunteer museum aides or as part-time ceramicists, as their presumably more aesthetically oriented female counterparts so often end up. As far as scholarship is concerned, how many men would really be willing to exchange their roles as teachers and researchers for that of unpaid, parttime research assistants and typists as well as full-time nannies and domestic workers?

It is only the extraordinarily enlightened or altruistic man who can really want to grant—the term itself is revealing—equality to women, and he will certainly not offer to switch places with one under present circumstances; on the contrary, he realizes that true equality for women will certainly involve considerable sacrifice of comfort, convenience, not to speak of ego-support and "natural" prerogatives, even down to the assumption that "he" is the subject of every sentence unless otherwise stated. Such sacrifices are not made lightly. It is unlikely that the French aristocracy in the eighteenth century would willingly have changed places with the Third Estate, or even granted its members a shred more privilege than they already had, unless forced to do so by the French Revolution; the working classes did not convince their capitalist employers that it would actually be to the latters' advantage to grant them a living wage and a modicum of security until after a long and bloody struggle when unions could reinforce such modest demands; certainly, the slaveowners of the South were willing to go to war to preserve their way of life with its still viable social and economic advantages, conferred by the possession of black slaves. While some of the more enlightened slaveowners may have granted freedom to their slaves, certainly none of them in their right minds could have ever suggested in anything but a spirit of black humor that he might prefer the carefree, irresponsible, watermelon-eating, spiritual-singing life of the darky to his own burdensome superiority. "I've got plenty of nothin'" is the tag-line of bad faith, coined by the uneasy conscience that would metamorphose the powerless victim into the lucky devil. It is through such bad faith that the holders of power can avoid the sacrifices that a truly egalitarian society would demand of all holders of privilege. It is no wonder that those who have such privilege inevitably hold on to it, and hold tight, no matter how marginal the advantage involved, until compelled to bow to superior power of one sort or another.

Thus, the question of women's equality—in art as in any other realm—devolves not upon the relative benevolence or ill-will of individual men, or the self-confidence or abjectness of individual women, but rather on the very nature of our institutional structures themselves and the view of reality that they impose on the human beings who are part of them. As John Stuart Mill pointed out more than a century ago: "Everything which is usual appears natural. The subjection of women to men being a universal custom, any departure from it quite naturally appears unnatural."[5] Most men, despite lip service to equality, are reluctant to give up this natural order of things in which their advantages so far outweigh their disadvantages; for women the case is further complicated by the fact that, as Mill astutely pointed out, theirs is the only oppressed group or caste whose masters demand not only submission, but unqualified affection as well; thus, women are often weakened by the internalized demands of the male-dominated society itself, as well as by a plethora of material goods and comforts: the middle-class woman has a great deal more to lose than her chains.

This is not to say that the oppression of women does not, in some way, disadvantage the dominant male in our society: male supremacist attitudes may distort intellectual matters in the same way as any unquestioned assumptions about historical or social issues. Just as a very little power may corrupt one's actions, so a relatively minor degree of false consciousness may contaminate one's intellectual position. The question "Why are there no great women artists?" is simply the top tenth of an iceberg of misinterpretation and misconception revealed above the surface; beneath lies a vast dark bulk of shaky *idées reçues* about the nature of art and its situational concomitants, about the nature of human abilities in general and of human excellence in particular, and the role that the social order plays in all of this. While the woman problem as such may be a pseudoissue, the misconceptions involved in the question "Why are there no great women artists?" point to major areas of intellectual obfuscation beyond the specific political issues involved in the subjection of women and its ideological justifications.

Beneath the question lie naive, distorted, uncritical assumptions about the making of art in general, much less the making of great art. These assumptions, conscious or unconscious, link together such unlikely superstars as Michelangelo and Van Gogh, Raphael and Jackson Pollock under the rubric of Great Artist—an honorific attested to by the number of scholarly monographs devoted to the artist in question—and the Great Artist is conceived of as one who has genius; genius, in turn, is thought to be an atemporal and mysterious power somehow embedded in the person of the Great Artist.[6] Thus, the conceptual structure underlying the question "Why are there no great women artists?" rests upon unquestioned, often unconscious, metahistorical premises that make Hippolyte Taine's race-milieu-moment formulation of the dimensions of historical thought seem like a model of sophistication. Such, unfortunately, are the assumptions lying behind a great deal of art history writing. It is no accident that the whole crucial question of the conditions *generally* productive of great art has so rarely been investigated, or that attempts to investigate such general problems have, until fairly recently, been dismissed as unscholarly, too broad, or the province of some other discipline like sociology. To encourage such a dispassionate, impersonal, sociological, and institutionally oriented approach would reveal the entire romantic, elitist, individual-glorifying, and monograph-producing substructure upon which the profession of art history is based, and which has only recently been called into question by a group of younger dissidents within the discipline.

Underlying the question about woman as artist, then, we find the whole myth of the Great Artist—unique, godlike subject of a hundred monographs—bearing within his person since birth a mysterious essence, rather like the golden nugget in Mrs. Grass's chicken soup, called genius or talent, which must always out, no matter how unlikely or unpromising the circumstances.

The magical aura surrounding the representational arts and their creators has given birth to myths since earliest times. Interestingly enough, the same magical abilities attributed by Pliny to the Greek painter Lysippos in antiquity—the mysterious inner call in early youth, the lack of any teacher but nature herself—is repeated as late as the nineteenth century by Max Buchon in his biography of the realist painter Courbet. The supernatural powers of the artist as imitator, his control of strong, possibly dangerous powers, have functioned historically to set him off from others as a godlike creator, one who creates being out of nothing like the demiurge. The fairy tale of the boy wonder, discovered by an older artist or discerning patron, usually in the guise of a lowly shepherd boy,[7] has been a stock in trade of artistic mythology ever since Vasari immortalized the young Giotto, whom the great Cimabue discovered drawing sheep on a stone, while the lad was guarding his flocks; Cimabue, overcome with admiration for the realism of the drawing, immediately invited the humble youth to be his pupil. Through some mysterious coincidence, later artists like Beccafumi, Andrea Sansovino, Andrea del Castagno, Mantegna, Zurbaran, and Goya were all discovered in similar pastoral circumstances. Even when the Great Artist was not fortunate enough to come equipped with a flock of sheep as a lad, his talent always seems to have manifested itself very early, independent of any external encouragement: Filippo Lippi, Poussin, Courbet, and Monet are all reported to have drawn caricatures in the margins of their schoolbooks, instead of studying the required subjects—we never, of course, hear about the myriad youths who neglected their studies and scribbled in the margins of their note-books without ever becoming anything more elevated than department store clerks or shoe salesmen—and the great Michelangelo himself, according to his biographer and pupil, Vasari, did more drawing than studying as a child. So pronounced was the young Michelangelo's talent as an art student, reports Vasari, that when his master, Ghirlandaio, absented himself momentarily from his work in Santa Maria Novella and the young Michelangelo took the opportunity to draw "the scaffolding, trestles, pots of paint, brushes, and the apprentices at their tasks," he did so so skillfully, that upon his return his master exclaimed: "This boy knows more than I do."

As is so often the case, such stories, which may indeed have a grain of truth in them, tend both to reflect and to perpetuate the attitudes they subsume. Despite the actual basis in fact of these myths about the early manifestations of genius, the tenor of the tales is itself misleading. It is no doubt true, for example, that the young Picasso passed all the examinations for entrance to the Barcelona, and later to the Madrid, Academy of Art at the age of fifteen in a single day, a feat of such difficulty that most candidates required a month of preparation; however, one would like to find out more about similar precocious qualifiers for art academies, who then went on to achieve nothing but mediocrity or failure—in whom, of course, art historians are uninterested—or to study in greater detail the role played by Picasso's art professor father in the pictorial precocity of his son. What if Picasso had been born a girl? Would Señor Ruiz have paid as much attention or stimulated as much ambition for achievement in a little Pablita?

What is stressed in all these stories is the apparently miraculous, nondetermined, and asocial nature of artistic achievement. This gratuitous, semi-religious conception of the artist's role was elevated into a true hagiography in the nineteenth century, when both art historians, critics, and, not least, some of the artists themselves tended to erect the making of art into a substitute religion, the last bulwark of higher values in a materialistic world. The artist in the nineteenth-century Saints' Legend struggles onward against the most determined parental and social opposition, suffering the slings and arrows of social opprobrium like any Christian martyr, and ultimately succeeds against all odds—generally, alas, after his death—because from deep within himself radiates that mysterious, holy effulgence: genius. Here we have the mad Van Gogh, spinning out sunflowers despite epileptic seizures and near-starvation, or perhaps because of them; Cézanne, braving paternal rejection and public scorn in order to revolutionize painting; Gauguin, throwing away respectability and financial security with a single existential gesture to pursue his calling in the tropics, unrecognized by crass philistines on the home front; or Toulouse-Lautrec, dwarfed, crippled, and alcoholic, sacrificing his aristocratic birthright in favor of the squalid surroundings that provided him with inspiration.

Of course, no serious contemporary art historian ever takes such obvious fairy tales at their face value. Yet it is all too often this sort of mythology about artistic achievement and its concomitants that forms the unconscious or unquestioned assumptions of art scholars, no matter how many crumbs are thrown to social influences, ideas of the times, economic crises, and so on. Behind the most sophisticated investigations of great artists, more specifically, the art history monograph, which accepts the notion of the Great Artist as primary, and the social and institutional structures within which he lived and worked as mere secondary "influences" or "background," lurks the golden nugget theory of genius and the free enterprise conception of individual achievement. On this basis, women's lack of major achievement in art may be formulated as a syllogism: if women had the golden nugget of artistic genius, then it would reveal itself. But it has never revealed itself. Q.E.D. Women do not have the golden nugget of artistic genius. Ig Giotto, the obscure shepherd boy, and Van Gogh, the epileptic, could make it, why not women?

Yet as soon as one leaves behind the world of fairy tale and self-fulfilling prophecy and instead casts a dispassionate eye on the actual situations in which important art has been produced, in the total range of its social and institutional structures throughout history, one finds that the very questions that are fruitful or relevant for the historian to ask shape up rather differently. One would like to ask, for instance, from what social classes, from what castes and subgroups, artists were most likely to come at different periods of art history? What proportion of painters and sculptors, or more specifically, of major painters and sculptors, had fathers or other close relatives engaged in painting, sculpture, or related professions? As Nikolaus Pevsner points out in his discussion of the French Acade-

my in the seventeenth and eighteenth centuries, the transmission of the artistic profession from father to son was
considered a matter of course (as in fact it was with the
Coypels, the Coustous, the Van Loos, and so forth);
indeed, sons of academicians were exempted from the
customary fees for lessons.[8] Despite the noteworthy and
dramatically satisfying cases of the great father-rejecting
révoltés of the nineteenth century, a large proportion of
artists, great and not-so-great, had artist fathers. In the
rank of major artists, the names of Holbein and Dürer,
Raphael and Bernini immediately spring to mind; even in
our more recent, rebellious times, one can cite the names
of Picasso, Calder, Giacometti and Wyeth as members of
artist families.

As far as the relationship of artistic occupation and
social class is concerned, an interesting parallel to "why are
there no great women artists?" might well be: "why
have there been no great artists from the aristocracy?" One
can scarcely think, before the antitraditional nineteenth
century at least, of any artist who sprang from the ranks
of any more elevated class than the upper bourgeoise; even
in the nineteenth century, Degas came from the lower
nobility—more like the *haute bourgeoise*, in fact—and
only Toulouse-Lautrec, metamorphosed into the ranks of
the marginal by accidental deformity, could be said to
have come from the loftier reaches of the upper classes.
While the aristocracy has always provided the lion's share
of the patronage and the audience for art—as indeed, the
aristocracy of wealth does even in our more democratic
days, it has rarely contributed anything but a few amateur-
ish efforts on the actual creation of art itself, although
aristocrats, like many women, have had far more than
their share of educational advantage and leisure, and,
indeed, like women, might often be encouraged to dabble
in the arts or even develop into respectable amateurs.
Napoleon III's cousin, the Princess Mathilde, exhibited at
the official salons; Queen Victoria and Prince Albert
studied art with no less a figure than Landseer himself.
Could it be possible that the little golden nugget—genius—
is as absent from the aristocratic make-up as from the
feminine psyche? Or is it not rather that the demands and
expectations placed on both aristocrats and women—the
amount of time necessarily devoted to social functions, the
very kinds of activities demanded—simply made total de-

votion to professional art production out of the question and unthinkable?

When the right questions are finally asked about the conditions for producing art (of which the production of great art is a subtopic), some discussion of the situational concomitants of intelligence and talent generally, not merely of artistic genius, has to be included. As Piaget and others have stressed in their studies of the development of reason and the unfolding of imagination in young children, intelligence—or, by implication, what we choose to call genius—is a dynamic activity, rather than a static essence, and an activity of a subject *in a situation*. As further investigations in the field of child development reveal, these abilities or this intelligence are built up minutely, step by step, from infancy onward, although the patterns of adaptation-accommodation may be established so early within the subject-in-an-environment that they may indeed *appear* to be innate to the unsophisticated observer. Such investigations imply that, even aside from metahistorical reasons, scholars will have to abandon the notion, consciously articulated or not, of individual genius as innate and primary to the creation of art.[9]

The question "Why the there no great women artists?" has so far led to the conclusion that art is not a free, autonomous activity of a superendowed individual, "influenced" by previous artists, and, more vaguely and superficially, by "social forces," but, rather, that art making, both in terms of the development of the art maker and the nature and quality of the work of art itself, occurs in a social situation, is an integral element of the social structure, and is mediated and determined by specific and definable social institutions, be they art academies, systems of patronage, mythologies of the divine creator and artist as he-man or social outcast.

THE QUESTION OF THE NUDE

We can now approach our question from a more reasonable standpoint, since it seems probable that the answer to why there are no great women artists, or so few women artists at all, lies not in the nature of individual genius or the lack of it, but in the nature of given social institutions and what they forbid or encourage in various classes or groups of individuals. Let us first examine such a simple, but critical issue as availability of the nude model to aspiring women artists in the period extending from the Renaissance until near the end of the nineteenth century, a period in which careful and prolonged study of the nude model was essential to the training of every young artist, to the production of any work with pretensions to grandeur, and to the very essence of history painting, generally accepted as the highest category of art. Indeed, it was argued by defenders of traditional painting in the nineteenth century that there could be no great painting *with* clothed figures, since costume inevitably destroyed both the temporal universality and the classical idealization required by great art. Needless to say, central to the training programs of art academies since their inception late in the sixteenth and early in the seventeenth centuries, was life drawing from the nude, generally from the male, model. In addition, groups of artists and their pupils often met privately for life-drawing sessions from the nude model in their studios. In general, while individual artists and private academies employed the female model extensively, the female nude was forbidden in almost all public art schools as late as 1850 and after—a state of affairs which Pevsner rightly designates as "hardly believable."[10] Far more believable, unfortunately, was the complete unavailability to the aspiring woman artist of *any* nude models at all, be they male or female. As late as 1893 "lady" students were not admitted to life drawing at the official academy in London; even when they were admitted after that date, the model had to be "partially draped."[11]

The very plethora of surviving "Academies"—detailed, painstaking studies from the nude studio model—in the youthful work of artists down through the time of Seurat and well into the twentieth century attests to the central importance of this branch of study in the pedagogy and development of the talented beginner. The formal academic program itself normally proceeded, as a matter of course, from copying from drawings and engravings, to drawing from casts of famous works of sculpture, to drawing from the living model. To be deprived of this ultimate stage of training meant, in effect, to be deprived of the possibility of creating major art works, unless one were a very ingenious lady indeed, or simply, as most of the few women aspiring to be painters ultimately did, restricted oneself to the "minor" and less highly regarded fields of portraiture, genre, landscape, or still life. It is rather as though a medical student were denied the opportunity to dissect or even examine the naked human body.

There exist, to my knowledge, no representations of artists drawing from the nude model that include women in any role but that of the nude model itself, an interesting commentary on rules of propriety: it is all right for a ("low," of course) woman to reveal herself naked-as-an-object for a group of men, but forbidden to a woman to participate in the active study and recording of naked-man-as-an-object, or even a fellow woman! An amusing example of this taboo on confronting a dressed lady with a naked man is embodied in Zoffany's group portrait of the members of the Royal Academy in London in 1772; all the distinguished members are gathered in the life room before two nude male models, with one noteworthy exception—the single female member, the renowned Angelica Kauffmann, who for propriety's sake, one assumes, is merely present in effigy, in the form of a portrait hanging on the wall. A slightly earlier drawing of *Ladies in the Studio* by the Polish artist Daniel Chodowiecki shows the ladies portraying a modestly dressed member of their own sex. In a lithograph dating from the relatively liberated epoch following the French Revolution, the lithographer Marlet has represented some women sketchers in a group of students working from the male model, but the model himself has been chastely provided with what appears to be a pair of bathing trunks, a garment hardly conducive to a sense of classical elevation; no doubt, such license was considered daring in its day, and the young ladies in question suspected of doubtful morals, but even this state of affairs seems to have lasted only a short while. In an English stereoscopic color view of the interior of a studio of about 1865, the standing, bearded male model is so heavily draped that not an iota of his anatomy escapes from the discreet toga, save for a single bare shoulder and arm: even so, he obviously had the grace to avert his eyes in the presence of the crinoline-clad young sketchers, who so clearly outnumber the men that one suspects this is a ladies' drawing class.

The women in the Women's Modeling Class at the Pennsylvania Academy were evidently not even allowed this modest privilege. A photograph by Thomas Eakins of about 1885 reveals these students modeling from a cow (bull? the nether regions are osbscure in the photograph),

a naked cow to be sure, perhaps a daring liberty when one
considers that even piano legs might be concealed beneath
pantalettes during this era; the idea of introducing a
bovine model into the artist's studio stems directly from
Courbet, who brought a living bull into his short-lived
studio academy in the 1860s.

The question of the availability of the nude model is but
a single aspect of the automatic, institutionally maintained
discrimination against women. It reveals both the universality of the discrimination and its consequences, as well as
the institutional rather than individual nature of but one
facet of the necessary preparation and equipment for
achieving mere proficiency, much less greatness, in the
realm of art. One could equally well have examined other
dimensions of the situation, such as the apprenticeship
system, the academic educational pattern that, in France
especially, was almost the only key to success; there was a
regular progression and set competitions, crowned by the
Prix de Rome, which enabled the young winner to work in
the French Academy in that city; this was unthinkable for
women, of course, and they were unable to compete for
the prize until the end of the nineteenth century, when the
whole academic system had lost its importance anyway. If
one uses as an example nineteenth-century France—a
country with the largest proportion of women artists—it
seems clear that "women were not accepted as professional painters."[12] In the middle of the century, there were
only a third as many women as men artists, but even this
mildly encouraging statistic is deceptive, when we discover
that even out of this relatively meager number, *none* had
attended that major stepping stone to artistic success, the
Ecole des Beaux-Arts; only 7 percent had received any
official commission or had held any official office—and
these might include the most menial sort of work—only
7 percent had ever received any salon medal; and *none*
had ever received the Legion of Honor.[13] Deprived of
encouragements, educational facilities, and rewards, it is
almost incredible that a certain percentage of women,
admittedly a small one, actually sought out a profession in
the arts.

It also becomes apparent why women were able to
compete on far more equal terms with men—and even
become innovators—in the field of literature. While art
making has traditionally demanded the learning of specific
techniques and skills, in a certain sequence, in an insti-

tutional setting outside the home, as well as becoming familiar with a specific vocabulary of iconography and motifs; the same is by no means true for the poet or novelist. Anyone, even a woman, has to learn the language, can learn to read and write, and can commit personal experiences to paper in the privacy of the home. Naturally, this oversimplifies the very real difficulties and complexities involved in creating good or great literature, whether by man or woman, but it still gives a clue as to the possibility of the existence of an Emily Dickinson or a Virginia Woolf, and the lack of their counterparts, at least until quite recently, in the visual arts.

Then, of course, there were the "fringe" requirements for major artists, which were for the most part both psychically and socially closed to women, even if they hypothetically could have achieved the requisite grandeur in the performance of their craft. In the Renaissance and after, the great artist, aside from participating in the affairs of an academy, might well be intimate with members of humanist circles with whom he could exchange ideas, establish suitable relationships with patrons, travel widely and freely, perhaps politic and intrigue; in addition he had to possess the sheer organizational acumen and ability required to run a major atelier-factory, like that of Rubens. An enormous amount of self-confidence and worldly knowledgeability, as well as a natural sense of well-earned dominance and power, was needed by the great *chef d'école*, both in running the production end of painting and in controlling and instructing the numerous students and assistants who might flock to his studio.

THE LADY'S ACCOMPLISHMENT

In contrast to the single-mindedness and commitment demanded of a *chef d'école*, we might set the image of the "lady painter" established by nineteenth-century etiquette books and reinforced by the literature of the times. It is precisely the insistence upon a modest, proficient, self-demeaning level of amateurism, the looking upon art, like needlework or crocheting, as a suitable "accomplishment" for the well-brought up young woman, who naturally would want to direct her major attention toward the welfare of others—family and husband—that militated, and still militates today, against any real accomplishment on the part of women. It is this emphasis that transforms serious commitment to frivolous self-indulgence, busy work, or occupational therapy, and today, more than ever, in suburban bastions of the feminine mystique, tends to distort the whole notion of what art is and what kind of social role it plays. In Mrs. Ellis's widely read *The Family Monitor and Domestic Guide,* a book of advice popular both in the United States and in England, published before the middle of the nineteenth century, women were warned against the snare of trying too hard to excel in any one thing. Lest we are tempted to laugh, we may refresh ourselves with more recent samples of exactly the same advice cited in Betty Friedan's *Feminine Mystique* or in the pages of recent issues of popular women's magazines.

It must not be supposed that the writer is one who would advocate, as essential to woman, any very extraordinary degree of intellectual attainment, especially if confined to one particular branch of study. "I should like to excel in something" is a frequent, and, to some extent, laudable expression; but in what does it originate, and to what does it tend? *To be able to do a great many things tolerably well, is of infinitely more value to a woman, than to be able to excel in any one. By the former, she may render herself generally useful; by the latter, she may dazzle for an hour. By being apt, and tolerably well skilled in every thing, she may fall into any situation in life with dignity and ease—by devoting her time to excellence in one, she may remain incapable of every other.*

So far as cleverness, learning, and knowledge are conducive to woman's moral excellence, they are therefore desirable, and no further. *All that would occupy her mind to the exclusion of better things, all that would involve her in the mazes of flattery and admiration, all that would tend to draw away her thoughts from others and fix them on herself, ought to be avoided as an evil to her, however brilliant or attractive it may be in itself.*[14]

This sound bit of advice has a familiar ring: propped up by a bit of Freudianism and some tag-lines from the social sciences about the well-rounded personality, preparation for woman's chief career, marriage, and the unfemininity of deep involvement with work rather than sex, it is the very mainstay of the feminine mystique until this day. Such an outlook helps guard the male from unwanted competition in his "serious" professional activities and assures him of "well-rounded" assistance on the home front, so that he may have sex and family in addition to the fulfillment of his *own* specialized talent and excellence.

As far as painting specifically is concerned, Mrs. Ellis finds that it has one immediate advantage for the young lady over its rival branch of artistic activity, music—it is quiet and disturbs no one (this negative virtue, of course, would not be true of sculpture, but accomplishment with the hammer and chisel simply never occurs as a suitable accomplishment for the weaker sex); in addition, says Mrs. Ellis, "it [drawing] is an employment which beguiles the mind of many cares. . . . Drawing is of all other occupations, the one most calculated to keep the mind from brooding upon self, and to maintain that general cheerfulness which is a part of social and domestic duty. . . . It can also be laid down and resumed, as circumstance or inclination may direct, and that without any serious loss."[15] Again, lest we feel that we have made a great deal of progress in this area in the last hundred years, I might bring up the remark of a bright young doctor who, when the conversation turned to his wife and her friends "dabbling" in the arts, contemptuously snorted: "Well, at least it keeps them out of trouble!" Amateurism and lack of real commitment, as well as snobbery and emphasis on chic on the part of women in their artistic "hobbies," feeds the contempt of the successful, professionally committed man who is engaged in "real" work and can, with a certain justice, point to his wife's lack of seriousness in her artistic activities. For such men, the "real" work of women is only that which directly or indirectly serves themselves and their children: any other commitment falls under the rubric of diversion, selfishness, egomania, or, at the unspoken extreme, castration. The circle is a vicious one, in which philistinism and frivolity mutually reinforce each other, today as in the nineteenth century.

In literature, as in life, even if the woman's commitment to art was apparently a serious one, she was naturally expected to drop her career and give up this commitment at the behest of love and marriage: this lesson is still inculcated in young girls, directly or indirectly, from the moment they are born. Even the determined and successful heroine of Dinah Craik's mid-nineteenth century novel about feminine artistic success, *Olive*, a young woman who lives alone, strives for fame and independence, and actually supports herself through her art—such unfeminine behavior is, of course, at least partly excused by the fact that she is a cripple and automatically considers that marriage is denied to her—ultimately succumbs to the blandishments of love and its natural concomitant, marriage. To paraphrase the words of Patricia Thomson, in *The Victorian Heroine,* Mrs. Craik, having shot her bolts in the course of her novel, is finally content to let her heroine, whose ultimate greatness the reader has never been able to doubt, sink gently into matrimony. "Of Olive, Mrs. Craik comments imperturbably that her husband's influence is to deprive the Scottish Academy of 'no one knew how many grand pictures.' "[16] Then, as so often is the case now, despite men's greater "tolerance," the choice for women seems always to be marriage *or* a career: solitude as the price of success *or* sex and companionship at the price of professional renunciation. If such were the alternatives presented to men, one wonders how many great artists, or even mediocre ones, would have opted for commitment to their art—especially if they had been constantly reminded from their earliest moments that their only true fulfillment *as* men could come from marriage and raising a family. That achievement in the arts, as in any field of endeavor, demands struggle and sacrifice, no one would deny; that this has certainly been true after the middle of the nineteenth century, when the traditional institutions of artistic support and patronage no longer fulfilled their customary obligations, is incontrovertible. One has only to think of Delacroix, Courbet, Degas, Van Gogh, and Toulouse-Lautrec, who all gave up the distractions and obligations of family life, at least in part, so that they could pursue their artistic careers more singlemindedly; yet none of them was automatically denied the pleasures of sex or companionship on account of this choice— on the contrary! Nor did they ever feel that they had sacrificed their manhood or their sexual role in order to achieve professional fulfillment. But if the artist in question happens to be a woman, a thousand years of guilt, self-doubt, and objecthood have been added to the undeniable difficulties of being an artist in the modern world.

An unconscious aura of titillation arises from a visual representation of an aspiring woman artist in the mid-nineteenth century. Emily Mary Osborne's heartfelt 1857 painting, *Nameless and Friendless,* a canvas representing a poor but lovely and respectable young girl at a London art dealers', nervously awaiting the verdict of the pompous proprietor on the worth of her canvases while two ogling "art lovers" look on, is really not too different in its underlying assumptions from an overtly salacious work like Bompard's *Debut of the Model*. The theme in both is innocence, delicious feminine innocence, exposed to the world. It is the charming *vulnerability* of the young woman artist, like that of the hesitating model, which is really the subject of Miss Osborne's painting, not the value of the young woman's work or her pride in it: the issue here is, as usual, sexual rather than serious. Always a model but never an artist might well have served as the motto of the seriously aspiring young woman in nineteenth-century art.

SUCCESSES

But what of the small band of heroic women, who, throughout the ages, despite obstacles, have achieved preeminence, if not the pinnacles of grandeur of a Michelangelo, a Rembrandt, or a Picasso? Are there any qualities that may be said to have characterized them as a group and as individuals? While such an investigation in depth is beyond the scope of this essay, we can point to a few striking characteristics of women artists generally: they all, almost without exception, were either the daughters of artist fathers, or generally later, in the nineteenth and twentieth centuries, had a close personal connection with a stronger or more dominant male artistic personality. Neither of these characteristics is, of course, unusual for men artists; it is simply true almost *without exception* for their feminine counterparts, at least until quite recently. From the legendary sculptor, Sabina von Steinbach, in the fifteenth century, who, according to local tradition, was responsible for the portal groups on the Cathedral of Strasbourg, down to Rosa Bonheur, the most renowned animal painter of the nineteenth century, and including such eminent women artists as Maria Robusti, daughter of Tintoretto, Lavinia Fontana, Artemisia Gentileschi, Elizabeth Chéron, Elisabeth Vigée-Lebrun, and Angelica Kauffmann—all without exception were the daughters of artists; in the nineteenth century, Berthe Morisot was closely associated with Manet, later marrying his brother, and Mary Cassatt based a good deal of her work on the style of her close friend, Degas. Precisely the same breaking of traditional bonds and discarding of time-honored practices that permitted men artists to strike out in directions quite different from those of their fathers in the second half of the nineteenth century enabled women, with additional difficulties, to be sure, to strike out on their own as well. Many of our more recent women artists, like Suzanne Valadon, Paula Modersohn-Becker, Käthe Kollwitz, or Louise Nevelson, have come from nonartistic backgrounds, although many contemporary and near-contemporary women artists have, of course, married fellow artists, a recourse impossible to their masculine contemporaries since there simply would not be enough women artists to go around.

It would be interesting to investigate the role of benign, if not outright encouraging, fathers in the formation of women professionals in the field: both Käthe Kollwitz and Barbara Hepworth, for example, recall the influence of unusually sympathetic and supportive fathers on their artistic pursuits. In the absence of any thoroughgoing investigation, though, one can only gather impressionistic data about the presence or absence of rebellion against parental authority in women artists, and about whether there may be more or less rebellion on the part of women, rather than men, artists. One thing, however, is clear: for a woman to opt for a career at all, much less for a career in art, has required a certain amount of unconventionality, both in the past and at present; whether or not the woman artist rebels against or finds strength in the attitude of her family, she must in any case have a good, strong streak of rebellion in her to make her way in the world of art at all, rather than conform to the socially approved role of wife and mother, the only role to which every social institution consigns her automatically, simply by virtue of her birth. It is only by adopting, however covertly, the "masculine" attributes of singlemindedness, concentration, tenaciousness, and absorption in ideas and craftsmanship for their own sake that women have succeeded and continue to succeed in the world of art.

ROSA BONHEUR

It is instructive to examine in greater detail one of the most successful and accomplished women painters of all time, Rosa Bonheur (1822-1899), whose work, despite the ravages wrought upon its estimation by changes of taste and a certain admitted lack of variety, still stands as an impressive achievement to anyone interested in the art of the nineteenth century and in the history of taste generally. In Rosa Bonheur's career, partly because of the magnitude of her reputation, all the various conflicts, all the internal and external contradictions and struggles typical of her sex and profession, stand out in sharp relief.

The success of Rosa Bonheur firmly establishes the role of institutions and institutional change as a necessary, if not a sufficient, cause of achievement in art. We might say that Bonheur picked a fortunate time to become an artist if she was, at the same time, to have the disadvantage of being a woman: she came into her own in the middle of the nineteenth century, a time in which the struggle between traditional history painting and the less pretentious and more free-wheeling genre painting, landscape, and still life was won by the latter group hands down. A major change in the social and institutional support for art itself was well under way: with the rise of the bourgeoisie and the fall of the cultivated aristocracy, smaller paintings, generally of everyday subjects, rather than grandiose mythological or religious scenes, were much in demand. To cite H. C. and C. A. White: "Three hundred provincial museums there might be, government commissions for public works there might be, but the only possible paid destinations for the rising flood of canvases were the homes of the bourgeoisie. History painting had not and never would rest comfortably in the middle-class parlor. 'Lesser' forms of image art—genre, landscape, still life—did."[17] In mid-nineteenth-century France, as in seventeenth-century Holland, there was a tendency for artists to attempt to achieve some sort of security in a shaky market situation by specializing, that is, making a career out of a specific subject. Animal painting was a very popular field, and Rosa Bonheur was no doubt its most accomplished and successful practitioner, followed in popularity only by the Barbizon painter Troyon, who was at one time so pressed for his paintings of cows that he hired another artist to brush in the backgrounds. Rosa Bonheur's rise to fame accompanied that of the Barbizon landscapists, supported by those canny dealers, the Durand-Ruels, who later moved on to support the work of the impressionists. The Durand-Ruels were among the first dealers to tap this expanding market of movable decoration for the middle classes (to use the Whites' terminology), and Rosa Bonheur, who because of her sex would have almost certainly been unable to succeed so brilliantly as a history painter, climbed on board the bandwagon of burgeoning specialization. Her naturalism and ability to capture the individuality—even the unique "soul"—of each of her animal subjects again coincided with bourgeois taste at the time. The same combination of qualities, with a much stronger dose of sentimentality and pathetic fallacy, to be sure, likewise assured the success of her animalist contemporary, Landseer, in England.

Daughter of an impoverished drawing master, Rosa Bonheur showed her interest in art early; at the same time, she exhibited an independence of spirit and liberty of manner that immediately earned her the label of tomboy. According to her own later accounts, her "masculine protest" established itself early; to what extent *any* show of persistence, stubbornness, and overwhelming vigor would be counted as "masculine" in the first half of the nineteenth century is, of course, conjectural. Rosa Bonheur's attitude toward her father is somewhat ambiguous: while realizing that he had been influential in directing her toward her life's work, there is no doubt that she resented his thoughtless treatment of her beloved mother; in her reminiscences, she half affectionately makes fun of his bizarre form of social idealism. Raimond Bonheur had been an active member of the short-lived Saint-Simonian community, established in the third decade of the nineteenth century by "Le Pere" Enfantin at Menilmontant. Although in her later years Rosa Bonheur might have made fun of some of the more farfetched eccentricities of the members of the community and might have disapproved of the additional strain that her father's apostolate placed on her overburdened mother, it is obvious that the Saint-Simonian ideal of equality for women—they disapproved of marriage, their trousered feminine costume was a token of emancipation, and their spiritual leader, Le Pere Enfantin, made extraordinary efforts to find a woman Messiah to share his reign—made a strong impression on her as a child and may well have influenced her future course of behavior.

"Why shouldn't I be proud to be a woman?" she exclaimed to an interviewer. "My father, that enthusiastic apostle of humanity many times reiterated to me that woman's mission was to elevate the human race, that she was the Messiah of future centuries. It is to his doctrines that I owe the great, noble ambition I have conceived for the sex which I proudly affirm to be mine, and whose independence I will support to my dying day . . ."[18] When she was still hardly more than a child, he instilled in her the ambition to surpass Elisabeth Vigée-Lebrun, certainly the most eminent model she could be expected to follow, and gave her early efforts every possible encouragement. At the same time, the spectacle of her uncomplaining mother's slow decline from sheer overwork and poverty might have been an even more realistic influence on her decision to control her own destiny and never to become the unpaid slave of a man and children through marriage. What is particularly interesting from the modern feminist viewpoint is Rosa Bonheur's ability to combine the most vigorous and unapologetic masculine protest with unabashedly self-contradictory assertions of "basic" femininity.

In those refreshingly straightforward pre-Freudian days, Rosa Bonheur could explain to her biographer that she had never wanted to marry for fear of losing her independence—too many young girls let themselves be led to the altar like lambs to the sacrifice, she maintained—without any awkward sexual overtones marring the ring of pure practicality. Yet at the same time that she rejected marriage for herself and implied an inevitable loss of selfhood for any woman who engaged in it, she, unlike the Saint-Simonians, considered marriage "a sacrament indispensable to the organization of society."

While remaining cool to offers of marriage, she joined in a seemingly cloudless, apparently completely platonic, lifelong union with a fellow woman artist, Nathalie Micas, who evidently provided her with the companionship and emotional warmth that she, like most human beings, needed. Obviously, the presence of this sympathetic friend did not demand the same sacrifice of genuine commitment to her profession which marriage would have entailed; in any case, the advantages of such an arrangement for women who wished to avoid the distraction of children in the days before reliable contraception are obvious.

Yet at the same time that she frankly rejected the conventional feminine role of her times, Rosa Bonheur still was drawn into what Betty Friedan has called the "frilly blouse syndrome," that innocuous version of the feminine protest which even today compels successful women psychiatrists or professors to adopt some ultrafeminine item of clothing or insist on proving their prowess as pie bakers.[19] Although she had early cropped her hair and adopted men's clothes as her habitual attire, following the example of George Sand, whose rural romanticism exerted a powerful influence over her artistic imagination, to her biographer she insisted, and no doubt sincerely believed, that she did so only because of the specific demands of her profession. Indignantly denying rumors to the effect that she had run about the streets of Paris dressed as a boy in her youth, she proudly provided her biographer with a daguerreotype of herself at sixteen years, dressed in perfectly conventional feminine fashion, except for her shorn head, which she excused as a practical measure taken after the death of her mother; "who would have taken care of my curls?" she demanded.[20]

As far as the question of masculine dress was concerned, she was quick to reject her interlocutor's suggestion that her trousers were a symbol of bold emancipation on her part. "I strongly blame women who renounce their customary attire in the desire to make themselves pass for men," she affirmed, thereby implicitly rejecting George Sand as a prototype:

If I had found that trousers suited my sex, I would have completely gotten rid of my skirts, but this is not the case, nor have I ever advised my sisters of the palette to wear men's clothes in the ordinary course of life. If, then, you see me dressed as I am, it is not at all with the aim of making myself interesting, as all too many women have tried, but simply in order to facilitate my work. Remember that at a certain period I spent whole days in the slaughterhouses. Indeed, you have to love your art in order to live in pools of blood. . . . I was also fascinated with horses, and where better can one study these animals than at the fairs, surrounded by horsecopers? I had no alternative but to realize that the garments of my own sex were a total nuisance. That is why I decided to ask the prefect of Police for the authorization to wear masculine clothing.[21] But the costume I am wearing is my working outfit, nothing else. The remarks of fools have never bothered me. Nathalie [her companion] makes fun of them as I do. It doesn't bother her at all to see me dressed as a man, but if you are even the slightest bit put off, I am completely prepared to put on a skirt, especially since all I have to do is to open a closet to find a whole assortment of feminine outfits.[22]

Yet at the same time, Rosa Bonheur is forced to admit: "My trousers have been my great protectors. . . . Many times I have congratulated myself for having dared to break with traditions which would have forced me to abstain from certain kinds of work, due to the obligation to drag my skirts everywhere ..." Yet the famous artist again feels obliged to qualify her honest admission with an ill-assumed "femininity": "Despite my metamorphoses of costume, there is not a daughter of Eve who appreciates the niceties more than I do; my brusque and even slightly unsociable nature has never prevented my heart from remaining completely feminine."[23]

It is somewhat pathetic that this highly successful artist, unsparing of herself in the painstaking study of animal anatomy, diligently pursuing her bovine or equine subjects in the most unpleasant surroundings, industriously producing popular canvases throughout the course of a lengthy career, firm, assured, and incontrovertibly masculine in her style, winner of a first medal in the Paris Salon, Officer of the French Legion of Honor, Commander of the Order of Isabella the Catholic and the Order of Leopold of Belgium, friend of Queen Victoria, should feel compelled late in life to justify and qualify her perfectly reasonable assumption of masculine ways, for any reason whatsoever, and should feel obliged to attack her less modest trouser-wearing sisters at the same time, in order to satisfy the demands of her own bad conscience. For her conscience, despite her supportive father, her unconventional behavior, and the accolade of worldly success, still condemned her for not being a "feminine" woman, since built in by the unconsciously incorporated prescriptions of society itself, it too was intractable to reasoned arguments of reality.

The difficulties imposed by these unconscious demands on the woman artist continue to add to their already difficult enterprise even today. The noted contemporary sculptor, Louise Nevelson, combines utter, "unfeminine" dedication to her work and conspicuously "feminine" false eyelashes; she openly admits that she got married at seventeen despite the certainty that she could not live without creating because "the world said you should get married."[24] Even in the case of these two outstanding artists —and whether we like *The Horse Fair* or not, we still must admire Rosa Bonheur's achievement—the voice of the feminine mystique with its internalized ambivalent narcissism and guilt, subtly dilutes and subverts that total inner confidence, that absolute certitude and moral and aesthetic self-determination demanded by the highest and most innovative work in art.

CONCLUSION

We have tried to deal with one of the perennial questions used to challenge women's demand for true, rather than token, equality, by examining the whole erroneous intellectual substructure upon which the question "Why are there no great women artists?" is based; by questioning the validity of the formulation of so-called problems in general and the problem of women specifically; and by probing some of the limitations of the discipline of art history itself. By stressing the *institutional*—that is, the public—rather than the *individual* or private preconditions for achievement in the arts, we have provided a model for the investigation of other areas in the field. By examining in some detail a single instance of deprivation and disadvantage—the unavailability of nude models to women art students—we have suggested that it was made *institutionally* impossible for women to achieve artistic excellence or success on the same footing as men, *no matter what* the potency of their so-called talent or genius, or their lack of this mysterious ingredient. The existence of a tiny band of successful, if not great, women artists throughout history does nothing to gainsay this fact, any more than does the existence of a few superstars or token achievers among the members of any minority group. A brief glance at the inner conflicts—and real difficulties— experienced by two highly successful women artists confirms the obvious truth that while great achievement is rare and difficult at best, it is still rarer and more difficult if you must wrestle with inner demons of self-doubt and guilt and outer monsters of ridicule or patronizing encouragement, none of which have any specific connection with the quality of the art work as such.

What is important is that women face up to the reality of their history and of their present situation, without making excuses or puffing mediocrity. Disadvantage may indeed be an excuse; it is not, however, an intellectual position. Rather, using their situation as underdogs in the realm of grandeur and outsiders in the realm of ideology as a vantage point, women can reveal institutional and intellectual weaknesses in general, and, at the same time that they destroy false consciousness, take part in the creation of institutions in which clear thought—and true greatness—are challenges open to anyone, man or woman, courageous enough to take the necessary risk, the leap into the unknown.

NOTES

1. "Women Artists," Review of Ernest Guhl's *Die Frauen in die Kunstgeschichte* in *The Westminster Review* (American Edition) 70 (July 1858): 91-104. I am grateful to Elaine Showalter for having brought this review to my attention.

2. See, for example, Peter S. Walch's excellent studies of Angelica Kauffmann or his unpublished doctoral dissertation, "Angelica Kauffmann," Princeton University, 1968, on the subject; for Artemesia Gentileschi, see R. Ward Bissell, "Artemesia Gentileschi—A New Documented Chronology," *Art Bulletin* 50 (June 1968): 153-168.

3. Mary Ellmann, *Thinking about Women* (New York: Harcourt Brace, 1968).

4. A misconception they share with the public at large, it must be added.

5. John Stuart Mill, *The Subjection of Women* (1869) in *Three Essays by John Stuart Mill* (London: World's Classics Series, 1966), p. 441.

6. For the relatively recent genesis of the emphasis on the artist as the nexus of aesthetic experience, see M. H. Abrams, *The Mirror and the Lamp: Romantic Theory and the Critical Tradition* (New York: Oxford University Press 1953), and Maurice Z. Shroder, *Icarus: The Image of the Artist in French Romanticism* (Cambridge: Harvard University Press, 1961).

7. A comparison with the parallel myth for women, the Cinderella story, is revealing: Cinderella gains higher status on the basis of a passive, "sex-object" attribute—small feet (shades of fetishism and Chinese foot-binding!), whereas the boy wonder always proves himself through active accomplishment. For a thorough study of myths about artists, see Ernst Kris and Otto Kurz, *Die Legende vom Künstler: Ein Geschichtlicher Versuch* (Vienna: Krystall-Verlag, 1934).

8. Nikolaus Pevsner, *Academies of Art, Past and Present* (Cambridge, England: The University Press, 1940), p. 96f.

9. Contemporary directions in art itself—earthworks, conceptual art, art as information—certainly point away from emphasis on the individual genius and his saleable products; in art history, Harrison C. and Cynthia A. White's *Canvases and Careers: Institutional Change in the French Painting World* (New York: Wiley, 1965), opens up a fruitful new direction of investigation, as did Nikolaus Pevsner's pioneering *Academies of Art*. Ernst Gombrich and Pierre Francostel, in their very different ways,

have always tended to view art and the artist as part of a total situation, rather than in lofty isolation.

10. Female models were introduced in the life class in Berlin in 1875, in Stockholm in 1839, in Naples in 1870, at the Royal College of Art in London after 1875. Pevsner, *op. cit.*, p. 231. Female models at the Pennsylvania Academy of the Fine Arts wore masks to hide their identity as late as about 1866—as attested to in a charcoal drawing by Thomas Eakins—if not later.

11. Pevsner, *op. cit.*, p. 231.

12. White and White, *op. cit.*, p. 51.

13. *Ibid.*, Table 5.

14. Mrs. Ellis, *The Daughters of England: Their Position in Society, Character, and Responsibilities* (1844) in *The Family Monitor* (New York, 1844), p. 35. My italics.

15. *Ibid.* pp. 38-39.

16. Patricia Thomson, *The Victorian Heroine: A Changing Ideal* (London: Oxford University Press, 1956), p. 77.

17. White and White, *op. cit.*, p. 91.

18. Anna Klumpke, *Rosa Bonheur: Sa vie, son oeuvre* (Paris, 1908), p. 311.

19. Betty Friedan, *The Feminine Mystique* (New York: Dell Publishing Co., 1963), p. 158.

20. Klumpke, *op. cit.*, p. 166.

21. Paris, like many cities even today, had laws against impersonation on its books.

22. Klumpke, *op. cit.*, pp. 308-309.

23. *Ibid.*, pp. 310-311.

24. Cited in Elizabeth Fisher, "The Woman as Artist, Louise Nevelson," *Aphra*, 1 (Spring 1970): p. 32.

22

WORKING IN "A MAN'S WORLD": The Woman Executive

Roslyn S. Willett

In most countries of the modern world the character of life is established by men's decisions. Thinking women have come to believe that a major reason for the social, economic, and political muddle in the world is precisely men's one-sided assumption of decision-making and responsibility. It is becoming clear that complementary decision-making that makes real use of the differences in temperament and talent of the two sexes is absolutely necessary.

It is generally accepted that males of most species tend to be more aggressive than females. Most women and men agree that men tend to fantasize more than women. The combination of the two, aggressiveness and fantasy, may be useful for developing ambitious plans and elaborating abstract systems and structures. But ambitious plans and abstract systems and structures are ineffectual without the counterbalance of a sensitive perception of what is really happening in the real world and a sustained interest in getting a real job done.

When they are solely responsible for making policy and decisions, men tend to overemphasize the aggressive and fantastic components of possible solutions to a problem. It

511

seems clear, however, that if women take on their proper responsibility as half of the human race, and contribute their organic awareness of what has to be done, all kinds of human needs will be met with less waste of energy. The male aggressiveness that has been overdeveloped for lack of feedback will be better proportioned to real-world requirements. The perceptions of women will be fully utilized, along with such male biological aggressiveness as must remain, to create a fine balance between the two complementary sides of the human temperament. With a righting of that balance, the probability of a saner, more wholesome society for *both men and women* is enormous, irrespective of the particular structures of the society.

This essay is an attempt to explore working relationships between men and women, the complementary distribution of working talent between the two sexes, and their possible relationships to biological differences. Its intention, finally, is to suggest fruitful ways of working together.

WORKING NOW

This is a time of transition in the working relationships between women and men, characterized by certain themes. One of them is women's poor image of themselves. Believing themselves to be lesser, smaller, more passive, weaker, more trivial, incapable of coping with men and other women as equals, incapable of taking hold of a *big* job, they behave as if they *are* this way and then get confirmation from others of their own beliefs.

Another theme is men's belief that women cannot really do big jobs, that women are not creative, and that women in offices, government, and industry should hold the jobs closest to housekeeping and a wife's duties. That is, that women should take care of the routine activities, the maintenance chores, the lubricating trivia while men do the big thinking and contact work. Men feel that in helping a man "do his thing," most women derive their satisfactions and feeling of being needed. And finally, they feel that any woman who does big jobs, is creative, and is successful must be a hard, nasty bitch, or sleeping with a guy who put her where she is.

These are myths. But they have been the operating myths of the working world, and they help to explain why it is that women are offered and accept low pay; that capable, educated women accept dead-end office-wife types of jobs; that women who work full-time also do virtually all the housework and child care without complaint in a family where a husband is also present. They also explain the "volunteer" syndrome in suburbs—the middle-class housewife who does not think she is worth much as a worker, but wants to work, and fritters her time away in volunteer chores where she feels "needed," but not *valued*.

Statistics from the Women's Bureau of the Department of Labor tell only part of the story. Incomes of women working full-time average about three-fifths of those of men working full-time; the gap has been widening rather than narrowing. Women clerical workers earn less than three-fifths of what men clerical workers earn; women sales workers earn about two-fifths of what men in similar positions earn; women managers, officials, and proprietors earn slightly more than half of what men in equivalent situations earn. The narrowest gap between the two is on the professional and technical level: women earn about two-thirds of what men earn. Some of the gap is attributable to the fact that women tend to drop out of work during the time that their children are young, so that their accumulated experience may be somewhat less. In addition, a higher proportion of black women than white ones are dependent on jobs; since black women's jobs tend to be low-paying and unskilled, their higher representation lowers the averages.

However, even among women and men of equal educational attainment, the median annual salary of women scientists in 1966 was about $3,000 a year lower than the median annual salary of all scientists of both sexes. Starting salaries offered for women whose qualifications were equal to those of men were usually lower. (Engineering shows the smallest gap—a difference of only a few hundred dollars a year.) One-third of all working women were in seven occupations in the late 1960's. One-fourth of them were in four: they were secretaries, retail saleswomen, household workers, or teachers in elementary schools; the next three occupations were bookkeeper, waitress, and nurse.

Myths about the working possibilities of men and women have been the foundation on which these atrocious figures rest. It would be easy to say that prejudice against women by men is the primary cause. It would be easy, but it would be only half the story. The trouble with working women lies also in themselves, in their definition of themselves and of each other.

Experiments reported in *Trans-Action* magazine several years ago showed that when an identical lecture was delivered by a female instructor and by a male instructor, women college students rated the male "better."

Most working girls and women, even young ones, have permitted their roles to be defined by others, even in contradiction of their own perceptions. Most working women perceive very clearly that their (male) bosses are not particularly bright. Over a period of time, they also become aware that they are themselves as capable as men, and in some areas—for example, responsiveness to situations, insights, and ability to carry a job through to completion—particularly good. They simply do not reach for the rewards of their capacity or even for ordinary equality. If they expected equitable evaluation on their merits and behaved as if they expected it, they would get it more often.

Considerable thought about the difference between the women who have "made it" and those who have not makes it clear that the women who *have* behave as if they expected to be treated as equal. They know the myths about women, but they do not believe them. They rely on their own perceptions of reality and respond directly to that reality. It is no wonder that over a period of time, they act on those perceptions with increasing confidence and become notable in a world of mythmakers for bluntness, directness, and effectiveness. These women have the fewest working "discrimination" stories to tell. They talk sense, and they are listened to. The problem for these women is that men *who do not know them* may not interview, hire, or promote them. They may not get as far, therefore, as men with similar capacities.

On the other hand, women who have been brainwashed early about the inferiority of women do not admit their own perceptions. The idea of equality has no meaning to them. For example, twenty-six years ago, a large company in midtown New York that was advanced enough to have hired an ordinary (not gorgeous) black woman as a receptionist, still required that women smoke cigarettes in the ladies' room, while men were permitted to smoke at their desks. My mere challenge to the personnel department sufficed to undo the ban on women's smoking. Why had the other women waited so long in such a ridiculous situation? It was obviously their feeling that despite the master's degrees in chemistry that a number of them had, they were only women.

Another example of women's bad self-image was in the questionnaire sent to successful women by two women authors of a book on careers for women. The questionnaire asked who had "helped" these women at a number of different stages. Would a man's career be defined by the "help" he had received along the way, making of him a passive recipient of favors? Should it not be as plain for women as for men that a career is not "helped"—that its advancement comes from others' recognizing capacity and making sensible economic use of it?

Demeaning images of women are even disseminated by educated women who are "experts." During the 1950's, a woman Ph.D., working for the then-largest advertising agency in the country as a market researcher, made a career for herself by defining women for the benefit of male marketers as emotional, trivial, and distractable—a great soap opera audience. These qualities could more readily be attributed to temporary isolation from meaning and responsibility than to feminine nature. But there was no differentiation in this analysis. Furthermore, it was extremely satisfying to her male audience, who developed marketing plans and advertising based on it. And handsome, young, married, gray-flannel-suit account men confessed with pleasure they could not "understand" women.

Home economists are among the few professional women employed in considerable numbers in industry. They have been charged by manufacturing and communications firms with interpreting women to their male bosses. Unfortunately, these women's training is more in specific technical areas—food, clothing, household maintenance—than in the liberal arts, psychology, or communication. In addition, home economics as a field of study has not attracted many high-powered women. The result, again, has until recently been a concentration on technical detail and further dissemination of clichés and conventional wisdom about women and their interests. Fortunately, these women have begun to see themselves differently, and a mutter of discontent may be heard at their professional meetings with male speakers whose lack of respect for these women's professional and business attainments expresses itself in silly sexual flattery.

Plainly women can and are beginning to think bigger about themselves and the work they can and should be doing. But, as I indicated at the beginning of this section, the trouble is more with men. Not all of them. Only enough to create difficulty. It is a matter of fact that in the scientific and engineering fields, into which few women have ventured, there is less discrimination than in fields that deal more with symbols. It may be that the habit of dealing with *things* realistically—a simple requirement for successful engineering—permits engineers to evaluate women's talents realistically, and let them work accordingly.

In areas where symbols and fantasy dominate work, women are more troubled by male misunderstanding and more subject to unexamined male prejudice, even if they hold good jobs. This is particularly true where what is being "sold" is image more than product, as it is in magazine publishing, advertising, and public relations. In 1950 when I was one of 140 applicants for a job as editor of a trade magazine and the only female applicant, I was hired because I had taken the trouble to look at the magazine before the interview and outline plans for changing it. The publisher disliked having a woman editor and was nervous about reader acceptance. I was introduced to the readership as "R. L. Willett, our new editor, who takes a tough shirtsleeves approach . . ."

One woman who is now president of her own manufacturing company tells a story of the difference between realism and fantasy in another area. In 1960 she had left a company where she had been in charge of systems design and development on a new computer for the American Stock Exchange. She was one of the few people in the country who had designed and built real-time systems and had the only experience in the country with the requirements of a stock exchange. She was interviewed by an official of the New York Stock Exchange for the job of administrator of their data-processing study group, and after extensive checking of her experience, hired. She accepted very happily; as she puts it, "enchanted with the prospect of another big system." However, because the job was a management job at a very high level, she had to be approved by the Executive Board of the New York Stock Exchange. This was generally a formality. In this case, it was not. The men on the board said no, to the considerable embarrassment of the man who had been delegated to find the best-qualified person in the country. His mortified explanation of their rejection was, "They said you might hear dirty words on the Exchange floor." As she tells it, they hired one man after another—including one who had been her junior in a previous work situation. None of them did the job adequately, and the New York Stock Exchange muddle continued for years.

Inability to believe that women are worth considering outside women's traditional jobs formerly characterized many employment agencies. In the mid-1950's, when I was running the major industrial accounts at a public relations agency, I registered with an employment agency that specialized in public relations executives. I put down my then salary, about $10,000, and the accounts I was working on (mostly in the institutional and packaging fields). The agency principal interviewed me briefly, deciding *a priori* that I was what was known in the trade as a "recipe peddler." (A woman who devises new consumer recipes for use with clients' food products and places them in newspaper and magazine food pages. This happens to be the most usual job for women in public relations, also the lowest paid.) I said I had *never* done that—my experience was entirely industrial, much broader, on a much higher level, and I was paid accordingly. The only job the agency ever offered me was one for a recipe peddler—at almost $3,000 less than I was earning.

Troubles like this continue. A short time ago I received a letter from a professor in the graduate school of business administration of the University of Colorado that read in part:

As you well know, it is a formidable obstacle to a woman graduating senior to get through the door into the business world. In twenty-nine years of doing what I can to help men and women find promising positions, I realize that women must have extra help. Most of our women graduates who have gotten into business have proven their ability to carry executive responsibilities, just as have our men graduates. I can point to many around the country.

More and more men and women executives recognize this and acknowledge that their acceptance is gradually improving, but it is still quite difficult for women to get through that first door. Legislation has not solved the problem.

Can you help? Will you make yourself available to these proven graduates who wish to start their careers in business? I am not soliciting lip-service, or clerk-type openings for these women, but am requesting your whole-hearted active effort to help a woman graduate when she, or I, contact you for your energetic help.

We want your name in our active file. The higher you stand in executive position, the more valuable is your personal availability and participation, just as theirs will be when they reach a level where they can help women graduates that follow. *You* will be greatly appreciated by all concerned, you may be very sure!

Also, we want names and addresses of those persons who you know will cooperate with this program. Please supply us with their names, and the details necessary for making contact with them.

The Wall Street Journal was impressed enough with this kind of effort (directed to only 200 women in the country!) to give it front-page mention a few weeks later.

Working women have had other kinds of problems in being treated as "equal." In the late 1940's I was promoted to a "man's job" in charge of technical service and development on food products in a company that sold colloidal materials to a number of different industries. I was promoted in the first place (from the job of technical and patents librarian) because I had the background, and because the technical director judged that I had the "guts" that the depression-wounded, MIT-educated chemical engineer I was replacing did not have. But, he said, very seriously, "Ros, one of the—things the job requires is that you drink with the boys. Can you do that?" As the single female member of the technical planning committee there, I had other problems. We met at the Chemists' Club, and women were not admitted to the bar. I was literally collared on my way out of the meeting room after a long morning by the company president demanding to know where I thought I was going. He had assumed I was heading to the bar. Far from it: I was heading for the ladies' room—which was almost equally inaccessible.

Other public accommodations problems present themselves: the Advertising Club, a professional, not social, organization, segregates members. Women members are only permitted to entertain in certain rooms, far from the nicest. Until recently United Air Lines ran an all-male executive flight to Chicago at 5 P.M. from Newark Airport. I make frequent trips to Chicago, and Newark is an hour closer to where I live than Kennedy, which was for years the only alternative. My secretary pointed out that I was an executive and so listed in several Who's Who's. No admission. I wrote to the Civil Aeronautics Board complaining about discrimination against women on this convenient plane. They said the all-male executive flight was entirely promotional, and that if women wanted an all-female executive flight that they would put one on. I pointed out the explosive black-white analogy, suggesting that they tell black people that they were not discriminated against on most flights, but on one flight a day, which was purely promotional, only whites were to be permitted; and if blacks wanted an all-black flight, all they had to do was create effective demand. United also said they scarcely ever had any complaints from women. This went on all through the 1960s until early 1970. I did not use United Airlines for any flight during that period and only use them now when they are the only airline into a city.

Inside organizations and even among male colleagues whom one likes, other kinds of experience indicate how hard it is for men to let women rise to their own level. Some years ago, I was a department head in a public relations agency, running several large industrial accounts. I was in a small office with a window, equipped with a standard office desk. The agency head learned of the availability, from a travel agency that was moving, of two tiny desks with drawers the size of those in a sewing machine cabinet—big enough to hold spools of thread. He bought the desks for five dollars each and then came into my office to tell me I was about to be the recipient of a "lady's desk," so that he could give my desk to a newly hired male writer. I pointed out that the folders and papers I used would not fit in the drawers of the "lady's desk," that my efficiency would be diminished by this inappropriate little table, that he would be wasting part of the pretty good salary I was being paid, that the work I did had nothing to do with being "female," and finally that I would not accept the little desk. He stomped out of my office virtually apoplectic with rage about "women." (He had another idea sometime later that my office, with its window, would be more appropriate for a man, who was my junior in age, experience, and responsibility. Again, my answer was no, with an explanation of why I felt it was wrong. The explanation was unheard. The response was that I was an irrational woman, exceptionally difficult to deal with.)

On other occasions where as an "expert" I have organized technical programs and delivered long, well-received talks to large audiences, the only comment from a "friendly" male colleague was that I said "hell" once and "damn" twice, during one speech. The implications were that he had a right to censure my unladylike behavior, and that the audience would be seriously disaffected by it. On another speech-making occasion, I was introduced to an audience of fellow consultants as "our cute, little, bright, girl consultant." When I said I was far from a little girl, being in my mid-forties, and that gender had nothing to do with this kind of work, I was labeled, again, "difficult"!

Another example of unthinking put-down is the story of a professional woman who had been employed as a regional dietitian, supervising the entire Midwestern area's school lunch programs and exercising her own initiative successfully for a number of years. She was hired to do similar work by the public relations agency at which I worked. She made her own schedules and handled her own correspondence and contacts with immense success for the years I was there. My successor was a man, a nice man. The head of the agency told him idly one day that he was to "boss" the school lunch representative, taking over her correspondence and contacts and making her travel schedule for her.

(It should be said, incidentally, to clarify what follows, that I was told while I was there that I was "boss" of a couple of very competent men, and expected to "boss" them. Since they were aware of their assignments and produced their work reliably, and since they knew I would be glad to help if they ran into any trouble with which I could help (technical or writing), I did not exercise my boss prerogatives in any noticeable way. Just saw to it that we got the work out.)

Nothing loath—my successor told the school lunch lady the news and asked that she turn her files and contact list over to him, thereby in one swoop making an independent and capable woman into his flunky. She refused. He called to tell me this story with the comment that she was as irrational as most women, very difficult to deal with. I pointed out to him that he had no real function to serve in this case that she was not already performing better, and that he could have said so to the agency head. Also that her response was direct and to the point. If a man had suffered this indignity, he might not have been so direct. A man might have said, "Yes, but we'll have to wait a few days till I get things in order," or devised some other scheme for evading the problem, and finally when it could not be avoided, disappeared into a bar or come down with a psychosomatic disorder that necessitated his absence until, hopefully, it was forgotten.

Men who can stand competent women as long as their biological differences can be ignored become terribly solicitous when biology comes to the fore. Every single woman who has looked for a job has been asked what she would do if she got married. (The responsibility for her departure always seems imminent to men who can ignore their own job turnover very comfortably.) If she is married, the probability of an instant baby overwhelms the interviewer. It required very blunt talks several times to lay that suspicion to rest in my own career. I had been married for ten years before I decided to have a child. When I changed jobs during that period, it was necessary to point out that I had a diaphragm and a fair amount of successful experience in using it.

Finally, when I did decide to have a child, most people, male and female, were "worried" about my continuing to work. I did work until the night before the baby was born, putting on a very successful client party less than two weeks before, at which I did not sit down at all. Two weeks after, I spent a day touring a client factory. My feeling about work was clued by my observation of pregnant alley cats. Belly or no, they continue to jump over fences and grub around in garbage cans. So can most women. When I was asked how I could continue to work with such a massive handicap, the answer was easy: a big belly only interferes with tying your shoelaces; it does not impair your intelligence. Ask any man with one.

Blunt, straightforward talk and action, and ad hoc responsiveness to real-world situations are very characteristic of women. But it is precisely because men do not want or expect directness—and often do not get it from each other, particularly in the white-collar world—that they find it incomprehensible. They prefer fantasies about what women are like and about what their work and organization are about.

A publishing affiliate of one of the best-known "thinking" corporations in the country asked me some time ago to write a book about dealing with women in industry and business for the benefit of male executives and middle management. I wrote to the editor and said they would not want the kind of book that I would write: describing many problems as men's problems with their own myths about women. I outlined a few. The answer was that I was right. It would comfort no executive to hear this kind of thing; he would not buy such a book.

But the situation is changing. The most serious business magazine in one field in which my firm works as consultants has for years been run mostly by women. But the title "editor" or "editorial director"—the magazine's public image maker—has always been awarded to a man of variable competence, who did not last long. Until lately. A year or two ago the farce ended. The woman "managing editor" became "editor." Other publications in the field have since followed suit as have at least some consumer publications, but the few latter only in the fields defined as "women's."

There are few women in contact positions in advertising and public relations agencies because the men who run them are worried about whether business*men* may not be disturbed at the idea of dealing with a woman. All other things being equal, agency heads have not wanted to disturb possible client prejudices, even in the interest of getting a good job done. Yet, when the question is treated on its merits—and a matter-of-fact evaluation of the requirement for getting a good job done is made—businessmen in heavy industry, high technology, and other fields can and do deal with women without comment. Agency fears have not been justified in my experience, and they are beginning to give way.

The question of competence and ability rarely comes up these days. Most men do not, in the face of evidence to the contrary, say that women *cannot* by their nature do a job; plainly they can and are doing many jobs exceedingly well.

Mary Wells Lawrence runs a dynamic and highly profitable advertising agency and is herself a very creative advertising person. Katherine Flack, administrator of institutional services for the New York State Mental Hygiene Department, has done the pioneering work on creation of a supplies system meeting the requirements of forty-six institutions which house and feed tens of thousands of people. Esther Conwell Rothberg, a physicist, did most of the theoretical work on the behavior of semiconductors. Vera Jenkins, a manufacturers' representative in the Southeast, has turned in the best sales record in the country for Amco Wire Products. General Electric has appointed a woman sales manager in New York for its commercial equipment. Marianne Moore is widely considered one of the country's foremost poets. Margaret Mead and Ruth Benedict have done as much creative thinking in anthropology as any man (and the results do not distort life so much as structural anthropology in the style of Lévi-Strauss). Louise Nevelson's and Marisol's works are as serious and consequential as any male's sculpture; Mary Bauermeister and Helen Frankenthaler, Bridget Riley, and Georgia O'Keeffe, are as creative as any male painter. Mme. Alexandra David-Neel is a fair mystic. Susanne Langer's contributions to philosophy are more important in my opinion than those of any other currently working philospher. Karen Horney's contribution to self-analysis and human typology are wearing better than much work done by male psychiatrists in the same period.

Geraldine Stutz, Dorothy Shaver, and Mildred Custin among others have been extraordinarily successful retailers. Katherine Meyer, Dorothy Schiff, and Alicia Patterson have been exceptionally creative publishers of very profitable newspapers. Margaret Chase Smith has a record of courage and good sense in the Senate equaled by few men. Female writers from Sappho to authors of virtually all the masterpieces of the Heian period of Japan, from Mary Wollstonecraft Shelley to George Eliot to Iris Murdoch, Sigrid Undset, Virginia Woolf, Doris Lessing, and Marguerite Duras, have produced creative work on a par with that of men. Martha Graham's dance compositions surpass those of any other choreographer now working.

Although the number of women physicians in the United States is not high (about 7 percent of the total), in Russia women are 75 percent of the total and they do not treat only women and children (see Solzhenitsyn's *The Cancer Ward*). The number of women lawyers in the United States is small, about 2½ percent; the number of woman lawyers in official positions is even smaller. But in 1959, a UN study quoted by Doris Sassower in *Trial* magazine showed that women were 14 percent of all lawyers in France, 9 percent of the public prosecutors in Hungary, 25 percent of the judges in Poland, and 50 percent of the law students in Denmark.

The trouble with advancement of women in business and industry no longer lies with the idea that they are incapable of doing the job. Plainly women can do well virtually anything there is to do. It lies instead in the male expectation or belief that women tend to be irrational and difficult to deal with. This is a self-serving myth perpetrated by those men who cannot cope with reality, but must impose fantasy on it. They define responsible women variously and pejoratively as, "a little nutty," domineering, masculine, aggressive, feminine, hard to get along with, and impossible to understand. So defined, few women can get past a middle level in any organization or be considered for public "image making" in non-sex-related jobs by the organization.

ARE THERE BIOLOGICAL AND BEHAVIORAL DIFFERENCES?

There are no absolute biological differences other than the clear-cut differences between primary and secondary sex organs (and even these seem to be blurred in a few unfortunate individuals). Human characteristics appear in distribution patterns like those of any other measurable factors—on a scale from "most" to "least," with a sizable group in the middle, and a trailing off of individuals to either side. This would be true of height, weight, muscularity, strength, and various specific abilities in verbal ability, math, games and strategies, peak-type energy output versus sustained energy output.

Since this is so for both men and women, it would be idiotic to say without qualification, "*All* men are good at math, strategy, peak-type pushes, have more mechanical aptitude, are better at manipulating spatial relationships; *all* women have better vocabularies, speak earlier and better, are higher in sensitivity and suggestibility, and can better sustain long energy outputs." Men and women vary; there are women who are stronger, more aggressive, and more capable of high-level mathematical abstraction than most men. There are men who are more aware and sensitive, have better vocabularies, and are more nurturing in their responses than most women. (This distribution of characteristics should not be regarded as making a man less male or a woman less female.) The distributions may be affected by social expectations as much as by biology. The precise etiology of human characteristics in inborn temperament or training is far from defined. But where measurements have been made, it would appear that the above differences are more likely to be true. Most of these differences are suggested by *Human Behavior: An Inventory of Scientific Findings* (Berelson and Steiner), by M. F. Ashley-Montagu, and others.[1]

Unquestionably, most people perceive that there *are* differences between men and women, although one should not demand them of any *individual* man or woman; if one examines the statistical distribution of characteristics, the median for men will be in a different place on the curve from the median for women. These differences manifest themselves early.

One of the easiest to see is musculature. Boys and men have, on the whole, larger, stronger muscles and considerably more muscle tension. This is clear, for example, in classical and folk dancing—where with equivalent or less training, men jump higher—and in athletics, where even the best women do not compete with men in track events.

There is an interplay between body structure and temperament. The tension in muscles requires release in activity. In our society boys are often called "immature" (in nursery and elementary school), "hyperactive," and other pejorative terms. The basic fact is that they are likely to require more activity to release perfectly normal muscle tensions that build up as a result of their normal structure and hormone supplies. Instead of seeing that the "trouble" lies in muscle tension that can be utilized physically and creatively, educators tend to equate maturity and the capacity for learning with the ability to sit still and look attentive. This may explain why girls get better marks in school until adolescence—when they discover that they are not supposed to be smart.

Any kind of tension, including normal muscle tension, is released by strenuous physical activity. It may be *expressed* by aggressive behavior. Our society tends to deplore acts it labels aggressive as if they were bad. But seizing a problem, attacking it with energy, and worrying it through to some kind of solution are all aggressive, human, and necessary. If, as is generally the case, men have more muscle tension and tend to be more aggressive as a result of biological structure, recognizing the biological base for such characteristics and planning to enjoy and use the results seem no more than common sense.

The paucity of research on any of these differences is pointed up by the few reports we do have. For example,

J. J. Gallagher makes the point that differences between boys and girls on written tests were undetectable.[2] They score about the same, except that the girls were *better* at giving solutions to hypothetical problems and the boys were more expressive (should we say aggressive?) in the classroom.

Another possibly biological difference between men and women that has not yet been adequately investigated, but seems to express itself in behavior, has to do with rhythmic cycling and peaking of activity. Possibly because of differences in muscle and hormone tensions, men seem to require a peak-type push and all-out activity at fairly short intervals, with all-out relaxation between. Observation indicates that most women prefer sustained activity without high peaks or deep drops of energy output. Women's activity preferences are much less on an "either-or" basis.

Many primitive societies take advantage of the probable difference in biological rhythms to divide the work between men and women accordingly. The intermittent, maximum-energy-output, then-relaxation jobs are usually men's jobs. In primitive society, hunting is the man's job. The men organize for a hunt, mobilize maximum energy and strategic capability in doing it, encounter very real danger and hardship, and come home with prizes. They then relax, tell stories, fantasize about hardships and danger, reconstruct heroic acts, eat, sleep, and gossip. Women in such societies handle the day-to-day activity, all the businesses, farming, and maintenance.

Aside from possible quantitative differences, there are qualitative differences, some of them perhaps because of training, but many at least partly inborn. One is the nature of perceived reality and how it is dealt with. For reasons that are not entirely clear, men seem to fantasize more than women. This may be one component of their biologically determined aggressiveness. And, perhaps in consequence of an innate difference in ability to perceive spatial relationships and of an interest in strategy and games, men tend to impose abstract structures on reality, and then to perceive reality in terms of their abstractions.

This could be, and often is, extremely fruitful. Abstractions are needed for thinking, for predicting, for developing new ideas. But if the map (the abstraction) does not match the territory (reality), it misleads and confuses. A great many masculine generalizations, abstractions, and "theories" are fake maps aggressively imposed on the real world. Their presence hampers perception of the real world and flexibility in response to it.

With a generally lesser component of aggressiveness and a generally smaller need for fantasy, women are often quite free to perceive the world as it is. The directness and organic wholeness characteristic of feminine perception is called "intuition," "earthiness," "common sense" in everyday affairs. It is also often strikingly new and insightful, creating great "maps" of previously uncharted "territory" like Susanne Langer's *Mind: An Essay on Human Feeling*.

Greater responsiveness to human situations—unvoiced and abstracted—may be somewhat more characteristic of woman *only* in consequence of the *absence* of the hormone and muscle tension that makes males aggressive. On the other hand, some investigators think there are real nervous system differences between men and women. Most women, however, are more likely to believe that sensitiveness and responsiveness are not necessarily positive, *feminine*, built-in characteristics, but qualities that are present in both sexes as part of the *human* endowment, but are covered up by tensions and aggressiveness in the male. The latter are reinforced socially and later become habitual. Possible innate female sensitivity is enhanced by women's experience of nurturing new life and of other *roles*—working and family—in which it is reinforced and deepened.

Apropos of biological differences, it is sometimes said that women are more emotional than men. It is more accurate to note that in our society it is not permitted to men to be as *expressive* of emotion. Women are permitted to be expressive in situations where men are not considered manly if they are expressive. Easy expression of feeling should not be assumed to correlate with intensity of feeling. Women are not necessarily more emotional than men; these things are individual. It may be that the habits of *repression* of feeling (which is masculine) and of imposing abstractions and fantasies on reality actually make men more "emotional." (Evidence exists in their fantasies, in their responsiveness to abstract stimuli for sex, in their preponderance in the crime and violence statistics.)

"Emotional behavior" by women may be related to frustration of their intelligence and capacities, to being put automatically in second place when they are capable of better. Women who work their way out of the second-place role tend not to have to be "emotional."

Granting the really minor differences between men and women, a question arises in the minds of both men and women as to why men have been permitted to dominate affairs for so long. There are several factors involved. First, most women know that the relationships are skewed, but they also know that men have been taught to relate their ego needs to their mythical superiority. Destroying the myths would be destructive of many men. Few women are willing to undertake a *destructive program* even for their own advantage. They know they themselves can readily make adjustment to reality. With their emotional affiliations to particular men, they cannot lightly countenance the possibility of damage to them. (This is not to say that in women's frustration and ambivalence toward the situation in which they find themselves they do not sometimes engage in destructive behavior. They do. But not with that avowed intent.)

Second, although most women perceive the masculine-imposed abstractions on the real world to be faulty, good new structures are not instantly available. In the meantime, it is extremely difficult to substitute for a dazzlingly simple structure (no matter how poorly it matches reality), a nonstructure, a set of ad hoc behaviors that cannot easily be taught or learned, but must be felt. Even discussion or argument about some male-made abstractions is difficult. As the semanticists would say, the formulations may be ultimately meaningless—not discussable.

The problems with the masculine imposition of not-necessarily-matching structure on the working world are all too evident. Economic theory is elaborated but quite often fails to be predictive, although that is its ostensible purpose. "Games" and "strategies" are pursued in business and politics, with immense waste of energy and loss of real purpose. Abstract structures are mistaken for reality, metastructures are imposed on the original abstractions. The whole male-dominated world shows symptoms of a progressive removal from the *real* world with its stubborn ad-hoc-ness and variability. The faulty abstractions aggressively imposed by men on the real world condition decision-making. The new nonverbal, reality-oriented "human potential" and "sensitivity training" movements suggest how urgently a counterbalance is needed.

WHERE DO WE GO FROM HERE?

The division of responsibility between men and women is beginning to right itself. Perhaps the recent progressive trivialization of women, in which a woman who could do effective work or even think was regarded as a freak, has run its course. The mere fact that a Gallup poll could question women recently as to whether they or men have a more "pleasant" life is a sign of change. The majority of women said that women have a more pleasant life. No one asked what has happened to their self-respect in accepting it.

It would be interesting to examine the death rates of men and women in societies in which work and responsibility are shared, comparing them with those in the United States, where women outlive men by seven or eight years. It seems probable that if the hazards of childbirth (which increase the death rate of young women in primitive societies) are not present, and work and responsibility are shared equally, the death rates should be more nearly equivalent.

Men die much earlier in industrial societies mainly because of undue stress. There are a number of factors involved in creating stress. One may be the unnecessary and excessive organization and routinization of work in modern society. This requires that men supplant their possibly more "natural" high-energy-output/relaxation cycle with sustained day-to-day routines that do not suit them as well. The other factor is the overload of responsibility they take on in most families.

Most married men take on the responsibility of earning most, if not all, of the family income. Where necessary, that may mean carrying *two* wage-earning jobs. Since most families are really economic arrangements, to which the money coming in is basic, this is an enormous responsibility. In addition, most men take on the responsibility for making major decisions about where to live, the kind of domicile, the kind of education for the children, the exterior and large-scale maintenance of housing and furnishings, as well as the care and repair of autos, dealings with government, and care of tax, legal, and financial matters. Women in such families do the shopping, take care of cleaning, cooking, laundry, children's errands, some bill-paying, and the social and cultural activities. They are generally under no time pressure. There is no demand that they politic in a hierarchical structure, waste time commuting, or live by the external pressures of the clock. They have reserved much of the very pleasant family business for themselves: the children, entertaining, and cultural activity.

In families where married women work full-time (fewer than half), they usually carry a double burden of household activity and work, and the responsibility may be more nearly shared. But often these women are doing too much of the routine work which should *also* be shared.

The result of this inequity in most families is tremendous responsibility and stress for the man, not enough responsibility for the woman. He may be ambivalent about the results, however gratifying they are to his sense of masculinity and power. He may want or need some time off from the treadmill. He may be envious of his wife's time for reading, for museum-going, or for children. He may resent how she uses "his" money—as if she earned no part of her own maintenance, in baby-sitting, cleaning, cooking, and shopping. He may actually feel that *he* works, and *she* spends. But he may also prefer to have it that way because he is thereby superior and she knows it.

Better arrangements can be made. If we define husband-and-wife as an equal partnership, then both should be expected to develop to their maximal potential at work and at home. In the partnership's domicile, maintenance activity should be shared. Housekeeping activities can easily be shared by two people on the basis of taste and time. If there are children they should learn that some of the maintenance chores are theirs. They should also be systematically taught as early as possible, how to fix simple meals for themselves, shop, use the phone, use public transportation, read a map, and pay attention to written messages directed to them as well as to record messages for other members of the family. In other words, they should be taught whatever adult competence they can learn.

Child care arrangements are far from ideal now, but Margaret Mead suggested many years ago that children raised with more than one adult reference point and with less tight one-to-one relationships with their parents tended to be less neurotic. Recent research by Stolz reported in *Child Development* magazine showed that children of employed mothers were likely to be neurotic only *one-third as often* as children of non-working mothers. The children in both studies were from intact homes. (Other studies have included the children of broken homes whose mothers were employed. The broken-home syndrome was a major factor in the report of neurosis in children of working mothers.)

It will take more than an equal assumption of responsibility by women to make a salutary change in working arrangements, as well as in economics and politics, but the assumption of decision-making power by women is indispensable to serious change.

It has been pointed out rather frequently in the past twenty years that industrial organization no longer requires the presence of large numbers of people in the same place at the same time. This was certainly the case in the primitive factories of the nineteenth century with their steam-powered machinery. With other sources of power such as electricity that are relatively easily disseminated, only certain process industries require centralization; others can be decentralized.

It is also the case that there is no particular rationale for a seven- or eight-hour day. Businesses and industries that arrange part-time schedules for their workers have found that they get *more* work per hour from part-timers, whose satisfactions in doing the job well are not dissipated by the requirement of spending the best part of their day on the spot. An examination of most jobs makes it clear that they are poorly planned on a management level, that most of them could be accomplished in less time. Part of the reason is that human energy and interest flag after a few hours, and the rest of the time on the job is devoted to fiddle-faddle for which the employer is paying. A rational working world would have people working on schedules they could choose for themselves in some measure, with employers paying for the fraction of the usual eight-hour day's work actually done in that period. Everyone would come out ahead—employer and employee—in terms of freedom, flexibility, and increased production.

This type of work scheduling, with increased sensitivity to human capacity, is something women understand very well. Attentiveness to human working rhythms could generate much greater productivity. I have had employees who could not get up in the morning, but could do a great job on a noon to 7 P.M. schedule. One young man worked best from midnight till 6 A.M. Why not?

With both members of the husband-and-wife team working sensible hours, neither of them need suffer the syndrome of being trapped in an economic rat race. Both could enjoy the freedom of thinking, reading, esthetic experiences, continuing education, and regular exercise. The tight family structure and land misuse that characterize the suburbs would go, in favor of more rational living arrangements near work (or more work at home) and better use of open land.

With equal partnership arrangements in families, another blow could be dealt to the rigid hierarchies that pass for organizational structure in most working places. Instead of bureaucratic pyramids with people walled into boxes in an organization chart, ad hoc structures could be developed for finite periods of time to do specific jobs. The resulting working flexibility and openness to new questions, problems, and activities would keep all human beings developing as individuals all their lives, making maximum personal and social use of potentials they scarcely know exist now.

NOTES

1. B. Berelson and G. A. Steiner, *Human Behavior: An Inventory of Scientific Findings* (New York: Harcourt, Brace and World, 1964); M. F. Ashley-Montagu, *The Natural Superiority of Women* (New York: Macmillan, 1953).
2. J. J. Gallagher, "Sex Differences in Expressive Thought of Gifted Children," *Personnel and Guidance Journal* 140 (November 1966).

23

WOMEN AND VOLUNTARISM

Doris B. Gold

Under the influence of the new feminism, one hears everywhere in the United States the battle cry, "Equal Pay for Equal Work!" The cutting edge, the powerful weapon, in this formidable struggle is the irrefutable fact of the inequity inherent in the economic life of American working women. But what of the more than thirteen million volunteers who "work" for no pay at all—a virtual underground of antlike burrowers in our social welfare institutions?[1] How are we to assess with the strange and powerful contradictions their situations represents?

Volunteering is beautiful sings out a new pop-art poster in the supermarket to the woman wheeling her consumer cart. Sooner or later, Mrs. Public is bound to respond, especially if her children are at school all day and she is over thirty-five. This appeal is directly bound up with one of the oldest, most subtle, most complicated ways in which women have been disengaged from the economy with their own eager cooperation—the well-known but little explored phenomenon of voluntarism.

The feminists of the late nineteenth and early twentieth century believed that as women became emancipated, they would seek the world of work. One of them, writing in 1903,[2] even envisioned apartment-house child-care hostels, cafeterias, and other social innovations making such freedom for women possible. But this anticipated evolution has not come to pass, and the nuclear age has found social welfare more in need of voluntary personnel than ever before.

533

In an era of greater leisure, the acute but submerged desires of women of all classes to find expression for their lives beyond the home have been met with a "new voluntarism," described as the fulfillment of one's social responsibility in this climate of national conscience. The designation is as timely as the need is urgent, and while young people and retirees of both sexes are also being sought for volunteer work, it is the women, due to their conditioning to serve and their long history of serving, who will naturally respond in droves, no matter who ostensibly is being addressed.[3]

In rural town, major city, and surrounding suburb, women volunteers in America perform a dizzying catalog of assignments without pay—from leading 4-H clubs to guiding visitors through art museums, from translating Braille to helping hospital therapists, from tutoring blacks and Puerto Ricans to teaching English to foreigners. They excel at collecting money—from cake sales for the PTA to funding symphonies and private schools. (As we shall see later, this involvement with money is one of their greatest hungers.)

Exact data on the genuine efficacy of the thousands of jobs these women perform are unavailable; yet everyone has at one time or another met a woman who has regularly or occasionally given her energies to an assignment.[4] In 1965 an economist estimated the monetary worth of volunteer work, at *14.2 billion* dollars.[5] Since recently young teenage and single women have joined the volunteer force, a feminist analysis may have special relevance and offer insight to the population as a whole. For women, who most often recruit each other into volunteer assignments,[6] consciousness-raising on the meaning of voluntarism in their lives is in order, especially since the Nixon administration is preparing a seven-million-dollar media campaign in 1971, under the National Center for Voluntary Action headed by George Romney, to persuade citizens to offer their services on the domestic front—in housing, health, education, rehabilitation, child care—while the national budget continues to give priority to defense and weaponry.

Why do women volunteer? Powerful social disapproval, coupled with their own psychological conditioning of self-negation and ambivalent self-realization, compels women to regard themselves as marginal jobholders except in times of family crisis or poverty. In addition, our free enterprise system is unable to guarantee full employment; women, along with youth, early retirees, and military personnel, are expendable. As a result, to fill this gap, women have created an impressive network of service systems, many over 100 years old.

While jobholding women are prominent on the feminist scene, the silent housewife-volunteer, often disapproving of her employed sisters with an air of superior compassion, raises many questions that feminists must consider. How did women come to be America's leading volunteers? Why do women so readily attach themselves to the Establishment in this way? Why do they so enjoy fundraising, for instance? How does their pseudowork function? Is it effective from the community's view, from the professionals' view, in women's own estimation? Why have trained, educated, "aware" women opted for voluntarism, instead of structured work or creativity, during or after child-rearing years? Curiously, these and other questions are rarely seriously considered in the writings of either male professional social workers or female administrators of volunteer bureaus; their concerns are mainly programmatic, statistical, and recruitment-oriented. Radical critiques now proliferating in education, the sciences, and sociology are absent. It is particularly strange that few professional writings on women volunteers are analytical in depth since until recently, "volunteer" was synonymous with "woman." Voluntarism remains a vast but hidden subculture of American women's lives, often not understood by the participants themselves; certainly, it deserves serious investigation in any formation of feminist ideology. As William L. O'Neill, historian-author of *Everyone Was Brave,* has pointed out, the basic conditions necessary for genuine female equality are radical and profound analysis of themselves, their social context and their possibilities, which has been so conspicuously absent up to this point.[8]

During the Civil War women first became volunteers as we now know them,[9] replacing the men who had left for the war front as "visitors to the poor." Earlier, during the colonial period, women had served in self-segregated religious groups preaching Christianity to the wayward and helping the sick and poor, in much the same way nuns in modern times have served Catholicism. (It is no wonder that so many of our first evangelists were women.) Later, the drive westward raised the status of women; pioneer society greatly needed their contributions on the frontier. By the Civil War, organizations such as the YMCA, Children's Aid, B'nai Brith, Society of St. Vincent de Paul, and Community Service Society were initiated to deal with the growth of cities and the problems spewed out by the Industrial Revolution—child labor, family disorganization, pauperism, and the like. By the turn of the century, a new profession, social work, was born. Its first practitioners were women volunteers; its philosophy was shaped by social reformers like Mary Richmond of Philadelphia, Zilpha Smith of Boston, and Jane Addams of Hull House in Chicago. The new profession never developed a coherent sense of labor and capital, for male bankers, industrialists, and philanthropists held the purse strings as members of the boards of directors. As early as 1860 some towns and cities had established governmental welfare boards, so a dual system of public and private social welfare emerged. The need for personnel was great, but it was believed that "good works" performed by citizen volunteers, working together with a few professionals, could do the vast job.

By World War I, a host of familiar service organizations had been established,[10] financed by the "men's world" and staffed by both women professionals and volunteers who were mainly wealthy. Various shifts in the division of labor between these volunteers and professionals eventually crystallized into a system where women volunteers did the paper work, freeing the social workers, particularly in private agencies, to offer counseling and other specialized services.[11] By the 1930s, when relief began to be doled out by government agencies, private agencies further narrowed their "clientele," and the public sector expanded with a host of New Deal innovations, in order to attend to the societal wreckage of the depression. Soon, professional social workers were unionized, forming the AFL and later CIO Social Service Employees' Unions which even asked for protection against their replacement by volunteers! Even today, the Red Cross carefully places hospital volunteers to avoid competition with the functions of health personnel who are union members.

World War II's use of eleven million Americans in a variety of crisis community tasks on the home front made the middle-class volunteer a visible factor. During that period women—from Rosie the Riveter to Diana the Draftsman—were also welcomed into the labor force;[12] many child-care services suddenly provided by private and industrial agencies made the freedom to work available for women. When "business as usual" resumed after Hiro-

shima, and young families left cramped city apartments
for one-story homes in spacious suburbs, the child-care
services disappeared. Women went back to their kitchens
and, ironically, yet another brand of voluntarism arose out
of their removal to the bedroom communities: do-it-
yourself school, community, and recreation "structures"
on the new frontier, where the rural enclaves had developed few services. Detouring from employment and
education into consumerism and a peak birth rate,[13]
women helped maintain the stagecoach era in suburbia—
though Sputnik was launched. Without any existing social
services to aid them, and in addition to domestic, chauffer-
ing, and gardening duties, women organized themselves to
plug every hole in the community dike. Professional social
workers were relieved of the need to initiate services.[14]
While voluntarism as a life style declined in the cities
where a female elite was weary of war canteen service, it
was given new life by middle-class women in suburbia,
who, as one sociologist said, needed "the relief of a new
anonymity." Another called voluntarism an attempt to
overcome "the suburban sadness."

Even a superficial overview of the one-hundred-year
history of women volunteers, with its peculiar interchange-
ability of layman and professional, coupled with social
work's beginnings as a woman's profession (somewhat
like teaching school) and its failure to demand a purse of
its own to fill its ranks (there is still a 30 to 40 percent
staff shortage), quickly makes it evident why the helping
professions seek volunteers as rocks invite moss.

While sophisticated, intricate technology has developed
in industry to accommodate the profit sector, congressman, philanthropists, and businessmen still control the
amount of capital allocated to the human services. Once
more voluntarism is being used as a placebo for a crash
program to combat current fiascos of poverty, welfare,
crime, and health. The 1965 federal study of voluntarism
surprisingly raises some basic questions in its conclusions:

What inadequacies in our social order is voluntarism
attempting to overcome? Could they be attacked more
suitably by other means? How does the work of the
volunteer stack up with that of the job-holder? Should the
volunteer attempt to find self-satisfaction, extend the program, or act as a catalytic agent for societal change? Can
he do all three?[15]

So far, there are few answers to the above,[16] which will doubtless set many a social agency director or university school of social work professor to scheduling seminars. In addition, planners, economists, and others must consider what effect the existence of a "volunteer pool" has on both the labor supply of the helping professions— beginning to attract young activists in the universities— and those unemployed being helped toward social mobility by the New Careers Act and other legislation under the Office of Economic Opportunity. Both feminists and social thinkers must question the long-range effects of applying volunteer "bandages" to "social hurts."

For our own purposes, a closer look at the women volunteers themselves is now in order. The middle-aged "classic" women volunteers, are familiar to most of us from personal encounter, news items, and the Helen Hokinson cartoons that appeared in the New Yorker in the 1940s and 1950s.[17] As a child in the 1930s, when I saw a woman visiting my mother at midday wearing an exceptional hat, I was told that she "worked for charity." Many years later as a staff member of a philanthropic organization, I observed that our "large givers" did wear hats; in fact, I was severely criticized by my woman boss when I appeared at a hotel luncheon, well-dressed (contrary to custom) and wearing my own hat! Though recent data show great differentiation of ages and cycles of service for women volunteers,[18] the woman over forty whose children no longer need her daily physical presence is still the one most likely to be found in the ranks of gala ball planners, luncheon givers, bazaar and county-fair throwers; in addition, she may perform a host of other useful work with the many disease foundations such as Cerebral Palsy, March of Dimes, and so forth, wherein those conditioned to view themselves as "more fortunate" help those "less fortunate." These "empty-nest"[19] women make up also the fundraising armies of countless voluntary clubs and organizations. As they grow older, they provide the work force for the thrift-shop operations of professionally staffed agencies.

In an earlier period, middle-aged women whose husbands were upper-class executives were expected to participate in these events out of noblesse oblige, as an aristocracy in a community "court." Thus, service cliques among women of the same class were created in the form of voluntary board elites with decision-making power as well—such as sectarian family services and Junior Leagues. These organizations gave wealthy woman an aura of superiority that they otherwise lacked since the world still indelibly defined them by their husbands' incomes, even as Jacqueline Kennedy Onassis is defined today.

Today middle-class women who seek to acquire status outside the home follow much the same paths as upper-class women of an earlier period, joining neighborhood organizations or forming new clubs and groups with women of kindred tastes and income levels. In fact, many women form structures disguised as "causes" and "needs" in order to fulfill their powerful social needs for adult contact. Those who go beyond their neighborhood to offer their services to established volunteer outlets (aside from disease foundations, most of the private-agency needs are unknown in neighborhoods because of poor public relations) tend to have more education and sophistication and a family tradition of female service. The loneliness they feel in their well-furnished homes and apartments, empty until 3 P.M. or dinner, is assuaged by their involvement with the self-created "work" that women without special training can do together with their trained and paid contemporaries in an office building or an institution.

A decade ago, "empty-nest" upper-class women like these became "Lady Bountifuls," who took their baskets to personally distribute the needed food to the poor family living on the wrong side of the railroad tracks. The recipients of this personal philanthropy, today disapproved by social work philosophy, never questioned these women's superiority; the poor invariably deferred to these representatives of benevolent capitalism in seeming appreciation for staving off hunger. Most men saw these women as meddling unsophisticates who should have stayed with their social teas and committees and kept out of those things in society they little understood. Wealthy husbands viewed, and often still view, their wives as parasitic, insufficiently interested in their domestic affairs, pampered with services and appliances of all kinds that they, the men, make possible through their daily sweat.[20] To the working professional, the ubiquitous woman volunteer, available for daytime hours (unlike the male volunteer who arrived for an evening decision-making meeting or influenced his peers on the outside of the agency), was a source of tension, sometimes a nuisance, always requiring deferential treatment and patience. The volunteers themselves often acted as though they deserved these evaluations: serving as a dedicated person without payment in a money culture invariably results in the assumption of attitudes of superiority and the halo of goodness; these are not easy to take in ordinary human relations.

While the external situation in voluntarism has changed today—men increasingly encourage women to take on interests beyond the home (gynecologists frequently recommend volunteer activity to women undergoing menopause, as do their traveling salesmen husbands), and understaffed social agencies value their presence more than ever—the motivations of the women who do volunteer work are still much the same as they have always been for those who have not used other options beyond domesticity.[21]

Let us speculate on some of the conscious and unconscious motivations that cause women to become unpaid volunteers. The most obvious reason is their legitimate need to leave the home and "see the world." The image of American women as preoccupied with homemaking, interior decor, shopping, bread-baking, animal and garden-loving, environment-creating, as well as mothering, is designed to lock her into place and it succeeds. However, neither the image nor the reality always satisfies woman's strong needs for achievement, despite her so-called "people orientation" as opposed to male's "thing-mindedness."[22] American women, it seems, *do* wish to leave the home whenever possible, to be with others. Because still-strong Puritan conditioning in American men sanctions her escape from the home only under favorable circumstances, such as all-female bridge or mah-jongg games or an innocuous sales job in the neighborhood, the American woman, especially if lower- or middle-class, avoids the hedonistic pleasures of real work away from her local area, feeling the unconscious disapproval which might view her behavior as tinged with egotism or sexuality. (This latter is particularly true of blue-collar wives.) Cultural or other explorations are made, using the rationale that it is "good for the children" when they are young. Perhaps the development of so many "separate but equal" women's voluntary organizations is a reflection of this conditioning.

Even if women leave the home, they act out the biblical helpmate tradition still central to our culture. As they turn from domesticity, they seek to perform in the larger society the same tasks of mothering and maintenance that they carry out inside the home; they become part of paternalistic institutional life—hospitals, schools, churches, synagogues, and other places where men's presence and influence has shaped a sense of family. This "need to be needed" when she is away from her kitchen is still quite strong in American women. Some have claimed this quality in her love is genetic and creates problems of possessiveness, but, more probably, it has been indelibly taught and overlearned. American woman's proclivity to disguise her own needs, even to herself, is striking; she is thoroughly imbued with the philosophy of "being busy means being happy." In fact, her astonishing hyperactivity in a limited sphere may make it difficult for her to recognize her social alienation or her need for self-development. For even in voluntary efforts women who serve are so highly praised by men that they accept rarely being included in the serious and expensive efforts that require decision-making or planning.[28]

Women who become volunteers because they want to "do something useful" are most often merely lonely and empty. Without special talents in music, art, theater, or entertaining and socialization, and without the inner resources to consciously set goals of learning or paid employment, or even to discover simple pleasures of living, these women continuously shop, attend TV screenings, play bingo, or go to luncheons requiring donations of small sums to this or that cause. They are also the planners of "benefits" and bazaars of bewildering variety and extraneousness—a major use of women's energies in voluntary organizations. Fundraising professionals realize that corporate or foundation giving in large amounts for necessary "causes" is less costly in terms of operating costs (and more efficiently spent), than small sums harvested from a wide base; however, since the involvement of so many available volunteers is a factor, the ends are determined by the means at hand—mostly women with time on their hands.

Psychiatrist Thomas Szasz recently remarked that women as a group are insecure because they lack power. Surely the making of money is the supreme act of personal power in our society. By allying themselves with this process, women must surely feel strength—even if counterfeit. Association with impressive looking buildings and institutions of venerable age that have the look of authority makes them feel at least symbolically included in pow-

er. Although she is still defined as her husband's economic
dependent, the married woman nevertheless regards herself as autonomous and unless there is economic need or a
desire for luxuries can find no reason to become part of
the economic machinery. It is far easier to do the pseudowork of "making money" than to earn it in any real
sense. Most women do not opt for the concomitants of
paid employment—fixed hours, rigid routines set by others, monotony, regularity, and particularly, men's control—
unless driven to do so by economic circumstances or
unless such self-discipline is necessary for a vocation chosen
prior to marriage. Women defer the "next logical step" after
mothering—job, education, political or social careers, creative work—and fail to consider the alternatives; more often
than not they assume the neighborhood life style. Even
women who are college graduates[24] display psychological
weakness in facing the implications of their groping for
sophistication; they are stifled by their own paralyzing
anxieties over failing or losing the esteem of the women
around them—representing society—who appear to cherish
motherhood as an all-embracing role. Husbands appear im-
possibly formidable opponents in the competition that
might result if their wives sought self-realization. In much
that American women do after marriage and child-rearing,
especially in their drift into this and that—taking courses,
traveling, voluntarism—their unconscious desire to appear
innocuous and uncontentious predominates.

Another reason why many women choose to be volunteers is obvious.[25] As women attempt to synthesize their
duties at home with their identification with a self-in-
society, they are confronted with an "all-or-nothing"
choice that is difficult for them to make. Except for
women with rare skills, part-time work on a broad scale is
not available beyond office, sales, reception, restaurant,
publishing, real estate and allied insurance fields. Voluntarism often seems like the only way that married women
can be involved in interesting work with and for others
outside the home. It is still very difficult to convince
American industry and technology that there is a labor
reservoir of women interested in a part-time schedule,
which businessmen still consider a burden to their routines.
CATALYST, a woman's organization founded in 1962, is
attempting to publicize the fact that over five million
women college graduates in the United States are not
utilizing their education, partially because of the "tradi-

tional employment pattern." Indeed, a part-time employment campaign for skilled married women is overdue; women's groups themselves have ignored the need for such an attempt. Newtime, a commercial agency in New York City, is attempting to place women in jobs between 9 A.M. and 3 P.M. to accommodate young mothers. The absence of part-time opportunities for women is one of the reasons for a recent rise in the number of hardy, independent women who sell arts and crafts products by mail order, establish boutiques, and conduct assorted "arts" forays with pin-money capital—self-initiated ventures that give women flexible hours for combining wifehood and motherhood. (A Women's Division within the N.Y. State Department of Commerce advises and guides such undertakings.) University programs in "continuing education" which promise certificates and degrees for part-time study, are quickly snapped up by women whenever they are offered.

Another motive for becoming a volunteer, not always guessed at by men, is the need for a changed self-image. After years of domesticity when the world has passed her by, a woman must bolster her confidence before seeking work; many times a "first step" in this process is becoming a volunteer. In social work, health, and welfare, women may find woman executives who serve as their models for future goals, in much the same way as female teachers serve as models for little girls. Since social welfare in general is "nonprofit," the woman feels less pressured for performance than she would with a profit-making company. Employment agencies know enough to describe prospective jobs as "low key" or "nonpressure" to the woman who has been at home for several years and is conditioned to feeling she could not handle a situation that demands speed. Instinctively, a woman feels safer where concrete measurement of results and specific achievement are not the goals; hence she frequents the "human services" scene which has vaguer expectations than other fields. If they dared, women would truly like to compete with men via achievement for their share of the wealth, but they avoid confrontation by evading the arena itself. Reared on principles of "pleasing a man" and "being nice," women escape self-knowledge through the constant reminder that their lives are to be fulfilled through their husbands' work; but the heaviest duties of their end of the partnership are generally performed during the first fifteen years of marriage, and then what? The woman volunteer often expresses her fundamental ambivalence either: (1) by working at an unpaid job where she demonstrates her superiority over others but does not reflect on her husband's earning power; or (2) by assuming a decision-making and planning role in the voluntary organization equal to her husband's at his job, where she creates her own organizational life and reflects on her husband's elevated status. She can thus have her cake and eat it too, psychologically speaking. The chronic inability of women to view themselves as individuals and their tendency to see themselves only through their husbands' occupations is noted by a current researcher:

> Not infrequently women have sought volunteer work so that they might be more interesting to their husbands. Others have sought volunteer activities which are in line with their spouse's business or profession as a way to increase their understanding of his work. The most obvious example of this is the hospital auxiliary, members of which are frequently wives of doctors.[26]

"Status-seeking" as a motivation for women volunteering their services is old-hat, but the middle-class American woman, with a new rationale for helping the "disadvantaged" in particular, is doing just that. By allying herself with causes for social justice, she makes it seem ruthless to deny "the nation's poor" an opportunity to "better themselves," albeit through her and others' efforts. The situation is faintly reminiscent of the colonial British era in India; women assume the white woman's burden to raise people up from welfare, complete with tutoring and housekeeping skills—but hope the objects of their benevolence keep out of "my neighborhood" or "my school."

Some women choose to become volunteers out of disillusionment with present employment opportunities for those who lack skills or dislike office or sales work—the staple of married women's labor. In health and welfare tasks, and in fields where experimental programs are under way—in education, geriatrics, museums, and municipal programs—many women find interesting and innovative niches for a changed self-image with new duties; these opportunities would be closed to them as paid employees in the same institutions because they lack the needed qualifications. The freedom thus offered these educated and/or adventurous volunteers to achieve their goals is sufficiently heady to attract a new breed of volunteer including fully employed men and young single women, who seek such opportunities on weekends. The increasing monotony and depersonalization of most white-collar jobs, depicted by David Riesman in *The Lonely Crowd* twenty years ago, has now intensified through the use of computer-related machinery in banks, insurance companies, and sales offices where women work, increasing their hunger for human relatedness. Feminists and "causists," volunteers themselves, must know the sense of achievement that results from working together with others to effect action—a feeling not easy to duplicate among coworkers in the context of a job. The experiences of brotherliness among union members in the heyday of trade-union formation was probably akin to this excitement. (Studies show that women workers still resist joining unions, consistent with their ambivalence in general. However, unions in the basic industries and crafts do have women's auxiliaries, to which nonworking wives of male union members belong.)

At least one investigation[27] indicates that women seek values different from men's when they work. A consistent need of all women of varying ages, in all socioeconomic groups and marital status, was found to be that of "mastery-achievement" or a "sense of accomplishment and satisfaction." Fulfillment of social needs was second. Women probably feel greater frustration than men because of their unproductive domestic chores and their missed opportunities for training or education; this frustration is felt as a nagging sense of inferiority—creating strong motivation to achieve at and master a job or volunteer assignment. Men seem to value economic rewards, management of others, recognition, independence, and prestige more. Guidance counselors rarely focus on girls' special needs when they are in high school, but steer a girl into volunteer work just as readily as toward regular employment "if her schedule is such that paid work is hard to obtain, or if she had a variety of diverse interests and finds it difficult to focus on a choice."

Since we contend that for women voluntarism is a hybrid of work and role playing, more closely linked to "occupational therapy" than to work accomplished in the economic sense, this psychodrama which has created a virtual subculture among women might seem to offer little else but "therapy" to the volunteer. From a feminist

and/or progressive unionist point of view, voluntarism is
clearly exploitative—in its implication that social justice
for all classes can be achieved through the moral "service" of some who are expendable, albeit out of "free
choice." Manipulating modern women's ambivalence
about their work participation in the economy and using
rationales of citizenship to maintain their loyalty to a
traditional system of human service does not seem eman-
cipating for women's long-term goals. While voluntarism
may have in fact helped to reinforce the fluidity of our
democratic society, wherein people of diverse socioeconomic groups interact with one another and manifest
brotherly love for their neighbors in action, it hardly aids
the development of women who are ready to move into
all aspects of our economic system to maintain them in
special enclaves of voluntarism. The helping professions
would probably demand capital funds to staff their houses
and develop auxiliary paid personnel, were they to exhibit
the same militancy as emerging women and agitate for
necessary changes.

Several volunteer leaders themselves agree that voluntarism is pseudowork, with the focus frequently on the
satisfaction of the volunteer rather than the job to be
accomplished.[28] In fact, one agency mentioned a totally
new youth recreation program it was launching (another
agency has a similar one already in operation); it felt such
a program could retain the younger women volunteers and
attract new ones in this age group. Agencies are now even
planning "careers" in voluntarism, ladders of service designed to present new and more challenging assignments
over the years, in order to reduce turnover. One wonders
how much activity in various social services is self-
perpetuating merely because women are available, and
how much is really needed in the objective sense. Cases in
point: A New York City family agency sponsors a program of volunteers as one-to-one teachers of English in a
ghetto of foreign-born adults, while little or no pressure is
exerted on the Board of Education to adapt its sleepy
archaism to the needs of thousands of new Americans. A
cultural institution uses volunteer assistants for its art
exhibitions, while simultaneously, art school graduates
trained for similar tasks where state funds might be available go unhired. Six volunteers—four of them women—
attempt to raise funds for a community narcotics addiction treatment center, where the placement of one

qualified person might make them eligible for foundation funds and/or municipal grants. A volunteer community relations woman is assigned to a low-income housing project to allay residents' fears after a "racial" incident, while at the same time a Police Department community relations officer and Youth Board assistant team up on the same problem. There are as many examples of such well-meaning extraneousness in voluntarism as there are instances of uniqueness of service and need, although much of the chaos is undoubtedly the result of the maze of urban life with its uncoordinated and unresponsive municipal structure. The insufficient expertise of many professionals is so marked that the urban social activist, functioning without professional staff, or the suburban "causist" is frequently more sophisticated about available resources and more aggressive in obtaining them.

There is more to the exploitative aspect of free woman-hours than woman's ambivalence about her role outside the home. Even the federal study questions the possibility of its becoming a "new panacea" for social ills.[29] For many years socialist thinkers tried to apply the ideology of labor to woman's work in the home as a way to rationalize "from each according to his (her) ability, to each according to his (her) need" payments by governments as recognition of domestic service. (Currently, a New York congressman is proposing legislation making housewives eligible for benefits under the Social Security Act.) Konrad Lorenz, the Austrian ethnologist, recently stated that ". . . some way ought to be found in society to compensate women for their 22 hour day."[30] As a European, he may already have become less conscious of work for economic gain as a major motivation of both men and women. It is not our intention to debate the many theories of economists concerning the ideology of labor, especially as it might apply to Americans in an advanced stage of evolving technocracy. The confusion in a capitalist economy over who shall receive the fruits of labor—especially as this applies to wages for married men and working wives—similarly appears in the use of volunteers as "real" workers. The U.S. Department of Labor itself grapples with the puzzling issue of payment, sparked by the various new federal programs that now include "expense reimbursements" to certain groups of volunteers among the poor and retired: ". . . the need for reimbursing volunteers in lower income brackets for expenses incurred . . . seems obvious. But when more than expenses yet less than the prevailing wage is paid, volunteers are in reality underpaid employed workers."[31]

While it is clear that unpaid volunteers have been responsible for large economies in the private and public sector, it is not generally recognized that many social experiments, such as the provision of sheltered workshops for handicapped workers, recreation for the aged, and progressive child-education programs like Head Start, were begun by women's voluntary organizations.[32] Most Americans know little of the interlocking between government and private agency programs accomplished by volunteers, particularly during times of war, in addition to the cooperation between popular agencies such as Red Cross, Salvation Army, National Jewish Welfare Board, and the newer federal agencies, Peace Corps, Vista, Neighborhood Youth Corps, and a host of Job Corps projects funded by government and administered by business to combat poverty. Elizabeth Koontz, director of the Women's Bureau of the U.S. Department of Labor, has indicated in one instance[33] the huge savings to the government for work done by WICS.[34] WICS spent an average of $44 for each Job Corps woman enrolled; the U.S. Employment Service spent $101 per recruit to do a less thorough job. (Obviously, the use of volunteers *saves*.) Fortunately, many women volunteer leaders are not always quiescent about the use of their energies, or those expectations that innovations in welfare work are not to be considered their sole responsibility. Mary Halloren, former WAC Director now with WICS, told government representatives at a recent meeting in Washington that staff funding rather than voluntary dedication was needed in order "to get something for nothing." At the same meeting, Mrs. Leonard Weiner, president of the National Council of Jewish Women, and also a board member of the Nixon administration's National Center for Voluntary Action, warned women volunteers against "dissipating ourselves all over the map." These indications of change, plus the Labor Department study's examples of volunteer assignments that might well become paid employment, call for swift reaction by both current and prospective women volunteers.

What constitutes work is generally undefined in American society with its advanced machine technology required in the manufacture of goods. Wages historically have always been associated with profits, but not with human needs. During the next thirty years, when according to sociologists, Americans will increasingly "play" at "work" and "work" at "play" with a loss of appetite for real labor at any price, the further development of unstructured work, much like that done by women volunteers now, may affect the labor force as a whole. At any rate, the market for volunteer pseudowork should be shrunk and many new part-time jobs should be developed, in order to place "services" in the same value system as the manufacture of profitable goods. In shaping new national health services, child-care centers, and the like, the helping professions must create many new job categories. This seems bound to occur as the New Careers program and others like it under the Office of Economic Oppportunity, VISTA, and so forth, grow and achieve success.[35]

There is a danger that polarization could take place, with middle-class volunteers withdrawing to a few private social services, while Puerto Ricans, Mexicans, blacks, and poor whites become paid paraprofessionals in "the human services," as new projects proliferate. Sensing this possibility—the crowding out of the "traditional unpaid volunteer"—a current volunteer professional writes:

> The struggles for professionalization of various groups of employees associated with community service delivery systems, as well as the more recent efforts to use these structures as a way to help the disadvantaged climb out of poverty (e.g. the New Careers Program) have often blinded professional and lay leadership ... to the needs of others in the community to participate ... and to the neglect of skills and abilities to be found among the interested citizenry ...[36]

While recognizing voluntarism's invalidity as a solution to the need of modern women to clearly define themselves as individuals with goals in society, unmanipulated by the Establishment for its own ends, it seems reasonable to assume that a new militancy and insight will not cause women to shut the doors on their homes at once, like so many Noras, and seek to find their identity "in the world." There will doubtless be many women in the years to come—along with retired men, students, and young adults of both sexes—who will remain marginal to the economy unless the cry of "full employment" is raised as it was at the close of World War II. It is evident that we may have a permanent reservoir of women who will out of circumstance or inclination continue to volunteer their unpaid services to the community, especially when appeals are made to their "need to be needed."

Voluntary organizations run by and for women can be faulted for serving everyone but themselves in the past. They need to be reminded of what Margaret Adams has called "the compassion trap." With attempts already begun to prod the government into sponsoring day-care centers, women themselves must begin to examine the other needs that welfare mothers and middle- and upper-class women have in common. In order to make the "voluntary system" responsive to true emancipation, they must become aware of how little they have demanded from both the social work and human services area and the government. They must insist *on being served themselves*, with the assistance of the "helping professions." Consciousness of women's busywork in many self-defeating and duplicating projects is in order. Most of all, women who wish to carry out an assignment must have a look-before-leaping approach, together with some sophistication beyond that of the professional.

"Liberation" should mean just that to women—self-experimentation, talent development, and vocational exploration without the spur of immediate income or success. Here voluntarism must be made to serve women, to help them break out of the mold of "suitable" jobs and the rigid lock-step system of "course" education that leaves many with vague talents and no skills. Voluntarism, viewed as a conscious opportunity to try out various environments, roles, and kinds of *real* work, *does* offer the chance at self-development both single and married women need. CATALYST, a women's organization previously mentioned, has already begun to explore the use of volunteer work as a structured training opportunity; it needs a dialogue with women volunteers to develop such a proposal for change. Already, federal civil service credit is extended to those having voluntary experience of like kind and responsibility, but this option is insufficiently used because of the women's undervaluation of their own past efforts. Teaching and/or private industry should also extend such credit. (It will surely make tutoring and other volunteer educational service as well as fundraising more meaningful and measurable.) The credo of women volunteers might become that *they should be served by the community which they themselves serve.*

How *should* women be served if they are contributing unpaid woman-hours to the community? They might demand full- or part-time training, education, or counseling, similar to the services the Veterans' Administration grants to returned soldiers. (Why not a Woman's Administration?) For "service hours performed" they might secure an income-tax deduction; the amount of credit granted would be determined by a national assignment of "priorities." (Perhaps working in health services might secure more credit deduction than, say, tutoring someone for high-school equivalency.) Women must persuade their legislators that according bonuses, leave pay, life-term insurance, and other fringe benefits to GI's separated from service sets a precedent for according various concrete privileges to women who have also "served." Women volunteers must now demand some form of the recognition our society confers on others who make a contribution to its well-being; but no honor certificate or ceremony of praise will suffice to make her a truly equal contributor in society.

One of voluntarism's most important advantages is that it can afford a critical view of society from the inside looking out, not possible by other means to nonemployed persons. If a feminist ideology is to be reaffirmed and strengthened among all levels of the female population, from welfare mothers to socialites, voluntarism, which already encompasses millions of American women, cannot be ignored on parochial grounds. An earlier generation of women created many of the present social services, which, in spite of their peripheral role in human affairs, expressed militancy and criticism of the Establishment in enabling change in the lives of individuals. The helping professions can again become responsive to women's needs in particular if those involved in the fermentation of the new grapes of feminism will share with them the wine of discontent over the status quo. Just as college students demanded inclusion on university boards of trustees; civil rights activists pushed for industry and banks in the ghetto, with ghetto residents involved in management; and welfare recipients insisted on representation on municipal staff committees, so must women demand participation in all functions purporting to serve their needs. Feminist women can use the volunteer structure for their own ends, experimenting with its training and mind-expanding "opportunities" to nourish a more conscious identity. Voluntarism in new dress—with mini, midi, or maxi, innovations and benefits to the women serving in it—must be judiciously altered to fit woman's growing need for real work in a real life.

NOTES

1. The U.S. Department of Labor, Office of Manpower Research, in a 1965 survey of U.S. volunteers (excluding political, religious, and fraternal organizations, so the actual figure is considerably larger), found that six of every ten American volunteers were women; in all, twenty-two million women served as volunteers. Three-quarters of the women were married; half were between twenty-five and forty-four; three-quarters served in youth and education programs. This study is reported in a U.S. government publication, *American Volunteer*, April 1969.
2. Charlotte Perkins Gilman, *Women and Economics* (Boston: Small, Maynard & Co., 1898).
3. Of 2,061 volunteers in New York City in 1970, 77 per cent were women, of whom 55 per cent were single and 22 per cent were married (a shift that bears watching). This is typical of large urban-center voluntarism, even where others were the target population. Reported in the June 1970 *News* of the Volunteer Coordinating Council of New York City.
4. To accommodate the special nature of voluntarism, one is not hired; recruitment or placement distinguishes this pseudowork. Since public relations skills and the history of voluntarism underlie this facet of social work, special courses are offered. Two universities have recently established centers devoted to the study and management of volunteers. The Nixon administration has established a data bank on voluntary projects under the National Center for Voluntary Action.
5. H. Wolozin of the University of Massachusetts, quoted by Helen B. Schaffer, "Voluntary Action: People and Programs," *Editorial Research Reports*, 1969.
6. In spite of public appeals, studies show that most women volunteer because of neighborhood styles or pressure from friends and relatives who are also volunteers.
7. There are no data on patterns of women's voluntarism among different religious and ethnic groups, although great variation is known to exist. More than one million Jewish women belong to women's divisions and all-female groups, for example. See my "Jewish Women's Groups—Separate—But Equal?" *American Jewish Congress Bi-Weekly*, February 1970.
8. William L. O'Neill, *Everyone Was Brave: The Rise and Fall of Feminism in America* (Chicago: Quadrangle Books, 1969).
9. Nathan E. Cohen, ed., *The Citizen Volunteer* (New York: Harper & Row, 1960), contains chapters on women volunteers as well as on the history of voluntarism.
10. Junior Leagues of America, National Council of Jewish Women,

Boys' Clubs, Girl Scouts, Campfire Girls, YWCA. Organizations like Red Cross developed earlier, before the Civil War; self-help groups among Jews and other immigrants reached a peak in the 1890s.

11. In one organization's organization even today, the women volunteers work alongside the staff in such profusion that one can distinguish them only because most volunteers wear hats.

12. During this period the United States had a woman cabinet member, Frances D. Perkins, who served as Secretary of Labor between 1933 and 1945. The only other woman cabinet member in U.S. history was Oveta Culp Hobby, Secretary of Health, Education, and Welfare under Eisenhower. (In passing one might note that the National Labor Relations Board ruled during World War II that a woman might not be called a draftswoman in order to evade the wage scale paid to draftsmen.)

13. This is detailed by Betty Friedan, *The Feminine Mystique* (New York: Dell Publishing Co., 1963).

14. When I lived in a suburb in 1953, there were more than 426 organizations, more than half for women, to serve 17,000 families. Professional writings barely mention voluntarism in suburbia, except for comments on its quality of local concern—PTA, home ownership, zoning, and so forth. My own observations show it has accounted for a large proportion of "caustists" (those who initiate social action) and "culturalists" (those who initiate cultural activities). Fundraising, which is self-initiated, without reference to established private agencies, and slow in following the population out of cities, has been especially important in the suburbs.

15. U.S. Department of Labor, *op. cit.*, p. 1.

16. A three-year study, begun in 1968 by United Funds and Community Councils of America, on volunteers in cities may deal with some of these questions.

17. American literature has virtually ignored the woman volunteer. The few exceptions include Sinclair Lewis' *Ann Vickers* and *Main Street* and, more recently, Jan de Hartog's *The Hospital*.

18. Women today volunteer even during child-rearing years; past thirty-five they volunteer for shorter periods; volunteers frequently move about to various agencies.

19. The term was coined by Sidonie Gruenberg, *The Many Lives of Modern Women* (New York: Doubleday, 1952).

20. Recently, I was asked by a busy male worker in a printing plant why I wasn't a JAP. I learned that this is an acronym Jewish men give their wives—Jewish American Princess.

21. There are few comprehensive analyses of women's motivation or behavior as volunteers, except for agency surveys on performance and satisfaction. One is Jean Beattie Tompkins, "A Study of Women's Voluntary Association Behavior," doctoral diss., University of Iowa, 1955.

22. Erik Erikson created a controversy two years ago with this analysis, which is still being debated by women in science. Erik Erikson, "Inner and Outer Space: Reflections on Womanhood," *Daedalus* 93 (1964): 582-606.

23. Women volunteer leaders, even socially prominent ones, are rarely included on foundation funding committees of any scope. For example, of the more than 100 members on the Committee for Economic Development's board of trustees, two are women —one a newspaper publisher, the other a former government

representative. Most of these think tanks do not include women known for "service."

24. Many women choose teaching after marriage because they can be home at 3 p.m. and take the summers off, not because teaching is their real choice.

25. As many as 200 different reasons were offered by men and women in the federal study. U.S. Department of Labor, *op. cit.*, p. 1.

26. Institute of Community Studies, United Community Funds and Councils of America, *Voluntarism and Urban Life Project*, April 1970.

27. Helen Bickel Wolfe, *Women in the World of Work* (Albany: New York State Department of Education, Division of Research, September 1969). The study involved 1,871 single, married, and divorced women in New York State during 1967, including volunteers between thirty-five and fifty-four years, in full-time and part-time work as well as homemaking.

28. Despite the tradition of women volunteers in hospitals, when serious solutions are proposed to tackle health personnel shortages, volunteers are seldom considered potential candidates. A recent example is the New York City plan to train retired firemen as nurses for understaffed city hospitals, with paid training periods and a special salary scale for the experiment.

29. U.S. Department of Labor, *op. cit.*, p. 1.

30. "A Talk with Konrad Lorenz," *New York Times Magazine*, July 5, 1970.

31. U.S. Department of Labor, *op. cit.*, p. 1.

32. This was originally initiated by the National Council for Jewish Women, currently under Mary Dublin Keyserling, making a national study of child-care facilities.

33. Elizabeth Koontz, "Voluteerism, A Vital Contribution," *A.A.U.W. Journal*, January 1970, pp. 66-68.

34. Women in Community Service, consisting of the National Council of Jewish Women, the National Council of Catholic Women, the National Council of Negro Women, and Church Women United.

35. Since 1960 as many as 10,000 paraprofessionals from various government programs have entered work in veterans' hospitals and other mental health services. Dr. Francine Sobey, *The Nonprofessional Revolution in Mental Health* (New York: Columbia University Press, 1970).

36. U.S. Department of Labor, *op. cit.*, pp. 18, 21.

24

THE COMPASSION TRAP

Margaret Adams

A good deal of the philosophy of women's liberation is widely accepted (if not universally acceptable) in America today; in more progressive political circles it is recognized as having significant meaning for other broader movements of social change. With increasing acceptance there is always a danger that a new idea and the term which embodies it may degenerate into an easy, simplistic catchword or petrify into a stereotyped dogma, inhibiting the very growth it is intended to promote. To avoid this danger of easy popularity, we must examine carefully the widely different, subtle, and often unperceived areas of peonage to which women are subjected with the same care and attention we expend on the more obvious exploitations. Therefore, instead of dealing with the more militant or politically sophisticated aspects of our common theme, which have been well publicized in a wide range of media, I want to analyze the social philosophy and thinking that has defined and shaped certain dominant characteristics of the feminine function, with which all Western women are saddled in one way or another. I shall describe the interacting forces that have developed and sustained the role despite its growing anachronistic inappropriateness, concentrating on the circular process by which biological endowment imposes a certain pattern of functioning, from which develops a self-perception that helps to reinforce, perpetuate, and extend the role.

The main target of my concern is the pervasive belief (amounting almost to an article of faith) that woman's primary and most valuable social function is to provide the tender and compassionate components of life and that through the exercise of these particular traits, women have set themselves up as the exclusive model for protecting, nurturing, and fostering the growth of others. Fundamental to this protective nurturing is the socially invaluable process of synthesizing diffuse and fragmented elements into a viable whole—a basic ingredient of any society's development and survival. This synthesizing operation informs the activities of every woman, whether it is expressed in a one-to-one personal relationship, in keeping more complex elements of a family cemented into a unity, or in actually maintaining the practical habitat of a home that eases the day-to-day living of those whom it shelters. This arbitrary social definition of woman's prime function (in value terms) has encouraged the hypertrophied growth of a single circumscribed area of the feminine psyche, while other qualities have been subjected to gradual but persistent attrition. This social manipulation of women's psychological resources is exploitation as blatant as the economic version that keeps them out of higher salaried jobs and pays them less than men at whatever level they are. Furthermore, it has much in common with the more grossly exploitative view of women as purely sexual objects.

The compassion trap, with its underpinning philosophy and social systems, is one of the strongest forces in today's world that subverts and distorts both the individual identities and the social roles of women. It represents a residual and anachronistic perception of their innate characteristics and social capacities; its uncritical perpetuation leads to an extremity of confused thinking as well as a great deal of frustrated and basically ineffectual activity. The resultant misplacement of vital energies has equally negative effects upon women, who are caught in these self-defeating trivialities, and upon society, which is deprived of the vital and significant contributions that women might make.

The basic framework within which the protective nurturing role of women has been developed and sustained is the social organism of the family, which originated from the biological imperative to ensure the successful repro-

duction of the species and the survival of the young into
independent maturity. This domestic paradigm illustrates
in sharpest relief the situation of women as reservoirs of
protective and nurturing forces. It is the primary device
for keeping women in both practical and emotional bondage. Less clearly realized is that the psychological main-
spring from which the woman's *family-centered* role draws
its staying power has an equally potent influence upon the
course and character of women's activities outside the
home. Briefly, the single woman, who is not tied to husband and children, or the married woman who has partially escaped into a professional role frequently finds herself
in the same sort of bind, confronting basically similar
demands and reacting with similar responses. To understand this seeming paradox, we need to look at the professional world that is open to women and understand how it
developed.

Educated women in employment tend to cluster in the
so-called helping professions. Although this type of work is
commonly thought to be most appropriate for, or congenial to, women's nature, the more significant and prosaic
explanation is that only these areas of professional employment have been open to women in any large numbers
until very recent times, when the strongholds of male-
dominated professions have begun to accept a token number of women. The most familiar of the women-dominated
professions are secretarial work, nursing, teaching, social
work, psychology, and the paramedical services of occupational, physical, and speech therapy; there is also some
controlled infiltration into the jealously guarded preserves
of medicine and the natural sciences. The position these
professions occupy in the hierarchy of social values, the
small degree of direct executive power they carry compared with that wielded by other more prestigious professions, and the sort of functions they involve all help to explain why they have been graciously ceded to women and
informally defined as their legitimate province. In order to
understand this sociological phenomenon more clearly, I
want to look at some other factors that may be associated
with the origin and purpose of these professions, particularly as they relate to some of the broader trends in social
and economic development.

The emergence of the helping professions on a significant scale from the middle of the nineteenth century can
be interpreted as the *psychosocial* counterpart of the gen-

eral trend in *economic* productivity that shifted the site of industrial activity from the small personal setting of individual homes to larger impersonal centers, usually factories, outside. This economic change made it easier to institute the division of labor that was a prerequisite for extracting the maximum profit from industrial enterprise; thus, it provided an opening for technological specialization and the eventual breaking down of complex productive processes into a mass of minute, separate repetitive activities. The helping professions followed a similar course; their proliferation into the complex array of different welfare services reflected an identical process of separating many of the more highly specialized aspects of the nurturing and protective functions from their original place within the home. This division of labor within the protective and nurturing sphere was necessary partly to keep pace with the social problems and issues that were an inevitable by-product of technological specialization in industry, in addition, when one or both parents were out of the home for a substantial part of the day, the acculturating functions they had previously discharged had to be delegated elsewhere. The helping professions were the institutionalized mechanisms by which a rapidly evolving society maintained its integrity and continuity. Education was needed to transmit technological skills to succeeding generations; more recently the emerging discipline of social work has been essential for interpreting the intangible effects of the dominant culture by which the overall functioning pattern of society is governed. In this way the synthesizing function traditionally discharged by women was translated to a wider sphere beyond the home and spread its influence through a broader range of activities; instead of (or in addition to) keeping the family intact and maximally functional, women became involved in housekeeping tasks on behalf of society at large and assumed responsibility for keeping its operation viable.

Outstanding historical examples of this sort of commitment are Jane Addams in Chicago, who helped immigrating foreigners to find their feet in the swiftly developing American society; Lillian Wald, who initiated a health and welfare service for the poor (again mostly immigrants) of New York City; Julia Lathrop, who first directed the U.S. Children's Bureau. Behind these famous figures was an increasingly large band of ordinary individuals (teachers, nurses, social workers), who carried the day-to-day responsibility for broadly conceived national projects and continued the protective, nurturing process at the more intimate level of face-to-face dealing with children, parents, and families.

In discharging this extramural formalized mandate of protection and succor, such women were, and have always been, subject to almost identical demands and standards of responsibility as their married counterparts experience in the more overtly, recognizably feminine setting of home and nursery. Both family and professional commitments incorporate the insidious notion that the needs, demands, and difficulties of other people should be woman's major, if not exclusive, concern and that meeting these must take precedence over all other claims. Implicit in the role that derives from this conviction is the virtue of subordinating individual needs to the welfare of others and the personal value and supposed reward of deriving a vicarious satisfaction from this exercise. This *indirect* expression of talents and skills and these rewards reaped secondhand are probably the chief features distinguishing women from men in their professional lives. Obviously, women's geographical shift out of the home away from domestic ploys did not involve a similar psychological emancipation from the pervasive concept of protection and nurturing. Thus, although women may appear to have achieved economic freedom by performing a job that is independent of the practical ties of children and husband, in terms of psychological commitment they are generally subject to the same sort of thinking; their *modus operandi* utilizes the identical resources and skills as the homebound wife and mother. This observation holds true of all the helping professions, but I am relating it specifically to social work because this is my own professional bailiwick and because the role of the professional social worker and the status of the profession have much in common with that of the housewife. For example, both have a broad mandate that is not clearly defined or specially visible to outsiders; neither on first sight appears to require skills recognizable as unique and essential to its successful operation; for both, the primary objective is to facilitate the growth and adjustment of others and help to make cohesive what is often fragmentary or disintegrating. The functions and skills of both social workers and home-based women are invariably seen as valuable only when their temporary absence results in disruption and malfunctioning, in either the small family or larger society. Prescience of these dangers and the nagging imperative to protect or rescue the vulnerable from their negative effects is the bait that has led most women into the trap where they are presently thrashing about in frustration.

The title of this essay was chosen to convey the idea that overemphasis on certain qualities and the social over-enforcement of functions associated with them have trapped women into a false and basically untenable position. A metaphor based on the karate match might be as apt. Just as the karate player's strength is turned back against him, woman's supposed social strengths have been gradually turned to her disadvantage and now are used to blunt her protest and to bar her escape from the confining role that their exclusive exercise has forced upon her. Women in general have been restrained from any uncompromising or threatening action on their own behalf for fear of negative repercussions on other individuals toward whom they stand in a protective role. In this way shaky and unsatisfactory marriages have been kept going for the sake of the children—this is the most commonly cited example—and in the case of unattached women, career opportunities have often been sacrificed because of some other dependent claims on their emotional resources, such as an aging or sick relative or a family of nieces and nephews that needs some buttressing from the outside. In the area of employment and industrial relations, women's claims for equal treatment and professional equity have often been weakened by their reluctance to apply the final sanction of walking out, for fear of the adverse effects on clients. In familiar situations, women find it extremely difficult to accept the short-term expediency of permitting (or even failing to prevent) harm to others, even when the long-term results may be highly beneficial. Occasionally, a brave wife walks out of an impossible family setup and leaves the other spouse to rally resources for the children, but such behavior is almost always heavily censured. In addition, the current pattern of family life, which dumps homemaking and child care exclusively upon the wife and gives the husband the sole responsibility for income maintenance, creates a realistic difficulty for the husband when the woman abandons her part of the contract.

Professionals in the helping areas have started to resist this sort of emotional blackmail by deliberately participating in boycotts, strikes, and walkouts. Both New York City's social workers and its public school teachers have rigorously demonstrated the necessity and value of forcibly protesting conditions that are inimical to employees (and therefore in the long run must also have an adverse effect upon the clients and children for whom they have a protective responsibility). Women as a whole need to feel justified in taking this stand when it is necessary; in order to insure that they are not constantly lured into the wrong sort of behavior for fear of doing harm, women need to examine their role in today's society, and particularly the psychological contribution that they make to the collusive pattern that so easily perverts their judgment and thinking.

To borrow a clinical metaphor, diagnosis has to precede treatment. Before women can put an end to this unsatisfactory situation, they must look into the reasons why it continues to persist even in the face of such frustrating consequences. One cogent explanation that is not immediately obvious has to do with the characteristics of society and the particular pressures they put upon women in their state of social transition. Today's fragmented and disintegrating world makes it essential for every individual and group of individuals to have an easily defined, clearly perceived, and socially reinforced role, which will preserve a sense of real identity and counteract the climate of futility and the relentless assault of status-conscious, competitive individualism. Because of their ambiguous status, women are especially prone to these socially alienating influences and find it very tempting to be designated as the person or group who has special understanding and insights, who can be relied upon to smooth away difficulties and reconcile warring elements, and who remains the willing repository for everyone else's unsolved problems. The overriding need to feel useful and wanted in a social system that in other respects does not accord women much, if any, value or opportunity for really significant participation makes most leap at this offer of involvement, even when it means stifling their underlying sense of frustrated disappointment with the soothing rationalization that personal ambition and success are corrupting, and that they remain the salt of the earth through adding savor and essential strength to the lives of others. The other side of the coin is that women's personal acculturation to the ideal of constant helpfulness and their early habit of thought that constrains them to this emotional indenture produce a high level of susceptibility to this very argument, particularly when extricating themselves from its premises takes so much intellectual effort and emotional fortitude. A lot is said and written about the exploitation of women as sexual objects to further the psychological needs of the male and the consumer needs of an overproducing economy, but what I am talking about is an exactly similar process in which not physical sexual attributes, but psychological ones, are subject to similar prostitution and misuse. This applies to the invaluable secretary, the personal assistant at the executive level, the woman physician in a rigidly structured medical hierarchy, the social worker, nurse, teacher (and many others in feminine jobs) who feed their skills into a social program that they have rarely designed and that, with few exceptions, is fundamentally geared to the maintenance of society's status quo in all its destructive, exploitative aspects. Emotional manipulation of this sort skews women's vision and creates the delusion that they are making a valuable contribution to society's well-being—which on examination is clearly impossible to maintain on several counts.

First, our society is primarily committed to destruction, of both obvious and subtle kinds; even benign social institutions (such as peace movements or progressive political groups) are riven by divisiveness and hostilities. Second, almost every human relationship operates from a baseline of exploitation and self-interest rather than mutual trust, and the social goals of most individuals and groups are guided by the profit motive. In this context, where piracy (or rugged individualism or freedom, whichever term you choose to describe the cutthroat interactive patterns of today) is the accepted and reinforced mode of operation, women face the devastating dilemma that their traditional commitment to invest their skills, ideas, emotional and practical energies in other peoples' enterprises must either be dispensed with or turned to the immoral and profitless end of advancing the personal ambitions of ruthless predatory individuals (or groups) or shoring up the crumbling efforts of inadequate ones. Third, the time-honoured function of reciprocal assistance, which is another means by which women discharged their synthesizing role, cannot be appropriately fulfilled today because it depends on a social cohesiveness and stability that are missing from today's scene.

Neither the practical patterns of social life nor its psychological undercurrents are conducive to awareness of interdependence and the common weal, both of which are based on the old assumption of geographical stability and historical continuity. Because of the frenetic pace of social mobility in this country, people move in and out of communities and neighborhoods with frightening rapidity; ongoing supportive relationships cannot be formed or sustained in the same way, either through informal social channels or the formalized intervention provided by social work. More disconcerting is the fact that the general disintegration of social values is creating a similar instability in emotional, social, moral, and political stances, so that mutual trust between people, which is the basis of social cohesiveness, is gradually being eroded. In such a social context, the organizing resources and concern for the well-being of others that have characterized women's function within the family, and also its derivatives, the helping professions, are being plundered, not in order to keep a basically healthy society in shape, but to prolong the moribund life of a corrupt and decaying social order.

In the field of social work, this pointless operation is particularly glaring, since as a profession we are asked to address ourselves to individual social problems which are only amenable to temporary alleviation, because of the social pathology from which they spring. In many areas of serious social maladjustment, the solution would be hastened if social workers withheld their remedial intervention and permitted critical stresses to mount to an explosive level; this would compel a drastic and more basic attack on the underlying problems, instead of a piecemeal concern with the more superficial symptomatic manifestations. Very few of us, either as individuals or as employees of a particular agency, would feel comfortable taking this seemingly ruthless path if it meant permitting the continuation of suffering that could be prevented, even though the long-range gains might be considerable. This short-range focus on social and personal problems, their origins and their cure, is another illustration of the compassion trap; it partially explains why women social workers do not occupy a high proportion of the profession's executive posts, which would give them power to plan basic long-range preventive services as well as those of the more immediate remedial kind. Instead, the majority have stayed at the practitioner level and concerned themselves with the narrower area of individual interpersonal problems, where their intuitive and empathetic qualities have had scope for expression to good particular effect, but with little total cumulative impact in proportion to the extent, nature, and complexity of the social problems that challenge the profession today. From another perspective, social workers, particularly women, are at a further disadvantage because their profession has a relatively low status: their expert formulations of diagnosis and treatment are liable to be ignored or overruled by colleagues who represent more dominant power groups in the professional arena.

The lack of acknowledged executive power at both planning and operational levels is psychologically very debilitating and probably accounts for certain features of the social-work profession that have been open to criticism. One of these is the long-standing preoccupation with the intrapsychic aspects of social maladjustment that has been at least partially responsible for the more practical aspects of social dislocation being overlooked or neglected. Being faced with overwhelming social problems without effective power to change them made social work just another more sophisticated housekeeping function. To escape from this burden of housekeeping chores, with their repetitive lack of essential creativity, social workers carved out an area for themselves in which they were able to develop the creative, imaginative aspects of their trade. Unfortunately, this heavy intellectual investment in the psychological and emotional factors of maladjustment has meant that the more overtly social components have not been well served.

A second feature of professional social work that directly reflects the profession's fundamental lack of power is the infantilizing system of supervision which, until recently, subjected the responsibilities and tasks of *fully-trained* workers to regular, continuous scrutiny and criticism by senior colleagues. The degree and duration of such surveillance far exceeded that practiced by other professions that carry equal responsibility for client welfare; more often than not the practice has been determined by the need to maintain a hierarchical structure rather than by the actual needs of workers. I cite this system as an illustration of the officious, busy, and basically trivial activities which people—in this case mainly women—have to resort to when more viable channels for expressing their basically sound and vigorous resources are systematically blocked. This assumption draws some support from the interesting fact that supervision tends to be most scrupulous (in the pejorative, obsessional sense) in regard to casework which concentrates on interpersonal problems and psychological activity, whereas workers who are concerned with organizing community resources to provide practical interventive services for real needs are often allowed to operate with greater independence and freedom for innovation. Very recently I attended a conference of social workers at which the main theme was advocacy for the mentally retarded and their besieged families—that is, the social-service responsibility for finding services to help compensate for their handicap and for exerting pressure to get such services developed when they are not in supply. Implicit in this function is the securing and protection of basic human rights. The most interesting feature of this meeting was the vigorous enthusiasm that this approach met with, as though it were novel and rather daring; less diverting were the persevering ruminations that went on about how to fulfill this role—what skills did it demand, how could they be inculcated in practice, what changes were needed in professional training to ensure competence in this task. Since the entire expertise of social work rests upon a fine and subtle understanding of human relations and the behavior they give rise to, it struck me as ironic that advocacy on behalf of an unquestionably weak and vulnerable client group should evoke such doubts; after all, the task requires attitudes and skills inherent to the profession. I think the explanation is that advocacy requires a more aggressive stance than the more familiar one of compassion and protection; in the last analysis it may demand confrontation and conflict. At first sight, this activity seems the antithesis of the nurturing and protective role, and it is not a coincidence that this new social-work concept has been borrowed from the almost exclusively masculine profession of law, which deals directly with balances of power.

However, the advocate's approach has been steadily gaining ground and is now recognized as the principal, if not only, way of securing equity and justice for the vast group of underprivileged and socially displaced individuals who are the profession's most needy clientele. This trend signifies an important stage in professional growth in that it implies a shift from a stance that is basically submissive to one that is potentially dominant. Social workers have generally been concerned with helping clients to gain insight into the dynamics of their problems, particularly the contribution made by their own personalities, so that with this understanding they can both modify their behavior and achieve a more satisfactory adjustment to the social pressures weighing upon them. The advocacy approach directs itself to understanding the dynamics of society that has disenfranchised so many citizens, regardless of personal strengths and weaknesses, and to establishing procedures that will secure their basic human and social rights. There is a marked parallel between this change of direction in social work and the new self-images and activities that women are assuming as part of the liberation movement; both groups encounter similar problems. The advocacy role, for example, is liable to involve negative repercussions for the client whose rights are involved. An obvious example of this is harassment by landlords when bad housing practices are exposed; within an institution, reporting staff for neglect or abuse of a patient may place the latter in the vulnerable position of hostage, unless there is sufficient administrative supervision to control aggressive staff behavior.

This second example illustrates my earlier point about the relative impotence of social work as a profession because it rarely negotiates from a position of equality or power. There are two main reasons for this: first, social workers' own attitude, already described, inhibits them from opposing the establishment framework within which they operate, even though this implicates them in policies and practices that represent a compromise of professional ethics and philosophy. The other reason is that social work is rarely accepted as a top-priority service because its function is never entirely clear to outsiders—in contrast to teaching or nursing—and in most instances its value is only manifested through its absence—that is when a social crisis develops that could have clearly been averted by earlier intervention. This fact highlights the features that this profession, which is a paradigm of feminine professional involvement, has in common with the condition of women in general; the more effective preventive aspects of both are subordinated to their remedial aspects, and both are usually involved when a mess has occurred that needs clearing up. Unfortunately, the brief moment of prominent and visible value that these crises offer to both groups colludes with their traditional self-image of indispensability and raises hopes that if they demonstrate their invaluable skills and strengths by retrieving precarious situations, they shall eventually be asked to participate at an earlier stage and in a more effective role.

I should like to elaborate on this by describing some hypothetical situations drawn from my current professional setting (a clinical and residential facility for the mentally retarded) to show the negative impact upon clients' welfare that often occurs because of the inferior status of social work and its diminished involvement in decision-making and framing policy. These illustrations pertain to social work's involvement in administration, medical counseling, and scientific research. To take the administrative sphere first, social workers can often apply their insights and experience of interpersonal relationships and social interactions to predict or interpret minor malfunctioning in the institutional system that is symptomatic of more serious disturbance and requires prompt and appropriate administrative intervention. The problem and the requisite action may be at the very simple and seemingly insignificant level of keeping the caretaking staff and residents in their charge informed about changes in organization that will affect the lives of both—for example, transfer from one residential unit to another. If the administration does not appreciate how crucial communication and explanation are to successful management, this rather rudimentary courtesy may be overlooked, with the resultant confusion, resentment, poor morale, and diminished efficiency inevitably having an adverse effect upon the residents' or patients' well-being. Invariably, social workers are not consulted on such changes, even though knowledge of the group dynamics involved and the theory of systems are part of their professional stock-in-trade.

Family counseling on serious medico-social issues is another instance in which the professional viewpoint of social work may be underestimated when it does not accord with the more dominant medical standpoint. The field of genetic counseling provides an interesting illustration. Certain hereditary anomalies affecting the nervous system can be diagnosed in utero by a new technique (amniocentesis) with the option of abortion. This is a very exciting medical discovery, making it possible to prevent the birth of babies with lifetime handicaps of a very serious and crippling nature. However, there is a danger that the relative ease and safety of this technique will promote a mechanical practice of repeated alternation of conception and abortion until a healthy pregnancy is confirmed. Such a possibility overlooks the serious social implications, particularly the emotional strain of interrupted pregnancies on the woman. In these circumstances the socially therapeutic measure of adoption might be a better solution to the couple's problem than a succession of bad trial runs. Unless, however, the physician in charge of the case has imagination, insight into the social implications, and enough professional humility to consider another colleague's perspective, this alternative of building up a family from existing children who are physically sound but socially risky may not be proferred with the same enthusiastic support as the clinical route of continuing to try to *produce* a new healthy child.

In the field of scientific research involving human subjects, there is an even greater divergence of viewpoint between the respective representatives of research and social work, with a corresponding gap between their relative power. In America research still carries disproportionate value and prestige because it fits the residual pioneer psychology that is always moving forward to new frontiers, and because such products as the flight to the moon are an excellent demonstration of conspicuous success and its correlate of power. The operational arena of social work is the exact opposite: its main preoccupation is with failure and with powerless people, who may be highly conspicuous as in the inner cities or chronically unobtrusive as in rural Appalachia. With scientific research and humanistic social issues occupying the polarized ends of the American value scale, it is not easy for the profession of social work to match its claims for consideration against the more socially esteemed claims of research. If an individual suffers from an unusual clinical condition, on which scientific data is greatly coveted, strong arguments will be advanced on the long-term value to medical research and future humanity, but less thought will be given to the emotional and psychological effects that the investigation may have upon the experimental subject. In the last analysis the suggestion that research be abandoned in preference to disturbing the psychological and social equilibrium of an individual would almost never be sustained; because of the profession's lack of power, the social worker's intervention does not get beyond persuasion or denunciation, and she cannot prevent the situa-

tion. Instead, the social worker involved is thrown back on
the all-too-familiar function of retrieving the damage and
trying to repair the shattered Humpty-Dumpty self-image
which research ambition has knocked off its rather precarious wall. This example illustrates perfectly the trap in
which social workers are caught through being without
power to prevent the catastrophe and through their almost
innate drive to rescue and reintegrate the pieces after it
has happened.

Earlier in this essay, I justified my theme by indicating
the need to explore the social and psychological origins of
the compassion trap concept before the patterns of personal and social behavior that have instituted and
maintained it could be changed. For a concluding note I
offer some cursory ideas on how the social definition of
women can be overhauled by a critical review of the
inventory of personal and social qualities generally
ascribed to them and a realistic assessment of how relevant they are now to the exigencies of society today.

The primary imperative for women who intend to assume a meaningful and decisive role in today's social
change is to begin to perceive themselves as having an
identity and personal integrity that has as strong a claim
for being preserved intact as that of any other individual
or group. This attitude will require women to develop an
explicit sense of the value of their own concerns, and, at
times, to insist that they take precedence. It will also
compel them to abandon the role of compassionate sibyl
at everyone's beck and call, because being permanently
available to other people's needs hinders women from
pursuing their chosen avocations with the steadfast concentration that is essential for their successful completion.

These new stances will differ greatly from women's
present circumstances, where they are constantly enmeshed in the conflict between the genuine claims of other
people for succor and protection and their own equally
urgent needs for personal development. This new situation
will raise the fundamental question of who will assume the
caretaking and healing tasks—which will always be needed
in any society—if women refuse to be meekly conscripted
for this vital but undervalued service. Although the prospect of women not in their accustomed place is daunting,
in fact it may lead to a reshuffling of roles and tasks based
on individual preferences and inclinations, rather than the

arbitrary division according to biological sexual endowment and social definitions.

This reorganization would speak to Ruth Benedict's concept of "congenial responses," which postulates that every individual has innate and personal tendencies that may be constructively exploited or underplayed according to how well they synchronize with the predominant value system of the prevailing culture. In our society's rigid pattern of stratification (grid would be a better word implying a mechanical rather than organic process) by sex, class, race, this very valuable principle has been violated to the extent that a large proportion of individuals have had no opportunity to recognize, let alone express, their "congenial responses." The roles and functions that have been imposed upon women illustrate this sort of social outrage: women have been compelled to contort their psychological and social make-up, so that certain features have been exaggerated into embarrassing prominence, while other more vital areas have been constricted almost beyond recognition.

An important task of the women's movement is to free women's congenial responses from the restrictive cultural regime and present them in a new and more functional shape. This demands that a great deal of thought be given to how women perceive and delineate themselves, so that they can project a living image to replace the lifeless and rigid stereotype that society dictates. The urgent—some might say strident—voice of the women's liberation movement is a much overdue attempt to redefine women in a fresh set of terms that reflects their congenial characteristics and portrays them from a series of different perspectives rather than a few highly selective angles. Implicit in the intellectual effort is the importance of defining women's characteristics in a culture-free way, as far as that is possible, and ensuring that we keep in mind a wide range of emotional, intellectual, and psychological options.

Women must not fall into the easy pitfall of delineating themselves solely in terms of their revolutionary protest, which, though it has crucial relevance to their current situation, cannot serve as a lasting definition. Further, though the plight of all women needs a drastic overhaul, not everyone will want the same style of improvement or espouse the same methods of bringing it about. Women who are currently the spokeswomen for their exploited sex must try to understand attitudes and aspirations that are

at variance with their own. Otherwise, one brand of doc-
trinaire tyranny will be exchanged for another, alienating
a substantial portion of women who are not yet ready for
total separation from the symbiotic relationship with the
"dominant" male sex to which they have been acculturated;
women will continue to set themselves into molds which
have different shapes but still represent a confining mode
of living.

It is imperative that an accurate assessment be made of
which of the so-called womanly characteristics have continued validity and can be used to useful social ends. This
may be rashly venturing into the heavily mined area of
controversy about whether differences between the sexes
are fundamental and real or artificially contrived by cultural forces. At the risk of expounding heresy, my feeling
is that, provided thoughtful analysis instead of global stereotyping is used, many of these questions can be disposed
of by pragmatically considering the tasks needing to be
done and who is best equipped to do them ("best" meaning the individual or group who can discharge them most
effectively through the maximum utilization of special
skills). Whether these skills are fundamental and innate or
have developed to a high level of proficiency through
long-accustomed use is relatively immaterial. In this respect two attributes particular to women have an increasingly important place in today's society: *flexibility of operation* and the *capacity for intuitive awareness* of personal
and social phenomena. Flexibility is a characteristic that
most women have had to foster in order to survive their
limiting circumstances without paralyzing frustration. Because their skills and creative energy have been mainly
expressed through promoting the successful growth and
functioning of others, they have developed unusual versatility concerning their own preferences and goals, a heightened ability to grasp opportunity when it occurs, an equal
capacity for withstanding disappointment when it is withdrawn, and unlimited competence in making things over,
whether these are food, clothing, furniture, the home
itself, or the total social situation within which they operate. In a period of rapid and major social change flexibility in thought and action is an extremely valuable quality;
one of the outstanding contributions that the women's
liberation movement can make to the overall revolutionary trend in this country is to set a model for nondoc-
trinaire policies and flexible goals. The other quality fre-

quently attributed to women is their apparent capacity for picking up subliminal clues which, when put together, can produce a diagnostic assessment of individuals or situations with more penetrating insight than is achieved by more usual processes of conscious thought. This celebrated characteristic is neither universally nor exclusively feminine, but it is likely to be developed to a higher level in women. When women's satisfactions and raisons d'être depend upon the skillful manipulation of other people's well-being, it is incumbent upon them to develop a very finely calibrated skill for tuning in to the needs and moods of those individuals (including the vulnerable, dependent, and inarticulate young) for whom they are responsible so that they may be ready with the appropriate response. The group tensions within family structure, the shifting of emphases and sites of power must all be picked up by the psychic radar equipment of women before they explode into consciousness and disrupt the group's functioning. *Mutatis mutandis,* this seismographic quality gives women an invaluable tool for divining subterranean stresses in larger group systems and alerting the participating individuals to their presence and to the possible courses they will take if not controlled. Men have not needed to develop this subtle influence to the same extent because their exercise of power has been overt and explicit; but in a social setting that is unstable and unpredictable, men's power tactics tend to be outmoded and lack the capacity for adroit maneuvering, rather like the Spanish Armada when naval warfare took on a new style.

One further point seems to have equal relevance to women and their self-perceptions and social roles, and to social workers, particularly women workers. Although both these subgroups have developed and practiced skills that are indispensable to the healthy functioning of society, neither has evolved a consistently systematic method for transmitting their arcane arts either to other individuals outside of their coterie or to successors in their own field. It was, for example, left to a masculine representative of a male-dominated profession to write the classic on childrearing, even though this knowledge and understanding form part of the repertoire of skills possessed sooner or later by most wives and mothers.

Another instance of the same phenomenon is a recent report in a leading social-work journal that the bulk of literary output in this field is produced by men. Among its observations on this phenomenon, the article mentioned that women favored teaching over writing as a channel for expressing their intellectual, as opposed to practical, concerns in social work. Teaching is one of the most conspicuous helping professions; it strikes me as significant that women social workers fall back on this outlet for their intellectual skills, thus demonstrating, perhaps unconsciously, their continued loyal adherence to the nurturing model. It represents also the persistent attraction of personal involvement as opposed to the more impersonal cerebral activity; however, the explanation for this preference is not an inborn and immutable tendency so much as the harsh fact that personal, concretely focused activities do not require the same kind of singleminded concentration as do writing and other creative ventures, and they suffer less from the interruption of external activities. In other words, women (and particularly women in social work) are less comfortable dealing with concepts than concrete problems, *not* because they lack imagination, insight, and conceptualizing skills, but because their self-perception does not permit them to give this item top priority. In a crisis which demands the full exercise of the compassionate mandate, women are much more ready to push aside a creative enterprise in its favor, even though in the long run the latter might well have represented a social contribution of more lasting value. The model for this sort of commitment to essential mundane needs was set by Martha in the New Testament, who chose to exercise her homemaking skills in a hospitable enterprise in preference to listening to divine wisdom. Her choice and the rebuke it drew forth evoke the question I have been trying, thus far unsatisfactorily, to solve in this essay: to what extent do women slide into the mold that society has shaped for them because they enjoy this useful self-effacement, and how much are they inextricably ensnared by firmly entrenched, outmoded patterns of social thinking and behavior, which are hard to break down and invariably involve hurt, harm, and at best the disruption of an accepted, smooth-functioning social regime. Since I cannot offer a satisfactory answer, I propose to end by recounting a small and outwardly inconspicuous incident that occurred a few weeks ago and provides an almost perfect illustration of the points I have been trying to make in this essay, particularly the trap into which women are so often forced, almost unwittingly, by expected social custom and observances.

I was spending the weekend with a family of close friends in which both parents are scientific writers. By common consent all three of us adults decided to reserve Saturday afternoon for a writing session; to that end we turned down all social engagements for that day, including one from a very favorite common friend. My hostess' elderly parents were staying in the house and were expecting a former pupil of the grandfather to visit them for tea—a very fitting activity that would make minimal demands upon the authors and yet provide a diversion for the house guests. So much for plans. Half an hour before the guest was expected, a car drew up, disgorging two young men, a young woman, and two small children. The former pupil had been driven over by his wife's sister and her family, so that what was designed as a quiet academic tête à tête mushroomed into a family party, involving the hospitable skills of all but one member of the household. Naturally, the elderly grandmother was not prepared to cope with four extra unexpected guests, so the two female writers of necessity abandoned their "scribbling" and reverted to their normal expected roles of dispensing tea, entertainment, and genial hospitality. Although reference was made to the various literary activities we were all engaged in, the invading party were completely oblivious of the major disruption they had caused, obviously seeing my hostess primarily as a wife, mother, and householder, not as a scientific woman of letters. Our third writer, the husband, fared better because he was permitted to remain cloistered in his study with tea being taken in and apologies for absence being relayed to the guests. This was quite justifiable since there was no point in three people's afternoons being ruined, but the point is that no one's comfort or peace of mind was disturbed by this behavior, nor was it regarded as anything unusual.

However, had my hostess and I adopted similar tactics a very different situation would have prevailed. The grandmother would have been flustered and upset at having to get tea and entertain four extra people, two of them young children. The carefully arranged interview between the grandfather and his former pupil would have been spoiled; the visiting family would have gone home embarrassed at having made a social gaffe instead of enjoying a pleasant afternoon in the country; the teenage daughter would probably have been intensely mortified to see her mother neglect guests. Thanks to the compassion trap and our susceptibility to its habitual claims, these vulnerable dependents were spared this painful experience. On the other hand, as so often happens with women's enterprises, our precious afternoon of creative activity was destroyed and our literary commitments had to be postponed.

This tale has a moral if we could only believe and act upon it.

REFERENCES

Beeton, Isabella. *Mrs. Beeton's Household Management.* Ward, Locke and Coy, 1861.

Benedict, Ruth. *Patterns of Culture.* Boston: Houghton Mifflin, 1961.

Brager, George. "Advocacy & Political Behaviour," *Social Work*, vol. 13, no. 2 (1968).

The Ad Hoc Committee on Advocacy. "The Social Worker as Advocate: Champion of Social Failure," *Social Work*, vol. 14, no. 2 (1969).

Klein, Philip. *From Philanthropy to Social Welfare: An American Culture Perspective.* San Francisco: Jossey-Bass, 1968.

Gospel According to St. Luke 10:38-42.

Reed, Evelyn. *The Myth of Women's Inferiority.* New England Free Press.

Rosenblatt, Aaron et al. Predominance of Male Authors in Social Work Publications. *Social Casework.* vol. 51, no. 7 (1970).

Scott, Peter. The Biological Need to Help. *New Society*, March 30, 1967.

Weisstein, Naomi. *Kinder, Küche, Kirche, as Scientific Law: Psychology Constructs the Female.* New England Free Press, 1968.

Wells, Lynn. *American Women: Their Use and Abuse.* New England Free Press.

IV:

SOCIAL ISSUES AND FEMINISM: EDUCATION, HOMOSEX- UALITY, RACE, AND RADICALISM

IV:

25

OUR FAILURES ONLY MARRY: Bryn Mawr and the Failure of Feminism

Liz Schneider

By upholding a standard of scholarship and culture that is difficult and not easy to attain, she will inevitably lose many students, but she will not regret the loss. Bryn Mawr has faith to believe that as long as her grey towers stand there will never be wanting youthful enthusiasm and youthful love of learning to inhabit them. Future generations will turn to her for inspiration. Be it her part never to betray her trust.—Alumnae Magazine, 1908.

Here are the voices of the women who followed, responding to the promise of meaningful education implicit in the feminist founding of Bryn Mawr:

I think that men's institutions are different from women's in that men's are constantly trying to build up their students; at Bryn Mawr I feel as though I'm being beaten down all the time. My mind is viewed as some kind of input-output mechanism; as though I'm being trained to perform well and be a good scholar so that I can come back and teach here. Bryn Mawr capitalizes on women's oppression by trying to give women the Truth.—Student, Class of 1970

The only thing that has made my last year at Bryn Mawr bearable has been women's liberation. Now I feel like I have something in common with other girls here, and that we have something that we are fighting for together. We are a community and I feel like I have real friends; I know that my problems are not only mine, and I want to work with other women, instead of competing against them, to solve those problems. Until women's lib, I thought of Bryn Mawr as a cloistered retreat from anything real.—Student, Class of 1972

The most outstanding part of my "Bryn Mawr experience" was Haverford[1]—to get a Haverford boy friend whom I could be an extension of and whose achievements and respect and friends I could acquire by association, and to be "known" at Haverford. My reputation at Haverford was of primary importance and fundamentally shaped my self-image.—Class of 1968

Everyone admitted to Bryn Mawr felt automatically that she was "superior," "exceptional," "chosen," "elite." I felt especially exceptional because I was superior not only to all the poor girls who "weren't accepted" or had merely B or C ratings, but also to most of the other Bryn Mawr students. The way I was superior to the superiors was by not even taking the place seriously. I was really above it all. I was (or pretended to be) casual instead of conscientious about studying and generally detached from the academic rat race (looking down on my classmates who would compare grades) except when I was successful, when I would make special efforts to find out who had done worse than I had and who was smarter than I was. But I was mostly "above it all" in my relationship to the school structure and traditions. Having grown up in an academic community, I was not intimidated by deans or even by having an interview with Miss McBride.[2] Having been to summer camp, I was scornful of the "traditional" activities such as Lantern Night and maypole dances and Hell Week. . . . In general, I think, I shared the attitude of Haverford students toward Bryn Mawr activities (on purpose, just as I had been "one of the guys" in high school by claiming to be disinterested in going to high school proms or graduation exercises of the Senior Class Day or the all-night party). I boasted that I slept through the strawberries-and-cream May Day breakfast, and that I didn't bother to memorize the words to the Lantern Night song. Thus, I disdainfully put down all my classmates who had become involved in such frivolity and silliness. My detached superiority and judgmental sarcasm must have made the girls who really enjoyed singing Greek songs and spinning May Day hoops very uncomfortable. (My Haverford boy friends, also social rebels, appreciated my superiority much as they appreciated my comparatively liberal sexual standards.)—Class of 1967

I don't know why they had all those traditional activities at Bryn Mawr. During Freshman Orientation Week I think the song-singing bit was a form of babysitting: they wanted organized but relaxing activities to keep us from getting bored, homesick, lonely, discouraged, or (worst of all) in trouble (especially with boys). I think it was insulting to treat us like kids at summer camp for early adolescents, although as I write this I find myself thinking "maybe it was necessary for some of the girls who didn't make friends easily." Bullshit. *It definitely was insulting.* Just as the mixers and song-sings and pole dancings were degrading and insulting and objectifying, just as sign-outs and lantern men and class attendance and gym class were absurd and insulting and passé and treating us like children, just as "Self-Gov"[3] was a total hoax and a lie and implicitly considered us idiots who couldn't see how phony all the rhetoric about "make your own decisions and rules, girls" really was.—Class of 1966

Hell Week was Something Else. Hell Week was Having It Both Ways. Hell Week had all the vicious sadism and cattiness and competitiveness and backbiting and popularity contests and class hierarchies and all the worst stereotypes of bitchy women and sororities, but then at the last moment was the surprise twist and after everyone had wallowed in the bitchiness and cattiness and competitiveness and sadism, and after the freshman victims had felt all the pain and guilt and fear and degradation of being made to be slaves to the upperclassmen and have intimate secrets about boy friends revealed and be picked on and teased according to their popularity, then everything was supposed to be magically forgiven and whitewashed by a bunch of crappy *flowers*. How trite can you get! How transparent can a double-bind message be? But no one seemed to question it. . . . I wonder at our naïveté, at our stupidity . . . we were totally brainwashed by *that place* to have this incredibly gullible self-image as part of a tradition which gave its alumnae competitiveness in the name of high standards, self-hate in the name of critical analysis, cocktail-party-ese in the name of well-rounded education, elitist snobbery in the name of talent and creative ability!—Class of 1968

Who were our models? Professors. The successful and popular and well-liked and intellectually respected professors. And except for a few token women (mostly eccentrics from another age) these professors were *men*. There were a few wonderful women, but most were faculty emeriti (over sixty) or low-level instructors (like in Baby Languages) but the really inspiring professors were known to be men, or at Haverford.—Class of 1965

We were taught that we were the select few to begin with and that we were then being given an exceptional education so that we could rise head and shoulders above our peers ... we were to be the best, after all. Bryn Mawr statistics were constantly available, comparing Bryn Mawr with the other Seven Sisters worth competing and comparing with. . . . Bryn Mawr had (percentage-wise) the most Ph.D's, the most advanced degrees, the highest percentage going on to graduate study, etc., etc., etc. So there we were, intended to go on and *achieve* and *be at the top*. There was no room for deviation. There were different paths one could take to *excellence* (as opposed to enlightenment) but only one direction to go. J. was brilliant but couldn't take the pressure to excel and did poorly on her written exams. She hated herself until she found another acceptable goal—to become a doctor (and if she had had trouble getting through Med school she would have hated herself more) ... —Class of 1967

Bryn Mawr helped its students live out the dreams of their middle-class and aspiring middle-class and upper-middle-class and nouveau riche parents for them ...

Social pressure. Friday and Saturday nights were miserable without a date. I had lots of dates, and I pretended to be "above" all that pressure, and most of the time I was having a passionate love affair by mail anyway, but I do not remember a single Friday or Saturday night when I didn't have a date which I enjoyed at all. It was much better to go out with any creep than to be alone in the dorm on a weekend. It was much better to have a date with a guy than to go out with one or a bunch of girls. If I didn't have a date I'd be really jealous of all the girls who did, and I'd go and read the sign-out book to see who went where with whom for how long.

One year some enterprising Princeton guys put out a *Guide to Women's Eastern Colleges* in which all the schools were stereotyped. I bet every girl at Bryn Mawr saw the guide with its cartoon of a long-legged, stooped, long-haired, bookwormish, bespectacled Bryn Mawr "type" and its tone of awe in describing the intellect of the "Bryn Mawr girl." Another double bind. You had to live up to that intellectual image and live *down* the negative aspects of the image. In other words, you must be clever and bright, but not intellectually aggressive or dully bookwormish; you must be knowledgeable, but not studious; you must be serious, but attractive, seductive, etc.—Class of 1964

Not only was the school classified into a "type" but each
dorm housed a "type." Rock girls were crazy and wild,
Radnor girls were quite and studious, (and sometimes
suicidal), Denbigh girls were wholesome and enthusiastic
and WASPy, Rhoads girls were sophisticated and New
Yorky (and artsy, I think). This typing was important for
roommates and for cliques getting "control" of certain
corridors and lots of competition in dorm applications and
assignments and getting the good people and avoiding the
despicable ones. But it was also important for the mixers,
... since the occupants of each dorm wrote the invitations
to the mixers, different types of men would come to each
dorm's annual mixer: if you wanted to meet a quiet, shy,
unsophisticated chemist you'd go to the Radnor mixer, etc.
Most Princeton guys were at the Rhoads mixer.

At mixers the man was totally in control. He would ask
you to dance, ask you your class and major during the
dance, and then disappear the instant the dance was over.
You'd see him half an hour later in an animated conversation with your roommate—or worse—with a girl you'd always admired for her poise or wit and you'd hate her (of
course, you'd never hate him, the real monster). He can
come and choose, pick over the "cheese" (as friends of
mine at Yale called it) and leave when he's had enough.

The double bind. You had to be intellectually assertive
(in class) and play dumb (with men). You had to be
ambitious and self-advancing but also supportive and submissive. You had to know when to speak up and when to
shut up and never get mixed up (the penalties for misjudg-
ing situations were severe: if you shut up in class you'd
get a lousy grade and if you spoke up on a date he'd never
ask you out again ... both major failures). You had to be
a good student and a good date and the standards for the
two were usually directly opposed to each other.—Class of
1969

Another contradiction: the trend was toward being liberal
in politics, especially on the civil rights issues currently
popular, but daily life at Bryn Mawr was like being part of
the master's family on a southern plantation. The maids
and porters were superb "house niggers" whose role was
rarely questioned by the students. The lantern men, who
were entrusted with the girls' virginity and the propriety of
their hours and good-night kisses and other moral details
were white: the maids and porters (black) were bag-
gage-carriers, floor-sweepers, kitchen-helpers, telephone-
answerers, and did other unnoticed shitwork. Widespread
("traditional") jokes circulated about how stupid one
maid was because she could never write out a telephone
message legibly, or how dumb another one was because
she always rang the wrong buzzer. A few times, I would

be ready to go through a door at the same time as a maid, and I would open the door to hold it open for her to walk through, but she would quietly refuse to walk through the doorway before me. . . . There was absolutely no way out; many of them had had their jobs for decades and they had been doing shitwork for "their girls" for years and they always held the door open for you . . .

The amazing thing to me is that we did manage to have some really good, honest, trusting relationships among us. Pitted together in that den of ruthless competitiveness (constantly, academically and socially), thriving on jealousy and cattiness and cliques, incessantly being wounded by feelings of failure and rejection and misery and self-hate, we actually managed, on occasion, to be friends, to dare to reach out to help each other and to trust each other, and to learn to accept ourselves. The best part of Bryn Mawr for me, in retrospect, was not Harverford, was not inspiring professors and stimulating courses, was not an academic tradition, was not going away from home but being supported by my father, was not the parties and getting high and the concert series and the Ivy League weekends and the dating scene, but the most rewarding part of Bryn Mawr was learning to love and trust a few women friends who, in spite of all the shit that turned us against each other all the time, were able to get together and support each other through all the bad times and share some of the happiness and growing of the good times.—Class of 1967

I feel insecure about myself here and I have for four years. I don't understand why Bryn Mawr has been so bad for me; it was supposed to be what I was working for for twelve years in school. I feel like the administration and faculty think that being a woman is something you are supposed to overcome. The expectations that they've placed on me are totally unrealistic. . . . They've told me that the world is my oyster and yet I feel unhappy being in the dorm and not being with a man. The conversations at dinner are so deadening and stupid, my classes are so boring. They tell me I'm supposed to go on to graduate school, but I feel like I'm being prepared to be a good conversationalist or make some man a good wife. The only good thing about Bryn Mawr is Haverford. In my Haverford classes professors keep on asking questions and I feel like some intellectual responsibility is being demanded of me.—Class of 1966

At first, in the abstract, it seemed like a fantastic prize to have won; soon after, in the reality of the situation, I became aware of how much I hated to be around only other women. It wasn't that I thought that they weren't interesting or exciting; for the most part they were the most interesting group of women that I had ever known. The most important thing was being desirable enough to get a boy friend, and/or doing brilliantly, both of which made all of us terribly competitive with each other. There was an obsession that prevailed each time I got involved with a new man; he was the Savior who would take me out of my all-girl cloister and save my mind and soul. I don't think that I ever felt capable of having a full, creative life on my own, without having something accrue to me vicariously through a man. The obsession with getting a boy friend began to disturb me more and more, if only because it seemed like something that I couldn't control as long as I was at Bryn Mawr. Moreover, I couldn't understand the reasons for my feeling this way except in the most personal, psychological terms, which indicated that my life would be a total failure. And then there was the intellectual atmosphere. I had been one of the smartest girls in my high school class. Suddenly I was only one of a myriad of very bright women, all of whom seemed infinitely brighter than I, all of whom seemed capable of doing better work that I was. There was an academic standard that I felt I could never meet. Classes were very boring and I never wanted to work, but what I did was to go through all the motions of working very hard, without being able to concentrate at all and learning almost nothing. I felt as though I were devoid of any interesting intellectual ideas, as though I had no mind or anything worthwhile to say. The only thing that I found interesting at all was sociology but even that seemed empty because it existed in a vacuum. The professor was very supportive, and he and a few others always had a coterie of the most political, active girls at Bryn Mawr around them. But all the good professors would always justify their feelings of depression and uselessness by the fact that they had to teach at a girls' school and that was a sad fate for any serious intellectual. True, they would criticize the passivity of women in their classes, and show special interest in those who showed signs of aggressiveness or imagination, but my American Social Structure course never once mentioned women as a subgroup, class, etc. In all my four years at Bryn Mawr I don't think the topic of women ever came up in a course. There were a few little discussion groups on "The Problems of Career and Marriage" which the Curriculum Committee led from time to time but they were few and far between and never related the issues of why we were all so miserable there to the problems and needs of an all-woman college.—Class of 1968

At an elite school like Harvard students can count on making contacts that will be useful to them in their later life. At Bryn Mawr we knew that we liked each other, but we never made plans for future activities. At men's colleges it is common for students to go out together to eat, to the movies, to do things, but at Bryn Mawr we felt that going places together was an inferior substitute for a date. Most of us would accept a date with anyone rather than stay in the dorm on a weekend night. I spent just about all my time studying in my boy friend's room at Haverford. Haverford was a more interesting place to be for several reasons. First of all men had more freedom, so we could come and go as we pleased there until we had to be back at two o'clock (if we were out with other women we had to be back at midnight). We could cook, smoke, drink, and make love in the guys' rooms but not in our own. There was always more action: loud music, frisbee games, water fights, interesting discussions, people coming and going. Bryn Mawr was always silent and still. (On a test that all freshmen had to pass before being admitted to the Self-Government honor system, most women said that they did not think we should be allowed to drink in our rooms because we would quickly become loud, rude and violently destructive.) Finally, Haverford was a better place to be because we would be with men and escape the oppressiveness of an all-female environment . . .—Class of 1968

The alienation that we felt from each other was inextricably bound with the alienation we felt from our education. We had heavy academic loads; four courses, all with long papers and exams. We sat in lecture classes, taking notes on the professors' wisdom. Rarely did we venture a differing opinion, fearing to be found wrong. We only felt confident in our ability to read extensively, digest the various facts and ideas, and organize them into lengthy, well-documented essays. The outstanding memory that remains from my philosophy course, an introductory survey required of everyone, is not any set of ideas, nor even a concept of what philosophy as a discipline is, but rather of the girl in front of me drawing an elaborate T.G.I.F. during every Friday lecture. We all commented on the recklessness of Haverford students who boldly challenged their professors whenever they disagreed or didn't understand. They seemed to feel that they had every right to an opinion and some even felt that they had to have an opinion to satisfy their egos. We accepted the authority of professors and books much too easily, but we didn't have the confidence to trust ourselves. We continued to be passive recipients just as we had been raised to be.—Class of 1963

The official rhetoric of Byrn Mawr College, an elite Seven Sisters school, reflects a firm commitment to feminism. Yet Bryn Mawr women, like their sisters in other female institutions, are discovering more and more that this rhetoric lacks substance, and they feel betrayed. The discrepancy between the official intellectual credo and the neurotic, hypersensitive, self-absorbed seriousness that pervades the college's atmosphere poses a problem. Its elitist rhetoric pretends that Bryn Mawr women are special, that their intellectual and class privilege and mobility transcend the political reality of their situation as women. Its emphasis on individual status and achievement denies that there is any collective problem for women in this society. Bryn Mawr women's supposed intellectual superiority places them above ordinary women. Its academic emphasis is accompanied by an intellectual rejection of all that is traditionally feminine—displays of emotion, signs of insecurity or fear, concern with practical good works or human suffering—and a snobbish attitude toward traditionally feminine professions such as teaching or social work, despite the existence of the Bryn Mawr School of Social Work. These attitudes are rarely made explicit but they are subtle and pervasive, and women at Bryn Mawr, if they do not already share them, soon internalize them in much the same way that women with working-class or regional accents learn to speak in a mellow, sophisticated style and voice.

Byrn Mawr's excellent academic reputation, which its founders fought so hard to establish in order to prove that women could take on the same intellectual work as men, now makes for an atmosphere of what is essentially pseudointellectualism, one in which scholarship is parroted, rather than realized. For the Bryn Mawr student finds herself primarily a study in twentieth-century female problems, and Bryn Mawr, founded as a feminist institution, does not permit feminism to exist as an issue. Bryn Mawr's nineteenth-century illusions of uniqueness and intellectual superiority make it unable to see the peculiar turn that its "special" situation as a woman's college has taken. In selecting a woman's college, students at Bryn Mawr may have been asking the school to relate to their needs and problems as women. However, trapped in the circularity of the "lets not admit that we're special, because then we'll be seen as inferior" problem that pervaded the black movement for so long, Bryn Mawr, in its cultural myopia, has become, if anything, antifeminist.

The reasons are complex and make Bryn Mawr an

instructive microcosm of the plight of educated women in sexist society. Obviously, the college itself cannot appreciably change the society for which it is educating its women. The education of women—no matter how rigorous or inspiring—cannot overcome the wholesale prejudice of a society entrenched in its belief that women are inferior and properly excluded from the positions a first-class education might prepare them for. Once it is made clear—and it is eminently clear in present-day America—that women will not be accorded positions of responsibility, their education begins to develop all the attributes of irrelevance: it becomes sterile, unspontaneous, academic, and ornamental rather than useful. The students themselves are acutely aware that their expensive educations will be of marginal use to society, and their already considerable feelings of uselessness (coexisting with traditional feminine desires for self-validation through altruism) are compounded by this apparent squandering of resources in pursuit of egotistical self-improvement. These feelings of guilt lead to further self-denigration and self-abnegation and produce strong conflicts with the competitiveness required for academic success. Thus, while creative and imaginative work is not unusual at Bryn Mawr and academic achievement quite common, the fact is that the Bryn Mawr woman who genuinely feels that her intellectual work is meaningful, or ultimately important, is rare.

In reality, a great deal of the Bryn Mawr woman's actual attention is focused on her emotional life, as well as on men and the need to find a husband. The atmosphere is charged with "sensitivity" and emotionalism. And yet the women learn to hate this—their emotions, their insecurities, their fears, their helpless concentration on all of it—because the college perpetuates the very functional myth that emotionalism is a sign of individual weakness. Thus, the Bryn Mawr woman finds herself in the classic female bind. Intellectualism is a constant—and unreached—goal, and therefore a cause for self-hatred. It functions to advance the pretense that "achievement means equality" (the line that the administration supports), while at the same time it deepens self-doubt and anxiety since intellectual pursuits never seem as satisfying as they should. The statement "Our failures only marry" (once made by M. Carey Thomas, the first president of the college) has long been distorted to "Only our failures marry"; this distortion reflects the real pressure the college exerts to deny such solely marital desires as do in fact exist. Most Bryn Mawr women are trapped in a fundamental ambivalence: do they want to be the doctor or the doctor's wife? In this confusion they are not different from most American women. But Bryn Mawr has only deepened the contradictions and failed to provide an environment in which these questions can be openly asked (or one in which it can be admitted that the question is even there).

Now, for the first time, Bryn Mawr has chosen a man as president, claiming that no "qualified" woman was able to free herself from her family commitments to take the job. Alumnae wrote in opposition, angry that the college had admitted failure on its own terms since it had not produced one woman graduate capable of serving as its president. Similarly, three women "who have lived with famous husbands" addressed the class of 1970 on Class Day. Thus, it is clear that the true condition of American women is now at Bryn Mawr's doorstep; the college's failure is only a grotesque expression of its time.

Bryn Mawr's early feminism has failed, but the real question is why? Bryn Mawr was founded to provide equal education for women; its first president was actively involved in the woman's suffrage movement and was known as the leading feminist educator of her time. The failure of feminism at Bryn Mawr is an illustration of the natural degeneration of nineteenth-century feminism; the history of Bryn Mawr's feminism provides a clear example of the class-bound contradictions and limited perspectives that resulted in the demise of nineteenth-century feminism. The inability to come to grips with the fundamental economic and social issues of marriage and the family and woman's position in those institutions, to analyze the institutional and psychological oppression of women, and to construct radical alternatives for socialized life—these were the vital failures, and they arose from the fundamental limitations of Bryn Mawr's early feminism.

Bryn Mawr's failure to maintain its position as a feminist institution is deeply connected to the failure of the larger feminist movement to transcend the suffrage issue with a more radical analysis of the structural causes of women's oppression. More basic, however, to the school's feminist confusions is the elite role which the founders of the college saw for it. The fundamental motivation for

Bryn Mawr's founding was the demand for education made by wealthy, leisured women who felt that their lack of a higher education was the barrier to the realization of their human potential. The men who first organized the college acted out of the Quaker belief that "women must be sensible and able; they should be equal to taking part in the thought and discussion of the vital things with which Friends were constantly occupied." Bryn Mawr was to be "a truly great experiment in American education, the proving of how far women's minds could go, once the limits of opportunity were removed," but it was, nonetheless, "a college for the advanced education and care of young women and girls of the higher and more refined classes of society."

M. Carey Thomas, the person most involved in the direction of Bryn Mawr College, was remarkable for the power of her vision and the strength of her commitment to the "advancement of women." Even as a child, she was enraged by the inferior position in which women were placed. "I can remember weeping over the account of Adam and Eve because it seemed to me that the curse pronounced on Eve might imperil girls' going to college. . . . I read Milton with rage and indignation; even as a child I knew him for the woman-hater he was." If she wrote "boys and girls" in her diary, she quickly crossed it out and substituted "girls and boys." Her anger reached a fevered pitch when a friend of her father walked home with her from a meeting talking about "the sacred shrine of womanhood."

> He said that "no matter what splendid talents a woman might have she couldn't use them better than by being a wife and mother" and then went off in some high-faluting stuff about the strength of women's devotion, completely forgetting that all women ain't wives and mothers, and they, I suppose, are told to fold their hands and be idle waiting for an eligible offer. Stuff! Nonsense![4]

Carey Thomas' commitment and single-minded devotion to building Bryn Mawr resulted from her own struggle to get an education. Her adolescent obsession with going to college was undoubtedly heightened by her fear that there might be some truth to the prevailing belief that women were made to be wives and mothers.

At twenty-seven she was determined to become pres-

ident of Bryn Mawr. Her father and uncle were on the
college's Board of Trustees; the three of them convinced
the board to appoint her professor of English and dean,
with the understanding that she would eventually become
president. Her motive in applying for the presidency, in
fact her whole purpose in life, is summed up by an entry
in her diary when she was ill as a child:

> If I ever live and grow up my one aim and concentrated
> purpose shall be and is to show that women can learn, can
> reason, can compete with men in the grand fields of
> literature and science and conjecture; that a woman can be
> a woman and a true one without having all her time
> engrossed by dress and society.[5]

Bryn Mawr became Carey Thomas' vehicle for realizing
her aim. She was determined to make its curriculum "just
as stiff as Harvard's," "to show that women could compete
with Harvard men." Her requirement that all faculty have
Ph.D.'s (except Woodrow Wilson) was mocked by Harvard's president, who claimed that "there was an intuitive
something in ladies of birth and position which enabled
them to do without college training, and make on the
whole better professors for women college students than if
they themselves had been to college." She even devised an
entrance exam every bit as rigorous as Harvard's, much to
the horror of other women's colleges.

Other features distinguished the early Bryn Mawr from
other women's colleges. Carey Thomas devised a self-
government system and also added a graduate school
whose students were to be integrated with undergraduate
students. Both the self-government system and the graduate school were intended to prove that education did not
turn women into invalids.

Basically, however, Carey Thomas shared the belief of
the men who helped to plan the college that the recipients
of this education should be "young women of the upper
classes." She established only one undergraduate scholarship, preferring, out of her own experience, to endow a
fellowship for one member of each graduating class to
study abroad. She believed that:

> The intellectual atmosphere of the college clearly must be
> such to set a standard; but the physical aspect and the
> social life too should have a certain graciousness and
> ceremony. Students should be shown as well as told of

those things which are beautiful and desirable. From the
smallest to the largest circumstance there should be as
little as possible to mislead their intellectual or aesthetic
perceptions for they must be accustomed to the best, so
that in the future they would recognize and demand and
work for it.[6]

To this end, Thomas spent generously on the design and
furnishings of each college building as it was added, and
had copies of European treasures, cloisters, and statues
made for the college.

Carey Thomas always perceived the need for good
education as the most important problem of women, but
after the college was successfully established, she turned
her attention to other aspects of the women's movement.
Her interests followed from her elitist perspective, but
then many activists shared her aristocratic attitude toward
women's rights. At the National American Woman Suffrage Association convention in Baltimore in 1906, she
became an active participant in the movement. In one of
her speeches she noted perceptively that the only true
objection to woman's suffrage is that women's enfranchisement "is the symbol of a stupendous social revolution and
we are frightened before it." In 1910 she actively partici-
pated in the liberal bloc at the NAWSA convention; in
1912 she sympathized with the Progressive party and
wrote sadly to Jane Addams that, although she had spoken
to the Bryn Mawr students in favor of Theodore Roosevelt, they had voted in their dummy presidential election
"two to one for Wilson . . . and Roosevelt only won over
Taft by four votes."

Her support of the suffrage movement was not entirely
disinterested; she saw it as a chance to enhance her own
prestige, to enhance Bryn Mawr's name, and to awaken
her students to new interests. Her interest in suffrage as an
issue was pragmatic; it had none of the "virtuous woman"
aura that suffused the rhetoric of other suffragists. Her
involvement in the woman's movement led her to initiate
three new projects at the college that reflect the contradic-
toriness of her conception of the woman's movement: the
founding of the Bryn Mawr School of Social Work, the
establishment of the Phoebe Anna Thorne Open Air
School, and the creation of the Bryn Mawr Summer
School for Industrial Workers.

In 1915 Carey Thomas founded the School of Social

Work to professionalize a field that many women were entering. She felt that professionalization would lend more prestige and respect to women and would also make the work they did more effective and scientific. The same motivation of professionalization led to the founding of the Phoebe Anna Thorne School as a "laboratory experiment in modern methods of teaching." She wanted to give both dignity and skill to women who entered the field of teaching (the field that most early women college graduates entered) and felt that practical teaching experience would be an effective part of the college curriculum. She appeared not to question whether "professionalization" would fundamentally change the nature of "woman's work."

At the same time, the working woman was becoming a matter of concern to those interested in women's rights. Women were being organized into unions; there was agitation over the working conditions of women and children in factories; women were fighting for equal pay. Carey Thomas, feeling that the most important thing she could do for women workers was to give them a smattering of a liberal arts education, translated this concern into the establishment of the Bryn Mawr Summer School for Industrial Workers. However, she felt no real sense of identity with working-class women, blind to the relationship between her own difficulties in getting an education and their problems in earning a decent wage, between her aversion to marriage and their difficulties in raising a family while they worked. Her lack of identification with working-class women is revealed in an excerpt from one of her speeches:

Rejoicing that British women had just been enfranchised and American women would soon be politically free, and wondering what would be the next great social advance . . . suddenly as in a vision, I saw that out of the hideous world war might come, as a glorious aftermath, international industrial justice and international peace, if your generation only had the courage to work for them as my generation worked for woman suffrage. I also saw as part of my vision that the coming of equal opportunity for the manual workers might be hastened by utilizing the deep sex sympathy that women now feel for each other before it had time to grow less, . . . then with a glow of delight as radiant as the desert sunset I remembered the passionate interest of the Bryn Mawr College students in fairness and

justice and the intense sympathy with girls less fortunate
than themselves and I realized that the first steps on the
path to the sunrise might well be taken by the college
women who, themselves just emerging from the wilder-
ness, know best of all women living under fortunate
conditions what it means to be denied things of the intellect
and the spirit.[7]

The Summer School was "to offer young women of
character and ability a further education, in order that
they might widen their influence in the industrial world,
help in the coming social reconstruction and increase the
happiness and usefulness of their own lives." Economics
and English were required, as well as art, hygiene, music,
and science. The students were to be women workers, not
supervisors, between the ages of eighteen and thirty-five.
The Summer School was run by a committee of labor
representatives and educators; it attempted to maintain an
"objective neutrality" with regard to such gut issues as
strikes and higher pay. From 1928 to 1939 it was highly
successful in educating women workers in those fields that
the school had deemed important; it seems unlikely that it
raised the consciousness of women workers themselves as
to the political implications of their situation. At the same
time, however, it represented a serious attempt on the
part of educated women to express their commitment to
improving the situation of women of other classes and was
a pioneer experiment, if not the only one of its kind.

Carey Thomas' view of feminism was complicated. Her
concern for the situation of women, regardless of class,
was real, but her understanding of the political responsibility of a college like Bryn Mawr, had been founded on
principles of feminism, and was, like the understanding of
most nineteenth-century feminists, confused. She did not
understand the basis of woman's degradation in her position in the family and underestimated the strength of
sexual conservatism in action throughout the society. This
limited her perspective on the college's function with regard to its students. She could not see that Bryn Mawr
existed in a vacuum, that the deeper truths of woman's
condition in society remained untouched, unaddressed,
unchanged. Her basic drive was to prove that women are
intellectually equal to men; Bryn Mawr was the vehicle
she used to prove it. Her belief in the intellectual capacities of women was radical at the time the college was

founded, and she was instrumental in changing the then widely held position that women were biologically and naturally unsuited to a life of the intellect. She was an unusual woman, for she let no one stand in the way of her goals. In order to get women admitted to Johns Hopkins Medical School, she raised $500,000 and contributed it to the school when they promised to take women students.

She did not, however, have a radical view of education. Bryn Mawr was designed to reinforce the symbols of education, the "good student" syndrome—"diligence, obedience, and complete faith in the school and its teachings."[8] Scholasticism was the rule at Bryn Mawr, but then again it may be true that "pedantry is not to be despised in an oppressed class as it indicates the first struggle of intellect with its restraints and is therefore a hopeful symptom."[9] Carey Thomas "never understood that she and her sister educators, at the same time that they made it possible for women to secure a first-class education, had helped establish a ceiling above which few women could rise. Carey Thomas' own accomplishments were born of rebellion; at Bryn Mawr there was no room for rebels."[10] It was exactly that "quality" education for which Miss Thomas had striven so hard that kept women down.

Furthermore, she did not see women's colleges as a permanent necessity; her real aim was—and always had been—integration. Bryn Mawr had been founded to meet an immediate crucial need, but Thomas did not think that women's colleges represented a long-range solution to the problems of education for women:

> The very first step (that university women should now take) seems to me to be the demand for unqualified, true, out-and-out coeducation. Only by having the schools and universities coeducational can we ensure the girls of the world receiving a thoroughly good education. There is not enough money in the world to duplicate schools and universities for women, and if we could duplicate them they would soon become less good. It requires endless vigilance to keep women's universities as good as coeducational universities. It would be tragic if now, after coeducation has been tried on a tremendous scale, we university women should accept separate universities for women.[11]

Women's colleges were to provide women with the intellectual skills to compete with men, yet Carey Thomas realized that there was no such thing as "separate but equal." Men had the power and their schools would always be better academically. To her the entire question of women's liberation turned on equal education. To her "the political and social aspects of women's struggle for equality commended themselves in particular only as they were allied to the educational side."

Bryn Mawr was an important institution during the years of the suffrage movement; Carey Thomas saw the school as an integral part of the women's struggle. She assumed, however, that both suffrage and the advent of educational opportunities for women would herald the coming of full freedom for women; in this respect she was representative of the larger feminist movement. She was not concerned with analyzing or changing the structural bases of women's oppression, and it was this failure that fostered the growth of an institution whose vestigial feminism had as its aim the development of a class of privileged women who would find a place in a male-dominated world. Miss Thomas' overinvolvement in academic achievement, her blindness to the political realities of sexism (which would prevent even women with "quality" educations from being equal to men), and her basic commitment to elite education obscured her vision.

Carey Thomas' feminism was unquestionably elitist. For the last forty years Bryn Mawr has maintained her elitism without her feminism. It is true that the women's rights movement was not sustained during these years, and that Bryn Mawr only succumbed to the general cultural atmosphere. Those members of the administration and faculty who retain feminist ideals have received little support or reinforcement from the society at large. Social history since World War II seemed to prove beyond contradiction that American women want nothing more out of life than a cloistered home, motherhood, and the role of loyal supporter of children, husband, and community. And certainly husbands, psychologists, sociologists, and pundits require nothing more for them. The students themselves have strongly internalized the social ideal of woman as supportive, altruistic, and self-sacrificing and thus have tended to view "old-fashioned" feminists as strident and selfish. Nevertheless Bryn Mawr had a distinctly feminist tradition and responsibility which it has subsequently failed to uphold.

Marion Park, Carey Thomas' successor as president of

Bryn Mawr, never showed any significant feminist concern; on the contrary, her feminist confusion was painful to behold, a perfect example of the degeneracy of the college's original ideas. She praised Virgina Woolf's *A Room of One's Own* as a book in which "a woman writes as a woman and presents her sex not in relation to men but in relation to all the other interests in the world, just as men are presented." At the end of this speech, Miss Park urged the students "to give this book to your woman friends and read it yourself. I only advise you not to give it to men because it is very much the sort of book that you can use and fit in delightfully in dinner conversations." A 1941 speech on the special problems of women's colleges further reveals her extraordinary ambivalence and its limitations with regard to feminism. Miss Park praised the anthropological discovery that the mental capacities of men and women are not fundamentally different and concluded that colleges should not act as though there were two homogeneous groups to be trained. She conceded that the problems of men and women are different; that professional women faced a more difficult time in their careers than men, and that "a woman who marries needs to be prepared to encounter interferences with her unified individual life and must be given intellectual techniques which will allow her to acquire interests readily after she has solved the immediate problems of bringing up a family." This fully stated recognition that Bryn Mawr's function is to train women to use their leisure time constructively while they assume full and primary responsibility for raising a family implicitly admitted the degeneracy of Bryn Mawr's feminism.

Two articles written by the students over the last fifteen years reflect the same degeneracy, and reveal the extent of the student body's acceptance of this position. Describing a conference in 1951 on "Women in the Defense Decade," a student writes that "the conference did not mention women's rights (thank god) but only women's responsibilities. It is time for women to stop complaining about lack of opportunity!" Most Bryn Mawr women probably feel this way during college, for they are told that they are "special," and they believe that their privilege makes feminism irrelevant to them. Another student, writing on "The New Feminism" in a 1963 issue of the Alumnae Magazine, describes her experience at Harvard Medical School:

The young men worried about us, rushed to protect us. . . .
They were young men who believed women should be
educated and should take up careers or jobs susceptible of
easy termination upon marriage or childbearing, and perhaps easy renewal at age 45 or so. They did not envisage a
man's world wanting to make a place for us on feminine
terms and so they feared the sacrifice of our femininity to
our careers in a man's world.

We were then what I like to call the New Feminists, no
longer militant but engaged in a sort of passive resistance
movement in a man's world, our personal difficulties
compounded by demands not only for professional acceptance . . . at least by one man per woman.

Bryn Mawr is . . . an ivory tower, an artificial temporary
community in which feminine capabilities can be expressed
fully without social pressure (and which) allows one to go
on even in the face of ordinary pressures and develop into
a feminine and attractive person. . . . Because it was taken
for granted that I was a person of serious purpose and
great ability, I acquired an enriched self-image.

At Bryn Mawr, no one, in class or out of class, ever
discusses what femininity means, what are the sources of
the problems faced by women, and what would be needed
to change the situation. Characteristically, the author does
not deal with any of those problems. She internalizes the
male image of her role, yet rebels against it. Passive
resistance would appear to mean a compromise for acceptance, based on the assumption that men could be cajoled
or seduced into accepting women as equals. Bryn Mawr
was an ivory tower that fooled her (and many other wom-
en) into believing that such a situation is possible and
workable. As a product of an elite school, the author was
able to secure one of the few places offered to women at
Harvard Medical School. What relevance does passive
resistance have for a secretary? For that matter, what
relevance does passive resistance have for the average
Bryn Mawr graduate?

Bryn Mawr's implied philosophy is that it is sufficient
for a woman's college to provide a haven for women so
that they can develop enough confidence to tackle the
obstacles facing them in a man's world. If Bryn Mawr
were providing that confidence-building haven to its students it would qualify as an important first-rank feminist
institution. But, in fact, Bryn Mawr has capitulated utterly
to society's regressive view of women and is actually
producing intellectual decorations, women of "sensitivity,"

who are rising to the challenge of "managing career and family" and developing into feminine and attractive people. Bryn Mawr as it is today is a metaphor for the discrepancy between women's apparent freedom and their actual social and psychological entrapments.

A woman's college that does not relate to the needs of its students and pretends that its education will solve the "inequalities" of women within the society is *dishonest*. Most prestige colleges train wives for the ruling and professional classes. If Bryn Mawr claims to do more, to train women to take a place alongside men in the present social structure, it is deluding its own students by not openly admitting and exposing the problems that women have faced and will continue to face until there is real liberation. Were the college to deal actively with sexism, the ramifications of their problems would begin to be apparent. Few women students would gear their struggle to their own self-interest so narrowly defined. Prestige education does offer the pretense of freedom and equality to many women; more important, however, is the distance that it creates between the "ordinary" woman and the Bryn Mawr woman. As long as the pretense of individual achievement (tokenism) is maintained, as long as the rhetoric of "uniqueness" is not exposed for the lie that it is, collective action will be made impossible by this very elitism.

Many of us as students believed that all of Bryn Mawr's problems could be solved by adding men, and the pressure for coeducation is still strong. Many women still feel that women (like blacks in the early stages of the civil rights movement) must integrate with men in order to prove that they are equal. How Bryn Mawr will deal with this pressure from many of its students and weigh it against its responsibilities as a woman's institution is unclear. What *is* clear, however, is that if Bryn Mawr chooses to remain an all-woman's college, it must radically redefine its responsibilities and choose to deal actively with the political and psychic oppression of its women students as a group.

Minimal steps toward becoming a feminist institution must be taken. The college must critically examine itself in order to deal honestly with sexism in its course and goal orientation, as well as in its own attitudes toward its students. It should devote resources toward developing a broad-based women's movement, whether through research, publication, or activism, and should establish a Women's Studies department which would include courses in history, sociology, psychology, and literature. The courses should be oriented toward developing ideas on structural change necessary for the liberation of women as a group, regardless of class.

At present, the reasons for remaining a woman's college are never discussed; they are justified purely by snobbery and tradition. The decline in the number of applications and the increase in the number of women who drop out or seek psychiatric help reflect the individualism that is a major stumbling block to Bryn Mawr's feminism. A woman's college, no matter how excellent it pretends to be, cannot evade its fundamental feminist responsibilities without doing serious damage to its students. Today, such a school can only genuinely reactivate its feminism by declaring active commitment to the struggle of all women for their liberation. Only by repudiating parochial interests can the school become a place where women can learn together, deal with their problems together, and act collectively in their struggle to assume their rightful positions as functioning adults in the world.

NOTES

1. A male Quaker college founded in 1833, one mile from Bryn Mawr.
2. President of Bryn Mawr from 1942 to 1970.
3. The student government organization.
4. Edith Finch, *Carey Thomas of Bryn Mawr.* (New York: 1947), p. 22.
5. *Ibid.*, p. 1.
6. *Ibid.*, p. 265.
7. *Ibid.*, p. 273.
8. William O'Neill, *Everyone was Brave: The Rise and Fall of Feminism in America.* (Chicago: Quadrangle, 1969), p. 113.
9. Harriet Martineau, quoted in *Everyone Was Brave,* p. 9.
10. *Ibid.*, p. 113.
11. *Carey Thomas of Bryn Mawr,* p. 278.

26

IS WOMEN'S LIBERATION A LESBIAN PLOT?

Sidney Abbott and Barbara Love

Those threatened by or irritated with women's liberation often dismiss the movement by saying, "Oh, they're just a bunch of dykes." The response of the women's liberation movement to this charge is vital to the feminists, the lesbians, the many who accept both identities, as well as to the life and the meaning of the movement itself.

The words "dyke" and "lesbian," especially when used by men, are charged words calculated to send shivers of horror up the spines of women who want a more independent life style. Men who pride themselves on their capacity for rational responses cannot keep a cool head on this subject. They are upset and confused by women who do not fit into categories they can handle: unmarried and seeking domination, married and dominated, frustrated career woman, or incomplete old maid or spinster. But a lesbian? "Let's face the truth," says one feminist, "the greatest threat to men is solidarity among women and 'lesbianism' epitomizes that solidarity." Few words carry as much emotional meaning, independent of context, as "dyke." The word brings a heavy load of prejudice with it and blocks any discriminating thought, preventing everyone—including the feminists—from discussing the real questions involved. When the word is used women usually respond with an uneasy silence.

Women need to think through the lesbian issue so that such name calling cannot be used to divide women who should be united in a common struggle. In their paper, "The Woman-Identified Woman," members of a new Women's Liberation group, the Radicalesbians, make it very clear: "As long as the word 'dyke' can be used to frighten women into a less militant stand, keep women separate from their sisters, and keep them from giving primacy to anything other than men and family—then to that extent they are dominated by the male culture."

<u>Lesbians have always been linked with women's liberation.</u> Articles on the movement by the mass media alluded to them long before feminists were even willing to acknowledge their existence. But the feminists were deluding themselves. The signs were clear. They had only to examine the life style of other women in the movement or listen to their friends to see there had to be a connection somewhere. Feminists who thought the lesbians were not there for legitimate reasons and would soon leave are disillusioned by now. Conservative elements in the movement are still trying to keep the lesbians in the closet by saying lesbianism is not important and at the same time, too dangerous to deal with. From motives of safety, not honest feeling, feminists dealing with the mass media still deny there are lesbians in women's liberation. The radical feminists, however, most of whom do not cooperate with the media, have never been afraid to discuss common objectives with lesbians, and now that the lesbian's sense of self has begun to flower through the women's movement and the Gay Liberation Front, to march with them, support them in public, even aspire to a genuine exploration of the lesbian way of life.

Who are lesbians? What kind of women are they? How does their experience, both in and out of the movement, shed light on women's liberation? What do they add to the movement? To the exploration of sexism? To the idea of cultural revolution as conceived by the feminists? To the idea of self-possession?

Lesbians are women who survive without men financially and emotionally, representing the ultimate in an independent life style. Lesbians are the women who battle day by day to show that women are valid human beings, not just appendages of men. Lesbians are the women whose relationships attempt a true break with the old sexual-emotional divisions. Lesbians are the women who are penalized for their sexuality more than any other women on earth. Thus, it is no wonder that lesbians are attracted to the women's liberation movement, are active in it, and feel that they are in the vanguard of it. If women's liberation does mean liberation from the dominance of men, lesbians' opinions should be actively sought out, for in many ways the lesbian *has* freed herself from male domination.

Lesbians are women who have chosen to love other women. They have a positive attitude toward women and do not think of their lives as an alternative, or as an aggressive rejection of men. Because they have little interest in pleasing men, lesbians are not usually man-haters, as the stereotype so often has it. They do not see men as a threat to them personally, as feminists often do.

Any kind of woman may be a lesbian, even concurrently with marriage and children. Lesbians may be rich, poor, good-looking, or homely. In short, they are like anybody else, except for their sexual preference. Research since Kinsey's day indicates that there are more women who are lesbians than men who are homosexuals. In one study 50 percent of the women queried had had intense emotional relationships with other women as adults, which is defined by some as homosexuality—while 27 percent admitted overt lesbian experience.[1] Other experts estimate that there are a large number of hidden lesbians among married women. There are probably more lesbians than male homosexuals.

Some feminists have reservations about supporting the militant lesbian feminists, and their reasons should be discussed. Some insist that lesbianism is merely a practice, not a political issue. However, Celestine Ware points out in her book *Woman Power* that "radical feminists believe that radical feminism is the only truly political cause now in existence. ... To achieve the elimination of dominance in human relationships, sex roles, i.e. stereotyped male and female identities, would have to be eradicated."[2] Peter Cohen comments that: "to live an alternative *that is totally outside the alternative of the culture* is a profoundly political act."[3]

One must look to the lesbians' oppression as part of women's oppression. One must look to the lesbians' desire to escape from the male power structure and achieve independent being. The penalties the feminist will face for openly denying her sex role will resemble those the lesbian now faces for showing an open preference for her own sex. To be a lesbian is unnatural—in men's eyes. To be a feminist is unnatural—in men's eyes. The price of rebellion against men's authority is living as an outcast without the approval and support of men.

The common enemy of feminists and lesbians is sexism. Sexism is not merely the preference of society for one sex, and the attribution to that sex of various preferred qualities and attitudes at the expense of the other sex. Sexism emerges from making reproduction rather than personal pleasure or personal development the goal of sexual intercourse. That society sanctions sex only for reproduction is clearly shown in various sex laws which make sex acts that do not lead to reproduction illegal, whether performed by two men, two women, or a man and a woman—married or unmarried. Clearly, these laws speak to our deepest fears of our own sexuality. Clearly too, these laws are obsolete, especially in light of our overpopulation problems and the growing popular belief that sex is acceptable for pleasure alone (evidenced by the widespread use of the pill and demand for repeal of abortion laws). This new acceptance of sexual liberation primarily benefits the most traditional male-female kind of sex. The homosexual is still considered perverted, although homosexual couples have not invented anything that heterosexuals cannot and do not do. Yet only the homosexual still bears the full burden of sexist fears.

Although women's liberation has insisted on the right of all women to control their own bodies, the subject has only been discussed in terms of abortion. In liberationist thinking the concept of the right to one's own body does not include freedom of sexual activities or freedom of sexual preference, which would logically seem to be a part of the kind of self-ownership and self-determination at the heart of feminist demands. This is probably because such a viewpoint would seem to come frighteningly close to actually endorsing lesbianism. Clearly, sexual freedom of all kinds would liberate women from guilt about sexual activities (heterosexual or homosexual), from performing on demand, and from the kind of sexual disappointment that comes from being held largely responsible for fulfilling sexual pleasure, as well as for conception, childbearing, and childrearing.

People outside the movement are questioning sexist customs and attitudes within the scope of women's liberation, particularly in regard to same-sex marriages. The blessings of God for homosexual unions are now given in some churches, and various individuals have urged that same-sex marriages be more acceptable and common in the future. Rita Hauser, the United States representative to the United Nations Human Rights Commission, speaking to the American Bar Association, on "Women's Liberation and the Law," argued that laws banning marriages between persons of the same sex were unconstitutional and were based on the outmoded notion that sex was for reproduction. Margaret Mead, the well-known author and anthropologist, has advocated for a long time two-career marriages, childless marriages, same-sex marriages, and communes of adults where sex is not the central organizing factor. Only one acknowledged feminist has made this case: Caroline Bird, author of *Born Female,* speaking to the Daughters of Bilitis, a lesbian group, predicted that "in the future we will see the stranglehold of reproduction on human relations broken, and numerous life styles will be possible."

Women's liberation's great importance is that it provides an opportunity for reexamination of modes of human behavior; this should include the idea that heterosexual relationships are the only acceptable life style. If, as some interpreters of the new Equal Rights Amendment point out, the new legislation would make homosexual marriages legal, this fact should be analyzed and accepted, even promoted, but not hidden.

The fight of all women against sexism is not the only common battleground of feminists and lesbians. Both groups are part of the larger struggle against oppression waged by all groups that refuse to be dominated by a hierarchical system in which certain groups are considered naturally superior, and others naturally inferior. In this battle, assimilation is the characteristic trademark. Lesbians who conceal their sexual preference are not persecuted; feminists who remain housewives and mothers are not rejected; prostitutes who conceal their occupations are not admonished; blacks who can pass for white are not discriminated against. It is only when oppressed people stand up and openly announce who and what they are that they are either pressured into assuming their correct roles and levels in society, or they are crucified.

Feminists who continue to live off their husband's incomes and perform the traditional duties of wife and mother *at the expense of their own development* are hiding and only paying lip service to their cause, much as lesbians who flirt with men in the office. They are trying to escape discrimination by appearing to perpetuate the system. But when a feminist truly joins the movement and steps off the pedestal, temporarily leaving men or defying them, she is moving from a recognized and valued position with certain kinds of privileges into a new, lonely place, one that may involve open hostility.

Today's cultural revolution consists of group after group saying, "We won't take it anymore. We want to be human." Lesbians are now emulating some of the tactics and the practices of women's liberation, even as that movement took its cues from black liberation. What is afoot here is a general rebellion of the dispossessed of the earth; as such, feminists and lesbians are deeply tied, one to the other. It was no accident that a 1970 meeting of revolutionary groups included the Black Panthers, homosexuals, and feminists.

Out of her activism in the feminist movement, more often than not, a new kind of lesbian has emerged, a lesbian who calls herself a lesbian activist or a radical lesbian and has learned most recently the enormous power and freedom of the open assertion of who and what one is. Not only is the radical lesbian no longer ashamed of her commitment to the lesbian way of life, but after some self-searching and self-analysis, she has come to realize that most of her problems are due not to any necessarily unhealthy traits in her personality, but rather to her social oppression.

The emotional development that enables the lesbian to throw off the sex roles and sex restrictions universally accepted in our society has been commonly described as a psychopathology: a mental sickness. It is assumed that something in the individual's family environment has caused the child's development to take a wrong turn. However, some progressive psychiatrists and social workers have begun to talk about a concept called sociopathology: a sickness in society. They have found that the individuals they have treated for so-called personal problems have real problems which they are in no position to control. The environment threatens them, even physically. This continual state of threat leads to tension, which leads to various emotional problems, which cannot be solved by treatment because they are perpetuated by real pressures from a hostile society. The concept of sociopathology fosters a need for systematic analysis of all women's behavior and sheds particular light on the society's rigidity and unwillingness to tolerate many life styles for women. It points to external reasons for lesbians' distress and emotional problems. The problems of lesbians—guilt, fear, self-hatred—can therefore be regarded as part of a sociopathology, part of what is wrong with our society, preventing whole categories of people from being happy and productive.

If women are generally dominated by men in all phases of their lives, from birth until death—and if this domination is unnatural—then all of women's modes of behavior are forms of evasive action or adjustment to survive the domination. They are all ways to live in a basically threatening environment. Thus, the clinging vine, the caretaker-housewife, and the child-woman are women who have succumbed to male dominance; the driving career woman, the feminist, and the lesbian are women who have struggled to reject male dominance. <u>Lesbianism is one reaction on the part of the growing female to the emotional understanding, shared by all females, of what it means to become a woman in our society.</u>

According to the Radicalesbians,

> The lesbian is the rage of all women, condensed to the point of explosion. She is a woman, who, often at an early age, acts in accordance with an inner compulsion to be a more complete human being than her society will allow her [to be]. These needs and conflicts, over a period of years, bring her into painful conflict with people, situations, and the accepted way of thinking, until she is in a continual state of war with everything around her, and usually with herself. She may not be fully conscious of the political implications of what for her began as personal necessity, but, on some level, she has not been able to accept the limitations and oppression laid upon her by the most basic role in society, the female role.

The lesbian often refused to play the game by rejecting dolls, kitchen playthings, sexual cunning, and instead showed an interest in the mental and physical pursuits reserved for boys—and later men. She knew that when boys said sneeringly that they didn't want to play girls' games and she mimicked them, saying she didn't want to

play boys' games, she was lying. She *did* want to play
boys' games. This was difficult to comprehend. As a child
she was natural; at the time of puberty, when she refused
to change, suddenly she was considered unnatural. When
her interests and feelings did not coincide with the demands of society, the pain, bitterness, and rejection began.
The pressure was on and would stay on until some force
greater than the individual—liberation or death—would
change it.

Women who have tried to adopt any of those human
qualities and attitudes not considered natural to a female
have always been labeled male-identified or lesbian. This
seems unfair since the man is allowed the status of a male
at the same time that he seeks all those very same human
qualities. To associate the woman or the lesbian with male
qualities, when she is simply trying to develop in a positively human way, is to consider both the feminist and the
lesbian inauthentic. That is to say, if a woman can never
be considered anything but less courageous, less intelligent, less creative, and less independent, we will only have
acceptable women who are less than males. Any woman
who is equal to or better than a man will be considered an
aberration—a non-woman.

It is generally recognized that career role playing is
unforgivable for feminists as well as for lesbians. And yet
some feminists say they once wanted to be generals, pi-
lots, lawyers, or senators. The women who were forced by
social pressure to give up these dreams are enraged.

Learning what careers or duties a woman could choose
was only one lesson in the psycho-social education of a
woman. She was also taught how to love men. During the
preteen years a crush on another girl was considered
natural, much the same as "immature" aspirations to
"men's" careers were considered natural. The girls would
grow out of both. But today, more and more, it appears
that women are socialized into sex roles as well as career
roles; there is nothing to prove that heterosexuality is any
more normal than homosexuality. Women's liberation has
not yet dealt with role playing in terms of sexual orientation.

Certainly by role playing, both in career aspirations and
in love relationships, the woman is not truly living. She is
living life much as an actress who assumes or is assigned a
part. She is not living a fully conscious life, making her
own choices. Role playing must be seen as an escape from

reality, much like the use of alcohol, drugs, or hypnosis. These are forms of half-death or semiconsciousness. Implicit in the act of jettisoning the role is the need to live a fully conscious life.

In *The Second Sex* Simone de Beauvoir expresses her conception of the natural response of women: "If nature is to be invoked, one can say that all women are naturally homosexual. The lesbian, in fact, is distinguished by her refusal of the male and her liking for feminine flesh; but every adolescent female fears penetration and masculine domination, and she feels a certain repulsion for the male body; on the other hand, the female body is for her, as for the male, an object of desire."[4]

People must come to realize and admit openly that there are varieties of sexuality, of which heterosexuality happens to be the most popular but not necessarily the most valid. Women's liberation must promote the issue as a nonissue of no more importance than a person's preference for Swiss or American cheese.

The return of those natural feelings for other women is a phenomenon that has certainly been released for investigation by the women's movement. It is expressed by two women from the Class Workshop who attended an all-women's dance held by the Gay Liberation Front. These feminists—not lesbians—published their reactions in the underground newspaper *Rat:* "I saw the possibility of having an experience that would counter the limited dance definition ... there would be present only women, in a social context of wanting to relate to women. What I experienced was a sense of emotional feeling without restriction, for women. When I danced close to another woman I was aware of how much feeling for one another we do have, yet are told not to express—and how this must stultify our personal relationships." The second reaction: "I was moved but experienced no great upheaval. It was not anything like a religious conversion. The idea of women loving other women just became more palpable and natural to me."

Because both feminists and lesbians lead independent lives, feminists are more likely to understand the lesbian point of view and accept their own homosexual feelings without the hysteria often seen in other women. It is also interesting to note that one of the few women recognized as a poet and a teacher in early Greek culture when women were confined to their homes was the "original" lesbian, Sappho, from the island of Lesbos.

The lesbian has taken the ultimate liberty heterosexual women are not permitted: to live and love exactly as she pleases. She does not make emotional tradeoffs for the privileges of being a lady. For this she is violently hated and tormented. Lesbianism is the one response to male domination that is unforgivable. The lesbian is labeled unnatural and forced to live unnaturally. As expressed blatantly by Simone de Beauvior in *The Second Sex*, "If there is a great deal of aggressiveness and affection in the attitude of Lesbians, there is no way they can live naturally in their situations; being natural implies being unselfconscious, not picturing one's acts to oneself. She can go her own way in calm indifference only when she is old enough or backed by considerable social prestige."[5]

Lesbians are doubly outcast, both as women and as homosexuals. Lesbians, like all women, are not encouraged to be independent or to educate themselves; as women they are always treated as inferior. On the other hand, they are denied the benefits of the sexist system: financial security, recognition in the home, maternal power. They suffer the oppression of all women but are not eligible for any of the rewards. Whereas heterosexual women are moving from a position in society that is privileged—wife and mother—to a freer position, lesbians are a minority fighting for the right to exist. The lesbian suffers the oppression of all women—only more so. Women get lower pay than men on the job, while lesbians are fired when their sexual preference is discovered. (Lesbians have not yet reached the level of tokenism.) A woman in college is fighting for grades equal to men's, but a lesbian is coping with fears and anxieties about being expelled. A divorced woman has a nearly unchallenged right to her children, but a lesbian's children are forcibly taken from her. Men are satisfied if a woman remains silent, but a lesbian triggers anger and hostility. A gigantic law suit should be instituted against schools, industry, and the psychiatric profession for severe psychic damage done to homosexuals, as well as to women.

Allies are difficult to find. Lesbians do not have the benefit of reliable support from straight sisters or gay brothers. Women—even those in women's liberation—are often sexist, in that they do not accept the lesbian's sexual preference; male homosexuals are often sexist, in that they often dismiss women or overlook them.

Male homosexuals who want unity with lesbians are being confronted with their sexism, but they do have other differences that keep them from identifying completely with lesbians. Male homosexuals are persecuted by police harassment and by legal sanctions. They suffer a fairly direct oppression, designed to limit their numbers or even eliminate them. Lesbians are spared much of this harassment, but they are ridiculed instead. Seen as imitation men, they are a laughingstock for both sexes. Although not considered important enough to harass and persecute very often, they live under an extreme form of psychological censure. Women who feel little or no threat from male homosexuals dread and are repulsed by lesbians, men who are not threatened by male homosexuals are curiously afraid of lesbians.

More than male homosexuals, lesbians are seen as a threat to the entire system based on sexual relationships. A male homosexual retains his male life style. In fact, he often views himself as a supermale, freed from the need for women and active in an all-male world not altogether different from that of a select men's club or sports team. He is promiscuous, and his promiscuity is a male privilege. He sometimes feels superior to the domesticated, suburban male. Lesbians try to live a stable life, more often they try to build a home life without men. Clearly, this is not permissible within the male sexist system. It is acceptable for a man to do without women, as in men's clubs, sports, or the army, but it is never acceptable for a woman to be without a man. A woman is defined in relationship to men and family. A female without a man and a family is not considered a complete woman, but rather a failed woman. The single man is a bachelor; the single woman is an old maid—or a lesbian.

Many women conceal parts of themselves from men, but as a homosexual, the lesbian suffers the pain of living entirely underground. In an article entitled "Gay Is Good," Martha Shelley explains:

Understand this—that the worst part of being homosexual is having to keep it a secret. Not the occasional murders by police or teenage queer-beaters, not the loss of jobs or expulsion from school, nor dishonorable discharges—but the daily knowledge that what you are is so awful that it cannot be revealed. The violence against us is sporadic.

Most of us are not affected. But the internal violence of being made to carry—or choosing to carry—the load of your straight society's unconscious guilt—this is what tears us apart, what makes us want to stand up in the office, in the factories, and in the schools and shout our true identity.

Some of the effects of living the lie are shown in the following excerpts taken from "Journals of Two Lovers," the story of a lesbian relationship. The first entry talks about the effects of trying to live without hiding: "The only way we can imagine living as lesbians together is to have a fast car and lots of money—to set up a temporary life for a few weeks before moving on—living an interim existence between discovery and discovery. Running, like fugitives. No way to settle down and live a productive life, no matter how great the desire, knowing that whatever we built would be ruined the instant our love was revealed." Another entry reveals the price of remaining silent: "I was sitting at the dinner table with my family ready to enjoy a beautiful meal—a virtual feast. We were celebrating a family reunion. My parents had just come back from Europe. Our hearts warmed as Pop stood up to give his traditional toast: 'When your mother and I were in Europe we had two boys at the next dinner table who were living together. It was very sad. The parents must suffer terribly. We thought how lucky we are that all of our kids are healthy. Skol.' My throat closed off and my whole body was racing. This meal was clearly not for me—a lesbian. It was for someone in my family who did not exist."

Any well-intentioned individual, including a lesbian, needs self-respect for a positive outlook on the world. Self-respect demands honesty. For a lesbian to have to deny who she is—outright or by default—is dishonest and destructive. The guilt associated with lying is tremendous, especially when that lying is for life. The lesbian has lived the lie because honesty means confronting society's hate alone. To declare oneself a lesbian is still tantamount to a Jew declaring himself in Nazi Germany. Maybe the lesbian will not be killed, but she risks losing everything and everybody important to her and putting a burden of suspicion or guilt on anyone who accepts her.

The lesbian is bombarded daily by society's thousands of little messages that insist her very life is a crime, just as heterosexual women absorb thousands of messages that insist they are not equal to men. The lesbian may carry guilt like a criminal; during the period called "coming out," when she begins to accept her lesbianism, she may feel very like Raskolnikov in *Crime and Punishment:* she wants to cry out to the world, but she dares not. As explained by Theodor Reik, "Something of the need for punishment finds partial gratification in the compulsion to confess." Fear of punishment creates tremendous anxiety, even though punishment may not occur. Lesbians have committed suicide rather than confess what should be a joyous and celebrated love. They still do. It is evidence of the individual courage of lesbians that they are not jumping out of buildings every day.

The one protection offered many lesbians is the possibility of hiding. It is relatively easy for perhaps 90 percent to "pass for white." The obvious lesbians, the ones who look boyish and are usually identified as lesbians, are a minority within a minority. The homosexual movement is different from other movements because of the *ease* of concealment. As a social movement fighting for acceptance, lesbians and male homosexuals will have to find a way to mobilize the many homosexuals who still feel they cannot afford to "come out" into the open.

Lesbians early saw women's liberation as a salvation—a movement that recognized women in a new way and seemed to advocate an independent life style similar to the lesbian life style. Lesbians not only needed better jobs, education, and pay, and the benefit of public accommodations laws, but also felt an affinity with the angry, struggling feminists who want their own identities. In fact, lesbians had a sense of déjà vu: they knew the frustration, the torn state of mind of the feminists very well. Their present life styles and outlook seemed to have a great deal in common. For lesbians who were still very alone and divided, it was intoxicating to be suddenly a part of a broad societal movement for human rights that could bring about lasting social change and a recognition of women's equality and independence. That was the strong pull. The push was that the Daughters of Bilitis, a fifteen-year-old lesbian organization, was not an activist group at a time when action became imperative. The DOB has always billed itself as "a home away from home"; it urges adjustment of the individual to society. When women's liberation opened the door to an activist role in the outside world, lesbians did not hesitate to step across that threshold, immediately joining NOW and other groups.

But there was one catch. Although active in a movement that touched on everything they lived and fought for, lesbians still had to remain silent. Early on, this silence stemmed from habit, tradition, and a sense of survival, as well as courtesy to the straight feminists, who were tense enough about the "dyke" accusations anyway. Later, lesbians hid because they were openly put down and fear was expressed that a large number of lesbians would join the movement. They were called the Achilles' heel of the movement and referred to by a star-studded NOW official as the Lavender Menace, a tag first given to Oscar Wilde. But the final blow was an open act of discrimination. A NOW official took the liberty of editing the one official press release from the first Congress to Unite Women, held in the fall of 1969. From the total of approximately fifteen organizations, she deleted the names of two lesbian groups. Then, in the report on the congress, she and another NOW woman described as "tabled" a workshop motion that was pro-lesbian. Other women recalled that the workshop motion had passed.

Discrimination was recognized in other feminist groups as well. A lesbian in Redstockings, for example, reported at the time that there was no interest in dealing with lesbian problems, no matter how often or how vehemently lesbians fought for abortion repeal and child-care centers. The lesbians became aware that only certain kinds of life styles were acceptable to the movement, and only the problems of those life styles would be considered.

Three volatile young women dropped out of NOW early in 1970. They made clear to everyone in the organization why they were leaving and published an addendum to the organization's newsletter at their own expense, damning NOW on several charges, including sexism. The notice stated in part: "We protest New York NOW's sexist viewpoint. The leadership constantly oppresses other women on the question of sexual preference—or, in plain words, enormous prejudice is directed against the lesbian. 'Lesbian' is the one word that causes the executive committee to have a collective heart attack ... the prevailing attitude is 'Suppose they flock to us in droves, how horrible.' May we remind you that this is a male-oriented image of lesbianism."

One of the three then called a meeting at her apartment

to discuss the discrimination against lesbians in women's liberation. The meeting was attended by some thirty women who were active in women's liberation and the Gay Liberation Front. Three consciousness-raising groups were formed. The GLF women proposed preparing a position paper on lesbianism for the women's liberation movement.

As work on the paper proceeded, the writers and others began to plan its presentation. Nothing seemed more natural than to bring it to the second Congress to Unite Women (this time the congress was not being run by NOW, but by a coalition of more radical feminists). The planning and writing group called themselves the Radicalesbians. As they grew and transformed themselves into an action group, they began to call themselves the Lavender Menace in memory of the NOW official's indictment.

At the opening Friday evening session of the congress, the lights in the public auditorium suddenly went out. When they flashed on again there were thirty Menaces in lavender T-shirts boldly lettered with the derisive name they had taken for their own. Much as the blacks had taken "Black is Beautiful" as a slogan to reverse their image, lesbians now said "Gay is Good" and used the words "lesbian" and "dyke" in a positive, fun-loving manner. Signs they carried read "Take a lesbian to lunch" and "Super-dyke loves you." The Menace liberated the microphone for the evening and led an open forum on sexism within the movement. One of the first to speak was a gray-haired feminist, Ruth Gage Colby. She said slowly: "This is an historic moment. For the first time in thousands of years, since the days of Sappho, these women, many of whom are intelligent and talented, and who have much to offer, have come out of hiding." Even the Menace had not expected this reaction. The next day lesbians held workshops on sexism in the movement, and they also invited the feminists to a dance after the congress.

Predictably, reactions to the weekend's activities were varied, but many women felt in their guts (and some verbalized it) that the lesbians' openness was a kind of bravery that provided an opportunity to reevaluate their own opinions of lesbianism and the genuine issues of sexism within feminism. The feminists' acceptance of the lesbians' action was the first *revolutionary* step toward ridding themselves of the sexist, male-identified, and overpowering sex-role system. The massive consciousness-raising among lesbians marked the beginning of a joint struggle, with women—both heterosexual and homosexual—fighting together openly for a social revolution that seeks to dissolve traditional sex roles and to bring about a new world of self-possession, one which must admit the emotional life of the homosexual and allow all women to live their lives as they themselves define them.

The new lesbian attitudes and actions are a kind of paradigm of the women's liberation movement: the lesbians decided to get up from the human garbage pile and walk away. As blacks had done and women had done, they took to the streets and marched for their rights. On June 28, 1970, 5,000 to 10,000 homosexuals (mass media estimates) marched up Sixth Avenue to Central Park in New York, proclaiming their new pride and solidarity and protesting laws that make homosexual acts between consenting adults illegal and social conditions that make it impossible for homosexuals to display affection in public, maintain jobs, or rent apartments. There were also marches in Los Angeles and Chicago and a Gay-in on the Boston Commons. The Rev. Troy Perry, pastor of the Metropolitan Community Church in Los Angeles, and two lesbians began a fast.

Lesbians in New York marched behind the banner "Lesbians Unite." One tall blonde girl, who marched with her shoulders back and a ready smile, wore a gigantic sign "I am a lesbian and I am beautiful"; her picture was carried by hundreds of papers across the country. Although the call was not put out to women's liberation groups, a few feminists—even members of NOW—did join the lesbians without the benefit of distinguishing banners or signs. One woman from WITCH was confronted in her apartment building about her participation. She refused to justify her actions by saying she was not a lesbian, but rather a feminist, realizing that such a distinction would be a put down of her lesbian sisters.

Women's liberation should consider lesbianism a total life style that is valid in itself, not simply a matter of sexual union. In terms of their experience, lesbians have a great deal to offer the women's liberation movement since they live independently of men and form bonds based on much more equitable relations. Also, a number of lesbians have been married or have children and so doubly understand the position of the lone woman.

The lesbian who unlearns or never learns what society tries to teach her about how to lead her life, and who lives as she wants and needs to live, indicates that sex roles and attributes are learned or arbitrary, not natural. The lesbian foreshadows a time when individuals will create themselves from the total range of human qualities and not limit themselves to those ascribed by culture's reading of their biology.

When faced with actually developing those male-identified traits necessary for independent survival, many women are ambivalent; they feel threatened; they have no idea of how to go about acquiring independence. The lesbian has learned the hard way. Now the feminist must start learning. Lesbians develop an awareness of the reality of independence at an early age. When you are in conflict with society, you need all the assets you can get. Independence from men means total responsibility for self, for a love relationship, and even for children.

Women who oppose the basic social notion that a woman should have a man must realize that what this actually means is: if you do not have a man around, you must be prepared to take total responsibility for your life. Women must set their own goals because they will no longer be merely supporters of men's goals. Therefore, a middle-class woman, for example, must consider higher education, study opportunities for promotions and pensions, and learn about real estate, insurance, politics, banking, and stocks. She will also have to respond to the smaller challenges like caring for a car, understanding simple mechanical and electrical appliances, painting, carpentry, and doing the budget. And naturally she will have to open her own doors and light her own cigarettes. Life becomes greatly expanded. Responsibilities both small and large multiply. Because the lesbian was not trying to interest men and probably rejected much limiting and damaging advice, she has an advantage over the feminist. She knows how to survive as a loner.

Equality in emotional-sexual relationships is another feminist ideal that makes an investigation of lesbian relationships important for women's liberation. Men find it difficult really to accept women as equals. Behind every man is a woman, men say, and that is the way it has always been. It will be a long time, it seems, before men will be willing to give up their positions of power, prestige, knowledge, and privilege. A few are trying and may be into men's liberation, but they are often ridiculed by other men who consider them less than men. Men want to be accepted in the male society of club-rooms; it is important for a man to be a man's man. That means being in control of one's family, not being equal partners. Thus, in the average heterosexual relationship the woman is still forced to give up many career and educational possibilities to support her husband and be a good wife. She is also expected to give up her friends and associate with the wives of her husband's friends, robbing herself of much stimulation in areas that might have interested her.

Feminists who have men in their lives and are free to demonstrate and fight for equality complain that the wonderful feelings of independence, self-possession, and self-determination they have around other women are shot down when they come home and are dominated by men in bed. No matter what the feminist does, the physical act throws both woman and man back into role playing: the male as conqueror asserts his masculinity and the female is expected to be a passive receiver. All of her politics are instantly shattered.

Love has only recently been analyzed in terms of power, a type of mass domination of women through personal domination in heterosexual love relationships. As long as women wait, accept, and succumb to domination physically, there is no hope that they will be free emotionally. Because there are very few men at this time willing to work at truly equal relationships, certain radical women's groups have turned with an almost religious dedication to celibacy or masturbation. Some have made a conscious or political decision to be lesbians.

Freedom from sexual domination by men has left lesbians free to pursue other areas of interest, albeit guilt and fear have in many ways kept them from achieving. Thus, when men call all women who succeed *lesbians*, there is an unconscious recognition that these women are not devoting 100 percent of their efforts to their duty of serving men. Man goes without love, puts it second, or treats it casually because his life is so much greater than the home. It extends to the community, the nation, the world, the universe. He not only brings the bacon home, he brings the outside world home for his woman to experience vicariously. He has a much greater love than that for his wife. The wife, on the other hand, may have no other love.

Love between equals provides the most fulfilling relationship. Anything short of equality in a love relationship is destructive, as one person usually gives always and lacks fulfillment. That one is almost invariably the woman. Total love is total vulnerability and unselfishness and should allow both parties to receive maximum pleasure. A mutual giving and taking provides a mutual renewal. If a woman always gives emotionally, which is her accepted role—in and out of love-making—her emotions are not replenished, certainly not through material goods, as the system would indicate. An equal experience is an enrichment shared by two lovers; this can be two women who instinctively know each other's needs and honor them.

The lesbian both expands and curtails her activities to work things out so that both partners have maximum opportunities. She sees very clearly that there are no specific roles, that the song-and-dance about men's jobs often merely keeps women from performing tasks that are stimulating and interesting. Lesbians have found that equality requires a great deal of honesty and understanding. In the absence of roles there is no prescribed way of thinking or acting. Everything is open for new consideration, from who will wash the dishes, to who will aggress in love, to who will relocate for whom. There are no traditional, social, legal, or moral statutes to base decisions on. Like all freedoms, freedom from role playing requires work. Each couple has to find its own way and there is no "how to do it" book available.

Unquestionably decisions made with the understanding of two people are more difficult than those made by a single person—the man. Decisions between equals are always difficult and can bring on a new kind of stress. But usually it is the kind of stress that results in healthy decisions and not in practiced reactions. The equality can lead to flexibility, change, and growth.

What happens when big decisions come along, such as one woman accepting a job promotion that requires moving? Because of the simplicity of the heterosexual role as it is currently structured, the woman would simply follow the man. However, in a homosexual relationship, where both women usually have careers, the second woman is not necessarily obligated to follow; with no marriage, no children, no common property, no legal binds, and no social pressures or supports to keep them together, lesbians can and often do split. What happens here is something for feminists to observe carefully, an object lesson for the future difficulties that will come with working out the most challenging relationship of all.

With equality in relationships with men so difficult, many woman are now considering separatism—in whole or in part—as a temporary way of life. This would mean that during the struggle men and women remain apart to discover who they are and what they are capable of. A frightening idea, perhaps, but separatism for a time may be healthy. In active relationships with men, women often spend more time and energy fighting old ways of relating and defining themselves, rather than creating new ones.

A vital relationship between lesbians and women's liberation is in their mutual interest in a time of changing relationships. Lesbians are the women who potentially can demonstrate life outside the male power structure that dominates marriage as well as every other aspect of our culture. Thus, the lesbian movement is not only related to women's liberation, it is at the very heart of it. The attitude toward lesbians is an indicator by which to measure the extent of women's actual liberation. On the other hand, women's liberation undoubtedly addresses the deepest interests of lesbians, who have the greatest stake in women's social, economic, and cultural progress, as they will never benefit from the rewards and privileges that normally come only with male relationships.

Del Martin, a founder of the Daughters of Bilitis, defines the interests lesbians have in common with women's liberation:

> By her very nature, the lesbian is cast in the role of breadwinner and will be a member of society's working force for the rest of her life. Because of (women's) traditionally low-paying work, the lesbian is very much concerned with equal job opportunities and equal pay. Because of her anticipated longevity in the working force, she is concerned with equal opportunities and for professional careers for women. Because she is taxed as a single person at the highest rate, regardless of commitments, the lesbian is also concerned with tax deductions for head of household. Because she may be a working mother and alone, she has a definite stake in proposals for child-care centers. Because of social pressures against manifestations of lesbianism, she may even have need for birth control information, and/or abortion. Economically and family-wise, the lesbian is very much tied to the Women's Movement.

With so many strong common grievances, women's liberation should expect lesbians to enter the movement in greater numbers than in other organizations and in greater proportion than in the general population. And they will be vocal, even on those relatively establishment-type demands that concern them. If the relationship between women's liberation and lesbianism can be dealt with intellectually and without emotional fear and prejudice, lesbians could become the bulwark of the movement instead of its Achilles' heel.

Recognition of the validity of the lesbian life style and acceptance of lesbian activism in women's liberation is crucial to the women's movement's ultimate goal—a new, harmonious, cooperative, nonauthoritarian society in which men and women are free to be themselves. To end the oppression of the lesbian is to admit of a wider range of being and acting under the generic name "woman." It is a cause that must be undertaken by women's liberation if women are truly to free themselves.

NOTES

1. The 2,200 women study quoted in *Female Homosexuality*, Frank S. Caprio (New York: Citadel Press, 1954), p. 56.
2. Celestine Ware, *Women Power* (Tower Public Affairs Book, 1970), p. 107.
3. Peter Cohen in *ibid.*, p. 18. Our italics.
4. Simone de Beauvoir, *The Second Sex* (New York: Bantam Books, 1961), p. 382.
5. Beauvoir, *op. cit.*, p. 396.

27

"THY NEIGHBOR'S WIFE, THY NEIGHBOR'S SERVANTS": Women's Liberation and Black Civil Rights

Catharine Stimpson

> Thou shalt not covet they neighbor's house, thou shalt not covet thy neighbor's wife, nor his manservant, nor his maidservant, nor his ox, nor his ass, nor anything that is thy neighbor's.—TENTH COMMANDMENT

The optimism of politics before a revolution is exceeded only by the pessimism of politics after one. One current optimistic theory sees all the oppressed classes of America joining together to storm the citadel of their oppressor. Black liberation and women's liberation as movements, blacks and white women as people, will fight together. I respect black liberation, and I work for women's liberation, but the more I think about it, the less hope I have for a close alliance of those who pledge allegiance to the sex and those who pledge allegiance to the skin. History, as well as experience, has bred my skepticism.

That blacks and women should have a common enemy,

white men and their culture, without making common cause is grievous, perhaps. They even have more in common than an enemy. In America they share the unhappy lot of being cast together as lesser beings. It is hardly coincidence that the most aggressively racist regions are those most rigidly insistent upon keeping women in their place, even if that place is that of ornament, toy, or statue. Of the ten states that refused to ratify the Nineteenth Amendment, giving women the vote, nine were southern. The tenth was Delaware. Gunnar Myrdal, in a brief appendix to *An American Dilemma,* his massive study of American blacks, tersely analyzed this peculiar national habit. Both blacks and women are highly visible; they cannot hide, even if they want to. A patriarchal ideology assigns them several virtues: blacks are tough; women fragile. However, the same patriarchal ideology judges them *naturally* inferior in those respects that carry "prestige, power, and advantages in society."[1] As Thomas Jefferson said, even if America were a pure democracy, its inhabitants should keep women, slaves, and babies away from its deliberations. The less education women and blacks get, the better; manual education is the most they can have. The only right they possess is the right, which criminals, lunatics, and idiots share, to love their divine subordination within the *paterfamilias* and to obey the paterfamilias himself.

The development of an industrial economy, as Myrdal points out, has not brought about the integration of women and blacks into the adult male culture. Women have not found a satisfactory way both to bear children and to work. Blacks have not destroyed the hard doctrine of their unassimilability. What the economy gives both women and blacks are menial labor, low pay, and few promotions. White male workers hate both groups, for their competition threatens wages and their possible job equality, let alone superiority, threatens nothing less than the very nature of things. The tasks of women and blacks are usually grueling, repetitive, slogging, and dirty. After all, people have servants, not simply for status, but for doing what every sensible person knows is unappetizing.

Blacks and women also live in the wasteland of American sexuality, a world which, according to W. E. B. DuBois, one of the few black men to work for women's emancipation, "tries to worship both virgins and mothers and in the end despises motherhood and despoils virgins."[2] White men, convinced of the holy primacy of sperm, yet guilty about using it, angry at the loss of the cozy sanctuary of the womb and the privilege of childhood, have made their sex a claim to power and then used their power to claim control of sex. In fact and fantasy, they have violently segregated black men and white women. The most notorious fantasy claims that the black man is sexually evil, low, subhuman; the white woman sexually pure, elevated, superhuman. Together they dramatize the polarities of excrement and disembodied spirituality. Blacks and women have been sexual victims, often cruelly so: the black man castrated, the woman raped and often treated to a psychic clitoridectomy.

These similarities in the condition of blacks and women add up to a remarkable consistency of attitude and action on the part of the powerful toward the less powerful. Yet for a white woman to say, "I've been niggerized, I'm just a nigger, all women are niggers," is vulgar and offensive. Women must not usurp the vocabulary of the black struggle. They must forge their own idiom by showing how they are, for instance, "castrated" by a language and a tradition that makes manhood, as well as white skin, a requisite for full humanity.

Women's protest has followed black protest, which surged up under the more intense and brutal pressure. Antislavery movements preceded the first coherent woman's rights movement, black male suffrage, woman's suffrage, the civil rights movement, the new feminism. For the most part, white women have organized, not after working *with* blacks, but after working *on behalf* of them. Feminism has received much of its impetus from the translation of lofty, middle-class altruism into the more realistic, emotionally rugged salvation of the self.

The relationship between black rights and woman's rights offers an important cautionary tale, revealing to us the tangle of sex, race, and politics in America. It shows the paradox of any politics of change: we cannot escape the past we seek to alter, any more than the body can escape enzymes, molecules, and genes. As drama, the story is fascinating. Blacks and white women begin generous collaborations, only to find themselves in bitter misalliance. At crucial moments, the faith of one in the other changes into doubt. High principles become bones of contention and strategies violate high principles. The movements use each other, betray each other, and provoke from each other abstract love and visceral hostility. The leaders are heroic—men and women of great bravery, resilience, intellectual power, eloquence, and sheer human worth whose energy is that of the Christians and the lions together. And the women of the nineteenth century, except for their evangelical Christianity, sexual reticence, and obsequious devotion to marriage, the family, home, or at least to heterosexuality, worked out every analysis the new feminism is rediscovering.

Unhappily, whenever white radical men control the agencies of black liberation, their feelings about women are unwittingly first-class tools in making feminists out of their wives, sisters, and lovers. Henry B. Stanton, Elizabeth Cady Stanton's husband, warned her that he would stay out of town if she took part in the 1848 Seneca Falls meeting (where American women first came together to organize against their oppression). She did take part; he did leave town. Ironically, Stanton, an agent for antislavery societies, wrote his business letters on paper embossed with the figure of a kneeling, manacled black female slave. That Stanton might be unsympathetic to feminism had been apparent for some time. Eight years earlier, Angelina Grimké Weld, the prominent white antislavery agitator from Charleston, South Carolina, had written: "We were very much pleased with Elizabeth Stanton who spent several days with us, and I could not help wishing that Henry were better calculated to mould such a mind."[3]

The editors of The History of Woman Suffrage summarized the trouble women radicals had. The most liberal of men, they said tartly, find it almost impossible "to understand what liberty means for woman. Those who eloquently advocate equality for a southern plantation cannot tolerate it at their own fireside."[4] To be fair, such failures of the masculine imagination, such needs of the masculine ego, were not present in several of the most notable male radicals. Nor were they limited to white men. In 1833 black students joined their white colleagues in an attempt to keep women out of Oberlin College. Nor were men the women's only opponents. Women themselves, even activists, denounced militant women, even before they were militant feminists. Catharine A. Beecher, an educator, exemplifies such failures of the feminine imagination, such weaknesses of the feminine ego. In 1837 she published An Essay on Slavery and Abolitionism, with

Reference to the Duty of American Females. This prim, stiff little tract tells an anonymous male friend why he should refuse to join an abolitionist society and a clearly labeled Angelina Grimké why she should refuse to urge women to join one. I loathe slavery, Miss Beecher sniffed, but those exasperating, divisive abolitionists simply refuse to recognize the necessity of *gradual* emancipation of the slaves. Women may work against slavery, but only if they appeal to kindly, generous, peaceful, benevolent principles. Their soft pleas must never go beyond domestic and social circles. After all, Miss Beecher said:

> Heaven has appointed to one sex the superior and to the other the subordinate station. . . . It is therefore as much for the dignity as it is for the interest of females, in all respects to conform to the duties of this relation.[5]

Miss Beecher, a rubber stamp of her age, never doubted her station. Only eccentric women did.

Antislavery work of women, even outside domestic and social circles, was magnificent. Obvious as organizers, fundraisers, and agitators, they were also an imperceptible moral force. The now misunderstood *Uncle Tom's Cabin* was written by a woman. In the last of his autobiographies, Frederick Douglass, the fugitive slave who became the most famous black leader of the nineteenth century and who had his own troubles with white male abolitionists, said:

> When the true history of the antislavery cause shall be written, women will occupy a large space in its pages, for the cause of the slave has been peculiarly woman's cause. Her heart and her conscience have supplied in large degree its motive and mainspring. Her skill, industry, and patience, and perseverance have been wonderfully manifest in every trial hour. Not only did her feet run on "willing errands," and her fingers do the work which in large degree supplied the sinews of war, but her deep moral convictions, and her tender human sensibilities, found convincing and persuasive expression by her pen and voice.[6]

The women had to be durable. During one national convention of the American Anti-Slavery Women in Philadelphia, they were physically attacked. They continued to speak as stones flew through the windows. That night a mob, maddened by the idea of the abolition of slavery and by the sight of women meeting, especially with black men, burned the meeting hall.

The reasons why women who later became America's great feminists were first active in antislavery work must have been complex, various, and deeply personal. Many of them, for example, came from slavery-hating families, and the antislavery movement was already there for them to enter. However, I think one overriding motive drove women into such work, making, in Douglass' words, "the cause of the slave ... peculiarly women's cause." In 1884 Frederick Engels decreed: "The modern individual family is founded on the open or concealed domestic slavery of the wife, and modern society is a mass composed of these individual families as its molecules."[7] Decades before that American women felt themselves to be slaves. Their society, unlike modern society, had forcefully reduced them to that social, legal, economic, and psychological state. Not only did women feel that they had always been slaves, but they clearly identified themselves with the American black slave. Recognizing the severe oppression of the black, they saw, perhaps for the first time, an image of themselves. The horrible biblical injunction, "Servants, obey your masters," became synonymous with "Wives, be in subjection to your own husbands."

The identification white women made with black slaves was pervasive. The wife of a southern planter described herself to Harriet Martineau, the traveling English intellectual, as "the chief slave of the harem."[8] The call for a woman's rights convention, the ante-bellum ancestor of teach-ins and consciousness-raising sessions, to be held in Worcester, Massachusetts, proclaimed:

In the relation of marriage (woman) has been ideally annihilated and actually enslaved in all that concerns her personal and pecuniary rights, and even in widowed and single life, she is oppressed with such limitation and degradation of labor and avocation, as clearly and cruelly mark the condition of a disabled caste.[9]

Elizabeth Cady Stanton, speaking before the New York State Legislature in 1860, hammered home the point:

The Negro has no name. He is Cuffy Douglas or Cuffy Brooks, just whose Cuffy he may chance to be. The Woman has no name. She is Mrs. Richard Roe or Mrs. John Doe, just whose Mrs. she may chance to be. Cuffy has no right to his earnings; he cannot buy or sell, or lay up. Mrs. Roe has no right to her earnings; she can neither buy nor sell, make contracts, nor lay up anything that she can call her own. Cuffy has no right to his children; they can be sold from him at any time. Mrs. Roe has no right to her children; they may be bound out to cancel a father's debt of honor. The unborn child, even by the last will of the father, may be placed under the guardianship of a stranger and a foreigner. Cuffy has no legal existence; he is subject to restraint and moderate chastisement. Mrs. Roe has no legal existence; she has not the best right to her own person. The husband has the power to restrain, and administer moderate chastisement.

Witty, passionate, Stanton went on:

The prejudice against color, of which we hear so much, is no stronger than that against sex. It is produced by the same cause, and manifested very much in the same way. The Negro's skin and the woman's sex are both *prima facie* evidence that they were intended to be in subjection to the white Saxon man. The few social privileges which the man gives the woman, he makes up to the (free) Negro in civil rights.[10]

The feminists saved their keenest empathy for black women. They showed an intuitive respect, a warmth, often missing in the white male radicals of the period. Angelina Grimké first rebelled against slavery when, a child, she saw a woman slave being mercilessly beaten. Perhaps the white women also felt some guilty relief at not being black, an impulse leading to moral action as well as to the more naive gestures of philanthropy. An anecdote about Elizabeth Cady Stanton is suggestive. One of Stanton's cousins, who ran a station on the Underground Railway, took her and some other young girls to visit a quadroon woman hiding on his third floor. The fugitive slave told her story. Somewhat pedagogically, Stanton asked if she did not find a similarity between being a woman and being a slave. "Yes," the fugitive allegedly answered, " ... but I am both. I am doubly damned in sex and color. Yes, in class too, for I am poor and ignorant; none of you can ever touch the depth of misery where I stand today."[11]

It is a measure of the deep sense of identification between women and black slaves that even the opponents of woman's rights used the analogy between the two. Their tone, of course, was one of self-righteous approval, not of righteous outrage. The *New York Herald* decreed in an 1852 editorial:

> How did woman first become subject to man as she now is all over the world? By her nature, her sex, just as the Negro is and always will be, to the end of time, inferior to the white race, and therefore, doomed to subjection; but happier than she would be in any other condition, just because it is the law of her nature.[12]

The ever-reliable Catharine Beecher had earlier given the game away. Asking the North to understand the South, she had written: "the Southerner feels (as irritated by the) interference of strangers to regulate his domestic duty to his servants as . . . a Northern man would . . . in regard to his wife and children."[13]

The more mature the feminist movement became, the more deftly it compared chattel slaves and white women for strategic gain. Once Susan B. Anthony, the unyielding mistress of civil disobedience, heard that a white man had incarcerated his wife and child in an insane asylum. Such locking up of rebellious wives, sisters, and daughters was not, it seems, an uncommon agent of repression. The woman, despite her family's testimony to her sanity, had been in the asylum for eighteen months. Anthony helped the woman and child to escape and to hide. Defending herself, Anthony drew upon public support for fugitive women. She reasoned: "In both cases an unjust law was violated; in both cases the supposed owners of the victims were defied, hence in point of law and morals, the act was the same for both cases."[14] Less dramatically, Lucretia Mott utilized the slaveholder to clarify the behavior of all men. She did not expect men, unlike women, to see how they robbed women. After all, slaveholders "did not see that they were oppressors, but slaves did."[15]

Inseparable from the psychological identification feminists had with slaves and the political use they made of it was a profound moral faith. All persons—men, women, whites, blacks—have certain inalienable rights; self-determination is one. In the Declaration of Independence and even in the Constitution, America organizes itself around those rights. When they protest, women and blacks are only seeking the simple human rights that they ought naturally to possess, but of which they have been unnaturally deprived. Moreover, any good person who fights for the freedom of one enslaved class must fight for the freedom of another. Liberation groups are all alike because all groups should be liberated. Loving the right for its own sake means loving the right everywhere.

The editors of the *History of Woman Suffrage* say flatly that the antislavery struggle was the single most important factor in creating the woman's rights movement in America—even more important than the material demands of an underdeveloped country and the spiritual support of a still-lively revolutionary tradition.[16] Certainly the antislavery struggle gave feminism its energetic, triumphant, articulate morality. In the company of "some of the most eloquent orators, the ablest logicians, men and women of the purest moral character and best minds in the nation," women learned the "a.b.c. of human rights," including their own. Angelina Grimké asserted:

> The investigation of the rights of the slave has led me to a better understanding of my own. I have found the Anti-Slavery causes to be the high school of morals in our land—the school in which *human rights* are more fully investigated, and better understood, than in any other.[17]

The antislavery movement taught women the austere disciplines of organizing for an unpopular cause, especially the need for patience in any long social struggle.

More important, women broke the near-psychotic taboo against their participation in public life. At first, the American Anti-Slavery Society would permit Angelina Grimké to speak only before small private groups of women. Then men began to sneak in surreptitiously to hear the lady abolitionist from the South. The Anti-Slavery Society saw it had a good thing going and scheduled Miss Grimké for large public meetings. Predictably, the churches were horrified. Theodore Dwight Weld, the abolitionist who was passionately in love with her, and whom she married in 1838, wrote that: " . . . folks talk about women's preaching as tho' it was next to highway robbery—eyes astare and mouth agape."[18] However, after hearing Miss Grimké, Sojourner Truth (called the "Lybian Sybil"), Lucretia Mott, Abby Kelley Foster, Mrs. Maria W. Stewart, and others, the "folks" became a more silent majority. In general, working against slavery made women stronger, more confident, and more responsible. Such qualities made their lack of rights even more implausible.

Ironically, the antislavery movement probably helped

feminism most by treating women so shabbily. It imposed independence upon them. Women had been part of the movement from the beginning. A Lydia Gillingham had been an officer of the first Anti-Slavery Society in America. Women were in Philadelphia on December 4, 1833, when a national convention of abolitionists formed the American Anti-Slavery Society. To its shame, the convention refused to seat women delegates. To their glory, the women, black and white, met together five days later in a schoolroom to found a separate Female Anti-Slavery Society. Rejection bred an unpredictable rebellion. Or, as the editors of the *History of Woman Suffrage* report grimly: " . . . through continued persecution was woman's self-assertion and self-respect sufficiently developed to prompt her at last to demand justice, liberty, and equality for herself."[19]

Feminists in the antislavery movement had two groups of enemies. The first were their friends. Sympathetic to woman's rights, they still asked antislavery women not to preach feminism for a while. In effect, the women were asked, as they are today, to sacrifice themselves in order to help others stop still others from sacrificing still others. Angelina Grimké and her intelligent sister Sarah, the second of the Grimké family's exiled and alien daughters, were early subjected to such pleas. Let your lives symbolize feminism, Theodore Weld told them at length, not your actual speeches. You are damaging the cause of the slave; you are losing your value as agitators. John Greenleaf Whittier, the radical poet, accused the sisters of splitting the left. His rhetoric should be hauntingly familiar to those who, for example, wish to work both against the Vietnamese war and for justice for the Panthers. "Is it necessary," he asked

> . . . for you to enter the lists as controversial writers on this question (of woman's rights)? Does it not *look,* dear sisters, like abandoning in some degree the cause of the poor and miserable slave. . . . Is it not forgetting the great and dreadful wrongs of the slave in a selfish crusade against some paltry grievance of our own?[20]

The Grimkés listened, consulted their consciences, and replied: "The *time* to assert a right is the *time* when *that* right is denied." If men were to reject them as antislavery agitators simply because they were women, then they had to defend themselves as women before they could be effective antislavery agitators. Appealing to his political self-interest, they asked Weld if he could not see that a woman *"could* do, and *would* do a hundred times more for the slave if she were not fettered?"[21] Angelina, defending Sarah, the more ardent feminist of the two, said:

> I am still glad of sister's letters (about woman's equality), and believe they are doing great good. Some noble-minded women cheer her on, and she feels encouraged to persevere, the brethren notwithstanding. I tell them that this is *a part* of the great doctrine of Human Rights, and can no more be separated from emancipation than the light from the heat of the sun; the rights of the slave and of woman blend like the colors of the rainbow. However, I rarely introduce this topic into my addresses, except to urge my sisters up to duty. Our *brethren* are dreadfully afraid of this kind of amalgamation.[22]

A second group of enemies of feminism among "the brethren" was nakedly hostile. They loathed woman's rights, either because they loathed woman or because they had a notion of her place in life that failed to include an antislavery movement. Their chauvinism helped to split the abolitionist movement in 1840. One group, led by William Lloyd Garrison, welcomed women, even letting them hold office; the other group excluded them. In that same year, in London, at the World Anti-Slavery Convention, male chauvinism enjoyed international triumph. Some American women asked to be seated as delegates. Yelped the Reverend Eben Galusha of New York: "I have no objection to woman's being the neck to turn the head aright, but do not wish to see her assume the place of the head." Intoned the Reverend A. Harvey of Glasgow: "if I were to give a vote in favor of females, sitting and deliberating in such an assembly as this, ... I should be acting in opposition to the plain teaching of the Word of God." The convention, after hours of debate, overwhelmingly voted to keep ladies out.[23]

Wendell Phillips, an American, assured the women that they could follow the convention with as much interest from their seats behind a curtain as they could from the floor. Would you say that, the women snapped back, to Frederick Douglass or to any other black man? That night Lucretia Mott, the Quaker moralist, who saw authority in truth, not truth in authority, walked down Great Queen

Street with Elizabeth Cady Stanton. They decided to hold a woman's rights convention in America as soon as they got back. The men to whom they had just listened were obviously in need of some education on the subject. Eight years later, in the Wesleyan Chapel of Seneca Falls, New York, the convention was finally held. Mott and Stanton, women of several causes, were to bring their greatest zeal to woman's rights. For the first time, their view of wrong was subjective, their vision a part of their own flesh.

The erratic bonds between women's rights and black liberation finally ruptured after the Civil War on the rough edges of the suffrage issue. Before the Civil War nearly all feminists were fierce abolitionists; during the Civil War they willingly stopped their arduous work on their own behalf. The last woman's rights convention was held in February 1861. There the invincible giants of early feminism—Mott, Anthony, Stanton—spoke for emancipation of the slaves, though crowds, as they often did, gave the women a hard time. Conventional war-relief tasks soon bored Anthony and Stanton, and the indifference to the war and to the principles of freedom on the part of many northern women appalled them. The women of America, Anthony said, "have been a party in complicity with slavery."[24] To stamp out that complicity, she and Stanton organized the Loyal League.

The Loyal League was to gather 400,000 signatures on petitions demanding emancipation for every slave. It was to turn the feminists into tough, efficient organizers. Yet its first meeting in New York in May 1863 foreshadowed the conflict between militant feminists, who said that justice for woman was a more important step in national safety than freedom or franchise for any race of men, and other women, who said several things. The New York gathering was more or less serene. However, a resolution linking the rights of women and those of blacks came up for a floor vote. It read, "There can never be a true peace in this Republic until the civil and political rights of all citizens of African descent and all women are practically established." Mrs. Hoyt of Wisconsin thought the resolution inexpedient. Bringing feminism into war work would frighten away war workers; the Loyal League should not involve itself "in any purely political matter, or any *ism* obnoxious to the people."[25] Sarah M. Halleck thought the resolution unfair to blacks. Their rights, she said, echoing prewar and postwar debate, have priority over women's rights. "The negroes have suffered more than the women, and the women, perhaps, can afford to give them the preference. ... It may possibly be woman's place to suffer. At any rate, let her suffer, if by that means, *man*kind may suffer less."[26] Halleck suggested that the words "all women" be deleted. From the audience came an anonymous cry, "You are too self-sacrificing." The older warriors supported the resolution. The orator Ernestine L. Rose, a Polish exile, declared that women must not be thrown out of the race for freedom. How, she asked rhetorically, can man be free if woman is not? Besides, she went on, women have been the equivalent of slaves. To support freedom for some slaves, and not for others, would be a foolish inconsistency. Then Angelina Grimké Weld spoke:

> I feel that we have been with the (Negro). . . . True, we have not felt the slaveholder's lash; true, we have not had our hands manacled, but our *hearts* have been crushed. . . . I want to be identified with the Negro; until he gets his rights, we never shall have ours.[27]

Eventually the resolution, which had a terrible prophetic truth, passed. The militants had taken the first, brief, parliamentary battle.

When the Civil War ended, many women had toiled to the point of exhaustion. Josephine Sophie Griffing, for example, had done relief work of an extremely systematic sort for freed slaves and she had also helped to found the ill-fated Freedman's Bureau. Feminists were legitimately convinced that their devotion to the Union, to blacks, and to the Republican party merited a reward. Their strategy was to act out the 1863 Loyal League resolution, to make black rights and woman's rights dependent upon each other. The next five years were to make paper boats of their hopes, mired in the mud of party politics and prejudice, luffing before the irresistable power of black claims.

The feminists also had to confront the fact that during the war, when only Susan B. Anthony had kept up even part of a guard, some legal rights for women, won at such expense of body and spirit, had been lost. The New York State Legislature, for example, had weakened a law of 1860 giving women the right to equal guardianship of their children. The amended law simply forbade a father to bind out or will away a child without the mother's written consent.

The immediate question was who in the great mass of the disenfranchised should obtain the ballot. The arena was a series of amendments to the Constitution. The Fourteenth Amendment provided that if the right to vote were denied to any "male inhabitants" of a state (excluding Indians not taxed), who were law-abiding citizens over twenty-one, that state's basis for representation in Congress would be proportionately reduced. Its purpose was to give the vote to black men. The militant feminists, led by Stanton and Anthony, furious that the word "male" should be put in the Constitution for the first time, sought to have it struck out. They would then claim the right to vote under the altered amendment.[28] According to the Fifteenth Amendment, the right to vote could not be abridged because of "race, color, or previous condition of servitude." Its purpose was to insure the vote for black men. The militant feminists wanted to add the word "sex." All else failing, the woman decided to press for a Sixteenth Amendment, specifically giving them the ballot.

Suffrage, a symbol of citizenship, is also a source of power and self-protection. Having it often seems irrelevant, but not having it is degrading. For women, who had to pay taxes, the vote meant that the old revolutionary American war whoop, "No taxation without representation," would finally have some substance. Perhaps the militant feminists would not have freely chosen suffrage as their do-or-die issue at this time, but suffrage as an issue was there. The women had to respond to the pull of the gravity of the black civil rights movement. The cannier strategists also figured that unless women took advantage of the current national concern about suffrage, they would have to spend years making the country interested in the question again.

Their demands were just. Freedom and civil rights were the natural property of everyone, not one sex. It was politically illogical and bitterly unfair to put two million black men into the polling places and to keep fifteen million black and white women out. Susan B. Anthony spoke out sharply against the oligarchy of sex that made men household sovereigns and women subjects and slaves. Arguments given in support of black male citizenship in debate and court were mimicked to support woman's full citizenship. In 1867 the great black woman Sojourner Truth put it all together:

There is a great stir about colored men getting their
rights, but not a word about the colored women; and if
colored men get their rights, and not colored women
theirs, you see the colored men will be masters over the
women, and it will be just as bad as it was before. So I am for
keeping the thing going while things are stirring; because
if we wait till it is still, it will take a great while to get it
going again. . . . I am above eighty years old. . . . I have
been forty years a slave and forty years free, and would be
here forty years more to have equal rights for all.[29]

As morally impeccable as the militant feminists position
was, its support was negligible. Facing the enmity of old
friends and of time itself, for it was the Negro's hour, they
were lonelier, more beleaguered than they had ever been
before and they were ever to be again. The Republican
party opposed them. Its more honorable members thought
that black men, for whom they had fought the Civil War,
deserved the vote; more cynical politicians figured that
freed slaves would gratefully feel that the Grand Old
Party deserved their vote. Democratic party maneuvers
added to Republican distrust. Democrats, including a notorious bigot, George Francis Train, used the question of
woman suffrage to embarrass the Republicans. Why not
give the women the vote, they taunted, if your concern
about civil rights is so pure that you wish to give it to
black men? (Their cute ploys foreshadowed those of
southern Democrats in 1964, who put women under the
protection of the Civil Rights Act. Their concern for
women was patently false, but their hope that taking care
of women would prevent people from taking care of
blacks was patently sincere.) Accepting the loud public
support of Train, the militant feminists damaged their
reputations and their cause among blacks and whites.

Nearly all the white male abolitionists, even those sympathetic to women, opposed woman's suffrage at this time.
They saw black male suffrage as the fitting triumph of
their decades of antislavery toil. They sensed that the
turbulent American political climate favored them at last.
They felt that the same climate did not favor women,
since too many people still irrationally believed that votes
for "strong-minded women" were simply the folly of
"weak-minded men." Fusing woman suffrage to black
suffrage would lead to anger, confusion, and defeat. Many
feminists agreed with them, perceiving themselves not as
suicidally self-abnegating, but as shrewd and ethical. They

reasoned that the advance of black men out of the pit of disenfranchisement would speed their own.

Necessarily, most black leaders also opposed the militant feminists. Among them was Frederick Douglass, who had long supported woman's rights. In Rochester, New York, he had founded an active Female Anti-Slavery Society, whose members included Elizabeth Cady Stanton, Susan B. Anthony, and Sojourner Truth. Arguing with Douglass from 1842 on, Stanton had swept away his arguments against woman's rights, until he came to believe that women had precisely the same right to participate in civil government as men and beautifully analyzed the reasons why women might not recognize their own unique oppression. His Rochester newspaper had supported woman's rights conventions; indeed, at Seneca Falls, he had been almost alone in supporting Elizabeth Cady Stanton's call for the vote for women, then thought, if not blasphemous or wildly daring, at the very least counterproductive. He had also insisted that meetings of black free men be open to women. Now he was as surprised by the militant feminist refusal to support suffrage for blacks before suffrage for women as they were angered by his refusal to make suffrage for women a condition for suffrage for blacks.

Douglass eloquently, repeatedly, stated his powerful case. The black man needed the vote more than the white woman, because the black man lacked the thousand ways a woman had "to attach herself to the governing power of the land." Woman might be "the victim of abuses . . . but it cannot be pretended . . . that her cause is as urgent as that of ours." In 1868 he wrote to Josephine Griffing in Washington to decline an invitation to speak for woman's suffrage. "The right of woman to vote is as sacred in my judgment as that of man," he said. However, for the moment, his loyalties were to his race:

to a cause not more sacred, certainly more urgent, because it is a life and death to the long-enslaved people of this country. . . . While the Negro is mobbed, beaten, shot, stabbed, hanged, burnt, and is the target of all that is malignant in the North and all that is murderous in the South his claims may be preferred by me without exposing in any wise myself to the imputation of narrowness or meanness towards the cause of women.[30]

The brief history of the American Equal Rights Association typifies the tension between the few who put woman's suffrage first and the many who put black suffrage first. The Eleventh National Woman's Rights Convention had bred the Equal Rights Association in May 1866. Its goal was nothing less than the reconstruction of the national sense of right; its hope was to "bury" the concepts of the black man and of the woman in the grander concept of the citizen. It worked vigorously for universal suffrage for a year. However, the Association nearly broke apart during its first national convention, held in the Church of the Puritans, New York, in May 1867. The fissure appeared in a floor fight over another of the resolutions irrevocably linking black suffrage to woman's suffrage. Elizabeth Cady Stanton and her faction supported it, those opposing it argued that anything that delayed getting the vote for black men was immoral and that black suffrage did not necessarily imply that the fight for woman's suffrage would be harder. The quarrel then degenerated into an odious squabble about whether blacks were more oppressed than women. Lucy Stone had written that black men, having legal and social rights women lacked, were better off. Nonsense, Abby Kelley Foster answered, "(The Negro is) without wages, without family rights, whipped and beaten by thousands, given up to the most horrible outrages, without that protection which his value as property formerly gave him."[31] Behind the competition for the unpleasant title of Most Oppressed Class in America lay a serious moral and political question. If history, which is so miserly about justice, is to help only one of several suffering groups, what standards can we possibly use to choose that group?

The resolution did pass. However, that autumn the citizens of Kansas generously voted *not* to amend their state constitution to permit either women or blacks to vote. The militant supporters of woman's suffrage, who had also campaigned for black suffrage, working nearly a year, traveling from twenty to forty miles a day under frontier conditions, facing down the hostility of liberal whites, suspicious blacks, and local Republicans, were blamed for the defeat of black male suffrage. The 1868 annual convention of the Equal Rights Association was bitter, and the 1869 annual convention divisive. The Association broke apart over the question of endorsing a woman's suffrage amendment. Frederick Douglass said:

When women, because they are women, are hunted down through the cities of New York and New Orleans; when they are dragged from their houses and hung upon lampposts . . . then they will have an urgency to obtain the ballot equal to our own.

A voice shouted, "Is that not all true about black woman?" Douglass, who loved human rights for all, put race before sex. "Yes, yes, yes," he answered, "it is true of the black woman, but not because she is a woman, but because she is black."[32] A black woman, Mrs. Francis Harper, a powerful orator, abolitionist, and feminist, concurred. Forced to choose between race and sex, she must let "the lesser question of sex go. Being black is more precarious and demanding than being a woman; being black means that every white, including every white working-class woman, can discriminate against you." Harper argued bitterly: "the white women all go for sex, letting race occupy a minor position."[33]

On May 14 friends of woman's suffrage, including delegates to the Equal Rights Convention, met separately in the Brooklyn Academy of Music. A few days later, they founded the National Woman Suffrage Association; a few months later, some of its members, motivated by personal animosities and a lesser devotion to militancy, created the more decorous American Woman Suffrage Association. The feminist movement, schismatic itself, was formally separated from the antislavery and black suffrage movement.

On March 30, 1870, Douglass celebrated the adoption of the Fifteenth Amendment. Using the considerable grace and power at his command, he immediately called for a campaign for woman's suffrage. He and his friends among the feminists resumed their old, warm ties. Perhaps American culture had exposed itself when it granted the vote to black men fifty years before it granted it to any woman. However, black men were soon virtually to lose the vote in the South. American culture also exposed itself in the fact that women never lost what they were eventually so laboriously to win.

On their own, the feminists still compared themselves to black slaves. One of the most intriguing, grotesque uses of the metaphor occurred at the Louisana Constitutional Convention in 1879. Mrs. Caroline E. Merrick, an able woman, was lobbying for either full or limited suffrage for her sex and the Convention asked her to address it. Her son encouraged her to speak, and her husband, the Chief Justice of the Louisiana Supreme Court before the Civil War, permitted her to do so. Perhaps, Mrs. Merrick suggested, men might find women's demands for their rights as surprising as a procession of slaves approaching "the lordly mansion of their master with several spokesmen chosen from their ranks, for the avowed purpose of asking for their freedom." Still, men must not refuse to give women the vote simply because they have never asked for it. Remember, Mrs. Merrick said:

> In old times most of our slaves were happy and contented. Under the rule of good and humane masters, they gave themselves no trouble to grasp after a freedom which was beyond their reach. So it is with us to-day. We are happy and kindly treated (as witness our reception here to-night) and in the enjoyment of the numerous privileges which our chivalrous gentlemen are so ready to accord; many of us who feel a wish for freedom, do not venture even to whisper a single word about our rights.[34]

It is hard to tell whether Mrs. Merrick's plea, during which she played the seemingly incongruent roles of slave, gentle rebel, and mistress of an old plantation, was sincere, spurious, or ironically cajoling.

However, the notion of woman as black slave slowly slipped from feminist thought and rhetoric. Soon the white working-class girl was to replace the slave as the object of the privileged woman's sympathy. The movement also turned against the black man: the once heroic slave became the besotted freedman. Women angrily compared themselves to the voting black. There was no reason, they argued, why an illiterate black man should exercise a power the educated woman lacked. "You have lifted up the slave on this continent," said Madam Anneke, an ardent German feminist from Milwaukee, "listen now to woman's cry for freedom."[35] The women also deeply resented the potential power a black man might exercise over them. Elizabeth Cady Stanton asked sardonically:

> Are we sure that the (Negro) once entrenched in all his inalienable rights, may not be an added power to hold us at bay? ... Why should the African prove more just and generous than his Saxon compeers?[36]

She also said, a strong elitism mingling with her racism:

Think of Patrick and Sambo and Hans and Yung Tung, who do not know the difference between a monarchy and a republic, who can not read the Declaration of Independence or Webster's spelling-book, making laws for Lucretia Mott, Ernestine L. Rose, and Anna E. Dickinson. Think of jurors and jailors drawn from these ranks to watch and try young girls for the crime of infanticide, to decide the moral code by which the mothers of this Republic shall be governed![37]

For a while most feminists preserved a vague ideal of sisterhood. They kept some faith with black women. Matilda Joslyn Gage, before a congressional committee in 1876, observed: "I know colored women in Washington far the superiors, intellectually and morally, of the masses of men, who declare that they now endure wrongs and abuses unknown in slavery."[38] Yet sisterhood proved fragile. The old moral solidarity between feminists and blacks gave way to a sexual solidarity, which, in turn, gave way to a primitive racial and class solidarity. A thoroughly ugly white supremacy infested the movement. Frederick Douglass had once said that "the government of this country loves women. They are the sisters, mothers, wives and daughters of our rulers; but the Negro is loathed."[39] The white Anglo-Saxon sisters, mothers, wives, and daughters, hoping for self-rule, or at the least a joint throne, used the loathing of their brothers, fathers, husbands, and sons for political gain. Transforming the Negro's hour into the woman's, they sacrificed the black.

White racism was consciously manipulated as early as 1867. Henry B. Blackwell, a New Englander married to Lucy Stone, wrote an open letter to southern state legislatures. Some of the arguments of "What the South Can Do" were blatantly expedient. Give women the vote, Blackwell urged, and rest in peace. The combined vote of white men and women will always outnumber the combined vote of black men and women. "In the light of the history of your Confederacy, can any Southerner fear to trust the women of the South with the ballot?" he crooned. If white supremacy were so guaranteed, the South could live with the Fourteenth Amendment. Neither its basis of representation in Congress nor its congressmen need be reduced. Moreover, "the Negro question would be forever removed from the political arena." The North would ignore southern politics, but confident of stable politics, it would invest in the South. Blackwell then gilded realpolitik with morality: "If you must try the Republican experiment, try it fully and fairly."[40]

The most leprous racism appeared in the last part of the nineteenth century as the movement suffered a serious ideological shift.[41] The older feminists lost their vision of a seamless web of human rights, and accepted the argument of younger women that the rights of women were separate from those of blacks. The movement also concentrated its energy on suffrage, since its members were convinced that unless women found the grail of the vote, they would lack both equality and the muscle to bring about reform. Suffrage would help women bring right into a wrongful world: northern women might abate the evils of industrialism, southern women might shore up white supremacy. Such ends would justify a number of shabby means. Feminism also simply reflected its age: the northern refusal to see the black, the southern demand to dominate him, and the gluttonous national need to expand, which used white hatred of blacks as a sick psychological rallying cry.

The more popular the movement became, the more conservative its leaders and members were. During the 1890s chapters of the National American Woman Suffrage Association were organized in the South despite rigid regional resistance.[42] In 1895 the National Association met in Atlanta; in 1896 the national board elected its first southern officers. The older feminists, some of them abolitionists, were quiescent. Susan B. Anthony attacked Jim Crow laws, in private. She spoke before the black Phillis Wheatley Club in New Orleans in 1903, unofficially. The club president, obviously a person of great dignity, told her guest that black women had "a crown of thorns continually pressed upon their brow, yet they are advancing and sometimes you find them further on than you would have expected." The president then assured Miss Anthony that she had helped the club to believe in the Fatherhood of God, the Brotherhood of Man, and "at least for the time being in the sympathy of women."[43]

The records of the feminists' national conventions make sorry reading. In 1899 in Grand Rapids, Michigan, the women refused to support the resolution of a black woman delegate, Mrs. Lottie Wilson Jackson, that protested Jim Crow laws on trains. In 1903 in New Orleans, the national board of directors promptly denied a local newspaper's charge that they were soft on race. The national association only cared about suffrage; state chapters could do what they wanted about race. The directors hastened to add:

> Like every other national association (we are) made up of persons of all shades of opinion on the race question and on all other questions except those relating to its particular object. The northern and western members hold the views on the race question that are customary in their sections; the southern members hold the views that are customary in the South. The doctrine of State's rights is recognized. ... The National American Woman Suffrage Association is seeking to do away with the requirement of a sex qualification for suffrage. What other qualifications shall be asked for it leaves to other states.[44]

On the last evening of the convention in New Orleans, Miss Belle Kearney, a famous Mississippi orator, spoke, advocating woman's suffrage as the national hope for government by the educated, propertied white. To great applause she warned:

> Just as surely as the North will be forced to turn to the South for the nation's salvation, just so surely will the South be compelled to look to its Anglo-Saxon women as the medium through which to retain the supremacy of the white race over the African.[45]

The response of the national president, Mrs. Carrie Chapman Catt, queasily allied a nod to principle and a low bow to pragmatism. She first affirmed the principle of state's rights. Then, as a woman who found Negrophobia Neanderthal, she added that Anglo-Saxons were "apt to be arrogant" about their blood. She reminded her audience that the Romans thought Anglo-Saxons too "low and embruted" to be slaves and suggested that Anglo-Saxons would cease to be dominant if they proved unworthy of the honor. Finally, she concluded brightly:

> ... the race problem is the problem of the whole country and not that of the South alone. The responsibility for it is partly ours but if the North shipped slaves to the South and sold them, remember that the North has sent some money since then into the South to help undo part of the wrong that it did to you and to them. Let us try to get nearer together and to understand each other's ideas on the race question and solve it together.[46]

In 1904 In Washington, D.C., Mary Church Terrell, the first president of the National Association of Colored Women, took the floor. The editor of the *History of Woman Suffrage,* exposing editorial pathology, describes Mrs. Terrell as "a highly educated woman, showing little trace of Negro blood."[47] Mrs. Terrell asked the feminists to support blacks:

> You will never get suffrage until the sense of justice has been so developed in man that they will give fair play to the colored race. Much has been said about the purchasability of the Negro vote. They never sold their votes till they found that it made no difference how they cast them. My sisters of the dominant race, stand up not only for the oppressed sex but also for the oppressed race.[48]

The convention, neatly juxtaposing present policy against past radicalism, swept on to adopt resolutions of regret for the death of many pioneer suffragists.

In other ways white feminists insulted black women and evaded the support of black organizations. Now and then, if black women seemed middle class, if black women escaped the white charge of sexual promiscuity, the movement patronized them. Ironically, the most ebullient white supremacists almost wrecked the national movement. Its grand strategy had been to make woman's suffrage a matter for state conventions and constitutions, but it became clear that it might be quicker to make woman's suffrage a matter for the federal Constitution. Some southern women deplored the notion of a federal amendment, because it might violate the principle of state's rights, might help Republicans hurt Democrats. In 1913 they organized the Southern States Woman Suffrage Conference with Kate M. Gordon, an energetic civic leader from New Orleans, who helped bring a sewer system to her city, as its prime mover. Only a revitalized national association, only a determined Mrs. Catt, fully committed to a federal amendment, subdued the Southern Conference.

The suffrage movement was no worse than other women's groups. Mrs. Josephine Ruffin, an early black suffragist in New England, the editor of a black newspaper, was verbally and physically attacked in 1900 in Milwaukee at a convention of the General Federation of Women's Clubs. The Women's Christian Temperance Union and the Young Women's Christian Association put black women in segregated units. The elite northern women's colleges, which had endured the most massive sexual prejudice, rarely rose above racial prejudice. By 1910 Smith and Radcliffe had each graduated four black women, Bryn Mawr, Mills, and Barnard none.[49] Nor, if such forces can be measured, was the women's racism as virulent as that of many of their opponents. Indeed, some women even clearly tried to shake off the disease.

What is sad is that woman's rights leaders, who had such a vivid sense of right, and woman's suffrage leaders, who worked so hard for a civil right, should have succumbed willfully to the corrupting gods in the Anglo-Saxon pantheon. What is instructive is that a coalition of the oppressed fell apart when the vital self-interest of one group collided with that of another. In 1865 blacks could hardly have been expected to wait for the vote for their men until the nation was willing to grant it to women. No group can reasonably be asked to stay either slaves or political beggars. What is appalling is how quickly morality and compassion went underground when anyone began to taste of power.

A black liberation movement has been active in America since the first black arrived in Virginia; only white belief in it has been erratic. The liberal civil rights movement which began in 1960, during the Greensboro, North Carolina sit-ins and ended around 1966, during the healthy purge of white power and participation, helped to generate contemporary women's liberation. The growth of women's liberation has imitated that of modern black protest. Civil rights activity, which demands equality within a system, breeds revolutionary activity, which demands a radically new system. Civil rights and liberation groups live together, more or less uneasily, their common enemy forcing a loose loyalty. The public, insensitive to bold differences of ideology and tactics, thinks of them as one.

There are really no formal bridges between integrated black civil rights groups and white women's liberation groups as there were in the nineteenth century, as there are in contemporary white radical gatherings. Reliable people also think that surprisingly few of the new feminists were seriously involved in civil rights. More came out of the New Left or in response to discriminatory post-World War II work conditions. The women who were committed to black causes, if they could shake loose from the roles of Lady Bountiful, Sister Conscience, or Daring Daughter, each in its way an archetypal woman's role, gained political and personal consciousness.

For many of us, civil rights activity was only a part of the interminable process of wooing knowledge, courage, and self-esteem. Other influences on our feminism may have been the psychological and moral need to have a cause, especially an impeccable but unconventional one; emotional or intellectual insults from the masculine world; and, to an interesting degree, a mother, grandmother, or aunt who, whether she wanted to or not, rebelled against woman's business as usual. For others, civil rights activity may have been crucial. It was, I am sure, different for northerners and southerners.

All learned something about the ideal of equality and how to organize to get it. Sensing the limitless possibilities of the protest movement also made us sense the impossible limits of old sex roles. Lillian Smith talks about the genteel church ladies who organized the Association of Southern Women for the Prevention of Lynching. No feminists, the ladies still helped to corrode the iron myth that white women were chaste butterflies. They had realized "that all a woman can expect from lingering on exalted heights is a hard chill afterwards."[50]

Like their ancestors in the antislavery movement, some women in the civil rights movement felt abused. They were given work supportive in nature and negligible in influence; they were relegated to the "research library and to the mimeograph machine."[51] If they were sexually exploited, their own sexual exploits were judged according to a double standard that let men sow wild oats but told women to reap the whirlwind. Not only did movement men tend to be personally chauvinistic, but many of the movement's ideals—strength, courage, spirit—were those society attributes to masculinity. Women may have them, but never more than men. The more paramilitary, the less nonviolent, black protest became, the less women and the putative womanly virtues were honored.

Still another pressure upon women in civil rights was the virility cult of white liberals officially concerned with the "Negro Problem." In 1965 the Moynihan Report made its notorious to-do about strong women and weak men. Behind its analysis lurked a grim belief in the patriarchal family. The Report declared:

When Jim Crow made its appearance towards the end of the 19th century, it may be speculated that it was the Negro male who was most humiliated thereby; the male was more likely to use public facilities, which rapidly became segregated once the process began, and just as important, segregation, and the submissiveness it exacts, is surely more destructive to the male than to the female personality. Keeping the Negro "in his place" can be translated as keeping the Negro male in his place; the female was not a threat to anyone.

Compounding its errors of fact and spirit, the Report went on:

Unquestionably, these events worked against the emergence of a strong father figure. The very essence of the male animal, from the bantam rooster to the four-star general, is to strut.[52]

A brief, appealing memo illustrated the complex mood of some women in the peace and freedom movements at this time. Written by Casey Hayden and Mary King to other women, it asked how we might "live in our personal lives and in our work as independent and creative people."[53] The women quietly admitted that working in the movement intensified personal problems, especially if people start applying its lessons to themselves and if women assume a new role which is only, ironically, the logical consequence of the ideology they have been preaching. Hayden and King, writing before the new feminism became a coherent force, felt alone. No one talked publicly about women; no one organized them. Few men took the issue seriously, even though it involved the "straitjacketing of both sexes," even though it involved the kind of private agony that the movement wishes to make a public responsibility. Lacking a "community for discussion," Hayden and King hoped to create a community of support.

Their ideas now seem mild. A few years ago they were whispers. Women, caught up in a sex caste system, must work around and outside of hierarchal structures of power. Their subordination is also assumed in their personal relationships. If they wish to struggle against their situation, they find few laws to attack; the enemy is more elusive. If they wish to work, they find only "women's" jobs. They have trouble asserting themselves against the world, let alone over others. Yet Hayden and King asserted that women cannot realistically withdraw from the system. A solution is to *rethink* the institutions of marriage and childrearing and the cultural stereotypes that bind.

The influence of black protest on women's liberation is more pervasive than the effect of one public event on the private lives of some valuable, interesting women. The civil rights movement scoured a rusty national conscience. Moral and political struggle against a genuine domestic evil became respectable again. The movement clarified concepts of oppression, submission, and resistance and offered tactics—the sit-ins, boycotts, demonstrations, proofs of moral superiority—for others to use to wrest freedom from the jaws of asses. Confrontation politics became middle class again as the movement helped to resurrect the appealing American tradition of rebellion. The real domino theory deals with the collapse of delusions of content. Once these delusions are exposed for one group, they tend to be obvious for others. The black became, as he had been before, the test of white good will. Being treated like blacks became proof of exploitation.

All of the women's liberation groups, even the more conservative, have drawn deeply on the inadvertent largesse of the black movement. Some women look to it for encouraging political lessons. It teaches that the oppressed must become conscious of their oppression, of the debasing folly of their lives, before change can come. Change, if it does come, will overthrow both a class, a social group, and a caste—a social group held in contempt. For those who place women's liberation into the larger context of general revolution, black people "have exposed the basic weakness of the system of white, Western dominance which we live under."[54] Brutal versions of the theory of the survival of the fittest have been refuted: the weaker can defeat the stronger. Their tactics will prove the virtue of flexibility, speed, and cunning. Those who were expelled from the civil rights movement are grateful for being forced to take stock of themselves, instead of taking stock of blacks. So isolated, they often go on to praise black models of the doctrine of separatism.[55]

Even more commonly, women use blacks to describe themselves. They draw strenuous analogies between themselves and blacks, between women's civil rights and black civil rights, between women's revolution and the black revolution. The metaphor litters even the most sensible, probing, and sensitive thought of the movement. One influential pamphlet, which I like, deploys it no less than eleven times:[56]

1. Women, like black slaves, belong to a master. They are property and whatever credit they gain redounds to him.

2. Women, like black slaves, have a personal relationship to the men who are their masters.

3. Women, like blacks, get their identity and status from white men.

4. Women, like blacks, play an idiot role in the theatre of the white man's fantasies. Though inferior and dumb, they are happy, especially when they can join a mixed group where they can mingle with The Man.

5. Women, like blacks, buttress the white man's ego. Needing such support, the white man fears its loss; fearing such loss, he fears women and blacks.

6. Women, like blacks, sustain the white man: "They wipe his ass and breast feed him when he is little, they school him in his youthful years, do his clerical work and raise him and his replacements later, and all through his life in the factories, on the migrant farms, in the restaurants, hospitals, offices, and homes, they sew for him, stoop for him, cook for him, clean for him, sweep, run errands, haul away his garbage, and nurse him when his frail body alters."

7. Women, like blacks, are badly educated. In school they internalize a sense of being inferior, shoddy, and intellectually crippled. In general, the cultural apparatus—the profession of history, for example—ignores them.

8. Women, like blacks, see a Tom image of themselves in the mass media.

9. Striving women, like bourgeois blacks, become imitative, ingratiating, and materialistic when they try to make it in the white man's world.

10. Women, like blacks, suffer from the absence of any serious study on the possibility of real "temperamental and cognitive differences" between the races and the sexes.

11. The ambivalence of women toward marriage is like the ambivalence of blacks toward integration.[57]

The potent analogy has affected the liberal conscience. A national news program declared that people who object to women entering an all-male bar are as reactionary as people who approve of Lester Maddox keeping blacks out of his chicken restaurant.[58] The analogy has also been the root of a favorite educational device. People are told to substitute the words "black/white" for the words "female/male" in their statements. Or, the person saying, "Women love having babies," is asked if he would burble, "Negroes love chopping cotton." The point is to use public disapproval of discrimination against blacks to swell public consciousness of discrimination against women.

However, I believe that women's liberation would be much stronger, much more honest, and ultimately more secure if it stopped comparing white women to blacks so freely. The analogy exploits the passion, ambition, and vigor of the black movement. It perpetuates the depressing habit white people have of first defining the black experience and then of making it their own. Intellectually sloppy, it implies that both blacks and white women can be seriously discussed as amorphous, classless, blobby masses. It permits women to avoid doing what the black movement did at great cost and over a long period of time: making its protest clear and irrefutable, its ideology self-sufficient and momentous, its organization taut. It also helps to limit women's protest to the American landscape. The plight of woman is planetary, not provincial; historical, not immediate.

Perhaps more dangerous, the analogy evades, in the rhetorical haze, the harsh fact of white women's racism. Our racism may be the curse of white culture, the oath of an evil witch who invades our rooms at birth. Or our racism may dankly unite culture and the way in which white infants apprehend their bodies, the real biological punishment in the myth of the Fall from the Garden of Eden. Whatever the cause, the virus has infected us all. One story may symbolize its work. Castration, when it was a legal punishment, was applied only to blacks during the period of Western slavery. In Barbados in 1693, a woman, for money, castrated forty-two black men. White men made the law. Their fear dictated the penalty. Yet a woman carried it out. White skin has bought a perverse remedy for the blows that sex has dealt.[59]

The racism of white women dictates more than a desire to dominate *something;* it also bears on her participation in what Eldridge Cleaver calls the "funky facts of life." For the black man she may be the sumptuous symbol of virtue, culture, and power, or she may be a sexual tempter and murderer, or she may be an object upon which revenge may fall. She may think of the black man as the exotic superstud, the magic phallus. A union with him may prove her sophistication and daring. She may perceive the black woman as a threat, a class and caste hatred rooted in sexual jealousy and fear.[60] I frankly dislike some of the assumptions about white women I find in black writers. I am neither the guiding genius of the patriarchy nor the creator of my conventional sex role nor a fit subject for rape. Being "cleanly, viciously popped," which LeRoi Jones says that I want, but which my culture provides for me only in "fantasies" of evil, is in fact evil. Yet white women do have deeply ambiguous sexual attitudes toward black people which often have very little to do with love.

My generalizations, which obviously ignore the idiosyncratic, subtle mysteries of the psychology of individual persons, may partly explain the tensions between members of the black movement and of the woman's movement. There are also political reasons for incompatability. The logic of the ideology of separatism is one. Blacks must liberate themselves from whites, including white women; women must liberate themselves from men, including black men. Everyone's liberation must be self-won. My brief narrative of the nineteenth century surely warns us against proxy fights for freedom. The result is that black liberation and women's liberation must go their separate ways. I would be ridiculously presumptuous if I spoke for black women. My guess is that many will choose to work for the black movement. They will agree with the forceful Sonia Sanchez Knight poem "Queens of the Universe":

> . . . we must
> return to blk/men his children full of our women/love/
> tenderness/sweet/blkness ful of pride/so they can shape
> the male children into young warriors who will stand along
> side them.[61]

They will accept the theory that "any movement that augments the sex-role antagonisms extant in the black community will only sow the seed of disunity and hinder the liberation struggle."[62] Any black woman's movement will also have a texture different from that of a white woman's movement.

The logic of the ideologies of class improvement also makes an alliance between blacks and white women seem ultimately unstable. Both classes suffer from irrational economic discrimination: black men the least, black women the most. If society rights this wrong, it may only multiply the competition among the outcast for the cushy jobs. More dangerously, society may fail to change its notions of work. It must begin to assume, especially in a technological age, that ability is an asexual happenstance; that doing housework and raising children are asexual responsibilities; that the nuclear family, in which a father, whose sex gives him power, guarantees the annual income, is only one of several ways of leading the good life. Changing these notions means uprooting our concepts of sex and power. Such assumptions are axioms to members of women's liberation. Whether they are or not to members of black liberation, or any other political force, is unclear to me.

Finally, those of us in women's liberation have tasks independent of those confronting black liberation. We must do much more arduous work to persuade women to recognize the realities of their life. Few blacks still need consciousness-raising. Our job is harder because white, middle-class women have so many privileges and because the national impetus toward suburbia makes each home, embracing its homemaker, not just a castle, but a miniature ghetto. Blacks have long celebrated their culture. We must discover if women have a commonly felt, supportive culture, a fertile, if academically disdained, luster of responses and beliefs. We must also confront the moral and strategic necessity of building a revolution that rejects violence. A black man, carrying a gun, despite horrified warnings that armed blacks make white blacklashes, is effective. A woman, carrying a gun, despite the fact that women can and do shoot, is politically ineffective in America. Our culture finds it bizarre, and I, for one, find it regressive.

However, people in the black movement and in the woman's movement can work together on civil rights. Nearly everyone, except the crackers of both sexes, professes belief in civil rights. However, getting them is still a matter of hard work, imaginative administration, gritty willfulnes, and often despair. Once, fighting miscegenation laws together would have been appropriate. Now raising bail money for Panther women is necessary. The movements can also form coalitions to struggle for specific ends. Such goals must appeal to the self-interest of both blacks and women. Among them might be decent day-care centers, humane attitudes toward prostitution, the organization of domestic workers, and the recognition of the dignity of all persons on welfare. Insisting upon these goals must lead to a real guaranteed annual income.[63]

What, at last, we have in common is a gift to America from its haphazard and corrupt revolution—the belief in human right that makes civil right imperative. We also share, if we are lucky, a vision of a blessed and generous and peaceable kingdom. If not for us, for our children. In *Prison Notes,* Barbara Deming, the poet and activist, talks about a feeling she had when she was in the city jail of Albany, Georgia, in 1964. She had been marching for peace between Quebec, Canada, and Guantanamo, Cuba. She writes:

> A kind of affection flows between us that I have known before only on other ventures like this—born in part of enduring together discomfort and danger ... and born in part of one thing more, too: our common attempt to act toward our antagonists with sympathy. This daily effort, however clumsy, to put from us not only our fear of them but our hostility draws us closer still, as we reveal ourselves to one another, disarmed and hopeful. I have never felt toward a group of people a love so sweet and so strange. The emotion of it is as sharp as though I were in love with each of them. It has astonished me to feel so sharp an affection that was not (a possessive love). And what astonishes me is to love so intensely so many people at the same time.[64]

Perhaps Deming is too tender for those immediately caught up in a violent struggle to survive. Yet the love she offers must surely be the heart and skeleton of any peaceable kingdom. The notion of such love, as well as a passion for liberty, are what women's liberation must keep alive during the turmoil and chaos which we call revolution and during which we long for companions which present realities must deny.

NOTES

1. Gunnar Myrdal, Appendix 5, "A Parallel to the Negro Problem," *An American Dilemma* (New York: Harper and Brothers, 1944), p. 1077.

2. W. E. B. DuBois, "The Damnation of Women," *Darkwater* (New York: Schocken Books, 1969), p. 164.

3. Gilbert H. Barnes and Dwight L. Dumond, eds., *Letters of Theodore Dwight Weld, Angelina Grimké Weld, and Sarah Grimké 1822-1844* (New York: D. Appleton-Century Company, 1934), 2: 842.

4. *The History of Woman Suffrage*, 1: 60-61. *History of Woman Suffrage* is the unique history of American feminism from its origins until the ratification of the Nineteenth Amendment. Elizabeth Cady Stanton, Susan B. Anthony, and Matilda Joslyn Gage edited the first three volumes; Susan B. Anthony and Ida Husted Harper the fourth; and Mrs. Harper the fifth and sixth. My citations from the first three volumes will be from the second edition (Rochester: Charles Mann, 1889); from the fourth volume (Rochester: Susan B. Anthony, 1902); from the last volumes (New York: The National American Woman Suffrage Association, 1922).

5. Catharine A. Beecher, *Essay on Slavery and Abolitionism, with Reference to the Duty of American Females* (Philadelphia: Henry Perkins, 1837), p. 99.

6. Frederick Douglass, *Life and Times of Frederick Douglass, Written by Himself* (1892) (New York: Collier, 1962), p. 469. Good accounts of Douglass' work for women's rights are Benjamin Quarles, "Frederick Douglass and the Woman's Rights Movement," *Journal of Negro History* 25 (January 1940): 39-44, and *Life and Writings of Frederick Douglass*, ed. Philip S. Foner, 4 volumes (New York: International Publishers, 1950).

7. Frederick Engels, *The Origin of the Family, Private Property, and the State* (New York: International Publishers, 1942), p. 65.

8. Harriet Martineau, *Society in America* (London: Saunders and Otley, 1837), 2: 118. Martineau's chapter, "The Political Non-Existence of Women," is acute and acerb.

9. *History of Woman Suffrage*, 1:222.

10. *Ibid.*, pp. 680-681.

11. *Ibid.*, p. 471.

12. *Ibid.*, p. 854.

13. Beecher, *op. cit.*, p. 144.

14. *History of Woman Suffrage*, 1:469.

15. *Ibid.*, p. 528.

16. *Ibid.*, p. 52.

17. Angelina Grimké, *Letters to Catherine E. Beecher* (Boston: Isaac Knapp, 1838), p. 114. A harassed, exhausted Miss Grimké answered *An Essay on Slavery*.

18. *Weld-Grimké Letters*, 1:403.

19. *History of Woman Suffrage*, 1:40.

20. In Catherine H. Birney, *The Grimké Sisters* (Boston: Lee and Shepard Publishers, 1885), p. 204.

21. *Weld-Grimké Letters*, 1:403.

22. In Birney, *op. cit.*, pp. 202-203.

23. *History of Woman Suffrage*, 1: 53-62.

24. *Ibid.*, 2: 58.

25. *Ibid.*, p. 60.

26. *Ibid.*

27. *Ibid.*, pp. 60-61.

28. Susan B. Anthony did try to vote in 1872. A nineteenth-century forerunner of Chicago Judge Julius J. Hoffman found her guilty for such heresy.
29. *History of Woman Suffrage*, 2 :193.
30. Douglass, *Life and Writings*, IV, 212-13.
31. *History of Woman Suffrage*, 2: 216.
32. *Ibid.*, p. 382.
33. *Ibid.*, pp. 391-392.
34. *Ibid.*, 3: 792-793.
35. *Ibid.*, 2:415.
36. *Ibid.*, p. 94.
37. *Ibid.*, p. 353.
38. *Ibid.*, 3:14.
39. *Ibid.*, 2:311.
40. A text of Blackwell's letter is in *ibid.*, pp. 929-931.
41. An excellent, full account of this is Aileen Kraditor, *The Ideas of the Woman Suffrage Movement 1890-1920* (New York: Columbia University Press, 1965).
42. The National American Woman Suffrage Association was the result of a merger in 1890 between the two older woman's suffrage groups.
43. *History of Woman Suffrage*, 5:60.
44. *Ibid.*, p. 59.
45. *Ibid.*, p. 83.
46. *Ibid.*
47. *Ibid.*, p. 105.
48. *Ibid.*, p. 106.
49. Eleanor Flexner, *Century of Struggle: The Woman's Rights Movement in the United States* (New York: Atheneum, 1968), p. 129. Miss Flexner's book remains the most lucid survey of the origins of feminism in America. An unpublished doctoral dissertation, K. E. Melder, "The Beginnings of the Women's Rights Movement 1800-1840" (Ann Arbor: University Microfilms, 1964), is also very useful.
50. Lillian Smith, *Killers of the Dream*, rev. (New York: W. W. Norton, 1961), p. 141.
51. Carol Hanisch, "Hard Knocks: Working for Women's Liberation in a Mixed (Male-Female) Movement Group," Shulamith Firestone and Anne Koedt, eds., *Notes from the Second Year: Women's Liberation* (New York, 1970), p. 60. Other white women veterans of the civil rights movement have less unhappy accounts of what happened, particularly in the South. They accuse some women of themselves using sex in order to gain power. They say that at least in the beginning women were influential. A white woman was the first administrator of the Student Non-Violent Co-ordinating Committee office in Atlanta. Jobs were given out on the basis of competence. Women could not have some simply because it would have been stupid and dangerous to have a white woman appear in public with a black man.
52. "The Negro Family: the Case for National Action," in Leon Friedman, ed., *The Civil Rights Reader* (New York: Walker and Company, 1967), p. 291.
53. The memo, written for private circulation, is dated November 18, 1965. It was later printed in *Liberation*, 11 (April 1966): 35-36. *Liberation*, 11 (December 1966) went on to print four more articles about the same problem, which gave some pro-

grams for women's liberation and which drew parallels between being a black and being a woman in America.

54. Roxanne Dunbar, "Female Liberation as the Basis for Social Revolution," Firestone and Koedt, *op. cit.*, p. 48. Dunbar says the Vietnamese have also done this.

55. The Honorable Shirley Chisholm discusses separatism: ". . . because of the bizarre aspects of their roles and the influence that nontraditional contact among them has on the general society, blacks and whites, males and females, must operate almost independently of each other in order to escape from the quicksands of psychological slavery." Her essay, "Racism and Anti-Feminism," *Black Scholar*, 1 (January-February 1970): 40-45 is a lucid account of the new feminism by an admirable black woman.

56. Beverly Jones and Judith Brown, "Toward a Female Liberation Movement" (Boston: New England Free Press, n.d.).

57. It should be noted that when many contemporary feminists compare themselves to slaves, they are speaking of historical slavery, not of black American chattel slavery, of which they have no personal knowledge. They are influenced not only by Engels but by John Stuart Mill's *The Subjection of Women* (1869).

58. Harry Reasoner, CBS early evening news, June 25, 1970. Reasoner was commenting on a court decision permitting women to enter McSorley's, a New York bar.

59. Joel Kovel, *White Racism: A Psychohistory* (New York: Pantheon, 1970), p. 193, gives a brilliant analysis of the way in which biology, economics, and cultural assumptions may have come together to breed American racism. He says that while the South enjoyed the black body and the North made it taboo, for both regions it was:

> the very incarnation of that fecal substance with which the whole world had been smeared by the repressed coprophilia of the bourgeois order. Here was the central forbidden pleasure that had become generalized into the pursuit of world mastery: the playing with, the reincorporation of lost bodily contents, the restoration of the narcissistic body of infancy, the denial of separation and the selfhood that had been painfully wrung from history. Here was the excremental body that had been hated, repressed, spread over the universe, but which was still loved with the infant's wish to fuse with the maternal image.

However, Kovel writes as if "man" meant both "man" and "woman," there being no difference between them, or as if writing about "man" were enough.

60. Such attitudes, once clandestine, are now much discussed in many places. Among them are Eldridge Cleaver, *Soul On Ice* (New York: Dell Publishing Co., Delta Book, 1968); E. Franklin Frazier, *The Negro Family in the United States*, rev. and abrd. ed. (Chicago: University of Chicago Press, 1966); Frantz Fanon, *Black Skin, White Masks*, trans. Charles Lam Markman (New York: Grove Press, 1967); Calvin C. Hernton, *Sex and Racism in America* (New York: Grove Press, 1966); Theodore R. Hudson, "In the Eye of the Beholder," *Negro Digest* (December 1969): 43-48; LeRoi Jones, *Dutchman and The Slave: Two Plays* (New York: William Morrow, Apollo Edition,

1964); LeRoi Jones, "American Sexual Reference: black male," *Home* (New York: William Morrow, Apollo Edition, 1966).

One of the most interesting studies of white women and black women is Archibald E. Grimké, "The Sex Question and Race Segregation," *Papers of the American Negro Academy* (Washington, D.C., December 1915). Grimké, a lawyer, writer, publicist, and diplomat, was asking white women to help create legal equality for blacks and to end the double standard which had so victimized black women. Yet he was dubious about the possibility of sexual solidarity because of the resentment white women felt toward black women. Grimké, born in 1849, was the illegitimate son of Henry Grimké, Angelina and Sarah's brother, and Nancy Weston, a family slave. After the Civil War, he left the South to educate himself in the North. His aunt Sarah, who accidentally discovered his existence and then deliberately discovered his blood relationship to her, helped him to go on to Harvard.

61. *Black Scholar* 1 (January-February 1970): 29.
62. Robert Staples, "The Myth of the Black Matriarchy," *Black Scholar* 1 (January-February 1970): 15. Staples, who thinks the black woman more aggressive, independent, and self-reliant than the proto-typical white woman, finds the myth of the black matriarchy a "cruel hoax," which the white ruling class has imposed in order to create internal dissensions within the black community.
63. Perhaps a transcendent ideal of modern socialism may unite elements of the two movements. However, I think that for the moment new feminism's allegiance to abolishing sexism and black liberation's allegiance to blackness are both too strong for that.
64. Barbara Deming, *Prison Notes* (Boston: Beacon, 1970), pp. 119-120.

28

CONSUMERISM
AND WOMEN

A Redstocking Sister

Perhaps the most widely accepted tenet of movement ideology, promulgated by many leftist thinkers, notably Herbert Marcuse, is the idea that we are psychically manipulated by the mass media to crave more and more consumer goods, thus powering an economy that depends on constantly expanding sales. It has been suggested that this theory is particularly applicable to women, for women do most of the actual buying, their consumption is often directly related to their oppression (for example, make-up, soap flakes), and they are a special target of advertisers. According to this view the society defines women as consumers, and the purpose of the prevailing media image of women as passive sexual objects is to sell products. It follows that the beneficiaries of this depreciation of women are not men but the heads of the corporate power structure.

The consumerism theory has not been subjected to much critical debate. In fact, it seems in recent years to have taken on the invulnerability of religious dogma. Yet analysis demonstrates that this theory is fallacious and leads to crucial tactical errors. This essay is offered as a critique of consumerism based on four propositions:

1. It is not psychic manipulation that makes people buy; rather their buying habits are by and large a rational

From Shulamith Firestone and Anne Koedt, eds., *Notes from the Second Year: Women's Liberation* (New York, 1970). Reprinted by permission of the author, c/o IFA, © 1970.

self-interested response to their limited alternatives
within the system.

2. The chief function of media stereotypes of women is
not to sell goods but to reinforce the ideology and therefore the reality of male supremacy—of the economic
and sexual subordination of women to men, in the
latter's objective interest.

3. Most of the "consuming" women do is actually labor,
specifically part of women's domestic and sexual obligations.

4. The consumerism theory has its roots in class, sex, and
race bias; its ready acceptance among radicals, including
radical women, is a function of movement elitism.

First of all, there is nothing inherently wrong with
consumption. Shopping and consuming are enjoyable human activities and the marketplace has been a center of
social life for thousands of years. The profit system is
oppressive not because relatively trivial luxuries are available, but because basic necessities are not. The locus of
the oppression resides in the *production* function: people
have no control over what commodities are produced (or
services performed), in what amounts, under what conditions, or how they are distributed. Corporations make
these decisions basing them solely on their profit potential.
It is more profitable to produce luxuries for the affluent
(or for that matter, for the poor, on exploitative install-
ment plans) than to produce and make available food,
housing, medical care, education, recreational and cultural
facilities according to the needs and desires of the people.
We can accept the goods offered to us or reject them, but
we cannot determine their quality or change the system's
priorities. In a truly humane society, in which all the
people have personal autonomy, control over the means of
production, and equal access to goods and services, consumption will be all the more enjoyable because we will
not have to endure shoddy goods sold at exploitative
prices by means of dishonest advertising.

As it is, the profusion of commodities is a genuine and
powerful compensation for oppression. It is a bribe, but
like all bribes it offers concrete benefits—in the average
American's case, a degree of physical comfort unparalleled in history. Under present conditions people are preoccupied with consumer goods not because they are brainwashed, but because buying is the one pleasurable activity

not only permitted but actively encouraged by our rulers. The pleasure of eating an ice cream cone may be minor compared to the pleasure of meaningful, autonomous work, but the former is easily available and the latter is not. A poor family would undoubtedly rather have a decent apartment than a new TV, but since they are unlikely to get the apartment, what is to be gained by not getting the TV?

Radicals who in general are healthily skeptical of facile Freudian explanations have been quick to embrace a theory of media manipulation based squarely on Freud, as popularized by market researchers and journalists like Vance Packard (Marcuse acknowledges Packard's influence in *One-Dimensional Man*). In essence, this theory holds that ads designed to create unconscious associations between merchandise and deep-seated fears, sexual desires, and needs for identity and self-esteem induce people to buy products in search of gratifications no product can provide. Furthermore, the corporations, through the media, deliberately create fears and desires that their products can claim to fulfill. The implication is that we are not simply taken in by lies or exaggerations—as, say, by the suggestion that a certain perfume will make us sexually irresistible—but are psychically incapable of learning from experience and will continue to buy no matter how often we are disappointed, and that in any case our "need" to be sexually irresistible is programmed into us to keep us buying perfume. This hypothesis of psychic distortion is based on the erroneous assumption that mental health and anti-materialism are synonymous.

Although they have to cope with the gypping inherent in the profit system, people for the most part buy goods for practical, self-interested reasons. A washing machine does make a housewife's work easier (in the absence of socialization of housework); Excedrin does make a headache go away; a car does provide transportation. If one is duped into buying a product because of misleading advertising, the process is called exploitation; it has nothing to do with brainwashing. Advertising is a how-to manual on the consumer economy, constantly reminding us of what is available and encouraging us to indulge ourselves. It works (that is, stimulates sales) *because* buying is the only game in town, not vice versa. Advertising does appeal to morbid fears (for example, of body odors) and false hopes (irresistibility), and shoppers faced with indistinguishable brands of a product may choose on the basis of an ad (what method is better?), but this is just the old game of *caveat emptor*. It thrives on naiveté and people learn to resist it through experience.

The worst suckers for ads are children. Other vulnerable groups are older people, who had no previous experience—individual or historical—to guide them when the consumer cornucopia suddenly developed after World War II, and poor people, who do not have enough money to learn through years of trial, error, and disillusionment how to be shrewd consumers. The constant refinement of advertising claims, visual effects, and so on, shows that experience desensitizes. No one really believes that smoking Brand X cigarettes will make you sexy. (The function of sex in an ad is probably the obvious one—to lure people into paying closer attention to the ad—rather than to make them "identify" their lust with a product. The chief effect of the heavy sexual emphasis in advertising has been to stimulate a national preoccupation with sex, showing that you can't identify away a basic human drive as easily as all that.) Madison Avenue has increasingly deemphasized motivational techniques in favor of aesthetic ones—TV commercials in particular have become incredibly inventive visually—and even make a joke out of the old motivational ploys (the phallic Virginia Slims ad, for instance, is blatantly campy). We can conclude from this that either the depth psychology approach never worked in the first place or that it has stopped working as consumers have gotten more sophisticated.

The argument that the corporations create new psychological needs in order to sell their wares is equally flimsy. There is no evidence that propaganda can in itself create a desire, as opposed to bringing to consciousness a latent desire by suggesting that means of satisfying it are available. This idea is superstitious: it implies that the oppressor is diabolically intelligent (he has learned how to control human souls) and that the media have magic powers. It also mistakes effects for causes and drastically oversimplifies the relation between ideology and material conditions. We have not been taught to dislike our smell in order to sell deodorants; deodorants sell because there are social consequences for smelling. And the negative attitude about our bodies that has made it feasible to invent and market deodorants is deeply rooted in our antisexual culture, which in turn has been shaped by *exploitative modes of production and class antagonism between men and women.*

The confusion between cause and effect is particularly apparent in the consumerist analysis of women's oppression. Women are not manipulated by the media into being domestic servants and mindless sexual decorations, the better to sell soap and hair spray. Rather, the image reflects women as men in a sexist society force them to behave. Male supremacy is the oldest and most basic form of class exploitation; it was not invented by a smart ad man. The real evil of the media image of women is that it supports the sexist status quo. In a sense the fashion, cosmetics, and "feminine hygiene" ads are aimed more at men than at women. They encourage men to expect women to sport all the latest trappings of sexual slavery—expectations women must then fulfill if they are to survive. That advertisers exploit women's subordination rather than cause it can be clearly seen now that *male* fashions and toiletries have become big business. In contrast to ads for women's products, whose appeal is "use this and he will want you" (or "if you don't use this, he won't want you"), ads for the male counterparts urge, "you too can enjoy perfume and bright-colored clothes; don't worry, it doesn't make you feminine." Although advertisers are careful to emphasize how *virile* these products are (giving them names like "Brut," showing the man who uses them hunting or flirting with admiring women—who, incidentally, remain decorative objects when the sell is aimed directly at men), it is never claimed that the product is *essential to masculinity* (as make-up is essential to femininity), only *compatible* with it. To convince a man to buy, an ad must appeal to his desire for autonomy and freedom from conventional restrictions; to convince a woman, an ad must appeal to her need to please the male oppressor.

For women, buying and wearing clothes and beauty aids is not so much consumption as work. One of a woman's jobs in this society is to be an attractive sexual object, and clothes and make-up are tools of the trade. Similarly, buying food and household furnishings is a domestic task; it is the wife's chore to pick out the commodities that will be consumed by the whole family. And appliances and cleaning materials are tools that facilitate her domestic function. When a woman spends a lot of money and time decorating her home or herself, or hunting down the latest in vacuum cleaners, it is not idle self-indulgence (let alone the result of psychic manipulation), but a healthy attempt to find outlets for her creative energies within her circumscribed role.

There is a persistent myth that a wife has control over her husband's money because she gets to spend it. Actually, she does not have much more financial autonomy than the employee of a corporation who is delegated to buy office furniture or supplies. The husband, especially if he is rich, may allow his wife wide latitude in spending—he may reason that since she has to work in the home she is entitled to furnish it to her taste, or he may simply not want to bother with domestic details—but he retains the ultimate veto power. If he doesn't like the way his wife handles his money, she will hear about it. In most households, particularly in the working class, a wife cannot make significant expenditures, either personal or in her role as object-servant, without consulting her husband. And more often than not, according to statistics, it is the husband who makes the final decisions about furniture and appliances as well as other major expenditures like houses, cars, and vacations.

The consumerism theory is the outgrowth of an aristocratic, European-oriented antimaterialism based on upper-class *ressentiment* against the rise of the vulgar bourgeois. Radical intellectuals have been attracted to this essentially reactionary position (Herbert Marcuse's view of mass culture is strikingly similar to that of conservative theorists like Ernest Van Den Haag), because it appeals to both their dislike of capitalism and their feeling of superiority to the working class. This elitism is evident in radicals' conviction that they have seen through the system, while the average working slob is brainwashed by the media. (Oddly, no one claims that the ruling class is oppressed by commodities; it seems that rich people consume out of free choice.) Ultimately this point of view leads to a sterile emphasis on individual solutions—if only the benighted would reject their "plastic" existence and move to East Village tenements—and the conclusion that people are oppressed because they are stupid or sick. The obnoxiousness of this attitude is compounded by the fact that radicals can only maintain their dropout existence so long as plenty of brainwashed workers keep the economy going.

Consumerism as applied to women is blatantly sexist.

The pervasive image of the empty-headed female consumer constantly trying her husband's patience with her extravagant purchases contributes to the myth of male superiority: we are incapable of spending money rationally; all we need to make us happy is a new hat now and then. (There is an analogous racial stereotype—the black man with his Cadillac and magenta shirts.) The consumerism line allows movement men to avoid recognizing that they exploit women by attributing women's oppression solely to capitalism. It fits neatly into already existing radical theory and concerns, saving the movement the trouble of tackling the real problems of women's liberation. And it retards the struggle against male supremacy by dividing women, just as in the male movement, the belief in consumerism encourages radical women to patronize and put down other women for trying to survive as best they can, and maintains individualist illusions.

If we are to build a mass movement, we must recognize that no personal decision, like rejecting consumption, can alleviate our oppression. We must stop arguing about whose life style is better (and secretly believing ours is). The task of the women's liberation movement is to collectively combat male domination in the home, in bed, on the job. When we create a political alternative to sexism, the consumer problem, if it is a problem, will take care of itself.

29

ON AMERICAN FEMINISM

Shulamith Firestone

In the radical feminist view, the new feminism is not just the revival of a serious political movement for social equality. It is the second wave of the most important revolution in history. Its aim: overthrow of the oldest, most rigid caste/class system in existence, the class system based on sex—a system consolidated over thousands of years, lending the archetypal male and female roles an undeserved legitimacy and seeming permanence. In this perspective, the pioneer Western feminist movement was only the first onslaught, the fifty-year ridicule that followed it only a first counteroffensive—the dawn of a long struggle to break free from the oppressive power structures set up by nature and reinforced by man. In this light, let's take a look at American feminism.

I. THE WOMAN'S RIGHTS MOVEMENT IN AMERICA

Though there have always been women rebels in history,[1] the conditions have never before existed that would enable women to effectively overthrow their oppressive roles. Women's capacity for reproduction was urgently needed by the society—and even if it hadn't

From Shulamith Firestone, *The Dialectic of Sex: The Case for Feminist Revolution* (New York: William Morrow, 1970), pp. 16-45. Copyright © 1970 by Shulamith Firestone. Reprinted by permission of William Morrow and Co., Inc. and Jonathan Cape.

been, effective birth control methods were not available. So until the Industrial Revolution feminist rebellion was bound to remain only a personal one.

The coming feminist revolution of the age of technology was foreshadowed by the thought and writing of individual women, members of the intellectual elites of their day: in England, Mary Wollstonecraft and Mary Shelley, in America, Margaret Fuller, in France, the Bluestockings. But these women were ahead of their time. They had a hard time getting their ideas accepted even in their own advanced circles, let alone by the masses of men and women of their day, who had barely absorbed the first shock of the Industrial Revolution.

By the middle of the nineteenth century, however, with industrialization in full swing, a full-fledged feminist movement was underway. Always strong in the U.S.—itself founded shortly before the Industrial Revolution, and thus having comparatively little history or tradition—feminism was spurred on by the abolitionist struggle and the smoldering ideals of the American Revolution itself. (The Declaration passed at the first national Woman's Rights convention at Seneca Falls in 1848 was modeled on the Declaration of Independence.)

The early American Woman's Right Movement[2] was radical. In the nineteenth century, for women to attack the Family, the Church (see Elizabeth Cady Stanton's *Woman's Bible*), and the State (law) was for them to attack the very cornerstones of the Victorian society in which they lived—equivalent to attacking sex distinctions themselves in our own time. The theoretical foundations of the early W.R.M. grew out of the most radical ideas of the day, notably those of abolitionists like William Lloyd Garrison and communalists like R. D. Owen and Fanny Wright. Few people today are aware that the early feminism was a true grass-roots movement. They haven't heard of the torturous journeys made by feminist pioneers into backwoods and frontiers, or door to door in the towns to speak about the issues or to collect signatures for petitions that were laughed right out of the Assemblies. Nor do they know that Elizabeth Cady Stanton and Susan B. Anthony, the most militant feminists of the movement, were among the first to stress the importance of organizing women workers, founding the Working Woman's Association in September, 1868. (Delegates to the National

Labor Union Convention as early as 1868, they later fell out over the short-changing of women workers by the— hasn't changed—male chauvinist labor movement.) Other pioneer female labor organizers such as Augusta Lewis and Kate Mullaney were in the feminist movement.

This radical movement was built by women who had literally no civil status under the law; who were pronounced civilly dead upon marriage, or who remained legal minors if they did not marry; who could not sign a will or even have custody of their own children upon divorce; who were not taught even to read, let alone admitted to college (the most privileged of them were equipped with a knowledge of embroidery, china painting, French, and harpsichord); who had no political voice whatever. Thus, even after the Civil War, more than half this country's population was still legally enslaved, literally not owning even the bustles on their backs.

The first stirrings of this oppressed class, the first simple demands for justice, were met by a disproportionate violence, a resistance difficult to understand today when the lines of sexual class have been blurred over. For, as often happens, the revolutionary potential of the first awakening was recognized more clearly by those in power than it was by the crusaders themselves. From its very beginning the feminist movement posed a serious threat to the established order, its very existence and long duration testifying to fundamental inequalities in a system that pretended to democracy. Working first together, later separately, the Abolitionist Movement and the W.R.M. threatened to tear the country apart. If, in the Civil War, the feminists hadn't been persuaded to abandon their cause to work on "more important" issues, the early history of feminist revolution might have been less dismal.

As it was, although the Stanton-Anthony forces struggled on in the radical feminist tradition for twenty years longer, the back of the movement had been broken. Thousands of women, at the impetus of the Civil War, had been allowed out of the home to do charity work. The only issue on which these very different camps of organized women could unite was the desirability of the vote— but predictably, they did not agree upon *why* it was desirable. The conservatives formed the American Woman Suffrage Association, or joined the sprouting women's clubs, such as the pious Woman's Christian Temperance Union. The radicals separated into the National Woman's

Suffrage Association, concerned with the vote only as a symbol of the political power they needed to achieve larger ends.

By 1890, further legal reforms had been won, women had entered the labor force in the service capacity that they still hold today, and they had begun to be educated in larger numbers. In lieu of true political power they had been granted a token, segregated place in the public sphere as clubwomen. But though indeed this was a greater political power than before, it was only a new-fangled version of female "power" of the usual sort: behind the throne—a traditional *influence on power* which took modern form in lobbying and embarrassment tactics. When, in 1890, with their leaders old and discouraged, the radical feminist National merged with the conservative American to form the National American Woman Suffrage Association (NAWSA), all seemed lost. Conservative feminism, with its concentration on broad, unitive, single-issues like suffrage, with its attempt to work within and placate the white male power structure—trying to convince men who knew better, with their own fancy rhetoric yet—had won. Feminism, sold out, languished.

Even worse than the conservative feminists were the increasing number of women who, with their new-found bit of freedom, jumped enthusiastically into all the radical-isms of the day, the various social reform movements of the Progressive Era, even when at odds with feminist interests. (Consider the old debate about discriminatory "protective" labor laws for women.) Margaret Rhondda, Britain's leading post-World War I feminist, put it this way:

> One may divide the women in the woman's movement into two groups: the Feminists and the reformers who are not in the least Feminists; who do not care tuppence about equality for itself. . . . Now almost every women's organi-zation recognizes that reformers are far more common than Feminists, that the passion to decide to look after your fellowmen, to do good to them in your way, is far more common than the desire to put into everyone's hand the power to look after themselves.

These "reformers," the women "radicals" of their day, were at best influenced by feminism. They were neither true feminists nor true radicals because they did not yet see the woman's cause as a legitimate radical issue in itself. By seeing the W.R.M. as only tangent to another, more important politics, they were in a sense viewing themselves as defective men: women's issues seemed to them "special," "sectarian," while issues that concerned men were "human," "universal." Developing politically in movements dominated by men, they became preoccupied with reforming their position within these movements rather than getting out and creating their own. The Women's Trade Union League is a good example: women politicos in this group failed at the most basic undertakings because they were unable to sever their ties with the strongly male chauvinist AFL, under Samuel Gompers, which sold them out time and again. Or, in another example, like so many VISTA volunteers bent on slumming it with an ungrateful poor, they rushed into the young settlement movement, many of them giving their lives without reward—only to become the rather grim, embittered, but devoted spinster social workers of the stereotype. Or the Woman's Peace Party founded to no avail by Jane Addams on the eve of American intervention in World War I, which later split into, ironically, either jingoist groups working for the war effort, or radical pacifists as ineffective as they were extreme.

This frenzied feminine organizational activity of the Progressive Era is often confused with the W.R.M. proper. But the image of the frustrated, bossy battle-ax derives less from the radical feminists than from the nonfeminist politicos, committeewomen for the various important causes of their day. In addition to the now-defunct movements we have mentioned—the Woman's Trade Union League, the National Federation of Settlements, and the Woman's International League for Peace and Freedom (formerly the Woman's Peace Party, begun by Jane Addams)—the whole spectrum of Organized Ladyhood was founded in the era between 1890 and 1920: The General Federation of Women's Clubs, the League of Women Voters, the American Association of Collegiate Alumnae, the National Consumer's League, the PTA, even the DAR. Although these organizations were associated with the most radical movements of their day, that in fact their politics were reactionary, and finally fatuous and silly, was indicated at first solely by their nonfeminist views.

Thus the majority of organized women in the period between 1890-1920—a period usually cited as a high point of feminist activity—had nothing in common with true feminism. On the one hand, feminism had been constricted to the single issue of the vote—the W.R.M. was (temporarily) transformed into a suffrage movement—and on the other, women's energies were diffused into any other radical cause but their own.

But radical feminism was only dormant: The awakening began with the return of Harriet Stanton Blatch, the daughter of Elizabeth Cady Stanton, from England, where she had joined the militant Woman's Social and Political Union—the English Suffragettes of whom the Pankhursts are perhaps the best known—in opposing the Constitutionalists (conservative feminists). Believing that militant tactics were needed to achieve the radical goals espoused by her mother, she recommended attacking the problem of the vote with the discarded strategy of the Stanton-Anthony faction: pressure to amend the *federal* Constitution. Soon the American militants split off from the conservative NAWSA to form the Congressional Union (later the Woman's Party), beginning the daring guerrilla tactics and uncompromisingly tough line for which the whole suffrage movement is often incorrectly credited.

It worked. Militants had to undergo embarrassment, mobbings, beatings, even hunger strikes with forced feeding, but within a decade the vote was won. The spark of radical feminism was just what the languishing suffrage movement needed to push through their single issue. It provided a new and sound approach (the pressure for a national amendment rather than the tedious state-by-state organizing method used for over thirty years), a militancy that dramatized the urgency of the woman issue, and above all, a wider perspective, one in which the vote was seen as only the first of many goals, and therefore to be won as quickly as possible. The mild demands of the conservative feminists, who had all but pleaded that if they won the vote they wouldn't use it, were welcomed as by far the lesser of two evils in comparison with the demands of the Woman's Party.

But with the granting of the vote the establishment co-opted the woman's movement. As one gentleman of that period, quoted by William O'Neill in *Everyone Was Brave,* summarized it, "Nevertheless woman suffrage is a good thing if only to have it over with." Mrs. Oliver Hazard Perry Belmont of the Woman's Party urged women to boycott the elections: "Husband your new power. Suffragists did not fight for your emancipation for seventy

years to have you become servants to men's parties."
Charlotte Perkins Gilman seconded this:

> The power women will be able to exercise lies with their
> not joining a party system of men. The party system of
> politics is a trick of men to conceal the real issues.
> Women should work for the measures they want outside of
> party politics. It is because the old political parties realize
> that woman's influence will be so negligible on the inside
> that they are so eager to get women to join them.

But none of this was to any avail. Even the formation of a
new Woman's Party on February 18, 1921, as an alternative to the major parties that were so rapidly absorbing
woman's new political strength, could not resuscitate the
dying movement.[3]

The granting of the vote to the suffrage movement
killed the W.R.M. Though the antifeminist forces appeared to give in, they did so in name only. They never
lost. By the time the vote was granted, the long channeling
of feminist energies into the limited goal of suffrage—seen
initially as only one step to political power—had thoroughly depleted the W.R.M. The monster Ballot had swallowed everything else. Three generations had elapsed from
the time of the inception of the W.R.M.; the masterplan-
ners all were dead. The women who later joined the
feminist movement to work for the single issue of the vote
had never had time to develop a broader consciousness:
by then they had forgotten what the vote was for. The
opposition had had its way.

Of all that struggle what is even remembered? The fight
for suffrage alone—not worth much to women, as later
events bore out—was an endless war against the most
reactionary forces in America at the time, which, as
Eleanor Flexner shows in *Century of Struggle,* included
the biggest capitalist interests of the North, i.e., oil, manufacturing, railroad, and liquor interests; the racist bloc of
southern states (which, in addition to their own bigotry
about women, were afraid to grant the woman's vote
because it would enfranchise another *half* of the Negro
race, as well as draw attention to the hypocrisy of "universal" male suffrage), and, finally, the machine of government itself. The work involved to achieve this vote was
staggering. Carrie Chapman Catt estimated that:

to get the word "male" out of the constitution cost the women of this country 52 years of pauseless campaign ... During that time they were forced to conduct 56 campaigns of referenda to male voters, 480 campaigns to get legislatures to submit suffrage amendments to voters, 47 campaigns to get state constitutional conventions to write woman suffrage into state constitutions, 277 campaigns to get state party conventions to include woman suffrage planks, 30 campaigns to get presidential party conventions to adopt woman suffrage planks in party platforms and 19 successive campaigns with 19 successive Congresses.

Thus defeat was so frequent, and victory so rare—and then achieved by such bare margins—that even to read about the struggle for suffrage is exhausting, let alone to have lived through it and fought for it. The lapse of historians in this area is understandable, if not pardonable.

But, as we have seen, suffrage was only one small aspect of what the W.R.M. was all about. A hundred years of brilliant personalities and important events have also been erased from American history. The women orators who fought off mobs, in the days when women were not allowed to speak in public, to attack Family, Church, and State, who traveled on poor railways to cow towns of the West to talk to small groups of socially starved women, were quite a bit more dramatic than the Scarlett O'Haras and Harriet Beecher Stowes and all the Little Women who have come down to us. Sojourner Truth and Harriet Tubman, freed slaves who went back time and again, with huge prices on their heads, to free other slaves on their own plantations, were more effective in their efforts than the ill-fated John Brown. But most people today have never even heard of Myrtilla Miner, Prudence Crandall, Abigail Scott Duniway, Mary Putnam Jacobi, Ernestine Rose, the Claflin sisters, Crystal Eastman, Clara Lemlich, Mrs. O. H. P. Belmont, Doris Stevens, Anne Martin. And this ignorance is nothing compared to ignorance of the lives of women of the stature of Margaret Fuller, Fanny Wright, the Grimké sisters, Susan B. Anthony, Elizabeth Cady Stanton, Harriet Stanton Blatch, Charlotte Perkins Gilman, Alice Paul.

And yet we know about Louisa May Alcott, Clara Barton, and Florence Nightingale, just as we know about, rather than Nat Turner, the triumph of Ralph Bunche, or George Washington Carver and the peanut. The omission of vital characters from standard versions of American history in favor of such goody-good models cannot be tossed off. Just as it would be dangerous to inspire still-oppressed black children with admiration for the Nat Turners of their history, so it is with the W.R.M. The suspicious blanks in our history books concerning feminism—or else the confusion of the whole W.R.M. with the (conservative) suffrage movement or the reformist women's groups of the Progressive Era—is no accident.

It is part of a backlash we are still undergoing in reaction to the first feminist struggle. The few strong models allowed girls growing up in the fifty-year silence have been carefully chosen ones, women like Eleanor Roosevelt, of the altruistic feminine tradition, as opposed to the healthily selfish giants of the radical feminist rebellion. This cultural backlash was to be expected. Men of those days grasped immediately the true nature of a feminist movement, recognizing it as a serious threat to their open and unashamed power over woman. They may have been forced to buy off the women's movement with confusing surface reforms—a correction of the most blatant inequalities on the books, a few changes of dress, sex, style ("you've come a long way, baby"), all of which coincidentally benefited men. But the power stayed in their hands.

II. THE FIFTY-YEAR RIDICULE

How did the Myth of Emancipation operate culturally over a fifty-year period to anesthetize women's political consciousness?

In the twenties eroticism came in big. The gradual blurring together of romance with the institution of marriage began ("Love and Marriage, Love and Marriage, go together like a horse and carriage . . ."), serving to repopularize and reinforce the failing institution, weakened by the late feminist attack. But the convalescence didn't last long: women were soon reprivatized, their new class solidarity diffused. The conservative feminists, who at least had viewed their problems as social, had been co-opted, while the radical feminists were openly and effectively ridiculed; eventually even the innocuous committeewomen of other movements came to appear ridiculous. The cultural campaign had begun: emancipation was one's private responsibility; salvation was personal, not political. Women took off on a long soul-search for "fulfillment."

Here, in the twenties, is the beginning of that obsessive modern cultivation of "style," the search for glamor (You too can be Theda Bara), a cultural disease still dissipating women today—fanned by women's magazines of the *Vogue, Glamour, Mademoiselle, Cosmopolitan* variety. The search for a "different," personal, style with which to "express" oneself replaced the old feminist emphasis on character development through responsibility and learning experience.

In the thirties, after the Depression, women sobered. Flapperism was obviously not the answer: they felt more hung up and neurotic than ever before. But with the myth of emancipation going full blast, women dared not complain. If they had gotten what they wanted, and were *still* dissatisfied, then something must be wrong with them. Secretly they suspected that maybe they really *were* inferior after all. Or maybe it was just the social order: They joined the Communist party, where once again they empathized mightily with the underdog, unable to acknowledge that the strong identification they felt with the exploited working class came directly from their own experience of oppression.

In the forties there was another world war to think about. Personal hangups were temporarily overshadowed by the spirit of the War Effort—patriotism and self-righteousness, intensified by a ubiquitous military propaganda, were their own kind of high. Besides, the cats were away. Better yet, their thrones of power were vacant. Women had substantial jobs for the first time in several decades. Genuinely needed by society to their fullest capacity, they were temporarily granted human, as opposed to female, status. (In fact, feminists are forced to welcome wars as their only chance.)

The first long stretch of peace and affluence in some time occurred in the late forties and the fifties. But instead of the predictable resurgence of feminism, after so many blind alleys, there was only "The Feminine Mystique," which Betty Friedan has documented so well. This sophisticated cultural apparatus was hauled out for a specific purpose: women had gotten hired during the war, and now had to be made to quit. Their new employment gains had come only because they had been found to make a convenient surplus labor force, for use in just such time of crisis—and yet, one couldn't now just openly fire them. That would give the lie to the whole carefully cultivated myth of emancipation. A better idea was to have them quit of their own volition. The Feminine Mystique suited the purpose admirably. Women, still frantic, still searching (after all, a factory job is no man's idea of heaven either, even if it is preferable to woman's caged hell), took yet another false road.

This one was perhaps worse than any of the others. It offered neither the (shallow) sensuality of the twenties, the commitment to a (false) ideal of the thirties, nor the collective spirit (propaganda) of the forties. What it did offer women was respectability and upward mobility— along with Disillusioned Romance, plenty of diapers and PTA meetings (Margaret Mead's Mother Nurture), family arguments, endless and ineffective diets, TV soap operas and commercials to kill the boredom, and if the pain still persisted, psychotherapy. *Good Housekeeping* and *Parents' Magazine* spoke for every woman of the middle class, just as *True Confessions* did for the working class. The fifties was the bleakest decade of all, perhaps the bleakest in some centuries for women. According to the 1950 version of the Myth, women's emancipation had already been tried and found wanting (by women themselves, no doubt). The first attempt to break away from a stifling "Creative Motherhood" seemed to have failed utterly. All authentic knowledge of the old feminist movement by this time had been buried, and with it the knowledge that woman's present misery was the product of a still-virulent backlash.

For the youth of the fifties there was an even more sophisticated cultural apparatus: "Teenagerism," the latest guise of that persevering romanticism so bent on shoring up, by cultural fiat, a crumbling family structure. Young girls of all ages dreamed of escaping the dull homes of their mothers through Teenage Romance. The parked car, an established tradition since the era of the flappers, became an urgent necessity, perhaps the one prop that best characterized the passions of the fifties (see Edward Keinholz's "environment" of The Parked Car). The rituals of the high school dating game compared in formality with the finest of Deep South chivalric tradition, its twentieth-century "belle" now a baton-twirling, Sweet Sixteen cheerleader. The highest goal that a girl could achieve was "popularity," the old pleasing "grace" in modern form.

But the boys couldn't take it. The cloying romanticism and sentimentality designed to keep women in their place had side effects on the men involved. If there was to be a ritual of girl-chasing, some males too would have to be sacrificed to it. Barbie needed a Ken. But dating was a drag ("Can I borrow the car tonight, Dad?"). Surely there must be an easier way to get sex. Frankie Avalon and Paul Anka crooned to teenage girls; the boys were tuned out.

In the sixties the boys split. They went to college and Down South. They traveled to Europe in droves. Some joined the Peace Corps; others went underground. But wherever they went they brought their camp followers. Liberated men needed groovy chicks who could swing with their new life style: women tried. They needed sex: women complied. But that's all they needed from women. If the chick got it into her head to demand some old-fashioned return commitment, she was "uptight," "screwed up," or worse yet, a "real bringdown." A chick ought to learn to be independent enough not to become a drag on her old man (trans. "clinging"). Women couldn't register fast enough: ceramics, weaving, leather talents, painting classes, lit. and psych. courses, group therapy, anything to get off his back. They sat in front of their various easels in tears.

Which is not to suggest that the "chicks" themselves did not originally want to escape from Nowheresville. There was just no place they could go. Wherever they went, whether Greenwich Village c. 1960, Berkeley or Mississippi c. 1964, Haight-Ashbury or the East Village c. 1967, they were still only "chicks," invisible as people. There was no marginal society to which they could escape: the sexual class system existed everywhere. Culturally immunized by the antifeminist backlash—if, in the long black-out, they had heard of feminism at all, it was only through its derogation—they were still afraid to organize around their own problem. Thus they fell into the same trap that had swallowed up the women of the twenties and thirties: the search for "the private solution."

The "private solution" of the sixties, ironically, was as often the "bag" of politics (radical politics, thus more marginal and idealistic than the official—segregated—arenas of power) as it was art or academia. Radical politics gave every woman the chance to do her thing. Many women, repeating the thirties, saw politics not as

a means toward a better life, but as an end in itself. Many
joined the peace movement, always an acceptable feminine pastime: harmless because politically impotent, it
yet provided a vicarious outlet for female anger. Others
got involved in the civil rights movement: but though
often no more politically effective than their participation in the peace movement, white women's numbered
days in the black movement of the early sixties proved to
be a more valuable experience in terms of their own
political development. This is easy to detect in the present-
day women's liberation movement. The women who went
South are often much more politically astute, flexible, and
developed than women who came in from the peace
movement, and they tend to move toward radical feminism much faster. Perhaps because this concern for the
suffering of the blacks was white women's closest attempt
since 1920 to face their own oppression: to champion the
cause of a more conspicuous underdog is a euphemistic
way of saying you yourself are the underdog. So just as
the issue of slavery spurred on the radical feminism of the
nineteenth century, the issue of racism now stimulated the
new feminism: the analogy between racism and sexism
had to be made eventually. Once people had admitted and
confronted their own racism, they could not deny the
parallel. And if racism was expungeable, why not sexism?

I have described the fifty-year period between the end
of the old feminist movement and the beginning of the
new in order to examine the specific ways in which the
Myth of Emancipation operated in each decade to defuse
the frustrations of modern women. The smear tactic was
effectively used to reprivatize women of the twenties and
the thirties, and thereafter it combined with a blackout of
feminist history to keep women hysterically circling
through a maze of false solutions: the Myth had effectively denied them a legitimate outlet for their frustration.
Therapy proved a failure as an outlet. To return to the
home was no solution either—as the generation of the
forties and the fifties proved.

By 1970 the rebellious daughters of this wasted generation no longer, for all practical purposes, even knew
there had been a feminist movement. There remained only
the unpleasant residue of the aborted revolution, an amazing set of contradictions in their roles: on the one hand,
they had most of the legal freedoms, the literal assurance

that they were considered full political citizens of society—and yet they had no power. They had educational opportunities—and yet were unable, and not expected, to employ them. They had the freedoms of clothing and sex mores that they had demanded—and yet they were still sexually exploited. The frustrations of their trapped position were exacerbated by the development of mass media in which these contradictions were nakedly exposed, the ugliness of women's roles emphasized by precisely that intensive character which made of the new media such a useful propaganda organ. The cultural indoctrinations necessary to reinforce sex role traditions had become blatant, tasteless, where before they had been insidious. Women, everywhere bombarded with hateful or erotic images of themselves, were at first bewildered by such distortion (Could that be Me?), and, finally, angered. At first, because feminism was still taboo, their anger and frustration bottled up in complete withdrawal (Beatnik Bohemia and the Flower/Drug Generation) or was channeled into dissent movements other than their own, particularly the civil rights movement of the sixties, the closest women had yet come to recognizing their own oppression. But eventually the obvious analogy of their own situation to that of the blacks, coupled with the general spirit of dissent, led to the establishment of a women's liberation movement proper. The anger spilled over, finally, into its proper outlet.

But it would be false to attribute the resurgence of feminism only to the impetus generated by other movements and ideas. For though they may have acted as a catalyst, feminism, in truth, has a cyclical momentum all its own. In the historical interpretation we have espoused, feminism is the inevitable female response to the development of a technology capable of freeing women from the tyranny of their sexual-reproductive roles—both the fundamental biological condition itself, and the sexual class system built upon, and reinforcing, this biological condition.

The increasing development of science in the twentieth century should have only accelerated the initial feminist reaction to the Industrial Revolution. (Birth control alone, for example, a problem for which the early feminists had no answer, has reached, in the period since 1920, its highest level of development in history.) The dynamics of the counterrevolution which in addition to temporal crises such as wars and depression obstructed the growth of feminism, I have attempted to describe. Because of such obstruction, new scientific developments that could have greatly helped the feminist cause stayed in the lab, while social-sexual practices not only continued as before but were actually intensified, in reaction to the threat. Scientific advances which threaten to further weaken or sever altogether the connection between sex and reproduction have scarcely been realized culturally. That the scientific revolution has had virtually no effect on feminism only illustrates the political nature of the problem: the goals of feminism can never be achieved through evolution, but only through revolution. Power, however it has evolved, whatever its origins, will not be given up without a struggle.

III. THE WOMEN'S LIBERATION[4] MOVEMENT

In three years, we have seen the whole political spectrum of the old women's movement recreated. The broad division between the radical feminists and the two types of reformists, the conservative feminists and the politicos, has reappeared in modern guise. There are roughly three major camps in the movement now, themselves subdivided. Let us summarize them briefly, keeping in mind that in such a formative period the politics, as well as the membership, of any one group is in a continual state of flux.

1. Conservative Feminists

This camp, though now proliferating into myriads of similar organizations, is perhaps still best exemplified by its pioneer (and thus more hardcore feminist than is generally believed) NOW, the National Organization of Women, begun in 1965 by Betty Friedan after her reverberating publication of *The Feminine Mystique*. Often called the NAACP of the woman's movement (and indeed, because it too is full of older professionals—career women who have "made it"—it is similarly attacked by the younger liberation groups for its "careerism"), NOW concentrates on the more superficial symptoms of sexism—legal inequities, employment discrimination, and the like.

Thus in its politics it most resembles the suffragist

movement of the turn of the century, Carrie Chapman Catt's National American Woman Suffrage Association, with its stress on equality with men—legal, economic, etc., within the given system—rather than liberation from sex roles altogether, or radical questioning of family values. Like the NAWSA, it tends to concentrate on the winning of single-issue political gains, whatever the cost to political principles. Like the NAWSA, it has attracted a wide membership, which it controls by traditional bureaucratic procedures.

However, already in the young movement, it is apparent that this position, untenable even in terms of immediate political gains—as witnessed by the failure of the last conservative feminist movement—is more a leftover of the old feminism (or, if you prefer, its forerunner) rather than a model of the new. The many women who had joined for lack of a better place to go soon shifted to radical feminism—and in doing so have forced NOW into an increasing radicalism, cf., where once the organization didn't dare officially endorse even abortion law repeal for fear of alienating those who could go no further than reform, now abortion law repeal is one of its central demands.

2. Politicos

The politicos of the contemporary women's movement are those women whose primary loyalty is to the Left ("The Movement") rather than to the Women's Liberation Movement proper. Like the politicos of the Progressive Era, contemporary politicos see feminism as only tangent to "real" radical politics, instead of central, directly radical in itself; they still see male issues, e.g., the draft, as universal, and female issues, e.g., abortion, as sectarian. Within the contemporary politico category is still a smaller spectrum, which can be roughly broken down as follows:

a. LADIES' AUXILIARIES OF THE LEFT. Every major faction on the left, and even some unions, by now—after considerable resistance—have their women's lib caucuses, which agitate against male chauvinism within the organization, and for greater decision-making power for women. The politicos of these caucuses are reformist in that their main objective is to improve their own situation within the limited arena of leftist politics. Other women are, at best, their foremost "constituency," strictly women's issues no more than a useful "radicalizing" tool to recruit women into the "Larger Struggle." Thus their attitude toward other women tends to be patronizing and evangelistic, the "organizer" approach. Here are some (female) Black Panthers in an interview in *The Movement*, an underground paper, stating it in a way that is perhaps embarrassing to the white left in its blatancy, but that nevertheless is typical of (because lifted from?) most white revolutionary rhetoric on the subject:

> It's very important that women *who are more advanced,* who already understand revolutionary principles, go to them and explain it to them and struggle with them. We have to recognize that women are backwards politically and that we must struggle with them. (Italics mine)

Or again, concerning an independent women's movement:

> They lose sight of the *Primary Struggle*. Some special organizing of women's groups is possible, perhaps, but dangerous: in terms of turning in on themselves, in terms of becoming petit bourgeois little cliques where they just talk about *taking care of the kids* all the time, or become a *gripe session*. (Italics mine)

We have here a complete denial by blacks (and women, no less) of their own principles of Black Power as applied to another group: the right of the oppressed to organize around their oppression *as they see and define it*. It is sad that the Black Power movement, which taught women so much about their political needs through the obvious parallels, should be the last to see that parallel in reverse. Grass-roots organizing, around one's own oppression, the end of leadership and power plays, the need for a mass base prior to bloody struggle, all the most important principles of radical politics suddenly do not apply to women, in a double standard of the worst order.

The women's liberation groups still attempting to work within the larger leftist movement haven't a chance, for their line is dictated from above, their analysis and tactics shaped by the very class whose illegitimate power they are protesting. And thus they rarely succeed in doing more than increasing the tension that already threatens their frayed leftist groups with extinction. If ever they do become powerful they are bought off with tokens, or, if necessary, the larger group quietly disintegrates and reorganizes without them. Often, in the end, they are forced to split off and join the independent women's movement after all.

b. MIDDLE-OF-THE-ROAD POLITICOS. Working separately from, but still under the protection of the male umbrella, these groups are ambivalent and confused. They vacillate. Their obvious imitation of traditional (male) left analysis, rhetoric, tactics, and strategy, whether or not they are suited to the achievement of their own distinct goals, is compensated for by a lot of sentimentalizing about the Oppressed Sisters Out There. Their own politics tends to be ambiguous, because their loyalties are: if they are no longer so sure that it is capitalism which directly causes the exploitation of women, they do not go so far as to intimate that *men* might have anything to do with it. Men are Brothers. Women are Sisters. If one must talk about enemies at all, why not leave it open and call it The System?

c. THE FEMINIST POLITICOS. This position describes perhaps the largest proportion of the anonymous cell groups of the women's liberation movement across the country: it is the position toward which many of the Middle-of-the-Roaders eventually drift. Basically it is a conservative feminism with leftist overtones (or perhaps, more accurately, it is a leftism with feminist overtones). While the feminist politicos admit that women must organize around their own oppression as they feel it, that they can best do this in independent groups, and that the primary concentration of any *women's* group should be on women's issues, every effort is still made to fit such activities into the existing leftist analysis and framework of priorities—in which, of course, Ladies never go first.

Despite the seeming diversity within such a spectrum, the three positions can be reduced to one common denominator: Feminism is secondary in the order of political priorities, and must be tailored to fit into a preexistent (male-created) political framework. The fear that if it isn't watched feminism will go off the deep end, to become divorced from The Revolution, gives away the politicos' fear that feminism is not a legitimate issue in itself, one that will (unfortunately) *require* a revolution to achieve its ends.

And here we have the crux of it: Politico women are

unable to evolve an authentic politics because they have never truly confronted their oppression *as women* in a gut way. Their inability to originate a feminist leftist analysis of their own, their need to tie their issue at all times to some "primary struggle" rather than seeing it as central, or even revolutionary in itself, is derived directly from their lingering feelings of inferiority as women. Their inability to put their own needs first, their need for male approval—in this case anti-establishment male approval—to legitimate them politically, renders them incapable of breaking from other movements when necessary, and thus consigns them to mere left reformism, lack of originality, and, ultimately, political sterility.

However, the contrast of radical feminism, the more militant position in the women's liberation movement, has forced the politicos, as well as the conservative feminists, into a growing defensiveness, and, finally, into an increasing radicalism. At first Cuban and NLF women were the unquestioned models, their freedom idolized; now there is a let's-wait-and-see attitude. Last year purely feminist issues were never brought up without tacking on a tribute to the blacks, workers, or students. This year spokesmen on the left instead talk pompously and importantly of the abolition of the nuclear family. For the Left Brotherhood have been quick to jump in to see what they could co-opt—coming up with a statement against monogamy, at which clear sign of male-at-work, feminists could only laugh bitterly. But still, where SDS didn't care a damn about a silly woman's movement a few years ago, it now has taken to giving its women a more and more glamorous role to keep them from bolting, e.g., the Women's Militia, the "longhair army" of the Weathermen faction of SDS. There are the beginnings of the official leftist acknowledgment of women as an important oppressed group in their own right; some shallow understanding of the need for an independent feminist movement; some degree of consideration of women's issues and complaints, e.g., abortion or day-care centers; and the growing tokenism. And, as with the early stages of Black Power, there is the same attempt to appease, the same nervous liberal laughter, the same insensitivity to how it feels to be a woman, disguised under a we're-trying-give-us-a-kiss grin.

3. Radical Feminism

The two positions we have described usually generate a third, the radical feminist position: The women in its ranks range from disillusioned moderate feminists from NOW to disillusioned leftists from the women's liberation movement, and include others who had been waiting for just such an alternative, women for whom neither conservative bureaucratic feminism nor borrowed leftist dogma had much appeal.

The contemporary radical feminist position is the direct descendent of the radical feminist line in the old movement, notably that championed by Stanton and Anthony, and later by the militant Congressional Union subsequently known as the Woman's Party. It sees feminist issues not only as *women's* first priority, but as central to any larger revolutionary analysis. It refuses to accept the existing leftist analysis not because it is too radical, but because *it is not radical enough:* it sees the current leftist analysis as outdated and superficial, because this analysis does not relate the structure of the economic class system to its origins in the sexual class system, the model for all other exploitative systems, and thus the tapeworm that must be eliminated first by any true revolution.

Offhand we may note that the radical feminist movement has many political assets that no other movement can claim, a revolutionary potential far higher, as well as qualitatively different, from any in the past:

1) Distribution: Unlike minority groups (an historical accident), or the proletariat (an economic development), women have always made up an oppressed majority class (51 percent), spread evenly throughout all other classes. The most analogous movement in America, Black Power, even could it instantly mobilize every black in the country, would command only 15 percent of the population. Indeed, all the oppressed minorities *together,* generously assuming no factional infighting, would not make up a majority—unless you included women. That women live with men, while on some levels our worst disadvantage— the isolation of women from each other has been responsible for the absence or weakness of women's liberation movements in the past—is, in another sense, an advantage: a revolutionary in every bedroom cannot fail to shake up the status quo. And if it's your wife who is

revolting, you can't just split to the suburbs. Feminism, when it truly achieves its goals, will crack through the most basic structures of our society.

2) Personal Politics: The feminist movement is the first to combine effectively the "personal" with the "political." It is developing a new way of relating, a new political style, one that will eventually reconcile the personal—always the feminine prerogative—with the public, with the "world outside," to restore that world to its emotions, and literally to its senses.

The dichotomy between emotions and intellect has kept the established movement from developing a mass base: on the one hand, there are the orthodox leftists, either abstract university intellectuals out of touch with concrete reality, or, in their activist guise, militantly into *machismo,* self-indulgent in their action with little concern for political effectiveness. On the other, there is Woodstock Nation, the Youth Revolt, the Flower and Drug Generation of Hippies, Yippies, Crazies, Motherfuckers, Mad Dogs, Hog Farmers, and the like, who, though they understand that the old leafletting and pamphletting and Marxist analysis are no longer where it's at—that the problem is much deeper than merely the struggle of the proletariat, which, in any case, is hardly the American vanguard—yet have no solid historical analysis of their own with which to replace it; indeed, who are apolitical. Thus the Movement is foundering, either marginal, splintered, and ineffective due to its rigid and outdated analysis or, where it does have mass movement appeal, lacking a solid base in history and economics, "drop out" rather than revolutionary. The feminist movement is the urgently needed solder.

3) The End of Power Psychology: Most revolutionary movements are unable to practice among themselves what they preach. Strong leadership cults, factionalism, "ego-tripping," backbiting are the rule rather than the exception. The woman's movement, in its short history, has a somewhat better record than most in this area. One of its major stated goals is internal democracy—and it goes to very great lengths to pursue this goal.

Which is not to claim that it is successful. There is much more rhetoric than reality on the subject, often disguising hypocritically the same old games and power plays—often with new and complex feminine variations. But it is too much to expect that, given its deep roots in sexual class and family structure, anyone born today would be successful at eliminating the power psychology. And though it is true that many females have never assumed the dominant (power over others) role, there are many others who, identifying all their lives with men, find themselves in the peculiar position of having to eradicate, at the same time, not only their submissive natures, but their dominant natures as well, thus burning their candle at both ends.

But if any revolutionary movement can succeed at establishing an egalitarian structure, radical feminism will. To question the basic relations between the sexes and between parents and children is to take the psychological pattern of dominance-submission to its very roots. Through examining politically this psychology, feminism will be the first movement ever to deal in a materialist way with the problem.

NOTES

1. For example, witches must be seen as women in independent political revolt. Within two centuries eight million women were burned at the stake by the Church—for religion was the politics of that period.
2. Hereafter abbreviated W.R.M.
3. The Woman's Party struggled on through a depression and several wars, campaigning for the next big legal boost to women's freedom, an Equal Rights Amendment to the Constitution. Fifty years later those who are still alive are still campaigning. The stereotype of the crotchety old lady with her umbrella obsessed with a cause already won is the product of the ossification of feminism created by The Fifty-Year Ridicule.
4. "Liberation" as opposed to "emancipation" to denote freedom from sexual classification altogether rather than merely an equalizing of sex roles. Nevertheless, I have always found the name heavy, too flavored with New Left rhetoric, and ashamed to acknowledge any relation to Feminism. I prefer to use "Radical Feminism."

Index